LIST OF DRILLS AND TIMED WRITINGS

---

[1] An alphabetic sentence appears in every Preparatory Practice, beginning on page 25.

[2] A figure sentence appears in many of the Preparatory Practices, beginning on page 33.

[3] A figure-symbol sentence appears in most of the Preparatory Practices, beginning on page 44.

[4] A fluency sentence appears

8TH EDITION
COLLEGE TYPEWRITING

D. D. LESSENBERRY *Professor of Education, Emeritus University of Pittsburgh*

S. J. WANOUS *Professor of Education, School of Education, UCLA (Los Angeles)*

C. H. DUNCAN *Head, Business Education Department Eastern Michigan University*

T 76
COMPLETE COURSE

SOUTH-WESTERN PUBLISHING CO.

Cincinnati   •   Chicago   •   Dallas
Burlingame, Calif.   •   New Rochelle, N. Y.

CONTENTS

Division 1
BASIC TYPEWRITING FOR COMMUNICATION

Division 2
INTERMEDIATE TYPEWRITTEN COMMUNICATION

Division 3
ADVANCED TYPEWRITTEN COMMUNICATION

COLLEGE TYPEWRITING, Complete Course, Eighth Edition, was specially designed to help students meet the requirements of top-level office jobs. The materials in the book are representative of those the students will type when they become employed. As nearly as possible, the materials are given to the students in the same form likely to be encountered on the job. The pace of the book and the content of the problems and timed writings are geared to college-level students.

ORGANIZATION OF THE BOOK

This book is organized into three divisions of 75 well-planned lessons each and a Reference Guide of useful typewriting information.

Division 1 provides materials for giving the students the "right start." Stressed are keyboard mastery; use of correct techniques and form; control of center-ing, tabulating, and other manipulative operations; and problem solving related to such commonly used personal and business papers as letters, memoran-dums, outlines, tables, and reports.

Division 2 covers basic information as well as many fine points of style on a representative sample of business papers. Emphasis is also placed on inte-grating spelling, punctuating, and capitalizing with typewriting, not only to make these skills more use-ful in an office setting but also to lay the foundation for careful proofreading.

The lessons in the first two divisions develop, under close guidance and direction, a basic under-standing of the requirements underlying the prepara-tion of personal and business papers.

Division 3 builds upon the foundations laid in the earlier lessons. The problems are presented in re-lated project form and sample the papers prepared in executive, accounting, professional, and government offices. The students develop good taste, judgment, and initiative by working through the projects with a minimum of direction repeating or reminding.

The first lessons of a division inventory basic skills and problem-solving competencies, giving the instructor an opportunity to fill in the training needs of his students before embarking on a new division of lessons.

Midway through each division and again at the end there are sections of lessons which focus on measurement of achievement in basic skill and pro-duction power. There are thus ample opportunities in the textbook to evaluate intensively a student's

Each section of lessons throughout the book stresses the development of basic skill through technique-building drills, skill-comparison and skill-transfer typing, guided practice, and timed writings. Goal setting and other uniquely devised procedures accompany these activities.

SPECIAL FEATURES OF THIS BOOK

1. The first edition of COLLEGE TYPEWRITING was published in 1930, as the first book prepared ex-clusively for college classes. The materials in this new Eighth Edition have thus gone through nearly forty years of testing, evaluating, writing and re-writing, selecting, and polishing.

2. The teaching experiences of more than 2,000 type-writing instructors have been woven into the pat-tern of this book. Before the revision got under way, college instructors across the country were asked to describe their classroom practices and preferences. Their responses provided invaluable assistance in tailoring the book to current needs.

3. Realistic, scientifically controlled copy is provided for building and measuring basic skill. Studies of copy difficulty, conducted by Dr. Jerry W. Robinson, led to the conclusion that (1) syl-labic intensity, (2) average strokes per word, and (3) percentage of high-frequency words were the three factors that affect the difficulty level of copy used in building and measuring skill. These factors were thus kept in mind in writing many of the skill-building drills and all the timed writings. As a result, an easy-to-difficult approach to skill build-ing is used, office-level copy is used for practice and timed writings, and a consistent measure of student progress is provided.

4. Composing skill is developed through drills and uniquely devised problems.

5. Clear, succinct, uniform directions are given for the first problems of each new group. Model illus-trations are provided. Thereafter, the directions are gradually diminished until the student makes most of the decisions on matters of procedure, based on his past experience in typing similar problems.

ACKNOWLEDGMENTS

The authors express their grateful thanks to the many instructors, students, and business workers who have contributed so generously of their ideas for the content and organization of this book. They have helped to make this book an effective aid to those who

LESSON 1

1A   Get Ready to Type

1. ARRANGE YOUR WORK AREA

a. Clear the work area of unneeded books and papers.

b. Place this textbook to the right of the typewriter on a bookholder, or put something under the top to raise it to better reading position.

c. Have the front of the frame of the typewriter even with the front edge of the desk or table.

2. INSERT THE PAPER

a. Adjust the **paper guide (8)** as directed on page iii.

b. Place a full-size sheet of paper on the desk to the left of the type-writer, turned so the long side of the paper is close to you.

c. Pull the **paper bail (11)** forward—toward you—with your right hand.

d. Grasp the paper with your left hand, the thumb under the sheet, as illustrated at the right.

e. Bring the paper to the **cylinder** or **platen (14)** and drop it between the cylinder and the **paper table (10)**, against the **paper guide (8)**; *at the same time*, bring the right hand to the **right cylinder knob (19)** and twirl the knob with a quick movement of the fingers and the thumb.

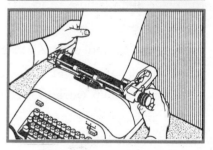

f. Snap the paper bail back with the thumb to hold the paper firmly against the cylinder. Place the **paper-bail rolls (13)** about 1½ inches from the side edges of the paper.

3. KNOW YOUR TYPEWRITER   • The numbers shown in boldface in the text above are those assigned to the machine parts illustrated below and on the diagrams presented on pp. i-ii.

```
        8              10              11              13              14
  PAPER GUIDE     PAPER TABLE     PAPER BAIL     PAPER-BAIL ROLL   CYLINDER (PLATEN)
   AND SCALE                      AND SCALE

7 MARGIN SET, LEFT                                            MARGIN SET, RIGHT 15
5 LINE-SPACE REGULATOR                                       PAPER-RELEASE LEVER 16
4 CARRIAGE RELEASE, LEFT                                   CARRIAGE RELEASE, RIGHT 18
2 CYLINDER
  KNOB, LEFT

1 CARRIAGE RETURN
  (Line-Space Lever)

                                                              CYLINDER KNOB, RIGHT 19

TYPEWRITER FRAME

KEYBOARD                                                                   KEYBOARD

                                                                      SPACE BAR 27
```

AVERAGE FAMILY INCOME, BEFORE TAXES[2]

1960–1970

1960	$ 6,900
1961	7,200
1962	7,500
1963	7,800
1964	8,300
1965	8,800
1966	9,400
1967	10,000
1968	10,600
1969	11,100
1970	11,700

(¶ 2) At least part of this increase in income might be traced to the nation's schools. As a result of the Vocational Act of 1963, our educational system has become more cognizant of the place and purpose of vocational education, of the importance of training young people to earn a living, and of the great necessity for providing business and industry with semi-skilled and skilled workers. The result: more people making more money. (¶ 3) Money, we have been told repeatedly, does not buy happiness; moreover, psychologists tell us that the lack of it does not always cause aggravation. A definite problem does arise, however, when, as Hopper[3] describes it, a family attempts to (1) determine the extent of its needs, (2) interpret and describe its wants, and (3) differentiate between the two. Food, clothing, and shelter have been enumerated as basic human needs; but there is little agreement as to how many suits of clothes are sufficient, how many rooms a home should have, or whether we should have steak or eggs—or steak and eggs—for dinner. Although each individual or family must make such decisions, they are often unprepared to do so wisely. (¶ 4) Wants involve discretionary spending. Theoretically they represent all the large and small luxuries with which a family seeks to indulge itself after basic needs have been met.[4] The questions they raise are sometimes agonizing. Do I want a color television set, or do I want a bank account? The young lady about to be engaged wants a diamond ring; her new home will need a refrigerator. Reason and emotion come into conflict; and decisions, once made, are very often inconclusive. (¶ 5) There is no magic formula to help us make wise decisions, but the study of consumer education will give us some guidelines that will be helpful with the ones that involve spending. Job training is important, of course, in that it helps to provide greater income with which to gratify our needs and wants. Consumer education, in addition, helps us to understand these needs and wants and teaches us how we can better satisfy them through wise use of the increased buying power that comes with higher income.

---

[1]Institute of Life Insurance, "Measuring Family Financial Progress," Topics, Vol. 17 (Spring, 1968), p. 1. (*26 words*)

[2]Ibid., p. 6. (*4 words*)

[3]Michael R. Hopper, Consumer Behavior: A Theory (Athens: Popular Press, 1968), p. 11. (*26 words*)

[4]Rennie W. Hurlbut, Climbing the Family Tree (Seattle: Beamon Publishing Co., 1968), p. 72. (*For Job 1: 23 words*)

Job 2: Leftbound Manuscript

Assume that you are typing the final page or pages of a manuscript that is to be bound at the left and that you are ready to begin the fifth page. Use the material in Job 1 that begins with ¶ 4. Place any footnotes on the page on which reference to them is made. (*226 words including the footnote*)

4. ADJUST THE LINE-SPACE REGULATOR

Set the **line-space regulator (5)** on "1" for single spacing the lines you are to type in this lesson.

(Set the regulator on "2" for double spacing and on "3" for triple spacing when such spacing is needed.)

The first two lines shown below are single-spaced (SS); the next line is a double space (DS) below the second line; and the last line is a triple space (TS) below that.

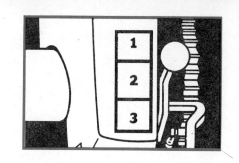

Line 1	This line and the next are single-spaced.	SS
2	This line and the next are double-spaced.	
3	(one blank line)	DS
4	This line and the next are triple-spaced.	
5	(two blank lines)	TS
6		
7	Set the regulator for correct spacing.	

5. SET THE MARGIN STOPS

Move the **left margin stop (7)** to approximately 25 spaces to the left of the center of the paper. Move the **right margin stop (15)** to the end of the scale. You will type the copy line for line and do not need the right margin stop to indicate the line ending.

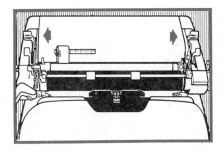

6. TAKE CORRECT TYPING POSITION (as illustrated)

EYES ON COPY

FINGERS CURVED; WRISTS LOW

ELBOWS NEAR THE BODY; FOREARMS PARALLEL TO SLANT OF KEYBOARD

SIT BACK IN CHAIR; BODY ERECT

TEXTBOOK AT RIGHT OF MACHINE, ELEVATED FOR EASY READING

TABLE FREE OF UNNEEDED BOOKS

FEET ON FLOOR, ONE JUST AHEAD OF THE OTHER

¶2
1.6 SI
5.8 AWL
75% HFW

Every human can think. The power to reason, anthropologists tell us, is a distinctive characteristic of man in the kingdom of animals. Although there appears to be little unanimity about why man can think, it seems evident that he does his best job of it when faced with the possibility of making a mistake. In such instances, he feels compelled to "act wisely," to "make a basic decision," to "use good judgment"––in other words, to THINK. The ability to think, therefore, is so valuable to man that he will, ideally speaking, take advantage of any chance to improve his capacity for it, assuming that in so doing he will promote his ability to avoid dangerous and expensive errors that could affect his family, his friends, his city, his employer––and himself.

1'	10'	
13	17	78
27	18	79
42	20	81
55	21	82
70	22	84
84	24	85
99	25	86
113	27	88
127	28	89
141	29	91
153	31	92

¶3
1.6 SI
5.8 AWL
75% HFW

While man has unique ability to apply reason in adapting himself to his surroundings, it does not follow that he actually enjoys making decisions. On the contrary, it will often appear that he actively seeks ways to avoid doing so. He can do this most easily by the formation of habits. As certain acts are repeated, the mind needs fewer directions with each repetition. As a result, many activities can become a matter of simple routine that we can finish successfully without any conscious thought. Any interruption of this routine will, at least momentarily, antagonize us. If, for example, we find someone sitting in a chair in which we are accustomed to sit, we resent seeing anyone else sitting there, even though we are free to sit in any chair we like.

13	32	93
27	33	95
42	35	96
56	36	98
70	38	99
85	39	100
99	41	102
113	42	103
128	43	105
141	45	106
153	46	107

¶4
1.6 SI
5.8 AWL
75% HFW

The act of thinking, of course, is not an end in itself. It needs to be purposeful; that is, it should look for a solution to a problem, explore phenomena, or even provide for our own amusement. In its best form it is a very efficient act. (Merely wondering about things accomplishes little; it is, as one author has put it, a kind of "intellectual vagrancy.") Freed of routine duties, the mind can engage itself in seeking, sorting, and assembling facts; make basic decisions; and plan positive action. It is thus that the act of thinking is elevated to its loftiest plane––the conception of human action based on a well-considered foundation of philosophy. It is man's way of conducting himself and his activities for his own and his neighbor's betterment.

13	47	109
28	49	110
42	50	111
56	52	113
71	53	114
84	54	116
98	56	117
113	57	119
128	59	120
142	60	122
153	61	123

1' GWAM | 1 | 2 | 3 | 4 | 5 | 6 | 7 | 8 | 9 | 10 | 11 | 12 | 13 | 14 |
10' GWAM | 1 | 2 |

225C Production Measurement: Manuscripts ㉚ 25' typing; figure n-pram

Job 1: Unbound Manuscript

Top margin: pica, 1½", elite, 2"; DS; 5-space ¶ indention; type footnotes on page where reference to them is made

Words

NEEDED: CONSUMER EDUCATION   5

(¶1) During 1960, a recent publication[1] has   13
reported, the income for the average Ameri-   22

can family was $6,900 for the year. The same   31
publication predicted the average American   39
family income for 1970 as $11,700, a remark-   48
able increase of almost 70 percent in only 10   57
years. The table below illustrates the year-   66
by-year growth of these income figures: (*SS;*   74
tabulate with spaced leaders)

1B Finger Position

Look at the keyboard shown below and locate **asdf** (*the home keys for the left hand*) and **jkl;** (*the home keys for the right hand*).

Look at your typewriter keyboard and locate the home keys. Place the fingers of your left hand on **asdf** and the fingers of your right hand on **jkl;** with your fingers curved and positioned upright (not slanting or leaning to the outside of the keyboard).

Remove your hands from the keyboard; then place your curved fingers in home position again, holding them *lightly* on the keys. *Repeat two or three times.*

1C Key Stroking and Spacing

For electric typewriters, turn ON-OFF switch to ON position.

Type **f** with the *left first finger*; then type **j** with the *right first finger*. Strike each key with a down motion and with the finger pulled slightly in to the palm of the hand, as illustrated below.

Type **fj** four times: **fjfjfjfj** Next, read how to space after typing a letter or group of letters.

To SPACE after typing a letter or between groups of letters, operate the **space bar (27)** with a quick down-and-in motion of the right thumb.

On the line on which you typed **fj** four times, type **f** (space) **j** (space) five times:

f j f j f j f j f j

Then on the same line, type:

asdf jkl; asdf jkl;

1D Carriage (or Element Carrier) Return

To space the paper forward and return to the beginning of the line, use the **lever (1)** on a non-electric (manual) typewriter or the **key (1)** on an electric one. Locate this part on your typewriter; then make the return as directed and illustrated below.

Nonelectric (Manual). Move the hand, fingers bracing one another, to the carriage return lever and move the lever inward to take up the slack; then return the carriage with a quick wrist and hand motion. Drop the hand to typing position without letting it follow the carriage across.

Electric and Selectric. Reach the little finger of the right hand to the return key, flick the key lightly, release it quickly, and return the finger to its typing position.

On the Selectric the return key returns the element carrier (*not the carriage*) to the left margin.

RETURN the carriage (or carrier). Then, operate the space bar several times and return again.

Job 3: Interoffice Memorandum

		Words
TO:	Emerson E. Erbe, Controller	7
FROM:	James Keene	10
DATE:	April 8, 19--	15
SUBJECT:	Travel Subsistence Expenses	22

(¶ 1) I have made an analysis of the travel 30
expense rates now in use to see how adequate 39
they are for current estimated costs. Several 48
important changes seem advisable. I have 57
listed the new rates below, and I think we 65
ought to put them into effect right away. Do 74
you agree? If not, will you let me have your 84
reasons as soon as possible. (¶ 2) For travel 92
of fewer than 24 hours, except for travel that 101
occurs wholly between 7 a.m. and 7 p.m. in a 110
single day, the following allowances may be 119
authorized: *(Type the following as a centered* 122
heading.)

SUBSISTENCE (OTHER THAN LODGING) 128

(Tabulate in 2 columns, headed Length of Travel
Time *and* Allowance) 141

Over 2 hours but not in excess of 4 hours 150
$2.00 | Over 4 hours but not in excess of 8 158
hours 3.75 | Over 8 hours but not in excess 167
of 12 hours 6.25 | Over 12 hours but not in 175
excess of 24 hours 8.75 180

LODGING 182

(¶ 3) For lodging, actual expenses are to be 190
paid to a maximum of $15.00 for a 24-hour 198
period. (¶ 4) The foregoing rates do not apply 206
to computation of fractional per diem for con- 215
tinuous travel of more than 24 hours. (¶ 5) 223
The per diem rates set forth above are in- 231
tended to be maximum allowances, and no 239
exceptions are to be made. 245

LESSON 225

225A Preparatory Practice (5) *each line at least three times*

Alphabet	An ugly villain quickly jerked the boxes from the dazed widow's grasp.
Figure-symbol	These new mahogany boxes--$8\frac{1}{2}$" x $7\frac{1}{2}$" x $26\frac{1}{4}$"--sell for $45.39, less 10%.
3d, 4th fingers	Phil and Zack quipped as piqued Paula quickened her pace on the piano.
Fluency	Seat yourself when you type so the arms slope down from hand to elbow.

| 1 | 2 | 3 | 4 | 5 | 6 | 7 | 8 | 9 | 10 | 11 | 12 | 13 | 14 |

225B Growth Index (15) *one 10′* control-level *writing; figure* nwam

All letters are used.

¶ 1
1.6 SI
5.8 AWL
75% HFW

Text	GWAM 1′	10′	
In several offices within our city sits a little sign carrying	13	2	63
what is surely a very significant message. The sign says quite simply,	27	3	64
THINK. Busy workers and customers hastily glance at the tiny sign, and	41	4	65
it is interesting to conjecture that maybe it says something just a wee	56	6	67
bit different to every one of them as they read it. To one, for exam-	70	7	68
ple, it might portend that he should exercise greater caution in his	84	8	70
work; to another, it could proffer encouragement to attack a pressing	98	10	71
problem that needs solving; while a third might interpret it as a note	112	11	73
of stimulation toward expanded creativity. That a five-letter word	126	13	74
printed on a sign should, like a tiny, mystical beacon, flash an indi-	140	14	75
vidual message to those who read it, is in itself thought provoking.	153	15	77

1′ GWAM | 1 | 2 | 3 | 4 | 5 | 6 | 7 | 8 | 9 | 10 | 11 | 12 | 13 | 14 |
10′ GWAM | 1 | 2 |

1E Home-Key Stroking Practice

DO: Type the typescript lines below. Single-space (SS) the two lines of copy; double-space (DS) between two-line groups, as shown.

Stroking Cue: Strike each key with a quick, snap stroke and release it immediately; then strike the next key without pausing.

| 1 | f j d k | ff jj ff jj fj fj fj dd kk dd kk dk dk dk fj dk fj | Return without |
| 2 | | ff jj ff jj fj fj fj dd kk dd kk dk dk dk fj dk fj | looking up |

DS (operate the return twice)

| 3 | s l a ; | ss ll ss ll sl sl sl aa ;; aa ;; a; a; a; sl a; sl | |
| 4 | | ss ll ss ll sl sl sl aa ;; aa ;; a; a; a; sl a; sl | |

DS (double-space)

| 5 | Home keys | a; sl a;sl dk fj dkfj a;sl dkfj a;sldk a;sldkfj a; | Space with a |
| 6 | | a; sl a;sl dk fj dkfj a;sl dkfj a;sldk a;sldkfj a; | down-and-in motion |

DS

| 7 | | a as ask ad lad ask lad all fall add lass all fall | |
| 8 | | a as ask ad lad ask lad all fall add lass all fall | |

DS

| 9 | Space once | a lad; ask dad; a lad asks dad; ask all; all fall; | |
| 10 | after ; | a lad; ask dad; a lad asks dad; ask all; all fall; | |

TS (triple-space)

1F Stroking Technique for H and E

1. Locate the new key on the keyboard chart.
2. Locate the new key on the typewriter keyboard.
3. Study the reach illustration for the new key.
4. Type the tryout drill for that key.

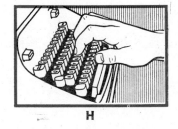

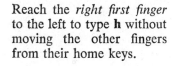

H

E

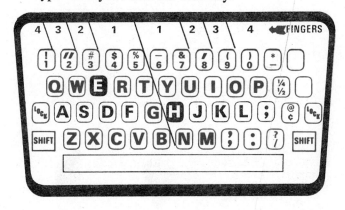

Reach the *right first finger* to the left to type **h** without moving the other fingers from their home keys.

Reach the *left second finger* up to **e**, lifting the first finger slightly to free the controlling finger.

Tryout Drills *type the lines as shown*

| 1 | h | hj has hash lash dash hj half all hall shall shall | Keep thumb close |
| 2 | | hj has hash lash dash hj half all hall shall shall | to the space bar |

DS

| 3 | e | ed led fled sale lake fled ee feel seek keel sleek | |
| 4 | | ed led fled sale lake fled ee feel seek keel sleek | |

DS

| 5 | h e | he led a lad; he has a sled; he seeks a safe deal; | |
| 6 | | he led a lad; he has a sled; he seeks a safe deal; | |

TS (triple-space)

Job 1: Outline in Rough-Draft Form

Top margin: 2″
Line length: pica, 6″; elite, 5″

PARPARING OFFSET MASTERS *(RE / AN / TS)*

I. MAKING *THE* NECESSARY PREPARATIONS
   A. Clean Type Faces, ~~and~~ Feed Rolls *and Platen*
   B. Move Paper Bail Rollers to Extreme End
   C. Use Special ~~Carbon~~ Ribbon
     1. Paper carbon
     2. Plastic carbon
     3. Special fabric "grease" ribbon
   D. ~~4.~~ Use Soft, Clean Eraser
     ① ~~5.~~ Pencil eraser
     ② ~~6.~~ Special offset eraser

II. TYPING THE MASTER
   A. Follow Visible Markings
   B. 1. Guides for 8 and 8½-inch-wide paper
     2. "Warning numbers" for 11 and 14-inch-long paper
   D C. Correct Errors Carefully
     1. ② Light strokes
     2. ③ Smooth surface
     ① ~~3.~~ Clean eraser

B. Type Directly on Master
C. Use Uniform Touch

III. Special Effects

   A. Offset Writing Implements
   B. Letters, Pictures, Signatures
   C. Illuminated Drawing boards

EQUIPMENT FOR

(Total number of words: 141)

Job 2: Proxy

Legal style (p. 323); 2 carbon copies

	Words
PROXY	1
THE MORTON COMPANY OF VIRGINIA	7

(¶ 1) The undersigned hereby appoints 14
TREVOR MOSTELLER and CHARLES ROBEY, 21
or either of them, who shall act, as proxies, 30
with power of substitution and revocation, to 39
vote all shares of Capital Stock of The Morton 49
Company of Virginia registered in the name 57
of the undersigned, at the Annual Meeting of 66
the Stockholders of the Company to be held 75
March 16, 19––, at 10 a.m., and at any adjourn- 84
ment thereof, with all powers the undersigned 93
would possess if personally present: (1) for 102
the election of Directors; and (2) at their 111
discretion, upon such other matters as may 120
properly be brought before the meeting. 128

Dated: February 19, 19–– 133

_____ 141
Signature of Stockholder 146

1G Stroking Technique Practice *type the lines as shown*

SPACING CUE: Space once after ; when it is used as a mark of punctuation.

Stroking Cue: Snap the finger quickly toward the palm of the hand as you release the key.

1	Home keys	ask a lad; a lad asks dad; a fall fad; ask a lass;
2		ask a lad; a lad asks dad; a fall fad; ask a lass;

DS

Return without spacing at end of line

3	h e	she has jade; he has a safe lead; he seeks a deed;
4		she has jade; he has a safe lead; he seeks a deed;

DS

5	All keys	lease a hall; sell all desks; a shelf held a safe;
6		lease a hall; sell all desks; a shelf held a safe;

DS

7		he held a lead; she sells jade; he has had a sale;
8		he held a lead; she sells jade; he has had a sale;

1H Remove the Paper and Center the Carriage

──────── **TO REMOVE THE PAPER** ────────

1. Raise or pull forward the **paper bail (11)**.
2. Operate the **paper-release lever (16)** with your right hand.
3. Remove the paper with your left hand. Return the lever to its position (or leave it in forward position if so directed).

TO CENTER THE CARRIAGE

Depress **right carriage release (18)** and hold it down. *At the same time,* grasp the **right cylinder knob (19)** firmly and move carriage to center.

LESSON 2

2A Get Ready to Type *for each lesson in this section*

1. Move the typewriter so the front of the frame is even with the edge of the desk.
2. Adjust **paper guide (8)** and **paper bail (11)**.
3. Have **paper release (16)** engaged.
4. Set **line-space regulator (5)** on "1" for single spacing (SS).
5. Set the **left margin stop (7)** about 25 spaces to left of center of paper; move the **right margin stop (15)** to end of scale. *Note the numbers on the margin scale or paper-bail scale (11) for stop settings and use these stop settings for this lesson and remaining lessons of this section.*

2B Preparatory Practice *type the lines as shown*

Correct Typing Position: Sit erect; feet on the floor; wrists low and relaxed; fingers curved. (See illustration on page 2.)

Stroking Cue: Begin to type at a slow, even pace. Strike the keys sharply; release them quickly. Hold your eyes on the copy as you type.

1	Home keys	fj dk sl a; fd jk fds jkl fdsa jkl; asdf ;lkj a;sl
2		fj dk sl a; fd jk fds jkl fdsa jkl; asdf ;lkj a;sl

DS

Eyes on copy as you return

3	h e	hj ed he she shed hj ed held hall shall sell shell
4		hj ed he she shed hj ed held hall shall sell shell

DS

5	All keys taught	he fled; she leads; he has a desk; she sells jade;
6		he fled; she leads; he has a desk; she sells jade;

TS

Job 3: Table with Braced Headings (Vertical Rules Omitted)

Reading position

Words

MAJOR OCCUPATION GROUPS, 1964 — 6

COMPARED WITH PROJECTED REQUIREMENTS, 1975 — 15

Major Occupation Group	Percent Distribution 1964	1975	Percent Change 1964-75	Words
				41, 45, 51, 56, 61, 74
Professional and technical	12.2	14.9	54	82
Proprietors and managers	10.6	10.4	23	89
Clerical workers	15.2	14.6	37	95
Sales workers	6.3	6.5	30	101
Craftsmen	12.8	12.8	27	105
Operatives	18.4	16.7	15	110
Laborers (except farm and mine)	5.2	4.2	--*	119
Service workers	13.2	14.1	35	125
Farm workers	6.3	3.9	–21	130
				143

*Less than 3 percent. — 147

LESSON 224

224A Preparatory Practice [5] *each line at least three times*

Alphabet The public was amazed to view the keen dexterity of the quick juggler.

Figure-symbol Is the new rate on our #8904 note for $3,500 (dated May 21) to be $7\frac{1}{4}\%$?

Long words The acceptability of the fiduciary examination will then be appraised.

Fluency We should take pride in our work if we have sincerely done our utmost.

| 1 | 2 | 3 | 4 | 5 | 6 | 7 | 8 | 9 | 10 | 11 | 12 | 13 | 14 |

224B Sentence Guided Writings [10] *two 1′ writings on each sentence with the call of the guide*

		GWAM 15″	12″	10″
1	In both money and friendship, making it may be easier than keeping it.	56	70	84
2	A person who is too old to learn was probably always too old to learn.	56	70	84
3	Clarity in writing is a quality which displays courtesy to the reader.	56	70	84
4	Many times common sense is just the ability to judge what is possible.	56	70	84

| 1 | 2 | 3 | 4 | 5 | 6 | 7 | 8 | 9 | 10 | 11 | 12 | 13 | 14 |

2C Shifting for Capitals: Left Shift Key

LEARN: To type a capital letter controlled by a finger of the right hand, as **H**, depress the **left shift key (28)** with the *left fourth (little) finger* without moving the other fingers from typing position. Hold the shift key down until the key for the capital has been *struck and released*; then release the shift key and return the finger to typing position quickly.

Tryout Drill. Study the illustration; then watch your left hand to see that it does not move out of position as you type **Hal** three times: Hal Hal Hal then type the following lines:

```
Ha Ja Ka La Ha Hal Ja Jake Ka Kahl La Ladd Ha Hall
                                                   DS
La Lake Ka Kale Ja Jade Ha Hale Jeff Leff Les Hess
                                                   TS
```

2D Continuity Practice

DO: Type each line twice, single-spaced (SS); then double-space (DS) before typing the next line. To double-space when the line-space regulator is set for single spacing, operate the return *twice*.

SPACING RULE: Space once after **;** when it is used as a mark of punctuation except that you will make the return without spacing if **;** is the last stroke in the line.

1 All letters taught are used
```
Ha Hale Hall Ja Jake Jeff La Ladd Ka Kale Les Jess
```
Return without looking up

2
```
Hal leads; Jeff led all fall; Hal has a safe lead;
```

3
```
Lee led; Les fled; Jeff had a sale; he sells jade;
```

4 Type on—one key at a time; do not pause or stop
```
Jake feels he has a safe lease; Jeff seeks a deed;
```

5
```
Hal Hall heads all sales; Jake Hess asks less fee;
```

6
```
Les Kade has had a fall sale; he has a sales lead;
```

7
```
Lee held a jade sale; Hal Leeds seeks a safe deal;
```

2E Know Your Typewriter

LEARN: The first line illustrated below and at the right is in *elite* type; the second, in *pica* type. Look at *your* typed lines. Does your typewriter have *pica* type? or *elite* type?

```
12 elite spaces to a horizontal inch
```
```
10 pica spaces to a horizontal inch
```

LEARN: *Center Point,* 50 for elite; 42 for pica.

Tryout Drill. Remove the paper from the machine. Place the left and right edges together. Make a slight crease at the exact center at the top.

```
12 elite spaces to a horizontal inch
```

1		2		3	
1		2		3	

```
10 pica spaces to a horizontal inch
```

Reinsert the paper with the center at 50 for elite type or at 42 for pica type (unless your instructor directs you to use another center point).

Move the paper guide against the left edge of the paper. Check to see that it is in this position at the beginning of each practice period.

223B Communication Aid: Proofreading ⑩ *after correction, four 1' writings*

thomas jefferson once stated that all men are created equal and an	14	82
infant republic rallied around an ideal. his words echo even today how-	28	96
ever anyone can easily see that few men remain equal. many are provided	43	111
with intellectual ability or physical energy and others are given the	57	125
gift of longivity. yet many enjoy none of these.	68	136

| 1 | 2 | 3 | 4 | 5 | 6 | 7 | 8 | 9 | 10 | 11 | 12 | 13 | 14 |

223C Production Measurement: Tabulated Reports ㉟ *30' writing; figure* n-pram

Job 1: Accounting Report with Leaders

Top margin: 2"; DS; 65-space line; 3-space indentions; Dates: Year A, this year; Year B, last year

	Year A	Year B	Words
ACE AERONAUTICS, INCORPORATED			6
Statement of Retained Earnings			12
For the Year Ended June 30, *Year A*			19
	Year A	*Year B*	22
Balance at beginning of period	$12,032,869	$ 7,406,032	35
Net income	5,423,617	5,391,029	48
Less:			49
Stock dividends and splits		(759,537)	59
Cost of treasury stock retired		(5,646)	68
Cash retained by predecessor company			93
to pay dissolution expenses	(649,998)		106
Balance at end of period	$16,806,488	$12,031,878	117

Job 2: Ruled Table

Reading position

Year	Number of Units	Value	Words
AUTOMOBILE FACTORY SALES[1]			5
Wholesale Values[2]			9
			31
			32
			36
			48
1900	4,192	$ 4,899,443	54
1910	181,000	215,340,000	60
1920	1,905,560	1,809,170,963	66
1930	2,787,456	1,644,083,152	72
1940	3,717,385	2,370,654,083	79
1950	6,665,863	8,468,137,000	85
1960	6,674,796	12,164,234,000	91
1970[3]	7,678,015	13,988,869,000	97
			108

[1] Table includes sales of military vehicles.   117

[2] Federal excise taxes excluded in all years.   127

[3] Estimated.   129

3A Get Ready to Type [5]*

Review Get Ready to Type, page 5:

1. Align machine with edge of desk.
2. Adjust paper guide.
3. Insert paper; adjust paper bail.
4. Set machine for SS (on "1").
5. Set margin stops at the numbers noted on the scale when you set machine for 2B, page 5 (25 spaces to left of center and at the end of the scale).

*A time schedule for the parts of this lesson and following ones is given as a guide for your minimum practice. If time permits, retype selected lines from various drills.

3B Preparatory Practice [7] *each line twice*

DO: Type the first line twice SS (single-spaced); DS (double-space), then type the next line twice; DS and type the final line twice.

Stroking Cue: Type with a light, quick motion and with the finger pulled slightly toward the palm of the hand as the key is released.

a; sl a;sl fj dk fjdk ed hj edhj Ha Ja Ka La Ha He — **Return quickly**

he she held all hall jell sell dell heed feel seek

Space once after ; — Hal fell; Lee led all; Jeff Hall held a fall sale;

3C Stroking Technique for I and T [10] *each line twice SS; DS after second typing of line*

I

Reach the *right second finger* up to **i**; lift the first finger slightly for improved stroking control.

T

Straighten the *left first finger* slightly and reach up to **t** without arching the wrist or moving the hand forward.

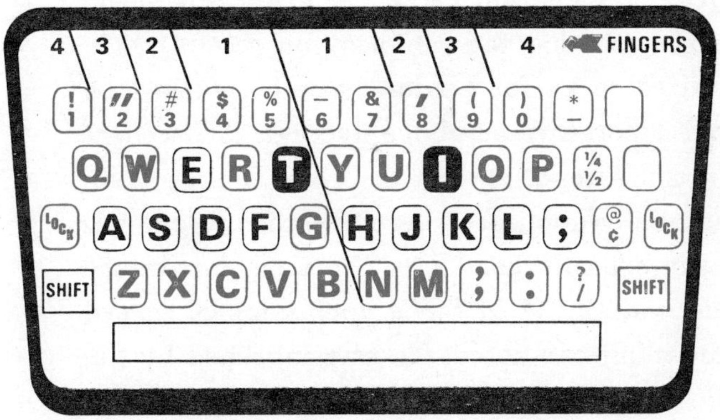

Curved Fingers. Keep the fingers curved and in home-key position except when a reach-stroke is to be made; then extend the controlling finger (relaxing the curvature only as much as you must to reach to the key). Make the reach-stroke without moving the hand forward or downward. Let the fingers do the typing!

Tryout Drills

i — k i ik if is his did side like life fill said file

t — f t tf at let set the tell take tale last that ate

i t — i t it fit its this list still; if it is; if I did

All reach-strokes taught are used — I had a list; Keith has left his list at the lake;

Job 2: Letter on Executive-Size Stationery (7¼″ x 10½″)

Modified block style; 1″ margins; open punctuation; indented ¶s

Words

october 14, 19–– mr p h dorrance president 9
brass belt manufacturing company 5600 17
diversey parkway chicago il 60639 dear mr 26
dorrance (¶ 1) I am pleased to report that 33
our company has purchased for cash all the 42
outstanding stock of United Electronics and 51
its subsidiary, Miracle Corporation of Amer- 59
ica. The two companies are engaged primarily 69
in the manufacture and sale of electronic com- 78
puters for industrial and scientific applications. 88
(¶ 2) These two companies have been operat- 95
ing profitably under the leadership of S. J. 104
Stahlsmith, who has agreed to continue to act 113
in this capacity. In addition, he will be in 123
charge of our growing foreign business for 131
computers and dictating equipment. (¶ 3) In 139
addition to our other services, therefore, we 148
can now work with you on your special cal- 156
culator problems. H. E. Leavenworth, who 165
has consulted with you in the past, will be in 174
touch with you soon to explain how you may 183
take advantage of our expanded services. 191
sincerely yours v lloyd smith vice president 200
in charge of sales 205/225

Job 3: Government Letter (Pages 339-340)

Words

may 22 19–– in reply refer to: LB-X-398 8
your reference: samples 87-B-3 mrs tommie 17
r johnson president randolph–hall woolen mills 27
inc 2014 hawthorne street brockton ma 02401 37
dear mrs johnson (¶ 1) We are happy to in- 44
form you that the samples you recently sub- 53
mitted to us for testing have been rated by 61
our laboratory as above average to excellent 70
in all categories tested. Our findings sub- 79
stantially duplicate, therefore, the preliminary 89
examinations conducted in your laboratory 97
last month. (¶ 2) Since your samples exceed 105
the minimum standards as established by the 114
Government Testing Bureau, we are now pre- 122
pared to discuss with you terms for the pur- 131
chase of approximately twenty-five thousand 139
yards of woolen fabric similar to the samples 149
you submitted. Mr. Sydney Shoemaker, of 157
our Boston office, will contact you soon to 166
discuss with you our specific requirements in 175
terms of bolt widths, colors, dates of delivery, 185
and so forth. (¶ 3) We hope that you and 192
Mr. Shoemaker will be able to arrive at terms 201
mutually satisfactory and that contract terms 210
can be completed shortly. sincerely yours 219
j p callahan superintendent, department of ac- 229
quisitions cc: Boston office LBeebe:(*your* 237
initials) 5-22––– 238

LESSON 223

223A Preparatory Practice [5] *each line at least three times*

Alphabet	Vince and Fay Baxter may work quite long to adjust the puzzling claim.
Figure-symbol	The United States Customs' gross receipts were $2,113,475,000 in 1968.
Direct reaches	My Uncle Bert graded the verses and sent only the best one to Harvard.
Fluency	Burning the midnight oil doesn't help much if it is burned in the car.
	| 1 | 2 | 3 | 4 | 5 | 6 | 7 | 8 | 9 | 10 | 11 | 12 | 13 | 14 |

3D Stroking Technique for C and . (Period) ⑩

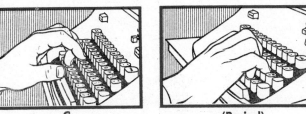

C

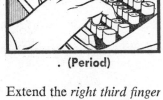

. (Period)

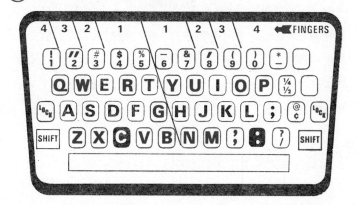

Reach down to c with the *left second finger* without twisting the elbow in or out or moving the hand down.

Extend the *right third finger* down to type . (period) without moving the hand downward or the elbow outward.

SPACING RULE: Space once after . (period) used at the end of an abbreviation; twice after . at the end of a sentence, except when it is the last stroke in the line; then return without spacing.

Tryout Drills

c	d c dcd cd cash call case lack deck each face sick
.	l . l.l .l adj. del. La. Ill. Lt. Jeff set a date.
c .	Jack called. He is sick. Lt. Heck has his check.
Review	Keith has cashed the checks. Jack is at his desk.

3E Continuity Practice ⑱   *each line twice SS; DS after second typing of line*

Home-Row Stroking: Strike each key firmly, release it quickly, and pull the finger toward the palm of the hand.

Third-Row Stroking: Reach to the third row (just above home row) with the finger without arching the wrist or moving the hand forward.

First-Row Stroking: Make the reach to the first (bottom) row without swinging the elbow out or changing the hand alignment.

All keyboard characters taught are used.

1	h and e	he she shed shelf heads shall fee feed feeds feels	Return without pausing
2	i and t	it is; he hit it; he is still ill; take this list;	
3	c and .	all call cash check chief cite each adj. etc. Ill.	
4	All letters taught are in Lines 4-8	I shall take the deed. I see Jack lists the cash.	
5		I see Keith is at his desk. Kit has a shelf safe.	
6		Let Jack take the file. He has set the lease fee.	
7		Kit Hale has a late date. Jeff has the last list.	
8		Lt. Keith said he cashed the checks that Kit left.	

TS

LESSON 222

222A Preparatory Practice [5] *each line at least three times*

Alphabet	Sixteen bags of quartz mix proved just enough to cover my garden walk.
Figure-symbol	Dane & Clark (479 Elm Drive) can't pay their $528.36 bill on March 10.
Long words	An experienced measurement consultant gave us a conservative estimate.
Fluency	The mind gets rusty with disuse; you can keep it sharp with new ideas.

| 1 | 2 | 3 | 4 | 5 | 6 | 7 | 8 | 9 | 10 | 11 | 12 | 13 | 14 |

222B Building Control [10] *three 2' writings on the* control level; *figure* nwam

65-space line
Listen for the bell

1.8 SI
6.0 AWL
70% HFW

All letters are used.

2' GWAM

Old philosophers, manipulating wispy chin whiskers with 6
bony fingers, tell us there is nothing upon which we can de- 12
pend for any continuity whatever except death and taxes. 18
Their admonition is ~~like~~ certainly a pessimistic, melancholy ~~lament~~ idea; 24
but perhaps they are ~~really~~ actually making us try to ~~believe that~~ realize we 30
should not be cajoled into ~~thinking~~ believing that in one of life's in- 38
numerable ruts, we can find security the kind so many people 42
appear to consider ~~to be~~ ideal habitats. Nothing is change- 47
less, they tell us, unless we allow our rut to fill up with 53
the mental quicksand of indifference. The equation "change 59
equals variety" emits the kind of wisdom we don't need any 65
whiskers to appreciate—for variety is truly the spice of life! 72

222C Production Measurement: Business Letters [35] *30' writing; figure* n-pram

Job 1: Average-Length Letter

Block style; mixed punctuation
Attention Sales Manager
Subject: Improving Your Company's Efficiency

Words

april 29 19-- heath-lyons corporation 3849 9
grove park drive durham nc 27705 gentlemen 18
(¶ 1) Here's a way to get better reports from 26
your field men--and in half the time it now 35
takes them to prepare these reports. Put a 44
Bell Dictator in their hands. Let them talk 53
their written work to you. You will be aston- 62
ished at how prompt and detailed their reports 71
will be. (¶ 2) The Bell Dictator is made espe- 79
cially for men in the field. It is light, compact, 90
sturdy. The cost--just a few cents a day. 98
Take your choice from the three models listed 108
below: (*tabulate in 3 columns*) Model J-115 111
Battery powered $360 | Model J-225 Elec- 117
tric powered $380 | Model J-335 Battery or 127
electric $420 (¶ 3) Just return the enclosed 135
card. See how you can get field reports that 144
talk. No obligation is intended, of course. 153
sincerely yours marlin c early advertising 162
manager 166/179

• Self-Improvement Practice

DO: Type the first line twice SS; then DS and type the next lines in the same way.

Return Cue: Return without spacing after the last stroke in the line; begin next line immediately.

1 he she the aid did is his it hit let jet tile till

2 as has led lead head each teach at ate hate checks

3 face late last desk sees fate heed seed this scale

4 last all fall ice side less fit add like fell tell

5 case call fill life list still skid had field felt

6 fill the case; he let it fall; each has had a desk

LESSON 4

4A Get Ready to Type [5]

Follow steps in Get Ready to Type, page 5. Center the paper; set the left margin stop 25 spaces to the left of the center of the paper for the beginning of a 50-space line; move right stop to end of scale.

4B Preparatory Practice [7] *each line twice SS; DS after second typing of line*

All letters taught are used

a;sl edhj tfik cd.l it fits he she sick deck still

Jeff called; Lee is ill. Jed cashed these checks. — Space quickly

I shall take the case. I see Jeff heads the list.

4C Stroking Technique Practice [15] *each line twice SS; DS after second typing of line*

First-Row Stroking: When typing a key in the first (lowest) row, make a direct finger reach without swinging the elbow out or changing the hand alignment with the keyboard.

Third-Row Stroking: When typing a key in the third (third from bottom) row, reach with the finger without arching the wrist or moving the hand forward. Snap the finger toward the palm of the hand.

All letters taught are used.

1 Curve your fingers — he flies a jet; he feels ill; she had aid; he held — Eyes on copy as you return

2 Strike and release quickly — cite the date; he leads the class; face this side;

3 it sticks; if she dials it; the chief has the file

4 Kit takes the checks; Jake seeks a safe cash deal.

5 Shift firmly — Jeff called it a chief skill; Keith has the facts.

6 Jack called. I had his list. Kit cashed a check.

7 Lee said Lt. Hill left the chief file at his desk.

considerably since the completion of the 146
new Reading General Hospital with 175 154
beds. The hospital is up to date in every 162
respect and is being efficiently managed by a 172
responsible, well-qualified board of medical 181
men. (¶ 4) My own practice has been grow- 188
ing steadily, to the point where I can no 196
longer give the time I wish to my research 205
and writing. To give you an idea of the finan- 214
cial picture of my practice, I am enclosing my 223
financial statement of last year. You will note 233
on the Statement of Financial Condition that 242
no value has been assigned to intangible 250
assets, so the statement is definitely on the 259
conservative side. I should mention, too, that 269
my office was closed for six weeks last year 278
while I was attending medical meetings at the 287
Universities of Rome and Bologna in Italy 296
and the University of Freiburg in West Ger- 304
many. (¶ 5) Although all aspects of the move 312
must be considered, I am sure that we could 321
come to an agreement on either a partnership 330
or a sharing-of-quarters basis should you de- 339
cide to return. If you like, I could stop in 348
Tacoma on my way to San Francisco to talk 356
with you personally about your coming to 364
Reading. I plan to make that trip on June 2 373
or 3. If you think such a conference would be 383
helpful, please write. (¶ 6) Turning to an- 390
other matter, I have been asked to prepare 399
and read a paper on automation in medicine 407
at the national convention in San Francisco 416
on June 6. As you have done some research 425
in this area, would you be good enough to 433
look over my tentative outline, which I am 442
enclosing. Please make any suggestions and 451
comments you feel are pertinent. If you know 460
of any recent articles in either lay or profes- 461
sional journals that you think might be useful, 479
please let me know about them. sincerely 487
yours t e sims m d 494/511

Job 2: Average-Length Letter

*Modified block style; blocked
¶s; mixed punctuation*

Words

november 23 19–– mr david r goodman vice 9
president hamilton–grantham manufacturing 17
company 5756 chesapeake road camden nj 26
08104 dear mr goodman (¶ 1) The Rapid 33

System 80 provides a radically new approach 41
to the automation of information handling 50
and control. Its one-second-selection capability 60
multiplies both the accessibility and the value 69
of records that are vital to your operations. 79
(¶ 2) The amazing ability of the new Rapid 86
System 80 to search by multiple characteris- 95
tics, either one at a time or in combination, 104
enables you to analyze and to control your 112
records with unprecedented ease and sophisti- 121
cation. (¶ 3) The Rapid System 80 builds on 129
a random-storage concept that eliminates re- 138
filing in the conventional sense. Misfiling 147
becomes a thing of the past, along with frus- 155
trating and unproductive searches for "lost 164
records." (¶ 4) At modest cost and with 171
techniques so simple and straightforward that 180
they can be learned in half a day, the Rapid 189
System 80 is a versatile, general-purpose man- 198
agement tool that may change your entire 207
way of thinking about data processing. (¶ 5) 215
The enclosed brochure describes some of the 223
highlights of the Rapid System 80. In half an 233
hour we can tell you enough about this can-do 242
business machine for you to appraise fully its 251
potential for your business. May we have that 261
opportunity? sincerely yours c e calhoun 270
branch manager 275/298

Job 3: Short Letter to Be Corrected

*Modified block style; indented ¶s; mixed
punctuation; capitalize and punctuate*

Words

september 6 19–– mr cleos s lucien manager 9
adelphi company 700 parkway drive hicksville 19
ny 11803 dear mr lucien (¶ 1) your letter re- 27
questing information about our new model 35
kj-90 electronic calculator came this morning. 45
we are pleased to learn of your interest in our 54
equipment. (¶ 2) our representative mr clif- 62
ford nivens will be in hicksville next tuesday 72
afternoon and can call at your office at 1 pm 82
to demonstrate this amazing calculator for 90
you. he will be happy to answer at that time 99
the questions you ask in your letter. (¶ 3) if 108
however you would prefer an appointment at 117
a different time please telephone me collect 126
of course and we can arrange an appointment 135
at a more suitable time. sincerely yours met- 145
ropolitan calculators alice brady manager 154/170

4D Shifting for Capitals: Right Shift Key ⑧

LEARN: To type a capital letter controlled by a finger of the left hand, as **A**, depress the **right shift key (26)** with the *right fourth (little) finger*. Hold the shift key down until the key for the capital has been *struck and released*; then release the shift key and return the finger to typing position without pausing.

Tryout Drill. Study the illustration. Watch your right hand to see that it does not move out of position as you type **Alf** three times: Alf Alf Alf then type the following lines twice each:

```
Al Sl Al Diehl Di Fl Dick Flack El Taft Ceil Slade
                                                   DS
Alf has the list.  Seth is sick.  Cal called Dick.
```

4E Continuity Practice ⑮ *each line twice SS; DS after second typing of line*

Continuity Cue: Begin to type at a slow, even pace. Increase your stroking rate gradually. Move from one letter to the next without pausing.

Shift-Key Cue: Hold the shift key down firmly until the capital letter is typed; then release the shift key and return the finger to home position.

All reach-strokes taught are used.

1	he held the dial; file each lease; date this side;	Hold the wrists low
2	a fast field; he cites the fact; Dee fits it least	
3	if I see; she had a safe lead; Ed heads his class;	
4	The staff sheet is late; Dick still takes the cash	
5 Shift firmly	Jack steals the last act. I shall tell his staff.	
6	Ceil has a check. Kit said it. Jeff flies a jet.	

● Self-Improvement Practice *each line twice SS; DS after second typing of line*

Stroking Cue: Type with easy, rhythmic stroking. Move from letter to letter without pausing between strokes.

Space-Bar Cue: Operate the space bar with a short, quick, down-and-in thumb stroke in rhythm with the typing without pausing between words.

All letters taught are used.

1 Relax—but don't slouch	Dick held a jade sale at Delf Lake late last fall.
2	Cliff asked Seth if he had set the last test date.
3	This is the file case that Cal let Lee Leith take.
4	Fae Dahl said Jack has left the test at Lake Heid.
5	Jack has the file that Cal said he left last fall.

SECTION 34 MEASUREMENT: Basic and Production Skills

LESSONS 221–225

Each lesson of Section 34 provides for 25 to 30 minutes of timed production typing. If you complete all jobs in a lesson before time is called, begin the first job again. Approximately 5 minutes will be allowed at the end of the period to figure *n-pram*.

Drill Copy: Full sheet; 70-space line; SS.

Paragraph Copy: Full sheet; 70-space line; DS; 5-space ¶ indention.

Production Copy: 1 carbon copy of all jobs unless more are specified. For letters, use your reference initials; type enclosure notations where appropriate; and address any envelopes required.

Special Supplies Needed: Letterheads or full sheets; executive-size and Government-size letterheads; interoffice memorandums; legal cap; envelopes of appropriate size.

LESSON 221

221A Preparatory Practice (5) *each line at least three times*

Alphabet	Peggy and Zola Mobray requested an extra week for their July vacation.
Figure-symbol	Ted Lee's note (plus 6½% interest), due May 19, amounts to $25,734.80.
Left hand	After the wet December weather, Eve's crabgrass grew excessively fast.
Fluency	Orderliness of ideas must be habitual if we want to achieve our goals.

| 1 | 2 | 3 | 4 | 5 | 6 | 7 | 8 | 9 | 10 | 11 | 12 | 13 | 14 |

221B Building Speed and Control (10) *four 1′ writings on the* exploration level*; then four 1′ writings on the* control level

1.8 SI
6.0 AWL
70% HFW

1′ GWAM

The success of a letter may depend upon your attitude as its writer. 14
Travel via the letter and introduce yourself to its recipient. Talk to 28
him in a natural way; avoid any stuffy rhetoric or quaint phrases. Try 43
to influence--but not necessarily to impress--him. An attractively 56
worded letter can develop sizeable profits; and a winning personality, 71
as exhibited by words you have chosen, can develop even bigger ones. 84

| 1 | 2 | 3 | 4 | 5 | 6 | 7 | 8 | 9 | 10 | 11 | 12 | 13 | 14 |

221C Production Measurement: Business Letters (35) *30′ writing; figure* n-pram

Job 1: Two-Page Letter

Block style; open punctuation

Words

march 15 19-- dr charles r mccallister tacoma 10
medical building 514 sunrise lane tacoma wa 19
98466 dear dr mccallister (¶ 1) Thank you for 27
your letter regarding your proposed return to 36
Reading to resume your practice here. When 45
David Morrow, representative of the Devens 54
Pharmaceutical Company, told me that you 62
were interested in returning, I immediately 71
hoped that you would decide to relocate in 79
this area. (¶ 2) As you probably know, our 87
immediate region has experienced a remarkable growth, with many upper-middle-income 95
104
families moving to this area as well as a great 113
number of workers and their families who 121
were brought in by the new industrial activity. (¶ 3) Hospital conditions have improved 130
138

LESSON 5

5A Get Ready to Type ③ *use standard procedure, page 5*

5B Know Your Typewriter ②

LEARN: The **ribbon-control lever (22)** can be set to type on the upper, middle, or lower part of the ribbon if there are four adjustments on the typewriter for this control. If there are just three adjustments, the typing will be on the upper or lower part of the ribbon. When the lever is set in stencil position, the ribbon is disengaged. This position is used to type stencils.

DO: Set the ribbon-control lever to type on the upper part of the ribbon.

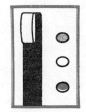

5C Preparatory Practice ⑦ *each line twice SS; DS after second typing of line*

DO: As you type the line the first time, note the awkward or difficult letter combinations. In the next writing of the line, try to smooth out the typing pace so you can type with continuity. Type a letter; turn loose of it; and type the next letter. Get rid of typing jerks or pauses; just keep on typing.

All letters taught are used in each line.

if it is; she called; Cliff sells jade; I like it.   Eyes on copy

Cal let Lee take all the jade; he is at Fell Lake.

Dick said that Cliff let Jack Hill take the files.

5D Stroking Technique for O and R ⑩ *each line twice SS; DS after second typing of line*

O

R

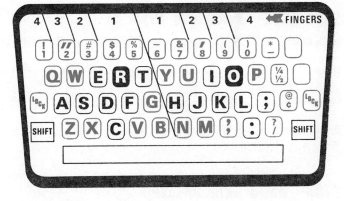

Reach the *right third finger* up to type **o** without moving the hand forward or the elbow outward.

Reach the *left first finger* to **r** without moving the other fingers from home-key positions.

Tryout Drills

o   l o lol so do to old sold fold told cold took look

r   f r frf air far sir are car cars heard clear chair

o r   or for cord road rock role frock force chord floor

Review Carl Ford left the horse for Dr. Rod Cole to ride.

LESSON 5   **Section 1: Letter Keys**   11

218D Production Skill Checkup [30]

Make a list of the jobs identified at the right which are to be typed in this lesson and in Lessons 219 and 220. Type as many jobs as you can in the time provided for each. When time is called, complete the line on which you are typing so that you can begin on a new line the next day. Make neat corrections and strive for neat, attractive copy.

When you have completed Lesson 220, type your name and the job and page number in the upper right corner of each job. Arrange the jobs in page-number order and fasten them in the upper left corner.

Page	Lesson Part	Job
271-272	157C	2
273	158D	3
288	168C	2
297-298	174C	2
309	181C	2
311	182C	2
327	190-191C	7
329	192-193C	1
339-340	199C	1
355	207-210D	6

LESSONS 219-220

219A-220A Preparatory Practice [5] *each line at least three times*

Alphabet	Jack Quinn used the exit from the Aztec Travel Agency to Bronson Park.
Figures	Reproduce 150 copies of page 49, 340 of page 268, and 570 of page 296.
Figure-symbol	The final cost of labor on Job #935 was $1,480.75 (26% of total cost).
Fluency	It is the duty of each individual in the firm to do the work assigned.
	| 1 | 2 | 3 | 4 | 5 | 6 | 7 | 8 | 9 | 10 | 11 | 12 | 13 | 14 |

219B-220B Technique Practice [8] *each line at least four times*

Double letters	I am sorry we cannot meet with the officials in Mississippi this week.
Stroke	Independent corporations immediately created additional conglomerates.
Combination	The regulation of television is of particular importance to all of us.
Word response	The five men met in the city to set the tax rate to pay off the bonds.
	| 1 | 2 | 3 | 4 | 5 | 6 | 7 | 8 | 9 | 10 | 11 | 12 | 13 | 14 |

219C Basic Skill Checkup [7]

Type three 1′ *exploration-level* writings on each ¶ of 218C, page 369. Figure *gwam.*

220C Basic Skill Checkup [7]

Type a 5′ *control-level* writing on 218C, page 369. Figure *nwam.* Compare score with that of the previous writing.

219D Production Skill Checkup [30]

Continue typing the jobs listed in 218D above. Unless instructed otherwise, retain all jobs until you have completed Lesson 220.

220D Production Skill Checkup [30]

Continue typing the jobs listed in 218D above. Unless instructed otherwise, retain all jobs until you have completed this lesson.

5E Stroking Technique for Z and N ⑩ *each line twice SS; DS after second typing of line*

Z

N

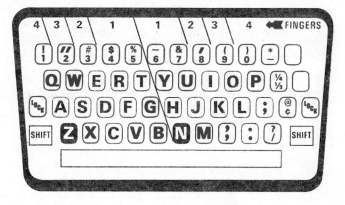

Reach the *left little finger* down to type **z** without moving the hand down or the elbow in or out.

Move the *right first finger* down to type **n** without moving the other fingers from their home keys.

SPACING SUMMARY: Space once after . (period) used at the end of an abbreviation; do not space after . within an abbreviation; space twice after . used to punctuate a sentence; and once after ; (semicolon) used as punctuation. At the end of the line, make the return without spacing after the final stroke whether this is a mark of punctuation or a letter.

Tryout Drills

z   a z aza za zeal haze size daze jazz raze doz. doze

n   j n jnj an can and hand not note once think chance

z n   Zoe has lots of zeal and zest; this drill is done.

Review   Dr. Nietz is in this first zone. The zoo is near.

5F Continuity Practice ⑱ *each line twice SS; DS after second typing of line*

Continuity Cue: Type at a steady pace without pausing between strokes, words, or lines.

Stroking Cue: Type with your fingers and with minimum hand or arm motion. Use snappy strokes.

All reach-strokes taught are used.

1   to do so; of the code; took a loss; food does cost

2   it is hers; take her car; it is fair; if there are

3   the food fair is here; their stock is off; too far

4   it is here to do; take her to the fair; do so here

5   an old hand; a size ten; in the end zone; seize it

6   The hard freeze forced the school to close at ten.

7   Roz and Liz think this last act has a fine chance.

8   Zahn had it sent there C.O.D. Jake left at three.

SECTION 33 BASIC AND PRODUCTION SKILLS CHECKUP

LESSONS 218–220

Drill Copy: Full sheet; 70-space line; SS.

Paragraph Copy: Full sheet; 70-space line; DS; 5-space ¶ indention.

Production Typing: When complete directions are not given, use your own judgment. Use the style of letter and punctuation you desire. Correct all errors. Make carbon copies as directed.

Special Supplies Needed: Letterheads, interoffice form, legal cap, appropriate envelopes.

LESSON 218

218A Preparatory Practice (5) *each line at least three times*

Alphabet	My job is to help answer questions and advise Z. K. Cage on tax forms.
Figures	The data you want can be found on pages 9, 60, 137, 152, 184, and 208.
Figure-symbol	The article, "Take 10%," will be found in Our Modern Taxes (page 316).
Fluency	They told both of us to send the original form to the downtown office.
	| 1 | 2 | 3 | 4 | 5 | 6 | 7 | 8 | 9 | 10 | 11 | 12 | 13 | 14 |

218B Technique Practice (8) *each line at least four times*

Direct reaches	She urged Becky to bring her serving tray for the center of the table.
Left hand	After a date was set for the meeting, a secretary addressed the cards.
Right hand	It is my opinion, not our policy, that we must limit our oil supplies.
Balanced hand	If they qualify, special aid may be given to the citizens of the city.
	| 1 | 2 | 3 | 4 | 5 | 6 | 7 | 8 | 9 | 10 | 11 | 12 | 13 | 14 |

218C Basic Skill Checkup (7) *one 5′* control-level *writing; figure* nwam

All letters are used.

		GWAM 1′	5′	
¶ 1	The major goal of an assistant to an executive is to free the boss	13	3	40
1.6 SI	of as many details as possible. Aside from the usual tasks of greeting	28	6	43
5.8 AWL	callers, using the telephone, and processing papers, this can be done	42	8	46
75% HFW	in many ways. An assistant can save his boss time by gathering data,	56	11	49
	preparing itineraries, arranging for meetings, scheduling the work of	70	14	52
	the office, and composing routine letters. In some cases, the tasks	84	17	54
	an assistant can do are limited only by his ability.	94	19	57
¶ 2	An assistant to an executive must be very well educated. He must	13	21	59
1.6 SI	have an insight of how business operates in general and possess special	28	24	62
5.8 AWL	knowledge of the firm for which he works. Technical ability is vital,	42	27	65
75% HFW	of course, but all executives emphasize the fact that personal traits	56	30	68
	are of equal value. Among the traits that are listed most often are a	70	33	71
	pleasant voice and manner, tact, poise, and initiative. Above all,	84	36	73
	though, an assistant must be loyal as well as discreet.	95	38	75
1′ GWAM	| 1 | 2 | 3 | 4 | 5 | 6 | 7 | 8 | 9 | 10 | 11 | 12 | 13 | 14 |			
5′ GWAM	| 1 | 2 | 3 |			

TYPING DOUBLE LETTERS / Nonelectric: Use a short, quick stroke. Do not allow full return of the key between strokes. **Electric:** Allow time for the key to return to position before striking it again.

TYPING ONE-HAND WORDS: Type by stroke response (one letter at a time) but pass from one letter to the next quickly. Speed up the typing by eliminating the pauses between strokes.

All letters taught are used.

1	Double letters	soon took fool tool root cook door cool noon floor
2	One-hand, double-letter words	see seed ill hill feed kill tree hook freed street
3	One-hand words	in as no at on are oil far kin set nil car ink add
4	Drill on z	zest size zone haze zinc raze daze fizz jazz sized
5	Drill on o and n	to do on no nor not note ton tone in kind one torn

LESSON 6

6A   Get Ready to Type ③ *use standard procedure, page 5*

6B   Preparatory Practice ⑦ *each line twice SS; DS after second typing of line*

All reaches taught are used.

Liz called; Ron heard her.   Ed thinks Jan is fine.

in it; as on; to do so; can find; Roz can find it;

o r n

Fritz and Frank North do not like to ride at noon.

6C   Stroking Technique Practice ⑮ *twice as shown*

Lines 1–2. Adjacent-key controls, such as **tr, oi, re,** and the like, need special attention. *Think* each letter vigorously.

Lines 3–4. Make a direct reach from **c** to **e, e** to **c,** and the like, without returning the controlling finger to home position.

Lines 5–6. Use a short, quick stroke. Center the stroking action in the fingers. Do not pause between strokes or between words.

All reach-strokes taught are used.

1	Adjacent	has said are her soil coil short trade heads sales
2	keys	Kier has a fine tire on sale; it has a safe tread.
		`DS
3	Direct	once force checks led deal lot old sold kits likes
4	reaches	Zach liked all the desks. Ceil checked each once.
5	Double	off add look fall need less staff loss steel skill
6	letters	He took a loss on the steel desk and lost the fee.
7	Speed-up	if it is he to do so or for the tie did then field
8	words	Jan lent a hand to Ken. Rod did it for Sid Field.

*For Year A, type this year;
for Year B, type last year*

Job 1: Financial Highlights of a Company

				Words
INTERNATIONAL MANUFACTURING COMPANY				7
Financial Highlights for the Year Ended December 31				18
	Year A	*Year B*	Increase	26
Sales	$66,170,213	$53,140,754	24.5%	33
Net income	8,582,730	6,731,465	27.5	41
Dividends paid	1,918,290	1,374,290	39.6	50
Total assets	55,987,597	45,105,400	24.1	58
Shareholders' equity	35,995,463	29,211,981	23.2	68
Per common share:				72
Net income	3.36	2.64		79
Dividends paid	.75	.54		87
Book value	14.08	11.45		94
Number of shareholders: *Year A*, 3,203; *Year B*, 2,432			31.7	105
Number of employees: *Year A*, 3,162; *Year B*, 2,996			5.5	114

Job 2: Model Letter for Stencil Duplication

Words

February 15, 19-- TO OUR SHAREHOLDERS: (¶1) This has been a banner year for our company! (¶2) Our performance again demonstrated the strength which results from our company's great diversity of markets and our continuous program of developing new products. (¶3) For the second consecutive year, the volume of our sales increased substantially, reaching a record total of $66,170,213. This 25 percent increase over last year came principally from continued growth and diversification in practically all product lines. (¶4) During the year, we added five enterprises of varying size in our merger and acquisition program. Each of these was selected with a view to broadening the base of our company's earnings while offsetting cyclical trends in some of the traditional industries we serve. (¶5) We are entering the new year with improved business conditions in most of the industries we serve, and we look forward to considerable improvement in both sales and earnings for the current year. We believe that through aggressive cost controls and the use of new automated equipment, we can continue to im- 8 15 23 32 41 49 57 65 75 84 93 102 111 120 129 138 148 156 165 174 183 191 200 209 217

prove our financial picture this year and in the years ahead. (¶6) We wish to express our appreciation to our stockholders, our employees, our suppliers, and our customers for their cooperation, support, and counsel during this exciting year. FOR THE BOARD OF DIRECTORS: C. Stephen Cunningham President 227 234 243 253 262 269 277

Job 3: Interoffice Memorandum

Words

TO: C. P. Snow, Director of Operations FROM: E. L. Stitt, President DATE: September 19, 19-- SUBJECT: Computerization of Procedures (¶1) The continued growth of the company has placed demands upon our administrative systems which can no longer be met. A preliminary report indicates that the computerization of certain procedures will solve the problem economically. (¶2) A meeting will be held in my office at 2 p.m., September 26, to discuss a long-range program to create new production and inventory control systems using computers. This program will parallel a similar program to use computers in processing customers' orders. (¶3) Please be prepared to discuss this matter in detail on September 26. 7 12 19 26 34 43 52 61 69 78 87 97 105 113 122 131 134

6D Sentence Guided Writing (25)

DO: Type each sentence three times without the guide. Increase the speed of stroking slightly when typing the sentence the second and third times.

DO: Type each sentence for a half minute. Pace your typing to complete the sentence in exactly a half minute (with the guide).

DO: Type each sentence as a 1' writing, trying to type the sentence twice. Your gross words a minute (*gwam*) are shown in Column 2 below.

Position Cue	Sit erect; feet on floor; fingers curved; wrists low.

Shift-Key Cue	Depress and hold shift key down firmly until capital letter has been typed.

All reach-strokes taught are used.

		Words in Line*	GWAM 30" Guide
1	Joe thinks I can do the drill.	6	12
2	Keith has laid all the tile he can.	7	14
3	Al can lend a hand to all those in need.	8	16
4	Zoe can teach Rod to dance; she said she can.	9	18
5	Ken has done one line of the drill for his friend.	10	20

| 1 | 2 | 3 | 4 | 5 | 6 | 7 | 8 | 9 | 10 |

---

*HOW TYPEWRITTEN WORDS ARE COUNTED

Five strokes are counted as one standard typewritten word. The figures in the first column at the right of the copy show the number of 5-stroke words in each of the lines. The scale beneath the copy shows the word-by-word count (5 strokes at a time) for each of the lines.

TO DETERMINE TOTAL WORDS TYPED

(1) List the figure at the end of each complete line typed during a writing. **(2)** Note in the scale the figure directly below the point at which you stopped typing. **(3)** Add these figures to determine the total gross words typed. (Gross words are the same as *gwam* for a 1-minute writing.)

● **Self-Improvement Practice**   *two or three times as shown*

All letters taught are used.

1	j and z	jet zinc jest zoo jazz join jade jot zeal oz. doz.
2		Zeke joins their jet set for jazz at the lake zoo.
3	k and c	coke risk lack check stock clerk thanks think once
4		Jack thinks a clerk needs to check the coke stock.
5	f and n	find facts off nine staff then front and of friend
6		All the staff think Fran can find half of the ink.
7	Double letters	fell tell sell jell call tall hall soon tool class
8		Nell can soon tell if the class did all the drill.

| 1 | 2 | 3 | 4 | 5 | 6 | 7 | 8 | 9 | 10 |

217A Preparatory Practice [5] *each line at least three times*

Alphabet	After Wade bought the zinnias, June quickly put them in an extra vase.
Figures	In March, 9,365 units were sold; in April, 17,028; and in May, 24,186.
Figure-symbol	Item #6320 (page 196) sells for $57.98; item #5801 (page 274), $63.49.
Fluency	The citizens of the town claim that the problems have not been solved.
	| 1 | 2 | 3 | 4 | 5 | 6 | 7 | 8 | 9 | 10 | 11 | 12 | 13 | 14 |

217B Growth Index [15] *one 10′* control-level *writing; figure* nwam

All letters are used.

		GWAM 1′	10′	
¶ 1 1.6 SI 5.8 AWL 75% HFW	American business offers a great many career opportunities for	13	1	38
	those who are ready to accept the challenge of helping to solve the	26	3	39
	many unique problems that exist in industry today. Openings may be	40	4	40
	found in the fields of chemicals, insurance, finance, sales, medicine,	54	5	42
	law, and utilities, to name but a few. The scope of modern business	68	7	43
	is second only to the wide variety of jobs that are open. The demand	82	8	44
	for those who are well trained ranges from typists, secretaries, and	96	10	46
	the operators of office machines to the managers who set the goals and	110	11	47
	direct the employees at all levels.	117	12	48
¶ 2 1.6 SI 5.8 AWL 75% HFW	In the choice of a career from among the many opportunities that	13	13	49
	are available, there are a number of factors to be considered. Your	27	14	51
	talent and schooling, of course, are primary factors. No one can hope	41	16	52
	to achieve success in an area for which he has little ability or no	55	17	53
	training. Experts in personnel agree that the interests of an employee	69	19	55
	play an equally essential role. Success comes more easily to those who	83	20	56
	enjoy the work they do than it does to those individuals who dislike	97	21	58
	or merely tolerate their jobs. In your search for a rewarding career,	111	23	59
	ascertain the area which interests you most; then, do your utmost to	125	24	61
	equip yourself for success through education.	134	25	62
¶ 3 1.6 SI 5.8 AWL 75% HFW	When it is time to choose a position within a specific industry or	13	26	63
	organization, there are also a number of factors that must be weighed	27	28	64
	very carefully. Obviously, the salary offered is an important aspect.	42	29	66
	In the long run, however, other factors may be more significant than	56	31	67
	the initial salary. The scale of wages must be examined as well as the	70	32	68
	chances for promotion. Another vital aspect is the opportunity accorded	85	34	70
	for training. Add to these factors the fringe benefits that are granted	99	35	71
	and you will have an overall estimate of the worth of the job.	112	36	73
1′ GWAM	| 1 | 2 | 3 | 4 | 5 | 6 | 7 | 8 | 9 | 10 | 11 | 12 | 13 | 14 |			
10′ GWAM	| 1 | 2 |			

LESSON 7

7A Preparatory Practice (8) *each line twice SS; DS after second typing of line*

● Beginning with this lesson and for all following lessons, getting ready to type will be a part of typing the Preparatory Practice.

All letters taught	Jack took the disk; Fitz needs it to send to Carl.
Direct reaches	led sled ode code once check tried shirt free tree
Shifting	Jeff Stone and Jack Firth stood drill in the rain.
	| 1 | 2 | 3 | 4 | 5 | 6 | 7 | 8 | 9 | 10 |

7B Sentence Guided Writing (5)

DO: Type each of the following sentences as two 1′ writings, or type each one three times if 1-minute timing is not used.

Reading Cue: Think and type the easy two-letter words, such as **to, do,** and **it**, as *words*. Think the word (not the letters) vigorously.

	Words in Line	GWAM 30″ Guide
Jane is to aid Hale as soon as she can do so.	9	18
Tod can do the three lines of the drill for Keith.	10	20
| 1 | 2 | 3 | 4 | 5 | 6 | 7 | 8 | 9 | 10 |		

7C Stroking Technique for U and W (10) *each line twice SS; DS after second typing of line*

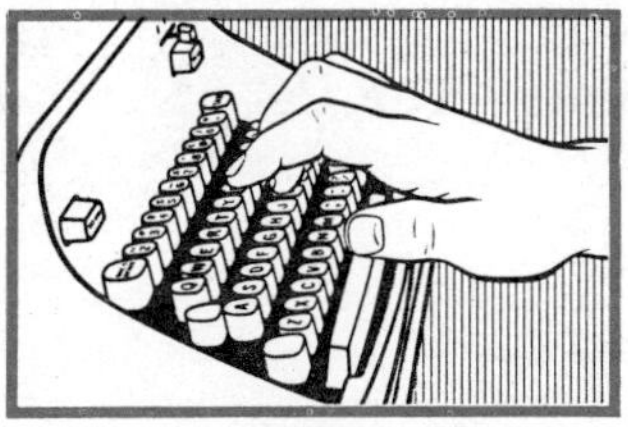
U

Reach the *right first finger* up to **u** without moving the other fingers from their home keys.

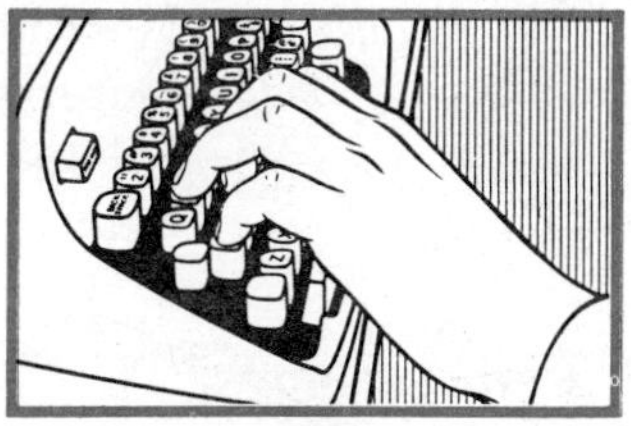
W

Reach the *left third finger* up to type **w** without moving the hand forward or arching the wrist.

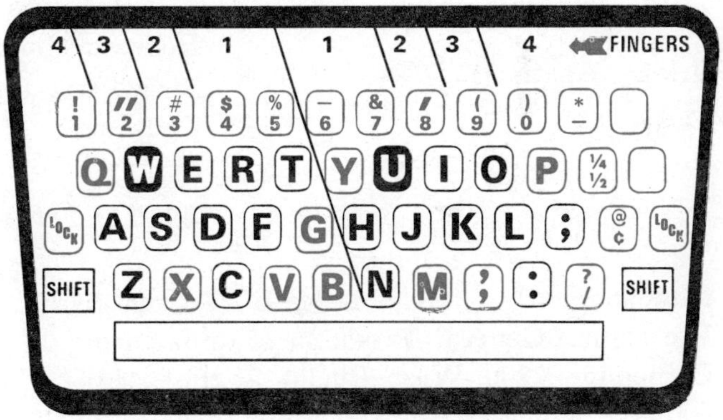

Tryout Drills

u	j u juj us use due jut sue fun sun cut cue hue nut
w	s w sws wit with worn sworn how show sow sown when
u w	four sure just turn thus with work wish want would
Review	We know June wants to show the house to us at two.

Job 10: Model of Dinner Program

Using the copy given below the illustrations, type a model copy for stencil duplication of the program for the annual employees dinner in a style similar to that illustrated.

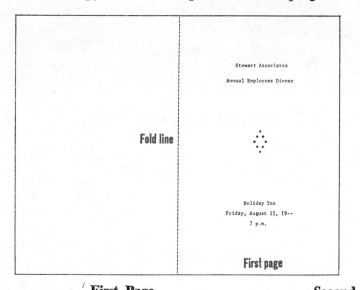

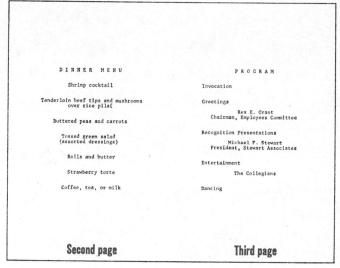

First Page

	Words
Stewart Associates	4
Annual Employees Dinner	9
*	9
* *	10
* *	11
* *	12
*	13
Holiday Inn	15
Friday, August 15, 19––	20
7 p.m.	22

Second Page

	Words
D I N N E R M E N U	26
Shrimp cocktail	29
Tenderloin beef tips and	34
mushrooms over rice	38
pilaf	39
Buttered peas and carrots	45
Tossed green salad	48
(assorted dressings)	53
Rolls and butter	56
Strawberry torte	59
Coffee, tea, or milk	64

Third Page

	Words
P R O G R A M	66
Invocation	69
Greetings Rex E. Grant	73
Chairman, Employees	77
Committee	79
Recognition Presentations	84
Michael F. Stewart	88
President, Stewart As-	92
sociates	94
Entertainment The Col-	98
legians	100
Dancing	101

Job 11: Letter with Carbon Copy

	Words
August 23, 19–– Mr. Charles B. Harrington,	9
President General Products Manufacturing	17
Company 7200 West Euclid Avenue Mil-	24
waukee, WI 53219 Dear Mr. Harrington	31
(¶ 1) As you suggested in our telephone con-	39
versation this morning, we shall present the	48
final report of the survey we made of your	56
organizational structure and managerial prac-	65
tices to you and your key executives on	73
August 31. Mr. Frank A. Stanton, Chief of	82
our Systems Analysis Branch, and Mr. Loren	90
O. Beggs, Chief of our Survey Branch, will	99
assist me in the presentation. (¶ 2) Our for-	107
mal presentation will take approximately two	116
hours. After that time, we shall be available	125
for any questions that you may wish to raise.	135
(¶ 3) We shall arrive in Milwaukee at 6:30	142
p.m. on August 30 on Eastern Flight 617. We	151
have arranged accommodations at the Med-	159
ford Inn. (¶ 4) It has been a pleasure for me	167
and my staff to work with you and your em-	175
ployees. We appreciate the wholehearted	183
cooperation you have given us. If you desire,	193
we shall be happy to assist you and your staff	202
in implementing our recommendations. Sin-	210
cerely yours	219/243

7D   Stroking Technique for B and , (Comma) ⑩

B

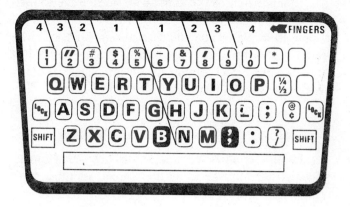

, (Comma)

Reach the *left first finger* down to type **b** without moving the hand from its typing position.

Reach the *right second finger* down to type , (comma). *Space once after a comma in a sentence.*

Tryout Drills

b	f b fbf bid fib fob rob rib job fbf both born bond
,	k, k, Kit, Fitz, and Ken took the bus; I can, too.
b ,	to be, we can be, on the job, be sure, it is best,
Review	Burt, not Bud, cashed the Club checks at the bank.

7E   Continuity Practice ⑰

DO: Type the copy as shown except that you are to type the last line of each group twice, double spacing after the second typing of the line. If time permits, use Line 10 for as many 1' writings as possible. Type without hurry, but type!

Reach Cue: Keep the correct hand alignment with the keyboard. As you make the down reach to , or b, for example, let the finger make a short, low, direct movement to the key without twisting the hand or the elbow out of position.

All reach-strokes taught are used.

1		but we job cut our wish both work just debts would
2	w u b ,	if we knew, cut our dues, four jobs, back to work,
3		Buck wants a job with the new branch of this bank.
4		jot kind down or for zone size their line short in
5	o r n z	jot it down; he has ten stores; he is a trade czar
6		Liz went to France in June; Zoe can join her soon.
7		of just task off face joke silk act jest code free
8	j k c f	face the fact; just file it; of the code; act fast
9		Jack has to face the fact that the job takes work.
10	1' writings	Buzz does not need luck to win if he works to win.

| 1 | 2 | 3 | 4 | 5 | 6 | 7 | 8 | 9 | 10 |

Job 7: Preparation of Roster

Using the cards typed in Job 6, prepare a double-spaced alphabetic roster of those who have signed up to donate blood. Type the last names first. Use the heading DONORS FOR RED CROSS BLOOD DRIVE ON JULY 10 and three column headings: Name, Department, and Blood Type. (*161 words*)

Job 8: Preparation of Special Roster

Using the cards typed in Job 6, prepare a single-spaced roster alphabetic by department of those who have signed up to donate blood. Type last name first. Use the heading DONORS FOR RED CROSS BLOOD DRIVE ON JULY 10, each department name as a secondary heading, centered and underlined, and two column headings: Name and Blood Type. (*207 words*)

Job 9: Model Copy for Spirit Duplicator

Type the following unbound manuscript with side headings as a model copy of material to be reproduced on the spirit duplicator. Use the heading GUIDES FOR ANALYZING ORGANIZATIONAL STRUCTURE AND PRACTICES. Side headings are underlined.

	Words
(¶1) An analysis of the structure of an organization must be based on sound principles.	19
	29
The principles which follow have evolved from	38
the lessons of operating experience and have	47
withstood the test of time. A comparison of	56
these principles with the existing organizational structure of a company should reveal	65
	73
most, if not all, situations which should be	82
remedied. In most instances, the principles	91
themselves suggest the corrective action to be	101
taken. Principle of Objective (¶2) All organizational elements and functions must	113
	121
contribute, directly or indirectly, to the accomplishment of the objective of the enterprise.	130
	140
Any function or organizational element not	148
required in the accomplishment of the overall	158
objective must be eliminated. In the analysis	167
of an organization, the value of each function,	177
each position, and each organizational unit	185
must be challenged. If the principles of organization were ranked in order of importance, the principle of objective would be	194
	202
	211
ranked first. Principle of Homogeneous Assignment (¶3) An effective organization	225
	233
should be designed so that only duties and	242

activities of a similar or related nature are assigned to an individual or group for accomplishment. Since specialization promotes efficiency, the duties of individuals and activities of organizational units must be scrutinized carefully to insure that they are similar or related in nature. Principle of Unity of Command (¶4) An individual should have only one boss and no one but that boss should give him direct orders. Violations of this principle lead to conflicts, confusion, and a loss of efficiency. The formal organizational structure often does not reveal the fact that an individual is required to answer to more than one person. Close questioning of employees is necessary to reveal violations of this principle. Principle of Delegation of Responsibility and Authority (¶5) There must be a clear line of formal authority running from the top to the bottom of every organization. This is often called the "chain of command." Ultimate authority and responsibility for a business lie at the top of the chain of command in the hands of the owners. If, however, a subordinate is to be held responsible for a certain task, he must be given the authority to carry out his responsibilities. This points up the necessity for clear-cut job descriptions which outline the authority inherent in the job as well as the duties and responsibilities. Principle of Span of Control (¶6) The number of individuals or units reporting directly to a supervisor should not exceed the number that can be feasibly and effectively directed. There is no "magic formula" to determine the optimum number of workers who can report to a given supervisor. The factors of distance, time, knowledge, and complexity of work must be analyzed for each supervisor in an effort to determine if the span of control has been exceeded. Principle of Coordination (¶7) The organizational structure must facilitate the development of close, friendly, and cooperative relations, particularly between line and staff activities. Effective coordination is dependent almost entirely upon adequate communication among all elements of an enterprise. The chief executive and his major subordinates must not only encourage and promote communication among all members of the organization, they must establish a climate which permits the free exchange of information and ideas at all times.

251
260
269
279
288
297
311
319
328
338
347
356
366
374
383
393
411
421
430
439
448
457
466
476
486
495
504
513
522
535
544
553
561
571
579
588
597
605
614
623
636
645
653
663
672
680
688
697
705
713
722
730
737

● **Self-Improvement Practice**   *each line three times SS; DS after third typing of line*

All reach-strokes taught are used.

Beth wrote a card to Nan and Sue, a note to Keith.

Dan said Ed is a whiz; and Jan, I know, thinks so.

A lad can be what he likes if he likes what he is.

It is their bid for the work. She held it for us.
| 1 | 2 | 3 | 4 | 5 | 6 | 7 | 8 | 9 | 10 |

LESSON 8

8A   Preparatory Practice (8)   *each line three times SS; DS after third typing of line*

All reach-strokes taught are used in the first line.

Bud, Tod, and Liz worked for an hour; so did Jack.

but who bad true blue when built black doubt board

We want to do all our work just as well as we can.
| 1 | 2 | 3 | 4 | 5 | 6 | 7 | 8 | 9 | 10 |

8B   Tab Mechanism Control (12)   *three times*

*SETTING TABULATOR STOPS

1. Move the carriage as far to the left as possible.

2. Clear previous settings to eliminate false stops by depressing the **tab clear key (31)** as you pull the carriage all the way to the right. *To remove a single stop without canceling other stops, tabulate to the stop and* operate the tab clear key. *Smith-Corona and Olympia typewriters have a Total Tab Clear key that clears all stops at one time without moving the carriage.*

3. To set a tabulator stop, move the carriage to the desired position; then depress the **tab set key (23)**. Repeat this procedure for each stop needed.

TABULATING TECHNIQUE

Nonelectric (Manual) Machines: Depress and hold the tab bar (right first finger) or key (right fourth finger) down until the carriage has stopped.

Electric Machines: Flick the tab key lightly with the little finger; return the little finger to its home position at once.

SET TAB STOPS
FOR THE DRILL:

1. Clear all tab stops. (See directions given above.)

2. For Column 2, set a tab stop 15 spaces from the left margin.

3. For Column 3, set a tab stop 15 spaces from first tab stop.

4. For Column 4, set a tab stop 16 spaces from second tab stop.

and	Tab	set	Tab	with	Tab	then
did		oil		work		wish
the		was		down		town
aid		ink		both		hand
wit		saw		lend		burn

Tab bar

Tab key

KEY | 3 | 12 | 3 | 12 | 4 | 12 | 4 |

SIGN UP FOR RED CROSS BLOOD DRIVE ON JULY 10

Name	Department	Blood Type
James Weaver	Drafting	O
Bruce Hickey	Systems Analysis	O
Richard Nelson	Systems Analysis	A
Judith Grant	Administration	O
John Russo	Administration	O
Jeanne Dunlap	Administration	O
Norma Boring	Executive	A
Patricia Rich	Administration	O
Michael Smith	Executive	B
Mary Nixon	Administration	O
Larry Adams	Drafting	AB
Dennis Holland	Drafting	O
Joseph Miller	Survey	O
Edward Cunningham	Survey	O
Donald Landis	Executive	A
Charles Craft	Survey	O
Albert Stover	Drafting	O
Dora Conklin	Administration	O
Garry Ogurchak	Systems Analysis	B
Stanley Zeleznok	Systems Analysis	O
Thomas Davidson	Survey	O
Kathleen Pescuric	Administration	O
Stefan Slater	Drafting	A
William Bromsky	Systems Analysis	O

8C Stroking Technique Practice ⑮ *twice as shown*

STROKING CUE / Home Keys: After striking the key firmly, pull finger slightly toward palm of hand.

Third-Row Keys: Reach with the finger; do not move the hand forward.

First-Row Keys: Make a direct reach without moving the elbow out or changing hand alignment.

Space-Bar Stroke: Use a quick, down-and-in motion. Release the bar quickly.

All reach-strokes taught are used.

1		all fall hall shall as ask had fad half dash flash	Space with
2	Home keys	shall add; had half; has a hall; ask all; as a fad	down-and-in
3		J. K. Dahl asks half. D. J. Hall adds a fall fad.	thumb motion

4		work tire wit out oil sure tried forth trust weeks
5	Third-row keys	use that route; write it; there were; short street
6		We were told to take the truck route for the tour.

7		nice back zinc bond corn zone branch czar none can
8	Bottom-row keys	has been in town, count the bonds, check the blank
9		Roz sent cash to the bank; the bank wants a check.

| 1 | 2 | 3 | 4 | 5 | 6 | 7 | 8 | 9 | 10 |

8D Paragraph (Continuity) Typing ⑮ *type the ¶s as directed; determine gwam*

DO: Clear tab stops; then set a stop for a 5-space ¶ indention. Use DS.

DO: Depress tab bar or key to indent the first line of each ¶.

DO: Type the ¶s as shown; then type 1' writings on each of the ¶s.

All letters taught are used.

Total Words
1' GWAM

Tab   •   4   •   8

¶1
*1.0 SI
4.2 AWL
97% HFW

----→All of us need to know how to talk and write   9

•   12   •   16   •

well, as we now do a lot of both. We are sure to   19

20   •   24   •   28

need these skills in the world of work, too.   28

•   4   •   8

¶2
1.0 SI
4.2 AWL
97% HFW

If we do not talk and write well now, we can   37

•   12   •   16   •

learn to do both well. We will need these skills   47

20   •   24   •   28

on the job if it is a job of the size to cause us   57

•   32 33

to show our worth.   61

| 1 | 2 | 3 | 4 | 5 | 6 | 7 | 8 | 9 | 10 |

*COPY DIFFICULTY: The ease or difficulty of copy to be typed is influenced greatly by three factors: (1) Syllable intensity (SI) or average number of syllables per word; (2) Stroke intensity or average word length (AWL); (3) Incidence of high-frequency words (HFW) or the percent of words used from among the 1,254 most-used words. In this section of lessons, the paragraphs are "very easy."

TO DETERMINE GWAM: The ¶s are marked with the 4-word count shown in figures and with an in-between count of 2 words shown by a dot (.) to aid you in determining your 1-minute *gwam.* If ¶ 1 is typed and a part or all of ¶ 2 in the 1-minute writing, use the cumulative total word count given in the column at the right plus the count for the incomplete line shown beneath the second paragraph.

Job 4: Itinerary

Type the following itinerary using two columns: Depart and Arrive. Use the heading ITINERARY FOR MR. MICHAEL F. STEWART. *(127 words)*

DEPART: New Rochelle 9:30 a.m.
July 21
(automobile)

ARRIVE: New York City 11:15 a.m.
July 21
(JFK airport)

DEPART: New York City 12:05 p.m.
July 21
TWA Flight 69*

ARRIVE: Pittsburgh 1:29 p.m.
July 21
(Hilton Hotel)

DEPART: Pittsburgh 8:55 p.m.
July 22
TWA Flight 499

ARRIVE: St. Louis 9:25 p.m.
July 22
(Sheraton Hotel)

DEPART: St. Louis 5:00 p.m.
July 23
American Flight 144

ARRIVE: Chicago 6:10 p.m.
July 23
(Palmer House)

DEPART: Chicago 6:45 a.m.
July 25
NW Flight 419

ARRIVE: Milwaukee 7:15 a.m.
July 25
(Medford Inn)

DEPART: Milwaukee 5:40 p.m.
July 26
NW Flight 224 **

ARRIVE: New York City 8:35 p.m.
July 26
(JFK airport)

*Luncheon flight

**Dinner flight

Job 5. Tentative Survey Schedule

Prepare the following Tentative Survey Schedule for the General Products Manufacturing Company as a model copy to be reproduced on a direct-copy machine. Use an appropriate heading and arrange the material in three columns headed: Date, Activity, and Personnel. *(135 words)*

July 25   Initial meeting with Mr. Harrington
Mr. Stewart

July 28   Planning conference
Mr. Stewart, Mr. Stanton, Mr. Beggs, Mr. Prennatt, Mr. Hall

August 3   Completion of survey plans
All personnel

August 6   Begin on-site survey
Mr. Willing, Mr. Johnson, Mr. Cooper, Mr. Eisenhart

August 16   Complete on-site survey
Survey Team

August 19   Begin preparation of report
Survey Team

August 23   Submission of draft of final report
Survey Team

August 28   Completion of final report
Survey Team

August 31   Presentation of final report to General Products Manufacturing Company
Mr. Stewart, Mr. Stanton, Mr. Beggs

Job 6: Typing 5- by 3-inch Lined Cards

Mr. Stewart has placed you in charge of the Red Cross Blood Drive. On page 364 are the signatures of those who have agreed to donate blood on July 10. For each individual type a 5- by 3-inch card. Typing the person's name (last name first) on the top line, his department on the third line, "Blood Type:" on the fifth line, followed by the person's blood type, and "Date Donated: July 10" on the seventh line. *(142 words)*

9A Preparatory Practice ⑧ *each line three times SS; DS after third typing of line*

All reach-strokes taught   Bud, John, and Cliff work with zest; so does Bill.

Double letters   Nell and Bill Hess will soon see Lee and Rob Reed.

Easy   It is just luck that Dick Burns can be with Keith.
| 1 | 2 | 3 | 4 | 5 | 6 | 7 | 8 | 9 | 10 |

9B Sentence Guided Writing ⑦

DO: Type each sentence as a 1' writing or type each three times if the 1' timing cannot be used. Study the Stroking Cue at the right before beginning to type the sentences.

Stroking Cue: Think the easy two- and three-letter words, such as **is, to, the,** and **and,** as words. Slow down slightly for such words as **was, were, looks, scared,** and so forth.

		Words in Line	GWAM 30" Guide
Easy	The work is to be done in an hour or so.	8	16
Difficult	We were sad when we saw that Fred was scared.	9	18
Easy	The suit is a fine fit, and it looks well on Jane.	10	20

| 1 | 2 | 3 | 4 | 5 | 6 | 7 | 8 | 9 | 10 |

9C Stroking Technique for Y and X ⑩ *each line three times SS; DS after third typing of line*

Y

X

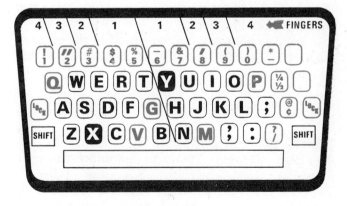

Reach the *right first finger* up to type **y**. Do not arch the wrist or move other fingers from their home keys.

Reach the *left third finger* down to type **x** without moving the hand downward. Reach with the finger!

Tryout Drills

y   jyj yj yet say jay hay jay lay jy fly way hay day

x   sxs xs xs ax six fix fox box nix next sixth fixed

y x   yes dry cry boy hay bay they next jinx lynx sixth

Review Jayne Clay can fix the next tax list for Rex Knox.

Use the following plan for these lessons. Unless otherwise instructed, retain all jobs until you have completed Lesson 216.

213-216A Preparatory Practice: (5') Type either 211A, page 358, or 212A, page 360, as directed there.

213-216B Technique Practice: (5') For Lessons 213 and 215, type each of the first three lines of 212B, page 360, as 1' *exploration-level* writings. For Lessons 214 and 216, type the same lines as 1' *control-level* writings.

213-216C Building Speed and Control: (10') For Lessons 213 and 215, type a 2' *exploration-level* writing on each paragraph of 212D, page 361. Determine *gwam* by dividing the 1' *gwam* by 2. For Lessons 214 and 216, type a 2' *control-level* writing on the same paragraphs. Determine *nwam* by subtracting 5 for each error from your 2' *gwam*.

213-216D Production Typing: (30') Type the jobs beginning below. Type as many jobs as you can in the time provided each day. When time is called, complete the line on which you are typing so that you can begin on a new line the next day. When complete directions are not given, use your own judgment. Strive for neat, attractive copy.

When you have completed Lesson 216, place your name and the job number in the upper right corner of each job. Arrange the jobs in numeric order and clip them together.

In these jobs, you are employed in the office of Michael F. Stewart, President of Stewart Associates, 500 Beaufort Place, New Rochelle, New York 10801.

Job 1: Letter on Executive-Size Stationery

Words

July 7, 19-- Mr. Charles B. Harrington, 8
President General Products Manufacturing 16
Company 7200 West Euclid Avenue Mil- 23
waukee, WI 53219 Dear Mr. Harrington 31
(¶1) Thank you for your letter of July 7. It 39
will be a pleasure for Stewart Associates to 48
survey the organizational structure and man- 57
agerial practices of your company. (¶2) Dur- 64
ing the week of July 21, I am planning a trip 74
to Pittsburgh, St. Louis, and Chicago. I can 83
fly to Milwaukee on July 25 for our initial 92
conference if this date is convenient for you. 101
(¶3) For our initial meeting, will you please 109
have available a copy of your latest organiza- 118

tion chart, copies of job descriptions, and any 128
procedures manuals you may have published. 137
(¶4) I am looking forward to meeting you 144
and hope that we may meet on July 25. Sin- 152
cerely yours 161/185

Job 2: Interoffice Memorandum

Words

TO: Ronald A. Hall, Director of Research 7
FROM: Michael F. Stewart, President **DATE:** 13
July 7, 19-- **FILE:** GPMC-1 **SUBJECT:** Sur- 18
vey of the General Products Manufacturing 26
Company (¶1) Mr. Charles B. Harrington, 33
President of the General Products Manufac- 42
turing Company, 7200 West Euclid Avenue, 50
Milwaukee, Wisconsin, has requested that we 59
survey the organizational structure and man- 67
agerial practices of his company. I plan to 76
meet with Mr. Harrington on July 25. (¶2) 84
In preparation for the survey, please prepare 93
a brochure of information about the General 102
Products Manufacturing Company which will 110
include the following information: (*enumer-* 117
ate) 1. History of the company 2. Biograph- 125
ical sketches of the key executives 3. Kinds 134
of products produced 4. Financial situation 143
5. Sales record and major customers (¶3) I 151
would appreciate it if you would have this 160
information available prior to my departure 169
on July 21. 172

Job 3: Letter on Executive-Size Stationery

Words

July 8, 19-- Mr. J. Orville Palmer, President 9
Hatcher Manufacturing Company 320 Oak- 17
hill Avenue Milwaukee, WI 53213 Dear 24
Orville (¶1) Many thanks for recommend- 31
ing Stewart Associates to Charles B. Harring- 40
ton of the General Products Manufacturing 48
Company. We have agreed to survey his 56
organization and will begin on July 25. (¶2) 64
I will be in Milwaukee on July 25 for the 72
initial meeting with Harrington. Unfortu- 81
nately, I must leave the following morning. 90
I hope that you and Anne can join me for 98
dinner, however, on the evening of July 25. 107
I have a reservation at the Medford Inn. (¶3) 115
Please give my best regards to Anne. I am 124
looking forward to seeing both of you again. 133
Sincerely 141/162

9D Stroking Technique for V and P ⑩ *each line three times SS; DS after third typing of line*

V

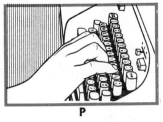

P

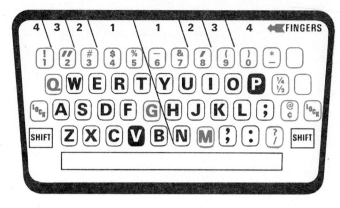

Reach the *left first finger* down to type **v**. Hold the elbow in position and the hand in alignment.

Straighten the *right fourth finger* slightly and move up to type letter **p**. Avoid twisting the elbow out.

Tryout Drills

v	fvf vf vie view vow vows five live rove love have
p	;p; p; up cup pay pen spend spent help paid prize
v p	van zip vote solve prove peace pound strive poise
Review	Steve and Paul say they leave for Spain next week.

9E Continuity Practice ⑮

DO: Type the six lines of drill twice as shown. (DS between two-line groups.) Use the ¶ for two or more 1' writings or type the ¶ twice if the 1' timing is not used.

Stroking Cue: Type with finger action. Hold the hands and arms quiet, almost motionless. Reach—don't hop—to the keys. Keep typing at a smooth and steady pace.

All reach-strokes taught are used.

1		by say yet year your why try six box tax next jinx
2	y and x	Dwayne will help Rex file his sales tax next year.
3		put part paid shop type keep five live have twelve
4	p and v	Van pays in cash and saves; it proves a fine plan.
5		you vex plans serve wax prove yes dye please price
6	y x p v	You and Paul have typed just five of the six jobs.

			1' GWAM
1.0 SI	Tab→As you work to learn, you will learn to work		9
4.5 AWL			
95% HFW	in such a way that skill will be yours. Work for		19
	speed with zest now and then, but know that speed		29
	is just a part of the plans you want to have next.		39

| 1 | 2 | 3 | 4 | 5 | 6 | 7 | 8 | 9 | 10 |

All letters are used.

	GWAM	
1'	10'	

¶ 1
1.6 SI
5.8 AWL
75% HFW

Managerial ability has led to better jobs and higher salaries for many who began as skilled clerks or secretaries. Most of us view a manager as someone who directs the work of others, but there is much more to it than that. Managers deal with materials, methods, machines, and money as well as with people. A manager is one who is eager to accept responsibility, to seek solutions to the varied problems that arise daily, and to initiate action quickly. Overall, the work of a manager can be broken down into the three major functions of planning, organizing, and controlling.

¶ 2
1.6 SI
5.8 AWL
75% HFW

Planning is a creative phase of a manager's job. It involves a determination of what is to be done, how and where it is to be done, and who shall be responsible. The initial and most vital step in planning is the establishment of goals or objectives. The fundamental objective of any business, naturally, is to realize a profit by providing goods or services to its customers. To achieve this objective, specific goals must be formulated. These goals not only provide a basis for action to be taken, they serve as yardsticks to assess the progress achieved.

¶ 3
1.6 SI
5.8 AWL
75% HFW

The plans of a business must be translated in terms of the exact resources necessary to carry out the plans. Duties and tasks must be combined to form work units and jobs, which leads, in turn, to the initiation of organizational structure and procedures. The organization of any business is of vital concern since it shows the relationships that are to exist among the work units and the people. Procedures set up the proper sequences for executing tasks so that the work is done efficiently. These are the steps that form the function of organizing.

¶ 4
1.6 SI
5.8 AWL
75% HFW

Controlling is the activity which is designed to insure that work is being executed as it was planned and organized. In simple terms, it consists of assuring that each person does the right thing, at the right time, at the right place, and with the proper resources. If not, corrective action must be initiated. Personal supervision is the most usual means of control, but reports of all kinds play a prominent role. Regardless of the means used, the aim of control is to facilitate the attainment of company goals in the most effective way feasible.

GWAM columns:

1'	10'
13	2 46
27	3 48
41	4 49
55	6 51
69	7 52
82	8 53
96	10 55
110	11 56
116	12 57
13	13 58
27	15 60
42	16 61
56	17 63
70	19 64
85	20 65
99	22 67
112	23 68
13	24 69
27	26 71
42	27 72
56	29 74
70	30 75
84	31 77
98	33 78
111	34 79
13	36 81
28	37 82
42	38 84
56	40 85
70	41 86
84	43 88
98	44 89
111	45 90

1' GWAM | 1 | 2 | 3 | 4 | 5 | 6 | 7 | 8 | 9 | 10 | 11 | 12 | 13 | 14 |
10' GWAM | 1 | 2 |

• Self-Improvement Practice   *each line three times SS; DS after third typing of line*

v   Dave Volp will have a leave of four or five weeks.

x   Rex fixed the box for Liz; next, he did your desk.

y   Kaye said you should stay with Faye for five days.

p   Pete has the pep, push, and poise for the top job.

Double letters   Lee will call Bill Cook to see if he has the book.

LESSON 10

10A   Preparatory Practice (8) *each line three times SS; DS after third typing of line*

All letters taught are used.

Clay Kane proved this size sox will just suit Dan.

in at on was you far kin eve hop red lab just zinc

Their work is done; they can leave when they wish.

| 1 | 2 | 3 | 4 | 5 | 6 | 7 | 8 | 9 | 10 |

10B   Tab Mechanism and Return Controls (12) *type twice*

1. Clear all tab stops.
2. For Column 2, set tab stop 15 spaces from left margin.
3. For Column 3, set a tab stop 15 spaces from first tab stop.
4. For Column 4, set a tab stop 16 spaces from second tab stop.

TABULATING CUE

Nonelectric (Manual): Depress and hold tab bar or key down until the carriage has completed its movement.

Electric: Flick the tab key lightly with the little finger; return the finger to home position quickly.

RETURN CUE

Nonelectric: Move lever inward to take up the slack; return with a quick wrist and hand motion. Do not follow carriage across.

Electric: Reach the little finger to the return key, flick the key lightly, and release it quickly.

Tab bar

for	Tab	act	Tab	hand	Tab	live
lay		lop		corn		your
but		wet		lend		have
cot		oil		lays		year
six		car		torn		vote
fox		pin		turn		size
win		sea		they		hunt
box		lop		wish		zone
fit		ate		laid		next

Tab key

KEY | 3 | 12 | 3 | 12 | 4 | 12 | 4 |

212A Preparatory Practice [5] *each line at least three times*

Alphabet — Judge Purvis ordered Nick Webb to fix the houses quickly or raze them.

Figures — The population of the city rose from 47,301 in 1956 to 78,250 in 1969.

Figure-symbol — The total of the 327 checks was $1,458.60 (or 94% of the May payroll).

Fluency — Send the names of those who are entitled to the stock dividend checks.

| 1 | 2 | 3 | 4 | 5 | 6 | 7 | 8 | 9 | 10 | 11 | 12 | 13 | 14 |

212B Technique Practice [10] *each line four times; then 1′ writings*

Stroke — Procedures announced yesterday include regulations regarding absences.

Combination — Miniaturization may be a possible solution to this perplexing problem.

Word response — It was my job to put the new files on his desk at the end of each day.

Fluency — The future of the company may depend on the sales they make this year.

| 1 | 2 | 3 | 4 | 5 | 6 | 7 | 8 | 9 | 10 | 11 | 12 | 13 | 14 |

212C Building Speed and Control [10]

Type two 2′ *exploration-level* writings; compute *gwam* on the faster writing. Then type two 2′ *control-level* writings and compute *nwam* on the more accurate writing.

All letters are used.

		GWAM 1′	2′
¶ 1 1.6 SI 5.8 AWL 75% HFW	The ability to communicate is an essential trait in any kind of	13	7
	job. There are very few people in the world of business who are not	27	14
	required to transmit ideas and facts clearly and effectively. This is	41	21
	decidedly true of those who work in an office. In an office, business	55	28
	activities are conducted chiefly through the media of oral and written	69	35
	communications. Your ultimate success in business may depend to a great	84	42
	extent on your ability to write and speak correctly.	94	47
¶ 2 1.6 SI 5.8 AWL 75% HFW	Writing is a great deal more than merely putting words on a piece	13	54
	of paper. You must develop the ability to write exactly what you mean	27	61
	so that everyone will understand precisely what you intended to say.	41	68
	Of equal value is oral expression. Business is conducted to a great	55	75
	extent through formal discussions or conferences. You must cultivate	69	82
	your capacity to verbalize your ideas clearly and concisely. If you	83	89
	improve your writing and speaking skills, you may be sure that you will	97	96
	derive gains in the form of better jobs and better pay.	108	102

1′ GWAM | 1 | 2 | 3 | 4 | 5 | 6 | 7 | 8 | 9 | 10 | 11 | 12 | 13 | 14 |
2′ GWAM | 1 | 2 | 3 | 4 | 5 | 6 | 7 |

10C Stroking Technique Practice ⑮ *three times as shown*

Lines 1 and 2: When the same finger controls two keys in succession, as the first finger controls **fr** in **front** and **br** in **branch**, move the controlling finger directly to the second key. Type without pausing between strokes.

Lines 3 and 4: To type adjacent keys, such as **re** in **here, poi** in **point,** and the like, think each letter vigorously and make each motion precisely. Train your eyes to see quickly the correct sequence of letters to be typed.

All reach-strokes taught are used.

1	Direct	why led side front once branch lots like kind just
2	reaches	Zahn holds the checks; Herb left the wharf; I like
3	Adjacent-key	has poor suit buy oil cards talk klatch point Yule
4	reaches	start here; few buy silk; we hope you trade; as we
5	All letters	Vance hopes to work with Jane for a day next week.
6	taught	Cal had a job for Roz to do, but she did not stay.
7		The skills you build you can prize as well as use.

| 1 | 2 | 3 | 4 | 5 | 6 | 7 | 8 | 9 | 10 |

10D Continuity Practice ⑮

DO: Type the six sentences three times each or use each sentence for two 1' writings with the 30" call of the line-ending guide. Use the ¶ for three or more 1' writings, or type it twice if 1' timing is not used.

Technique Summary: Sit erect, feet on floor. Curve the fingers. Hold eyes on the copy as you type. Type at a steady pace, with hands and arms quiet and stroking action centered in the fingers. Space quickly with a down-and-in motion of the right thumb.

All letters taught are used.

		Words in Line	GWAM 30" Guide
1	Vern fixed the barn for Clay Zilch.	7	14
2	Ruth wrote that you are to pay your way.	8	16
3	Jake said a lad fell when he rushed to class.	9	18
4	Do not put off for an hour what you should do now.	10	20
5	Keith paid for the work with his half of the cash.	10	20
6	Fred and Dave Hays have to pay a tax on the prize.	10	20

		1' GWAM
1.0 SI	Tab ───→If you work well, you can soon type what you	9
4.4 AWL	have had to write with a pen up to now. Try hard	19
93% HFW	to build a skill you can prize for years. On the	29
	next try just do your best to top your last speed.	39

| 1 | 2 | 3 | 4 | 5 | 6 | 7 | 8 | 9 | 10 |

number of people. (¶ 5) The spirit master set 288
consists of two basic parts: a master sheet 297
and a sheet of special carbon, as shown in the 306
illustration. The use of a backing sheet will 315
improve the consistency of the type impres- 324
sion. If a specially prepared master set is not 334
available, simply place the special carbon 342

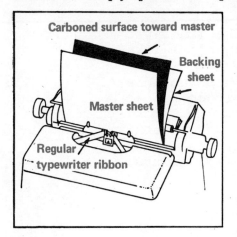

paper be- 344
tween the 346
master and 348
the back- 350
ing sheet 352
with the 354
glossy side 356
toward 357
you. As 359
you type, 361
the carbon 363
copy will 365
be on the 367
back of the 370
master 372

sheet. (¶ 6) For better spirit duplicator mas- 380
ters and copies, follow these suggestions: 389
(enumerate) 1. Prepare a model copy of the 395
material to be typed on the master. Check 404
the copy for accuracy of form and typing. 412
2. Clean the type. Inasmuch as a heavy ribbon 422
causes broad impressions and filled-in charac- 431
ters, the ribbon should be lightweight. 3. Use 441
a firm, even stroke on a nonelectric machine. 450
On an electric typewriter, one of the lower 459
pressure settings is usually best. 4. If you 468
make an error, scrape off the letter or word 477
on the back of the master sheet with a knife 487
or razor blade. Rub the scraped area with a 496
correction pencil. Then, place a small piece 505
of carbon (torn from an unused section) 513
under the area to be retyped, with the glossy 522
side toward you. Type over the incorrect 531
letter or word. Remove the piece of carbon 540
as soon as you have corrected the error. 548

Stencil Duplication 556

(¶ 7) The stencil duplication process can be 564
used to reproduce more than a thousand clear, 573
dark copies of material. A stencil, illustrated 583
at the left, consists of three basic parts: a 592
stencil sheet, a backing sheet, and a cushion 601
sheet. The cushion sheet is placed between 610
the stencil and the backing sheet to absorb 619
the impact of the striking keys. A typing film 628

may be placed over the stencil if darker copies 638
are desired. This film also protects the stencil 648
sheet from letter cutout when the typeface is 657
extremely sharp. (¶ 8) Before typing the sten- 665
cil, follow these steps: (enumerate) 1. Type a 673
model copy of the material. Check it for accu- 682
racy of form and typing. 2. Clean the type 691
thoroughly. 3. Move the ribbon-control lever 700
to the stencil position. 4. Insert the cushion 710
sheet between the stencil sheet and the back- 719
ing sheet. 5. Set the touch control at the point 729
that will insure the sharpest outlines without 738
cutting out the characters. 6. Push the paper- 748
bail rollers to the extreme left and right sides 758
of the bail so that they will not roll on the 767
stencil sheet. 7. Place the top edge of the 776
model copy at the corner marks of the stencil 785
to see where to type the first line of copy. 794
The scales at the top and sides of the stencil 804
will help you position the copy correctly. 813
(¶ 9) Insert the stencil into the typewriter 820
and align it properly. Use a firm, uniform, 829
staccato touch as you type. If you make an 838
error, you can correct it easily with correction 848
fluid. If there is a film over the stencil, this 858

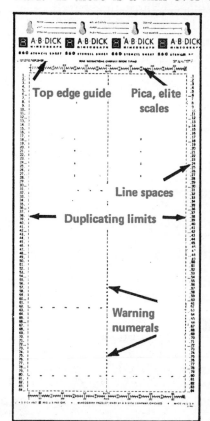

must be de- 860
tached until 863
you resume 865
typing. Use a 874
glass bur- 876
nisher or a 878
paper clip to 881
rub the sur- 883
face of the 885
error on the 888
stencil sheet. 891
Place a pencil 894
between the 897
stencil sheet 899
and the cush- 902
ion sheet and 905
apply a light 908
coating of the 911
correction 914
fluid over the 917
error. Let it 920
dry and make 922
the necessary 925
correction, us- 928
ing a light 930
touch. 931

LESSON 11

11A   Preparatory Practice ⑧ *each line three times SS; DS after third typing of line*

All reach-strokes taught are used.

```
The boy played jazz for Vic for six weeks in June.

to be; for us; can do; we like; pay the; they can;

He can do the drill in an hour or so, I feel sure.
|  1  |  2  |  3  |  4  |  5  |  6  |  7  |  8  |  9  | 10  |
```

11B   Stroking Technique Review ⑩ *each line three times SS; DS after third typing of line*

All letters taught are used.

```
1    boy axe owns says drop hue seeks laws top two yard

2    puff bulb lieu bulk fraud writes yield width snail

3    Jay can pay the two debts or seek a new bank loan.

4    Len felt that the size of the vote would help Ned.

5    Its style and tone have kept this harp at the top.
     |  1  |  2  |  3  |  4  |  5  |  6  |  7  |  8  |  9  | 10  |
```

11C   Stroking Technique for Q and M ⑩ *each line three times SS; DS after third typing of line*

Q

M

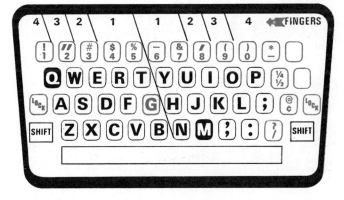

Reach the *left fourth finger* up to type **q** without swinging the elbow out or arching the wrist.

Reach the *right first finger* down to type **m**. Do not move the hand down or swing the elbow out.

Tryout Drills

```
q        qa quit qa quit quiz quack quick quell quote quite

m        mj am jam ham sum rum mix firm form harm come much

q m      quiz quack quest qualm much must myth mixed mosque

Review   Max made out a quiz for me to mail to Mr. Squires.
```

LESSON 211

211A Preparatory Practice (5) *each line at least three times*

Alphabet	Jim made several dozen quaint wicker baskets with wax fruit for Peggy.
Figures	Of the 5,920 employees, 271 are 65 or older; only 34 are less than 18.
Figure-symbol	Invoice #7590 (May 13) totaled $2,146, less discounts of 12½% and 8¼%.
Fluency	It is the right and the duty of all citizens to vote in the elections.
	| 1 | 2 | 3 | 4 | 5 | 6 | 7 | 8 | 9 | 10 | 11 | 12 | 13 | 14 |

211B Technique Practice (10) *each line four times; then 1′ writings*

Direct reaches	I am unable to make any progress on the service contract for my truck.
Long words	Administration representatives defended the transportation facilities.
Double letters	The booklets will be shipped as soon as the account has been approved.
Fluency	The firm must show signs of vigor if it is to make a profit this year.
	| 1 | 2 | 3 | 4 | 5 | 6 | 7 | 8 | 9 | 10 | 11 | 12 | 13 | 14 |

211C Production Typing: Preparing Layout of Copy (35)

The following material on duplicating processes will be included in an office procedures manual as Section VII. Type a layout of the material in the form of a leftbound manuscript, using single spacing. The illustrations on page 359 will be included in the manual.

Center the section number and the heading DUPLICATION PROCESSES. Type the side headings and list the enumerated items in the appropriate form.

For the first illustration, draw a box 2¼ inches square in the lower right corner of the first page, using the margins as guides. When you reach the box, adjust your right margin accordingly. For the second illustration, draw a box 2 by 4¼ inches in the lower left corner of the second page, using the margins as guides. When you reach the box, reset the left margin 2 spaces to the right of the box.

Words

(¶ 1) Economy and convenience are the major 12
factors to be considered in selecting the proper 22
duplication process. Three means of duplica- 31
tion are available in the office: direct-copy 40
machines, spirit duplicators, and stencil dupli- 49
cators. To insure that the appropriate process 59
is selected for each job and that the material 68
for duplication is prepared properly, the fol- 77
lowing guides are provided for each process. 87

Words

Direct-Copy Process 94

(¶ 2) The direct-copy process is used primar- 102
ily for making from one to ten copies. Copy 111
machines are especially useful in making ad- 120
ditional copies of incoming documents such as 129
customers' orders and bills of lading. They 138
may also be used when a few additional copies 147
of correspondence are required. (¶ 3) In pre- 155
paring materials for copy machines, follow 163
these simple rules: (*enumerate*) 1. Clean your 171
type; be certain that the ribbon will produce 180
dark print. 2. Type the material to be copied 189
on plain paper, letterhead, or special form. 199
3. Erase errors neatly or cover them with 207
opaque white ink; then, correct them in the 216
usual manner. 219

Spirit Duplication 226

(¶ 4) Although up to 300 copies can be made 234
from a single spirit master, the spirit process 244
is generally used for runs of 10 to 100 copies. 253
It can be used to reproduce copies of memo- 262
randums, minutes of meetings, notices, or 270
other material that is to be distributed to a 279

11D Stroking Technique for G and ? (Question) ⑩

G

? (Question)

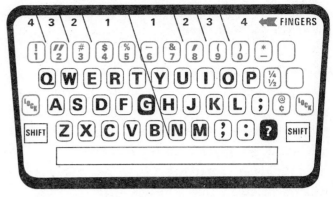

Reach the *left first finger* to the right to type **g** without moving the other fingers from their home keys.

Type **?** with the *right fourth finger.* Remember to shift to type **?** *Space twice after* **?** *at the end of a sentence.*

Tryout Drills

g	fgf gf go got fog fig rug dug big flag right fight
?	;?; ?; ?; Is he? Is he next? Did Sam go to town?
g ?	Is Mat right? May Tom and I go? Am I to see Max?
Review	Has Zeke packed my box with just five grown quail?

Do not space after ? at end of line

11E Continuity Practice ⑫

DO: Type the first four lines three times each; DS after the third typing of the line. Use the ¶ for three or more 1′ writings, or type it twice if 1′ timing is not used.

Technique Summary: Sit erect. Curve the fingers. Space quickly. Strike each key with a quick, sharp stroke; release it quickly. Snap the finger slightly toward the palm of the hand as you release the key.

All letters are used.

my gym fog rug put eggs must mark hymn guess eight

large small quote square quick growth valves sighs

terms dodge bring length slight lymph signs flings

q m g ?   May Gregg make a quick trip to the square for Meg?

		1′ GWAM
	Tab ----→ The man who wants to get to the top must pay	9
1.0 SI	a high price. It may take work to learn to type;	19
4.2 AWL	but if you just keep on and do not quit, the next	29
93% HFW	try may add a word. Have you the zeal to make it?	39

| 1 | 2 | 3 | 4 | 5 | 6 | 7 | 8 | 9 | 10 |

Job 9: Vacation Schedule

Margins: 2" top, 1½" side
Heading: VACATION SCHEDULE FOR SUMMER, 19—
SS; DS between items

	Words
(¶1) The vacation schedule for summer,	14
19—, is given below. In preparing the sched-	23
ule, every effort was made to give each em-	31
ployee the week of his choice. When conflicts	41
arose, the employee with the greatest senior-	49
ity was given preference. (¶2) No changes	57
will be made in this schedule without prior	66
approval.	68

Week of	Employee	
		74
June 29	Roberta Taylor	79
July 6	Rita Schellenberg	84
July 13	Connie Carroll	89
	Louis Perry	91
July 20	Jeanne Baily	95
	Diane Cochran	98
July 27	Betty Fischer	102
Aug. 3	Lois Hall	106
Aug. 10	Charles Burns	110
Aug. 17	Terry Brenneman	115
Aug. 24	Mary Halligan	120
Aug. 31	Karl Greenfield	124
Sept. 7	Margaret Tillman	129

Job 10: Reminders on Plain Paper

Margins: 2" top and side
Heading: REMINDERS FOR JULY
SS; DS between items

	Words
1. July 7 is your wife's birthday. 2. The week-	14
end of July 15 is "Parents' Day" at your son's	23
summer camp. 3. On July 18, you are invited	32
to speak at a dinner meeting of the Industrial	42
Management Club in Shorewood. 4. You are	50
to be the host at the July 21 meeting of your	59
investment club. 5. You have accepted an	68
invitation from Dr. Lewis to be a guest lec-	77
turer in the School of Business at Denton	85

	Words
University on July 25. 6. Your parents' 50th	94
wedding anniversary is July 29.	101

Job 11: Long Letter

1 carbon copy

	Words
June 30, 19— Mr. Michael F. Stewart Stew-	8
art Associates 500 Beaufort Place New	16
Rochelle, NY 10801 Dear Mr. Stewart (¶1)	23
The Board of Trustees of our company has	31
authorized me to engage a management con-	39
sultant to survey our organizational structure	48
and managerial practices. Your firm has been	57
recommended to me by Mr. J. Orville Palmer,	66
President of the Hatcher Manufacturing Com-	75
pany in Milwaukee. (¶2) The General Prod-	82
ucts Manufacturing Company began as a	89
single proprietorship in 1939 when Brooks A.	98
Eastwood, now Chairman of our Board of Trus-	107
tees, began manufacturing resistors for the	116
Government. He built his first plant in 1943	125
and a second plant in 1951. In 1953, the enter-	134
prise was incorporated. (¶3) At the present	142
time, we produce a variety of electrical and	151
electronic parts for the aerospace industry	160
with gross sales in excess of $20,000,000 a	169
year. We have nine shops with over 600 em-	177
ployees engaged in independent but related	186
production. In the near future, we plan to	195
erect a third plant which will include a mod-	204
ern research facility. (¶4) The organizational	212
structure of the company has been permitted	221
to grow somewhat haphazardly. New offices	230
and departments have been added as needed	238
—often on a crash basis. This has led not	247
only to confusion and overlapping of functions	256
but, I fear, to a decided reduction in efficiency.	266
(¶5) If you are interested in undertaking a	274
survey of our company, I would appreciate it	283
if you or a member of your staff would visit	292
us in Milwaukee so that we may discuss the	301
matter in more detail. Sincerely yours	316/336

• Self-Improvement Practice *each line three or more times SS; DS after third typing of line*

Line 1: Clear all tab stops. Set tab stops to have 5 blank spaces between words.

Tabulator	make held hand work them eight
Space bar	he we am up as it or an by to of my on and few man
Shift keys	Don Ames and Zoe Foss played May Janz and Tod Hay.
Alphabet	May Vern Fox help Jack Wolds on the next big quiz?

LESSON 12

12A Preparatory Practice [8] *each line three times SS; DS after third typing of line*

Alphabet	Joe gave my boy five quick trips with Max and Liz.
q m g	Gus quit my team. Doug may go to Rome quite soon.
Easy	George said Tom Squires is the man to do the work.

| 1 | 2 | 3 | 4 | 5 | 6 | 7 | 8 | 9 | 10 |

12B Know Your Typewriter: Backspacing [5]

Backspacing: To fill in an omitted letter or to position the carriage, depress the **backspace key (30)**. Locate the key on the keyboard.

Electric: Reach with the little finger; make a light, quick stroke. Release the key quickly to avoid a double backspace. Hold the key down for repeat backspacing.

Nonelectric (Manual): Straighten the finger and reach it to the backspace key with minimum hand motion. Depress the key firmly; release it quickly.

1. TYPE the first word; backspace and type over the final letter. Type the other words in the same way.
2. Type the first word again; backspace and type over the first letter. Type the other words in the same way.

it go by up as on we my am of cue fix pay men quit

12C Stroking Technique Review [12] *each line three times SS; DS after third typing of line*

1	z j q x	fix jobs quit size next quite jazz quote jinx quiz
2	k v b g	bank like have big kind gave talk serve black save
3	w p m f	firm hope know flip owns put from zip few my views
4	y u c d	cut why did buy act day used your type court place
5	Alphabet	Del Fox just quit my show and gave back his prize.

| 1 | 2 | 3 | 4 | 5 | 6 | 7 | 8 | 9 | 10 |

Job 7: Summary of Telephone Conversation

Type the following summary of a telephone conversation between Mr. Harrington and Mr. Barnes in the form of a memorandum. Center the heading SUMMARY OF TELEPHONE CONVERSATION. Indent the enumerated items 5 spaces from both margins. Prepare a carbon copy for Mr. Barnes.

	Words
DATE: April 17, 19---	4

SUBJECT: Contract Negotiations   11

(¶ 1) With the permission of both parties, the   19
telephone conversation of April 17, 19--, be-   28
tween Charles B. Harrington, President of   36
General Products Manufacturing Company,   44
and J. T. Barnes, Business Agent of Local   52
289, Independent Mechanics Union, regarding   61
contract negotiations was recorded. The fol-   70
lowing is a summary of the major points dis-   79
cussed. (enumerate) 1. Contract negotiations   86
between the company and the union will begin   95
at 9:30 a.m. on May 15, 19--. The site of all   104
negotiations will be Suite 1208 of the Hotel   113
American. The company will be the host.   121
Discussions on May 15 will deal primarily   130
with matters of procedure. 2. On May 16,   138
the union will present its formal contract pro-   148
posals. A detailed, written statement of the   157
proposals will be provided. 3. On May 18, the   166
company will reply to the proposals made by   175
the union and offer additional items for discus-   185
sion. 4. Mr. Barnes stated that the union will   194
be prepared to discuss a three-year contract   203
to replace the current one-year contract. He   213
also asked that the company give close atten-   221
tion to fringe benefits, especially those deal-   231
ing with health insurance and improved   238
retirement plans. 5. Mr. Harrington stated   247
that the company is vitally interested in dis-   256
cussing the introduction of automated equip-   265
ment in any new plants that may be constructed   274
in the future. He requested that the union   283
study the use of automation in the facilities of   293
competitors and present the union's views on   302
automation during the negotiations. 6. It was   312
agreed that, in the event the parties cannot   321
reach an agreement upon a new contract   328
within 30 days after the start of negotiations,   338
all matters in dispute will be referred to a   347
panel of arbitrators, as provided in the current   357
contract.   359

Job 8: Press Release

Type the following press release in the form illustrated at the right. Type an original copy for the *Morning Press*, the *Evening Gazette*, and TV station KQMU. At the bottom of the page, center ### to indicate the end of the release.

	Words
FROM: General Products Manufacturing	8
Company	9
DATE: June 15, 19---	13
For Immediate Release	18

(¶ 1) The General Products Manufacturing   25
Company will begin the construction of a new   34
plant in Easton, Wisconsin, within the next   43
two months according to an announcement   51
made today by Charles B. Harrington, Presi-   59
dent of the company. General Products, one   68
of the nation's leading manufacturers of elec-   77
trical and electronic components, now oper-   85
ates two plants in the Milwaukee area. (¶ 2)   93
Easton was selected for the site of the new   102
General Products plant, according to Mr. Har-   111
rington, because of the many advantages it   119
offers from the standpoint of water, labor, and   129
transportation. Although the plant will be   138
semiautomated, more than 100 employees will   147
be required by the third year of operation.   156
The annual payroll at that time will exceed a   165
half-million dollars. (¶ 3) An outstanding   172
feature of the new plant will be one of the   181
most modern research facilities in the United   190
States. "Although great progress has been   199
made, electronics is still in its infancy," Har-   208
rington stated. "Initially, our new research   218
facility will be limited to the small-scale ex-   227
perimental production of several different de-   236
signs of integrated circuits, with the objective   246
of developing miniaturized components for   254
the ever-expanding aerospace industry." (¶ 4)   262
The General Products Manufacturing Com-   270
pany was founded in 1939 by Brooks A. East-   278
wood, now Chairman of the Board of Trustees.   287

288

12D Paragraph (Continuity) Typing ⑮

Each ¶ is marked with the 4-word count shown in figures and with an in-between count of two words shown by a dot (.) to aid in determining your 1′ *gwam*. (Use figure or dot nearest last word typed.)

¶ 1: TYPE two 1′ writings. The figure or dot (.) above the last word typed (ignoring errors temporarily) will be your 1′ *gwam*.

¶ 2: TYPE as directed for ¶ 1.

¶s 1 and 2: TYPE a 2′ writing, beginning with ¶ 1 and typing as much of ¶ 2 as you can. Divide 1′ *gwam* (figures at right plus incomplete sentence, if any) by 2 for your 2′ *gwam*.

All letters are used.

		1′ GWAM
¶1 1.0 SI 4.6 AWL 95% HFW	Make up your mind to put first things first;	9
	and if you try to mix work and fun, be quite sure	19
	you do the work first; then do what you wish, for	29
	you did first that which was first.	36
¶2 1.0 SI 4.6 AWL 95% HFW	When you work, work as hard as you can; when	45
	you play, you can do just what you wish. Do both	55
	with zest to be at your best. Right now let your	65
	work come first, and you will learn to type well.	75

| 1 | 2 | 3 | 4 | 5 | 6 | 7 | 8 | 9 | 10 |

12E Stroking Skill Checkup ⑩

DO: Type each sentence as a 1′ writing, typing it as many times as you can until time is called.

DO: Type Sentences 1, 3, and 5 for 1′ each; compare the *gwam** for the writings.

Stroking Cue: Make low, quick reach-strokes. Keep the hands and arms quiet—almost motionless.

All letters are used.

		Words in Line
1	Is there work for each of us to do?	7
2	Do you think you can learn to type well?	8
3	Wish for what you want, but work for it, too.	9
4	The six girls do not have quite the zeal you have.	10
5	All of them know they must put first things first.	10
6	He needs to know just the way to write your check.	10

| 1 | 2 | 3 | 4 | 5 | 6 | 7 | 8 | 9 | 10 |

*TO DETERMINE GWAM:

1. List the figure at the end of each complete line typed during the timed writing.

2. Note in the scale the figure directly below the point at which you stopped typing.

3. Add these figures to determine the total gross words typed, known as *gwam*.

Type the following report of the Planning Committee with 1-inch top and side margins, single-spaced; double-space the table.

	Words
PRELIMINARY REPORT OF THE PLANNING COMMITTEE	9
ON THE PROPOSED PLANT IN EASTON	15

Projected Net Income for First Three Years — 24

The following table is a summary of anticipated gross sales. antici- 37 pated expenditures, and anticipated net income for the first three-year 52 period of operation at the proposed Easton Plant. 62

	First Year	Second Year	Third Year	Words
				75
Gross sales[1]	$2,000,000	$3,000,000	$4,500,000	90
Expenditures:				93
Purchases[2]	560,000	590,000	940,000	100
Wages and salaries[3]	200,000	300,000	500,000	109
Other direct costs	120,000	180,000	270,000	118
Indirect costs	150,000	275,000	295,000	125
Taxes[4]	250,000	390,000	520,000	138
Total expenditures	$1,280,000	$1,735,000	$2,525,000	154
Net income[5]	$ 720,000	$1,265,000	$1,975,000	179

[1]Projected sales are based on the assumption that increased sales 192 will necessitate an expansion of 35% in production capacity each year 206 after the first. 210

[2]In addition to the purchase of materials required for increased 223 production, a factor of 2% a year has been included in the cost of mate- 237 rials based on an anticipated rise in prices. 246

[3]Labor costs are based on the assumption that a 3-year contract with 260 the union will be signed and that labor conditions will remain relatively 275 stable during the 3-year period. 281

[4]Since Congress has initiated a detailed study of the Federal tax 294 structure, it is extremely difficult to project taxes. This study, how- 309 ever, was made on the assumption that there will be no major revision in 324 corporate tax rates during the period covered. 334

[5]The net income represents a 36% return on gross sales the first 347 year, 42.2% the second year, and 43.9% the third year. This will equal 361 a return on capital investment of 8% the first year, 8.6% the second 375 year, and 9.1% the third year. 381

Respectfully submitted, 386
DS
J. Thomas VonClay, Chairman 392

SECTION 2 ▶ IMPROVING BASIC SKILLS

LESSONS 13–15

Purpose. The purpose of this section is to improve your typing techniques and stroking skill. You will also learn to type longer words. *All letters are used in every drill of this section.*

Machine Adjustments. Line: 60—left margin stop 30 spaces to left of center, right stop at end of scale. Single-space (SS) word and sentence drills; double-space (DS) and indent paragraphs 5 spaces.

LESSON 13

13A Preparatory Practice ⑧ *each line three times SS; DS between groups*

Alphabet   My friend Jack would just love to pass up his next big quiz.

2-syllable words Begin typing at a very easy pace. Speed up as you go along.

Fluency   Do the work you like to do and like the work you have to do.
| 1 | 2 | 3 | 4 | 5 | 6 | 7 | 8 | 9 | 10 | 11 | 12 |

13B Manipulative Parts Drill: Shift Keys ⑩ *each line at least twice SS; DS between groups*

1 Left shift   Kathy and Nat Kelso left for Nepal; the Harts went to Japan.

2 Right shift C. Q. Roberts may open an office above A. X. Sill Supply Co.

3 Both shifts Ask Jan Ellis, Don Maze, and Glenn Markel to help Mrs. Bell.

4 Both shifts Will Clyde Coe or Rick Dye enter the race at Le Mans in May?

5 Both shifts Use AL for Ala., WI for Wis., MA for Mass., and CO for Colo.
| 1 | 2 | 3 | 4 | 5 | 6 | 7 | 8 | 9 | 10 | 11 | 12 |

13C Technique Practice: Response Patterns ⑮ *each line at least twice SS; DS between groups*

Word-Level Response. Some short, frequently used words (like **to, and, the,** and **work**) are so easy to type they can be typed as words instead of letter by letter. *Think and type the word.*

Letter-Level Response. Many words (like **only, state, exceed,** and **extra**) are not so easy to type even though they are often used. Such words are typed letter by letter. *Think the letter; type it.*

Combination Response. Most normal copy is composed of both word- and letter-level sequences that require variable speed: high speed for easy words, low speed for hard ones. *Learn to recognize the difference.*

1 Word-level   is to for do an may work so it but an with and them she with
2 response   if he is to go; she did the work; he may work with the panel
3   He may go with us and make them do the work by the big dock.

4 Letter-level only state jolly zest date plump verve extra join rate taxes
5 response   you saw a great race; my only free dates are; get a tax case
6   You exceeded the stated rate; only the street guard saw you.

7 Combination it up so at for you may was but him work were they best into
8 response   the case is, the great city, date the card, quit my best job
9   If it is up to you to get the best rate, look into it today.
| 1 | 2 | 3 | 4 | 5 | 6 | 7 | 8 | 9 | 10 | 11 | 12 |

Job 5: Rough Draft of a Report

Type the following report of the Planning Committee as an unbound manuscript with a 1-inch top margin. Prepare an original and four carbon copies.

PLANNING COMMITTEE PRELIMINARY REPORT OF   8

Feasability of Locating A Plant in Easton, Wisconsin   19

1. <u>Labor</u>. Easton is a buyer's market for industrial firms ~~which use~~ utilizing workers   35

     with relatively ~~only a few~~ skills. The ~~exceptionally~~ high rate of local unemploy-   47

     ment (10.6% of the work force) contributes to the advantageous position of   62

     local industry in the labor ~~field~~ market.   69

2. POWER & FUEL. Easton is located in an ~~era~~ area in which fuel and power costs are   86

     "average." Electricity is the ~~major~~ main source of power. An atomic energy   100

     plant to generate electricity to be built ~~sometime in the near future~~ within the next two years,   114

     should reduce power costs ~~to a great extent~~ considerably.   122

3. WATER. Because of it's proximity to ~~a number of~~ numerous small lakes, water supply   137

     is abundant and relatively cheap. This is one of the ~~main~~ major advantages   152

     of locating ~~a new manufacturing plant~~ in Easton.   156

4. TAXES. Tax concessions are made to new industries only after ~~negotiations~~ stet   172

     with ~~the~~ local ~~governments~~ officials. In the past, the city and county have   184

     ~~been generous in granting concessions~~ granted reductions in the assessment ratio of up to   19?

     ~~twenty-five percent~~ 25% for the first three years. Last year, city taxes   206

     on ~~land and buildings~~ real property were 17 mills on 40% of the ~~selling price~~ market value.   217

     County and school taxes were ~~2.2%~~ 22 mills.   225

5. TRANSPORTATION. Easton is situated favorably with regard to national mar-   241

     kets. The availability of excellent high ways is a ~~element~~ factor which favors   255

     plant location. Excellent local facilities exist for air-freight   281

     service, although motor freight is the primary means of transportation,   283

6. ANTICIPATED RETURN ON INVESTMENT. See confidential   294

     summary.   296

13D Continuity Practice: Guided Writing ⑰ ½', 1', and 2' writings as directed

Paragraph 1. Type two ½-minute writings. Determine *gwam* for the better writing (1' *gwam* times 2). Use this as your ½-minute base rate when setting a new goal. Ignore errors temporarily.

New Goal: Add 2 *gwam* to your ½-minute base rate; then type two ½-minute and two 1-minute writings at the new goal rate.
Paragraph 2. TYPE ¶ 2 as directed for ¶ 1.

Paragraphs 1 and 2. Type a 2-minute writing without the guides. Begin with ¶ 1 and type as much of ¶ 2 as you can. Determine *gwam*. Ignore errors. If time permits, type a second 2-minute writing.

All letters are used.

		GWAM *1'
¶1	The person who cannot do at least one thing quite well	11
1.2 SI 4.8 AWL 94% HFW	finds it hard to move ahead in any job. So work on; do not	23
	give up. Value your new skill. Try daily to improve it.	34
¶2	Size up the kind of job you want, and build the skills	45
1.2 SI 4.8 AWL 94% HFW	it requires. If typing is one of them, try to develop high	57
	speed next. Direct your effort to a new goal day by day.	69

1' GWAM | 1 | 2 | 3 | 4 | 5 | 6 | 7 | 8 | 9 | 10 | 11 | 12 |

*The figures in the GWAM Column at the right of the ¶s show the total words as well as the 1' *gwam*. The scale beneath the final ¶ indicates the 1' *gwam* for the incomplete line.

To Determine the 2' GWAM: Determine the 1' *gwam*, using the figures at the right of the ¶s and the scale beneath the final ¶; then divide the 1' *gwam* by 2.

LESSON 14

14A Preparatory Practice ⑧ *each line three times SS; DS between groups*

Alphabet   Karl and Jack served with Gus Fox in La Paz but quit in May.

2-syllable words   Cyrus will go into the city for the copy only if he is able.

Fluency   If we have the get up and go, can we go where we want to go?

| 1 | 2 | 3 | 4 | 5 | 6 | 7 | 8 | 9 | 10 | 11 | 12 |

14B Manipulative Parts Drill: Space Bar ⑩ *each line at least twice SS; DS between groups*

he was by the pier; call for my yacht; then get a quick deed

try to do your best now; send us an order; fold the end next

Just keep on, word by word. That is the way to build skill.

See if you can take the prize, for you must have skill then.

| 1 | 2 | 3 | 4 | 5 | 6 | 7 | 8 | 9 | 10 | 11 | 12 |

You are employed in the office of Charles B. Harrington, President of the General Products Manufacturing Company, 7200 West Euclid Avenue, Milwaukee, Wisconsin 53219. Strive for neat, attractive copy.

Job 1: List of Appointments

Type the appointments made by Mr. Harrington for March 23, 19--. Use the heading APPOINTMENTS FOR MARCH 23, 19--. Arrange the material neatly in two columns: Time and Appointment. Make a carbon copy for your use.

Words

9:30 a.m. Courtesy call by J. T. Barnes, the 22
new Business Agent of Local 289, Independ- 30
ent Mechanics Union (schedule for new con- 38
tract talks may be discussed). 10:15 a.m. 46
Coffee with Bill Cervo, Chief of Production, 55
in his office (routine review of current opera- 65
tions). 12:15 p.m., Kiwanis luncheon, Blue 73
Room of the Hotel American (Kiwanis Presi- 81
dent Shaffer has invited you to sit at the head 90
table). 2:00 p.m., Meeting with Planning 98
Committee in Conference Room 203 (agenda 106
attached). 3:15 p.m., Presentation of Service 115
Awards in Shop A (Salvatore Russo, 25 123
years; Barry O'Donnell, 20 years). 6:30 p.m., 132
Dinner meeting of the Executive Secretary 140
Association in the McKinley Room of the 148
Royal York Hotel (black tie). A copy of your 157
speech is attached. 161

Job 2: Partial Text of Speech

The copy in 206C, page 351, and 206D, page 352, is a partial text of a speech Mr. Harrington will make. Type the copy as a leftbound manuscript, *triple-spaced*. Use the heading REVOLUTION IN THE AMERICAN OFFICE. (*406 words*)

Job 3: Topic Outline of Speech

Type the following topic outline of the speech on 8- by 5-inch cards. Use the heading given in Job 2.

Words

I. PERIOD OF GREAT AND DYNAMIC CHANGE 15
A. Revolution in Business Caused by Com- 23
puter (tell story of computer with hiccups) 31
1. Capacity to process information at amazing 41
speed (more than a million bits a second) 49
2. Growing use in routine operations and to 58
solve complex business problems B. Fear That 67

Words

Computer Will Cause Loss of Office Jobs 75
(tell story of lost push button) 1. Routine 84
office operations of computer a. Process orders 94
b. Compute invoices c. File d. Type letter in 104
3 seconds 2. Increased need for clerks and sec- 113
retaries C. Effect of Computer on Quality of 122
Clerks and Secretaries (tell robot story) 131
1. Need for workers to perform routine tasks 140
down 2. Demand for employees with man- 148
agerial abilities up, especially executive secre- 157
taries II. EXECUTIVE SECRETARY ONE OF 165
HIGHEST PAID EMPLOYEES IN OFFICE (give 173
examples) A. Basic Skills Needed 1. Type 181
2. Take notes 3. Answer telephone 4. Other 191
skills B. Managerial Abilities Needed 1. Think 200
analytically 2. Make sound decisions 3. Solve 210
problems 4. Organize effectively 217

Job 4: Letters on Executive-Size Stationery

Type the following letter to each member of the board of trustees listed below. Mr. Harrington prefers that an original copy be sent to each member of the board. Make a carbon of the first letter only and list the other addressees on the back of the carbon copy. (*The word count is given separately for the letter address, envelope address, and salutation for each addressee.*)

Mr. Brooks A. Eastwood, 3479 Lowell Drive, Madison, Wisconsin 53715 (*28 words*)

Mr. Owen Pearson, 201 Edgewater Avenue, Fairview, Wisconsin 53719 (*27 words*)

Mr. Phillip J. Ellsworth, 16 South Pine Avenue, Milwaukee, Wisconsin 53207 (*31 words*)

Dr. C. Earl Hammon, Medical Arts Building, 700 North Tenth Street, Milwaukee, Wisconsin 53233 (*37 words*)

Dr. Milton Lewis, President, Denton University, Greenfield, Wisconsin 53220 (*30 words*)

Words

March 24, 19-- (*Use an appropriate salutation*) 3
(¶ 1) The regular meeting of the Board of 10
Trustees will be held in the company Execu- 19
tive Suite on Monday, May 2, 19--, at 2 27
p.m. (¶ 2) The major item of discussion at 34
the meeting will be the Planning Committee's 43
report of the feasibility of locating a new 52
plant in Easton, Wisconsin. A preliminary 61
report of the committee is enclosed for your 70
study. A copy of the complete agenda will be 79
mailed to you within the next week. Sin- 87
cerely yours (*Provide appropriate closing lines.*) 99

14C Technique Practice: Stroking ⑭ *each line at least twice SS; DS between groups*

1	Home row	Alf Lakas had Sal add half a glass. I shall stash all cash.
2	Third row	Your typewriter is a useful tool; it helps you perform well.
3	Bottom row	Mac gave all six men a chance to act as foremen in my plant.
4	Adjacent keys	Mr. Leeds had his store open, but Sal quit buying art there.
5	Direct reaches	A host of friends is just a myth; true friends are numbered.
6	Double letters	Will Buzz and Lee carry the express carton to my booth soon?
7	One-hand words	After my new rate was set, a decrease in taxes was detected.
8	Balanced-hand words	It is right for them to sign the forms; Ken may do so, also.

| 1 | 2 | 3 | 4 | 5 | 6 | 7 | 8 | 9 | 10 | 11 | 12 |

14D Continuity Practice: Guided Writing ⑱

DO: Type ½- and 1-minute writings on each ¶ as directed in 13D, page 28.

Then, type a 2-* and a 3-minute writing, beginning with ¶ 1 and typing as much of ¶ 2 as you can.

All letters are used.

		GWAM	
		1'	3'

¶1
1.2 SI
4.8 AWL
94% HFW

	1'	3'
The major aim of this book is to help you learn how to	11	4 · 35
type. Its second aim is to help you improve how you write,	23	8 · 39
for you will not always be able merely to copy all the work	35	12 · 43
you need to prepare. You will have to compose, also.	46	15 · 46

¶2
1.2 SI
4.8 AWL
94% HFW

	1'	3'
As you practice to learn how to type, try to develop a	57	19 · 50
writing skill, too. The next time you are asked to compose	69	23 · 54
a paper for class, size up the job and set about writing it	81	27 · 58
on the machine. It may be quite slow at first, but keep on.	93	31 · 62

1' GWAM | 1 | 2 | 3 | 4 | 5 | 6 | 7 | 8 | 9 | 10 | 11 | 12 |
3' GWAM | 1 | 2 | 3 | 4 |

*To determine the 2' rate, divide the 1' rate by 2.

LESSON 15

15A Preparatory Practice ③ *each line three times SS; DS between groups*

Alphabet	Was Dale quick to give him a box just the size for my plant?
2-syllable words	Many of the women are away today to study a new money offer.
Fluency	A man can grow out of a small job and come to fit a big one.

| 1 | 2 | 3 | 4 | 5 | 6 | 7 | 8 | 9 | 10 | 11 | 12 |

All letters are used.

		GWAM	
		1'	5'

¶ 1
1.6 SI
5.8 AWL
75% HFW

Though it is true that the use of the computer has not reduced the
need for clerical and secretarial personnel, it has had a decided effect
on the quality of office workers hired. The need for clerks who can
perform only repetitive jobs has declined since the computer can execute
routine operations far more efficiently than humans. On the other hand,
the demand for the employee with managerial skills has grown rapidly.
This is especially true of those who work in an executive office.

1'	5'	
13	42	81
28	45	84
42	47	87
56	50	89
71	53	92
85	56	95
98	59	98

¶ 2
1.6 SI
5.8 AWL
75% HFW

The executive secretary is one of the highest paid employees in an
office. To attain one of these jobs, you must know how to type, take
notes, file, use the telephone, and perform other tasks. In addition,
you must be adept in the skills of management. You must know how to
think analytically, how to make sound decisions, how to solve problems,
and how to organize effectively. These are the qualities that separate
the executive secretary from a typical clerk and command higher pay.

1'	5'	
13	61	100
27	64	103
42	67	106
55	70	109
70	73	112
84	75	115
98	78	117

1' GWAM | 1 | 2 | 3 | 4 | 5 | 6 | 7 | 8 | 9 | 10 | 11 | 12 | 13 | 14 |
5' GWAM | 1 | 2 | 3 |

206E Sustained Skill Building (15) *two 5' timed writings; determine average* nwam

Begin with the paragraphs of 206C, page 351;
continue with the paragraphs of 206D, above. If necessary, repeat the paragraphs of 206D, above. The 5'
gwam count is continued from page 351 to page 352.

LESSONS 207-210

LESSONS 207 AND 209

Use the following plan for Lessons 207 and 209.
Retain all jobs until you have completed Lesson 210.

207, 209A Preparatory Practice: (5') Type either
206A, page 351, or 211A, page 358, as directed
there.

207, 209B Technique Practice: (5') Type each of
the first three lines of 206B, page 351, as 1'
exploration-level writings.

207, 209C Building Speed: (10') Type two 2'
exploration-level writings on each ¶ of 206D, above.
Determine your *gwam* by dividing the 1' *gwam* provided by 2.

207, 209D Production Typing: (30') Type the jobs
beginning on page 353. Type as many jobs as you
can in the time provided each day. When time is
called, complete the line on which you are typing so
that you can begin on a new line the next day. Follow
the directions carefully.

LESSONS 208 AND 210

Use the following plan for Lessons 208 and 210.
Retain all jobs until you have completed Lesson 210.

208, 210A Preparatory Practice: (5') Type either
206A, page 351, or 212A, page 360, as directed
there.

208, 210B Technique Practice: (5') Type each of
the first three lines of 206B, page 351, as 1' *control-
level* writings.

208, 210C Building Control: (10') Type two 2'
control-level writings on each ¶ of 206C, page 351.
Determine *nwam* by dividing the 1' *nwam* by 2.

208, 210D Production Typing: (30') Continue typing the jobs. When you have completed Lesson 210,
place your name and the job number in the upper
right corner of each job. Arrange the jobs in numeric
order and fasten them with a paper clip.

15B Manipulative Parts Drill: Tabulator and Return ⑩ *twice as shown*

Machine Adjustments. Line: 60. Clear all tabulator stops; set a tab stop 5 spaces to the right of the left margin; then, set three additional tab stops 5 spaces apart.

Procedure. Begin the first line of the drill at the left margin. Tabulate once (5 spaces) to type Line 2; 10 spaces to type Line 3, and so forth. Learn to tab, release, and type quickly.

1	Margin→	Set a new goal for each drill and push yourself to reach it.
2	Indent 5 ----→	A new goal and renewed zeal may be all you need to win.
3	Indent 10 --------→	If more speed is your goal, keep your hands quiet.
4	Indent 15 ------------→	Do not quit; just keep on; give it your best.
5	Indent 20 ----------------→	Ask much of yourself; next, work for it.

15C Technique Practice: Stroking ⑮ *each line three times SS; DS between groups*

1	Long words	deftly together clarity express ideas puzzling message today
2	Weak fingers	exact size; top tax plan; quick stop; pop quiz; I was amazed
3	Awkward reaches	extra plaque; only jazz; excess nylon; was razed; exact copy
4	One-hand	Are you on my tax case? My tax rates are, in fact, average.
5	Balanced-hand	It is the duty of the six girls to work with the audit firm.
6	Combination	He based the case upon the data shown on the express ticket.

| 1 | 2 | 3 | 4 | 5 | 6 | 7 | 8 | 9 | 10 | 11 | 12 |

15D Growth Index ⑰ *three 3' writings; determine average gwam*

All letters are used.

		GWAM 1'	GWAM 3'
¶1	How well you write means just how deftly you put words	11	4 | 36
1.2 SI 4.8 AWL 94% HFW	together to say what you want to say. It does not mean how	23	8 | 40
	well you can use a pen. If you learn to type well, you can	35	12 | 44
	improve the clarity as well as the manner of your writing.	47	16 | 48
¶2	When you next try to express an idea, reduce the haze;	58	19 | 52
1.2 SI 4.8 AWL 94% HFW	say what you want to say in such a way that the reader will	70	23 | 56
	know your meaning quickly. Do not leave him to puzzle over	82	27 | 60
	your message. A top typing job will help him on his way to	94	31 | 64
	what you mean, too.	97	32 | 65

| 1' GWAM | 1 | 2 | 3 | 4 | 5 | 6 | 7 | 8 | 9 | 10 | 11 | 12 |
| 3' GWAM | | 1 | | 2 | | 3 | | 4 | | | |

SECTION 32 TYPING IN AN EXECUTIVE OFFICE

LESSONS 206–217

Drill Copy: Full sheet; 70-space line; SS.
Paragraph Copy: Full sheet; 70-space line; DS; 5-space ¶ indention.
Production Copy: When complete directions are not given, use your own judgment. Choose letter and punctuation styles; correct errors; make carbon copies as directed.
Special Supplies Needed: Executive-size letterheads, appropriate envelopes, 8- by 5-inch and 5- by 3-inch cards.

LESSON 206

206A Preparatory Practice (5) *each line at least three times*

Alphabet	Jack and Marge Sawyer explored the queer caves in Arizona before dawn.
Figures	The factory produced 3,876 units on May 19 and 4,529 units on June 20.
Shift keys	J. T. Kane will visit Jamaica, N.Y., Altoona, Pa., and Lake Shore, Md.
Fluency	The quality of the work done is much more important than the quantity.
	| 1 | 2 | 3 | 4 | 5 | 6 | 7 | 8 | 9 | 10 | 11 | 12 | 13 | 14 |

206B Technique Practice (10) *each line four times; then 1′ writings*

One hand	In effect, we agree with his opinion regarding the great oil monopoly.
Direct reaches	I must include in my article the data from that issue of the magazine.
Double letters	I feel that good manners are essential to success in business affairs.
Balanced hand	The panel may work with the auditor to check the finances of the firm.
	| 1 | 2 | 3 | 4 | 5 | 6 | 7 | 8 | 9 | 10 | 11 | 12 | 13 | 14 |

206C Building Speed (10) *three 1′* exploration-level *writings on each ¶; compare* gwam

All letters are used.

		GWAM 1′	GWAM 5′
¶ 1 1.6 SI 5.8 AWL 75% HFW	We are living in a period of great and dynamic change. We are	13	3
	in the midst of a revolution in business which was brought about by the	27	5
	introduction and employment of the computer. The value of the computer	41	8
	lies in its capacity to process information at amazing speeds. It is	55	11
	no problem whatever for a computer to process more than a million bits	70	14
	of information a second. From routine operations to the solution of	83	17
	complex business problems, the importance of the computer is growing.	97	19
¶ 2 1.6 SI 5.8 AWL 75% HFW	Many people are quite sure that the use of the computer will cause	13	22
	a great number of office workers to lose their jobs. The computer has	28	25
	the ability to execute many of the routine operations in an office.	41	28
	It can process orders, compute invoices, and file all records. It can	56	31
	even type a personalized, full-page letter in less than three seconds.	70	33
	Despite the extensive use of the computer, the need for skilled clerical	85	36
	and secretarial personnel has grown steadily in the past ten years.	98	39
1′ GWAM	| 1 | 2 | 3 | 4 | 5 | 6 | 7 | 8 | 9 | 10 | 11 | 12 | 13 | 14 |		
5′ GWAM	| 1 | 2 | 3 |		

Purpose. The basic purpose of this section is to develop your figure-typing skill. You will also build your basic skills to higher levels.

Machine Adjustments. Line: 60; SS all drills, unless otherwise directed; DS and indent ¶s 5 spaces.

Self-Improvement Practice. Select from page 39 material correlating with the appropriate lesson.

Copy Difficulty. Up to now you have typed very easy copy. You will now type longer, less frequent words that contain more syllables.

Some of the drills may be more difficult, but the straight-copy ¶s you will type are rated *Easy.*

You will also type some copy that contains figures and still other material in handwritten or script form.

LESSON 16

16A   Preparatory Practice ⑧ *each line twice SS; DS between two-line groups*

Alphabet	Four jets zoomed up quickly, leaving six white trails below.
x and p	Rex put six stamps on a tiny box for the next postal pickup.
y and q	Ilya Myers quietly began her quest for quaint styles Monday.
Fluency	They kept the rug on the theory that they had a right to it.

| 1 | 2 | 3 | 4 | 5 | 6 | 7 | 8 | 9 | 10 | 11 | 12 |

16B   Stroking Technique Practice for 5, 8, and 1 ⑮

5—Left first finger

8—Right second finger

1—Left fourth finger
(Special Figure 1)

1—Right third finger
(Letter *l* for 1)

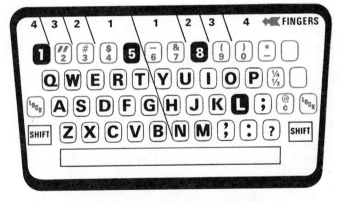

1. Locate the new key on the keyboard chart.
2. Find the key on your typewriter keyboard.
3. Study the appropriate reach illustration, at left.
4. Watch your finger make the reach a few times.
5. Type the tryout drill, below, for that key.

Tryout Drills *each line at least twice*

1	5	f f5f 5f 5f 551 555	All 55 students took 5 tests in 5 days.
2	8	k k8k 8k 8k 881 888	Kate may play the 88 from 8 until late.
3	Figure 1	a ala la la 111 111	My 11 men worked from May 1 to June 11.
4	Letter l as 1	1 11 .1 1. .11 1.1.	My 11 men worked from May 1 to June 11.
5	Consolidation	Is it Channel 5, 8, or 11? Was the score 5 to 8, or 8 to 5?	
6		Three of the 158 men are absent; the other 155 arrived at 8.	

| 1 | 2 | 3 | 4 | 5 | 6 | 7 | 8 | 9 | 10 | 11 | 12 |

Job 1: Government Letter

	Words
march 9 19–– in reply refer to Order 8561–XL	10
your reference CfLtr 3–1 lester imprint com-	18
pany 1450 parramore street abilene tx	26
79601 gentlemen (¶ 1) Please disregard	33
Paragraph Three, Contract AB–89357–K, as	42
it pertains to our most recent order placed	50
with your company. All other paragraphs	59
should remain in effect, and delivery will be	68
accepted in accordance therewith. (¶ 2) Due	76
to recent changes in postal regulations, specifi-	85
cations as treated in Paragraph Three will no	94
longer be required in filling our orders. (¶ 3)	103
Please inform us if there is a price differential	113
due to this change. sincerely yours max r hel-	122
pern chief federal supply service DPly-	130
mouth:	134

Job 2: Military Letter

	Words
(*Reference*) AB–157 (*date*) 26 April 19––	4
SUBJECT: Removal of Command to Fort	12
Benning Commanding Officer 25th Brigade	20
Fort Lincoln Springfield, IL 62703 (¶ 1)	27
1. Within five days, orders will be issued to	36
move your command from its present barrack	45
to Fort Benning, GA. Copies of these orders	54
will be delivered to you through the Com-	62
manding General, Fort Lincoln. (¶ 2) 2. Upon	70
receipt of these orders, will you please inform	79
this office, through the CG Fort Benning, of	88
your proposed schedule of movements in order	97
to be established on your new post on or be-	106
fore 1 June. (¶ 3) 3. Inform this office, through	115
CG Fort Lincoln, of transportation needed to	124
accomplish this movement. Air travel will be	133
furnished only in case of emergency. Use	142
Form AB–65, a copy of which is inclosed.	150
BY ORDER OF THE COMMANDING GENERAL:	158
1 Incl REGIS L. BIXBY	162
as Lt. Col., CAV.	166
Troop Supply and Services	171
CF:	172
CG, Fort Lincoln	175
CG, Fort Benning	178

Job 3: Approval Copy of Directive

1" top and side margins; center and DS heading; 5-space ¶ indentions; SS ¶s

	Words
U.S. DEPARTMENT OF HEALTH, EDUCATION,	8
AND WELFARE | OFFICE OF EDUCATION |	14
Washington, D.C. 20202 (*DS; type the current*	19
date at the right margin. Space 6 times; type the	
following as a salutation.) TO DEANS AND	21
DIRECTORS OF RESEARCH PROJECTS: | SUB-	29
JECT: Cooperative Research Program | (¶ 1)	36
Enclosed are four reports as follows: (*Indent*	44
the following 10 spaces from each margin; DS	
between items.) (¶ 2) 1. A general statement	48
of purpose and authority regarding the pro-	57
gram. (¶ 3) 2. Criteria for evaluating pro-	64
posals. (¶ 4) 3. General instructions for	72
preparing an application for support of a co-	81
operative research project. (¶ 5) 4. Instruc-	89
tions for preparing a budget for the project.	98
(¶ 6) Please note that 30 copies of a research	106
proposal are now required, instead of the for-	115
mer 20. Also, a one-page abstract of the pro-	124
posal is to be included as part of the applica-	134
tion. (¶ 7) Please destroy earlier versions of	142
the four reports. If you need additional copies	152
of the revised reports, you may write to this	161
office for them. (*TS and start at center.*) Wil-	165
liam B. Bayless Research Coordinator Co-	173
operative Research Branch (*at left margin*)	178
Enclosures: Form CR–29(69) Form CR–30	186
(69) Form CR–1(69) Form CR–1.1(69).	192

Job 4: Government Letter with Changes

Retype Job 1. Address the letter to:

	Words
A & D Stationery, Inc.	5
480 Madison Avenue	9
Paterson, NJ 07524	13

(*regarding Contract AB–89330–K*)

16C Tab Mechanism and Figure Practice ⑫ *type the drill three times as shown*

PROCEDURE FOR SETTING TAB STOPS	TECHNIQUE EMPHASIS
1. Clear all tab stops. (See page 17, if necessary.)	**Nonelectric:** Depress and hold the tab bar or key down until the carriage stops. Move quickly back to home position and type the next item.
2. For Column 2, set a tab stop 8 spaces from the left margin.	
3. For Column 3, set a tab stop 8 spaces from the first tab stop.	**Electric:** Flick the tab key or bar lightly; return the controlling finger to its home position at once.
4. Set stops for remaining columns in similar manner.	

Reach with the fingers									Eyes on copy during return
	it	to	if	do	go	so	the	and	
	85	15	88	55	51	18	581	858	
	we	in	as	no	be	on	was	pin	
								DS	
	58	88	51	85	55	15	518	115	
	by	of	an	is	me	am	oz.	lb.	
	81	55	18	88	85	58	181	151	
KEY	2 6	2 6	2 6	2 6	2 6	2 6	3 6	3	

16D Skill-Transfer Typing ⑮

Skill-transfer typing is a procedure used to determine how well you are able to transfer your straight-copy skill to other types of copy: script (handwritten copy) and statistical copy, for example. **Goal:** To equal your straight-copy rate.

1. Type each ¶ as a 1′ writing. Compare *gwam*. If your script rate does not equal your straight-copy rate, type two additional 1′ writings on ¶ 2.

2. Type each ¶ again as a 1′ writing. Compare *gwam*.

3. Type a 3′ writing on ¶s 1 and 2 combined.

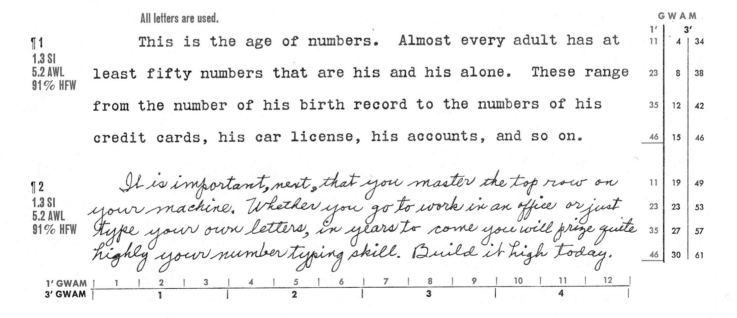

All letters are used.

		GWAM		
		1′	3′	
¶1 1.3 SI 5.2 AWL 91% HFW	This is the age of numbers. Almost every adult has at	11	4	34
	least fifty numbers that are his and his alone. These range	23	8	38
	from the number of his birth record to the numbers of his	35	12	42
	credit cards, his car license, his accounts, and so on.	46	15	46
¶2 1.3 SI 5.2 AWL 91% HFW	It is important, next, that you master the top row on	11	19	49
	your machine. Whether you go to work in an office or just	23	23	53
	type your own letters, in years to come you will prize quite	35	27	57
	highly your number typing skill. Build it high today.	46	30	61

1′ GWAM | 1 | 2 | 3 | 4 | 5 | 6 | 7 | 8 | 9 | 10 | 11 | 12 |
3′ GWAM | | 1 | | 2 | | 3 | | 4 | |

GWAM
1′ 10′

All letters are used.

¶ 1
1.6 SI
5.8 AWL
75% HFW

One of the important reasons for gaining a college education is that it can prepare us for life of a nature that is not possible with lesser educational levels. While a college degree does not automatically open doors, it can provide a set of keys that will. Hopefully, in our set would be found such keys as Appreciation, Logic, Technology, and Flexibility. But in an age that moves as fast as the present one, locks change rapidly; our educational keys will need constant attention.

¶ 2
1.6 SI
5.8 AWL
75% HFW

One of the easier ways we can keep up to date is with a well-planned reading program. A local daily newspaper, read thoroughly, can keep us abreast of daily occurrences. Studying a current events magazine can give us the in-depth comprehension we need on topics of vital interest. For exercising our mental facilities, what can beat a good book? A daily newspaper, a weekly magazine, a monthly book, all read from cover to cover, can help us stay alert, interested, and interesting.

¶ 3
1.6 SI
5.8 AWL
75% HFW

The educated man has learned, also, that he can discover important details through the simple act of listening. The secret, however, as is well known, is to listen with discretion. His usual ability to hear forces him to tune in thousands of noises, while his keen listening ability lets him select what is vital from what is minutiae. Often his only contribution is a question; and if his listening post is an important television program, he doesn't have to make any comment at all.

¶ 4
1.6 SI
5.8 AWL
75% HFW

The classroom is still useful even if we may have completed a formal part of our education. Higher degrees are possible--and desirable. For the person who does not wish to enter a degree program yet needs to obtain some additional, perhaps specialized, education, classes are often offered. Adult classes in a locality, for example, have been known to run from interior design to judo, from art to philately. Some of these classes are fun; but learning can be fun as well as useful.

¶ 5
1.6 SI
5.8 AWL
75% HFW

An intelligent man looks for education in activities. He sees and does things, he goes places; and he learns by seeing, doing, and going. Anything new is of interest to him--in foods, in music, in hobbies, in sports, in nearly everything. He can probably attend either a concert or a basketball game with the same quiet enthusiasm because he knows how to understand and enjoy both. He figures that life provides things and ideas to be sampled, understood, and appreciated--for his own benefit.

¶ 6
1.6 SI
5.8 AWL
75% HFW

Then, too, for the educated man there are those rewarding moments in his life that are meant for quiet meditation. If, through his activities, he is learning, his enhanced education must continue to answer questions and solve problems connected with his life. Simply to react to his environment is not enough for him--he wants to reason. If his education is to be at all meaningful to him, it must be given meaning by integrating it into his existence, maybe even via his philosophy.

1′	10′
13	1	60
27	3	61
41	4	63
55	6	64
69	7	66
83	8	67
98	10	69
14	11	70
28	13	71
42	14	73
57	16	74
70	17	76
85	18	77
97	20	78
13	21	80
28	22	81
42	24	82
55	25	84
70	27	85
84	28	87
98	29	88
13	31	89
28	32	91
42	34	92
56	35	94
69	36	95
84	38	96
97	39	98
13	40	99
28	42	101
42	43	102
56	45	103
71	46	105
85	48	106
99	49	108
13	50	109
27	52	110
42	53	112
56	55	113
70	56	115
84	57	116
98	59	117

1′ GWAM | 1 | 2 | 3 | 4 | 5 | 6 | 7 | 8 | 9 | 10 | 11 | 12 | 13 | 14 |
10′ GWAM | 1 | 2 |

17A Preparatory Practice (8) *each line twice SS; DS between two-line groups*

Alphabet   Having just made six quick points, we simply froze the ball.

z and o   Zed overshot their end zone, leaving the score zero to zero.

Figure   Her flight, No. 158, lands at 8 p.m. on Thursday, August 15.

Fluency   Did the firm pay the fares for the men, women, and children?

| 1 | 2 | 3 | 4 | 5 | 6 | 7 | 8 | 9 | 10 | 11 | 12 |

17B Stroking Technique Practice for 2, 0 (Zero), and : (Colon) (15)

2—Left third finger

0—Right fourth finger

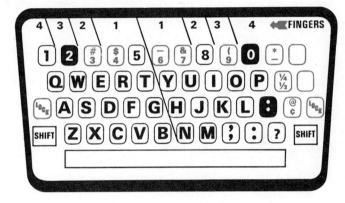

Typing : (Colon). Type : (the shift of ;) with the *right fourth finger*. Do not space after : used to separate hours and minutes in stating time. Space twice after : in other uses.

Tryout Drills *each line at least twice*

1	2	s s2s 2s 2s 22 222 Andrew is 21; Keith, 22; and Walter, 25.
2	0	; ;0; 0; 0 00 000 Use 0, 00, or 000 steel wool for the job.
3	:	; ;:; :; 1:15 8:01 5:10 Call me at 5:15 and arrive at 8:20.
4		Get there by 8:00 or 8:05; the opera begins at 8:15 or 8:20.
5	Consolidation	Whether you are 20 or 50, each workday begins at 8:15 there.

17C Tab Mechanism and Figure Practice (15) *twice with SS; DS between typings*

Set left margin stop; set tab stops to leave 7 spaces between columns.

the	150	work	5810	eight	11,200
for	201	then	1580	handy	58,201
did	885	with	2285	right	21,822
and	551	town	2058	their	20,581
man	820	much	1150	girls	55,220
due	112	firm	8201	chair	18,250
aid	582	land	2805	field	52,815

KEY | 3 | 7 | 3 | 7 | 4 | 7 | 4 | 7 | 5 | 7 | 6 |

Job 4: Letters with Copies Furnished Notation

CF: is used in place of the nonmilitary cc:

	Words
(*Reference*) AXTJ (*date*) 27 April 19-- SUB-	4
JECT: Accounting for Rations During Opera-	13
tion Pioneer Commanding Officer Fort Riley	21
Fort Riley, KS 66442 (¶ 1) 1. Effective this	30
date, the use of Form AXTJ-5100, Accounting	38
for Rations, will be instituted within your	47
command and continued until completion of	56
Operation Pioneer. A completed sample of	64
this form is inclosed for your use. (¶ 2) 2. Pro-	73
cedures necessary for providing required in-	81
ventory figures should be started at once. You	91
will notice that while no statement of disposi-	100
tion of rations is requested, an accurate ac-	109

	Words
counting for those on hand will be needed.	118
(¶ 3) 3. Form AXTJ-6000, Annual Report of	125
Rations, Supplies, and Materiel Consumed,	134
will be continued as a part of your Command-	142
ing Officer's Annual Report. Procedures nec-	151
essary for the completion of this report,	159
therefore, should not be altered.	166

		Words
BY ORDER OF THE COMMANDING GENERAL:		174
1 Incl	E. L. BRITTON	178
as	Colonel, AGC	181
	Adjutant	183
CF:		184
DA, OGS		186
CO, FMS		187

Job 5: One-Paragraph Military Letter

Single ¶s are not numbered

	Words
(*Reference*) ELL-15-J (*date*) 7 September 19--	5
SUBJECT: Lost, Stolen, or Not-Received	13
Checks Commanding Officer First United	21
States Army Fort George G. Meade, MD	28
20755 (¶ 1) Prompt notification by telephone	36
to the Office of Finance will allow a Request	45
for Stop Payment, Form 2749, to be initiated	54

	Words
to the Treasury Department without delay.	63
Claimant will receive a copy. Such notification	73
must be confirmed by a statement personally	81
signed by the owner.	86

	Words
BY ORDER OF THE ADJUTANT GENERAL:	93
B. J. CLEMENTS	96
Major, FC	98
Finance Officer	101

Job 6: Indorsement on a Military Letter

An *indorsement* is a reply or forwarding statement typed on the bottom, back, or second page of a
letter that has been received. Type the indorsement
below on the original and courtesy copy (first carbon
copy) of the letter for Job 5. Single-space; double-
space between items as shown.

	Words
(*Reference*) BRGPA-AA-V	2
DS	
(*from*) DA, OIC, HQ, Fort George G. Meade,	9
Maryland 20755 23 Sept. 19--	15
DS	

	Words
TO: The Adjutant General, ATTN: OSF, De-	23
partment of the Army, Washington	30
DS	
Request supply of Form 2749 be sent this	38
command immediately.	43
DS	
FOR THE COMMANDING OFFICER:	48
LYLA V. RHOERS	51
Lt., WAC	53
Chief, Office Services	58

LESSON 205

205A Preparatory Practice (5) *each line at least three times*

Alphabet
My half dozen flavorful new soup mixes are in big, quick-to-open jars.

Figure-symbol
Their letter of May 21 states, "We shall ship 80 #479 files @ $86.35."

Awkward reaches
Exactly two dozen executives attended the evening exercises in Quebec.

Fluency
What power can be as mighty as the truth, or what can be more strange?

| 1 | 2 | 3 | 4 | 5 | 6 | 7 | 8 | 9 | 10 | 11 | 12 | 13 | 14 |

17D Skill-Transfer Typing ⑮

DO: Type a 1' writing on each ¶. Compare *gwam*. Then type another 1' writing on each of the two slower ¶s.

DO: Finally, type a 3' writing on ¶s 1, 2, and 3 combined. Determine *gwam*. Compare your 3' *gwam* with your best 1' *gwam* on each of the three ¶s.

All letters are used.

	GWAM 1'	3'	

¶1
1.3 SI
5.2 AWL
91% HFW

Will you enjoy working, or will you merely consider it   11 | 4 | 42

something you must do? Your attitude may give the answer.   23 | 8 | 46

Did you enter school to learn in order that you might go   34 | 11 | 50

forth to serve? If so, you may well enjoy your work.   45 | 15 | 54

¶2
1.3 SI
5.2 AWL
91% HFW

At what age will you begin work? If you attend college,   11 | 19 | 58
you will probably be over twenty. Your next major effort may   24 | 23 | 62
bring a sizable job. Will you quit, or will you keep on?   35 | 27 | 66

¶3
1.3 SI
5.2 AWL
91% HFW

Even though the working life of most men is less than 50   11 | 31 | 69

years, more than a few plug along until they exceed 51 or 52.   24 | 35 | 74

In about 18 years, our retirement age may drop by 10 percent.   36 | 39 | 78

1' GWAM | 1 | 2 | 3 | 4 | 5 | 6 | 7 | 8 | 9 | 10 | 11 | 12 |
3' GWAM | 1 | 2 | 3 | 4 |

LESSON 18

18A Preparatory Practice ⑧ *each line twice SS; DS between two-line groups*

Alphabet   One judge was baffled as five boys quickly mixed the prizes.

c and y   Can you come by my office at once to approve your contracts?

Figures   Read: Unit 5, 8 pages; Unit 8, 20 pages; Unit 10, 12 pages.

Fluency   Did the auditor see the bids for this work on the city dock?
| 1 | 2 | 3 | 4 | 5 | 6 | 7 | 8 | 9 | 10 | 11 | 12 |

18B Tab Mechanism and Figure Practice ⑦ *twice as shown; DS between typings*

121	111	1582	12.50	8:15	11,500
212	222	2158	15.20	5:00	25,000
515	555	2085	28.00	2:50	85,205
818	888	8200	22.55	8:20	18,200

KEY | 3 | 7 | 3 | 7 | 4 | 7 | 5 | 7 | 4 | 7 | 6 |

18C Skill-Transfer Typing ⑫ *repeat 17D, above, as directed*

DEPARTMENT OF THE ARMY
OFFICE OF SPECIAL SERVICES
WASHINGTON, DC 20310

S-10 March 19-- DS   3

Fifth line below
letterhead ——→ BL-BMA   Fifth line below
                              letterhead ——→ 12 February 19--   8
        DS

SUBJECT: Format for a Military Letter   16

3 blank lines

Commanding General   20
8th Infantry Division   24
Fort Carson, CO 80913   29

4 blank lines

1. The letter style illustrated here is used for correspond-   41
ence by the agencies of the Departments of the Army, Navy,   52
Air Force, Defense, and the United States Coast Guard.   64

2. Note that it follows generally the modified block style.   76
Allow about one inch for the side margins and at least 1¼   88
inches for the bottom margin.   94

3. Number each paragraph consecutively when more than one   106
paragraph is used.   110

4. Leave four blank lines above the blocked signature lines.   123

5. Type an inclosure notation at the left margin on the same   135
line as the first signature line, showing the total number of   147
inclosures and the abbreviation Incl (with no period). If   159
the inclosures have been identified in the body of the letter,   172
directly below the notation type as (for as stated). If the   184
inclosures have not been identified, number and list each one   197
as shown in the inclosure notation below.   205

Authority line   FOR THE COMMANDER: 209

4 blank lines

                    Robert B. Harris

Enclosure notation   2 Incl   ROBERT B. HARRIS   214
                      1. DBA 270-115   Colonel, AGC   220
                      2. Ltr AF61 7 Oct --   Chief, Manpower Division   230

Margins: side, at
  least 1 inch;
  bottom, at least
  1¼ inches

Military Style Letter (Pica Type)

18D Stroking Technique Practice for 3, 6, and / (Diagonal) ⑬

3—Left second finger

6—Right first finger

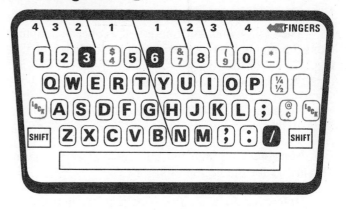

Typing the Diagonal (/). Move the *right fourth finger* down to **?** and *without shifting* type /. Use / to type fractions for which there are no keyboard symbols, as 2/3 and 3/4.

Tryout Drills *each line at least twice*

1	3	d d3d 3d 3d 3d 33 333 Type 31, 38, 53, 30, 23, 58, and 201.
2	6	j j6j 6j 6j 6j 66 666 Reach for 61, 56, 16, 26, 68, and 66.
3	/	; ;/; /; / 1/8 or 1/5 Type these fractions: 1/8, 5/8, 2/5.
4		What is the sum of 136 and 63? of 20 and 58? of 3/5 and 2/3?
5	Consolidation	In 1868, we had just 215 workers; today, we have over 1,300.

18E Stroking Review and Skill Building ⑩

DO: Type each of the four drill lines twice: once for speed; once for control.

DO: Type two 2' writings on the ¶. Determine *gwam* on the better writing.

All figures taught	You must pay Edit, Inc., Invoices 163, 186, and 203 at once.
All figures taught	Order these items: 2 doz. 513A; 3 lbs. 268X; 10 gal. 360DC.
Alphabet	Dolly Webb seeks her next prize for quince jam at Big River.
Alphabet	Milford J. Zorn will give a trophy to the six quickest boys.

| 1 | 2 | 3 | 4 | 5 | 6 | 7 | 8 | 9 | 10 | 11 | 12 |

All letters are used.

		2' GWAM
1.3 SI 5.2 AWL 90% HFW	The advice to write as you talk has a lot going for it,	6 48
	provided you have an effective manner of speech. Some persons	12 54
	who can talk in a clear, friendly way, however, will often	18 60
	freeze up when they have to dictate a letter or report or	24 66
	write one on the typewriter. The way to write as you talk is	30 72
	really quite simple: Just forget about trying to impress or	36 78
	express and simply try to inform with a free and easy manner.	42 84

2' GWAM | 1 | 2 | 3 | 4 | 5 | 6 |

Production Typing Information

MILITARY LETTERS

The following information has been adapted from the manual for preparing correspondence of the Department of the Army. Study it carefully before you type the jobs in the next two lessons.

Letter Style. Modified block with blocked ¶s (on 8- by 10½-inch stationery)

Margins. One inch for side margins and at least 1¼ inches for the bottom margin

Reference Symbol. Begin at the left margin on the fifth line below the last line of the letterhead.

Date. Type the day, month, and year, in that order and without punctuation, on the same line as the reference symbol, ending at the right margin.

Suspense Date. This date is used only when a reply must be received by a certain—or *suspense*—date. It is typed a double space above the date, preceded by the designation *S-* and ending at the right margin.

Subject Line. Started at the left margin a double space below the reference symbol; SUBJECT in all caps

Inside Address. Started at the left margin on the fourth line below the subject line and followed by four blank lines. State names may be abbreviated or spelled out, but ZIP Codes must be used with all domestic mailings.

Salutation and Complimentary Close. Omitted in military correspondence

Paragraphs. With letters of more than one paragraph, each paragraph is numbered consecutively with all lines blocked at the left margin.

Subparagraphs. Only the first line of a subparagraph is indented four spaces; subsequent lines are blocked. The first order of subparagraphs are designated by lower case letters (a., b., c., and so on). The next order of subparagraph is designated by numbers enclosed in parentheses, but with only the first line of each indented four spaces.

Authority Line. Used to indicate the authority under whom the letter is being written; typed in all caps at the left margin a double space below the last line of the body of the letter

Inclosures (Military Spelling). At the left margin on the fifth line below the authority line, type the number of inclosures with the abbreviation *Incl*. If inclosures have been identified in the letter, type *as* (for *as stated*) on the next line. If not, identify each on a separate numbered line.

Signature Block. Four blank lines below the authority line, in the modified block style, the name (in all caps), rank, and other identification of the writer is typed.

Copies. A courtesy copy for the addressee is generally sent with the letter but not listed as an inclosure; a copy is made for the files; and a copy is made for each agency to receive a copy. The copy notation is *CF:* (for *copies furnished*) and is typed a double space below the last preceding line with a list below of those to receive copies. Copy notations on military letters may be shown on the original copy or on only the carbon copies.

Job 3: Military Letter with Suspense Date

	Words
(*Reference*) R-1778 (*suspense date*) S–30 January 19-- (*date*) 5 January 19-- SUBJECT:	3 / 7
Change in Monthly Accounting Procedures	15
Commanding General 25th Infantry Division	23
Fort Dix, NJ 08640 (¶ 1) 1. The Accounting	31
Department of the Office of General Services	40
has recently moved to a new location in conjunction with the implementation of plans for	49 / 58
centralizing the various functions of the Adjutant General's Office. (¶ 2) 2. Since this move	67 / 76
is part of the second phase of the transition	85
from manual to computerized accounting, it is	94

	Words
essential that the inclosed Manual for Reporting Accounting Data be used in preparing the	107 / 120
appropriate officers for the new accounting	129
procedures that go into effect the first of next	138
month. (¶ 3) 3. If there are questions or comments regarding these procedures, please contact this office immediately for clarification.	147 / 155 / 165

FOR THE ADJUTANT GENERAL: 171

1 Incl   HARMON E. CLOWER   175

as   Colonel, GS   178

         Chief, Accounting Service   183

19A   Preparatory Practice ⑧ *each line twice SS; DS between two-line groups*

Alphabet   Pride in his work quickly gave Jim Fitz his next big chance.

Fractions   Type these fractions: 1/3, 5/6, 2/5, 3/8, 1/6, 8/15, 10/13.

Figures   Type these figures: 58, 20, 15, 11, 55, 38, 22, 10, 33, 85.

Fluency   She paid the firm the usual price for the six formal chairs.
            | 1 | 2 | 3 | 4 | 5 | 6 | 7 | 8 | 9 | 10 | 11 | 12 |

19B   Stroking Technique Practice for 4, 9, and Shift Lock ⑬

4—Left first finger

9—Right third finger

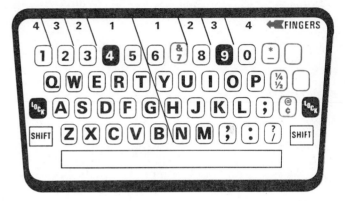

Using the Shift Lock (29). To type in ALL CAPS or to underline several words, use the shift lock. Depress the shift lock and leave it down until the typing is done. Operate the shift key to release it.

Tryout Drills *each line at least twice*

1	4	f f4f 4f 4f 14 44 444 Study Unit 14, pages 144 through 164.
2	9	l 191 91 91 91 99 999 All pools opened at 9:15 during 1969.
3	Shift lock	Vol. XXXVIII Check Vol. XXIX, No. 10, of the YMCA magazine.
4		Her ZIP Code is 49128. Did Jan and Ed say theirs was 63015?
5	Consolidation	The clerk checked Items 24, 36, and 58 on pages 190 and 201.

19C   Tab Mechanism and Figure Practice ⑫ *twice SS; DS between typings*

was	491	were	3649	after	13,462
yes	144	have	2992	yours	95,846
yet	191	best	3829	month	20,400
way	290	able	4059	today	16,396
let	490	next	1289	daily	52,609
off	958	plan	5395	story	41,200

KEY | 3 | 7 | 3 | 7 | 4 | 7 | 4 | 7 | 5 | 7 | 6 |

Job 6: Approval Copy of Directive

8″ by 10½″ plain paper; 1″ top margin; DS the 3-line heading; SS and indent *the ¶s; follow instructions shown for special vertical spacing*

Words
U.S. DEPARTMENT OF HEALTH, EDUCATION, 8
AND WELFARE | OFFICE OF EDUCATION | 14
Washington, D.C. 20202 *(DS; type the cur-* 19
rent date at the right margin; TS; center and SS
the lines of the following heading) Announce- 20
ment of Institutional Research Grants | Title 29
VII, NDEA, P.L. 840864 *(TS)* (¶ 1) The 35
scope of the research program of Title VII, 44
National Defense Education Act, has been 52
enlarged to permit the award of grants to 60
schools and universities for research on the 69
planning, production, and utilization of new 78
media to improve institutional curricular or 87
instructional programs. (¶ 2) Some examples 95
of studies that might be supported are: *(In-* 103
dent 10 spaces from both margins; DS between
items) 1. The use of filmstrips for independent 112
study in American history 2. How to use a 120
filmed science course in team teaching 3. Op- 129
timum use of a professor's time when a self- 138
instructional course is used (¶ 3) Application 146
deadlines are February 1 and August 1. In- 155
structions for preparing projects will be the 164
same as those for the traditional grant re- 172
search program. *(Leave 3 blank lines and* 175
block signature lines, starting at page center.)
william b. bayless research coordinator coop- 184
erative research branch 189

LESSONS 203-204

203-204A Preparatory Practice [5] *each line at least three times*

Alphabet	Judge Zerb will not acquit the expert; the key witness may have proof.
Figure-symbol	Boone & Strong paid Invoice #3698 totaling $250.74, less 10% discount.
Double letters	A bookkeeper will tell the association to settle all accounts in full.
Fluency	The quantity of work we do may depend on how soon we get around to it.

| 1 | 2 | 3 | 4 | 5 | 6 | 7 | 8 | 9 | 10 | 11 | 12 | 13 | 14 |

203-204B Skill-Comparison Typing [10]

First Day. Type two 1′ writings on each line of 203-204A; compare *gwam.*

Second Day. Type two 1′ writings on each line of 203-204A; correct all errors; compare rates.

203-204C Production Typing: Military Correspondence *(two days)* [35]

Study carefully the Production Typing Information about military letters on page 346 and the illustration of a military letter on page 347. Then type Jobs 1 through 6 as time permits.

Job 1: Military Letter

Type the letter shown on page 347.

Job 2: Military Letter with Subparagraphs

Words
(Reference) RADS-L *(date)* 2 October 19–– 4
SUBJECT: Paragraph Designations for Mili- 13
tary Letters | Commanding Officer, Fourth 21
United States Army | Fort Sam Houston, TX 29
78234 (¶ 1) 1. Reference is made to: (¶ 2) 35
(indent first line 4 spaces) a. Department of 39
the Army Memorandum 87-6, dated 15 May 47
19––, subject as above. (¶ 3) b. Department 55
of the Army Manual DD–821–FY. (¶ 4) 61
c. Letter, HCS, HQ, 20 September 19––, 69
SUBJECT: Military Correspondence (¶ 5) 76
2. With military letters of more than one para- 85
graph, each paragraph should be numbered 94
consecutively. Subparagraphs of the first 102
order are designated by letters of the alphabet 112
and indented as shown above. The second and 121
succeeding lines of subparagraphs are typed 130
at the left margin. FOR THE COMMANDING 138
GENERAL: 140

3 Incl — A. P. CHILLWORTH 144
as — Captain, GS 147
Director of Services 151

19D Skill-Transfer Typing ⑰

DO: Type a 1' writing on each ¶. Compare *gwam*. Then type two 1' writings on each of the two slower ¶s.

DO: Finally, type two 3' writings on ¶s 1, 2, and 3 combined. Determine average *gwam*. Compare average *gwam* with your best 1' *gwam* on each ¶.

All letters are used.

		GWAM 1'	3'	

¶1
1.3 SI
5.2 AWL
91% HFW

How many GWAM can you type today: 16, 18, 19, 20, or 22? | 12 | 4 | 49

With thoughtful attention to your typing habits, you can soon | 24 | 8 | 53

type 25 to 30 GWAM. Try to improve your speed by at least 20 | 37 | 12 | 58

to 24 GWAM before the end of this quarter. | 45 | 15 | 60

¶2
1.3 SI
5.2 AWL
91% HFW

A big secret to speed is to type without pausing, word by | 12 | 19 | 64
word. As you complete a word, do not freeze to it. Instead, | 24 | 23 | 68
turn loose of it immediately, space quickly, and begin the next | 37 | 27 | 73
word at once. Force yourself to keep on. | 45 | 30 | 75

¶3
1.3 SI
5.2 AWL
91% HFW

Have a special goal for each writing. If the immediate | 13 | 34 | 79

goal is to improve speed, move quickly from word to word. If | 24 | 38 | 83

the new aim is control, drop back in rate to type with greater | 36 | 42 | 87

ease. Adjust the rate to the purpose of practice. | 46 | 45 | 91

1' GWAM | 1 | 2 | 3 | 4 | 5 | 6 | 7 | 8 | 9 | 10 | 11 | 12
3' GWAM | | 1 | | 2 | | 3 | | 4

LESSON 20

20A Preparatory Practice ⑧ *each line twice SS; DS between two-line groups*

Alphabet   Quig Flynn will have the boxes packed with my prize jellies.

Shift lock   Have you read THE PERSISTENT TRUTH and THE PRICE OF FREEDOM?

Figures   My test covers 156 pages in 4 chapters: 28, 29, 30, and 31.

Fluency   Major cities are rich with problems but poor with solutions.
    | 1 | 2 | 3 | 4 | 5 | 6 | 7 | 8 | 9 | 10 | 11 | 12 |

20B Skill-Transfer Typing ⑳

DO: Repeat 19D, above. Type the 1' writings in reverse order: ¶3 first, then ¶2, and finally ¶1. Begin the 3' writing with ¶1; *circle errors*.

GOALS: To improve skill in handling script and statistical copy; to increase percentage of transfer from straight copy to other kinds of copy.

Job 4: Partial Copy of a Research Proposal

8" x 10½" plain paper; unbound-report form; top margin, 2"; heading in 3 DS lines; SS ¶s; 5-space ¶ indentions

	Words
INTENSIVE SURVEY AND STUDY CONFERENCE	TO REVIEW PRESENT AND NEEDED DEVELOPMENTS	IN EDUCATIONAL DATA PROCESSING	7 13 20 22

TS

I. Statement of Problem — 31

DS

There is a recognized need for a study preliminary to the undertaking of support for new programs in the general area of educational data processing. This need is for an assessment of the kinds of programs, facilities, and data processing equipment already in use throughout the nation's schools. — 39 48 56 65 75 84 91

TS

II. Objectives — 96

The object of the proposed study is to answer the following broad, general questions: — 104 112 114

DS

A. What is the present state of knowledge about automated school information systems? — 121 128 131

DS

B. What kinds of research and development in school information systems should be stimulated? — 139 146 151

C. What are the general criteria by which funding agencies can evaluate research projects? — 158 165 169

III. Related Research — 177

At Purdue University, the assignment of students to a predetermined schedule of classes is operational, and more than 18,000 students can be scheduled to classes in fewer than six hours. — 185 193 202 212 215

IV. Procedure — 220

A. By direct inquiry, the project staff will identify relevant research and development projects under way throughout the nation. — 228 235 242 246

B. Participants at the proposed colloquy will be requested to prepare concise written summaries of their position respecting the general problems central to the study. — 255 262 269 276 280

Job 5: Outline for Paper to be Prepared by Conferees

8" x 10½" plain paper; standard outline form; 2" top margin

	Words
OUTLINE FOR PAPER TO BE PREPARED BY CONFEREES	7 9

I. INTRODUCTORY DATA — 14

A. Name, Position, Title — 19

B. Institution, Agency, or Association Affiliation — 27 29

II. BRIEF BACKGROUND STATEMENT — 36

A. Relationship to Developments in Educational Data Processing
1. Direct or indirect
2. Kinds of equipment used — 43 48 53 59

B. Institutional or Agency Responsibility for Data Processing — 67 71

III. PRELIMINARY STATEMENT OF GENERAL QUESTIONS — 78 81

A. What is your assessment of the present state of knowledge about automated school information systems? — 89 95 102

B. What kind of research and development in school information systems should be stimulated? How? — 110 117 123

C. What are the general criteria by which funding agencies can evaluate proposals for research projects? — 130 137 144

IV. PRESENTATION OF DATA — 149

V. CONCLUSIONS AND PROJECTIONS — 156

20C Stroking Technique Practice for 7, – (Hyphen), and –– (Dash) ⑫

7—Right first finger   ––Right fourth finger

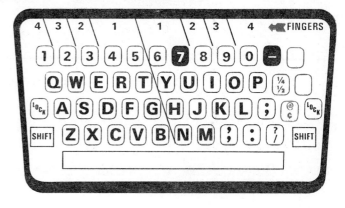

Typing the Dash (––). Type the dash with two hyphens without spacing either before or after; as in:

a 6-room house--2 bedrooms--at 12 Elm Ave.

Tryout Drills *each line at least twice*

1   7   j j7j 7j 7j 17 77 777   On May 27, 1970, 77 tags were issued.

2   –   ; ;-; -; co-op   This up-to-date edition is first-class work.

3   ––   ; -- ; -- Use a 6-inch line--60 pica spaces--for your paper.

4   I bought a 7-room house--3 bedrooms--at 6 1/4 percent today.

    Consolidation
5   FOR SALE: 8-room, 3-bath house--4/5 acre at 290 Elm Circle.

20D Growth Index and Skill Building ⑩

DO: Type a 3′ writing on the following ¶s. Determine *gwam* and errors.

DO: Type additional 3′ writings as time permits, trying to improve your speed or control, as appropriate.

All letters are used.

	GWAM 1′	3′

¶1
1.3 SI
5.2 AWL
91% HFW

	1′	3′
Just how well are you able to speak and to write? Is	11	4 / 43
it difficult for you to put your ideas into words that others	23	8 / 47
can easily understand? If so, you must learn how to use words	36	12 / 51
with greater ease and control. Choose each one with extreme	48	16 / 55
care. Control your use of words.	55	18 / 58

¶2
1.3 SI
5.2 AWL
91% HFW

Some people think that it is essential to use complex	11	22 / 61
terms to impress others; but it is the right word, not the	23	26 / 65
size of the word, that is important. Be as concise as possible	35	30 / 69
in your quest to improve your writing. Use as many words as	48	34 / 73
are necessary, but as few as you must, to state your thought	60	38 / 77
in familiar terms.	63	39 / 79

1′ GWAM | 1 | 2 | 3 | 4 | 5 | 6 | 7 | 8 | 9 | 10 | 11 | 12 |
3′ GWAM | 1 | 2 | 3 | 4 |

201-202C Production Typing: Government-Office Papers (*two days*)

Job 1: Government Memorandum

Words

DATE: (*current*) — 3

TO: Leland M. Foss — 6

FROM: William B. Bayless, Research Coordinator — 14

SUBJECT: Summary of Cooperative Research Program Accomplishment, July 1, 1967, to June 30, 1969. — 21, 29, 32

(¶ 1) The summary below provides an indication of the accomplishments of the Cooperative Research Program from July 1, 1967, to June 30, 1969. (*Tabulate with spaced leaders.*) — 39, 47, 56, 59

Proposals received . . . 192 | Proposals recommended to the Commissioner . . . 43 | Projects signed into contract . . . 41 | Projects completed . . . 29 | Total Federal funds obligated to bring 41 projects to completion . . . $253,192 — 73, 78, 90, 104, 117

(¶ 2) The proposals recommended to the Commissioner in the tabulation above include 12 projects that were approved earlier but which have not yet been signed into contract. (¶ 3) Funds for projects continuing beyond the current fiscal year are included but are contingent on the appropriation of funds. — 124, 133, 141, 149, 157, 165, 174, 176

Job 2: Transmittal Memorandum

Words

DATE: August 22, 19–– — 3

TO: Chancellor Myron R. Bayer — 8

FROM: Gray L. Downey — 11

SUBJECT: Educational Data Processing Survey — 18

(¶ 1) Enclosed are 46 copies of a request for funds for the project named above. Upon — 26, 35

approval, 30 copies of this request should be presented to the U.S. Department of Health, Education, and Welfare. (¶ 2) The total amount requested is $18,570 for a one-half-year period. The submission deadline is August 26, 19––. (¶ 3) The 15 percent of the total direct costs allowed as overhead by the grantor has been included. The University contribution is $2,000. — 44, 53, 60, 68, 76, 84, 94, 102, 107

Job 3: Telephone Memorandum

On plain 8- by 10½-inch paper, type the memorandum below in the style used for Job 2, but add the heading TELEPHONE MEMORANDUM, 1 inch from the top of the paper at the left margin.

Words

DATE: September 14, 19–– — 9

CALL FROM: William Bayless — 15
U.S. Office of Education — 20

TO: Gray L. Downey — 24

SUBJECT: (*Same as Job 2.*) — 33

(¶ 1) Some slight changes in the budget sub- — 40

mitted with the subject application were discussed. It was agreed that overhead be computed at 33 percent of salaries and wages, including salaries paid consultants, instead of the 15 percent originally submitted in the application. (¶ 2) Dr. Downey said that he was not sure that the category "consultants" listed in the budget was allowable and that instead of consultants, the personnel involved may be hired as research assistants, in which case the overhead application would be allowable. — 49, 58, 67, 77, 85, 93, 102, 111, 120, 129, 138, 139

Self-Improvement Practice

The following lines of drill material are correlated with the five lessons that constitute Section 3, with two lines of drill provided for each lesson.

The lines designated for a specific lesson emphasize the figures presented up to and including that lesson. *Reach* with the *fingers*.

Lesson 16
5 8 1
The 5 women and 18 men took Flight 158 to New York on May 5.
Did 15 of the 55 boys make a grade of 88 on the June 8 test?

Lesson 17
2 0 :
Each of the 2 men worked 250 hours from March 5 to April 20.
Check these flights: Delta 285 at 8:05; United 120 at 8:12.

Lesson 18
3 6 /
Ken is 36 years and 10 months old, and he weighs 266 pounds.
Buy 3 preferred shares at 38 1/8; 6 common shares at 26 3/8.

Lesson 19
4 9 Shift lock
What is the sum of 9 and 94 and 403 and 649 and 138 and 492?
The overall OLYMPIAN record: WON, 494; TIED, 49; LOST, 199.

Lesson 20
7 - --
Did Flight 277 arrive at 7:37 p.m., or was it delayed again?
Forty-six boys took the test--a 5-minute writing--on May 17.

| 1 | 2 | 3 | 4 | 5 | 6 | 7 | 8 | 9 | 10 | 11 | 12 |

COMMON PROOFREADER'S MARKS (CORRECTION SYMBOLS)

Study carefully the following proofreader's marks, their meanings, and their applications. They will be encountered in Section 4 and subsequent ones.

CORRECTION	SYMBOL AND ILLUSTRATION	
Add space	#	We should get underway by noon tomorrow.
All caps	≡≡≡	He requested a copy of Economics by Morganroth.
Cap letter	Cap or ≡	She selected an unusual oriental rug at Clossons.
Close up space	⌒	Letters of good will exert great influence today.
Delete (take out)	ℰ	The morning sessions begin at 9 a.m.
Insert	∧ ∨	"We meet on Monday, the 15th of June," she said.
Insert parentheses	( )	Take these steps: (1) Assemble a 4-carbon pack;
Insert period	⊙	Your interest is appreciated. Every effort . . . . .
Lower-case letter	l.c. or /	She received a set of exquisite China as a gift.
Move left	⊏	⊏ Your interest in our new product is very . . . . .
Move right	⊐	Your interest in our product is very gratifying . . . .
Paragraph	¶	. . . on your next visit. ¶ Please let me know . . . .
Transpose	tr or ∽	Ask Rita to back order the four last items on the list.
Underline	ital or —	He is an editor for Reader's Digest, or so he says!

200C Production Typing: Government Form Letter [35]

Production Job: Form Letter

Use the form paragraphs below to type letters to the four addresses shown. Add an appropriate salutation and any special information given for each one.

Use the letter style illustrated on page 340. Type the notation *FL29* before your reference initials as typist. Mr. Helpern will sign the letters.

		Words
¶ 1	Tests on items selected at random from your most recent shipment indi-	14
	cate that standards as specified in our contract with your firm have	28
	not been met. The entire shipment, therefore, has been returned to you.	42
¶ 2	A copy of the report on our laboratory tests will be forwarded to you	56
	under separate cover. If after studying the report you believe it to	70
	be in error, you may file an exception (Form B–801/33) with our office.	85
¶ 3	As you know, our contract with you specifies that any failure to main-	99
	tain minimum-standard requirements must be remedied within 90 days or	113
	the contract becomes subject to review. We encourage you, therefore,	127
	to take prompt action in this matter.	134

Letter 1. Send the letter to Mr. E. Waldo Johnston, President, Precision Instrument Company, 4700 Widmer Road, Shawnee Mission, KA 66216.

In reply refer to: LB–X–78
Your reference: A–588201–12–73
(*Add 40 words for these lines.*)

Letter 2. Send the letter to Mr. Harry R. Davenport at D–R–B Machine Tool Corporation, 6080 Del Amo Way, Bakersfield, CA 93305.

In reply refer to: LB–X–79
Your reference: B–183023–66–60
(*Add 39 words for these lines.*)

Letter 3. Send the letter to Mr. Lewis F. McGinnis, President, Naval Tool and Supply Company, 800 New Jersey Avenue, Norfolk, VA 23508.

In reply refer to: LB–X–88
Your reference: A–604302–00–41
(*Add 40 words for these lines.*)

Letter 4. Send the letter to Mr. William A. Gilbreth, President, Michigan Tool and Die Corporation, 5000 Imperial Highway, Detroit, MI 48240.

In reply refer to: LB–X–93
Your reference: A–200123–18–10
(*Add 41 words for these lines.*)

Add a final ¶ to Letter 4 stating that one of the Government inspectors, Mr. Albert Tilbot, will be in Detroit within the next week or two and will be available to confer with the company officials at their convenience. Arrangements can be made through Mr. Helpern's office. (*45 words*)

LESSONS 201-202

201-202A Preparatory Practice [5] *each line at least three times*

Alphabet	Jake Morgan said that there will be a quiz in physics at exactly five.
Figure-symbol	Make your payment of $8,497.65 in 10 days (May 3) for the 2% discount.
Long words	A reference symbol is given on Government and military communications.
Fluency	It takes insight to find the right goal; it takes patience to gain it.
	| 1 | 2 | 3 | 4 | 5 | 6 | 7 | 8 | 9 | 10 | 11 | 12 | 13 | 14 |

Purpose. To learn to type symbols, improve number control, and build higher basic skill. You will also learn to type corrected copy.

Machine Adjustments. Line: 60; SS word and sentence drills, unless otherwise directed; DS and indent ¶s 5 spaces.

Self-Improvement Practice. Select from page 48 material to type that meets your need. Two lines are provided for each lesson.

LESSON 21

21A Preparatory Practice ⑦ *each line twice SS; DS after second typing of line*

Alphabet   Pam questioned why Vic Bortz must make six more jet flights.

Figures   The box is 6 5/8 by 9 1/2 feet and weighs 375 to 400 pounds.

Shift keys Dr. Clayton moved to Atlantic City, New Jersey, on April 26.

Fluency   Did Keith make the six boys sign the form when he paid them?

        | 1 | 2 | 3 | 4 | 5 | 6 | 7 | 8 | 9 | 10 | 11 | 12 |

21B Stroking Technique for ' ! " _ (Underline) ⑧ *each tryout drill twice*

' (Apostrophe). *Nonelectric:* Type ' (shift of **8**) with *right second finger:* k'k 'k 'k
Electric: Type ' (to right of ;) with the *right fourth finger:* ;'; '; ';

! (Exclamation Point). Type ' and backspace; then type a period (!). (If the machine has a key for ! type it with the *left fourth finger*.) Space twice after the exclamation: Try! Don't stop! Keep on!

" (Quotation). *Nonelectric:* Type " (shift of **2**) with *left third finger:* s"s "s "s
Electric: Use *right fourth finger* to type " (shift of '): ;"; "; ";

_ (Underline). *Nonelectric:* Type _ (shift of **6**) with *right first finger:* j_j _j _j
Electric: Use *right fourth finger* to type _ (shift of –): ;_; _; _;

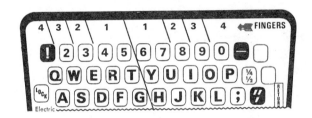

To Underline: Backspace (or move by hand) to first letter of the word; then type the underline once for each letter in the word.

21C Stroking Technique Practice ⑮ *each line three times SS; DS after third typing of line*

Words

1 ' (Nonelectric) k'k 'k 'k It's so. I'm next. It's accuracy that is needed. 12
   ' (Electric)   ;'; '; '; It's so. I'm next. It's accuracy that is needed.

2   Try! Don't stop! Keep right on typing! Type with control! 12

3 " (Nonelectric) "s "s Sue typed "lose" for "loose" and "chose" for "choose." 12
   " (Electric)   "; "; Sue typed "lose" for "loose" and "chose" for "choose."

4 _ (Nonelectric) _j _j _j Use a quick stroke. Keep the eyes on the copy now. 12
   _ (Electric)   _; _; _; Use a quick stroke. Keep the eyes on the copy now.

5 Review   The principal said, "It's right! Stand by your principles!" 12

Job 3: Government Letter

Words

march 29 19–– in reply refer to Ltr 3–29 8
HETCO your reference Ship Order 1855Y the 17
halliburton company 1900 louisville avenue 25
lubbock tx 79410 gentlemen (¶ 1) Your recent 34
shipment of generators arrived at our receiv- 42
ing dock in Alexandria this morning. It was 51
complete as per your shipping memorandum 60
dated March 21. According to our contract 68
with you, half of the requested number of 77
generators have now been received. (¶ 2) We 84
must inform you, however, that three crates 93
were broken open and their contents exposed. 102
Fortunately, no damage was incurred; but 111
future shipments should be packaged in a 119
manner certain to protect against loss. (¶ 3) 127
Examination revealed that insufficient buffer 136
material allowed the generators to slide against 146
the sides of the crates causing the wooden 155
slats to splinter. Nailing the generators to a 164
wooden track at the bottom of these crates 173
should prevent shifting, and we now request 182
that all future shipments be crated in this 190
fashion. sincerely yours max r helpern chief 200
federal supply service cc Dock Superintendent | 210
Legal Officer *(E. Mays wrote the letter.)* 216

LESSON 200

200A Preparatory Practice [5] *each line at least three times*

Alphabet — Quivering and almost frozen, the six boys crawled over a jutting peak.
Figure-symbol — All $5,000 4½% bonds (Series 3E) were sold for a profit of $12,568.79.
Drill on exa — I am exasperated at the exact number of examples that are exaggerated.
Fluency — Men who give thought to small things are likely to achieve big things.

| 1 | 2 | 3 | 4 | 5 | 6 | 7 | 8 | 9 | 10 | 11 | 12 | 13 | 14 |

200B Communication Aid: Capitalization and Punctuation [10]

70-space line; DS; use the book copy for all writings; compare gwam

1. Copy the ¶; insert necessary capitalization and punctuation.
2. Type three 1′ writings on the *control level.*
3. Copy the ¶ twice, changing all written numbers to typed figures.

All letters are used.

1.8 SI
6.0 AWL
70% HFW

GWAM 1′

of the sixteen men who started on that well reported january second 14
voyage to the estuary of the amazon three were natives of guayaquil 28
ecuador four had lived at one time or another in rio de janeiro eight 42
were bostonians and one although few of the others actually believed 56
him indicated reykjavik was his birthplace and hometown. veteran trav- 71
elers all yet none of them had ever visited macapa an interesting old 85
city of approximately twenty seven thousand citizens spread over the 99
equator on the northern bank of the great amazon. 109

1′ GWAM | 1 | 2 | 3 | 4 | 5 | 6 | 7 | 8 | 9 | 10 | 11 | 12 | 13 | 14 |

(The gwam *in the column is for the writing with numbers spelled out. The word count given above the lines is for the writing with typed figures.)*

21D Skill-Transfer Typing ⑩ *a 1' writing on each line*

DO: Compare the rates on Sentences 1 and 4, 2 and 5, 3 and 6. The difference in rates may show the "cost" of typing from script.

DO: Type additional 1' writings on the script sentence for which the widest difference is shown between typing from script and typescript.

SPACING RULE: Space once after an exclamation point used within a sentence. See Line 6.

			Words
1	Easy	A light touch is the right touch to use to build good skill.	12
2	Figures	Ken read aloud pages 137, 264, and 389 of the 450-page book.	12
3	Figure-symbol	My 1967-68 report read, "This year's earnings are our best!"	12

| 1 | 2 | 3 | 4 | 5 | 6 | 7 | 8 | 9 | 10 | 11 | 12 |

4	Easy	*The good workman always does what he does as well as he can.*	12
5	Figures	*On June 2, Flight 159 left at 7:20 with 36 men and 48 women.*	12
6	Figure-symbol	*I typed 37 words; then Sue said, "Don't stop!" and I didn't.*	12

21E Skill-Progression Typing ⑩

DO: Type two 1' writings on each ¶. Try to complete the ¶ before time is called. Determine *gwam*.

Stroking Cue: Make low, quick reach-strokes; keep hands and arms almost motionless.

All letters are used.

		3' GWAM
¶1 1.3 SI 5.2 AWL 90% HFW	Time is important. It is the one constant in daily life,	4
	for all have the same amount of it. The way we use time is	8
	what makes for our unequal accomplishments.	11
¶2 1.3 SI 5.2 AWL 90% HFW	How time is used can determine the limit of our success,	14
	for time is as important for work as it is for getting the	18
	most enjoyment out of free hours. Time should be prized	22
	highly and used wisely to gain maximum success.	25
¶3 1.3 SI 5.2 AWL 90% HFW	The chance of having to do our work over is increased	29
	by starting to do it before we have thought through all the	33
	problems involved. Thinking takes time and time is one of	37
	our most valuable commodities, but we will save time if we	41
	will take time to think before we begin our work.	44

3' GWAM | 1 | 2 | 3 | 4 |

Words

GENERAL SERVICES ADMINISTRATION
FEDERAL SUPPLY SERVICE
WASHINGTON, DC 20025

Margins: side and
bottom, at least
1 inch

Started a DS be- → February 6, 19--   3
low letterhead
and 2½ inches   In reply refer to: 7
from right edge   OPFA-29-1 DS   SS   11

Line 12   AIRMAIL

Line 14 regardless Mr. Jerome R. Wiley   18
of letter length Office Services Company   26
2543 Alexander Street   Your reference:
Charleston, WV 25302   Letter styles   30
35

Closed punctuation Dear Mr. Wiley: 38

Thank you for your recent inquiry about standard procedures   50
for typing Government letters. The style and form of this   62
letter will illustrate for you the format generally used by   74
Government offices.   78

Letter styles, however, differ somewhat within the divisions   90
of the Government. The branches of the armed forces, for   102
example, have a standard style of their own. If you study   114
the enclosed material, you will find the standard procedures   126
for the various written communications as defined by the   137
Department of the Air Force.   143

We are glad to send you the enclosed materials to illustrate   156
further the procedures used in typing Government letters.   167
If we can help you again, please let us know.   176

Standard closing   Sincerely yours,   180

Max R. Helpern

MAX R. HELPERN   183
Chief, Federal Supply Service   189

Enclosure notation Enclosures: 191
Preparing and Processing Written Communications   211
Report E27-R, Duplication Processes   218

Carbon copy nota- cc: 219
tion Regional Civil Service Director   225
District 1 Supply Office   ← Not shown on the   230
original copy

Reference notation DPlymouth:av 2-6---   234

Government Letter (Pica Type)

LESSON 199   **Section 31: Typing in a Government Office**   **340**

LESSON 22

22A   Preparatory Practice ⑦   *each line twice SS; DS after second typing of line*

Alphabet   Why not have Judge Burt Kumpf quiz the six local boys today?

Figures   I built 7-room houses--28 in all--on 36th Street in 1949-50.

Symbols   Shouldn't we show and also tell the "how" and "why" of this?

Fluency   The six girls can handle the quantity of forms without help.

| 1 | 2 | 3 | 4 | 5 | 6 | 7 | 8 | 9 | 10 | 11 | 12 |

22B   Sustained Skill Building ⑩

DO: Type a 3′ writing on the ¶s of 21E, page 41 (preceding page). Determine *gwam*. Practice difficult words by typing each one four or five times.

DO: Type a second 3′ writing on the ¶s, trying to increase your speed and maintain your control. Determine *gwam*.

Continuity Cue	Reduce the time interval between strokes. Use a "rippling" (not metronomic) rhythm in typing short and easy words. Type long words with a quick, smooth, and flowing movement from one letter to the next and from one word to the next.

22C   Stroking Technique for $ & ( ) [Left and Right Parentheses] ⑧   *each tryout drill twice*

$ (Dollars). Type $ (shift of **4**) with the *left first finger:* f$f $f $f

& (Ampersand or "and"). Type & (shift of **7**) with the *right first finger:* j&j &j &j

([Left Parenthesis]. Type ([shift of **9**] with the *right third finger:* l(l (l (l

) [Right Parenthesis]. Type) [shift of **0**] with the *right fourth finger:* ;);););

22D   Stroking Technique Practice ⑧   *each line twice SS; DS after second typing of line*

1    $ and &   A check for $2,375 was sent to Nietz & Johnson on August 14.

2   (and)   We sold the short-term (due in 91 days) U.S. Treasury Bills.

3    $ & ( )   North & Owen's note for $1,850 (due 6/4) was paid on May 27.

4   Review   We mustn't use "it's" (contraction) for "its" (the pronoun).

5   Consecutive/ direct   Fred Hunt hauled many hundred pounds of freight in my truck.

| 1 | 2 | 3 | 4 | 5 | 6 | 7 | 8 | 9 | 10 | 11 | 12 |

Production Typing Information

GOVERNMENT LETTERS

In typing the Government letters in Lessons 199-202, use the modified block style with blocked paragraphs and mixed punctuation. Make further modifications as explained below and as shown on page 340. Prepare three carbon copies of each letter.

Special-Size Stationery. Agencies of the United States Government use 8- by 10½-inch stationery.

Margins. 1-inch (at least) side margins; at least 1-inch bottom margins

Date. Typed a double space below the letterhead and started 2½ inches from the right edge of the paper

Reference Lines. Printed or typed a double space below the date and blocked with it, the items single-spaced but separated by a double space

In reply refer to: The *writer's* identifying code, symbol, or subject
Your reference: The *recipient's* identifying code, symbol, or subject

Special Mailing Instructions. Typed on Line 12, a double space above the inside address

Inside Address. Started on Line 14 to position the address for use with window envelopes

Enclosure Notation. At the left margin a single space below the word *Enclosure*, list by name anything being sent with the letter. (Remember to underline titles of publications.)

The following information is not shown on the original copy. To exclude the information from the original, turn the cylinder knob toward you, rolling the carbon pack backwards. Insert a half sheet of fairly transparent paper in front of the original to cover the area where notations are to be typed; then turn the pack back to typing position. Type the notations in the proper position.

Carbon Copy Notation. The notation symbol is *cc:* Below the symbol list the names or titles of those who are to receive copies.

Reference Initials. The writer's first initial and surname, the typist's initials, and the date are typed at the left margin in one line; for example:

EMason:st 7-5-69

MEMORANDUMS

Informal correspondence within and between Government agencies is written in the form of a *memorandum* on a printed form. The basic style of Government letters (1-inch margins, SS blocked ¶s) is used.

199C Production Typing: Government Letters ㉟

Job 1: Government Letter

Type the letter shown on page 340. At the end, fill in the current year, as 2-6-70.

Job 2: Government Letter with Enclosures

	Words
(*Current date*) in reply refer to FSO-479-AP	9
(72) your reference GSS-2700 mr w e washington president mt troy manufacturing company 2391 denbigh street newark nj 07105	17 / 26 / 35
dear mr washington (¶1) Four copies of Contract A-579436-00-69 are enclosed with this letter. They are complete in all details except for additional provisions listed as required on page 47A of the Manual of Form for Government Contracts. (¶2) In order to expedite completion of this contract, we have	42 / 50 / 60 / 69 / 78 / 89 / 98

typed and signed as an addendum the required provisions on page 8. Our legal office informs us that these addenda items must now be signed by the officers of your company. (¶3) All other terms of the contract are agreeable to our office; and with the return of our copies of the signed contract, we can accept delivery of our preliminary order entered with you when contract negotiations began. sincerely yours max r helpern chief, federal supply service enclosures 4 copies of Contract A-579436-00-69 | Manual of Form for Government Contracts cc: GSS Legal Officer 215/218

107 / 116 / 124 / 133 / 142 / 152 / 161 / 169 / 178 / 187 / 195 / 207

J. Galey wrote the letter for Mr. Helpern's signature; use Mr. Galey's name, your initials, and the date, as illustrated on page 340.

22E Skill-Transfer Typing ⑩

1. Type two 1' writings on each ¶. Determine your *gwam* for the better writing on each ¶.

2. Type a 3' writing beginning with ¶ 1 and typing as far as you can until time is called. Compare 3' *gwam* with best 1' rate on each ¶.

Difficulty controls for "mixed" copy (words and figures) are determined for the words only. Punctuation marks and symbols used with words, such as quotation marks and parentheses, are considered to be a part of the word with which they are typed. See ¶ 2.

All letters are used.

	3' GWAM
¶ 1 Most men can do just about anything they think they can,	4
1.3 SI for belief is magic. If they think they are not equal to	8
5.2 AWL	
90% HFW what is expected of them, they won't be able to use the	11
wonder-working power of faith in themselves to realize the	15
true success they should have.	17
¶ 2 Many workers are retired by the time they are 65 or 70	21
1.3 SI years old. The so-called "golden age" (more age than gold)	25
5.2 AWL	
90% HFW will come more quickly than we realize. We must have a	29
hobby for our present enjoyment and for the days to come	33
when we may have considerable free time.	35

22F Rough Draft ⑦ *study the correction symbols; then type each drill line once or more*

Rough Draft: Copy corrected with pencil or pen and ink. Some of the most common correction symbols are shown at the right.

Correction Symbols

Cap. or ≡ means capitalize
∧ means insert
⅌ means delete (take out)
⊏ means move to left

means add space
/ or l.c. means lower-case letters
_____ means underline

		Words
1	use a light, quick strokes to build the highest typing skill.	12
2	Many men mentioned the points fred listed for us to discuss.	12
3	l.c. The Principal said, "It's the Principle of (rule) to follow."	12
4	Typing Cue: keep your eye on the copy; use a quick strokes!	12
5	Bart will read the cards on which the date of the Trade was given.	12

198E Alertness Training [10]

1. Copy the ¶ below, inserting a 1-syllable word of your choice in place of each blank.
2. Using the book copy, type two 1′ writings, inserting the words that you remember choosing when you first typed the ¶.
3. Type the ¶ again with 5-stroke underlines where they appear below. In addition, replace three more words of your choice with blanks.
4. Using your copy typed with the blanks, type two 1′ writings.

	1′ GWAM
Words do not mean what you think they _____; they mean what those	13
who read or _____ them think they mean. Keep on in your search for the	28
right _____ so that no one will fail to _____ just what you mean when you	42
write or _____. Skill in the use of _____ will grow with use, but it	56
will call for some good hard _____ on your _____ to find just the right	71
_____ to say what you want to say.	78

1′ GWAM | 1 | 2 | 3 | 4 | 5 | 6 | 7 | 8 | 9 | 10 | 11 | 12 | 13 | 14 |

198F Sentence Guided Writings [10] *two 1′ guided writings on each sentence*

		GWAM 15″	12″	10″
1	When a person has little education, he may be forced to use his brain.	56	70	84
2	Forests would be quiet places if all birds except the best were quiet.	56	70	84
3	Life may depend less upon what you make than upon what you make of it.	56	70	84
4	You need a good memory to remember what worried you so much last week.	56	70	84

| 1 | 2 | 3 | 4 | 5 | 6 | 7 | 8 | 9 | 10 | 11 | 12 | 13 | 14 |

LESSON 199

199A Preparatory Practice [5] *each line at least three times*

Alphabet	Ben Marvin requested exactly a dozen jackets for the long winter trip.
Figure-symbol	Your final quotation of October, 1968, read: 59# @ $3.74, 2/10, n/30.
Long words	Many recommendations were drafted for professional research personnel.
Fluency	Work for the fine gift of using words that give life to your thoughts.

| 1 | 2 | 3 | 4 | 5 | 6 | 7 | 8 | 9 | 10 | 11 | 12 | 13 | 14 |

199B Skill-Transfer Typing [10] *two 1′ writings on each sentence; compare* gwam*; try to reach the rates set on the goal sentence*

65-space line; DS

			Words
1	Goal sentence	They wrote a law protecting the innocent by punishing the guilty.	13
2	Shift key	Alexis Cooper works for the Amos Shoe Company in Portland, Maine.	13
3	Script	*To hold our world together, we require the adhesive "friendship."*	13
4	Rough draft	Maria was per plexed by ~~Cy's~~ Jim's appar~~a~~ent lack of aptitude~~s~~ for ~~the~~ a job.	13

LESSON 23

23A Preparatory Practice (7) *each line twice SS; DS after second typing of line*

Alphabet   Did Peter Wallington quiz Evelyn Jackson about her tax form?

Symbols   "Truth," a man once said, "doesn't hurt unless it <u>ought</u> to!"

Figure-symbol   Hunt & Dwyer's $623.75 check (Check 1489) is dated April 10.

Fluency   The firm holds the usual title to the visual aids they sell.

    | 1 | 2 | 3 | 4 | 5 | 6 | 7 | 8 | 9 | 10 | 11 | 12 |

23B Stroking Technique for # * % (6) *each tryout drill twice*

 # (Number or Pounds). Type # (shift of **3**) with the *left second finger:* d#d #d #d

Note. Before a figure, # is the symbol for *No.;* after a figure, it is the symbol for *pounds.* See Line 1 of 23C, below.

* (Asterisk). *Nonelectric:* Type * (shift of **–**) with the *right fourth finger:* ;*; *; *; *Electric:* Type * (shift of **8**) with the *right second finger:* k*k *k *k

% (Percent). Type % (shift of **5**) with the *left first finger:* f%f %f %f

23C Stroking Technique Practice (10) *each line three times SS; DS after third typing of line*

                                                                         Words

d#d #d #d Ship Order #165 for 437# of Compound #98 on May 2.   12

* (Nonelectric)   *; *; *; My first * refers to page 290, ** to pages 305-307.   12
* (Electric)   *k *k *k My first * refers to page 290, ** to pages 305-307.

%   f%f %f Will the 6% rate be changed to 5% or possibly 5 1/2%?   12

Review   Smith & Carey's account is $2,957.83 (for 5/30 Order #1460).   12

23D Rough Draft (7) *study the correction symbols; then type each line twice*

Correction Symbols

⌒ means close up   *tr or* ∪ means transpose   ] means move to right

                                                                           Words

1   Don't space between figures and symbols: #, $, %, /.   12
2   Shift when typing # (no. or lbs.), % (per cent), and " (quote).   12
3   Use the * (asterisk) for your foot note to refer to Page 264.3   12
4   never let the fear element keep you from doing your best.   12
5   Order #1460 from Dieckman Muncy (dated 3/29) is $1,570.85.   12

SECTION 31 TYPING IN A GOVERNMENT OFFICE

LESSONS 198–205

Section 31 contains examples of communications typed in Government offices.

Drill Copy: Full sheet; 70-space line; SS.
Paragraph Copy: Full sheet; 70-space line; DS; 5-space ¶ indention.
Production Copy: Unless otherwise directed, make 1 carbon copy. (The directions for government and military letters will call for 3 carbon copies.)

Since the jobs in Section 31 are technical in their construction, be sure to read carefully all directions, notations, and other instructional material. As you type the illustrated government and military letters, make an extra carbon copy of each to use as a guide for similar jobs on other pages.

LESSON 198

198A Preparatory Practice [5] *each line at least three times*

Alphabet	Jody Quinn packages frozen vegetables for shipment by Railway Express.
Figure-symbol	I said, "Pay Bill #48502 for $671.98, but first add 3½% to the total."
Adjacent keys	Drew returned the funds without reading the directions in the booklet.
Fluency	Guide your life by the standards you admire when you are at your best.
	| 1 | 2 | 3 | 4 | 5 | 6 | 7 | 8 | 9 | 10 | 11 | 12 | 13 | 14 |

198B Skill-Comparison Typing [5] *one 1′ writing on each line of 198A; compare* gwam

198C Action Typing [10] *type twice; as you type, follow the directions in the ¶s*

Words

When you have typed this paragraph, center (in all capitals) the 13
following headings, "guesstimating" their position as closely as pos- 27
sible. Triple-space after each heading. 35

cost of equipment 39
probable savings with equipment 45
estimate of time saved 50
installation costs 54
installation time 57

Now use the backspace-centering method to center each heading below 71
its first typing; compare the first typing with the second. 83
(The last word count includes the second typing of the headings.) 105

198D Communication Aid: Capitalization and Punctuation [10]

Capitalize and punctuate each sentence as you type it. Check your work with your instructor; then retype the sentences.

1 yes i received a quick courteous reply from the well known director
2 when the books are ready please send them to joe curtis old address
3 "in this world said jackson a man must be either anvil or hammer
4 in 1968 403 firms adopted the sylvester plan 275 are still using it
5 h e fosdick said "sooner or later every man finds his boundaries
6 these 45 60 and 90 day trips to africa will be discontinued today
7 kay bell our teacher is a little known authority on spanish history
8 frank will speak to the rotary club on friday april 15 at 1215 pm

| 1 | 2 | 3 | 4 | 5 | 6 | 7 | 8 | 9 | 10 | 11 | 12 | 13 | 14 |

23E Skill-Comparison Typing ⑳

1. Type a 1' writing on each ¶. Determine *gwam* for each writing. Compare rates.

2. Type two more 1' writings on each of the two ¶s on which you had the lowest *gwam*.

3. Type two 3' writings, starting with ¶ 1 and typing as far as you can until time is called. Determine *gwam* and compare with your best 1' rate.

Return Cue: *Make the return without looking up at the end of the line.*

All letters are used.

	3' GWAM
¶1 1.2 SI 5.0 AWL 96% HFW	

¶1
1.2 SI
5.0 AWL
96% HFW

Up to now, much of your typing has been from quite easy 4

copy. Many of the words came from the list of common words 8

with two to five letters and just one syllable. This simple 12

copy was used to help you to build a good typing skill. 15

¶2
1.4 SI
5.4 AWL
86% HFW

From now on, try to type such short and simple words as 19

two-letter balanced-hand words by word-recognition response 23

and not by letter response. To do this, you must think the 27

word with real vigor, but not think the individual letter. 31

¶3
1.5 SI
5.8 AWL
76% HFW

This progressive-difficulty copy has a few long and less 35

frequently used words and a few words of many syllables. From 39

your experience in typing these specialized paragraphs, you can 43

learn to vary your stroking pattern for the copy to be typed. 47

3' GWAM | 1 | 2 | 3 | 4 |

LESSON 24

24A Preparatory Practice ⑦ *each line twice SS; DS after second typing of line*

Alphabet Wilbur Jamieson packed the very large box of quartz mineral.

Figure-symbol Orr & North's Check #2035 for $648.10 should be for $864.10.

Shift key Dick Webb and Max King will go with Jim Carr to Zurich soon.

Fluency In May, the ancient jewels can be seen at the downtown shop.

| 1 | 2 | 3 | 4 | 5 | 6 | 7 | 8 | 9 | 10 | 11 | 12 |

24B Typing for Control ⑩

Type two 3' writings of 23E, above, on the *control level*. Type at a rate that is 4 to 8 words lower than your best 1' rate made when typing the ¶s as 23E.

Job 1: Certificate of Business, Fictitious Name

2 carbon copies

Words

CERTIFICATE OF BUSINESS, 5
FICTITIOUS NAME 8

(¶ 1) The undersigned do certify they are con- 16
ducting a business at 1348 Euclid Street, City 25
and County of San Diego, State of California, 35
under the fictitious name of INGRAD AUTO- 43
MATIC DOORS, and that said firm is composed 51
of the following persons, whose names in full 61
and places of residence are as follows: (*Indent* 69
10 spaces from both margins; SS items; DS be-
tween them.)

Charles Ingle, 148 Kearny Mesa 75
Road, San Diego, California 92111 82

Richard Radford, 79 Gardena Ave- 88
nue, San Diego, California 92110 95

Dated: August 15, 19-- 100

_____ 106
Charles Ingle 109

_____ 115
Richard Radford 118

Note. At the end of the document, type an
acknowledgment similar to the one in Lessons 190-
191C, Job 3, page 325. Use the names of the partners and make any necessary changes to the plural
form in wording the acknowledgment. Date the document August 15, 19--. (*78 words*)

Job 2: Medical History Report

Words

MEDICAL HISTORY 3

Name. E. E. Laughlin Age. 29 Sex. M Date. 14
9/19/-- 16

Address. 9299 Bainbridge Avenue, Provi- 25
dence, Rhode Island 02909 30

Entrance Complaint. Pain in shoulder 41

Present Illness. Patient fell a week ago. Since 54
he noticed no immediate discomfort, he as- 62
sumed he had not injured himself and did not 71
seek medical help. No other injuries have 80

been sustained since. Present symptoms are 89
especially apparent at night, and the patient 98
reports loss of sleep due to a dull ache along 107
the back of the left shoulder. 114

Past History. Usual childhood illnesses. No 125
fractures or serious injuries reported. Treat- 134
ment for jaundice at age 9. 140

Systems Review. 146

Gastrointestinal. Appetite good. Pa- 156
tient reports a slight recent weight 164
gain, but his weight is not excessive 171
for his height and build. Appendix 179
was removed at age 19. 183

E.N.T. Patient was suffering from 191
slight nasal congestion. Tonsils and 199
adenoids missing. 203

Cardiovascular. Negative 210

Locomotor. No cogent history 218

Family History. Only child. Parents well. 230

Social History. Patient is a married male em- 242
ployed as a county surveyor. He has no chil- 250
dren. He does not use tobacco. 257

Job 3: Short Letter

1 carbon copy; block style

Words

june 29, 19-- darwin electronic supplies 890 9
unity avenue, north minneapolis, mn 55422 17
gentlemen (¶ 1) Please send us your best 24
prices on the following equipment: 32

500 Cadmium sulfide photoconduc- 38
tive cells, Type CL-2P 42

50 Self-generating selenium photo- 49
cell and sun batteries, Type 55
B2M 56

100 Multiple-contact relays, Type 62
KL 63

(¶ 2) Orders for this equipment will be placed 71
within the next thirty days. very truly yours 81
albert w carson purchasing agent 88/103

24C   Stroking Technique for ½ and ¼ ⑥ *each tryout drill twice*

½ **(Fraction Key).** Type ½ (at right of letter **p**) with the *right fourth finger* and without shifting: ;½; ½; ½;

¼ **(Fraction Key).** Type ¼ (shift of ½) with the *right fourth finger:* ;¼; ¼; ¼;

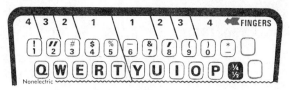

24D   Stroking Technique Practice ⑩ *each line three times SS; DS after third typing of line*

		Words
½	Type fractions in the same way: 1/2 and 2/3--not ½ and 2/3.	12
¼	Peter Lopez said the total of 25¼, 36¼, 47¼, and 90¼ is 199.	12
Figure-symbol	Don's 4¼% note (for $750) was paid on May 26 by Check #1839.	12
Symbols	Don't hurry or worry--just type <u>right</u> to learn to typewrite!	12

| 1 | 2 | 3 | 4 | 5 | 6 | 7 | 8 | 9 | 10 | 11 | 12 |

24E   Rough Draft ⑦ *each line twice SS; DS after second typing of line*

		Words
1	[l.c. The Half] sheets of paper (8½ by 5½ inches) has just 33 lines.	12
2	Roy--as the would-be leader--was is gifted with 20-20 hindsight!	12
3	Their Teachers said, use quick strokes; <u>keep eyes on copy</u>! "	12
4	In 1967, Weyth and Pointer stock sold at 25½; and in 1968, at 40¼.	12
5	[Add these words to the list: <u>generally</u>, shipments, handled,	12

24F   Skill-Transfer Typing ⑩ *a 1' writing on each sentence*

DO: Compare the rates on Sentences 1 and 4, 2 and 5, 3 and 6. The difference in rates may show the "cost" of typing from rough draft.

DO: Type additional 1' writings on the rough draft sentences for which the widest difference occurs between it and typescript.

			Words
1	Easy	The auditors for their firm can make their report on May 26.	12
2	Figures	On July 25, Flight 480 had 37 women, 18 men, and 9 children.	12
3	Figure-symbol	O'Neil & Long's $750 note (due 3/26) was paid by Check #481.	12

| 1 | 2 | 3 | 4 | 5 | 6 | 7 | 8 | 9 | 10 | 11 | 12 |

			Words
4	Easy	[l.c. An Elements of doubt kept them from help ing the Project with.	12
5	Figures	Didn't 46 of the 350 boys and of the 89 girls 27 pass the test?	12
6	Figure-symbol	Jim Webb's fare is #234.50 (less 6%--net cost of $220.43.	12

LESSON 197

197A Preparatory Practice (5) *each line at least three times*

Alphabet	A puzzled male executive sat by his desk wondering if Jeanne had quit.
Figure-symbol	Invoice #483–5967, due on October 10, gave the discount for cash @ 2%.
One hand	Address my letters in care of Bret Edwards or John Baxter in Honolulu.
Fluency	Counting time, however, is not nearly so important as making it count.

| 1 | 2 | 3 | 4 | 5 | 6 | 7 | 8 | 9 | 10 | 11 | 12 | 13 | 14 |

197B Growth Index (15) *one 10′* control-level *writing; figure* nwam

All letters are used.

		GWAM 1′	10′	
¶ 1	Perhaps you did not realize that there are several basic principles	14	1	48
1.6 SI	of learning that are used to gain typewriting skill. An expert typist	28	3	49
5.8 AWL	does not acquire his rapid and highly accurate score simply by chance.	42	4	51
75% HFW	He realizes how necessary it is for him to take advantage of each of	56	6	52
	these common principles of learning if he is to perform with maximum	70	7	53
	efficiency.	72	7	54
¶ 2	It is not unusual, for example, for a learning typist to reach a	13	9	55
1.6 SI	"plateau" in his quest for increased speed. To continue typing at his	27	10	56
5.8 AWL	present rate is no problem, but it appears impossible for him to climb	41	11	58
75% HFW	to a higher level. When this happens, it seems necessary to dedicate	55	13	59
	some practice drills to speed development, even though a temporary	69	14	61
	accuracy drop is incurred.	74	15	61
¶ 3	We can safely consider that improper stroking habits are respon-	13	16	62
1.6 SI	sible for a failure to achieve above a certain figure. This is a basic	27	17	64
5.8 AWL	cause of plateaus; but you can find material especially designed to	41	19	65
75% HFW	develop quick, sharp stroking. Use a segment of the drill period work-	55	20	67
	ing on the exercises. You may notice no immediate, drastic change;	69	22	68
	but it will come if you work for it.	76	22	69
¶ 4	Among other essential ideas to keep before us is the advice that	13	24	70
1.6 SI	all drills must be practiced with a definite aim in mind. Unless a typ-	27	25	71
5.8 AWL	ist realizes what he is striving to attain, he cannot hope to achieve	41	27	73
75% HFW	any particular degree of success. Flailing away weekly at a keyboard	55	28	74
	in the hope that practice makes perfect is inadequate. Practice should	70	29	76
	be approached with specific goals in mind.	78	30	76
¶ 5	The need for having goals is not limited to a student working for	13	31	78
1.6 SI	speed improvement. We arrive safer and quicker at any destination if	27	33	79
5.8 AWL	we use a reliable road map. Certainly a worker who aspires to a higher	42	34	81
75% HFW	position works diligently toward that end. Sound learning principles--	56	36	82
	especially knowing the why, where, and how of our activities--might be	70	37	83
	applied to a great many facets of our daily lives.	80	38	84
¶ 6	Not much is accomplished on our planet simply by accident. Behind	13	39	86
1.6 SI	any major achievement is a plan of attack. Many people admittedly have	28	41	87
5.8 AWL	a limited amount of luck "going for them"; but relying too heavily on	42	42	89
75% HFW	luck is foolish. If your typewriting skill needs improvement, learn	56	44	90
	what you need to practice. Use any aids available to you; but, above	70	45	91
	all, take responsibility for your own growth--and take pride in it, too.	84	46	93

1′ GWAM | 1 | 2 | 3 | 4 | 5 | 6 | 7 | 8 | 9 | 10 | 11 | 12 | 13 | 14 |
10′ GWAM | 1 | 2 |

25A   Preparatory Practice ⑦ *each line twice SS; DS after second typing of line*

Alphabet   Will my box be packed with quick-frozen foods by Jim Vaughn?

Figures   Our address will be 14867 West 35th Street after October 29.

Figure-symbol   Will Mr. Link's $5,000 Policy #23-678 expire on May 6, 1974?

Fluency   Ken paid for the work with his half of the sale of the land.
　　　　| 1 | 2 | 3 | 4 | 5 | 6 | 7 | 8 | 9 | 10 | 11 | 12 |

25B   Stroking Technique for ¢ (Cent or Cents) and @ (At) ⑥ *each tryout drill twice*

¢ (Cent or Cents). *Nonelectric:* Type ¢ (an unshifted character to the right of ;) with the *right fourth finger:* ;¢; ¢; ¢;
Electric: Type ¢ (shift of **6**) with the *right first finger:* j¢j ¢j ¢j

@ (At). *Nonelectric:* Type @ (shift of ¢) with the *right fourth finger:* ;@; @; @;
Electric: Type @ (shift of **2**) *with the left third finger:* s@s @s @s

SPACING RULES: 1. Space before and after typing @, which is used in typing bills. **2.** Do not space between ¢ and the figure it follows.

Note. These spacing rules apply when the symbols are used in a sentence or in typing bills, but not when used in typing drills, such as the tryout drills.

25C   Stroking Technique Practice ⑩ *each line three times SS; DS after third typing of line*

¢   I paid 98¢ for a pen and 16¢ for a pencil, a total of $1.14.

@   Eleanor bought 12 7/8 yards @ $6.75 and 9 2/3 yards @ $5.40.

¢ and @   Use ¢ and @ when typing bills; as, Ship 647 lbs. @ 89¢ a lb.

¢ and @   Space after @, but not between the figure and ¢, *, #, or $.
　　　　| 1 | 2 | 3 | 4 | 5 | 6 | 7 | 8 | 9 | 10 | 11 | 12 |

25D   Rough Draft ⑩ *each line three times SS; DS after third typing of line*

Words

1   ~~Miss~~ *Zelma* Quigley (will) have *some* lunch fixed at Koffpe *for Bryan?*   12

2   ~~When is~~ Kent & Clayton's note *of #38,765* (plus 5½% interest) *is* due ⦿   12

3   [Sam Werder said Myna munson sold Five Hundred desks *in July.*   12

4   The elements of dang⌒er on this Job will make *workmen* ~~them very~~ careful.   12

5   The *last* sale of 9 *doz* note⌒books @ 18⌒¢ *each* came to $19.44.   12

Words

Thermoelectric Effects 684

DS

(¶ 9) If the two ends of a capsule switch are 692
kept at the same temperature, all thermal 700
electromotive forces cancel; and no resultant 709
electromotive force is generated. When, how- 718
ever, a gradient exists, the output voltages may 728
easily be the same order as those from the 737
thermocouple being measured. The thermo- 745
electric force, generated by a gradient of 122° 754
F. between the ends of the switch, was 1.9 763
millivolts. This voltage was primarily due to 772
the junction between the #52 stainless alloy 781
and the copper leads. 786

TS

Conclusions 790

TS

(Indent and single-space the enumeration.)

1. From the point of reliability, current- 799
carrying capacity, low overall resistance, and 808
freedom from vibration or altitude effects, the 818
Concord Electric Capsule Switch is a suitable 827
switching device; however, for some low- 835
impedance circuits, the percentage-variation 844
in resistance between operations might be 853
objectionable. 2. In conjunction with a small 862
coil, the switch is suitable for general relay 872
service. 874

---

[1]Inasmuch as the axial length of the coil is large compared to its diameter, the values so computed are correct within engineering accuracy. *(32 words)*

[2]The time required for a mechanical movement of the switch is less than 0.5 milliseconds, including the contact bounce. *(28 words)*

Job 2: Title Page for Technical Report

Prepare a title page for the technical report prepared as Job 1. Include the information given below, arranged appropriately. Staple the report, with title page, ½ inch from the left edge.

Words

PERFORMANCE TEST OF CONCORD ELECTRIC CAPSULE SWITCH 10

Report No. E-547 14

April 15, 19-- 17

Solex Electronic Research Company 24

Baton Rouge, Louisiana 28

LESSON 196

196A Preparatory Practice [5] *each line at least three times*

Alphabet Elizabeth just accepted the quick excuse which Ivy made for Genevieve.

Figure-symbol The cabin will take 67 8-ft. 2 x 4's (standard grade) @ $139.50 per C.

Double letters Nannette Ellis passed the difficult cooking quiz held in Battle Creek.

Fluency If you want to know about the road, question the turtle--not the hare.

| 1 | 2 | 3 | 4 | 5 | 6 | 7 | 8 | 9 | 10 | 11 | 12 | 13 | 14 |

196B Skill-Comparison Typing [10] *two 1' writings on each line of 196A; compare* gwam

196C Production Skill Building [35]

Type for 30 minutes on these problems. Compute *n-pram.*

Page 324, Job 1; page 329, Job 2; Page 330, Job 4; page 331, Job 5

25E Growth Index ⑰

1. Type a 3′ writing. Determine *gwam* and number of errors.
2. Type two 1′ writings on each ¶, typing once for speed and once for accuracy.
3. Type a second 3′ writing on the *control level*. Determine *gwam* and number of errors. Compare your rate and control with the first writing. Be guided by this comparison in your next practice.

All letters are used.

		1′	3′
¶1 1.3 SI 5.2 AWL 90% HFW	To the extent that men of good skill and good will want	11	4
	to work and can work, jobs must be made available to them; but	24	8
	business and industry are not welfare agencies, and workers	36	12
	must have both good skill and good will. Most men realize	48	16
	that this is so, but not all are adequately prepared for work.	60	20
	The need is for far more and far better education for all.	72	24
¶2 1.3 SI 5.2 AWL 90% HFW	More and better education may not be the final answer to	11	28
	the problem of matching men and jobs, for automation has made	24	32
	the question of jobs a difficult one. How will workers keep	36	36
	their jobs when machines can do the work as well as the workers	48	40
	can? This is recognized by the experts as the big problem	61	44
	we must face in the years just ahead.	68	47

1′ GWAM | 1 | 2 | 3 | 4 | 5 | 6 | 7 | 8 | 9 | 10 | 11 | 12 |
3′ GWAM | 1 | 2 | 3 | 4 |

● Self-Improvement Practice   *each line three or more times*

1 *Lesson 21* Tom's father said, "Might won't make right!" He's so right!
2 ' ! " _   Mrs. O'Donovan just won't pay for this book, Technique Cues!

3 *Lesson 22* Was King & Jordan's check (or was it Mr. King's) for $5,200?
4 $ & ( )   Cole & Meade, Inc., gave $750 to the cause (the Boys' Club)!

5 *Lesson 23* The * refers to Item #9, the 6% charge on Ed's $25,000 note.
6 # * %   The 2% discount on Bill #467 (for *** Pads) comes to $38.90.

7 *Lesson 24* The $5\frac{1}{4}$% rate has been changed to $5\frac{1}{2}$% and will go to 6% soon.
8 $\frac{1}{2}$ $\frac{1}{4}$ Take full sheets ($8\frac{1}{2}$ by 11") or all half sheets ($8\frac{1}{2}$ by $5\frac{1}{2}$").

9 *Lesson 25* Mark sold a pen @ 89¢, pad @ 27¢, and 24 pencils @ 15¢ each.
10 ¢ @   Note the correct spacing: 24 @ 9¢ each, $2.16; Order #97-A.

| 1 | 2 | 3 | 4 | 5 | 6 | 7 | 8 | 9 | 10 | 11 | 12 |

LESSON 25   Section 4: Symbols   48

Note No. 2. The material below contains an equation in which you must make insertions in ink. At the right of the equation, type its explanatory key, positioned so that the 2 items together are centered on the line length of your report. When you type the equation, use the variable line spacer for the vertical alignment and leave a blank space for the *pi* symbol. Later, insert in ink both the *pi* symbol and a lower-case letter *l* in script (to avoid possible confusion with a typewritten figure *1*). Use this procedure for the letter *l* in the key also.

(Type the following key at the right of the equation.)

A	Amperes	381
T	Total number of turns	386
l	Length of coil in centimeters	392

TS

(¶ 6) The same electrical circuit was used to check variation in switch resistance with changes in magnetizing force. To obtain these data, the current was held constant at 0.3 amperes, and potential was measured with a Brown Potentiometer. Contact resistance change was calculated from changes in this potential with different values of coil excitation. 400 408 418 426 435 443 452 461 463

TS

Tests for Thermal Effects 473

DS

(¶ 7) Inasmuch as the Concord Electric Capsule Switch is composed of several different metals, thermal electromotive forces can be generated by temperature gradients along the switch and at the terminals. To measure the thermal electromotive force at the terminals when normal copper leads were attached, an oil bath was prepared and heated to 122° F. (50° C.) above ambient temperature. With the switch completely immersed and held closed by a permanent magnet, no voltage could be read on the Leeds and Northrup K-2 Bridge. 480 489 498 507 516 525 533 542 551 559 567 576 577

TS

Discussion and Results 586

TS

Normal Performance 594

DS

(¶ 8) Application of any magnetizing force greater than 32 oersteds closes the switch reliably in an operating time of less than 3 milliseconds.[2] The contact resistance is 14 to 20 milliohms. Larger magnetizing forces do not materially reduce the contact resistance. The switch closes upon application of 32 oersteds. The contact resistance varies erratically for exciting fields of less than 32 oersteds. 601 610 620 629 638 647 657 666 675

---

to and supported by lead wires sealed into the ends of the glass tube. The inner extremities of the beams overlap but are separated from each other by approximately 0.005 inches. The overlapping surfaces are infused with gold to provide a good electrical contact surface. 184 194 202 212 221 230

TS

Procedure 234

TS

(¶ 4) Inasmuch as the switch is sealed, it is not anticipated that the low air pressures and temperatures encountered at high altitudes could have deleterious effects upon its operation. The factors arising during use in flight which may affect the performance of the switch are: *(Indent and single-space the enumeration.)* 242 251 260 269 278 286 289

1. Changes in supply voltage that vary the magnetic field excitations 296 303
2. Thermal gradients that admit electromotive forces spurious to the signal under observation 310 317 322

TS

Tests for Normal Performance 333

DS

(¶ 5) An apparatus was built to determine the minimum closing and opening field strength. The current through the coil was measured and the magnetizing force (H) was calculated, using the following formula:[1] 341 350 359 368 374

$$H = \frac{4\pi AT}{10l} \text{ oersteds}$$

379

SECTION 5 ▶ IMPROVING BASIC SKILLS

LESSONS 26–30

Purpose. To improve stroking, response patterns, and use of machine parts.

Machine Adjustments. Line: 60; SS drills, unless otherwise directed; DS and indent ¶s.

Self-Improvement Practice. Selected lines from page 54 until you can demonstrate control.

LESSON 26

26A Preparatory Practice ⑧ *each line three times SS; DS between three-line groups*

Alphabet   Vern Flynn made six quick shots to win the Jets a big prize.

Figures   The 43 men, 67 women, and 125 children sailed today at 8:09.

Figure-symbol   Coe & Lowe's bonus in 1967-8 was $252; in 1969, it was $340.

Fluency   May they pay for the big sign with half the profit due them?
    | 1 | 2 | 3 | 4 | 5 | 6 | 7 | 8 | 9 | 10 | 11 | 12 |

26B Technique Practice: Response Patterns ⑮ *each line three times; practice difficult word groups*

Lines 1-2: Type at a controlled pace: read a letter, type it; then read and type the next letter.

Lines 3-4: Try for a "chained" response: read and type a *word* or a *syllable* at a time; then the next.

Lines 5-7: Type short, easy words by word response; longer or more difficult ones letter by letter.

1   Letter-level response   only after you; refer my tax case; my opinion; extra reserve

2   As you are aware, my estate tax case was, in fact, deferred.

3   Word-level response   visit the city; fix the chair; the proxy is; if the chairman

4   It is the duty of men to work; their wish, to make a profit.

5   if you care to, when you try it, if only he, she refers also

6   Combination response   you may see; get the facts; the opinion of; refer the reader

7   He treated the data with care; he gave the facts with vigor.
    | 1 | 2 | 3 | 4 | 5 | 6 | 7 | 8 | 9 | 10 | 11 | 12 |

26C Manipulative Parts Drill: Space Bar, Shift Keys, and Shift Lock ⑩

Type each line at least twice for precise control of machine parts.

1   Space bar   we pay for it; plans to send half; many a man offers to work

2   Set your sights for the top; then do your best to get there.

3   Shift-keys   1-I; 5-V; 10-X; 30-XXX; 40-XL; 50-L; 75-LXXV; 100-C; 1,000-M

4   Our guests are: Pam and Don; Sylvia and Harl; Roz and Jack.

5   Shift lock   she is a new CPS; join the AMS; define quixotic and charisma

6   A critique of Bey's book, OMEGA, appears in Literary Review.
    | 1 | 2 | 3 | 4 | 5 | 6 | 7 | 8 | 9 | 10 | 11 | 12 |

Job 1: Technical Report with Handwritten Insertions

Leftbound manuscript style

1. The first page of the report you will type is shown below in pica type in correct form. Type it as it appears (or as nearly so as possible); then type the remainder of the material in similar form.

2. Type on all subsequent pages the information that appears at the top of the first page. This includes a page number, the report number, and the title underlined as shown. Type the page number on the

fourth line space from the top, all pages. Type the report title 2 inches from the top of the first page; 1 inch from the top of subsequent pages. Triple-space after the title.

3. The footnotes for this report appear at the end of the problem. Type them on the pages on which their reference figures appear.

Note No. 1. The word count for this report does not include the heading to be typed on each page. To add the count for a heading *through the underline*, use the number correct for your typewriter.

For elite type: Add 36 words
For pica type: Add 32 words

Words

Page 1 | Report No. E-547

PERFORMANCE TEST OF CONCORD ELEC-
TRIC CAPSULE SWITCH
TS

Summary   3
TS

(¶ 1) The low contact resistance, rapid action,   11
high natural frequency, and sealed construc-   20
tion of the Concord Electric Capsule Switch   29
indicate that it should have several useful   38
applications. The following limitations, how-   47
ever, apply: (*Indent and single-space the   49
enumerated items.*)

  1. The current should not exceed 0.3   57
    amperes.   59
  2. The contact resistance is subject   67
    to a maximum variation of about   73
    2.0 milliohms in a total contact re-   80
    sistance of 14 to 20 milliohms.   87
  3. The exciting magnetizing force   94
    should be more than 32 oersteds.   100
TS

Introduction   105
TS

(¶ 2) The investigation was undertaken to   113
determine whether the Concord Electric Cap-   121
sule Switch is a suitable switching device for   130
use under conditions encountered during flight.   140
(¶ 3) The switch consists of two pieces of   148
ferromagnetic material formed into thin rec-   156
tangular beams enclosed in a hydrogen-filled,   165
sealed glass envelope. These beams are welded   175

Page 1
Report No. E-547

PERFORMANCE TEST OF CONCORD ELECTRIC CAPSULE SWITCH

Summary

    The low contact resistance, rapid action, high natural frequency, and sealed construction of the Concord Electric Capsule Switch indicate that it should have several useful applications. The following limitations, however, apply:

    1. The current should not exceed 0.3 amperes.

    2. The contact resistance is subject to a maximum variation of about 2.0 milliohms in a total contact resistance of 14 to 20 milliohms.

    3. The exciting magnetizing force should be more than 32 oersteds.

Introduction

    The investigation was undertaken to determine whether the Concord Electric Capsule Switch is a suitable switching device for use under conditions encountered during flight.

    The switch consists of two pieces of ferromagnetic material formed into thin rectangular beams enclosed in a hydrogen-filled, sealed glass envelope. These beams are welded to and supported by lead wires sealed into the ends of the glass tube. The inner extremities of the beams overlap but are separated from each other by approximately 0.005 inches. The overlapping surfaces are infused with gold to provide a good electrical contact surface.

First Page of a Technical Report

26D Skill-Comparison Typing 🔟

1. Type a 1′ writing on each ¶; compare *gwam*.

2. Type one or more 1′ writings on the slower ¶, trying to exceed the rate on the faster ¶.

3. When your rate on one ¶ exceeds that on the other, switch to the slower ¶ for additional practice.

4. Type a 3′ writing on both ¶s; determine *gwam*.

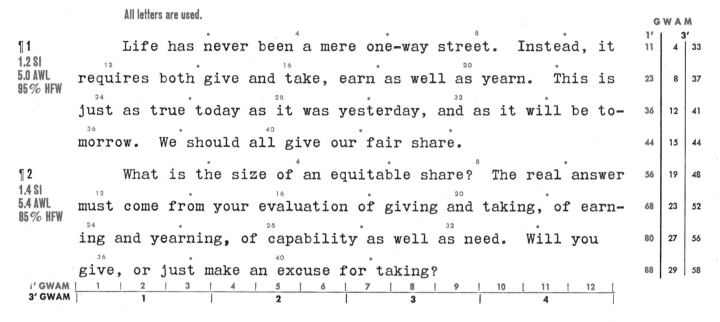

All letters are used.

		GWAM		
		1′	3′	
¶1 1.2 SI 5.0 AWL 95% HFW	Life has never been a mere one-way street. Instead, it requires both give and take, earn as well as yearn. This is just as true today as it was yesterday, and as it will be to-morrow. We should all give our fair share.	11 23 36 44	4 8 12 15	33 37 41 44
¶2 1.4 SI 5.4 AWL 85% HFW	What is the size of an equitable share? The real answer must come from your evaluation of giving and taking, of earn-ing and yearning, of capability as well as need. Will you give, or just make an excuse for taking?	56 68 80 88	19 23 27 29	48 52 56 58

1′ GWAM | 1 | 2 | 3 | 4 | 5 | 6 | 7 | 8 | 9 | 10 | 11 | 12 |
3′ GWAM | 1 | 2 | 3 | 4 |

LESSON 27

27A Preparatory Practice 🔠 *each line three times SS; DS between three-line groups*

Alphabet   Quick approval by Rex Evans might "sew it up" for Don Jantz.

Figures   Type these figures: 28, 46, 39, 57, 208, 840, 196, and 375.

Figure-symbol   Can you make 10% profit on #3849 @ $6.72 a dozen (56¢ each)?

Fluency   The eight men who work on the dock come in during the night.

| 1 | 2 | 3 | 4 | 5 | 6 | 7 | 8 | 9 | 10 | 11 | 12 |

27B Typing from Dictation ⑦ *once with the book open; once with the book closed*

Do not type the color dividers

also city busy duty body visit panel title vigor civic angle

of the | is the | by the | and the | to the | to them | for the | for them

to 59 the 573 fix 482 work 2948 held 6393 spend 20373 social

00 22 88 44 99 33 77 55 66 11 50 121 391 846 390 551 205 691

27C Skill-Comparison Typing 🔟

1. Type ¶1 of 26D, above, as a 1′ writing to establish a base rate.

2. Type two 1′ guided writings on ¶1 for speed (base rate plus 6-8 *gwam*); then two slightly slower writings for precise control.

3. Repeat Steps 1 and 2 for ¶2 of 26D, above.

4. Type a 3′ writing on both ¶s combined. Determine *gwam* and errors.

5. Compare the 3′ *gwam* with that typed in Lesson 26.

Job 5: Long Business Letter

Words

march 30, 19-- e sanders cunningham m d 9
northern clinic 335 northern boulevard albany 18
ny 12204 dear dr cunningham (¶ 1) I appre- 25
ciate your having made an appointment to see 34
Mr. Arnold Sweeney in your office on Thurs- 43
day, April 5, at 3 p.m. I shall be happy to give 53
you a brief summary of his medical history, as 62
I indicated in our recent telephone conversa- 71
tion. (¶ 2) This young man was first seen in 79
my office on Monday, March 15, complaining 87
of palpitations, shortness of breath, intoler- 96
ance for exercise, and swelling of feet and 105
ankles. The symptoms had been present for 114
approximately three weeks, and he had previ- 122
ously not sought medical care. (¶ 3) A review 130
of the patient's past history revealed that at 140
the age of eight he had suffered migratory 148
joint pains, chiefly in the wrists, elbows, 157
ankles, and feet. At that time, he was treated 167
by his physician for rheumatic fever and was 176
kept out of school and on bed rest for four 185
months. He was advised that there was some 193
heart damage as a result of the rheumatic 202
fever and that he should continue under close 211
medical observation. (¶ 4) As the family 218
moved to another area soon, Mr. Sweeney 226
lost contact with his previous physician; and 235
since he appeared to be well, medical assis- 244
tance was not sought. He received no medical 253
care, such as prophylactic antibiotic therapy, 263
for the past ten years. This young man now 271
presents himself with classical findings of con- 281
gestive heart failure, resulting from far- 289
advanced mitral valvular disease. (¶ 5) I shall 298
appreciate your seeing and evaluating this 306
patient. Please forward your findings and rec- 316
ommendations to me as soon as possible. 324
sincerely yours oscar ryan m.d. 331/348

Job 6: Abstract of Medical Research

Type the abstract below on an 8- by 5-inch card or paper of that size. Arrange the material for easy reading.

Words

IMPLANTATION OF HETEROLOGOUS PARA- 6
THYROID TISSUE | by E. L. Kryzer and J. C. 15
Porter | Northeastern J. Med., 312:115, 1967 | 23
Condensation in Medical Review, Vol. 5 (May, 35
1968), p. 80. 38

Heterologous parathyroid tissue was trans- 46
planted to a woman of 49 years who had been 55
hypoparathyroid for 8 years. Judged by remis- 64
sion of symptoms and elevation of serum 72
calcium levels, the response obtained was 80
excellent, though microscopic examination of 89
the transplant revealed no identifiable para- 98
thyroid cells; and the biochemical response of 107
the patient to a calcium infusion was charac- 116
teristic of hypoparathyroidism. It is assumed 126
that the transplant led to improved adaptation 135
of the patient to her hypoparathyroid state. 144

LESSONS 194-195

194-195A Preparatory Practice [5] *(each day)* *each line at least three times*

Alphabet When judging books and movies, she frequently awarded exciting prizes.

Figure-symbol Book #E-18493 (which once sold for $13.50) contains 276 illustrations.

Double letters Bill cannot succeed unless he applies the rule to all those attending.

Fluency A major pain to some of us is the pain that comes with a weighty idea.

| 1 | 2 | 3 | 4 | 5 | 6 | 7 | 8 | 9 | 10 | 11 | 12 | 13 | 14 |

194-195B Production Skill Building [10] *(each day)*

First Day. Use Job 5, above, for a 3′ and a 5′ writing. Use correct letter style and placement. Do not correct errors. Compare *gwam.*

Second Day. Use Job 2, page 329, for three 3′ writings. Use regular-size paper and average-length letter placement. Do not correct errors. Compare *gwam.*

27D   Manipulative Parts Drill: Tabulator and Backspacer ⑱ *three or more times SS*

Tabulating Cue: *Reach* to the tab bar or key; tab and type without pausing.

Backspacing Cue: *Reach* with the little finger to backspace; move back quickly and type.

↓ Margin	↓ Tab	↓ Tab	↓ Tab	↓ Tab	↓ Tab	1' GWAM
2,731	213	▶ 6¼	759	◀ 4,290	5.00	6
9,594	▶ 58½	947	286	115¼	6.34	12
▶ 620	847	▶ 65	◀ 3,621	337	◀ 12.50	19
4,837	◀ 1,500	◀ 2,048	▶ 64½	▶ 98	7.98	26

KEY | 5 | 6 | 5 | 6 | 5 | 6 | 5 | 6 | 5 | 6 | 5 |

LESSON 28

28A   Preparatory Practice ⑧ *each line three times SS; DS between three-line groups*

Alphabet
Janice kept two quiet prize lynx she got from Bev in Dallas.

Figures/shift keys
Use area codes: Waco, 817; Hays, 913; Enid, 405; Mesa, 602.

Figure-symbol
That check, #4639, for $1,582.40 is dated February 21, 1970.

Fluency
Go to the city for the auto signs and pay the firm for them.

| 1 | 2 | 3 | 4 | 5 | 6 | 7 | 8 | 9 | 10 | 11 | 12 |

28B   Technique Practice: Stroking ⑧ *each line three times SS; DS between three-line groups*

Double letters
Russ will see that the staff accounts for all food supplies.

Consecutive/direct
June ordered a gross of tax receipts from a Fort Myers firm.

Adjacent keys
We saw column upon column of troops poised for quick action.

First/third rows
Many a man never quite wins the big prize of complete peace.

| 1 | 2 | 3 | 4 | 5 | 6 | 7 | 8 | 9 | 10 | 11 | 12 |

28C   Typing from Dictation ⑥ *once with the book open; once with the book closed*

it is, to do, of us, by me, or go, if he, is so, do an, I am

by 46; do 39; for 495; when 2736; girls 58412; height 638574

if we, go in, is my, go up, is in, for you, she was, and are

Do not type the color dividers
Jack & Jill's|1720 Elm|at 9:30 a.m.|lend at 6½%|get 5# @ 48¢

| 1 | 2 | 3 | 4 | 5 | 6 | 7 | 8 | 9 | 10 | 11 | 12 |

28D   Manipulative Parts Drill: Tabulator and Backspacer ⑫

DO: Repeat the drill of 27D, above, typing it only twice. Work for improved control of machine parts.

DO: Type a 1' writing on the drill. Determine *gwam*. GOAL: Approximately ⅓ of your straight-copy rate.

Job 3: Letter with Changes

Use executive-size paper. Send the letter typed as Job 2 to Dr. Werner L. Jenssen, 1300 Prestwick Street, Houston, TX 77025, changing the first sentence of ¶ 2 to read: At recent meetings I have been asked to suggest the projects most worthy of "getting off the ground" this year.

Job 4: Medical History Report

If no form is available, type the medical history on plain paper in standard report form: SS the copy under each heading; DS between sections of the report.

MEDICAL HISTORY

<u>Name</u>. James Davisson   <u>Age</u>. 19   <u>Sex</u>. M   <u>Date</u>. 3/26/--

<u>Address</u>. 5775 Pasqualito Drive, Pasadena, CA 91108

<u>Entrance Complaint</u>. Red spots on chest and abdomen for one day.

<u>Present Illness</u>. Patient was well and healthy upon retiring the evening of March 25, 19--. Upon arising and showering the following morning, he noted a faint rash over the abdomen and chest. This was not associated with itching. The patient also noted nodules at the base of the skull and behind both ears. Upon taking his temperature, he found that it had elevated to 100.4°.

	Words
MEDICAL HISTORY	3

<u>Name</u>. James Davisson <u>Age</u>. 19 <u>Sex</u>. M <u>Date</u>. 15
3/26/--   17

<u>Address</u>. 5775 Pasqualito Drive, Pasadena, CA 28
91108   29

<u>Entrance Complaint</u>. Red spots on chest and 41
abdomen for one day.   46

<u>Present Illness</u>. Patient was well and healthy 58
upon retiring the evening of March 25, 19--. 67
Upon arising and showering the following 75
morning, he noted a faint rash over the abdo- 84
men and chest. This was not associated with 93
itching. The patient also noted nodules at the 103
base of the skull and behind both ears. Upon 112
taking his temperature, he found that it had 121
elevated to 100.4°.   125

<u>Past History</u>. Mumps and chicken pox as a 136
child. Tonsillectomy at age 8, poliomyelitis 145
at age 12. No fractures or serious injuries. 155

<u>Systems Review</u>.   161

(Indent 5 spaces from both margins.)

    <u>Gastrointestinal</u>. Appetite good. No 171
recent weight loss and no history of 179
indigestion. Patient had one episode 186
of acute abdominal pain at age 10, 193
which was observed by his physician 201
for possible acute appendicitis. The 208
condition subsided spontaneously. 215

    <u>E.N.T</u>. Tonsillectomy at age 8. 223

    <u>Cardiovascular</u>. Negative 231

    <u>Locomotor</u>. Temporary weakness of 239
the right arm resultant from polio- 246
myelitis. Arm has since returned to 254
normal. 255

<u>Family History</u>. Both parents are living and 267
well. One brother died at age 3 following an 276
automobile accident. Two sisters are living 285
and well. 288

<u>Social History</u>. Patient is a single male em- 299
ployed as a service station attendant. He does 309
not use tobacco or alcohol. 314

28E Skill-Comparison Typing ⓰ *as directed in 26D, page 50*

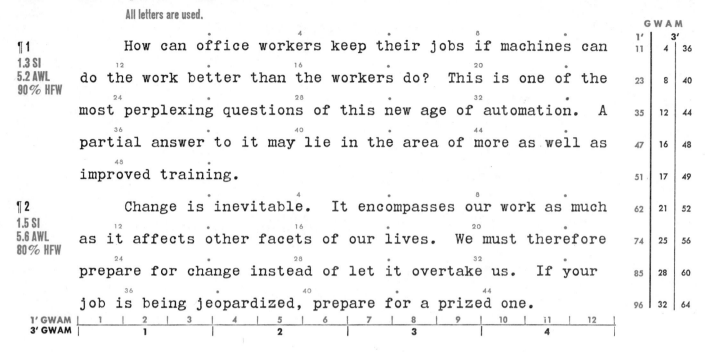

All letters are used.

		GWAM
		1' · 3'

¶1
1.3 SI
5.2 AWL
90% HFW

How can office workers keep their jobs if machines can   11 | 4 | 36
do the work better than the workers do? This is one of the   23 | 8 | 40
most perplexing questions of this new age of automation. A   35 | 12 | 44
partial answer to it may lie in the area of more as well as   47 | 16 | 48
improved training.   51 | 17 | 49

¶2
1.5 SI
5.6 AWL
80% HFW

Change is inevitable. It encompasses our work as much   62 | 21 | 52
as it affects other facets of our lives. We must therefore   74 | 25 | 56
prepare for change instead of let it overtake us. If your   85 | 28 | 60
job is being jeopardized, prepare for a prized one.   96 | 32 | 64

1' GWAM | 1 | 2 | 3 | 4 | 5 | 6 | 7 | 8 | 9 | 10 | 11 | 12 |
3' GWAM | 1 | 2 | 3 | 4 |

LESSON 29

29A Preparatory Practice ⑧ *each line three times SS; DS between three-line groups*

Alphabet   Jack Heintz now plans a daily quota of six very big mallard.

Figures   You may call my residence, 571-2639, or my office, 281-4600.

Figure-symbol   In a call-in campaign, 13,480 (57%) said "No" on Issue #926.

Fluency   If they sign the union form, may they then see the chairman?

| 1 | 2 | 3 | 4 | 5 | 6 | 7 | 8 | 9 | 10 | 11 | 12 |

29B Manipulative Parts Drill: Tabulator and Return ⑦ *at least twice*

Center + 10 ↓

Tab ---→Reach the finger to   Return

the tabulator bar or key.------Tab------→Depress it quickly,   Return

then move back to home position.------→Reach to the return

lever or key quickly, too.

29C Skill-Comparison Typing ⓰

1. Type ¶ 1 of 28E, above, as a 1' writing to establish a base rate.

2. Type two 1' guided writings on ¶ 1 for speed (base rate plus 6-8 *gwam*); then two writings at a slightly slower rate for precise control.

3. Repeat Steps 1 and 2 for ¶ 2 of 28E, above.

4. Type a 3' writing on both ¶s combined. Determine *gwam* and errors.

5. Compare the 3' *gwam* with that in Lesson 28.

Job 1: Outline of Paper

Job 2: Letter on Executive-Size Stationery (7¼" x 10½")

1" side margins; do not indent enumerated items but use hanging indentions (type the item number; space twice; block all lines of the items on this point)

Words

dr r e williams haplin clinic 4875 ruth street 13 winston-salem nc 27105 dear dr williams 22 (¶ 1) Congratulations on your election to the 30 office of president of your local medical 38 society. Although the work load is heavy, the 47 satisfaction from services rendered will make 57 this a memorable year. (¶ 2) At our meeting 64 last month, you asked me to suggest the projects 73 most worthy of "getting off the ground" 82 this year. Here are a few that were discussed 92 at our board meetings last year. (¶ 3) 1. Set 100 aside funds for resuscitator devices to be given 110 to our public swimming pools. Appoint members 118 to instruct the lifeguards at the pools in 128 the proper use of these resuscitators. (¶ 4) 136 2. Hold a clinic for athletic coaches in high 145 schools of the area. (¶ 5) 3. Increase the number 154 of members serving in the well-baby 162 clinics. (¶ 6) Feel free to call on me if I can 170 be of any assistance. cordially yours oscar 179 ryan m.d. 182/197

Skill-Transfer Typing ⑳ *three 1' writings on each ¶; determine* gwam

To determine percents of transfer: Divide your straight-copy rate into your statistical rate, your script rate, and your rough-draft rate.

Your statistical rate should approximate 65-75% of your straight-copy rate; your script rate, 75-85%; and your rough-draft rate, 70-80%.

		1' GWAM
¶1 1.4 SI 5.4 AWL 85% HFW	The purposes of business letters are many and varied.	11
	Letters are used to seek or inform, to direct or explain, to	23
	gain or retain goodwill, to name only a few functions. Their	36
	value is great; the cost is vital, too.	43
¶2 1.4 SI 5.4 AWL 85% HFW	A 1967 study revealed that an average first-class letter	11
	cost $2.49 as compared to only $1.83 in 1960--an increase of	24
	over 36%. The cost stood at just $1.17 apiece through 1953.	36

1' GWAM | 1 | 2 | 3 | 4 | 5 | 6 | 7 | 8 | 9 | 10 | 11 | 12 |

¶3 1.4 SI 5.4 AWL 85% HFW *More than twenty billion pieces of mail are dictated each* — 12
year in American business offices. Based on the cost of just — 24
a few years ago, you can see with great ease that the size of — 36
our annual letter budget is fantastic. — 44

¶4 1.4 SI 5.4 AWL 85% HFW ¶The ~~largest element~~ *biggest factor* in letter cost is labor. # Reduce Lower the — 12
[cost of this *human* factor--increase the production of the One — 24
who dictates and, *the one who* makes notes and types, and you ~~immediately~~ — 36
reduce *a major* ~~the greatest~~ cost of writing letters. — 44

LESSON 30

30A Preparatory Practice ⑧ *each line three times SS; DS between three-line groups*

Alphabet	When Ziggy Bux joined my squad, five players took more care.
Figures	Add ZIP to your letters: 15213, 90024, 45227, 85026, 33116.
Figure-symbol	Purchase 275 units @ 30¢ ($82.50) and 140 units @ 65¢ ($91).
Fluency	If a man is paid a high fee, he may work with improved zest.

| 1 | 2 | 3 | 4 | 5 | 6 | 7 | 8 | 9 | 10 | 11 | 12 |

30B Typing from Dictation *once with the book open; once with the book closed*

if it is; and to do; by the way; do the work; lend me a hand

sow 20#; paid 6%; make $73; 8:15 p.m.; 4/6 or 2/3; a #9 sock

we may; if you were; try to get; they are in; she was at the

Do not type the color dividers 10% 475# $89.50 #66│7:15 p.m.│2' x 6"│30# @ 12¢│Kelso & Cole

LESSONS 192-193

192-193A Preparatory Practice [5] *(each day)* *each line at least three times*

Alphabet	A jury asked puzzling questions of an expert on his views about music.
Figure-symbol	On May 7, 1968, the rate on Ted's $3,820 note went up from $4\frac{1}{2}\%$ to $5\frac{1}{4}\%$.
Long reaches	We were wholly unaware that he was acting in behalf of this syndicate.
Fluency	We know it is always best to forgive and not to try to obtain revenge.

| 1 | 2 | 3 | 4 | 5 | 6 | 7 | 8 | 9 | 10 | 11 | 12 | 13 | 14 |

192-193B Paragraph Guided Writings [10] *(each day)*

First Day. Type a 1′ writing on the *control level* to establish your base rate. Then type three 2′ writings, trying to hit the exact letter of your base rate in each writing. The half minutes will be called as a guide.

Second Day. Type a 2′ writing on the *exploration level*; then type three additional 2′ writings with a drop back in speed of 4 to 8 words. Note the *gwam* for your best writing.

1.7 SI
6.0 AWL
70% HFW

	GWAM 2′	GWAM 3′	
Adjustment letters are a vital part of business. No one is perfect,	7	5	51
so errors occur that need to be remedied. The seller and the buyer must	14	9	56
handle each end of the communication rapidly and politely. It must be	22	14	61
recognized that a well-written adjustment letter fosters better business	29	19	66
relations. A customer can get speedier action if he sends a clear, posi-	36	24	70
tive letter explaining his problem. The man who composes a reply must	43	29	78
picture himself in the sender's place if he is to answer any criticism	50	33	80
fairly, exactly, and without violating any of the basic principles in-	57	38	85
volved. Tact, honesty, and empathy are needed if a company's reputation	65	43	90
is to be retained or, hopefully, even to be improved.	70	46	93

2′ GWAM | 1 | 2 | 3 | 4 | 5 | 6 | 7 |
3′ GWAM | 1 | 2 | 3 | 4 | 5 |

192-193C Production Typing: Medical Reports and Correspondence [35] *(each day)*

In typing the jobs in Lessons 192 and 193, assume you are secretary to Dr. Oscar Ryan, 491 Greenwood Road, Reading, PA 19602. When a date is not given in a letter, use the current date. Erase and correct all errors. Add enclosure notations when needed. Prepare a carbon copy and an envelope for each letter. Use the block letter style and open punctuation.

30C   Growth Index ⑩ *type a 3' writing; practice words or word groups that caused hesitation or error; type another 3' writing; determine gwam on the better writing*

All letters are used.

	GWAM	
	1'	3'

¶1
1.4 SI
5.4 AWL
85% HFW

There is an old saying which suggests: Take care of the ... 11 | 4 | 40
pennies and the dollars will take care of themselves. This ... 23 | 8 | 44
is very good advice in handling money, and it can be applied ... 36 | 12 | 48
quite directly to other phases of life, also. ... 45 | 15 | 51

¶2
1.4 SI
5.4 AWL
85% HFW

For instance, if you learn to accept or conquer each of ... 56 | 19 | 55
your little frustrations as they occur every day, you will ... 68 | 23 | 59
develop the ability to face personal crises if and when they ... 80 | 27 | 63
arise. You will also learn to maintain a clear head and not ... 92 | 31 | 67
be panicked by the size of the next major problem that might ... 104 | 35 | 71
block your progress. ... 108 | 36 | 72

1' GWAM | 1 | 2 | 3 | 4 | 5 | 6 | 7 | 8 | 9 | 10 | 11 | 12 |
3' GWAM | 1 | 2 | 3 | 4 |

30D   Skill Building ㉕

DO: Type the two ¶s of 30C, above, without being timed. Try to increase control and reduce errors.

DO: Type a 1' guided speed writing on each ¶ of 30C, with your instructor calling the guide.

DO: If time permits, type the four ¶s of 29D, page 53, without timing. Try for improved control.

● **Self-Improvement Practice**

Space bar | The man who plans for success is already well on his way up.

Shift keys | He shifts to type: @ (at), * (asterisk), and & (ampersand).

Shift lock | He knows what the abbreviations PBX, AMS, CPA, and ZIP mean.

Tabulator | 56021 ⟦5⟧ 8742 ⟦5⟧ 2973 ⟦5⟧ 9954 ⟦5⟧ 2835 ⟦5⟧ 2146 ⟦5⟧ 82470

Center + 8 ↓

Tabulator and return | Tab - → Return without spacing   Return
at the end of the line.

Backspacer | The words to and too are still too frequently misused today!

Short words | to do so is he by she and the for with work lend forms their

Long words | fantastic progress themselves frustrations maintain chairman

| 1 | 2 | 3 | 4 | 5 | 6 | 7 | 8 | 9 | 10 | 11 | 12 |

Job 7: Notice to Creditors

NOTICE TO CREDITORS

(¶ 1) In the Superior Court of the State of California, for the County of San Diego. In the matter of the Estate of THOMAS GEORGE LANDELL, deceased. (¶ 2) Notice is hereby given to creditors having claims against the said decedent to file said claims in the office of the clerk of the aforesaid court or to present them to the undersigned at the office of William R. Biel, 1435 Thorn Street, in the City of San Diego, in the aforesaid County, which latter office is the place of business of the undersigned in all matters pertaining to said Estate. Such claims, with the necessary vouchers, must be filed or presented as aforesaid within six months after the first publication of this notice.

Dated: November 17, 19—

Norman Weedon Landell
Executor of the Will

William R. Biel   (*SS the attorney's*
Attorney-at-Law   *name and address.*)
1435 Thorn Street
San Diego, California   92103

Job 8: Notice of Hearing of Petition for Probate of Will

**NOTICE OF HEARING OF PETITION
FOR PROBATE OF WILL**

No. 943497

(¶ 1) In the Superior Court of the State of California, for the County of San Diego. In the matter of the Estate of THOMAS GEORGE LANDELL, deceased. (¶ 2) Notice is hereby given that the petition of NORMAN WEEDON LANDELL, for the probate of the Will and Codicil to the Will of the above-named decedent and for issuance of Letters Testamentary thereon to the Petitioner to which reference is hereby made for further particulars, will be heard at 9:30 o'clock a.m., on November 23, 19—, at the court room of the Superior Court of the State of California, for the County of San Diego, City of San Diego.

Dated: November 17, 19—

JOHN R. ALCORN
County Clerk and Clerk of the Superior Court of the State of California, for the County of San Diego

Note. Type Mr. Biel's name, his title as attorney for petitioner, and his address here as in Job 7, above.

Job 9: Notice of Sale by Lien Claimant

**NOTICE OF SALE OF PERSONAL PROPERTY
BY LIEN CLAIMANT**

(¶ 1) Notice is hereby given that, in accordance with provisions of the Warehouse Receipts Act, the undersigned will sell at auction to the highest bidder for cash at undersigned's place of business, 9890 Swidler Place, Santa Ana, California, on Wednesday, February 19, 19—, at 9 a.m. and continuing each following weekday at the same time and place until all goods are sold, or until lien is satisfied, the following unclaimed and uncalled-for personal property consisting of household goods, boxes, barrels, cartons, etc., to wit:

Mr. V. J. Hart	$ 79.80
Mr. C. K. Lester	296.78
Mr. W. H. Dwyer	780.00
Mrs. Lyla Penn	687.09

stored by the above named to satisfy a lien in the amounts stated and due the undersigned for rent, storage, and incidentals together with the cost of advertising and expenses of sale. (¶ 2) Dated: January 29, 19—.

BELL'S VAN AND STORAGE

By: Harold Bell, President

Loren F. Telman
Attorney-at-Law
1200 Sugar Street
Santa Ana, California   92704

Purpose. To apply basic skill to typing simple communications, and to improve basic techniques.

Machine Adjustments. 70-space line; SS drill lines; DS when directed to do so.

Self-Improvement Practice. Type selected lines from page 65 and repeat as time permits.

LESSON 31

31A Preparatory Practice ⑧ *each line three times SS; DS after third typing of line*

Alphabet	A new gold plaque may be awarded at the next Schuylkill Jazz Festival.
Figures	You may contact Evelyn and Pat by calling either 631–9460 or 257–8273.
Figure-symbol	The 2% discount on Todd's Bill #963 (for $1,450.87) amounts to $29.02.
Fluency	If these girls handle the work right, Mr. Clayborne may make a profit.

| 1 ' 2 | 3 | 4 | 5 | 6 | 7 | 8 | 9 | 10 | 11 | 12 | 13 | 14 |

31B Technique Practice: Stroking ⑮ *each line three times; then 1' writings on Line 5*

First-row keys	Have Benny, Mac, and Zora Nixon been on vacation in Brazil and Panama?
Home-row keys	Gladys Skaggs was glad she had some of Hal Hall's fad jewelry to wear.
Third-row keys	We try to treat the young workers as we treat the top men of our firm.
Figures	The typed line of 8 1/2 inches has 85 pica spaces or 102 elite spaces.
Fluency	The busy city authorities have to handle many civic problems promptly.

| 1 ' 2 | 3 | 4 | 5 | 6 | 7 | 8 | 9 | 10 | 11 | 12 | 13 | 14 |

31C Problem Typing: Informational Memorandums ⑳

Problem 1: Memorandum on the Block Style

*Half sheet; line: 60; 1½"
top margin; block style; SS*

Type the following memorandum. Use current date. Circle errors.

Note. Three words (15 strokes) are counted for the date.

			Words
Down 9 spaces; type date on	1½" (9 line spaces) top margin		
Line 10	*Current date*	Operate return mechanism 4 times (3 blank line spaces)	3
11			
12			
13			
14	SUBJECT: The Block Style		8
15		DS	
16	This memorandum is typed in the block style. Note that all		20
17	lines begin flush with the left margin, with double spacing		32
18	(one blank line space) between paragraphs.		41
19			
20	The use of the block style for typing letters, memorandums,		53
21	and other personal or office communications is common today		65
22	and will probably grow in favor as its value is recognized.		77
23	Since lines begin at the left margin, the date and subject,		89
24	when used, are typed to begin at this point.		98

Job 5: Will

Retype the entire will if you make errors on names, dates, or amounts. ¶ 7 can be either single- or double-spaced for acceptable paging.

	Words
LAST WILL AND TESTAMENT OF	5
THOMAS GEORGE LANDELL	10

(¶ 1) I, THOMAS GEORGE LANDELL, residing (17) in the City of San Diego, State of California, (26) hereby publish and declare this to be my Last (35) Will and Testament, and I revoke all former (44) Wills and Codicils made by me. (¶ 2) FIRST: (52) I declare that I am married, and my wife's (61) name is HAZEL JONES LANDELL. I have two (69) children now living; namely, THOMAS GEORGE (78) LANDELL, JUNIOR, and HEATHER DIANE (85) LANDELL. (¶ 3) SECOND: I direct that all my (92) just debts and funeral expenses be paid as (101) soon as convenient after my decease. (¶ 4) (109) THIRD: I give, devise, and bequeath all my (117) property, real and personal and wherever (126) situated, to be divided as follows: one half to (135) my wife, HAZEL JONES LANDELL, one fourth (144) to my son, THOMAS GEORGE LANDELL, (150) JUNIOR, and one fourth to my daughter, (158) HEATHER DIANE LANDELL. In the event that (167)

my wife should predecease me, then her portion is to be divided equally between my son (184) and my daughter. (¶ 5) FOURTH: I do hereby (192) name and appoint my wife, HAZEL JONES (199) LANDELL, executrix of this my Last Will and (208) Testament, to serve without bond. (¶ 6) IN (216) WITNESS WHEREOF, I have hereunto set my (224) hand and seal to this my Last Will and (232) Testament, on this the tenth day of July, (240) 19—, at San Diego, California. (246)

_____L.S. (253)

(¶ 7) The foregoing instrument was signed by (261) the testator, THOMAS GEORGE LANDELL, in (269) our presence, we being present at the same (278) time, and he then declared to us that such (286) instrument was his Last Will and Testament; (295) and we, at the testator's request and in his (304) presence and in the presence of each other, (313) have signed such instrument as witnesses. (321)

_____residing at_____ (342)
_____residing at_____ (363)
_____residing at_____ (384)

Job 6: Codicil

A *codicil* may be attached to a will as a means of modifying the terms of the will in some particular.

Retype the entire codicil if you make errors on names, dates, or amounts. ¶ 5 can be either single- or double-spaced for acceptable paging.

	Words
FIRST CODICIL TO WILL OF	5
THOMAS GEORGE LANDELL	9

(¶ 1) I, THOMAS GEORGE LANDELL, of the (16) City of San Diego, State of California, do (25) make, publish, and declare this to be the first (34) codicil to my Last Will and Testament, dated (43) the tenth day of July, 19—. (¶ 2) I do hereby (52) name and appoint my brother, NORMAN (59) WEEDON LANDELL, of the City of San Diego, (67) State of California, executor, to serve without (77) bond, of my Last Will and Testament. (¶ 3) (84) I hereby ratify, republish, and reaffirm said (94) Will and Testament in all respects, except as (103) modified by this Codicil thereto. (¶ 4) IN (110)

WITNESS WHEREOF, I have hereunto set my (118) hand and seal this fifteenth day of October, (127) 19—. (129)

_____L.S. (136)

(¶ 5) Signed, sealed, published, and declared (144) by THOMAS GEORGE LANDELL, the above- (151) named testator, as and for a Codicil to his (160) Last Will and Testament, dated July 10, 19—, (169) in the presence of us, who at his request and (178) in his presence and in the presence of one (187) another, have hereunto subscribed our names (196) as witnesses, this fifteenth day of October, (205) 19—. (206/268 *)

Note. Type lines for names and addresses of three witnesses as you did in typing the Will in Job 5.

_____

*This figure includes the lines for the names and addresses of the witnesses.

Problem 2: Memorandum on Typing Paper

Half sheet; line: 60; block style; SS

Type on the control level with a 1½″ top margin. Circle errors. Retype if time permits.

REMEMBER to leave 3 blank lines below the date and to DS before and after paragraphs.

	Words

Line 10 — *Current date* — 3

SUBJECT: Center Point — 8 (Line 14)

Most typing paper is 8½ inches wide and 11 inches long with 66 lines to the page; a half sheet (8½ by 5½ inches) has 33 lines. A line has 102 elite or 85 pica spaces. — 20 / 32 / 41

The exact horizontal center of the paper is at 51 for elite or 42½ for pica type. Unless otherwise directed, use 50 for the elite center (instead of 51) and 42 for the pica center (instead of 42½). — 53 / 66 / 78 / 81

(Line numbers shown at left: 10, 11, 12, 13, 14, 15, 16, 17, 18, 19, 20, 21, 22, 23)

31D   Skill-Transfer Typing ⑦ *each line as two 1' writings, or each typed four times; line: 60*

	Words
A majority of the women questioned the chairman's authority.	12
This paper, 8½ inches wide, has 85 pica or 102 elite spaces.	12
The ~~An~~ 11-inch sheet ~~is~~ has 66 lines (~~long;~~) half of the sheet, 33 lines	12

LESSON 32

32A   Preparatory Practice ⑧ *each line three times*

Alphabet	When is J. C. Paxton required to move his zoology lab from Room K-261?
Figures	On April 18, Elizabeth moved to Apartment 36-A, 2450 West 79th Street.
Figure-symbol	Is Frohm & Kelly's $12,750 note (with 5½% interest) due on January 19?
Fluency	The author is skeptical of the authenticity of those formal documents.

| 1 | 2 | 3 | 4 | 5 | 6 | 7 | 8 | 9 | 10 | 11 | 12 | 13 | 14 |

32B   Technique Practice: Response Patterns ⑮ *each line three times; then 1' writings on Line 5*

Stroke	The executive expects the expert to explain his action to the auditor.
Combination	Six of the states do not have the same wage and tax laws that we have.
Stroke	Flight 476 left Rome at 8:15 a.m. and arrived in New York at 3:29 p.m.
Combination	Nine seniors pointed to the easy quiz questions to support their case.
Word-recognition	The aid the men got from us did much to help them get their work done.

| 1 | 2 | 3 | 4 | 5 | 6 | 7 | 8 | 9 | 10 | 11 | 12 | 13 | 14 |

32C   Problem Typing: Memorandums ⑳

Problem 1: Type Problem 2 of 31C, above, as directed. Review learning elements. Circle errors.

Job 3: Power of Attorney with Acknowledgment and Legal Back

Legal backs for first two copies; see illustration on p. 323

A *power of attorney*, a formal written authorization by one party for another to act as his agent or attorney, must be *acknowledged* before a notary public if the document is to be recorded. An acknowledgment (shown at the end of Job 3) certifies the identity and the authority of the executor of a document. Single-space the acknowledgments called for in the jobs that follow.

	Words
POWER OF ATTORNEY	4

(¶ 1) KNOW ALL MEN BY THESE PRESENTS, that I, MONTGOMERY A. BRIEM, of the City and County of San Diego, State of California, by these presents do make, constitute, and appoint DONALD HYDE, of the City of Jamul, County of San Diego, State of California, my true and lawful attorney, for me and in my name, place, and stead, to negotiate for the purchase of the structure and property situated at 111-113 West Main Street, City and County of San Diego, State of California, known as Mission Towers; and I hereby ratify

	Words

and confirm all that my said agent or attorney will lawfully do, or cause to be done, in connection with this purchase. (¶ 2) IN WITNESS WHEREOF, I have hereunto set my hand and seal this (*current day*) of (*current month*), 19--.

———————————————— L.S.
Montgomery A. Briem

STATE OF CALIFORNIA)
: ss.
County of San Diego)

(¶ 3) On (*current date*), before me, a Notary Public, in and for said County and State, personally appeared MONTGOMERY A. BRIEM, known to me to be the person whose name is subscribed to the within instrument, and acknowledged that he executed the same. (¶ 4) WITNESS my hand and official seal.

————————————————
Notary Public

Words	
115	and confirm all that my said agent or attorney
124	will lawfully do, or cause to be done, in con-
132	nection with this purchase. (¶ 2) IN WITNESS
140	WHEREOF, I have hereunto set my hand and
147	seal this (current day) of (current month),
148	19--.
155	L.S.
159	Montgomery A. Briem
163	STATE OF CALIFORNIA
164	: ss.
169	County of San Diego
177	(¶ 3) On (current date), before me, a Notary
186	Public, in and for said County and State, per-
193	sonally appeared MONTGOMERY A. BRIEM,
202	known to me to be the person whose name is
210	subscribed to the within instrument, and
218	acknowledged that he executed the same.
225	(¶ 4) WITNESS my hand and official seal.
231	
234	Notary Public

Job 4: Warranty Deed

Add an acknowledgment

	Words
WARRANTY DEED	3

(¶ 1) FOR A VALUABLE CONSIDERATION, receipt of which is hereby acknowledged, I, GLEN MINTON, grant to JOSEPH BEARD, all that real property situated in the City of Tustin, County of Orange, State of California, described as follows: (*Indent 10 spaces from both margins; SS.*)

Lot 510 of Tract 2798, as per map recorded in Book 797, at pages 51-53 of Maps, in the records of the County Recorder of said County.

(¶ 2) I hereby covenant with JOSEPH BEARD that I am seised in fee simple of the property; that JOSEPH BEARD shall have quiet enjoy-

ment of the same without lawful disturbance; that the same is free from all encumbrances; and I warrant said real property to JOSEPH BEARD against every person lawfully claiming the same. (¶ 3) To have and to hold the above granted and described premises unto said JOSEPH BEARD, his heirs and assigns, forever. (¶ 4) IN WITNESS WHEREOF, I have hereunto set my hand and seal this (*current day*) of (*current month*), 19--.

————————————————— L.S.
Glen Minton

Note. At the end of the Warranty Deed, type an acknowledgment similar to the one in Paragraph 3 in Job 3, but change the name of the county to *Orange* and the name of the person to *Glen Minton*. (*Add 72 words.*)

Problem 2: Memorandum on Centering Information

Half sheet; line: 60; block style; SS

Type current date on Line 10; subject on Line 14. Circle errors. Retype if time permits.

Note. Paragraph headings are emphasized by capitalizing important words and by underlining.

Words

Current date   3

SUBJECT: Horizontal Centering   9

<u>Get Ready to Center.</u> Move both margin stops to the ends of   25
the scale. Clear the tabulator stops; move the carriage or   37
carrier to the center of the paper. Set a tabulator stop.   49

<u>Steps for Centering.</u> Tabulate to the center of the paper.   65
From this center point, backspace once for each two letters   77
(or letter and space) in the line. If the line has one odd   89
or leftover letter, disregard it and start typing where the   101
backspacing ends.   104

32D Drill on Typing Outside the Margins ⑦ *right margin: center + 30*

1. Depress the margin release or margin bypass (25) and backspace 5 spaces into left margin.
2. Type the 71-space sentence, below, three times,

typing until the carriage locks (ignore the ringing of the bell); then depress the margin release (bypass) and complete the typing.

Set right margin stop 3 or more spaces beyond the line ending you want.

LESSON 33

33A Preparatory Practice ⑧ *each line three times*

Alphabet   Was Len Burke amazed by the very excellent report given by Jeff Quinn?
Figures   My 174-page research report has 28 tables, 6 graphs, and 53 footnotes.
Figure-symbol   Was the rate on Dodd & Boyd's note of $5,000 (date 2/8/69) 6½% or 7%?
Fluency   Try to improve the quality without reducing the quantity of your work.
                | 1 | 2 | 3 | 4 | 5 | 6 | 7 | 8 | 9 | 10 | 11 | 12 | 13 | 14 |

33B Problem Typing: Horizontal Centering ⑳

Problem 1

1. Get ready to center. (See ¶ 1 of Problem 2, above.)
2. Study HOW TO CENTER, below.
3. Center and type each line at the right.

> HOW TO CENTER: From center of paper, backspace *once* for each *two* letters, figures, spaces, or punctuation marks in the line. Do not backspace for a leftover stroke. Start to type where the backspacing ends.

Half sheet; DS; 1½″ (9 line) top margin

Words

FREE TUTORING SERVICE   5
IS

Honors Society   7

offers   9

Free Tutoring to Freshmen and Sophomores   17

Mondays and Thursdays, 3:45 p.m.   24

Rooms 206 and 208, Royce Hall   30

First Session on Monday, October 10   37

Job 1: Partnership Agreement

Words
PARTNERSHIP AGREEMENT 4
(¶ 1) THIS AGREEMENT, made in the 10
City of San Mateo, State of Califor- 17
nia, on the tenth day of August, 24
19––, between ALBERT BELL and 30
RANDALL EDWARDS, both of San 35
Mateo, California, (¶ 2) WHEREIN 41
IT IS MUTUALLY AGREED, AS FOL- 47
LOWS: (¶ 3) 1. That the parties 52
hereto shall, as partners, engage in 60
and conduct the business of buying, 67
selling, and installing automatic at- 74
tachments for opening doors. (¶ 4) 80
2. That the name of the partnership 87
shall be SUNSET AUTOMATIC DOORS. 94
(¶ 5) 3. That the capital of the part- 101
nership shall be the sum of Forty 107
thousand dollars ($40,000); and 114
each party shall contribute thereto, 121
contemporaneously with the execu- 128
tion of this agreement, the sum of 135
Twenty thousand dollars ($20,000) 141
in cash. (¶ 6) 4. That at the end of 148
each calendar year the net profit or 155
net loss shall be divided equally be- 163
tween the parties hereto, and the 169
account of each shall be credited or 177
debited as the case may be, with his 184
proportionate share thereof. (¶ 7) 190
IN WITNESS WHEREOF, the said par- 197
ties have hereunto set their hands 204
the day and year first above written. 211

Words
____________________ 218
Albert Bell 220
____________________ 226
Randall Edwards 229
Signed and delivered 234
in the presence of 237
____________________ 242
____________________ 246

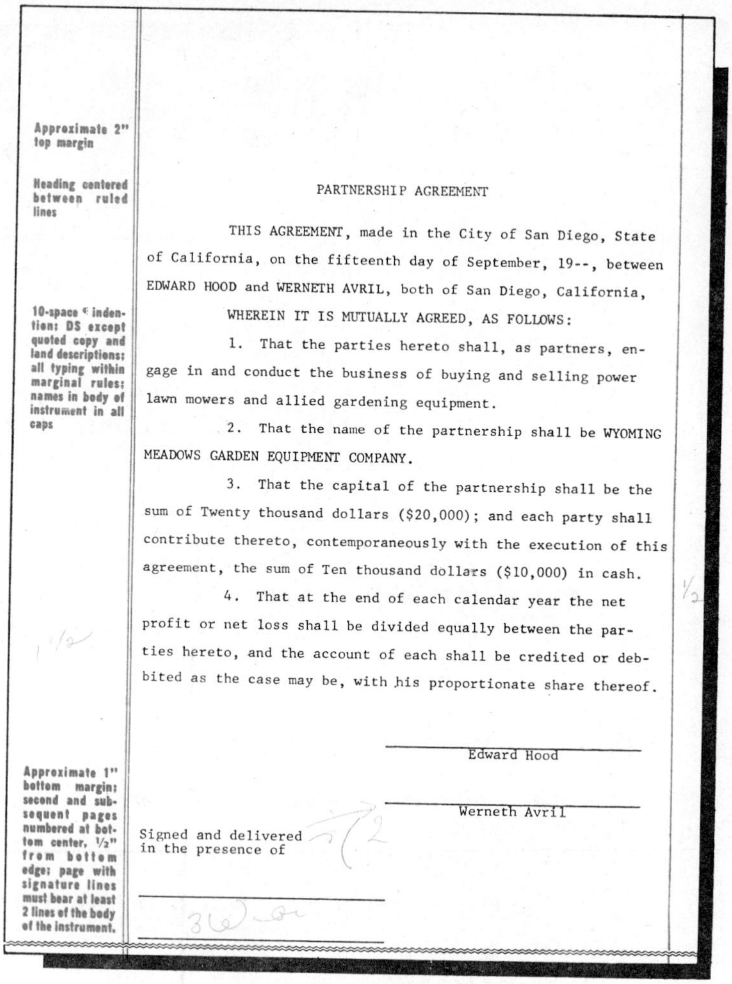

Approximate 2" top margin
Heading centered between ruled lines
10-space ¶ indention; DS except quoted copy and land descriptions; all typing within marginal rules; names in body of instrument in all caps
Approximate 1" bottom margin; second and subsequent pages numbered at bottom center, ½" from bottom edge; page with signature lines must bear at least 2 lines of the body of the instrument.

PARTNERSHIP AGREEMENT

THIS AGREEMENT, made in the City of San Diego, State of California, on the fifteenth day of September, 19--, between EDWARD HOOD and WERNETH AVRIL, both of San Diego, California,

WHEREIN IT IS MUTUALLY AGREED, AS FOLLOWS:

1. That the parties hereto shall, as partners, engage in and conduct the business of buying and selling power lawn mowers and allied gardening equipment.

2. That the name of the partnership shall be WYOMING MEADOWS GARDEN EQUIPMENT COMPANY.

3. That the capital of the partnership shall be the sum of Twenty thousand dollars ($20,000); and each party shall contribute thereto, contemporaneously with the execution of this agreement, the sum of Ten thousand dollars ($10,000) in cash.

4. That at the end of each calendar year the net profit or net loss shall be divided equally between the parties hereto, and the account of each shall be credited or debited as the case may be, with his proportionate share thereof.

Edward Hood

Werneth Avril

Signed and delivered
in the presence of

Partnership Agreement

Job 2: Bill of Sale

BILL OF SALE 3
(¶ 1) KNOW ALL MEN BY THESE PRESENTS, 9
that the undersigned for valuable considera- 18
tion does hereby grant, sell, transfer, and de- 27
liver to CHARLES W. CARTER (Grantee), 34

Words
residing at 1275 Crescent Bay Drive, Laguna 43
Beach, California 92651, the following de- 52
scribed original paintings, at the prices listed: 62
"Seascape" by Alexander Fisher $450 69
"Canal en Automne" by Peter Lely $650 77
(¶ 2) To have and to hold all and singular the 85
said paintings to said Grantee, his successors 94
and assigns. The undersigned covenants with 103
said Grantee that the undersigned is the law- 112
ful owner of said paintings; that they are free 122
from all encumbrances; that the undersigned 130
has a good right to sell the same; that the 139
undersigned will warrant and defend same 147
against the lawful claims and demands of all 156
persons. (¶ 3) IN WITNESS WHEREOF, I have 164
hereunto set my hand this 15th day of Janu- 172
ary, 19––. 174

____________________ 181
Seller 182

Problem 2: Centered Lines

Half sheet; DS; 1" top margin; center each line horizontally

	Words
HORIZONTAL CENTERING	4
TS	
Move Margin Stops to Ends of Scale	11
Clear Tab Stop Settings	16
Set Tab Stop at Center	21
From Center, Backspace "Once for Two"	28
Disregard Leftover Stroke	33
Begin to Type at Point Backspacing Ends	41
Type the Line	44
Tabulate to Center	48
Center and Type Each Remaining Line	55

Problem 3: Centered Lines

Half sheet; DS; 1½" top margin; center each line horizontally

	Words
Dinner Dance	3
TS	
Benefit of Scholarship Funds	8
LEADERSHIP CLUB	11
music by Alphonse Garcia and Orchestra	19
Saturday, 19 November, 19--	25
Sussex House	27
Twelve Dollars, a Couple	32

Problem 4: Centered Lines

Retype Problem 3, but in all capital letters.

33C Building Control ⑧ *one 1' and two 2' writings on the* control level; *circle errors*

70-space line; 5-space ¶ indention; DS

1.4 SI
5.4 AWL
85% HFW

All letters are used.

When typing, think the word, or think the sequence of letters if the word is long or unusual. Adjust your speed to the kind of material you are to type. Emphasize an even and flowing motion, and type without pausing between one word and the next.

	GWAM		
	1'	2'	
	13	6	31
	27	14	38
	42	21	46
	50	25	50

1' GWAM | 1 | 2 | 3 | 4 | 5 | 6 | 7 | 8 | 9 | 10 | 11 | 12 | 13 | 14 |
2' GWAM | 1 | 2 | 3 | 4 | 5 | 6 | 7 |

33D Setting the Margin Stops ⑦

1. Set the margin stops for an exact 60-space line (left: center — 30; right, center + 30).
2. Type the sentence, below, at a slow rate; stop as soon as the bell rings. Instead of typing the remainder of the sentence, type the figures 123 (etc.) until the machine locks. The last figure typed is the number of spaces the bell on your typewriter rings before the carriage locks.
3. Subtract 3 from the number of bell cue spaces (Step 2) and move the right stop to the right that far: center + 30 + 3 to 7 or more.

4. Type the sentence again. If the bell rings as you are typing a word, complete it, make the return, and continue to type. If the machine locks as you are typing a word, depress the margin release (margin bypass) and complete the word.

If the bell rings on the space between words, make the return at once or type the next word before making the return if it is a short word. This is often desirable because of your typing momentum.

When the carriage locks, depress the margin release and type on.

33E Listening for the Bell ⑦

60-space line; 5-space ¶ indention; DS

Type the ¶ of 33C, above, as two 1' and one 2' writings on the *control level*. Listen for the ringing of the bell to warn of the line ending. Your typed lines will not be the same as the lines appearing in the ¶ in 33C.

PAPER

Printed forms are available for many legal instruments. If such forms are not available, use legal paper, which is 8½ by 13 or 14 inches with ruled left and right margins.

TITLES ON LEGAL FORMS

Type the title in all capital letters centered between the marginal rulings.

MARGINS AND SPACING

On legal paper, type within the vertical marginal rulings. If you are using plain paper, set the margin stops for a 1½-inch left margin and a ½-inch right margin. Indent paragraphs 10 spaces; double-space the copy with the exception of land descriptions and quoted matter, which should be single-spaced and indented 10 spaces from both margins.

Begin the first line of typing on all pages about 2 inches (12 blank lines) from the top of the paper. Leave a bottom margin of approximately 1 inch.

PAGE NUMBERS

The first page is usually not numbered, except on a will, but subsequent page numbers are centered between the marginal rulings a half inch (3 blank lines) from the bottom of the page. Type a hyphen before and another after the page number.

SIGNATURE LINES

The maker or makers of an instrument sign at the right of the page. Witnesses, if any, sign at the left. Type signature lines approximately 3 inches long. Leave 2 or 3 blank lines between them.

At least 2 lines of typing must appear on the page that contains the signature of the maker and those of the witnesses.

LEGAL BACKS AND ENDORSEMENTS

While the practice is not common, legal documents may be bound in a cover that is slightly heavier and larger than the sheets on which the documents are typed. These covers are referred to as *legal backs*. On them is sometimes typed information (called the *endorsement*) giving the name of the paper and the names of the parties thereto. You will prepare legal backs for a number of the problems in this section.

PREPARING A BACK FOR THE ENDORSEMENT

1. Fold down the top 1 inch. This fold will later be the binding for the legal papers.

2. Bring the bottom edge of the sheet even with the creased top edge and crease neatly.

3. Bring the folded bottom edge to the top and crease. The legal back has now been folded into 4 equal parts, not counting the 1-inch binding fold.

4. Type the endorsement on the back of the sheet, confined within the second fold from the top. To be sure the endorsement is typed right side up, place the sheet in the typewriter with the top 2 folds exposed and the 1-inch binding fold at the left.

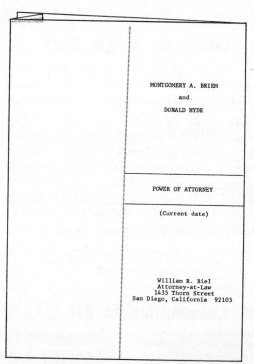

POWER OF ATTORNEY

KNOW ALL MEN BY THESE PRESENTS, that I, MONTGOMERY A. BRIEM, of the City and County of San Diego, State of California, by these presents do make, constitute, and appoint DONALD HYDE, of the City of Jamul, County of San Diego, State of California, my true and lawful attorney, for me and in my name, place, and stead, to negotiate for the purchase of the structure and property situated at 111-113 West Main Street, City and County of San Diego, State of California, known as Mission Towers; and I hereby ratify and confirm all that my said agent or attorney will lawfully do, or cause to be done, in connection with this purchase.

IN WITNESS WHEREOF, I have hereunto set my hand and seal this _____ day of _____, 19--.

_____ L.S.
Montgomery A. Briem

STATE OF CALIFORNIA)
            : ss.
County of San Diego)

On (current date), before me, a Notary Public, in and for said County and State, personally appeared MONTGOMERY A. BRIEM, known to me to be the person whose name is subscribed to the within instrument, and acknowledged that he executed the same.

WITNESS my hand and official seal.

_____
Notary Public

Power of Attorney

MONTGOMERY A. BRIEM
and
DONALD HYDE

POWER OF ATTORNEY

(Current date)

William R. Biel
Attorney-at-Law
1435 Thorn Street
San Diego, California 92103

Endorsement on Legal Back

34A Preparatory Practice ⑧ *each line three times*

Alphabet — Jean and Gladys quickly won several prizes at the Foxburgh track meet.
Figures — Flight 590 left for Paris with 34 girls, 16 boys, and 28 men on May 7.
Figure-symbol — My letter read, "Wire best price on 9 cars 4/4 C & B Oak f.o.b. Erie."
Fluency — It will pay you to take the needed time to learn to control your mind.

| 1 | 2 | 3 | 4 | 5 | 6 | 7 | 8 | 9 | 10 | 11 | 12 | 13 | 14 |

34B Building Control ⑫ *two 1' and two 3' writings on control level; circle errors*

70-space line; 5-space ¶ indention; DS

The ringing of the bell is a signal that you will have just a few more strokes to type before the machine will lock. Listen for it, and it will tell you, even without your looking up from the textbook, when to make the return. Acquire the habit of paying attention to the bell, and you will realize an immediate gain in your typing power.

	GWAM	
	1'	3'
	13	4	27
	27	9	32
	42	14	37
	56	19	41
	68	23	45

1' GWAM | 1 | 2 | 3 | 4 | 5 | 6 | 7 | 8 | 9 | 10 | 11 | 12 | 13 | 14 |
3' GWAM | 1 | 2 | 3 | 4 | 5 |

34C Problem Typing: Announcements ⑳

Problem 1: Announcement with Centered Line

Half sheet; 60-space line; block style; 1½" top margin

October 26, 19---   Words 3

3 blank line spaces

The first in our exciting series of Fall FORUMS is to be on   15
Wednesday, November 6, at 8:15 p.m. in Science Hall. The   27
subject will be   30

"Radioactive Isotopes"   35

The speaker, Dr. Anton Szechenyi, of the Nuclear Science   46
Service, Inc., will discuss some biological and biomedical   58
applications of isotopes to the space program.   67

Problem 2: Centered Announcement

Half sheet; DS; 1½" top margin; center each line

Words

SCIENCE FORUM *TS*   3
Lecture on "Radioactive Isotopes"   10
By Dr. Anton Szechenyi   14
of *the*   16
Nuclear Science Service, *Inc.*   22
in Science Hall   25
Wednesday, November 6, *8:15 p.m.*   31

Problem 3: Alertness Training

Type Problem 2 again as directed, except that you will type it in capitals. (To type in capitals, depress the shift lock.)

Alertness cue: Don't let the figures trip you!

The textbook may not always warn you by an "alertness cue" that there is a problem in the material to be typed. It is your responsibility to see that all your work is correct in form, content, and meaning. This is why alertness training is important.

34D Listening for the Bell ⑩ *two 3' writings on the control level; circle errors*

60-space line; 5-space ¶ indention; DS

Type 34B, above. Your typed lines will not be the same as those in the ¶. If typing a word when the bell rings, complete it; if the machine locks, depress the margin release (margin bypass) and complete the word.

190-191A Preparatory Practice (5) *(each day)* *each line at least three times*

Alphabet	Excited voices kept buzzing as qualified members of the jury withdrew.
Figure-symbol	Mark's term policy #862380 (for $7,000) will expire on August 4, 1975.
Long words	The recommendations are based exclusively on recent research evidence.
Fluency	All men who succeed in life can focus their minds on a single problem.
	| 1 | 2 | 3 | 4 | 5 | 6 | 7 | 8 | 9 | 10 | 11 | 12 | 13 | 14 |

190B Communication Aid: Proofreading (10) *use 190B the first day and 191B the second.*

Capitalize and punctuate each sentence as you type it. Check your work with your instructor; then type the sentences a second time.

1 the question confronting mary is this when should she sell the bond
2 on may 1 1968 the new rules were adopted by our dayton ohio plant
3 some believe 100 pilgrims sailed on the mayflower others 101 or 102
4 a middle aged worker for example may elect to take two 10 day trips
5 moreover the industry which supplies their fuel is the coal industry
6 mr jones our manager visited our plants in iowa texas and kansas
7 john said "if you want to use time wisely begin now but we didnt
8 read first for meaning afterwards check your work for typing errors

| 1 | 2 | 3 | 4 | 5 | 6 | 7 | 8 | 9 | 10 | 11 | 12 | 13 | 14 |

191B Communication Aid: Proofreading (10)

Correct the paragraph as you type it. Check your work with your instructor; then use the paragraph for 1′ writings as time permits. Determine your *gwam* after each writing.

	1′ GWAM	
a letter of application must be accurate concise and thorough.	13	27
outline in it the extent of your education any vocational experience	27	54
you have had and other pertinent facts about yourself. if you attach	41	82
a data summery you can usually keep the letter relatively brief. site	56	113
three or four references obtaining permission to use each one before	70	140
you send the letter. make it easy for an employer to contact you.	83	166

1′ GWAM | 1 | 2 | 3 | 4 | 5 | 6 | 7 | 8 | 9 | 10 | 11 | 12 | 13 | 14 |

190-191C Production Typing: Legal Papers (35) *(each day)*

Lessons 190 and 191 contain examples of work typed in a legal office. Make two carbon copies of each document.

Legal documents are usually typed on 8½- by 13- or 14-inch paper called "legal cap." The workbook provides 8½- by 11-inch legal cap. If a job should require a longer sheet, you may use the reverse side of the paper provided.

When carbon copies are a part of the job, take care not to change the original order of the papers.

Before you type Job 1, study page 323 carefully.

35A Preparatory Practice ⑧ *each line three times*

Alphabet Were quite big loans applied for by J. H. McVay and Baxter K. Ziegler?

Figures   A half sheet is 8½ by 5½ inches and has 33 lines (6 lines to an inch).

Figure-symbol Items marked 26-A, 345-X, and 789* sell at 10% discount until April 7.

Fluency   Nancy and Henry worked on the problem with their usual vigor and zeal.

| 1 | 2 | 3 | 4 | 5 | 6 | 7 | 8 | 9 | 10 | 11 | 12 | 13 | 14 |

35B Problem Typing: Report on Centering ⑳

Full-size sheet; 70-space line; 5-space ¶ indention; DS; 3" (18-space) top margin

Problem 1

Words

CENTERING ON SPECIAL-SIZE PAPER TS   6

To center *a line* on special-size paper or card, *first* determine   19

the center of the paper (or card). To do this, add the numbers *from* at   33

the scale at the Left and Right edges of *the* paper; divide by 2.   46

The resulting number will be the center of the paper (or card)   59

¶ *When you are and type lines* To center on special-size paper (or card), *follow the rules summarized* do these things: *below:*   81 / 84

Insert the paper

Center each line ℓℓ𝒮   Add scale numbers at left and right edges of paper   94

Divide sum by 2 for center   100

Follow steps for getting ready *to center*   108

Back space from center *"once for two"*   115

Center (the line and type)   120

Problem 2: Centering on Special-Size Paper

1. Insert a half sheet (5½" by 8½") with the *long edge at the left*. Use DS; 2" top margin.
2. Determine the center and set tab stop.
3. Center horizontally and type only the main heading and centered lines of the body of Problem 1, above.

Problem 3: Centering on Special-Size Paper

1. Fold the half sheet used in Problem 2 from bottom to top.
2. Insert the folded sheet, creased edge at left.
3. Use a 1½" top margin.
4. Center and type the heading of Problem 1.

35C Listening for the Bell ⑩

Full-size sheet; 60-space line; 5-space ¶ indention; DS; 3" top margin

Type Problem 1 of 35B, above, with a 60-space line. Listen for the bell to warn of the line ending. Your typed lines of the ¶s will not be the same as those of the problem, but it will not be necessary for you to divide any word when typing with the shorter (60-space) line. The centered lines can be typed without changing the margin stops. Type at less than your top speed and listen for the bell.

188E Paragraph Guided Writing [10]

Type a 1′ *control-level* writing to establish your base rate. Type three 2′ writings, trying to hit the exact letter of your base rate each time. Regulate your rate by a signal given at half-minute intervals.

All letters are used.

1.7 SI
6.0 AWL
70% HFW

	GWAM 2′	3′	
Would you enjoy being a secretary in a law firm? Would you like	7	4	52
managing the work and assuming responsibilities that such a job demands,	14	9	56
where basic prerequisites are the ability to type and take dictation	22	14	61
accurately? Due to the nature of the business transacted in most legal	28	19	66
firms, a secretary must use added caution in examining all work. It	35	23	70
must be accurate--absolutely accurate--to the final comma. The duties	42	28	75
of such a secretarial position differ, depending on the size of the	49	32	80
firm and the varieties of legal affairs handled. Without exception,	56	37	84
though, such work is fascinating and challenging to anybody who enjoys	63	42	89
dealing with the unusual, working behind the scenes for the man who	70	46	94
goes to court.	71	47	95

2′ GWAM | 1 | 2 | 3 | 4 | 5 | 6 | 7 |
3′ GWAM | 1 | 2 | 3 | 4 | 5 |

LESSON 189

189A Preparatory Practice [5] *each line at least three times*

Alphabet	Judy explained the law requiring the man to have his back fence razed.
Figure-symbol	Mr. Day's notes (due May 14 and 23) for $97,850 were discounted at 6%.
Hyphen	My son-in-law won the first-place award in the coast-to-coast contest.
Fluency	To improve, be big enough to admit that perhaps you have a few faults.

| 1 | 2 | 3 | 4 | 5 | 6 | 7 | 8 | 9 | 10 | 11 | 12 | 13 | 14 |

189B Skill-Comparison Typing [10] *two 1′ writings on each sentence in 189A; compare* gwam

189C Paragraph Guided Writings [10]

1. Using the paragraph in 188E, type a 2′ writing on the *control level* to establish your base rate.
2. Choose a rate 4 to 8 words above this base rate.
3. Type three 2′ writings, trying to reach the higher rate on each writing while maintaining the *control level*. The half minutes will be called as a guide.

189D Typing Figures [10] *70-space line; three 3′ writings*

Beginning with 100, type consecutive numbers separated by the word *and*. When time is called, subtract 2 for each typing error from the last number typed. This is your score.

189E Building Speed and Control [15] *two 5′ writings on 187B, page 317*

35D Special Characters ⑫ *each line three or more times*

' Minutes, Feet (apostrophe)
" Seconds, Inches, Ditto (quotation mark)
× Times, By (lower-case x with a space before and after)
− Minus (hyphen with space before and after)

+ Plus (diagonal; backspace; hyphen)
÷ Divided by (hyphen; backspace; colon)
= Equals (hyphen; backspace; roll platen forward slightly; hold it in position; type hyphen; return platen to line position)

1   The 2' speed range, typed with the 15" call of the guide, is 30 to 46.

2   A rug 15'6" x 18'9" will be just right for a room that is 20'6" x 25'.

3   His problem is 27 x 89 − 364 ÷ 2. What is the sum of 157 + 509 − 263?

4   Ed said 5 x 90 − 62 + 136 ÷ 2 = 262 and 7 x 284 − 965 + 301 ÷ 2 = 662.

5   If 32 x 564 − 897 + 109 equals 17,260, what would 57 + 509 − 63 equal?
| 1 | 2 | 3 | 4 | 5 | 6 | 7 | 8 | 9 | 10 | 11 | 12 | 13 | 14 |

LESSON 36

36A Preparatory Practice ⑧ *each line three times*

Alphabet   Did Frank expect to solve the jigsaw puzzle more quickly than Bob Lee?

Figures   Move 90 to 100 chairs to Rooms 236-8 for the 4:15 lecture on the 27th.

Special symbols   Check this problem: 20 x 367 − 541 + 891 ÷ 2 = 3,845. Is that right?

Fluency   You can speed up your typing by thinking the word rather than letters.
| 1 | 2 | 3 | 4 | 5 | 6 | 7 | 8 | 9 | 10 | 11 | 12 | 13 | 14 |

36B Centering on Typed Lines ⑦ *DS; follow steps of 35B, page 60*

1. Type a 5½" line with the underline.
2. Type a 3" line with the underline.
3. Center and type your name on the 5½" line.
4. Center and type the date on the 3" line.

36C Problem Typing: Memorandum and Postal Cards ⑳ *half sheet; 2 postal cards*

Problem 1: Memorandum with Subject Line

Half sheet; 50-space line; 1½" top margin; block style; SS

October 29, 19--

SUBJECT: Typing Postal Cards

A postal card is 5½ by 3¼ inches and has a total of 19 lines. Since both top and bottom margins require 2 or 3 lines each, there will be just 12 to 15 lines for typing.

Each line has 55 pica or 66 elite spaces, but the left margin will take 3 or 4 spaces and the right margin 2 or 3 spaces. The writing line, then, is limited to 48 to 50 pica or 59 to 61 elite spaces.

Words
3
9
19
29
39
44
54
64
74
83

Section 30 contains examples of communications to be typed in legal, medical, and scientific offices.

Drill Copy: Full sheet; 70-space line; SS.

Paragraph Copy: Full sheet; 70-space line; DS; 5-space ¶ indention.

Production Copy: Unless otherwise directed, use the current date. Correct all errors.

LESSON 188

188A   Preparatory Practice (5)   *each line at least three times*

Alphabet   John's famous bazaar required exhausting work, patience, and vitality.
Figure-symbol   She noted the price change of item #254 from 10 @ $9.76 to 12 @ $9.83.
Long words   Management has preferred the qualitative to the quantitative approach.
Fluency   Send the prints to her as soon as you find that you are able to do so.
                 | 1 | 2 | 3 | 4 | 5 | 6 | 7 | 8 | 9 | 10 | 11 | 12 | 13 | 14 |

188B   Skill-Comparison Typing (10)   *two 1' writings on each sentence in 188A; compare gwam*

188C   Communication Aid: Word Choice (10)

Read the sentences at the right; then, from the words at the left, select the correct one to insert at the point of the blank space. Supply the correct word and capitalize and punctuate each sentence as you type it. After checking your work with your instructor, retype the sentences.

1	you, your	we regret ____ having to ask us for mr browns address a second time
2	principal, principle	the ____ reason we believe for retaining any position is skill
3	capital, capitol	if assets are overstated ____ figures i think are also affected
4	affects, effects	my fundamental act was simple however the ____ were most complex
5	advice, advise	the councils ____ favors the development of a simple novel answer
6	access, excess	all corporations that make ____ profits will normally pay dividends
7	accept, except	do not ____ packages between 915 am and 530 pm on february 25
8	formally, formerly	my business teacher who was ____ an office manager is efficient
9	ascent, assent	it is required that all parties ____ to the dissolution she said
10	altar, alter	when working with legal material one must be careful not to ____ it

188D   Unarranged Tabulation (15)   *DS; erase and correct all errors*

Align and type the figures below in columns as indicated. Place the problem in the exact center of the top half of the sheet.

In the exact center of the bottom half of the sheet, retype the problem with the amounts in each column arranged from the largest to the smallest.

Column 1:	$24.84	316.21	502.97	183.12	344.00
Column 2:	$956.93	46.87	5.98	.75	76.20
Column 3:	$3.16	9.07	804.32	500.00	93.54
Column 4:	$154.87	96.80	191.80	23.45	57.60

Problem 2: Message Typed on a Postal Card

1. Use 2 postal cards (or paper cut to size of a 5½- by 3¼-inch card).
2. Insert card; determine center; then set stop for a 48-space line.
3. Type the date on Line 3; then type the postal card message given below.

Note. The salutation and complimentary close are omitted because of limited space for the message.

4. Remove the typed card; turn it message side down; then insert the second card; and type the same message.

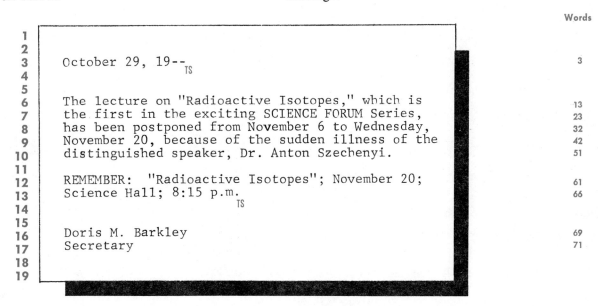

	Words
October 29, 19-- TS	3
The lecture on "Radioactive Isotopes," which is	13
the first in the exciting SCIENCE FORUM Series,	23
has been postponed from November 6 to Wednesday,	32
November 20, because of the sudden illness of the	42
distinguished speaker, Dr. Anton Szechenyi.	51
REMEMBER: "Radioactive Isotopes"; November 20;	61
Science Hall; 8:15 p.m. TS	66
Doris M. Barkley	69
Secretary	71

Problem 3: Addressing Postal Cards

LEARN:

1. SS and block both the return and the postal card addresses.
2. The new state abbreviations are two capital letters typed without a period or space between. For automatic sorting into destination bins by the Optical Character Reader, the ZIP Code *must* be used. (See the Reference Guide, page viii, for a complete list of the new two-letter state abbreviations.) It is still permissible, however, to spell the state name in full or to use standard abbreviations.
3. Type the return address in the upper left corner of the card on the address side, beginning on Line 2 from the top edge and 3 spaces from the left edge.
4. Type the address about 2" from the top edge of the card and begin it 2 inches from the left

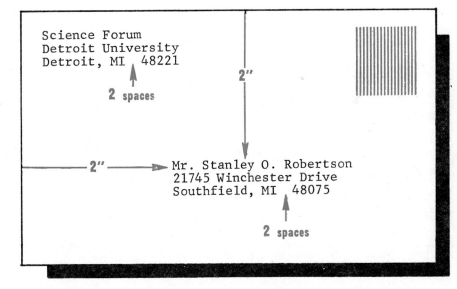

edge. Have 1 or 2 spaces between the state abbreviation and the ZIP Code.

DO: 1. Insert the first card typed as Problem 2, above, and type the address side of the card as shown.

2. Insert the second card typed as Problem 2, above. Address the card to:

Miss Elfreda Trimble
1609 Pontchartrain Blvd.
Detroit, Mich. 48203

Job 2: Capital Statement

Full sheet; DS; reading position; all dates current year

		Words
FORSTMANN BROTHERS COMPANY		5
CAPITAL STATEMENT		9
For Year Ended December 31, 19--		16
Capital, January 1, 19--	$56,500.00	26
Net income for the year $32,178.14		36
Less withdrawals 24,178.14		48
Increase in capital	8,000.00	60
Capital, December 31, 19--	$64,500.00	74

Job 3: Letter with Tabulations

Words

bent–craft envelope company 387 coyier lane 12
madison wi 53713 gentlemen (¶1) Your cata- 19
log for January of last year quoted prices as 29
shown below for the following envelope sizes: 38

#85056	3 5/8" x 6 1/2"	$5.00 per M	45
86135	5 1/8" x 9 1/2"	8.20 per M	52
89980	9" x 12"	9.60 per M	57
98097	12" x 18"	0.18 each	62

(¶2) This catalog also included the following 70
statement on the inside front cover: (*Indent* 78
quotation) Prices quoted here are final, sub- 84
ject to date of order. Prompt, postpaid ship- 93
ment of goods is assured. (¶3) We have re- 101
ceived no more catalogs from you; therefore, 110
we need substantiation of these prices and a 119
statement of your present shipping policy. If 128
prices quoted are still in effect, you may enter 138
the following order for us: (*Calculate and* 144
type the amounts for each item and the total.)

5M	#85056	$	147
1M	86135		152
2M	89980		155
50 only	98097		159
		————	160
		$	162

Words

(¶4) If these prices are no longer valid, please 171
disregard our order and send quotations for 179
the items indicated. very truly yours pur- 188
chasing agent (*A. C. King is the purchasing* 193/205
agent.)

Job 4: Letter with Changes

Capitalize and punctuate

Words

mr and mrs newton b arden 3348 bingham 11
drive portsmouth va 23703 dear mr and mrs 20
arden (¶1) robert podesta who serviced your 28
account until recently has been transferred to 38
our yorktown office, which will be open in 47
about three weeks. charles e cooper will take 56
his place in the portsmouth office and will 65
handle your account. after reviewing your ac- 74
count mr cooper will call to see how he may 83
best serve you. (¶2) as a result of recent 91
growth we shall be adding another registered 100
representative to our office in about one 109
month. we are pleased that the portsmouth 117
office is growing and i personally want to 126
thank you for the business that you have given 135
us. (¶3) should you have any questions re- 143
garding this change or any other matter please 152
call me and i shall do my best to assist you. 162
sincerely yours albert e hibbard branch 170
manager 172/186

36D Special Characters [10] *each line three or more times*

/ Insert (Type / between words at point inserted material is to go; then roll platen backward (toward you) and type inserted matter. Return platen to line position.)

! Exclamation (see page 40).
\# Pounds (see page 44).
° Degree (Roll platen backward a half space; hold in position; type small o.)

                       of the   very
1 Have most/students tried quite hard to learn to type/well?

2 Paul said, "The box weighs 310#." I exclaimed, "Never. It couldn't."

3 The boiling point of water is 212° F. and the freezing point is 32° F.

4 Morris said this problem is correct: 936 x 7 – 458 + 170 ÷ 2 = 3,132.

5 The problem is 27 x 89 – 364 ÷ 2. What is 157 x 409 – 263 + 238 ÷ 12?

| 1 | 2 | 3 | 4 | 5 | 6 | 7 | 8 | 9 | 10 | 11 | 12 | 13 | 14 |

36E Errorless Typing [5] *each line once without error or three times with not more than 1 error a line*

All of us will have problems to be solved at some period in our lives.

Each day's work calls for the application of preceding days' learning.

Since I can't escape problems in life, I must learn how to solve them.

| 1 | 2 | 3 | 4 | 5 | 6 | 7 | 8 | 9 | 10 | 11 | 12 | 13 | 14 |

LESSON 37

37A Preparatory Practice [8] *each line three times*

Alphabet May Jack provide a few extra quiz questions or problems for the girls?

Figures In 1965, Lynn & Beard had 84 salesmen; in 1967, 230; and in 1968, 491.

Figure-symbol Does 30 x 156 – 374 + 928 ÷ 4 = 1,308½? Does 40 x 516 + 273 = 20,913?

Fluency The duties of the chairman have been taken over by Elvis until August.

| 1 | 2 | 3 | 4 | 5 | 6 | 7 | 8 | 9 | 10 | 11 | 12 | 13 | 14 |

37B Technique Practice: Manipulative Parts [10] *each drill three times*

Center →

Tabulator and return Depress the tab bar (or flick your electric key) to move from column to column.

Margin release Use the margin release (or margin bypass) to type outside the margins.

Shift lock To assure the fastest service, we use the <u>National ZIP Code Directory</u>.

Hyphen and dash The editor-in-chief--if that's his new title--used an up-to-date list.

Centered line Backspace-from-Center Method

| 1 | 2 | 3 | 4 | 5 | 6 | 7 | 8 | 9 | 10 | 11 | 12 | 13 | 14 |

¶4
1.6 SI
5.8 AWL
75% HFW

¶5
1.6 SI
5.8 AWL
75% HFW

A fine education is one that includes in its purposes the type of ideas that can be sorted out, arranged, stored, and recalled as they are needed to handle new situations. Such an education will supply qualities that are uniquely human--those of morality, of creativity, of pride, and, if you will, of compassion--that cannot be copied by a machine.

Total responsibility for education, though, does not reside with institutions. Schools are just one source of education; and each individual must undertake sole responsibility for his own development as a citizen, as a worker, as a parent--for each role in life he is looked upon to play. To a large extent, we are what we cause ourselves to be.

	GWAM		
	1'	5'	
	13	44	114
	28	47	117
	42	50	120
	57	53	123
	70	56	126
	13	58	128
	27	61	131
	41	64	134
	55	67	137
	70	70	140

1' GWAM | 1 | 2 | 3 | 4 | 5 | 6 | 7 | 8 | 9 | 10 | 11 | 12 | 13 | 14 |
5' GWAM | 1 | 2 | 3 |

187C Production Measurement ㉚ 25' typing; figure n-pram

Job 1: Schedule of Accounts Receivable

Exact center; DS

ANDERSON–ROBEK CARPETS, INC.

SCHEDULE OF ACCOUNTS RECEIVABLE

June 30, 19--

Debtor	Amount Due	Original Amount	Age in Months	Words
				6
				12
				15
				41
				45
				51
				64
James K. Braemmer	$ 72.50	$ 115.50	2	72
Ellis W. Jones	90.00	125.00	2	80
Clark W. Lawson	140.00	140.00	1	87
Patricia Patterson	43.85	93.85	2	96
Mary Recupero	162.35	162.35	1	103
Regent Theater	2,500.00	3,000.00	3	110
St. Mark's Church	1,425.00	1,425.00	1	118
James K. Tuscuro	482.25	482.25	1	126
T. James Walker	612.10	1,000.00	3	134
Claretta Wister	175.00	500.00	5	141
Gary B. Van Ryn	190.35	750.00	4	149
Alan Worpler	72.20	172.20	3	156
David E. Young	8.12	212.12	12	165
Total	$5,973.72			172
				185

Problem 1

Type the problem once on a half sheet, SS, in exact center; and once on a full-size sheet, DS, in reading position. Center the problem vertically (see Basic Rule at right); and center each line horizontally.

REVIEW OF CENTERING ELEMENTS

TS

Block Style
Spaces in Horizontal Inch
Center of Paper
Lines in Vertical Inch
Basic Rule for Horizontal Centering
Centering on Special-Size Paper
Setting Margin Stops
Postal Cards
Backspace-from-Center Vertical Centering
Special Characters
Bell Cue

Vertical Centering: Backspace-from-Center Method

BASIC RULE. From vertical center of paper, roll platen (cylinder) back once for each two lines, two blank line spaces, or line and blank line space. Ignore leftover line.

Steps in Vertical Centering

1. To insert paper to vertical center, start spacing down from *top edge of paper*:
   a. *Half sheet*: Down 6 TS — 1 SS (to Line 17).
   b. *Full sheet*: Down 11 TS + 1 SS (to Line 34).

2. From vertical center:
   a. *Half sheet*, SS or DS: Follow Basic Rule (back 1 for 2).
   b. *Full sheet*, SS or DS: Follow Basic Rule (back 1 for 2); then back 2 SS for *reading position.**

REMEMBER: TS (2 blank line spaces) after main heading.

NOTE: The mathematical method of vertical centering is taught on page x.

*About 2 line spaces above actual vertical center.

Problem 2: Postal Card with Centered Heading

48-space line; block style

	Words
ATTENTION CLUB TENNIS PLAYERS	6
TS	
The Mixed Doubles Tennis Match now scheduled for	16
May 18 will be rescheduled for May 25 because of	26
conflicts in area sports activities.	33
DS	
All entries should be in not later than May 21.	43
Call 621–4630 to be entered in the match.	52
TS	
Loren T. Parker, Chairman	57
Athletic Club Tennis Committee	63

Problem 3: Announcement

Half sheet; 60-space line; current date on Line 8; block style

Type Problem 2 as an announcement with 3 blank line spaces between the date and the centered heading. It will not be necessary for you to divide any words when typing the problem with the 60-space line, but your lines will not be the same as those shown in Problem 2. Let the bell indicate the line ending.

Job 2: Outline from Rough Draft *142 words*

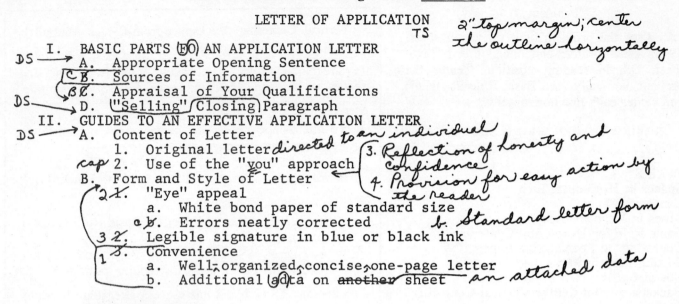

```
                    LETTER OF APPLICATION                2" top margin; center
                                       TS                the outline horizontally
     I.  BASIC PARTS (FO) AN APPLICATION LETTER
DS →     A.  Appropriate Opening Sentence
        C B.  Sources of Information
        B C.  Appraisal of Your Qualifications
DS →     D.  "Selling" Closing Paragraph
    II.  GUIDES TO AN EFFECTIVE APPLICATION LETTER
DS →     A.  Content of Letter
             1.  Original letter directed to an individual
     cap     2.  Use of the "you" approach
                                  3. Reflection of honesty and confidence
                                  4. Provision for easy action by the reader
         B.  Form and Style of Letter
           2 1.  "Eye" appeal
                 a.  White bond paper of standard size
               a b.  Errors neatly corrected      b. Standard letter form
           3 2.  Legible signature in blue or black ink
           1 3.  Convenience
                 a.  Well-organized, concise, one-page letter
                 b.  Additional (ad)ta on another sheet   an attached data
```

LESSON 187

187A Preparatory Practice [5] *each line at least three times*

Alphabet	Max and June Zachary saw the aquatic show in Bigsville Park on Friday.
Figure-symbol	Their March 25 estimate of $689.37, less 10%, includes a 4% sales tax.
3d, 4th fingers	A person who never makes a mistake is not checking his work very well.
Fluency	This is the way we learn; and it is the right way, most of us believe.
	| 1 | 2 | 3 | 4 | 5 | 6 | 7 | 8 | 9 | 10 | 11 | 12 | 13 | 14 |

187B Growth Index [15] *two 5′ writings; compare* nwam

All letters are used.

		GWAM 1′	5′	
¶ 1	Perhaps the most evident impact of the trend to automation involves	14	3	73
1.6 SI	a vital need for better education. Qualified workers must be found, and	28	6	75
5.8 AWL	our education system must make them available. Moreover, a time may be	43	9	78
75% HFW	imminent when more insight about automation will be needed by almost	56	11	81
	everyone—and it will then be the duty of the schools to provide it.	70	14	84
¶ 2	Education for living in an automated age should mean more for us	13	17	86
1.6 SI	than merely taking some technological courses. A liberal education to	27	19	89
5.8 AWL	comprehend the broad implications of automation is essential. It is not	42	22	92
75% HFW	enough just to know how the computer runs; we should appreciate, also,	56	25	95
	the effects it might have on man and on the world in which he lives.	70	28	98
¶ 3	Education is man studying man, his history, his relationships, his	13	31	100
1.6 SI	societies, and the globe he inhabits. Yet, education must do more than	28	33	103
5.8 AWL	inspect man; it should train him to use his brain, not only for memori-	42	36	106
75% HFW	zation but also for creativity; it should educate him to live as well	56	39	109
	as to make a living in an increasingly complex and perplexing world.	70	42	112
1′ GWAM	| 1 | 2 | 3 | 4 | 5 | 6 | 7 | 8 | 9 | 10 | 11 | 12 | 13 | 14 |			
5′ GWAM	| 1 | 2 | 3 |			

187B is continued on page 318.

		GWAM	
	1′	3′	5′

70-space line;
5-space ¶ in-
dention; DS

All letters are used.

When you type, concentrate on what you are typing and how you are to type it. If you find this difficult to do while people around you are talking and moving about, block out the noise by becoming involved in what you are doing and nothing can distract you. Realize the need for and the importance of concentration and think of how you can focus your undivided attention on what you are typing no matter what is going on around you.

¶ 1
1.4 SI
5.4 AWL
85% HFW

1′	3′	5′
13	4	3
27	9	5
41	14	8
55	18	11
70	23	14
84	28	17
87	29	18

¶ 2
1.4 SI
5.4 AWL
85% HFW

Concentration cannot be given to you as a gift by a teacher, parent, or friend. You must decide, on your own, whether learning to type well is to become one of your major goals. Once this decision has been reached, the next step is to address yourself to the problem of concentrating on one single goal at a time until eventually you are able to utilize the power that is latent within you.

1′	3′	5′
12	33	20
26	38	23
40	42	25
54	47	28
67	51	31
78	55	33

```
1′ GWAM  |  1  |  2  |  3  |  4  |  5  |  6  |  7  |  8  |  9  | 10 |  11  |  12  |  13  |  14  |
3′ GWAM  |         1         |         2         |         3         |        4        |       5       |
5′ GWAM  |              1              |              2              |            3            |
```

● **Self-Improvement Practice** *each line three or more times*

		Words in Line	GWAM		
	All letters, figures, and symbols are used in the sentences.		20″	15″	12″
1	Lead a boy to college where they try to make him think.	11	33	44	55
2	With faith enough and work enough, we can do about anything.	12	36	48	60
3	We may not be born great, but we can try to work up to greatness.	13	39	52	65
4	A good many of the workers of this world need to have a faith lifting.	14	42	56	70
5	Use * for a footnote, and use ¢ and @ in typing a bill.	11	33	44	55
6	He wrote, "Sam's Policy 765432, due in 1980, is for $2,500."	12	36	48	60
7	Check #453 (dated July 29) is for $167.80, but Paul owes $176.80.	13	39	52	65
8	Lane & Roth gave a 2% discount on Bill #345 (dated May 6) for $789.10.	14	42	56	70
9	Do some distance thinking--far ahead of where you are!	11	33	44	55
10	A man may be <u>down</u>, but he's never OUT until he gives up.	12	36	48	60
11	The next goal to be realized: a gain of a word or two each week.	13	39	52	65
12	James has quite as much zeal for his work as he has for his pay check.	14	42	56	70
13	The year's high for Manox was 89½; it sold at 82 today.	11	33	44	55
14	Be uniform in typing fractions: 1/2 and 1/4--not 1/2 and ¼.	12	36	48	60
15	If 109 x 6 − 57 + 83 = 680, what will 902 x 3 − 754 + 183 ÷ 2 be?	13	39	52	65
16	I say the following problem is right: 360 x 4 − 854 + 710 ÷ 12 = 108.	14	42	56	70

186B Speed and Accuracy Checkup ⑮ *two 5' writings on 184B, page 312; compute* nwam

186C Production Measurement ㉚ *25' typing; if time permits, repeat Job 1*

Job 1: Unbound Manuscript with Footnotes

Top margin: 2"; heading, LETTERS OF APPLICATION

	Words
(¶ 1) The letter of application is your personal	18
representative. Those interested in employ-	22
ing you will study it carefully. Employers	31
know that a competent applicant may write an	40
unimpressive letter, but they also know that	49
an outstanding letter is seldom written by an	58
incompetent person.	62

Basic Parts of an Application Letter — 77

(¶ 2) Hanna, Popham, and Beamer state that	84
an application letter should consist of four	93
parts:[1] (¶ 3) Appropriate opening sentence.	106
The opening sentence is often the most diffi-	115
cult one to write well. A good letter starts	124
with the business at hand. Tell your reader	133
just what position you are applying for and	142
how you learned about it. (¶ 4) Appraisal of	153
your qualifications. Emphasize your qualifi-	165
cations that particularly fit the job as you see	175
it. Be direct; be specific. Tell the reader what	185
training and experience you had that specifi-	194
cally qualify you for that position. Try to	203
convince the reader that he should see you.	212
(¶ 5) Sources of information. Make it easy	224
for the reader to obtain additional objective	233
information about you if a position is open	242
with his firm. (¶ 6) A closing ("selling")	254
paragraph. You should try to "sell" yourself	265
in the closing paragraph by suggesting an	273
appointment. This gives the employer an	282
opportunity for definite action toward hiring	291
you.	292

Guides to an Effective Application Letter — 309

(¶ 7) There is no pat formula for writing a	317
strong application letter, but the following	326
guides will help you.[2]	330

(Indent and list enumerated items; SS; DS between items.)

	Words
1. Write an original letter. Study other appli-	345
cation letters, but never copy one as your own.	355
The reader is interested in employing you, not	364
the original writer of a letter you may copy.	373
2. Address your letter to the individual. If at	391
all possible, obtain the employer's name and	400
personal title. Using his name personalizes	409
an application letter. 3. Use the "You" ap-	421
proach. Since the application letter is a per-	431
sonal sales letter, you cannot avoid using the	441
personal pronoun "I." Do not overpraise your	450
ability, however. 4. Be honest and confident.	464
Be specific. State your qualifications accu-	473
rately. Don't apologize for shortcomings.	482
5. Make it easy for the reader to act. Let the	498
reader know where and how he can reach	506
you. If your letter obtains an interview for	515
you, it has done all that an effective letter is	525
expected to do. 6. Keep the letter short.	538
Stress the ways in which your qualifications	547
fit you for the position. For detailed informa-	556
tion on your training and experience, include	566
a personal data sheet with your letter. 7. Give	576
the letter eye appeal. Use a standard-size	589
paper. English usage and typing must be	597
flawless. 8. Sign the letter properly. Type	611
your name after the complimentary close. A	620
woman should indicate her marital status.	628
Remember to sign your letter in ink.	636

---

[1] J Marshall Hanna, Estelle Popham, and Esther K. Beamer, Secretarial Procedures and Administration (5th ed.; Cincinnati: South-Western Publishing Co., 1968), pp. 649-652.
(46 words)

[2] Ibid. *(6 words)*

Purpose. To learn to type personal notes and letters, to address envelopes, and to compose at the typewriter (think and type).

Machine Adjustments. Line: 70 spaces, unless otherwise directed; SS drills and problems; DS and indent timed writing ¶s 5 spaces.

Self-Improvement Practice. Type selected lines from page 76, or type each line as directed and as time permits.

LESSON 38

38A Preparatory Practice ⑧ *each line three times; Line 4 for 1' writings as time permits*

Alphabet	Jack will be quite vexed when Troy Gilman buzzes the fine new airport.
Figures	18 24 539 670 100 4,281 3,596 1,700 2,344 12,485 96,703 82,314 610,597
Figure-symbol	Check #803 for $914.56 (dated February 27) was mailed to Dodge & Sons.
Fluency	The eight girls may want a ride to the game if the bus is not on time.

| 1 | 2 | 3 | 4 | 5 | 6 | 7 | 8 | 9 | 10 | 11 | 12 | 13 | 14 |

38B Building Speed and Control ⑫

1. Type each ¶ of 37D, page 65, as a 1' *exploration-level* writing. Speed up the stroking for these writings.

2. Type the ¶s as a 5' *control-level* writing. Reduce the speed of stroking for this writing.

38C Problem Typing: Personal Note in Block Style ⑳

2 half sheets; line: 50; block style; SS

1. Type the following note as illustrated. Circle your errors.

2. Type the note a second time, but address it to Elsie. Circle your errors.

Line			Words
7	Date	October 18, 19––	3
8		*Operate return 4 times*	
9			
10			
11	Salutation	Dear Frank	6
12			
13		The Homecoming Queen and her court will be chosen	16
14	Body	by the student body on November 16 in an election	26
15		to be held in Student Center from 8 a.m. to 4 p.m.	36
16			
17		The Student Government Committee asked me to get	46
18		some students to supervise the polls on election	56
19		day. I hope you will be willing to help do this.	66
20		We need you very much. Call me at 621–3078 to let	76
21		me know we can count on you.	82
22			
23	Complimentary	Sincerely yours	85
24	close	*Operate return 4 times*	
25			
26			
27	Writer's name	*Your name*	89
28			
29			

Job 2: Interoffice Memorandum

Half sheet of plain paper; 1" top and side margins; type headings

Words

TO: lyman t edwards west coast manager 8
FROM: albert f gianola sales manager 16
DATE: *(current)* 21
SUBJECT: sale of company vehicles 28
(¶ 1) You are hereby authorized to place the 36
following vehicles on sale: *(list)* Buick 43
LeSabre, 1967, 2-door | Cadillac Eldorado, 51
1966, convertible | Ford Galaxie, 1968, 4-door 60

Words

(¶ 2) The sale of these vehicles, as is, will be 68
on a fixed-price basis, plus sales tax. The 77
selling price will be established at the time of 87
sale. A deposit of $50 will hold any vehicle 96
for five days, at which time the selling price 106
must be paid in cash or by cashier's check. 115
(¶ 3) These vehicles are to be sold without 122
guarantee except for clear titles. 130

Job 3: Three-Column Table

Reading position; DS; rule the column heads

Words

JOB STATUS OF EMPLOYEES AFTER INSTALLATION 9
OF DATA PROCESSING EQUIPMENT* 15
(One Year After Installation) 21

Type of Job Change	No. of Employees	Percent	Words
			22
			36
No Change in Position	1,498	53.3	43
Reassigned	552	19.7	47
Transferred	331	11.8	52
Resigned	238	11.7	56
Retired or Died	42	1.5	61
Granted Leave	35	1.2	66
Discharged	13	.5	70
Laid Off	9	.3	76
All Employees	2,808	100.0	82
			85

*Data relate to employees in affected units of 20 offices. 97

LESSON 186

186A Preparatory Practice [5] *each line at least three times*

Alphabet	Jeff Goodwin's book and the subsequent movie were criticized expertly.
Figure-symbol	During your term of office (1963 to 1968), sales increased by $45,720.
Adjacent reaches	As we discovered, the money was not deposited to our account in Ghent.
Fluency	The prize goes to the man who does the right job in the very best way.

| 1 | 2 | 3 | 4 | 5 | 6 | 7 | 8 | 9 | 10 | 11 | 12 | 13 | 14 |

38D Composing and Typing: Sentence Completion ⑩ *line: 50; 5-space ¶ indention; DS*

1. Type the sentences in ¶ form and fill in the needed information. The line endings will not be the same as those in the copy. Ignore any typing errors you make.

(¶ 1) **My name is** (*your name*). **My home is in** (*city or town and state*). **My home address is** (*street number and name or P.O. Box, city, state, and ZIP Code*). **I am a student at** (*name of your school*), **in** (*city and state*). **I am now living at** (*street address, dormitory, or other*).

2. When you have completed the typing, remove the paper, make pencil corrections, and retype the material on a half sheet with an appropriate top margin.

(¶ 2) **The name of the typewriter I use is** (*type the name*) **and the title of my textbook is** (*underline the title or type it in all CAPS*). **I type at approximately** (*state rate in figures*) <u>gwam</u>. **My greatest difficulty seems to be** (*too many errors, not enough speed, poor techniques, etc.*).

LESSON 39

39A Preparatory Practice ⑧ *each line three times; 1' writings on Line 4*

Alphabet   Rex Quig watched jet airplanes flying above the haze in the amber sky.

Figures   We are to study Section 2, pages 95-180, and Section 5, pages 274-360.

Figure-symbol   I sold 1 punch @ $4.50; 72 pencils @ 8¢ each; and 37 rulers @ 9¢ each.

Fluency   Many of the new problems are to be solved when we come to the meeting.

  | 1 | 2 | 3 | 4 | 5 | 6 | 7 | 8 | 9 | 10 | 11 | 12 | 13 | 14 |

39B Problem Typing: Memorandum; Personal Note ⑳

Problem 1: Memorandum on Word Division

Half sheets; line: 60; SS; 1½" top margin

Type the main heading centered horizontally. After typing the first line, reset the left margin stop 4 spaces to the right. To type the numbers for ¶s 2 and 3, move the carriage (or carrier element) outside the left margin. (See 32D, page 57.) Circle errors; then retype the problem.

	Words
GUIDES FOR WORD DIVISION	5
TS	

Reset margin

1. Divide a word between syllables only. (Do not divide a word of five or fewer letters).   17 / 24

Use margin release; then backspace

2. When a syllable is added to a word that ends in double letters, divide after the double letters (as, express-ing); but if the final consonant is doubled in adding a suffix, divide between the double letters (quit-ting).   36 / 47 / 58 / 69

3. Do not divide from the remainder of the word (a) a one-letter syllable at the beginning or end of a word, or (b) a syllable without a vowel (as, couldn't), or (c) a two-letter syllable at the end of a word (neat-ly).   82 / 93 / 104 / 114

SECTION 29 MEASUREMENT: Basic and Production Skills

LESSONS 185–187

Each lesson of Section 29 provides for 25 to 30 minutes of timed production typing. If you complete all the jobs in a lesson before time is called, begin the first job again. Approximately 5 minutes will be allowed at the end of the period to figure your *n-pram.*

Drill Copy: Full sheet; 70-space line; SS.

Paragraph Copy: Full sheet; 70-space line; DS; 5-space ¶ indention.

Production Copy: Unless otherwise directed, use the following styles and procedures.

For *letters*, use modified block style with blocked paragraphs, open punctuation, the current date, your reference initials, one carbon copy, and the appropriate envelope.

For *tabulated reports*: Decide spacing between columns; no carbon copies.

For *manuscripts*: Follow the binding form indicated; no carbon copies.

LESSON 185

185A Preparatory Practice [5] *each line at least three times*

Alphabet	Dave made his way back to an exit after analyzing part of a job quote.
Figure-symbol	We ordered 59 @ 26½¢ and 8 @ 42¼¢ but received 7 @ 39½¢ and 60 @ 41¼¢.
Long words	We studied improvement of data processing through work simplification.
Fluency	Consider the chance to do a major job a chance to grow in proficiency.

| 1 | 2 | 3 | 4 | 5 | 6 | 7 | 8 | 9 | 10 | 11 | 12 | 13 | 14 |

185B Skill-Comparison Typing [5] *1′ writing on each line of 185A; compare* gwam

185C Communication Checkup: Capitalization and Punctuation [10]

Capitalize and punctuate as you type. Check your work with your instructor; then use the paragraph for 1′ writings as time permits. Determine your *gwam* for each writing.

	1′ GWAM	
situated among many rather ordinary buildings in new yorks wall	13	26
street area is the home office of the chase national bank its enormous	28	57
aluminum and glass facade making a beautiful addition to a famous sky-	41	82
line. when the banks big computer center is finally in operation it	55	110
will analyze over a million checks daily.	64	129

1′ GWAM | 1 | 2 | 3 | 4 | 5 | 6 | 7 | 8 | 9 | 10 | 11 | 12 | 13 | 14 |

185D Production Measurement [30] *25′ typing; figure* n-pram

Job 1: Short Letter

	Words
mr charles rusiewicz 386 raphael perea way	12
el paso tx 79922 dear mr rusiewicz (¶ 1)	19
Missed anything lately? We have. (¶ 2) We	27
have missed receiving those payments that	35
you regularly sent us for the past four months.	45
Probably you simply overlooked last month's	54
payment. Such things happen, we know. Our	63
accountants, however, never overlook any-	71
thing; and they report to me that your ac-	79
count has now been stamped PAST DUE. (¶ 3)	87
Although I know––and you know––that the	95
payment is forthcoming, accountants are a	103
difficult group to convince. But there is one	112
good way to convince them––just mail your	121
check directly to my office. Let me send them	130
a carbon copy of your receipt. yours truly	139
b j scatterlein, credit manager	146/159

Problem 2: Personal Note

Type the note given at the right, double spacing between single-spaced ¶s. See 38C, page 66, for form.

The | in the copy indicates the end of the 60-space line, or other special line. Do not type it; but when you come to it, make the return without looking up and keep on typing. The title of a book may be typed in all CAPS or underlined. (See ¶ 1.)

Half sheet; line: 60; block style; SS; date on Line 7; reset margin stops in 5 spaces to type quoted ¶ 2; then reset at original margins

	Words
October 20, 19—	(*Operate return 4 times*) Dear Tom	(¶ 1) Let	6
me answer your question about freedom of speech on the	campus	18
by quoting from the <u>College Handbook</u>:		30
(¶ 2) The College wants speakers invited to the campus		39
for an open forum to express their ideas freely.		59
(¶ 3) The purpose of an institution of higher learning must		60
always	be the free exchange of ideas. The College adheres to		73
this	purpose at all times.	Sincerely yours	(*Operate return 4*		81
times) E. M. Brownfield		85

39C Skill-Transfer Typing ⑫ *line: 70; ¶ indention: 5; DS*

1. Type a 1′ *exploration-level* writing on each ¶. Try to maintain the same speed on the more difficult second and third ¶s (figures and rough-draft copy).

Do this by forcing your fingering speed.
2. Type a 5′ *control-level* writing on all ¶s. Determine *gwam* and errors.

All letters are used.

		GWAM	
		1′	5′

¶ 1
1.4 SI
5.4 AWL
85% HFW

Too many young people make the big mistake of postponing the very 13 | 3 | 30

difficult decision of the choice of a career. Much thought should be 27 | 5 | 33

given to this matter long before college work is begun, yet a final 41 | 8 | 36

decision need not always be made by this time, of course. 52 | 10 | 38

¶ 2
1.4 SI
5.4 AWL
85% HFW

By 1964, career guidance was given to a few kindergarten classes 13 | 13 | 41

and in Grades 1, 2, and 3 to children 5 to 7 or 8 years old, but many 27 | 16 | 43

schools wait to give this guidance until children are about 10 years old. 42 | 19 | 46

¶ 3
1.4 SI
5.4 AWL
85% HFW

Guidance Experts say that (students should/all) plan to have a their programs 13 | 21 | 49

of study to equip them for the jobs of the next coming generation. They will 27 | 24 | 52

[work more zealously, also, if they enjoy the work and in are able to do 41 | 27 | 54

it very well. 44 | 28 | 55

1′ GWAM | 1 | 2 | 3 | 4 | 5 | 6 | 7 | 8 | 9 | 10 | 11 | 12 | 13 | 14 |
5′ GWAM | 1 | 2 | 3 |

39D Composing and Typing ⑩ *half sheets; line: 60; SS; 1″ top margin; date: October 20, 19—*

1. Compose and type a short note to Frank to express your pleasure that he has accepted your invitation to supervise the polls on election day. (See 38C, page 66.)

2. Compose and type a short note to Elsie to express your regret that she cannot accept your invitation to supervise the polls on election day.

Job 1: Table with Leaders

ESTIMATED PER CAPITA
GROSS NATIONAL PRODUCT PROJECTIONS
For Selected Western European Countries

	1955	1970	Percent of Increase	Job 1	Job 2
				4	4
				11	11
				19	19
				21	
				29	60
WESTERN EUROPE	$ 747	$1,067	42.8	39	67
Belgium	1,076	1,569	45.8	49	73
France	932	1,400	50.2	59	78
West Germany	850	1,180	38.8	69	84
Italy	454	747	64.5	79	89
Netherlands	732	1,072	46.4	89	95
Spain	276	403	46.0	99	100
Switzerland	1,281	1,817	41.8	109	107
United Kingdom	1,047	1,362	30.1	119	113
					123

Job 2: Table with Horizontal Rulings

Retype Job 1. Omit the leaders and type a double rule (across the entire table) above the columnar headings and a single rule below them and below the table. (*You may wish to reposition the table.*)

Job 3: Table with Braced Headings

GROSS CAPITAL FORMATION PER CAPITA
AND AS PERCENT OF GNP

Country	Per Capita		Percent of GNP		Words
					7
					11
					23
	1955	1970	1955	1970	28
					37
					41
					53
WESTERN EUROPE	$151	$197	20.2	18.5	60
Denmark	160	217	17.1	16.5	65
Luxembourg	298	284	24.9	17.0	72
Netherlands	170	207	23.2	19.3	78
Norway	288	274	30.2	20.1	83
Portugal	30	42	14.5	14.5	89
Spain	50	59	18.1	14.6	94
Sweden	263	323	21.9	18.1	100
Switzerland	284	354	22.2	19.5	106
United Kingdom	170	211	16.2	15.5	113
					125

LESSON 40

40A Preparatory Practice ⑧ *each line three times; 1' writings on Line 4*

Alphabet   Pat Ford and Sam Oxford will solve the big jigsaw puzzle very quickly.

Figures   24 63 17 80 95 821 624 731 805 1,000 9,376 472,116 2,047,890 6,337,425

Figure-symbol   Bowen's Check #978 is for $211.27 for Invoice #161 ($234.75 less 10%).

Fluency   Some of the other men thought that Sue would be right for the new job.
| 1 | 2 | 3 | 4 | 5 | 6 | 7 | 8 | 9 | 10 | 11 | 12 | 13 | 14 |

40B Word-Division Drill ⑫ *half sheets; line: 70; DS; 10 spaces between columns; 1½" top margin*

1. Type the hyphen (–) to show all acceptable word divisions in typewritten work, as in Line 1.
2. Check your work.
3. Retype the drill, correcting any errors you made.

WORD DIVISION

TS

					Words
couldn't	cen-tered	care-fully	com-mis-sion		11
enough	children	completed	compelling		20
finger	mortgage	knowledge	connection		28
aligned	numbered	preferred	controlling		37
hyphen	students	problems	professing		45
only	transfer	thousands	preferring		52

Tabulate from column to column

KEY | 8 | 10 | 9 | 10 | 10 | 10 | 13 |

40C Problem Typing: Personal Notes ⑳

Problem 1: Note with Centered Line

	Words
October 21, 19--	(*Operate return 4 times*)	3
Dear Larry	(¶1) Phi Eta Sigma has sched-	10
uled an open meeting for 12:15 next	Thurs-	19
day. The speaker is to be Professor O'Connor,	28
who will	talk on		32

DS

"Business Cycles in the U.S." 38

DS

(¶2) Professor O'Connor is always interest- 45
ing and informative. | I hope you can go with 54
me to the meeting. We may get some | use- 62
ful information for our midterm paper. Can 71
you join me? | (DS) Yours | (*Operate return 4* 75
times) *your name* 79

Problem 2: Note on Special-Size Paper

Half sheet with long edge at the left; line: 40; date on Line 14; block style; SS (Refer to 35B, p. 60, for centering on special-size paper)

	Words
October 21, 19--	Dear Dick	(¶1) The foot-	7
ball game of the season will be	played in	16
Kent on the 30th. I have four	good seats and	25
want you to come for the	weekend. Several	33
choice parties are to	be given, any one of	42
which we'll enjoy.	(¶2) Fly over late Friday	50
or early Saturday	morning. Just let me know	59
your arrival	time and flight number so I can	68
meet you.	Yours	*your name*	76

Problem 3: Alertness Training

Insert a half sheet with long edge at the left. Line: 40; date on Line 14. Retype Problem 1.

40D Skill-Transfer Typing ⑩

Type two 1' writings of each ¶ of 39C, page 68, the first on the *exploration* and the second on the *control* level. Compare the *gwam* and errors of the *exploration* and *control* writings.

LESSON 184

184A Preparatory Practice [5] *each line at least three times*

Alphabet	Extensive adjustment of the zoning law quickly boosted property taxes.
Figure-symbol	Bell & Down $5\frac{1}{2}$% bonds (due May 26, 1984) sold at 102 to 107 on June 3.
Long reaches	My brother may bring the unbroken bronze statue to the British Museum.
Fluency	A nice smile is a good thing to own since it makes other people happy.
	1 | 2 | 3 | 4 | 5 | 6 | 7 | 8 | 9 | 10 | 11 | 12 | 13 | 14

184B Growth Index [15] *two 5′ writings; figure* nwam

All letters are used.

		GWAM 1′	5′	
¶ 1 1.6 SI 5.8 AWL 75% HFW	Since time began, man has tried to make his labor less tiring, his	13	3	75
	mental and physical efforts more endurable, his heavy work more bearable.	28	6	78
	Over the ages, he has been calling upon his ingenuity to guide him along	43	9	81
	the way to a more productive life. From a very crude hand tool to quite	58	12	84
	simple and then more complex models, man has now erected machines that	72	14	87
	can run themselves. The recent developments in the evolution of machin-	86	17	90
	ery are known to the civilized world as "automation."	97	19	92
¶ 2 1.6 SI 5.8 AWL 75% HFW	The advent of automated equipment is changing the modern office	13	22	94
	as surely as did the invention of the typewriter more than one century	27	25	97
	ago. New data processing equipment is helping to solve the problems of	41	28	100
	handling tedious and repetitive, though highly vital, jobs that are done	56	31	103
	in the office today. As the use of the typewriter eliminated the need	70	33	106
	for long hours of effort with pen and ink, automated machinery will do	84	36	109
	away with scores of similar low-level jobs.	93	38	111
¶ 3 1.6 SI 5.8 AWL 75% HFW	Even as commerce the world over has grown at a fantastic rate, so	13	41	113
	has the need for more information increased. Executives everywhere want	28	44	116
	massive amounts of data upon which to base their decisions; they want	42	46	119
	the data faster. Transactions must be recorded rapidly. Just as auto-	56	49	122
	mation in the factory helped to produce goods more efficiently, now it	70	52	125
	is developing in the office to help keep pace with a huge demand for	84	55	127
	more and more paper work.	89	56	128
¶ 4 1.6 SI 5.8 AWL 75% HFW	It is human nature to resist change. A century ago, for example,	13	58	131
	many people said that the invention of the cotton gin would cause unem-	27	61	134
	ployment problems far greater than any benefits that might derive from	42	64	137
	such a shift toward agricultural mechanization. Even today we find a	56	67	139
	few people who are afraid of what may happen to the role of the clerical	70	70	142
	worker as high-speed machinery becomes more commonplace in an office.	84	73	145
1′ GWAM	1 | 2 | 3 | 4 | 5 | 6 | 7 | 8 | 9 | 10 | 11 | 12 | 13 | 14			
5′ GWAM	1 | 2 | 3			

LESSON 41

41A Preparatory Practice ⑧ *each line three times; 1' writings on Line 4*

Alphabet Dick will make a quick flight to La Paz, Bolivia, next July or August.

Figures Get ready for the April 16 test by studying pages 258-307 and 489-502.

Figure-symbol Leman & Ward's Catalog 70 lists Item #482 at $960 (less 10% for cash).

Fluency It is well for us to aim high so we can reach somewhere near the mark.
| 1 | 2 | 3 | 4 | 5 | 6 | 7 | 8 | 9 | 10 | 11 | 12 | 13 | 14 |

41B Errorless Typing ⑦ *each line twice without error or three times with not more than 1 error to a line*

1 One-hand We are aware that the union monopoly case is exaggerated by the staff.

2 Fluency A man should want work enough to do and strength enough to do it well.

3 Shift keys Jean, Alvin, and Carl saw the "Late Midnight Show" on TV Station QJEO.
| 1 | 2 | 3 | 4 | 5 | 6 | 7 | 8 | 9 | 10 | 11 | 12 | 13 | 14 |

41C Problem Typing: Modified Block Letters ⑳

Problem 1: Style Letter 1, Page 71

Full sheet; line: 60; tab stop at center; return address on Line 14

Type the letter shown on page 71; tabulate to the center point to type the return address and the closing lines.

Problem 2: Speedup in Typing Letters

Type a 1' writing on each of the following parts of Style Letter 1, page 71; then retype the letter:

1. Return address, date, and letter address

2. Salutation and ¶ 1

3. Last ¶ and closing lines

Problem 3: Addressing Small Envelopes

Study the directions and the illustration at the right; then address an envelope for the letter typed as Problem 1.

1. **Return Address.** Type in block style, single spaced, the writer's name, street number and name (or box number), city, state, and ZIP Code in the upper left corner of the envelope. Begin on the second line from the top and 3 spaces from the left edge of the envelope.

2. **Envelope Address.** Begin about 2 inches (on Line 11 or 12) from the top and 2½ inches from the left edge of the envelope. Type the address in block style with single spacing, no matter how many or how few lines are used. *Type the city, state name or abbreviation, and ZIP Code on the last line of the address.*

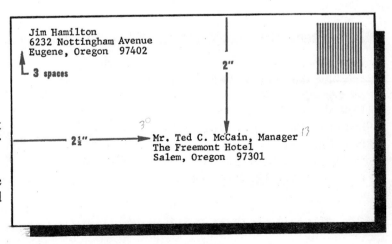

Job 2: Table Typed Sideways with Horizontal and Vertical Rulings and Braced Headings

Braced Headings. A heading that applies to two or more column headings is called a *braced heading*. Type it by leaving the necessary vertical space, typing the column heads to which the braced head applies, and then rolling back the cylinder to type the braced head. Center it as follows: (1) Move the carriage to the first space of the area to be bracketed; note the number on the cylinder scale. (2) Move to the last space of the area to be bracketed; note the number on the scale. (3) Add the two numbers; divide by 2 for the number on which to center the heading. Draw vertical rules with a ruler in ink.

Full sheet inserted sideways; center vertically; DS; 4 spaces between columns

ESTIMATED PER CAPITA CONSUMPTION EXPENDITURES

Country	Total		Food		Clothing		Other		
	1955	1970	1955	1970	1955	1970	1955	1970	
WESTERN EUROPE	$490	$ 719	$177	$251	$ 60	$ 89	$ 52	$ 79	
Denmark	646	932	184	265	78	113	64	92	
France	631	915	239	335	82	119	48	90	
West Germany	499	740	167	240	72	107	60	97	
Norway	590	933	187	295	97	154	60	99	
Sweden	745	1,154	229	355	102	158	100	149	

Words: 9, 25, 31, 45, 53, 69, 81, 90, 100, 111, 120, 130, 146

LESSON 183

183A Preparatory Practice (5) *each line at least three times*

Alphabet You took extra effort to pass the long, major quiz covering big words.

Figure-symbol The assets of Bell & Johns, Inc., amounted to only $14,023.75 in 1968.

Direct reaches Ed Fry swears he expects to swim the swift Sweetbriar stream Thursday.

Fluency Hit each key with a sure stroke, but let go of it like a red-hot coal.

| 1 | 2 | 3 | 4 | 5 | 6 | 7 | 8 | 9 | 10 | 11 | 12 | 13 | 14 |

183B Technique Improvement: Judgment Placement in Centering Headings (5)

1. Triple-space the headings at the right in what you consider the approximate horizontal center of the paper.
2. Roll the paper back to one line below the first heading. Center the heading by the backspace-centering method. Type the remaining headings in the same manner. Compare your "guesstimated" placement with the exact placement.

YOUR FUTURE IS WHAT YOU MAKE IT

EVOLUTION OF AN IDEA

PRODUCTION--THE KEY TO CONSUMER ABUNDANCE

FOUNDATIONS OF THE MASS PRODUCTION SYSTEM

SELLING FUNDAMENTALS

WRITING WHAT COMES NATURALLY

183C Production Skill Building (40) *35' writing from jobs below; compute n-pram*

Lesson 176D, Job 3, page 303, Job 5, page 304; **Lesson 182C**, Job 2, above

*Tabulate to center to type
return address and date*

6232 Nottingham Avenue
Eugene, Oregon 97402
October 23, 19-- *Operate return 4 times*

4	4
9	9
12	12

Address

Mr. Ted C. McCain, Manager
The Freemont Hotel
Salem, Oregon 97301
DS

17	17
21	21
25	25

Salutation

Dear Mr. McCain
DS

3   29

Thank you for an interesting summer of work at the Freemont.
My assignment in the dining room brought me into contact with
people under many different conditions, some happy and some
difficult. I gained much from my experiences, not the least
of which is an added awareness of the complexity of human
relationships.

16	41
28	53
40	65
52	77
64	89
67	92

Body

It is possible that I may apply for a part-time job later in
the semester. This will depend on the amount of study time
that will be required for my college courses. If I should
apply for a job, may I use your name as a reference?

12	104
24	116
36	128
46	138

Your offer of work for next summer is sincerely appreciated.
If I do not attend the summer session, I shall be happy to
return to the Freemont where I had so many interesting and
worthwhile experiences this past summer. I shall let you
know my plans very soon. In the meantime, thank you again
for a pleasant summer and all good wishes to you personally.

12	151
24	163
36	174
48	186
59	198
71	210

*Tabulate to center to type
complimentary close*

Sincerely yours *Operate return 4 times*

Jim Hamilton

75   213

*Tabulate to center to type
writer's name*

Jim Hamilton

77   215

In the modified block style, the return address, date, complimentary close, and writer's name are typed at the horizontal center of the paper; the inside address, salutation, and lines of the paragraphs are begun at the left margin.

When open punctuation is used, marks of punctuation are omitted after the opening and closing lines unless an abbreviation ends the line.

STYLE LETTER 1: *Personal Letter in Modified Block Style (Typed in Pica Type)*

your stockholders. The figures, as presented on the enclosed table, can probably be inserted in their present form into your annual report. (¶ 2) Two additional employment data are given below for your use if page space permits. The first column of figures is for last year; the second, for year before last. The monetary amounts are stated in thousands of dollars. (*Tabulate*) Average number of employees 47,961, 48,081 Total payroll and employee benefits $420,332 $402,939 (¶ 3) If you need additional figures or compilations for your report, we can provide them in one or two days, unless you wish a written analysis to accompany them. very truly yours frank ekas chief accountant

Words
85
100
112
126
140
156
168
183
197
211/230

LESSON 182

182A Preparatory Practice (5) *each line at least three times*

Alphabet	Marcia Jacques will be taking the plane back to Vera Cruz next Friday.
Figure-symbol	Your Invoice #8579 for $102.64 is subject to a 3% discount in 10 days.
Long words	Several data processing systems provide a means of intercommunication.
Fluency	Hold your wrists not more than an inch from the frame of your machine.

| 1 | 2 | 3 | 4 | 5 | 6 | 7 | 8 | 9 | 10 | 11 | 12 | 13 | 14 |

182B Skill-Comparison Typing (5) *a 1' writing on each line of 182A; compare* gwam

182C Production Typing: Letter, Table with Braced Headings (40)

Job 1: Letter with Tabulation

Modified block style; blocked ¶s; arrange the tabulation attractively

(*Current date*) mr bruce e mcgivern vice president in charge of advertising general exporters, incorporated 3500 burnett street youngstown oh 44502 dear mr mcgivern (¶ 1) The enclosed table is an exact copy of the figures we cited in our Bulletin #32, THE RISING LEVEL OF LIVING: HOW MUCH? Since this bulletin is now out of print, we regret that we cannot honor your request for 25 copies. The enclosed table, however, conveys the information you sought; and you may duplicate it in any way that will serve your purpose. (¶ 2) The following bulletins are still in print. They are available in quantity at the prices shown.

Words
15
30
44
58
74
88
102
115
125

Bulletin No.	Title	Bulletin Prices	
		Single Copies	100 or More
54	PROJECTIONS FOR SELLING TOYS	.05	.03
56	A LOOK AT THE AMERICAN SHOPPER	.08	.06
57	THE PACKAGING REVOLUTION	.08	.06
58	THE RISING COST OF CREDIT	.08	.07
59	JUNE BRIDE: MARKETING BOON	.10	.08

131
135
140
154
162
171
178
185
193

(¶ 3) Address your requests to me; I shall be happy to see that your needs are promptly met. sincerely yours h r beaumont general manager

207
223/250

41D Drill on X-ing Out Words [5]

When composing and typing a first draft, you may ignore misstrokes that do not make the word unreadable and may x-out unwanted words. To x-out words, strike the x and m alternately with the first or second finger of each hand unless you use an electric machine with a repeat x key.

1. Type: The job interview was my undoing.
2. X-out the last two words of the sentence; then space forward and complete the sentence to read:

   The job interview was difficult for me.

41E Composing and Typing [10] *full sheet; line: 60; 5-space ¶ indention; DS; 2½" top margin*

Assume you are living A.D. 3000 and know nothing about our present civilization. You find a 1-cent piece of 1968 coinage. After studying the coin, type a description of what the coin tells you about our civilization; then make needed corrections and retype the composition with appropriate top margin.

LESSON 42

42A Preparatory Practice [8] *each line three times; 1′ writings on Line 4*

Alphabet	Clay Jenkins will have the money required for our next big cash prize.
Figures	The serial number of his 1968 typewriter is either 2503740 or 2053740.
Figure-symbol	McNeil's Invoice #4296 (our Order #750B dated 10/18) comes to $942.30.
Fluency	The title to the land is now in the hands of the chairman of the firm.
	| 1 | 2 | 3 | 4 | 5 | 6 | 7 | 8 | 9 | 10 | 11 | 12 | 13 | 14 |

42B Problem Typing: Modified Block Letters [20]

Problem 1: Letter with Line Endings Indicated

Full sheet; line: 60; tab stop at center; return address on Line 16. Address an envelope. Place typed letter under flap of addressed envelope, address side up.

Words

842 Hibiscus Drive | Tampa, Florida 33617 | 8
October 24, 19-- | *(Operate return 4 times)* 12
Mr. Raymond Lawrence | 920 Pinetree Road | 19
Orlando, Florida 32804 | Dear Ray (¶ 1) 26
I'm no golf pro, I must confess, but I must 35
be better than | I thought because I've sur- 43
vived the Qualifying Round for the | Men's 51
Club Championship. Next comes the big 59
Tournament. | 62

(¶ 2) The whole Tournament will be played 69
week after next, but I | shall play just one 78
match on Thursday of that week, with the | 86
semifinals following on Friday and the finals 95
on Saturday. | 98

(¶ 3) Can you come for a visit with me from 105
Thursday to Monday of | Tournament Week? 113
Win or lose, after the Tournament ends on | 121
Saturday, we'll celebrate with a party at our 131
house. I hope | you can come for the long 139
weekend. | 141

(¶ 4) Write or telephone to say when you'll 148
arrive--or just come | on, but in time for 156
the match on Thursday. | Yours | *(Operate re-* 162
turn 4 times) Alvin Morgan 165/188

Problem 2: Alertness Training

Type the letter of Problem 1 with the following changes: (1) Begin the return address on Line 18; (2) address the letter to Mr. Lee Flaherty | 962 Flamingo Drive | Miami, Florida 32803 | (3) add an appropriate salutation; (4) omit the final ¶; and (5) address an envelope. 97/119

Job 1: Statement of Financial Highlights

Dates: main heading, this year; for Year A, type this year; for Year B, type last year. See p. 311 for instructions for typing the column heads; use 3-space indentions for each order.

UNITED MOTOR TRANSIT CORPORATION

AND CONSOLIDATED SUBSIDIARIES

19—— Financial Highlights

	Amounts in Thousands of Dollars	
	Year A	*Year B*
Net sales	1,369,683	1,265,062
Income before Federal and other taxes	135,516	114,409
Net income after taxes	71,591	62,109
Return on sales		
Before taxes: *Year A*, 9.9% ; *Year B*, 4.0%		
After taxes: *Year A*, 5.2% ; *Year B*, 4.9%		
Earnings per share of common stock:		
Year A, $4.18; *Year B*, $3.61		
Dividends		
On preferred stock	2,908	2,908
Per share of preferred stock:		
Year A, $1.75; *Year B*, $1.75		
On common stock	36,143	33,562
Per share of common stock:		
Year A, $2.20; *Year B*, $2.05		
Income reinvested in business	32,540	25,639
Book value per share of common stock:		
Year A, $35.82; *Year B*, $33.83		
Replacement and new facilities	90,433	62,890
Depreciation and depletion	51,762	50,911
Taxes of all kinds	92,434	77,070
Total taxes per share of common stock:		
Year A, $5.62; *Year B*, $4.70		
Number of stockholders		
Common stock: *Year A*, 117,667; *Year B*, 117,656		
Preferred stock: *Year A*, 6,278; *Year B*, 6,449		

Words
7
13
18
20
28
32
45
59
73
76
83
90
98
103
105
118
124
129
142
148
153
167
174
180
193
207
221
229
234
238
247
256

Job 2: Letter with Tabulation and Enclosure

Modified block style; indented ¶s; arrange tabulation attractively

april 17, 19—— mr john e sheard treasurer united motor transit corporation 187 baker avenue cleveland oh 44102 dear mr sheard (¶ 1) In accordance with your request of April 14 for material for a statement of last
year's financial highlights, our staff has compiled from those available
the figures they believe would be most meaningful and interesting to

14
28
43
57
71

Problem 3: Folding and Inserting Letters into Small Envelopes

Study the directions and illustrations for folding and inserting letters into a small envelope; then fold and insert into their addressed envelopes the letters typed as Problems 1 and 2, page 72.

FOLDING A LETTER FOR A SMALL ENVELOPE

Step 1. With the letter face up on the desk, fold from the bottom up to ½ inch of the top.

Step 2. Fold right third to left.

Step 3. Folding from left to right, fold left third to ½″ of last crease.

Step 4. Insert last creased edge first.

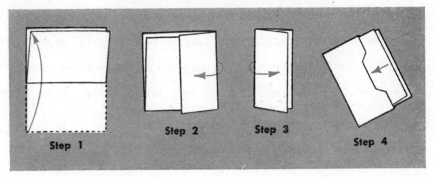

Step 1   Step 2   Step 3   Step 4

42C Guided Writing for Control ⑩

1. Type two 1′*control* writings. Determine average *gwam*. Divide by 2 for ½′ goals. Identify six ½′ goals for a 3′ writing.

2. Type a 3′ *control* writing. Your instructor will call the ½′ guides. Determine your *gwam* and errors.

All letters are used.

		3′ GWAM
1.4 SI	A good deal of time must be given to the actual process of securing	5
5.4 AWL	one's very first full-time position. Some make the mistake of accepting	9
85% HFW	the first job that is offered. Others see the importance of using an	14
	approach that will get the jobs that are best for them. Use all the	19
	extra aids you have to find out which jobs are open for which you might	23
	qualify. We do hear about jobs from our relatives, friends, and other	28
	citizens. The services of the public and private employment agencies	33
	can also be of immense aid.	35

3′ GWAM | 1 | 2 | 3 | 4 | 5 |

42D Drill on Erasing ⑫

Type the sentences as shown, omitting the numbers. Study the guides for erasing given at the right. Erase and correct each error in your typescript.

1 Turn paper froward ro vackward.

2 Ersae lightly; vrush eraser dirt awah.

3 don't dampen eth eraser.

4 Erase thoroughyl; retype the wrod lightyl.

GUIDES FOR ERASING

1. Lift the paper bail.
2. Turn the paper forward if the error is on the upper two thirds of the page or backward if it is on the lower third.
3. Use a plastic shield and a hard eraser.
4. Move the carriage to the left or right as far as you can to keep dirt out of mechanism.
5. Erase lightly—don't "scrub" the error. Brush eraser particles away from page.
6. Return the paper to writing position and type.

LESSON 180

180A Preparatory Practice (5) *each line at least three times*

Alphabet	Jeff Kobac took quite extensive trips through Switzerland and Germany.
Figure-symbol	Call Frank on Tuesday, February 17, at 9:30 a.m. (830–6459, Ext. 852).
Long reaches	Many executives may attend the evening exercises in Myron–Bryson Hall.
Fluency	They will not get very far until they have learned to make time count.

| 1 | 2 | 3 | 4 | 5 | 6 | 7 | 8 | 9 | 10 | 11 | 12 | 13 | 14 |

180B Communication Aid: Capitalization and Punctuation (10) *as directed for 178B, page 307*

	1' GWAM	
	13	87
do you realize it was the industrial revolution that started a	13	87
change from the use of hand labor to the use of power tools. yes quite	27	101
a few of the initial ideas for automation really appear in machines as	41	115
early as evans continuous flour mill babbages calculator jacquards	56	130
card controlled loom and watts automatic control of his steam engine	70	144
odd as it may seem	74	148

1' GWAM | 1 | 2 | 3 | 4 | 5 | 6 | 7 | 8 | 9 | 10 | 11 | 12 | 13 | 14 |

180C Production Typing (35) *continue typing 176D, page 301, as directed*

LESSON 181

181A Preparatory Practice (5) *each line at least three times*

Alphabet	Rex Bella enjoyed Kim Switzer's big banquet before leaving Copenhagen.
Figure-symbol	Send $26.95 for 180 copies of "Investments"; only 347 copies are left.
Balanced hand	The gowns worn by the girls lent an air of enchantment to the evening.
Fluency	The man who makes his mind work for him is sure to go far in his work.

| 1 | 2 | 3 | 4 | 5 | 6 | 7 | 8 | 9 | 10 | 11 | 12 | 13 | 14 |

181B Skill-Comparison and Transfer Typing (10) *a ½' and a 1' writing on each sentence*

Reach for the rate set on the goal sentence in typing the succeeding sentences.
Type additional writings on sentences on which you need the most improvement.

			Words
1	Goal sentence	To write well, determine what it is you want to say; then say it.	13
2	3d, 4th fingers	A puzzling allegory in the avant-garde poetry was explained well.	13
3	Rough draft	When writing a manuscript, be sure to use some source materials.	13
4	Script	Source materials include such items as books, records, and notes.	13

LESSON 43

43A   Preparatory Practice (5)   *each line three times; Line 4 for 1' writings*

Alphabet   H. J. Wexler amazed Cal by reporting so quickly on my five test items.

Figures   On May 9, the 15 girls typed 203 letters, 46 reports, and 78 invoices.

Figure-symbol   Dexter & Marcy's check for $967.20 (Check #1035) was cashed on June 4.

Fluency   It did not take Sue more than six hours to do the work for Mr. Worley.

     | 1 | 2 | 3 | 4 | 5 | 6 | 7 | 8 | 9 | 10 | 11 | 12 | 13 | 14 |

43B   Determining the Cost of an Error (10)

1. Type the ¶s of 42C, page 73, as a 3' *control* writing. Hold your speed to a rate you can maintain with good control. Determine *gwam* and errors.

2. Type the ¶s again for 3', but erase and correct each error as you type. Determine your corrected *wam* and compare with the first writing.

43C   Problem Typing (32)

Problem Typing Review

Problems 1 and 2

Make pencil notations of the problems and page numbers listed below. Place the notation sheet beside the typewriter. Type each problem once only and, as you type, correct any errors you make. Before removing the typed problem, proofread it and correct any errors you find.

> Problem 1, page 67, centered on full sheet in reading position. (See 37C, page 64.)
>
> Problem 1, page 70, as directed

Problem 3: Modified Block Letter

60-space line; return address on Line 16

Erase and correct errors. Address an envelope; fold and insert the letter into the envelope.

	Words
7701 Harrison Place | Gary, Indiana 46410 |	8
October 26, 19-- | Miss Elizabeth Turner |	16
North High School | 2319 Stringtown Road |	24
Evansville, Indiana 47711 | Dear Miss Turner | (¶ 1) When I studied English with you,	32
ner | (¶ 1) When I studied English with you,	39
there must have been times | that you despaired of my learning anything except by	47
spaired of my learning anything except by	56
rote | memory. I learned more than you	63
realized, for what you are | as well as what	72
you taught, influenced me greatly. |	79

	Words
(¶ 2) My courses here at the University are	86
often challenging and | sometimes exciting. I	95
think I am doing well this first year | in the	104
"academic halls of learning." For this, I	113
thank my | high school teachers, and I thank	122
you most of all. | Sincerely yours | Nancy	130
McDonald	131/160

Problem 4: Modified Block Letter

Use the return address, date, signature, and directions for Problem 3, except that you will begin the return address on Line 18. Listen for the ringing of the bell to indicate the line endings.

	Words
Miss Mary Alice Knox | 921 Southland Blvd.,	20
E. | Louisville, Kentucky 40214 | Dear Mary	28
Alice | (¶ 1) My "thank you" letter to your	35
mother was sent by airmail the day after I	44
got back from my weekend with you. The	52
delay in writing you has been caused by a cold	61
I developed two days after I got back here.	70
I am still blowing and wheezing, but I'll live,	80
I am sure! (¶ 2) I shall long remember this	88
visit to your home. It was most delightful,	97
and I am grateful to all of you for giving me	106
such a happy time. (¶ 3) Exams are coming	113
up, and I have much to do to get ready for	122
them. I shall write a longer letter soon. In	132
the meantime, my grateful thanks to all of	140
you for a wonderful weekend. Sincerely	151/176

LESSON 178

178A Preparatory Practice [5] *each line at least three times*

Alphabet	Maxine Jason saw a folk dance near the gray villa by the quaint plaza.
Figure-symbol	The 5% note for $36,489 is dated February 15. It matures in 120 days.
Shift keys	Miss Janet Sue Brown lives on East Second Avenue, Minot, North Dakota.
Fluency	A quick, light, firm stroke of each key will make you a better typist.
	| 1 | 2 | 3 | 4 | 5 | 6 | 7 | 8 | 9 | 10 | 11 | 12 | 13 | 14 |

178B Communication Aid: Capitalization and Punctuation [10]

Capitalize and punctuate as you type. Check your work with your instructor; then use the paragraph for 1′ writings as time permits. Determine your *gwam* after each writing.

Full sheet; 70-space line; DS

	1′ GWAM	
to overrate the authority of a great orator is difficult. it was	13	84
clay who suggested that probably no power is like that of true oratory.	28	98
as caesar dominated men by agitating their fears cicero dominated them	42	113
by capturing their affection and moving their passion. the authority	56	127
of the one died with its owner that of the other continues to this day.	71	141
1′ GWAM | 1 | 2 | 3 | 4 | 5 | 6 | 7 | 8 | 9 | 10 | 11 | 12 | 13 | 14 |		

178C Production Typing [35] *continue typing 176D, page 301, as directed*

LESSON 179

179A Preparatory Practice [5] *each line at least three times*

Alphabet	A shy zebra jumped when five peacocks quickly extended giant feathers.
Figure-symbol	Order #1958 amounted to $362.70 and was paid by Check #4960 last week.
Double letters	His business success occurred suddenly when it hardly seemed possible.
Fluency	Do not be afraid to tackle new problems or any that are tough for you.
	| 1 | 2 | 3 | 4 | 5 | 6 | 7 | 8 | 9 | 10 | 11 | 12 | 13 | 14 |

179B Technique Improvement: Response Patterns [10] *each line at least three times*

Type the first lines using the response pattern suggested. Type the last two lines on the *control level.*

1	Word recognition	The time will come when each of us can show what he has learned to do.
2	Word recognition	Those who do good work do not spend their time informing others of it.
3	Stroke	Their newest modular furniture components are designed for efficiency.
4	Stroke	The latest catalogue illustrates a great number of award-winning cars.
5	Combination	The type of flexible equipment that we all need is the hydraulic lift.
6	Combination	You can get out the mail more efficiently with the use of this system.
7	Double letters	He succeeded in attracting the attention of a committee to the matter.
8	Long words	A revolutionary new experimental compressor unit is being constructed.
		| 1 | 2 | 3 | 4 | 5 | 6 | 7 | 8 | 9 | 10 | 11 | 12 | 13 | 14 |

179C Production Typing [35] *continue typing 176D, page 301, as directed*

LESSON 44

44A   Preparatory Practice ⑧ *each line three times; Line 4 for 1' writings*

Alphabet   Dwight Mystroni lives in a quiet area just six blocks from Jasper Zoo.

Figures   The show was at 1946 E. 37th Street on April 25 and began at 8:30 p.m.

Figure-symbol   Mr. Smith (of Idaho) sold Items #29, #41, and #39* to Jim for $572.69.

Fluency   Lena paid cash for the yams, but I gave them a check for the six hams.

  | 1 | 2 | 3 | 4 | 5 | 6 | 7 | 8 | 9 | 10 | 11 | 12 | 13 | 14 |

44B   Word-Division Drill ⑩ *half sheets; line: 70; DS; 10 spaces between columns; 1½" top margin*

1. Center WORD DIVISION as the main heading.
2. Type the hyphen (–) to show all acceptable word divisions in typewritten work, as in Line 1.

3. Refer to 39B, page 67, and to the dictionary to check your divisions.
4. Retype the drill.

				Words
Tabulate	didn't	con-cluded	per-formed	pro-fes-sion	11
from col-	abroad	centrally	supposed	transcribed	19
umn to	lighted	compelled	transmits	performance	28
column	across	specially	transcend	conditioned	37
	upon	schedule	troubled	referring	44

KEY | 7 | 10 | 10 | 10 | 10 | 10 | 13 |

44C   Growth Index ⑩ *5' control writing; determine gwam and errors; 1' control writings on each ¶ as time permits*

All letters are used.

	GWAM		
	1'	5'	

¶ 1
1.4 SI
5.4 AWL
85% HFW

Our economic system is one in which individuals have the right to produce goods and services to be sold to the public at a profit to the producer. Since there are laws that govern the operation of a business, our "free enterprise" system is subject to those laws and thus is "free" just to the extent that the laws allow.

13 | 3 | 42
27 | 5 | 45
42 | 8 | 48
57 | 11 | 51
64 | 13 | 53

¶ 2
1.4 SI
5.4 AWL
85% HFW

Under our economic system the customer can choose from many products and services what he wants to buy. The producer may set the price of the product; but if it is too high, the customer will not buy it and so, in effect, he controls the price that business can charge for its product. The business that does not win customers, fails.

14 | 16 | 55
28 | 18 | 58
42 | 21 | 61
56 | 24 | 64
67 | 26 | 66

¶ 3
1.4 SI
5.4 AWL
85% HFW

A business of any size is often owned by many people. They buy stock in the hope of earning a profit. If the business prospers, they get quarterly dividends, as a rule; and the remainder of the profits may be used to expand plant, create new jobs, pay interest on bank loans, pay taxes, labor, and other costs of operating a business.

13 | 29 | 69
27 | 32 | 71
41 | 34 | 74
54 | 37 | 77
67 | 40 | 80

1' GWAM | 1 | 2 | 3 | 4 | 5 | 6 | 7 | 8 | 9 | 10 | 11 | 12 | 13 | 14 |
5' GWAM | | 1 | | 2 | | 3 |

Job 10: Typing Labels

Typing Labels: Insert a sheet of paper so that the top edge is ½″ above the ribbon. Place the label back of the top edge of the paper and against the cylinder. Roll the cylinder toward you until the label is in position for typing the first line; type the information.

Prepare a label to be attached to each folder. On the labels type the information given at the right.

	Words
HOLMES MEDICAL CENTER	4
ANNUAL FINANCIAL REPORT	9
MAY 31, 19--	12
Prepared by Gladys H. Flaugher	18
Certified Public Accountant	24

LESSON 177

177A Preparatory Practice [5] *each line at least three times*

Alphabet	Jack will ship by express the quantity of goods that we have itemized.
Figure-symbol	They can send the #6079 tacks in these sizes: 1/4, 3/8, 1/2, and 3/5.
One hand	Only Edward Johns saw Fred Street win the award at the bazaar in Lyon.
Fluency	It pays to let good manners show in both your letters and your speech.

| 1 | 2 | 3 | 4 | 5 | 6 | 7 | 8 | 9 | 10 | 11 | 12 | 13 | 14 |

177B Squeezing and Spreading Letters [5]

Type these sentences as shown; then erase and correct the errors by squeezing or spreading letters.

There is no "right" for anyo ne without a corresponding responsibility.

A man doesn't lose his tem per until he feels he has lost the argumnt.

Anyone can be a leader--if hecan just convince someone to fol low him.

177C Building Speed and Control [5] *two 1′* exploration-level *writings; then two 1′* control-level *writings*

	1′ GWAM	
The work in an accounting function is usually as engrossing as it	13	87
is varied. There are a variety of accountancy firms that make it a busi-	28	102
ness to audit and to manage the accounting work of other concerns; or	42	116
a firm may hire one or more accountants whose responsibilities are to	56	130
handle its bookkeeping work, to analyze procedures, and to write the	69	143
reports for management.	74	148

1′ GWAM | 1 | 2 | 3 | 4 | 5 | 6 | 7 | 8 | 9 | 10 | 11 | 12 | 13 | 14 |

177D Production Typing [35] *continue typing 176D, page 301, as directed*

44D Problem Typing ㉒ *2' to get ready; 20' to type, with errors erased and corrected*

Problem 1: Modified Block Letter

60-space line; return address on Line 14; address envelope; fold and insert letter

	Words
1368 Forest Green Drive | Ogden, Utah	7
84403 | October 30, 19-- | Mrs. Rubye Man-	15
ville | Emerson College | 1121 Washington	22
Blvd. | Ogden, Utah 84404 | Dear Mrs. Man-	30
ville | (¶1) You asked me to let you know	37
the nature of the interview and | tests I took	46
yesterday at the Briggs Chemical Company. |	55
(¶2) The employment test included English,	62
spelling, arithmetic, | and typewriting. I think	72
I did well on these tests; but I | was nervous	81
when taking the typewriting test and made	89
some | errors, I am sorry to report. |	96
(¶3) In the interview, I was asked about my	104
club activities, my | hobbies, and my com-	112
munity involvements. Attitudes, I was | told,	121
are considered as important as aptitudes; and	130
the job | interview is used to evaluate the	139
applicant's attitudes as | the tests are used to	148
evaluate her skill competence. |	155
(¶4) I shall let you know the results of my	162
interview if I get a | call from the Company.	171

	Words
I thank you for all the help you have | given	180
me, and it has been more than you probably	189
know. | Sincerely yours | Lorna Jane Crawford	
	197/225

Problem 2: Alertness Training—Personal Letter Without Addresses

60-space line; date on Line 20

	Words
October 30, 19-- | Dear Kathie | (¶1) Let me	7
tell you about my job interview and tests at	16
Briggs | Chemical Company yesterday. | (¶)	23
(For ¶2, type ¶3 of Problem 1.)	82
(For ¶3, type only the first sentence of ¶2.)	93
(¶4) I shall let you know the results of my	105
interview if I get a | call from the Company. |	114
Yours | (*Signature in ink: Lorna Jane*)	117

Problem 3: Alertness Training

Type the letter of Problem 1, addressing it to Mr. R. N. Heilman \| 1062 Elberta Drive \| Ogden, Utah 84404. Add an appropriate salutation.

(192 words)

● Self-Improvement Practice *each line at least three times*

1	Balanced-hand	Six of their girls may go on the right lane by the lake if they do go.
2	One-hand	Bart Kimmon was aggravated after only a few union cases were referred.
3	Combination	The staff at the car lot wanted him to make a trade after ten minutes.
4	Adjacent-key	The guides were in columns as we went over the trails after the lions.
5	Double letters	Bill and Ann will soon see the bookkeeping committee from Mississippi.
6	Number-symbol	Call 701 771-4084 or 701 771-4085 at 2:30 p.m. about Shipment #29-468.
7	Special symbols	Frank is sure this problem is correct: 369 x 7 + 125 − 840 ÷ 4 = 467.
8	Degree symbol	It was 82° in Miami, 4° below zero in Missoula, and 36° in Pittsburgh.
9	Number-symbol	Approximately 10% of the #139 machines were priced incorrectly at $89.
10	Combination	He must often make a choice between the easy wrong and the hard right.
11	Balanced-hand	The auditor for the firm of Burns & Mantleman can make a report today.

| 1 | 2 | 3 | 4 | 5 | 6 | 7 | 8 | 9 | 10 | 11 | 12 | 13 | 14 |

Job 7: Schedule of Land Holdings

*Insert rules as shown in Job 5; use 5-space indentions;
place footnote below last line of table in standard form.*

HOLMES MEDICAL CENTER
SCHEDULE OF LAND HOLDINGS*
May 31, 19--

Location	Current Market Value	Original Purchase Price	% Increase in Value	
3177 Flamingo Drive	$14,000	$12,800	9.38	41
87 Granada Court	9,000	8,000	12.50	48
9690 Flowers Avenue	10,500	8,000	31.25	55
56 Grace Street	9,000	8,606	4.58	66
Totals	$42,500	$37,406	13.62	72

*Exclusive of buildings

Job 8: Funds Flow Statement

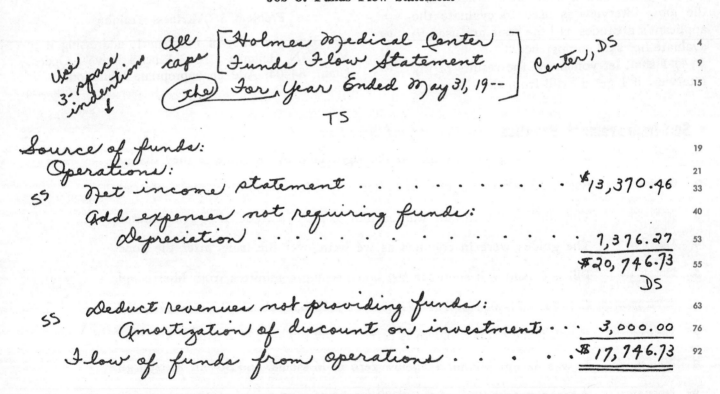

Use 3-space indentions
All caps [Holmes Medical Center
Funds Flow Statement
(the) For Year Ended May 31, 19--] Center, DS
TS

Source of funds:
  Operations:
ss   Net income statement $13,370.46
      Add expenses not requiring funds:
        Depreciation 1,376.27
                                             $20,746.73
                                             DS

ss Deduct revenues not providing funds:
      Amortization of discount on investment . . . 3,000.00
  Flow of funds from operations $17,746.73

Job 9: Arranging Copies

Collate in order of completion the copies of the schedules, statements,
and the letters into three groups—original, first carbon copy, and second
carbon copy. Fasten each group of papers at the left into a folder or a binder.

Purpose. To build skill in tabulating; to learn the principles of word division; and to improve typing speed and control.

Machine Adjustments. Line: 70. Drills: SS. Timed writings: DS, 5-space ¶ indention. Problems: as directed.

Self-Improvement Practice. Type the Alertness Training paragraphs as directed in Self-Improvement Practice, page 96.

LESSON 45

45A   Preparatory Practice ⑧ *each line three times; then 1' writings on Line 4*

Alphabet	Maude Parker will visit the Chicago zoo before joining Alexis Quigley.
Figures	On May 28, 158 boys and 347 girls took a history test on pages 69-102.
Figure-symbol	Add the 4% sales tax of $7.22 (on $180.56) to Webb & Orr's Bill #8390.
Fluency	Ruth did not blame her neighbor for being skeptical about the visitor.

| 1 | 2 | 3 | 4 | 5 | 6 | 7 | 8 | 9 | 10 | 11 | 12 | 13 | 14 |

45B   Tabulating Drills ⑫

Drill 1. Arrange the following 4 words in 2 columns with 12 spaces between columns. (Follow Guides 1, 2, and 3 at right.)

accommodate   bookkeeping
controlled   definite

Drill 2. Arrange the 3 groups of figures in 3 columns with 8 spaces between columns. (Follow Guides 2 and 3.) **Note.** Space forward or backspace to align figures at the right.

432,165	78,234	9,061
82,560	4,397	16,203

Preparing to Tabulate

1. Preparatory Steps
   a. Move margin stops to extreme ends of scale.
   b. Clear all tab stop settings.
   c. Move carriage to center of paper.
   d. Decide spacing between columns—preferably an even number of spaces (4, 6, 8, 10, etc.).
2. Setting Left Margin Stop

   From center of paper, backspace 1 space for each 2 letters, figures, symbols, and spaces in longest line of each column and for each 2 spaces left between columns. *Set the left margin stop at this point.* **Note.** Carry forward to the intercolumn the extra space that may occur at the end of the longest line of a column; to the next column the extra space that may occur in an intercolumn. If an extra space occurs at the end of the longest line of the final column, drop it.

3. Setting Tab Stops

   From left margin, space forward once for each letter, figure, symbol, and space in longest line in the first column and for each space to be left between first and second columns. *Set tab stop at this point for second column.* Follow similar procedure for additional columns. TABULATE FROM COLUMN TO COLUMN.

45C   Problem Typing ⑳

Problem 1: Two-Column Tabulation

Half sheet; SS; 10 spaces between columns

Center the problem vertically (page 64), the heading horizontally (page 57), and the columns horizontally (Guides 2 and 3, above).

		Words
WORD STUDY		2
	TS	
already	all right	6
bathroom	bank draft	10
bondholders	bona fide	14
cupful	de facto	17
northeast	dining room	22
percent	inasmuch as	26
postman	post office	30
wastebasket	price list	34

KEY | 11 | 10 | 11 |

Job 5: Schedule of Accounts Receivable

HOLMES MEDICAL CENTER

SCHEDULE OF ACCOUNTS RECEIVABLE

May 31, 19--

Debtor	Amount Due	Original Amount	Age (in Months)	
				4
				11
				13
				17
				33
George E. Burkridge	$ 87.80	$100.00	3	41
Juanita Connors	8.00	8.00	2	49
Edward L. Edwards	15.00	15.00	1	56
Harold S. Isbell	27.00	45.00	18	64
Adam V. Krubinoff	8.00	8.00	2	72
E. Donald Loiseau	250.00	300.00	1	80
Norman M. O'Lafferty	187.60	325.00	9	88
Preston C. Orange	240.00	300.00	6	96
Charles T. Quittman	8.00	8.00	1	104
B. A. Rounciman	92.45	92.45	1	111
Luke Seibert	1.00	22.30	14	118
Walther V. Ubermann	38.60	55.60	8	126
Elizabeth Wilson	15.00	75.00	4	134
Tracey Rae Xavier	15.00	25.00	17	142
R. J. Young	75.00	75.00	1	148
Frank D. Zink	8.00	8.00	1	157
Total	$1,076.45			164

Job 6: Schedule of Accounts Payable

Current year for all dates

HOLMES MEDICAL CENTER

SCHEDULE OF ACCOUNTS PAYABLE

May 31, 19--

Creditor	Amount Owed	Due	
			4
			10
			13
			14
			22
Amory Surgical Instrument Company	$ 718.00	August 31, 19--	34
Bostwith Printing and Supply Company	37.50	June 30, 19--	46
Internal Revenue Service	700.00	September 14, 19--	57
Lancer Bank & Trust Company	597.00	June 30, 19--	67
Montgomery Publishing Company	265.00	Currently	79
Total	$2,317.50		86

Problem 2: Three-Column Tabulation

Half sheet; SS; 8 spaces between columns

Center the problem vertically (page 64), the heading horizontally (page 57), and the columns horizontally (page 77).

Technique cue: Tabulate from column to column without looking up from the copy. Reach to the tab bar or key without moving the hand out of typing position.

WORDS FREQUENTLY MISSPELLED

TS

accessible	accidentally	accommodate	13
announced	appearance	athletic	19
believable	benefited	consensus	25
definitely	disappointed	dissatisfaction	33
eligible	existent	extraordinary	40
governor	gauge	guarantee	45
independent	inoculate	insistence	51
judgment	justifiable	knowledgeable	58
laid	liaison	likelihood	63
maintenance	manageable	miscellaneous	70
occasionally	occurrence	personal	77
permissible	personnel	pertinence	83
precede	principle	privilege	89
procedure	prominence	questionnaire	96
recommend	referring	resistance	102
singular	smooth	soluble	107
transferred	truly	various	112
vicinity	withhold	zoology	117

KEY | 12 | 8 | 12 | 8 | 15 |

45D   Building Speed and Control ⑩ *two 1' writings for speed; two 1' writings for control* *one 2' writing for speed; one 2' writing for control*

All letters are used.

1.4 SI
5.4 AWL
85% HFW

	GWAM 1'	2'	
As tabulating is an extension of centering, which you have been	13	6	46
doing for quite some time, it is not new to you. When you were typing	27	13	53
words or figures in columns at different times, you were told how many	41	21	60
spaces to leave between the columns. From now on, you will use guides	55	28	67
for the horizontal placement of columns but must often use judgment as	69	35	74
to how many spaces should be left between them.	79	40	79

1' GWAM | 1 | 2 | 3 | 4 | 5 | 6 | 7 | 8 | 9 | 10 | 11 | 12 | 13 | 14 |
2' GWAM | 1 | 2 | 3 | 4 | 5 | 6 | 7 |

LESSON 46

46A   Preparatory Practice ⑧ *each line three times; 1' writings on Line 4*

Alphabet   Our unexpected freezing weather may have killed John Quinley's shrubs.

Figure   Paul typed page 27 on May 9, page 34 on May 10, and page 56 on May 18.

Figure-symbol   "All the world's a stage" is from Act II, Line 139, of As You Like It.

Fluency   The total endowment is not big enough to meet the needs of the school.

| 1 | 2 | 3 | 4 | 5 | 6 | 7 | 8 | 9 | 10 | 11 | 12 | 13 | 14 |

46B   Building Speed and Control ⑩

Type 45D, above, as directed except you will determine *gwam* and errors for the 2' *control writing*.

Words

HOLMES MEDICAL CENTER

STATEMENT OF EARNINGS

For the Year Ended May 31, 19--

	Year to May	May	Total	
				23
Income				
Rents received	$42,218.20	$4,228.12	$46,446.32	26 / 44
Expenses				47
Accounting	1,250.00	125.00	1,375.00	60
Depreciation	6,705.70	670.57	7,376.27	72
Furnishings	325.00	--	325.00	85
Garbage disposal	290.50	33.00	323.50	97
Insurance	995.78	--	995.78	109
Interest paid	2,497.05	220.82	2,717.87	122
Legal fees	125.00	--	125.00	134
Miscellaneous	124.98	4.90	129.88	147
Office supplies	37.26	--	37.26	159
Operating supplies	1,112.94	115.29	1,228.23	171
Rental collection	65.00	--	65.00	184
Repairs	829.31	270.92	1,100.23	196
Salaries and wages	7,110.00	622.00	7,732.00	209
Taxes	6,857.40	19.44	6,876.84	221
Transportation	18.00	--	18.00	233
Utilities	2,310.22	339.78	2,650.00	252
Total Expenses	$30,654.14	$2,421.72	$33,075.86	268
Net Income	$11,564.06	$1,806.40	$13,370.46	291

Job 4: Statement of Retained Earnings

Proofreader's marks are shown on page x.

Use spaced leaders between Cols. 1 & 2

All caps; center each line; DS

Holmes Medical Center
Statement of Retained Earnings

19-- (This year)   19-- (Last year)

Balance, June 1	$36,448.40	$28,425.50
& Net Income (, May)	13,730.00 → 46	8,425.90 → 022
Balance (31	49,818.86	448
	$ 50,178.40	$ 36,851.40

For the Year Ended May 31, 19--   *Center & DS below main heading*

4
11
20
28
39
54

46C Drill on Spacing Main and Secondary Headings ⑫

LEARN: Double-space between main and secondary headings, if both are used; triple-space between last line of heading (whether main or secondary) and first line of columns (or columnar headings).

Type the drill at right with 12 spaces between columns; set margin and tab stops as directed on page 77; center the headings horizontally.

			Words
Main heading → TELEPHONE AREA CODE NUMBERS			5
DS			
Secondary heading → Ten Major Cities			9
TS			
New York	New York	212	13
Chicago	Illinois	312	17
Los Angeles	California	213	23

KEY | 11 | 12 | 10 | 12 | 3

46D Problem Typing: Three-Column Tabulations ⑳

Problem 1

Half sheet; SS; 12 spaces between columns

Center the problem vertically (page 64), the headings horizontally (page 57), and the columns horizontally (page 77).

Tabulating cue: Tabulate from column to column.

			Words
TELEPHONE AREA CODE NUMBERS			6
DS			
Ten Major Cities			9
TS			
New York	New York	212	13
Chicago	Illinois	312	18
Los Angeles	California	213	23
Philadelphia	Pennsylvania	215	29
Detroit	Michigan	313	33
Houston	Texas	713	37
Baltimore	Maryland	301	41
Cleveland	Ohio	216	45
Dallas	Texas	214	49
Washington	D.C.	202	52

KEY | 12 | 12 | 12 | 12 | 3

Problem 2

Half sheet; SS; 8 spaces between columns

Center the problem in exact vertical center and the headings horizontally.

Type Column 1 as shown; in Column 2, type the words of Column 1 with the diagonal (/) to indicate all syllables; in Column 3, type the words of Column 1 with the hyphen (–) to indicate the preferred point of division. (See Guides, pages 67 and 80).

			Words
SYLLABLE IDENTIFICATION AND WORD DIVISION			8
Application of Page 67 Guides			16
anoints	a/noints	anoints	19
beginner	be/gin/ner	begin-ner	25
doubted			30
dropped			35
equalled			40
ideas			44
children			50
controlled			57
described			63
destined			69
knowledge			75
manuscript			83
possessed			89
separates			96
transferred			103
transcripts			111

KEY | 11 | 8 | 12 | 8 | 12

Problem 3

Full sheet; DS

Type Problem 2, above, centered in reading position. (See page 64.)

Use 3-space indentions for each order of indention shown

			Words
HOLMES MEDICAL CENTER			4
BALANCE SHEET			7
May 31, 19--			10
TS			
ASSETS			11
DS			
Current Assets			17
Cash on hand and in bank		$ 4,796.97	24
Accounts receivable		1,076.45	33
Total current assets			$ 5,873.42	39
			DS
Land. Buildings. and Equipment			52
Land		$ 37,406.00	55
Medical buildings	$213,448.10		61
Less depreciation res.	64,837.72	148,610.38	73
Reception-office equipment	$ 1,562.95		80
Less depreciation res.	1,149.60	413.35	92
Work under construction		1,261.43	101
Total land, buildings,			106
and equipment			187,691.16	113
			DS
Total Assets			$193,564.58	123
			TS

LIABILITIES AND OWNERS' EQUITY — 129

			Words
Current Liabilities			137
Accounts payable	$ 2,317.50		143
Payroll tax deductions	107.28		150
Group insurance	36.30		157
Total current liabilities		$ 2,461.08	165
Long-Term Liabilities			174
Trust deed, due 4/26/80		51,284.64	183
Total Liabilities			$ 53,745.72	189
Owners' Equity			195
Capital stock issued			199
9,000 shares @ $10		$ 90,000.00	205
Retained earnings			208
Balance June 1, 19--	$ 36,448.40		216
Net income	13,370.46		223
Balance May 31, 19--		49,818.86	232
Total owners' equity			139,818.86	241
Total Liabilities and Owners' Equity			$193,564.58	255

LESSON 47

47A   Preparatory Practice ⑧ *each line three times; 1' writings on Line 4*

Alphabet   Won't Judge Robb have to quiz Mr. Kruptman and five or six local boys?

Figures   Don Parker moved from 2479 East 135th Street to 2628 West 60th Street.

Fractions   Can John Webb add these fractions: 2/3, 3/4, 4/5, 5/6, 7/8, and 9/10?

Fluency   The authority of those in power should be used for the benefit of all.
| 1 | 2 | 3 | 4 | 5 | 6 | 7 | 8 | 9 | 10 | 11 | 12 | 13 | 14 |

47B   Technique Practice: Stroking ⑩ *each line three times*

Home-row keys   Hal Skaggs had a bad fall as he made a gallant dash to raise the flag.

First-row keys   Anna Mae McVay became excited when Calvin Bixmont raced over the line.

Third-row keys   Is it true that you were the ones who raised the issue of party lines?

Adjacent keys   As we were saying, it is our opinion that power belongs to the people.

Direct reach   Myrtle looked for a place to hide the junk Fred Hunt left in the yard.
| 1 | 2 | 3 | 4 | 5 | 6 | 7 | 8 | 9 | 10 | 11 | 12 | 13 | 14 |

47C   Problem Typing: Guides for Word Division ⑳

Problem 1

Full sheet; line: 60; SS

Center the problem vertically in reading position; center the heading horizontally.

After typing the first line of ¶ 1, reset the left margin stop 4 spaces to the right. Backspace into left margin to type the numbers 2, 3, and 4.

Alertness cue: Don't let the hyphen in the heading trip you.

Words

WORD-DIVISION GUIDES 4

TS

1. Type a hyphen at the end of the line to indicate the division. Try to put enough of the word on the line to suggest what the completed word will be. Type the remainder of the word on the succeeding line. 17, 28, 39, 47

2. Divide after a one-letter syllable in a word (as, separate) unless the word ends with able, ible, or ical—the two-syllable endings you must keep as a unit (as, deplorable). If 2 one-letter syllables come together, divide between the vowels (as, continu-ation). 59, 73, 85, 96, 104

3. When dividing words ending in cial, tial, cion, sion, or tion, keep the endings as a unit (as, expres-sion). 119, 131

4. When the final consonant in a word is doubled in adding a suffix, divide between the double letters (as, compel-ling); but when a syllable is added to a word that ends in double letters, divide after the double letters (as, will-ing, dismiss-ing). 144, 155, 167, 178, 182

176C Communication Aid: Word Choice ⑩

Half sheet; 70-space line; DS

Read the sentences at the right; then, from the words at the left, select the correct one to insert at the point of the blank space. Capitalize and punctuate each sentence as you type it. After checking your work with your instructor, retype the problem.

1   personal, personnel   the _____ manager mr daley hires typists clerks and salesmen

2   cite, site   please _____ the sources you used in compiling the facts for the graph

3   extant, extent   the _____ of damage is not known the reports did not give estimates

4   canvas, canvass   robert said "we shall _____ the offices to find efficient typists

5   council, counsel   when you are asking for _____ do not assume a know it all attitude

6   principal, principle   according to mr white the _____ denied that he saw the accident

7   adherence, adherents   meanwhile however edwards _____ read the clear concise report

8   lose, loose   if you are absent mr hunt you will _____ the decision to mr wilson

9   adverse, averse   _____ circumstances prevented sylvia from going but i shall attend

10 moral, morale   all agreed however that even though we lost we won a _____ victory

| 1 | 2 | 3 | 4 | 5 | 6 | 7 | 8 | 9 | 10 | 11 | 12 | 13 | 14 |

176D Production Typing: Accounting Papers ⑳ (*each day*)

The jobs in this and the next four lessons of this section are grouped for continuous typing. Daily skill-building exercises for Lessons 177-180 begin on page 306.

Type as many jobs as you can in the time provided each day. When time is called, complete the line on which you are typing so that you can begin a new line the next day.

These jobs cover portions of an accounting report to be bound at the left. Type each one on a separate sheet with two carbon copies. Use the current year with all May 31 dates; use last year with all June 1 dates.

Retain all papers until you have completed Jobs 1-10; then bind them according to the instructions in Jobs 9 and 10.

Job 1: Auditor's Statement

Remember to plan for binding at the left for this letter and all other parts of the report

	Words
july 14, 19-- board of directors holmes medi-	9
cal center 9750 forest circle orlando fl 32803	19
gentlemen (¶ 1) I have examined the records	27
and financial transactions of the Holmes	35
Medical Center for the year ended May 31,	43
19--. My examination was made in accor-	51
dance with generally accepted auditing stan-	60
dards and accordingly included such tests of	69
the accounting records and such other audit-	77
ing procedures as I considered necessary in	86
the circumstances. (¶ 2) In my opinion the	94
accompanying statements present fairly the	102
financial position of Holmes Medical Center	111
on May 31, 19--, in conformity with generally	120
accepted accounting principles applied on a	129
basis consistent with that of the preceding	138
year. respectfully submitted gladys h flaugher	148
certified public accountant	154

Full sheet; line: 60; SS

Words

WORD DIVISION   3

"Do Not" and "Avoid" ~~Rules~~ *Guides*   TS   8

Center the problem vertically in reading position; center the headings horizontally.

After typing the first line of ¶ 1, reset the left margin stop 4 spaces to the right. Backspace into left margin to type the numbers 2, 3, 4, and 5.

Note. Study Problems 1 and 2 so that you will know how to divide words when it is necessary for you to do so.

1. To avoid dividing *a* words, *& you may have* a line ~~may be~~ approximately   21
five ~~5~~ strokes longer or shorter than the desired ending.   33

2. Avoid dividing *after* a two-letter syllable at the beginning of a   47
~~—~~ word. *Try to divide elsewhere in the word.*   56

3. Avoid dividing initials, proper names, numbers, or abbre-   69
viations. *Initials or a given name may be separated*   80
from a surname when necessary.   86

4. Do not divide a word of five or fewer letters.   98

5. Do not divide from the remainder of the word: 109
l.c. A. A one-letter syllable at the beginning or end of a   120
word; as, against, steady.   126
l.c. B. A syllable without a vowel; as, shouldn't.   136
c. A two-letter syllable coming at the end of a word;   147
as, strongly.   150

47D   Aligning and Typing Over Words ⑫ *line: 60; SS*

Locate the variable line spacer (3) and the aligning scale (33).

1. Type the sentence below but do not make the return:

   Use the alignment scale to align your copy.

2. Move the carriage (or element) so a word with the letter "i" is above the scale. Note that a white line points to the center of the letter "i" in the word.

3. Study the relation of the top of the scale to the bottom of the letters with down stems.

It is important for you to get an eye picture of the exact relation of the typed line to the top of the scale so you will be able to adjust the paper correctly to type over a word with exactness.

4. Remove the paper; reinsert it. Gauge the line so the bottoms of the letters are in correct relation to the top of the aligning scale. Operate the variable line spacer (3) if necessary to move the paper forward or backward. Operate the paper release (16) to move the paper to the left or right if necessary when centering the letter "i" over one of the white lines on the scale.

5. Check the accuracy of your alignment by setting the ribbon control (21) for stencil position and typing over one of the letters. If necessary, make further alignment adjustments. *Return the ribbon control to typing position.*

6. Type over the words with the letter "i" in the sentence, moving the paper forward or backward, to the left or right, as necessary for correct alignment.

7. Type the following sentence; remove the paper; then reinsert it; gauge the line and letter; and type over the first and final words.

   It is wise for this firm to dismiss the men.

8. Repeat the entire drill if time permits.

175E Typing Figures (5) *three 1′ writings; proofread each writing carefully; circle errors*

DS; 8 spaces between columns

				Words
78.14	27.33	51.00	1,369.24	6
32.27	5.12	403.65	89.14	11
395.64	46.89	1.87	20.07	17
1.01	10.00	29.23	647.58	22

175F Building Speed (15)

1. Use ¶ 1. Type two 1′ writings. Use the higher *gwam* as your goal rate.
2. Use ¶ 2. Type three 1′ writings. Try to reach your goal rate.
3. Use ¶s 1 and 2. Type three 3′ writings. Try to reach your goal rate.

All letters are used.

	Text	GWAM 1′	3′	
¶ 1 1.6 SI 5.8 AWL 75% HFW	Expansion in a firm can mean specialization for its employees.	13	5	57
	Customers may become just faces to them. An office worker may not sell	27	9	62
	directly to a customer; yet, he can make or break a sale as surely as	41	14	67
	the salesman. When a firm can lick worker indifference, then quality,	55	18	72
	job morale, and customer relations are promoted.	65	22	75
¶ 2 1.8 SI 6.2 AWL 70% HFW	The bigger a commercial enterprise, the heavier reliance it will	13	26	79
	place upon personnel removed from the centralized function of manage-	27	31	84
	ment. Removed from the motivation for profit, such personnel may rely	41	35	88
	on a paycheck that they believe will arrive whether they take a personal	56	40	93
	interest in a job or not. The result is a form of compensated slavery,	70	45	98
	satisfying to nobody--a situation that, unless remedied, can be dis-	84	50	103
	astrous to a business and ultimately to its employees.	94	53	106

1′ GWAM | 1 | 2 | 3 | 4 | 5 | 6 | 7 | 8 | 9 | 10 | 11 | 12 | 13 | 14 |
3′ GWAM | 1 | 2 | 3 | 4 | 5 |

LESSON 176

176A Preparatory Practice (5) *each line at least three times*

Alphabet	Zoe Poe requested five tax blanks in May; the wrong ones came in June.
Figure-symbol	In technical papers, you may use this form: 350′4″ x 217′9″ x 216′8″.
Long words	He reflects the critical observations made by advertising specialists.
Fluency	Try to keep the front of your machine even with the edge of your desk.

| 1 | 2 | 3 | 4 | 5 | 6 | 7 | 8 | 9 | 10 | 11 | 12 | 13 | 14 |

176B Building Control (15) *use 175F, above, as directed, but erase and correct errors*

48A Preparatory Practice ⑧ *each line three times; 1' writings on Line 4*

Alphabet   Will Judge Alexander Vonrique permit the seizure of your bank records?

Figure-symbol   On May 17, we shipped Lukin & Decker 6 cars of #923Y valued at $5,840.

Shift keys   Edward Kuhn and George Lyon flew to Italy, Greece, and Spain on May 2.

Fluency   Ken may find that some elements of their problems are hard to isolate.

| 1 | 2 | 3 | 4 | 5 | 6 | 7 | 8 | 9 | 10 | 11 | 12 | 13 | 14 |

48B Errorless Typing ⑦ *each line twice without error or three times with not more than 1 error to a line*

	GWAM		
	Words	15"	12"
If you have lots of pluck, you won't need to depend on luck.	12	48	60
Appreciation of their work is of first importance to the workers.	13	52	65
A man must learn to control himself before he tries to control others.	14	56	70

| 1 | 2 | 3 | 4 | 5 | 6 | 7 | 8 | 9 | 10 | 11 | 12 | 13 | 14 |

48C Problem Typing ⑳

Problem 1

Full sheet; DS; determine space between columns

Center the problem in reading position; center the headings horizontally.

Type Column 1 as shown; in Column 2, type the words of Column 1 with the diagonal to indicate all syllables; in Column 3, type the words of Column 1 with the hyphen to indicate the preferred point of division. Check the divisions in Column 3 with a dictionary or your instructor. (Do not type the numbers beside Column 1 words.)

Tabulating cue: Tabulate from column to column.

				Words
	SYLLABLE IDENTIFICATION AND WORD DIVISIONS			8
	Application of Guides, Pages 80-81			15
1	educated	ed/u/cat/ed	edu-cated	22
2	paragraph			28
3	graduation			36
4	dependable			43
5	physically			50
6	mechanical			58
7	impartially			66
8	impression			73
9	condition			80
10	expelling			86
11	progressing			94
12	progression			102
13	imply			106
14	abounds			111
15	wouldn't			117
16	strangely			123
17	greedy			127

KEY | 11 | 7 | 14 | 8 | 13 |

Problem 2: Composing and Typing

Half sheets; line: 60; SS

Compose and type a brief explanation of why each of the last five words of Column 1, Problem 1, (13-17) should not be divided. Type the ¶s in block form similar to Problem 1, page 80, numbering each ¶ (1 to 5). Check your explanations with pages 80 and 81. Make pencil corrections as needed; then retype.

SECTION 28 TYPING IN AN ACCOUNTING OFFICE

LESSONS 175–184

Drill Copy: Full sheet; 70-space line; SS.

Paragraph Copy: Full sheet; 70-space line; DS; 5-space ¶ indention.

Production Copy: For tabulated reports, decide number of spaces between columns, use of DS or SS, exact placement or reading position, and (for short reports) exact placement or 2-inch top margin. DS all multiple-line main headings in this section.

Special Supplies Needed: Letterheads, carbon paper, second sheets, folders or binders for accounting report, gummed labels, and envelopes.

LESSON 175

175A Preparatory Practice (5) *each line at least three times*

Alphabet	Jim Nix, the vibrant goalie, zipped the spinning puck forward quickly.
Figure-symbol	The only fee for a 102-week course covering 36 basic areas is $984.75.
One hand	Afterwards, we saw John West get an award for making the best address.
Fluency	The past is of use to us only as it can make fuller the life of today.
	| 1 | 2 | 3 | 4 | 5 | 6 | 7 | 8 | 9 | 10 | 11 | 12 | 13 | 14 |

175B Technique Improvement: Judgment Placement in Centering Headings (10)

1. Triple-space the headings at the right in what you consider the approximate horizontal center of the paper.
2. Roll the paper back to one line below the first heading. Center the heading by the backspace-centering method. Type the remaining headings in the same manner. Compare your "guesstimated" placement with the exact placement.
3. Type the exercise again on another sheet.

TYPEWRITERS WITH SPECIAL TALENTS

COMPUTERS AND HOW THEY WORK

EFFECTIVE BUSINESS COMMUNICATION

BUSINESS CYCLES AND FORECASTING

AUTOMATED ACCOUNTING

AUTOMATION OFFICE PRACTICE

175C Sentence Guided Writings (10) *two 1′ writings on each line with the call of the guide*

		GWAM 15″	12″	10″
1	Any man is as old as he feels, or at least as he feels like admitting.	56	70	84
2	Advice is what some ask for when they want someone to agree with them.	56	70	84
3	There are mighty few traffic problems on the straight and narrow path.	56	70	84
4	The joints in the body will not allow you to pat yourself on the back.	56	70	84
	| 1 | 2 | 3 | 4 | 5 | 6 | 7 | 8 | 9 | 10 | 11 | 12 | 13 | 14 |			

175D Communication Aid: Capitalization and Punctuation (5)

Each of the following lines is a single sentence. Capitalize and punctuate as you type; then check the sentences with your instructor.

1 the firms budget you see must first be discussed costs are rising
2 i think the team is ready nevertheless lets review the plans again
3 we wanted front row seats of course and that is what harvey ordered
4 phil reports that the information is not up to date and cant be used
5 unfortunately captain wyeth not captain rudofman will be in charge
| 1 | 2 | 3 | 4 | 5 | 6 | 7 | 8 | 9 | 10 | 11 | 12 | 13 | 14 |

48D Drill on Drawing Lines at the Typewriter ⑮

To Draw Pencil Lines: Place the pencil point on the type bar guide (36) above the ribbon, in the cardholder (12) notch, or against the aligning scale (33). Hold the pencil firmly against the paper.

Horizontal Line. Place the pencil in position, depress the carriage-release lever, and draw the carriage across to make the line of whatever length is desired

Centering on Lines. To determine the center of a line, (1) read and add the numbers on the cylinder scale at the beginning and end of the line; (2) divide by 2. The resulting number is the center of the line.

Vertical Line. Operate the automatic line finder or ratchet release (6). Place the pencil in position, and turn the cylinder (platen) forward (away from you) for the length of line desired. Return the automatic line finder to its normal position.

Drills on Drawing Horizontal Lines

1. Type the following sentence:

   They played quite a good game.

2. Draw a pencil line under the sentence, leaving a little space between the down-stem letters and the line. Note the relationship of the line to the typed letters.

3. Draw an approximate 4″ pencil line; then center and type the sentence of Drill 1 correctly placed on the line. Be sure the letters with down stems do not cut through the line.

4. Type a 3″ underline; remove the paper; reinsert it; align; then center and type the sentence of Drill 1 correctly placed on the line.

Drills on Drawing Vertical Lines

5. Draw two vertical pencil lines about 2″ long and about 4″ apart. (Return the finder to normal position.) Near the top of the space between the lines, center and type the following heading:

   DRAWING VERTICAL LINES

6. Draw a pencil line under the heading just typed.

7. Draw two vertical pencil lines about 2″ long and 3″ apart. (Return the line finder to normal position.) Near the top of the space between the lines, center and type your name; then DS and center and type the current date.

8. Repeat Drills 4, 5, and 6.

LESSON 49

49A Preparatory Practice ⑧ *each line three times; 1′ writings on Line 4*

Alphabet   Zora and John Voight played a number of quiet games with Chuck Baxter.

Figures   Your Certificates 36285A and 47190C bear the date of January 20, 1969.

Figure-symbol   Didn't Mr. Lee wire, "Ship 6 cars of 4/4 C&B Oak on West's Order #96"?

Fluency   The civic group may ask for a formal audit of the records in February.
| 1 | 2 | 3 | 4 | 5 | 6 | 7 | 8 | 9 | 10 | 11 | 12 | 13 | 14 |

Note. Remove the paper; then reinsert it, gauge the line and letter, and type over the first and last word of the last line typed.

49B Drill on Drawing Lines at the Typewriter ⑩

Repeat Steps 3, 4, and 5 of 48D, above. Appraise the accuracy of your centered lines and of the placement of the typing on the horizontal lines.

more than half the employees in the auto- 97
mated departments remained in the same posi- 105
tions. Fewer than one percent, however, had 114
been discharged. 2. More than 80 percent of 123
the employees who were affected held routine 132
jobs involving record maintenance. Only four 142
percent were in stenographic, secretarial, or 151
correspondence jobs. 3. About one third of 160
those assigned to a new job were promoted 168
to jobs of a higher grade. 4. Some new posi- 177
tions were created to operate the computers. 186
The average number employed to fill these 195
new positions by the 20 companies studied 203

was 29. Most of these new employees were 212
engaged in programming and planning. On 220
the whole, the salary rates set for these new 229
jobs were at or near the top of the scale. 238
5. Almost all the employees in new positions 247
were selected from within the offices. On-the- 256
job training sessions were provided for those 266
who were selected for the new jobs. (¶ 2) 273
This study is reported in full in Bulletin No. 285
1287 of the United States Department of 294
Labor. It is available at your local library if 303
you care to study it further. 309

Job 2: Invoice from Unarranged Data

Prepare an original and 2 carbon copies in the form shown on page 293, but capitalize all important words, as is done in some offices. Compute and type the total price for each item and the total for all items.

Words

Invoice No. 8039112 **Sold To** Hollowwell Book Supplies, 130 Adams Street, Portsmouth, VA 13
23703 **Terms** Net 30 **Date** (current) **Our Order No.** AD–7045 **Cust. Order No.** 83904 **Shipped Via** 21
Midwest Transport **Salesman** 700 26

Quantity	Stock No.	Description	Price	Total	
10	174812	single board easels	13.50		34
10	173716	friction wheels	2.25		42
20	177311	educational clock dials	1.25		51
20	160923	trimming boards, 12″ x 12″	12.00		61
10	164498	eyelet punches	4.15		69
			———		70
					71

Job 3: Tabulation

Full sheet; DS

Rearrange the terms into two vertical columns in alphabetic order. To do this, type the first and second columns as your first column and the third and fourth columns as your second one. (Total words: 54)

SELECTED VOCABULARY TERMS
Electronic Data Processing

access time	hardware	optical scanner	software
alphanumeric	input	output	sorter
binary code	instruction	printer	system
bug	keypunch	processing	updating
computer	loop	program	verifier
console	memory	random access	write

49C Problem Typing ⑳

Problem 1: Memorandum with Tabulated Items

			Words
	THE ZIP CODE SYSTEM		4
	DS		
	The Zoning Improvement Plan		10
	TS		

Full sheet; DS; 2" top margin; 65-space line; 5-space ¶ indention; SS tabulated lines; decide spacing between columns

ZIP Code divides the country into delivery units, each desig- 22
nated by a five-digit number. The first digit represents one of 35
ten geographic areas; the second digit, a specific portion of a 48
geographic area; the third digit, one of the 553 sectional center 61
areas for sorting mail; and the last two digits, today's delivery 74
zone numbers. Here are some examples of the ZIP Code numbers and 87
the new two-letter state abbreviations recommended for use with 100
the ZIP numbers: 104

Reset margin stop

Deerfield	MA	01342	107
Jamestown	KS	66948	111
Las Cruces	NM	88001	115
McGregor	TX	76657	119
Marble City	OK	74945	123
Forest Hill	MD	21050	127

Type the ZIP Code number on the line with the city and the 139
state name or abbreviation with two spaces between them. The ZIP 152
Code number should be included in the letter address as well as 165
in the envelope address. 170

Problem 2: Letter with Tabulated Items

Full sheet; 60-space line; tab stop at center; return address on Line 16; modified block style (see page 71); decide on the spacing between tabulated items

Words

(*Your return address; current date*) Miss Eloise Leffingwell | 20
President, Alpha Chapter | Delta Pi Epsilon | New York University | 32
New York, New York 10003 | Dear Miss Leffingwell | At a recent meeting 44
of business teachers, I talked with three | members of other DPE 57
chapters who now live in nearby cities. | Each of these teachers 70
expressed an interest in transferring | their DPE membership to 82
Alpha Chapter. Their names, chapters, | and chapter numbers are 94
given below: | 97

Roger N. Fitzhugh	Beta	561	103
Lera B. Jackson	Gamma	389	108
Estelle Norabach	Gamma	72	113

What is the procedure for transferring membership from one | 125
DPE chapter to another? I shall be glad to get this informa- | 137
tion to these DPE members and to invite them to our next Alpha | 149
Chapter meeting if you wish me to do so. | Sincerely | *Your name* 164

LESSON 174

174A Preparatory Practice [5] *each line at least three times*

Alphabet	Jud may give gifts to persons who can quickly open the new puzzle box.
Figure-symbol	I need 760 feet of 3/4 plywood and 912 feet of 5/8 plywood by tonight.
Long reaches	Five hunters told my uncle they were cold and hungry much of the time.
Fluency	Let your goal be to get ahead of yourself, not to get ahead of others.

| 1 | 2 | 3 | 4 | 5 | 6 | 7 | 8 | 9 | 10 | 11 | 12 | 13 | 14 |

174B Growth Index [15] *two 5′* control-level *writings; figure* nwam

		GWAM 1′	5′	
¶ 1	A letter is one of the truly powerful elements that may be employed	14	3	61
1.6 SI	in modern business. The men in the companies that use letters and fol-	28	6	63
5.8 AWL	low them up promptly are certain to reap rich rewards. A man who aspires	43	9	66
75% HFW	to a satisfying business career should fully realize the benefits that	57	11	69
	accrue as a result of effective correspondence.	66	13	71
¶ 2	Writing a letter that is friendly in tone and has the right corre-	13	16	74
1.6 SI	lation of ideas and words ranks no less important as a business asset	27	19	77
5.8 AWL	than as an element in general culture. The effective letter is prepared	42	22	79
75% HFW	with a sense of "reader impact." It conveys the information it intends	56	24	82
	to convey without wasting words or violating rules of correct grammar.	70	27	85
¶ 3	Why do many letters land on target while others usually land in	13	30	88
1.6 SI	the incinerator? Why does one letter acquire for its author a job, a	27	33	91
5.8 AWL	crucial order, a deposit, or a smile from an agitated customer? Why	41	35	93
75% HFW	does another lose business, create ill will, and drive customers away?	55	38	96
	A businessman must discover answers to these questions if he wishes to	69	41	99
	remain in business long.	74	42	100
¶ 4	The expert manager in today's business world can get the facts, fix	14	45	103
1.6 SI	them in logical order, and discuss them satisfactorily. He can reason	28	48	106
5.8 AWL	well; he can relate his ideas to words with ease; and he can speak and	42	50	108
75% HFW	write clearly and forcefully. Ability to express himself gives him the	56	53	111
	confidence he needs to meet a problem effectively. Usually he can name	71	56	114
	his own salary in the business community.	79	58	116

1′ GWAM | 1 | 2 | 3 | 4 | 5 | 6 | 7 | 8 | 9 | 10 | 11 | 12 | 13 | 14 |
5′ GWAM | 1 | 2 | 3 |

174C Production Measurement [30] *25′ writing; figure* n-pram

Job 1: Leftbound Manuscript with Carbon Copy

	Words
EFFECTS OF AUTOMATION	4
Allen M. Woods	7
(¶ 1) From time to time we have discussed the	15
effect on office personnel of installing elec-	24
tronic computers. Some interesting data on	33
the subject are available from the Bureau of	42
Labor Statistics, which has completed a study	51
of 20 offices that have installed electronic com-	61
puters for processing business information.	70
Here are the general findings of the study.	79
(Arrange enumerated items in listed form.)	
1. A year after the installation of computers,	89

49D Skill-Comparison Typing ⑫ *Line: 70; 5-space ¶ indention; DS*

1. Type easy ¶ 1 as a 1' control writing to determine your base *gwam*.
2. Type two 1' writings of ¶ 2 on the *exploration level*, trying to reach your base rate. **Note.** The 1' rate will be twice the 2' rate shown in Column 1 at the right.

3. Type a 2' writing on the *control level*.
4. Type a 3' writing on the *control level*.
5. Circle errors on the 2' and 3' writings and compare the *gwam*.

All letters are used.

	2'	3'	
			GWAM

¶ 1
1.3 SI
5.2 AWL
90% HFW

Text	2'	3'	
The typewriter has changed the place of women in the world, for	6	4	46
it opened the doors of the business office to them. They now fill many	14	9	50
jobs that used to be for men only. That the need for women in business	21	14	55
is recognized is shown by the many ads for competent women workers that	28	19	60
are found in the daily papers.	31	21	62

¶ 2
1.6 SI
5.8 AWL
75% HFW

Text	2'	3'	
Numerous positions are available in the local offices of diversi-	38	25	66
fied companies. Duties such as typing, taking shorthand, and filing	44	29	71
are very common. Those who apply for jobs with these companies must	51	34	76
be aware of the skills that a job requires, as they will be expected	58	39	80
to use them as well as related skills.	62	41	83

2' GWAM | 1 | 2 | 3 | 4 | 5 | 6 | 7 |
3' GWAM | 1 | 2 | 3 | 4 | 5 |

LESSON 50

50A Preparatory Practice ⑧ *each line three times; 1' writings on Line 4*

Alphabet   For the chemical test, J. K. Pew may request a large-size box and vat.
Figure-symbol   Is the up-to-date report on Bill #6753–48 on Profits due May 19 or 20?
One-hand words A few dead trees were scattered among the great grove of orange trees.
Fluency   The auditor said the profit due you should have been paid before this.
                | 1 | 2 | 3 | 4 | 5 | 6 | 7 | 8 | 9 | 10 | 11 | 12 | 13 | 14 |

50B Skill-Comparison Typing ⑫ *type 49D, above, as directed*

50C Skill-Transfer Typing ⑩ *line: 60; SS; each line for two 1' writings; compare gwam*

	Words
Straight copy The six girls who are in our office do their work with ease.	12
Figure-symbol Order #836 comes to $197.50 and is to be shipped by July 24.	12
Script The new chairman may not want you to sign the amendment now.	12
Rough draft lc. Will Rodney handle the problems of form for your firm today.	12

Job 1: Interoffice Memorandum

		Words
TO:	All Department Heads	4
FROM:	Controller's Office	8
DATE:	October 25, 19––	12
SUBJECT:	New Account Numbers	16

(¶1) For several months, Atwater–Kern, a 23
consulting firm, has been working with our 31
office in an attempt to facilitate the flow of 41
paper work required to maintain an efficient 50
account record of the activities of our com- 58
pany. By the first of next year, this study 67
should be completed; and a complete summary 76
will be issued to you for your use in account- 85
ing for departmental budgets. In the mean- 94
time, however, we shall continue with our 102
present procedures, except for a few minor 111
changes that are needed at the present time 119
to overcome several bottlenecks that have 128
prevented our giving you up-to-date informa- 136
tion quickly. (¶2) Effective November 1, 144
therefore, the following expense account num- 153
bers will be added to the accounting system. 162
Will you please use these numbers when you 170
report expense items to this office. These 179
numbers will be punched as code to activate 188
the accounting machine (or tabulator) and 196
record the expense item directly to the appro- 205
priate account. 208

Code	Item	
		212
611	Advertising charges	217
617	Automotive repairs	221
634	Postage	224
635	Telephone and telegraph	229
637	Miscellaneous	233

Job 2: Summary of Expenses

Petty Cash Disbursement

No. 38   Date 3/1   Code 153
Pay from petty cash $1.00
To A. & B. Delivery Co.
For C. O. D. charge
Disbursed by _____

The illustration above shows a petty cash voucher that was completed when money from the petty cash fund was disbursed. For unit record data processing, the voucher would be considered a *source document*; and the data from a number of such vouchers would be punched directly into cards. A tabulator would automatically update the amounts in the proper accounts according to code numbers and, in addition, print a summary of all disbursements similar to the one shown below.

On a full sheet with double spacing, type the summary in duplicate as shown.

			Words
PETTY CASH DISBURSEMENTS FOR MARCH			7
Code 153	Voucher 38	1.00	12
33	39	1.50	14
401	40	4.75	17
611	41	3.50	19
617	42	3.50	21
153	43	5.80	24
627	44	7.25	26
634	45	2.75	29
635	46	4.25	31
634	47	4.25	33
		34.45	35

Job 3: Composing a Letter

Type a personal letter of at least three paragraphs to a friend describing the unit of study you have just completed in typewriting. Try to summarize a few of the things you have learned; give your general impressions about the desirability of more study or even employment in the area of data processing.

Problem 1: Rough Draft of Manuscript

Full sheet; line: 65; 5-space ¶ indention; DS; 1½" top margin; DS between enumerated items; SS table; 4 spaces between columns; correct errors

Words

Center in all caps   Abbreviating in Business Correspondence   TS   8

"When in doubt, write it out" once was an admonition to students of   22

shorthand that applied equally to other business writers, too. There is   35

evidence, however, that "long" shorthand is not very efficient and that ab-   50

breviating is no longer taboo in business communication. Modern   63

business practice is based on the new concept of efficiency, and the judicious   78

use of abbreviations adds to efficiency without offending the   91

equally important human relation aspect of business correspondence.   105

Here are some basic principles of abbreviating: 115

1. Use only those abbreviations that are commonly known.   127
2. Spell out all words that would be conspicuous if   137
   abbreviated in formal typewritten text.   146
3. Use abbreviations in informal writing and also in tables,   159
   footnotes, records, and technical writing.   168

Listed below are some types of abbreviations that are commonly   181

used in both personal and business correspondence: 191

Personal Titles	Doctor	Dr.	197
Company names	Incorporated	Inc.	203
Street names	Boulevard	Blvd.	209
Department names	Department	Dept.	215
Association names	Delta Pi Epsilon	DPE	222
State names	California	Calif.	229

Problem 2: Three-Column Table

Half sheet; SS; 12 spaces between columns; center the heading and the columns horizontally; center the problem vertically

Words

SOME STATE NAMES, THEIR REGULAR ABBREVIATIONS, 9
AND TWO-LETTER ZIP CODE ABBREVIATIONS 17

Arizona	Ariz.	AZ	20
California	Calif.	CA	24
Colorado	Colo.	CO	28
Illinois	Ill.	IL	31
Indiana	Ind.	IN	34
Massachusetts	Mass.	MA	39
Michigan	Mich.	MI	43
Mississippi	Miss.	MS	47
New York	N.Y.	NY	50

Job 5: Purchase Order

DREXALL COMPANY
2143 HIGHLAND AVENUE
ELGIN, ILLINOIS 60124
Telephone 835-4442
Area Code 312

Order No. 54189

To Atkins Boyd Calculator Company
455 Jefferson Street, N.E.
Peoria, IL 61603

Date March 25, 19--

Terms 1/10, n/30

Shipped Via Best way

Quantity	Description	Price	Total
1	Model AB-607 calculator	519.50	519.50

BY E. A. Fox
Purchasing Agent

As shown at the left, type a purchase order in duplicate for the items from Jobs 3 and 4. Order the quantities indicated; include the unit price (cost per dozen); calculate the total cost for each item and type it in the Total column; compute and type the total cost at the foot of the Total column.

		Words
To:	Dodge–Duval Company	4
	317 Council Crest	8
	Madison, WI 53711	11
Order No.:	54271	13
Date:	April 7, 19--	15
Terms:	1/10, n/30	18
Ship Via:	United Trucking Lines	22

Quantity	Description	Price	Total	
10 doz.	Potentiometers, 50K ohms, 1 watt	18.60		33
30 doz.	Resistors, Size 1.8K ohms, 1 watt	5.40		44
20 doz.	2N293 transistors	36.00		53
20 doz.	2N187 transistors	60.00		61
20 doz.	2N1265 transistors	21.60		69
50 doz.	1.5V Pen-Lite cells	12.00		78
			———	80
				81

LESSON 173

173A Preparatory Practice (5) *each line at least three times*

Alphabet	Viewed by many as lazy speech, excessive jargon shows lack of quality.
Figures	There were 14 A's, 23 B's, 58 C's, 30 D's, and 7 F's on the 1969 test.
Long words	The morning speaker outlined the characteristics of digital computers.
Fluency	In general, any man shows what he is by what he does with what he has.

| 1 | 2 | 3 | 4 | 5 | 6 | 7 | 8 | 9 | 10 | 11 | 12 | 13 | 14 |

173B Communication Aid: Capitalization and Punctuation (10)

Capitalize and punctuate as you type. Check your work with your instructor; then use the ¶ for 1′ writings as time permits. Determine your *gwam* after each writing.

Full sheet
70-space line
DS

	1′ GWAM
over 250 years ago gottfried leibniz a clever german mathemati-	13
cian invented the way of writing numbers we know as the binary system.	28
at that time it had little value. today however it is highly useful	42
in operating electronic computers. the binary system uses only two	56
numerals the 1 and 0 as compared to our decimal system which uses ten.	70

1′ GWAM | 1 | 2 | 3 | 4 | 5 | 6 | 7 | 8 | 9 | 10 | 11 | 12 | 13 | 14 |

51A Preparatory Practice (8) *each line three times; 1' writings on Line 4*

Alphabet   Dr. Foxburgh and Mr. Jackson quit Paris and are in Vevey, Switzerland.

Figure-symbol   Order #590-C read, "Ship 30 doz. #621 ** Star Brand at $4.78 a dozen."

Drill on sw   The Swede swore he saw the swords swung swiftly at the Swiss swimmers.

Fluency   The chairman of the Endowment Fund said a big check had been received.

| 1 | 2 | 3 | 4 | 5 | 6 | 7 | 8 | 9 | 10 | 11 | 12 | 13 | 14 |

51B Drill on Typing Columnar Headings (12)

To Determine Center of Column: Method 1. (1) Read and add the numbers on the scale at the left and right edges of the column; (2) divide the total by 2 for the center point.

Note. This method is not new to you, for you used it to determine the center of special-size paper (35B, page 60).

Method 2. From point at which column begins, space forward once for each two letters, figures, or spaces in the longest line (the line that requires the most strokes to type). Disregard a leftover stroke.

To Type a Columnar Heading: From center of column, backspace once for each two letters or spaces in the heading. Disregard a leftover stroke. Begin to type where the backspacing ends.

Drill 1. Draw vertical pencil lines approximately 4" apart and 2" long. Use Method 1 (at left) to determine center; then center and type between the lines the following heading:

TYPING COLUMNAR HEADINGS

Drill 2. Use Method 2; 10 spaces between columns.

Name	Birthday
George Washington	February 22, 1732

Drill 3. Repeat Drill 1 with vertical lines 3 inches apart; Drill 2 with 6 spaces between columns.

51C Problem Typing (20)

Problem 1: Tabulation with Columnar Headings

Half sheet; SS; 8 spaces between columns

Center the problem vertically; center the headings and the columns horizontally.

In Column 2, type the words of Column 1 but show all syllables; in Column 3, type the same words, but show the preferred point or points of division.

Check your syllabication and word division; then retype the problem to include any corrections you have made.

			Words
WORD DIVISION			3
DS			
Syllable Identification and Preferred Divisions			12
		TS	
Word	Syllables	Divide	21
		DS	
alignment	a/lign/ment	align-ment	27
comparable			35
correction			42
contractual			51
crucible			57
feasible			63
mystical			69
possible			75
syllable			82
expressing			89
expression			96
expressive			103

KEY | 11 | 8 | 14 | 8 | 13 |

Production Typing Information

A computer programmed to do so can maintain a constant, up-to-date inventory for a business. Fed information concerning future needs for an inventory of items, such a computer could have prepared automatically any of the following forms you will type as Jobs 3, 4, and 5.

Job 3: Purchase Requisition

Type the requisition in duplicate in the same form as the illustration below.

	Words
Deliver To: Department G	3
Location: Loading Dock 127	6
Job No. 7391	7
Requisition No. 1102	8
Date Issued: April 1, 19—	11
Date Required: May 15, 19—	13

Quan-tity	Description	Words
10 doz.	Potentiometers, 50K	19
	ohms, 1 watt	22
30 doz.	Resistors, Size 1.8K	27
	ohms, 1 watt	30
20 doz.	2N293 transistors	35
20 doz.	2N187 transistors	40
20 doz.	2N1265 transistors	46
50 doz.	1.5V Pen-Lite cells	51

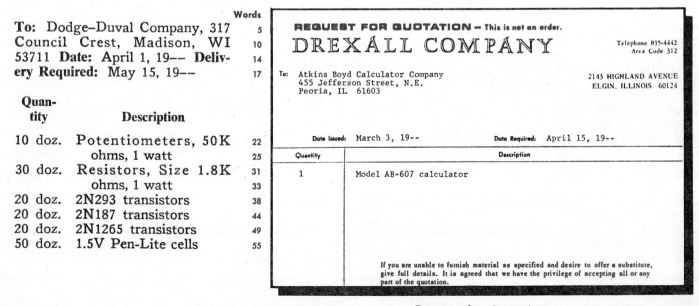

Purchase Requisition

Job 4: Request for Quotation

Type in duplicate the following request for quotation as illustrated below.

	Words
To: Dodge–Duval Company, 317	5
Council Crest, Madison, WI	10
53711 **Date:** April 1, 19— **Deliv-**	14
ery Required: May 15, 19—	17

Quan-tity	Description	Words
10 doz.	Potentiometers, 50K	22
	ohms, 1 watt	25
30 doz.	Resistors, Size 1.8K	31
	ohms, 1 watt	33
20 doz.	2N293 transistors	38
20 doz.	2N187 transistors	44
20 doz.	2N1265 transistors	49
50 doz.	1.5V Pen-Lite cells	55

Request for Quotation

Problem 2: Rough-Draft Tabulation

Half sheet; DS; 12 spaces be-
tween columns; center the copy
both vertically and horizontally

Center heading (DIFFERENTIATED VOICE QUALITIES (ING TONE inserted)   7

Telephone Tips TS   10

	Good	Bad	14

Problem 3

Retype Problem 2, correcting all errors
as you type.

Good	Bad	
Pleasant	Expressionless	18
Friendliness (Friendly)	Mechanical (Robot-like)	22
Cap cordial	Indifference (to)	26
Cheerfulness (Cheerful)	Impatient	30
Interesting	Inattentive	35

51D Building Speed and Control (10) *line: 70; ¶ indention: 5; DS*

1. Type three 1' writings: first, for control; second, for speed; and third, for control. Control writings: circle errors; note *gwam*.

2. Type two 2' writings: first, for speed; next for control. Determine errors and *gwam* for the control writing. Compare with 1' control writing.

All letters are used.

1.5 SI
5.6 AWL
80% HFW

	2' GWAM
Always try to put first things first in every job you decide to do,	7	44
and you can win the prize you seek. This is especially important if you	14	51
have the goal of improving your skill in typewriting. Many things go	21	58
into developing expertness at the typewriter, but first is the use of	38	65
right techniques, including the efficient use of all the operative parts	35	73
of the typewriter.	37	74

2' GWAM | 1 | 2 | 3 | 4 | 5 | 6 | 7 |

LESSON 52

52A Preparatory Practice (8) *each line three times; 1' writings on Line 4*

Alphabet   J. B. Deckers, from the next floor, gave away grapes on the quiz show.

Figures   The population of Houston in 1950 was 596,163; in 1960 it was 938,219.

Long words   Today, car buyers are knowledgeable about performance characteristics.

Fluency   How well did the eight boys do the problems you assigned for homework?

| 1 | 2 | 3 | 4 | 5 | 6 | 7 | 8 | 9 | 10 | 11 | 12 | 13 | 14 |

52B Building Speed and Control (10) *type 51D, above, as directed*

LANDIS Office Supplies & Equipment

TELEPHONE 321-9732

2100 TRAVIS ST., HOUSTON, TEXAS 77002

INVOICE No. 37742

Sold	KOHRS OFFICE SUPPLIES	Date 7 25 —	7
To	299 WEST 21ST STREET	Our Order No. B42378	13
	AUSTIN, TX 78705	Cust. Order No. 578318	18
		Shipped Via AMERICAN EXPRESS	21
Terms	NET 30	Salesman 51	23

Quantity	Description	Cat.No.	Unit Price	Total	
48	STAPLERS	59380	4.50	216.00	29
24	PAPER PUNCHES	59461	2.50	60.00	36
48	PENCIL SHARPENERS	59330	2.10	100.80	44
72	CANVAS RING BINDERS	48187	1.20	86.40	52
24	DRAFTING SETS	39195	7.80	187.20	59
				650.40	60
	LESS 10% DEALER DISCOUNT			65.04	66
				585.36	68

Invoice prepared on an electronic typewriter-calculator.
Amounts in color are printed automatically.

Job 2: Typing a Summary of Sales by District and Salesman

This is an example of a summary report prepared by a tabulating unit, automatically, from punched cards. You are to type it for this job.

Full sheet; reading position; DS

SUMMARY OF SALES BY DISTRICT AND SALESMAN
WEEK ENDING NOVEMBER 5, 19--

SALES-MAN	AMOUNT	DISTRICT	AMOUNT	TOTAL	Words
30	1,734.80				24
31	2,247.90				27
32	925.70				29
		1	4,908.40		31
36	1,877.50				34
37	1,747.20				36
38	2,474.10				39
40	1,170.60				41
		2	7,269.40		43
50	2,671.30				46
51	1,955.30				48
		3	4,626.60		50
				16,804.40	52

52C Problem Typing ⑳

Problem 1: Two-Column Tabulation

Full sheet; DS; 8 spaces between columns; reading position; correct errors

		Words
RANK OF VOCATIONAL TRAITS		5
DS		
OF		6
DS		
OUTSTANDINGLY SUCCESSFUL SECRETARIES		13
TS		
Accuracy	1	15
Responsibleness	2	19
Dependability	3	22
Intelligence	3	25
Courtesy	5	27
Initiative	5	30
Judgment	5	32
Personal Pleasantness	9	37
Personal Appearance	9	41

Problem 2: Composing and Typing

Modified block; open punctuation; your return address; current date

Compose and type a letter to your instructor to say that you found a reference to the 1924 study typed as Problem 1 and that the study is now out of print. Tabulate the first four traits and their ranking and indicate your amazement that "Honesty" is not among these.

Add a final paragraph stating your opinion as to the probable reason "Honesty" was not ranked among the first four traits of outstandingly successful secretaries.

Type your name in signature position; then make pencil corrections as needed, and retype the letter in acceptable form.

Problem 3: Letter with Enclosure

Letterhead (or full sheet); 60-space line; modified block; open punctuation; current date

If a letterhead is used, type the date on Line 16. If plain paper is used, type Westminster College on Line 14; New Wilmington, Pa.   16142 on Line 15; and the current date on Line 16.

~~~~~~
still, send your check for this year's contribution and help
Westminster maintain its role as a college of distinction.

                              Sincerely yours

                         Student Chairman
                         ANNUAL ALUMNI FUND

Enclosure
~~~~~~

	Words
Mr. Anton J. Gabbert | 237 Radcliffe St. |	11
Bristol, Pa. 19007 | Dear Mr. Gabbert | (¶ 1)	18
As Student Chairman of Westminster College	27
Alumni Fund, I hope to interest you in join-	36
ing other distinguished alumni in an "invest-	45
ment in youth." You can do this through your	54
contribution to the Annual Alumni Fund.	62
(¶ 2) The enclosed copy of part of an editorial	70
from the Alumni News tells something of our	81
needs and our hopes. Please réad it; then	89
send in your pledge of support for your col-	99
lege. Better still, send your check for this	108
year's contribution and help Westminster	116
maintain its role as a college of distinction.	126
Sincerely yours | (*Operate return 4 times*) Stu-	130
dent Chairman | ANNUAL ALUMNI FUND |	136
Enclosure	138

52D Technique Practice ⑫ *each line twice without error*

Left shift	Henry and I are going to Maryland in May, but Paul is going to Norway.
Right shift	Dick West left for Greece, but Clay Spillman went to France with Carl.
Both shifts	Were Paul and Robert asked to imitate Leslie's typewriting techniques?
Both shifts	"Get SPEED and ACCURACY," Mr. Ward said, "for real typewriting power."
Both shifts	John and Frank spent April in Mexico City and June and July in Brazil.

| 1 | 2 | 3 | 4 | 5 | 6 | 7 | 8 | 9 | 10 | 11 | 12 | 13 | 14 |

171-172A Preparatory Practice [5] *each line at least three times*

Alphabet	Our clever expert justified his fee by equalizing his weekly payments.
Figure-symbol	John said, "In our 1968 class of 573 seniors, 204 won various awards."
Shift keys	Violet Springer flew to France on Thursday and later goes to Portugal.
Fluency	Send the title form so the men can finish a formal audit by the tenth.
	1 | 2 | 3 | 4 | 5 | 6 | 7 | 8 | 9 | 10 | 11 | 12 | 13 | 14

171-172B Building Speed and Control [10]

Type two 2′ *exploration-level* writings; compute *gwam* on the faster writing. Then type two 2′ *control-level* writings and compute *gwam* on the more accurate writing.

		GWAM 1′	GWAM 2′
¶ 1	By accepting employment, you become a partner in an enterprise.	13	7
1.8 SI	You agree to provide talent, energy, expertise, intelligence, and any	27	14
6.2 AWL	other qualifications needed for the job. The employer provides essen-	41	21
70% HFW	tial rooms and machinery and agrees to show you all you need to know	55	27
	about his enterprise. He invests in your professional ability; you	68	34
	participate in any income he earns. You can realize, nevertheless,	82	41
	that the position costs an employer a sizeable sum of money; so he must	96	48
	make a reasonable return on his investment, or you may be in the part-	110	55
	nership only temporarily.	115	58
¶ 2	Expense items are of major significance to any company, for they	13	64
1.8 SI	usually represent the difference between success and failure. As an	27	71
6.2 AWL	employee, you are an element of expense. You represent a cash outlay.	41	78
70% HFW	The efficient employee, however, contributes over what he costs; and any	56	86
	economist or auditor will tell you that such money is a wise investment.	70	93
1′ GWAM	1 | 2 | 3 | 4 | 5 | 6 | 7 | 8 | 9 | 10 | 11 | 12 | 13 | 14		
2′ GWAM	1 | 2 | 3 | 4 | 5 | 6 | 7		

171-172C Production Typing: Business Forms [35] *(each day)*

Preliminary Information

The remaining jobs in this section provide further examples of work that might be handled with data processing equipment. Some forms might be typed on a typewriter-calculator, a tape-punching typewriter, or a keypunch; others might be produced by equipment such as a tabulator or printer.

As you complete these jobs, therefore, keep in mind that such work exemplifies the terms *data* (as input) or *information* (as output) as a part of a data processing system and that probably hundreds of such forms could be prepared with data processing equipment while you are typing one.

Job 1: Invoice Typed on a Typewriter-Calculator

When a form such as an invoice is prepared on a typewriter-calculator, only part of the typing is done by the operator. All calculations are made and typed automatically. In the illustration on page 293, the copy in black was typed by the operator; that in color was added automatically.

Punched cards or punched paper tape may be prepared automatically as the invoice is being typed. Only selected information is punched on the card or tape.

Type the invoice from the illustration on page 293. Type all the information, using a one-color ribbon. Prepare a carbon copy.

53A Preparatory Practice ⑧ *each line three times; 1' writings on Line 4*

Alphabet   Mr. Brown was dazzled by the quick jumps of the five or six young men.

Figure-symbol   Does the 10% discount on Bedford & Hunt's Invoice #469 come to $23.58?

One-hand words   The union referred only a few of my cases to the referee for decision.

Fluency   They did not include in the report the profits due the firm in August.

| 1 | 2 | 3 | 4 | 5 | 6 | 7 | 8 | 9 | 10 | 11 | 12 | 13 | 14 |

53B Building Control ⑫ *line: 70; ¶ indention: 5; DS*

1. Type a 1-, a 3-, and a 5-minute writing on the *control level.* Pace your typing at a rate you can control with a high degree of accuracy.

2. After each writing, determine an appropriate goal for the next writing—fewer words and greater accuracy or more words with the same accuracy—and type to achieve that goal.

All letters are used.

1.4 SI
5.4 AWL
85% HFW

	GWAM 3'	GWAM 5'	

Learning the "time cost" of correcting errors in typing is best   4 | 3 | 42

done by making a check of the time you require to erase and correct an   9 | 5 | 44

error on an original and carbon copy. When this was done with some   14 | 8 | 47

typists, it was found that the most proficient required twenty-six   18 | 11 | 50

seconds; most required about forty-five seconds; and some required a   23 | 14 | 53

complete minute to erase and correct one error on an original and carbon   27 | 16 | 55

copy. The assumption can be made, then, that it will take you about   32 | 19 | 58

thirty seconds to make each correction. If you type a three-minute   37 | 22 | 61

writing at forty-eight words a minute but make and correct two errors,   41 | 25 | 64

your actual typing time will be just two minutes. You must realize the   46 | 28 | 67

high price you pay for the errors you make, and then you must learn to   51 | 31 | 70

type with a high degree of accuracy. You will type more when you type   56 | 33 | 72

with control even though you seem to be typing at a slower speed. Type   61 | 36 | 75

as fast as you can but as slow as you must to type with accuracy.   65 | 39 | 78

3' GWAM	1	2	3	4	5
5' GWAM	1	2	3		

170C Production Typing: Arranging Data ㉟

Job 1: Arranging Data by Customer Account Number

This job and the two that follow it are examples of the kinds of task that can be done quickly by unit record equipment. Once the addresses are punched into cards, the equipment can sort and print them in any order desired.

Type each of the addresses shown below on a 5 x 3 card. Type them exactly as they appear, with the customer number on the line above the firm name.

Then arrange the cards so that the lowest customer number is on top, the rest of the cards being in sequential order so that the last, or bottom, card has the highest customer number. In this sequence, type the data in two columns in vertical order. Single-space the items and double-space between them. Title the page MARCH SHIPMENTS BY CUSTOMER ACCOUNT NUMBER.

Job 2: Arranging Data by Company Name

Arrange the cards used for Job 1 in alphabetic order by company name. Then type the list in two vertical columns as you did for Job 1. Continue to include the customer's account number. Title the page MARCH SHIPMENTS BY COMPANY NAME.

Job 3: Arranging Data by ZIP Code

Arrange the cards used for Job 1 so that the lowest ZIP Code number is on top and the highest is the last, or bottom, card. In this sequence type the list in two columns as you did for Job 1. Title the page MARCH SHIPMENTS BY ZIP CODE NUMBER.

082087
Adrion Electronics, Inc.
4743 Mitchell Road
Waco, TX   76710

029361
Research Corporation of America
21 Spring Forest Drive
Pittsburgh, PA   15238

029369
Trevellis Brothers
Attention Mrs. Rose Graham
2220 Miner Avenue, East
Stockton, CA   95205

062738
Arkansas Systems
One Duff Lane
Little Rock, AR   72204

073868
Rockford Laboratories, Inc.
9500 Eggleston Road
Rockford, IL   61108

056668
Roundex Equipment Company
3948 Concord Road
Beaumont, TX   77703

087355
Watson & Kingman, Inc.
800 Sperry Street
Waterbury, CT   06710

040676
S & S Electric Company
5500-5550 Sierra View Way
Sacramento, CA   95820

086492
Electromechanics, Inc.
900 Avila Road
San Mateo, CA   94402

060237
Unity Electric Products Co.
1850 Jefferson Street
Concord, NH   03301

090465
National Instrument Corp.
2900 Cliff Avenue, South
Sioux Falls, SD   57105

094366
Ravanall Corporation
600 Apache Street, West
Tulsa, OK   74127

020533
Bruce-Elliott Systems, Inc.
125 Florence Avenue, West
Inglewood, CA   93701

099023
Rexon Business Forms
6565 Ann Arbor Avenue, North
Oklahoma City, OK   73132

035354
Peerless Reduction Company
2207–2219 Mayflower Avenue
New Rochelle, NY   10801

Full sheet; DS; 65-space line; 5-space ¶ indention; 2" top margin; correct errors

Alertness cue: Your typed lines will not be the same as those in the copy.

	Words
all caps To Our Partners in Education	6
¶ A College such as Westminster ∧now faces two major *(triple-space)*	16
problems: ~~in common with~~ *better prepared and more* highly motivated	26
students, ~~and~~ *as well as* the "knowledge explosion." We	37
have too many students ∧ *for our present facilities.* We need more classrooms,	52
dormitories, laboratories, professors, library	61
books, and space to meet the needs of our	70
students and those "knocking at our doors."	79
Alumni News quotes our President as	88
saying, that ¶ Ours is a college of distinction	96
SS and indent quotes ¶ in spite of our many needs. We maintain	104
the high educational ideals and standards	112
set by the distinguished men ∧ *and women* who studied	123
at ~~this college~~ *Westminster* before the present deluge of	131
students. We now need their help. ~~They~~ *Let's*	140
~~must be our partners in education~~ tell them so.	143
They ~~will~~ *won't* fail us in this time of need.	151
¶ The honor roll for this year's partners in	160
education goes to the printer soon. Space	168
has been reserved on it for your name.	176
Let us put it there! Send your check	184
or pledge NOW.	187

Job 2: Compiling a List

2 full sheets; unbound manuscript form; title, DATA PROCESSING TERMS; *TS between items*

The following terms and their definitions are to be arranged in alphabetic order and typed on full sheets. One way to proceed would be to type only the terms in rough form in alphabetic order; then, using your list as a guide to correct order, type the terms and their definitions in final form.

HARDWARE: A <u>system</u> of equipment or machinery

FORTRAN: FORmula TRANslation--a mathematical language for programming computers

ON-LINE, OFF-LINE: The operation of equipment in direct communication with a computer (<u>on-line</u>) or with peripheral equipment (<u>off-line</u>)

ACCESS TIME: The time used by a computer to locate data in its <u>memory</u> section

BUG: An error in the design of a <u>program</u>

COBOL: COmmon Business Oriented Language-- a language for programming computers

ALPHANUMERIC: A combination of letters and numerals used as a code

CONSOLE: A panel through which the operator controls the flow of data and instructions to and from a computer

BINARY CODE: A number system using Base 2; there are two symbols--1 and 0

WRITE: To transfer data from the <u>memory</u> to the <u>output</u> section of a computer

OUTPUT: Information produced by a computer

UNIT RECORD EQUIPMENT: Equipment that utilizes the punched card

PRINTER: The device that types the <u>output</u> from a computer

SYSTEM: A network of related procedures for performing a major activity

RANDOM-ACCESS STORAGE: A process of using <u>memory</u> in which parts of data can be located quickly

COMMON LANGUAGE: A term used to describe punched paper tape, edge-punched cards, punched cards, or magnetic tape that can be "read" by and used to activate various office machines

INSTRUCTION: A coded statement that causes a computer to perform

UPDATING: The process of bringing information in <u>memory</u> up to date

PROGRAM: <u>Instructions</u> that tell a computer how to perform

SOFTWARE: The parts of a <u>system</u> exclusive of equipment (<u>hardware</u>)

MEMORY: Devices for storing data for later use; also referred to as <u>storage</u>

LOOP: A sequence of instructions to be repeated a number of times

---

LESSON 170

170A Preparatory Practice (5) *each line at least three times*

Alphabet   Quick victory was assured if the excited boys jumped into a goal zone.

Figure-symbol   Mount Everest (29,028 feet) was not climbed by man until May 29, 1953.

Long words   They organized symposiums for the programming of electronic computers.

Fluency   Anyone who gets ahead can handle people as well as he can handle jobs.

| 1 | 2 | 3 | 4 | 5 | 6 | 7 | 8 | 9 | 10 | 11 | 12 | 13 | 14 |

Alertness cue: Your typed lines will not be the same as those in the copy.

WESTMINSTER COLLEGE

Office of Vice-President
for Development

(814) 555-1212
New Wilmington, PA 16142

	Words
December 6, 19--	3
Mr. Edward O. Babcock, Esq.	8
3176 State Street, W.	12
Boise, Idaho 88703	16
Dear Mr. Babcock	20

Idaho doesn't seem so far away now that we have received your letter with your check for $500 as your "investment in our youth" program. We thank you for your generous gift, and Even more, we thank you for your continued interest in and concern for Westminster College and its continued growth.

Last year we had gifts from two other alumni who reside in Boise, Idaho, but we have not had any response to our letters this year asking for their continued support. The names of these alumni and the amount each gave are listed below:

Mrs. Leonora Moore Judd	$ 500	
Edward Kimmon	1,000	

Will you be good enough to try to contact Mrs. Judd and Mr. Kimmon to see if you can get them to make a contribution to the College again this year. We very much want to add their names to the honor roll where your name heads the list for Idaho and nearby states.

Again, thanks you for your check and good wishes. Thanks, you too, for any help you can give us in contacting Mrs. Judd and Mr. Kimmon.

Sincerely yours

Student Chairman
Vice-President for Development
All caps → Annual Alumni Fund

	Words
	31
	42
	52
	60
	72
	84
	95
	106
	118
	124
	128
	137
	149
	159
	171
	180
	193
	204
	207
	210
	213
	217

LESSON 169

169A Preparatory Practice [5] *each line at least three times*

Alphabet	Mazie Raye just displayed a fashionable, exquisite black evening gown.
Figure-symbol	Report #6 was not correct; I saw errors on pages 36, 89, 105, and 247.
Rhythm	The busy social chairman took the time to solve the big quota problem.
Fluency	Form the habit of using time well, and you will profit from your work.

1 2 3 4 5 6 7 8 9 10 11 12 13 14

169B Building Control [10] *¶s of 165E and 166B on page 283 for two 3′* control-level *writings; compare* gwam

169C Production Typing: Tabulated Report; List [35]

Sideways on a full sheet; center vertically and horizontally; decide on spaces between columns

Job 1: Wide Tabulation

EDUCATION REQUIRED FOR COMPUTER OCCUPATIONS

	High School	Technical	College	Special Study	Words
					9
					26
Card-Tape-Converter Operator	Preferred	. . .	. . .	. . .	37
Chief Console Operator	Required	Desirable	. . .	(Experience)	49
Coding Clerk	Required	. . .	. . .	. . .	57
Computer Engineer	. . .	. . .	Phys. sci. or	Math	67
			engineering		69
Console Operator	At least	Desirable	. . .	Data processing	81
Data Typist	Preferred	. . .	. . .	Typewriting	90
Director, Data Processing	. . .	Required	Helpful	Data processing	103
Electronics Mechanic	. . .	Two years	. . .	Electronics	114
Engineering Analyst	. . .	. . .	Phys. sci.	Math	124
High-Speed-Printer Operator	Required	. . .	. . .	. . .	135
Junior Programmer	Required	Desirable	. . .	. . .	144
Keypunch Operator	Preferred	Desirable	. . .	Typewriting	156
Lead Programmer	. . .	Required	Helpful	Accounting and	166
				math	167
Operations Research Analyst	. . .	. . .	Doctorate	Higher math	180
Programmer	. . .	Required	Helpful	Accounting and	190
				math	191
Sorting-Machine Operator	Required	. . .	. . .	. . .	201
Systems Analyst	. . .	. . .	Business	Accounting	211
Systems Engineer	. . .	. . .	Engineering	. . .	220
Tape Handler	Required	Desirable	. . .	. . .	229
Tape Librarian	Required	. . .	. . .	Business	238
Verifier Operator	Required	. . .	. . .	Typewriting	248

252

Source: U.S. Department of Labor, Occupations in Electronic Computing Systems, 1965. 278

Problem 3: Three-Column Tabulation

Full sheet; DS; reading position; 8 spaces between columns

			Words
WESTMINSTER COLLEGE BUILDING FUND			9
Contributions Received in Third Quarter			15
Name	**State**	**Amount**	
George W. Anderson	Pennsylvania	$ 1,750.00	24
Edward O. Babcock	Idaho	500.00	30
Myron T. Buffington	Pennsylvania	1,500.00	39
Marilyn O. Crawford	Indiana	2,000.00	47
D. Wesley Dodds	Ohio	500.00	53
Arlene N. Ruskin	Utah	275.00	58
Marjorie McC. Thomas	Ohio	425.75	65
Arthur N. Tomasson	California	15,000.00₁₀	74
Alexander R. Trexler	West Virginia₁₃	375.00	82
Norton C. Wallingford	Ohio	3,500.00	90
Edward O. Wilson	Pennsylvania	225.00	97
Robert H. Woodside	New York	75.00	104
T. N. Woolson	Maine	50.00	109
Henry Harrington Young	Michigan	100.00	117

PROOFREADING PRACTICE

It takes time to proofread carefully, but it is time well spent, for you will then know by your own proof that your work is right or wrong. Before you can correct your errors, you must find them. Before you can claim competence in proofreading and correcting your errors, you must find ALL your errors and correct them, preferably BEFORE you remove the work from the typewriter.

Double-check the accuracy of your typing. Give special attention to checking the spelling of names and check numbers to see that no inaccuracy gets by you. A misspelled name can irritate the recipient and an inaccurate figure can confuse the records. Demonstrate evidence of your proofreading competence. Recheck all work in today's typing to see if you have corrected all errors.

THE ELECTRONIC COMPUTING SYSTEM — 5

Allen M. Woods — 8

(¶ 1) In 1945, few businessmen would have [14] risked their reputations for clear thinking by [22] predicting the appearance in offices of elec- [29] tronic data processing. Today, many of those [37] same men could not make the decisions they [44] do without the aid of a computer system. In [52] fact, electronic data processing has become so [60] commonplace that anyone who works in an [67] office must know how the system works if he [74] is to understand his job. (¶ 2) Three basic [83] steps. Stripped of its glamour and mystery, [91] the computer system includes the following [98] basic steps: (*Indent 10 spaces from both margins and SS these items.*) [101]

1. The input or source data are written [109] into the system. DS [112]

2. The data are processed within the [118] system. [120]

3. The end result or output is written [128] out.[1] [129]

(¶ 3) Input and output media. Data process- [139] ing machines do not generally read regular [147] print. Input data, therefore, can be recorded [155] in cards and paper tape as punched holes; on [162] magnetic tape, discs, or drums as magnetized [170] spots; on documents as characters printed in [177] magnetic ink or printed in certain type fonts.[2] [186] The processed data coming from the computer [193] are printed on paper or recorded in cards, in [201] paper tape, or on magnetic tape. Special units [209] can convert recorded data from one medium [216] to another automatically. (¶ 4) Data entering [223] the system are stored, sorted, and analyzed. [230] Calculations are performed. These functions [238] are performed by three major units of the [245] computer; namely, the storage, control, and [252] processing (arithmetic) units. (¶ 5) The stor- [259] age feature is the unique characteristic of elec- [267] tronic computers. Two types of information [275] are stored in the computer: (1) the data to [282] be processed and (2) the detailed instructions [290] needed to process them, commonly referred to [298] as the program. (¶ 6) Control unit. When [308] processing starts, each instruction in a pro- [315] gram that has been stored in the computer [322] enters the control unit where it is interpreted [330] and carried out.[3] It is obvious that the pro- [338] gram must be carefully worked out in detail [345] if chaos is to be avoided, as the computer [352] works with lightning speed. (¶ 7) Processing [361] unit. Computations are made in the process- [369] ing unit of the computer. Any problem for [376] which a program can be devised can be solved; [384] but to obtain the correct answer, the steps in [392] the program must be carefully and logically set [400] down. [401]

---

[1] S. J. Wanous, E. E. Wanous, and A. E. Hughes, Introduction to Automated Data Processing (Cincinnati: South-Western Publishing Co., 1968), p. 97. (*35 words*)

[2] John J. W. Neuner and B. Lewis Keeling, Administrative Office Management (5th ed.; Cincinnati: South-Western Publishing Co., 1966), p. 709. (*29 words*)

[3] Ibid., p. 711. (*7 words*)

Job 3: Composing

Prepare five or six good discussion questions to use as a second page for the outline (Job 1). Be sure the questions can be answered from the facts included in the outline. Title the questions QUESTIONS ON AUTOMATED SYSTEMS and arrange them attractively on the page. Do not number the page.

LESSON 54

54A **Preparatory Practice** ⑦ *each line three times; then 1' writings on Lines 2 and 4*

Alphabet	Jane Fox owns a copy of the book Zelma Quade has given to all members.
Figures	On May 5, we added 7 stations: 358, 359, 360, 361, 362, 363, and 364.
Figure-symbol	Send the following items: 3 sets K-217F @ $6.75; 4 prs. M826 @ $9.20.
Fluency	We mailed your statement to the address given on the card you sent us.

| 1 | 2 | 3 | 4 | 5 | 6 | 7 | 8 | 9 | 10 | 11 | 12 | 13 | 14 |

54B **Growth Index** ⑧ *one 5' writing; determine* gwam *and errors*

All letters are used.

		GWAM 1'	5'	

¶ 1
1.4 SI
5.4 AWL
85% HFW

If climbing the ladder to success is vital to you, you possess an advantage over many who have no strong feeling one way or the other. This is just as true in college as it is on the job. Your instructors can guide you, but you must do the work. History is filled to the brim with great men who had harsh strikes against them in health, education, and even intelligence. But one asset they did possess. They wanted to learn; they wanted to win the prize; they expected to reach their goal. Desire and action are effective qualities. Put them to work for you immediately.

1'	5'	
13	3	49
27	5	52
42	8	55
56	11	57
70	14	60
85	17	63
99	20	66
113	22	68
116	23	69

¶ 2
1.4 SI
5.4 AWL
85% HFW

Do you ever feel that you are in the wrong place as you try to master a difficult problem or succeed in a new job? You usually have these feelings because you have not prepared well enough. The way to eliminate the difficulty is to master every new learning and every new skill that will help you past some hurdle that may lie ahead. Do you think you might want to establish your own business some day? Then learn to analyze; learn to communicate well; learn to make decisions. Improve each of the skills required in your work or study, and you will feel in the right place.

1'	5'	
13	26	72
27	28	75
41	31	78
55	34	80
69	37	83
82	40	86
97	42	89
111	45	92
116	46	93

1' GWAM | 1 | 2 | 3 | 4 | 5 | 6 | 7 | 8 | 9 | 10 | 11 | 12 | 13 | 14 |
5' GWAM | 1 | 2 | 3 |

54C **Problem Typing Measurement:** Tables and Word Division ㉟

Get Ready to Type	5'
Timed Production	25'
Proofread	5'

Type the problem at the right and those on page 95 as directed. Correct errors as you type. Give each problem a quick final check *before you remove it from the typewriter* and correct any errors you have not already corrected.

Problem 1: Word Division

Half sheet; line: 60; DS; 1" top margin; columnar spacing as indicated

			Words
PREFERRED POINTS TO DIVIDE WORDS			7
Word	**Syllables**	**Divide**	15
advertisement	ad/ver/tise/ment	adver-tise-ment	24
agreements			31
carefully			38
determination	*(Indicate all syl-*	*(Indicate preferred*	48
self-propelled	*lables for all*	*division point or*	57
synonymous	*words.)*	*points for all words.)*	64

KEY | 14 | 6 | 17 | 6 | 16 |

Job 1: Outline

1½" top, 1" side margins

	Words
DATA PROCESSING SYSTEMS	5
I. UNIT RECORD SYSTEM	9
A. Application	13
1. Tabulation of information	19
2. Recording, transmitting, computing, and reproducing information	31
tion by punched tapes or cards	37
B. Components of System	42
1. Keypunch machine	47
2. Verifier	49
3. Sorter	51
4. Calculator	54
5. Tabulator	57
II. INTEGRATED DATA PROCESSING SYSTEM	65
A. Application	68
1. Processing and transmitting data to other machines	79
2. Use of items of recorded data repeatedly for various purposes	91
poses	92
B. Components of System	97
1. Tape- or card-punching typewriter	105
2. Teletypewriter	109
III. ELECTRONIC DATA PROCESSING SYSTEM	117
A. Application	120
1. Processing data in a continuous chain from input item to final	133
printed document	137
2. Storing data for repeated use when needed	146
B. Components of System	151
1. Equipment to produce input items	158
a. Office machines (typewriters, calculators, cash registers)	171
that produce punched tape	176
b. Office machines that produce printed tape	185
c. Keypunch machines that produce punched cards	195
2. Input units	198
a. Tape readers	202
b. Optical Character Readers	208
c. Punched-card readers	213
3. Control center	217
4. Central processing unit	222
5. External storage unit	227
6. Printer-output unit	232

Problem 2: Memo with Table

Half sheet; 65-space line; block style; SS; begin on Line 7; leave 8 spaces between columns

Add the following headings over the three columns: Year, Winner, NWAM.

February 28, 19-- | SUBJECT: Some Typewriting Champions | (¶ 1) Championship typewriting contests were great sport for typewriter companies during the first half of the 20th century. The highest speeds attained in these one-hour contests are given below.

1922	George Hossfield	144
1923	Albert Tangora	147
1941	Margaret Hamma	149

(¶ 2) Winners of other contests (at lower speeds or for shorter periods of time) include: Stella Pejunas, Cortez Peters, Grace Phelan, Norman Saksvig, and Stella Willins.

Words count: 11, 25, 41, 50, 55, 60, 65, 78, 92, 98

Problem 3: Letter with Table

Modified block, blocked ¶s; open punctuation; return address on Line 11; 60-space line; center table, leaving 4 spaces between columns

Words

761 Fairfield Avenue | Bridgeport, Connecticut 06604 | February 28, 19-- Dr. John B. Sheppard | Educational Services, Inc. | 240 Madison Avenue | New York, New York 10016 | Dear Dr. Sheppard

(¶ 1) The series of typewriting workshops you conducted during the past year proved to be most rewarding and motivating to Connecticut teachers. It was reassuring to see that your skill-building procedures had a dual base: experimental as well as experiential.

(¶ 2) Please send the indicated number of copies of the three items you used in demonstrating effective teaching procedures.

20	Timed Homework Practice Record, T	$20.00
25	High-Speed Typewriting Drills	6.25
2	Guided Writing Record, T	4.00

(¶ 3) The teachers in Trumbull High School were most enthusiastic about being able to give more guided writings without depending on a stopwatch to indicate quarter-minute guides. We plan to make one of the guided writing records available to students for extra practice in one of our small typewriting labs.

(¶ 4) I know you travel nationally to help teachers improve typewriting instruction, but I hope your schedule will permit you to return to Connecticut soon to demonstrate again that "learning can be fun."

Cordially yours | Howard Prentice

Words count: 13, 26, 36, 49, 64, 79, 88, 101, 112, 121, 129, 136, 149, 163, 177, 192, 197, 210, 223, 237, 243

Problem 4: Table on Postal Card

Type the table in Problem 2 on a postal card (or on paper cut to that size: 5½" x 3¼"), using SOME TYPEWRITING CHAMPIONS as the main heading. Leave 4 spaces between columns. DS the items in the table.

Words

on cards with a pencil. Marked cards similar 499
to those used in the punched-card process acti- 508
vate the machine. This method makes it pos- 516
sible to record data on cards in the plant or 526
field, thus eliminating the rewriting of these 535
records in the office. (¶ 8) Magnetic tape. 546
Information recorded on tapes similar to those 555
used in ordinary tape recorders can be read 564
and processed by certain electronic data pro- 572
cessing equipment. Magnetized spots, which 581
are invisible, create electronic impulses that 591
tell the computer what to do. (¶ 9) Magnetic 600
ink characters. Some of the machines that 612
can process printed data require that informa- 621
tion be printed in distinctive style in magnetic 631
ink. Such a procedure is often used by banks 640
for handling checks and deposits. The numer- 649
ical information on these forms is printed in a 658
style that the human eye may find difficult to 668
decipher. (¶ 10) Data processing by automa- 675
tion begins with the information in plain 683
language. It ends in a report or business 692
paper in plain language. Between these two 701
steps, however, the data must often be con- 709
verted to some code that can be understood 718
by the data processing equipment being used. 727

Job 2: Composing

After you have completed typing Mr. Ogden's notes, type five or six questions that could be answered by anyone who read or listened to the material in the notes. Use the heading DISCUSSION QUESTIONS, and position the material to match the style used in typing the notes. Attach the questions as the final page of the notes with two staples. Be sure to number the page as you did the others.

LESSON 168

168A Preparatory Practice (5) *each line at least three times*

Alphabet	Faye Wilken capitalized quite a bit on her deluxe Jamaican Glove Shop.
Figure-symbol	Please call 370–6291 between 5:15 and 8:40 p.m. Saturday for the data.
Double letters	I planned to accept a better offer unless the matter was soon settled.
Fluency	To type in the right way, one must get rid of the jerks in his typing.
	| 1 | 2 | 3 | 4 | 5 | 6 | 7 | 8 | 9 | 10 | 11 | 12 | 13 | 14 |

168B Paragraph Guided Writings (10)

1. Type a 1′ writing on the *control level* to establish your base rate.
2. Type three additional 1′ writings; try to reach the exact letter of your base rate in each writing.
3. Raise your rate 8 words. Type three or four 1′ writings; try to reach the exact letter of the new rate.

5.8 AWL
1.6 SI
75% HFW

Some words will produce miracles as readily as others will result in disagreement or enmity. Words create ideas that otherwise would not exist. Every time you write or talk, you may be saying or writing a thought which had not been phrased just that way before. Think of the potential that is yours if you capitalize on chances to develop an adequate vocabulary to express your own creative ideas.

● Self-Improvement Practice: Alertness Training

5 half sheets; 70-space line; DS; 5-space ¶ indention; 1½" top margin

In Alertness Training you must pay attention to what is typed and to do what you are told to do in the sentence you type. Always type the entire sentence before you follow any directions given in the sentence you are typing.

For example, the second sentence of Alertness Training 1 directs you to type the first sentence again at a speed slower than your first typing. As the third sentence, then, retype the first sentence; then continue to type the paragraph.

1 Type at a speed that is well within your zone of control. Type the first sentence again, but type at a speed that is 8 to 10 words slower than your first typing. Type with quiet, even stroking. Underline the preceding sentence with an unbroken line; then start a new paragraph. Center and type the next sentence in all capital letters on a separate line, with a blank line space before it, and without typing the period. Think as you type.

2 Pay attention to what you type. Move the carriage to the first word of the paragraph, and type over the first sentence. Without changing the margin stops, type the next sentence on one line to begin 5 spaces outside the left margin and with a double space before it. It is the duty of a typist to check each typed page and to correct all errors.

3 Center ACTION TYPING 3 as a heading a triple space above this line, remembering to release the shift lock before typing the figure 3. When typing, underline words that are printed in *italics*, so underline the italicized word in this sentence. Beginning at the left margin a double space below this completed sentence, type the alphabet in all capitals and the figures 1 to 10, with a space after each letter and figure; then remove the paper, reinsert it to type on the reverse side, and type your own return address and current date in correct position for a 60-space line personal letter.

4 Lock the shift key when you type the next sentence in all capital letters. Type with ease. Add an exclamation point to the preceding sentence. Position the carriage and underline the second sentence; then reposition the carriage and continue to type the paragraph. As you type the next sentence, correct the misspelled words. The reply to our questionnaire does not warrant our recommending him for promotion. Remove the paper, reinsert it, and type over the first word of the paragraph.

5 Center and type your name in all capital letters a triple space above this line. Type the following sentence as rapidly as you can type with a sense of ease and control. It is up to me to build my skill in typing to as high a level as possible. Remove the paper, reinsert it, and type over your name centered above the paragraph; then continue to type the remainder of this paragraph. Center and type the current date a double space below this line.

167B Communication Aid: Spelling ⑩

1. Type the words in double-spaced columns, a separate column for each section; but as you type each word, make the change indicated at the left.

2. Check your work with your instructor; then type the words a second time, incorporating any necessary changes.

Adding

dine cross-section permit chase run forget get quiz enclose rattle appraise remit fascinate begin refer

Change to past tense

intern combat* equip collect quarrel* prescribe transmit circumvent answer mail punish commit offend travel* pay

Change to plural

niece century stencil by-pass footnote employee press copy brother-in-law premise alumnus calf analysis frogman basis

*There are two equally correct spellings of the past tense of these words.

167C Production Typing: Manuscript; Composition ㉟

First page: 2" top margin

Production Job: Unbound Manuscript

NOTES ON OFFICE AUTOMATION — 5

Wendell E. Ogden — 9

(¶ 1) <u>Chief aim of automation</u>. Automation in the office attempts to eliminate the handling and writing of records countless times in order to get needed information or to make reports available. Automation cuts down or eliminates manual duplication. The exact procedure for doing this will vary from system to system. Certain of these systems will be discussed at a later time. (¶ 2) Throughout our discussions, however, you should keep in mind that "automatic" office systems are never wholly automatic. They depend upon humans. Someone must gather data, prepare them for use in a form the machinery can handle, and interpret the results. Without intelligent direction, even the most sophisticated equipment loses its utility. (¶ 3) <u>Codes and input media</u>. Some equipment—the Optical Character Reader, for example—can "read" printed information; usually, however, special codes are used. Such codes are made a part of a medium upon which the machine feeds. Examples of such media are punched cards, magnetized tape, mark-sensed cards, and the special business forms that have been printed

21 31 40 49 58 66 75 84 92 101 110 119 127 136 145 154 165 174 183 192 201 209 217 226 235

with magnetic ink. (¶ 4) <u>Punched cards and tape</u>. Machines can interpret and process data that have been punched as holes in cards. The punched card is so widely used for this purpose that it is often referred to as the "workhorse of automation." (¶ 5) The holes in the cards represent figures and letters of the alphabet. Once data have been punched into cards, the machines can sort, classify, calculate, and print the data. As a rule, anyone who can operate a typewriter or a 10-key adding machine has the skill needed to punch the holes into the cards. (¶ 6) Machines can also interpret and process information punched as holes in paper tape. Paper tape is a continuous medium, whereas punched cards are of fixed length. The holes punched in paper tape appear in real or imaginary channels that run the length of the tape. Each vertical row of punches represents one letter, digit, or symbol. The tapes are usually produced simultaneously with the completion of a document on a typewriter, billing machine, calculator, or other piece of equipment. This tape is then fed into equipment that can perform additional functions with it, such as calculating and printing. (¶ 7) <u>Mark-sensed cards</u>. Some machines can read and process data marked

246 256 265 274 283 291 300 308 317 327 336 345 353 362 371 379 388 398 407 416 425 434 443 452 460 470 481 489

Purpose. To learn to type business letters neatly and quickly, to prepare carbon copies, to address envelopes, and to fold letters.

Machine Adjustments. Line: 70, unless otherwise directed; SS drills and problems; DS and indent timed writing ¶s 5 spaces.

Self-Improvement Practice. Type phrases of 55B, below, of 57B, page 100, of 58B, page 102, or the Self-Improvement Practice, page 107.

LESSON 55

55A   Preparatory Practice (7) *each line three times; then 1' writings on Line 4*

Alphabet   Dr. Robert Wachs received a quaint onyx ring from Jack Pelz of Venice.

Figures   Please turn to page 350 and answer Items 2, 4, 6, 7, 8, 9, 10, and 16.

Symbol-shift   "Have sunglow all winter," she said, "with a Magic Sun Lamp by Solco."

Fluency   It is the wish of the chairman to have all the workmen at the meeting.
                | 1 | 2 | 3 | 4 | 5 | 6 | 7 | 8 | 9 | 10 | 11 | 12 | 13 | 14 |

55B   Technique Practice: Response Patterns (10) *each line once from the book, twice from dictation*

The phrases presented below and in subsequent lessons are among those most often used in business communication. Learn to type them rapidly and accurately.

Technique Cue: Read a phrase with one sweep of the eye and type it as a unit, with no perceptible pause between words. *Space quickly.*

to you | to your | to our | to have | to him | like to | to be | of the | in the | to us
to the | for the | on the | with the | and the | from the | that the | at the | by the
is the | you will | you have | you are | you can | and you | that you | to you | it is
for your | of your | to your | in your | we are | we have | we will | we would | to be
of the | of our | this is | of this | one of | we can | in this | should be | that the
if you | with you | that you | may be | do not | in our | in your | can be | have been

55C   Drill on Assembling and Inserting a Carbon Pack (13) *full sheet; Line: 65; SS; 3" top margin*

1. Read ¶ 1 below and assemble a carbon pack as directed there.

2. Read ¶ 2, then insert the pack as instructed.

3. Type the following material in the form illustrated.

Copy sheet
Carbon paper
Original

		Words
ASSEMBLY AND INSERTION OF A CARBON PACK		8

TS

After typing the first line, reset left margin stop 4 spaces in.

		Words
1.	Place the sheet on which the file (or carbon) copy is to be	21
	made flat on the desk; then place a sheet of carbon paper,	33
	carbon side down, on top of the paper. (If you desire more	48
	than one carbon copy, add another plain sheet and another	60
	carbon sheet for each copy.) Finally, place the sheet for	72
	the original on top of the carbon paper.	80

Use the margin release and backspace 4 times to type "2."

		Words
2.	Pick up the papers and tap them lightly on the desk (with the	94
	glossy side of the carbon paper toward you); then insert the	106
	pack into the machine (carbon side toward you as you insert	125
	the papers). Roll the pack in far enough for the feed rolls	139
	to grip the papers; finally, operate the paper-release lever	151
	to release the pressure and eliminate the wrinkles.	161

166C Typing Figures [10] *use 165D, page 282*

Preliminary Information

When specific directions are unavailable, it becomes necessary to study a job carefully before you begin to type it. Check first for known facts about the job. The instructions for binding a manuscript, for example, indicate the margin settings to be used. The preliminary instructions that are given before the first lesson of a section will help you with other decisions.

Your primary responsibility will be to place material on a page in such a way that it will be attractive and easy to use. Learn to be a critical judge of your own work.

166D Production Typing: Interoffice Memorandum; Notice [20]

Job 1: Interoffice Memorandum

Words

TO: Henry E. Erb **FROM:** Allen M. Woods 6
DATE: July 19, 19-- **SUBJECT:** Course for 13
Employees in Automated Data Processing 18

(¶ 1) Upon receipt of your memorandum of 25
July 10, our department began a study to de- 34
termine the need for and the feasibility of 43
offering an in-plant training course in data 52
processing for our office employees. (¶ 2) 59
Wendell Ogden and Arthur Webb assisted me 68
in surveying the staff as to their wishes about 77
such a course. Many of them were highly in 86
favor of participating in an ADP class (as you 96
said you thought they would be) and indicated 105
they would be willing to remain after work if 114
necessary if the class time did not extend be- 123
yond six o'clock. (¶ 3) Accordingly, beginning 131
September 6 and running until December 13, 140
the three of us will hold a two-hour lecture- 149
and-discussion meeting every Thursday after- 158
noon from four until six in the staff lounge. 167
In a sense, the firm is "giving" an hour of 176
working time that the employee will match 184
with an hour of his own time. (¶ 4) We hope 192
you will join us for as many of these meetings 202
as you can. 205

Job 2: Notice of Course in Data Processing

Using the interoffice memorandum you completed for Job 1 as your source document, type an announcement for the bulletin board that gives the important details about the course in automated data processing. Use a full sheet; make the notice brief, attractive, and informative.

LESSON 167

167A Preparatory Practice [5] *each line at least three times*

Alphabet	A zoo keeper showed Joan a very big ox, a calf, and some little quail.
Figure-symbol	Order #5719 from Adams & Robb for 830 pens was filled on May 24, 1969.
Double letters	Billie Williams is planning to accept all offers for swimming lessons.
Fluency	Though it is not an easy job, you can learn to type a word as a whole.

| 1 | 2 | 3 | 4 | 5 | 6 | 7 | 8 | 9 | 10 | 11 | 12 | 13 | 14 |

55D Building Speed and Control ⑳

1. Type each of the following ¶s as two 1′ writings, once for *speed* and once for *control*.

2. Use all three ¶s for two 5′ writings. Determine *gwam* and errors for the better writing.

All letters are used.

	GWAM 1′	5′	

¶ 1
1.4 SI
5.4 AWL
85% HFW

Words are the tools we use to communicate. They must be selected — 13 | 3 | 33
wisely and used with care. A short, simple word is generally preferred — 28 | 6 | 36
to a long one. You must not, however, be afraid to use any word that — 42 | 8 | 39
conveys the precise meaning you want to get across. — 52 | 10 | 41

¶ 2
1.4 SI
5.4 AWL
85% HFW

Be quick to realize that a large vocabulary is vital to success- — 13 | 13 | 44
ful writing. The more extensive your store of usable words and word — 27 | 16 | 46
meanings, the more precise your message is likely to be. On the topic — 41 | 19 | 49
of words, be sure you have the right ones at hand. — 51 | 21 | 51

¶ 3
1.4 SI
5.4 AWL
85% HFW

You must try hard to build a good vocabulary. You must read ex- — 13 | 23 | 54
tensively, look up the meanings of unfamiliar words, and actively use — 27 | 26 | 57
those words. In this way you can learn to produce quickly the exact — 41 | 29 | 59
word to get just the effect you seek in your writing. — 51 | 31 | 62

1′ GWAM | 1 | 2 | 3 | 4 | 5 | 6 | 7 | 8 | 9 | 10 | 11 | 12 | 13 | 14 |
5′ GWAM | 1 | 2 | 3 |

LESSON 56

56A Preparatory Practice ⑦ *each line three times; then 1′ writings on Line 4*

Alphabet Daryl Javits was quick to pick a green Mercedes–Benz for his next car.
Figures Fred had 160 at the 3-, 5-, and 7-day workshops on June 8, 14, and 29.
Symbol-shift Is the notation on this memorandum Bob's, Neal's, Chuck's, or R. D.'s?
Fluency The right chance at the right time may make a big profit for the firm.
| 1 | 2 | 3 | 4 | 5 | 6 | 7 | 8 | 9 | 10 | 11 | 12 | 13 | 14 |

56B Building Speed and Control ⑳ *repeat 55D, above*

56C Problem Typing: Business Letters in Modified Block Style ㉓

1. Study Style Letter 2, page 99. Note the placement of the date and the closing lines. Read the brief explanation of *mixed punctuation*.

2. Use a 60-space line; modified block style with block paragraphs; mixed punctuation; date on Line 14.

3. Set a tabulator stop at the horizontal center point to indent to the position for typing the date and the closing lines.

4. When the letter has been typed once, make pencil corrections as needed; then retype the letter, *preparing two carbon copies*.

	GWAM 1'	3'	
added knowledge about business management can be found in small	13	4	46
bits of information that can be taken from a variety of sources. the	27	9	50
alert manager will hold an isolated item for use here or there in solv-	41	14	55
ing his companys problems. the paragraph below is a good example of	55	18	60
these "bits of knowledge.	60	20	62
growth and profits require the use of written policies. contrary	13	24	66
to some executive opinion they are not a straitjacket. they do not	27	29	71
lessen flexibility nor immobilize a company with delayed decisions. they	42	34	75
may be twisted ignored and left to age but a good policy is still one	56	39	80
of the best tools the manager can have.	64	41	83

1' GWAM | 1 | 2 | 3 | 4 | 5 | 6 | 7 | 8 | 9 | 10 | 11 | 12 | 13 | 14 |
3' GWAM | 1 | 2 | 3 | 4 | 5 |

165F Creative Timed Writing [5]

70-space line

Using the general subject "My School," type for three minutes about your high school or the college you are attending. Type your thoughts as freely as you can; and when time is called, estimate (14 words to a line) your *gwam*.

LESSON 166

166A Preparatory Practice [5] *each line at least three times*

Alphabet	David Jackson will take the final quiz in geography before next month.
Figure-symbol	Henry ordered 57 copies at 8¢ each, 36 at 9¢ each, and 24 at 10¢ each.
Drill on min	The minister was mindful that the minor spent a minimum of one minute.
Fluency	Experience is a great teacher and also part of the pay I get for work.

| 1 | 2 | 3 | 4 | 5 | 6 | 7 | 8 | 9 | 10 | 11 | 12 | 13 | 14 |

166B Communication Aid: Capitalization and Punctuation [15] *continue as directed in 165E, page 282*

	GWAM 1'	3'	
if a company allows the higher costs of benefits--especially for	13	4	51
medical provisions to keep older workers off its payroll it may be	27	9	56
making a most serious mistake in judgment. an expert who has studied	41	14	61
the pros and cons of hiring capable senior citizens says that such	54	18	65
workers are worthy of the increases in payroll costs that may result.	68	23	70
all men who want victory in the business arena must learn to use	13	27	74
psychology. pleasing customers creating on the job harmony knowing	27	32	79
the exact time to ask for a raise giving credit where it is due and	41	36	83
asking advice from your assistant are situations that call for applica-	55	41	88
tions of psychology. psychology in short is the oil that can make a	69	46	93
firm run smoothly.	73	47	94

1' GWAM | 1 | 2 | 3 | 4 | 5 | 6 | 7 | 8 | 9 | 10 | 11 | 12 | 13 | 14 |
3' GWAM | 1 | 2 | 3 | 4 | 5 |

		Words in Parts	5' GWAM

Begin date at center on Line 14

Date line   October 20, 19--   3   1

3 blank lines (4th line space)

Address
Miss Janet Wellington   8   2
Republic Supply Company   13   3
2670 Queen City Avenue   17   4
Cincinnati, OH 45238   22   5
DS

Salutation
Dear Miss Wellington: 26   6
DS

Body
The modified block style has some distinctive features, as   12   8
shown by this letter and described in the enclosed pamphlet.   24   10

The date, complimentary close, and name and official title of   37   12
the dictator are begun at the horizontal center of the page.   49   15
These can be placed correctly with one tabulator adjustment.   61   17

Special lines (reference, enclosure, and carbon copy notations)   74   20
are placed at the left margin, a double space below the last   86   22
of the closing lines. If the dictator's name is part of the   99   25
closing lines, only the typist's initials are required in the   111   27
reference. If the dictator's initials are used, they precede   123   30
those of the typist and are usually typed in capital letters.   136   32

The modified block style, about which you inquired yesterday,   148   35
is widely used by the clients for whom we prepare letters.   160   37
We think you will like it, too.   167   38

Complimentary close   Sincerely yours,   3   39

3 blank lines (4th line space)

Randall B. Parkhurst (signature)

Typed name   Randall B. Parkhurst   8   40
Official title   Communications Director   12   41
                                            DS

Reference initials   lkd   13   41
                         DS
Enclosure notation   Enclosure   15   42
                         DS
Carbon copy notation cc Mr. John R. Rodgers, Jr.   21   43

STYLE LETTER 2: *Modified Block Style, Block Paragraphs; Mixed Punctuation (Typed in Pica Type)*

Mixed Punctuation. With *mixed punctuation*, as illustrated above, a colon follows the salutation and a comma follows the complimentary close.

Open Punctuation. With *open punctuation*, no punctuation follows the opening and closing lines unless one of them ends with an abbreviation.

SECTION 27 TYPING IN A TECHNICAL OFFICE

LESSONS 165–174

Drill Copy: Full sheet; 70-space line; SS
Paragraph Copy: Full sheet; 70-space line; DS; 5-space ¶ indention.
Production Copy: For interoffice memorandums, use blocked ¶s; SS. For manuscripts, use margins appropriate to binding instructions given; DS; make no carbon copies unless so instructed.
Special Materials: Full sheets, 5 x 3 cards, interoffice-memorandum forms, special business forms (such as invoices, requisitions, purchase orders) as required.

LESSON 165

165A Preparatory Practice (5) *each line at least three times*

Alphabet	By refining techniques, Jane will realize excellent skill development.
Figure-symbol	Flight #679 leaving here at 12:30 is scheduled to reach Berne at 8:45.
Drill on eve	Almost everyone eventually attends these events––even in the evenings.
Fluency	When writing a term paper, be concise; for there is no weight to wind.

| 1 | 2 | 3 | 4 | 5 | 6 | 7 | 8 | 9 | 10 | 11 | 12 | 13 | 14 |

165B Skill-Comparison Typing (5) *each line of 165A for a 1′ writing; compare* gwam

165C Building Control (10) *each line three times without error*

1	Adjacent fingers	George Fervre decided to try for a record number (67) of hurdle jumps.
2	3d, 4th fingers	At six o'clock, Professor Cryzer arose; he smiled. Was the quiz over?
3	One hand	Kimon dreaded seeing me trade my best pony cart for Polly's Essex car.
4	Double letters	I am sorry we cannot keep the dresses referred to in your last letter.
5	Long reaches	I was undoubtedly nervous until the mysterious symbols were uncovered.
6	Shift keys	Mr. Clarence R. Collins left New York for Rome in either June or July.
7	Long words	Several honor students recently compiled comprehensive bibliographies.
8	Stroke response	The manager heartily subscribes to the philosophy expressed yesterday.
9	Word recognition	When he finds that he has to pay on time, he will find a way to do it.
10	Combination	As you see, the auditor's office is no longer located in the building.

| 1 | 2 | 3 | 4 | 5 | 6 | 7 | 8 | 9 | 10 | 11 | 12 | 13 | 14 |

165D Typing Figures (10) *70-space line; SS*

Type two 3′ writings, starting with the number 11 and alternating consecutive numbers with the word *and* as shown below. If you reach 100 before time is called, begin again with 11.

Scoring: From the last number (or total number if you started to repeat) in your writing, deduct 1 for each error. Try to improve your score on the second writing.

11 and 12 and 13 and 14 and 15 and 16 and 17 and 18 and 19 and 20 and
21 and 22 and 23 and 24 and 25 and 26 and 27 and 28 and 29 and 30 and

165E Communication Aid: Capitalization and Punctuation (15)

1. Read the ¶s at the top of page 283; then type them with correct capitalization and punctuation.
2. Check your corrected ¶s with your instructor. Using your corrected copy, type two 1′ writings from each ¶.
3. From the book, type two 1′ writings from each ¶. Compare *gwam*.

LESSON 57

57A Preparatory Practice ⑦ *each line three times; then 1' writings on Line 4*

Alphabet   Hal's quick flip to the Bronx end zone went just above Myers' fingers.

Figures   Invoices 4997 and 5023, both dated November 16, are due on December 8.

Figure-symbol   Lenz & O'Brien's Invoice #4956 for $738 (less 2% discount) is now due.

Fluency   May five of the big men work with the foreman for the next eight days?

| 1 ' 2 | 3 | 4 | 5 | 6 | 7 | 8 | 9 | 10 | 11 | 12 | 13 | 14 |

57B Technique Practice: Response Patterns ⑦ *each line once from the book, twice from dictation*

I am | I have | I would | I will | I hope | I can | that I | that we | and we | with you

will be | would be | to us | to make | to do | to me | able to | as to | is to | wish to

up to | and to | as the | about the | have the | you may | you would | as you | is not

for you | from you | with your | on your | and your | we do | we hope | if we | all of

which we | as we | not be | as to | be able | be in | is to | is in | there is | are not

57C Guides for Erasing Original and File Copies ⑬ *full sheet; Line: 65; SS; 3" top margin*

Make 1 carbon copy: original
carbon sheet
file copy sheet

First, study the Guides below. Then erase and correct any errors you make as you type the Guides as shown. Before removing the paper from the typewriter, proofread; then correct any errors not already corrected.

                                                   Words

GUIDES FOR ERASING ORIGINAL AND FILE COPIES   9

TS

After typing the first line, reset left margin stop 4 spaces in.

1. Move the carriage to the extreme left or right to prevent   21
eraser crumbs from falling into the well of the typewriter.   33
(This step is not necessary on the Selectric.)   43

2. Pull the original sheet forward and place a 5" x 3" card   56
(or one slightly larger) in front of the first carbon sheet.   68

3. Return the original sheet and make the erasure on it with a   81
hard (typewriter) eraser. Brush the eraser crumbs away from   93
the typewriter. An eraser shield is helpful but not essential.   106

4. Remove the protective card (unless more than one carbon copy   120
is being made, in which case place the card in front of the   132
second carbon sheet). With a soft (pencil) eraser, erase the   144
error on the carbon (file) copy.   151

164C Production Measurement ③⓪ 25′ typing; figure n-pram

N-PRAM. *N-pram* (net production rate a minute) refers to the rate on production copy on which errors are erased and corrected.

$$N\text{-}PRAM = \frac{\text{Gross (total) words} - \text{Penalties}}{\text{Length (in minutes) of writing}}$$

PENALTIES FOR UNCORRECTED ERRORS. Deduct the following penalties for errors not corrected during the production period:

Deduct 10 words......for each error not erased on an original copy

Deduct 5 words.......for each error not erased on a carbon copy

---

Job 1: Agenda for a Special Meeting *70-space line*

	Words
YOUNG MANUFACTURING COMPANY	6
Agenda for Special Meeting of the Board of Directors	16
June 29, 19--	19
1. Call to Order . . . . Wayne A. Young	33
2. Statement of Purpose . . . . Henry D. Rico	46
3. Special Reports ·	50
Proposal to Purchase Husse Patent . . . . David H. Van Zant	63
Proposal to Continue Company Research . . Douglas James	75
4. Discussion . . . . Henry D. Rico	88
5. Adjournment	91

Job 2: Interoffice Memorandum

	Words
TO: Board of Directors **FROM:** Wayne A.	6
Young, President **DATE:** June 22, 19-- **SUB-**	12
JECT: Special Meeting of June 29 (¶1) The	18
Board of Directors will hold a special meeting	27
on Friday, June 29. (¶2) We have received	35
a letter from Mr. Lawrence Husse, the holder	44
of a patent for a successful method of	52
striating metal rods, saying that he has de-	60
cided to sell his patent outright rather than	70
begin his own business. If our company is	78
interested, he will consider our bid. (¶3) As	87
you know, however, we have been perfecting	95
our own striating process with a considerable	104
investment of money in the venture. A deci-	113
sion needs to be made, and Mr. Van Zant and	122
Mr. James will present alternative proposals	131
for our consideration. (¶4) The meeting will	139
begin promptly at 1:30 in the Board Room.	148

Job 3: Letter on Executive-Size Stationery

	Words
july 2, 19-- mr lawrence husse 27 la brea	9
st billings mt 59102 dear mr husse (¶1)	18
Our Board of Directors has directed me to	26
inform you that Young Manufacturing Com-	34
pany will not at this time enter a bid for the	43
purchase of rights to your Patent #64068355.	52
(¶2) As you perhaps know, our company has	60
been working on a process that results in the	69
same type of striation as does that covered by	78
your patent; and the amount we have invested	87
to perfect our process, the Board feels, indi-	96
cates that we should complete the work. (¶3)	105
If, however, the bids you receive are unsatis-	114
factory, you may wish to propose a leasing-	122
agency arrangement. We shall be happy to	131
discuss any proposals you may care to	138
make. very truly yours wayne a young	146
president	149

Job 4: Agenda with Changes

Retype the Job 1 agenda. Substitute F. Eugene Young for Henry D. Rico.

57D Problem Typing: Business Letters in Modified Block Style ㉓

Problem 1

Line: 60; date on Line 14; standard spacing of 3 blank lines between date and address. After reviewing Style Letter 2, page 99, type the following letter. Erase and correct errors on the original and the file copy.

	Words
October 21, 19--	3

	Words
Mr. Gary R. Fischer, Office Manager	10
Wright–Patterson Manufacturing Co.	17
1867 Memorial Parkway	22
Newport, KY 41075	26

Dear Mr. Fischer:	29

Office Aides walk right in and help you out ^{38} during those rush periods when your work ^{46} piles up and your workers bog down. ^{54}

Whatever the paperwork bottleneck--order ^{62} handling, billing, letter or report preparation, ^{72} data processing--Office Aides, Inc., has a staff ^{82} of top-flight personnel to help you move the ^{91} work along with maximum efficiency. And ^{99} unlike many temporary-employee firms, Office ^{108} Aides will work wherever it is most conve- ^{116} nient for you--in your offices, or in ours. ^{127}

Although new to the Cincinnati area, Office ^{135} Aides, Inc., is well known and widely used in ^{145} New York, Chicago, Atlanta, and Miami. In ^{153} Cincinnati we have already supplied temporary ^{162} office help to such firms as General Plastics ^{172} Corp., Merry Toy Company, Queen City ^{179} Printing Company, and Hilton–Jennings. ^{187}

The enclosed brochure describes our services ^{196} and methods of operation. Get ready now for ^{205} your next rush season by dialing 271–8811 and ^{214} discussing your temporary-help needs with ^{223} Mr. Seybold, one of our work relations coordi- ^{232} nators. He is well qualified to fit the man ^{241} (or woman) to the job. ^{245}

Sincerely yours, ^{249}

John D. Morganroth ^{253}
Assistant Sales Manager ^{257}

slr ^{258}

Enclosure ^{260}

Problem 2

Line: 60; date on Line 14; standard spacing of 3 blank lines between date and address. Prepare two cc's, one for Mr. K. L. Stewart. Type the enclosure and carbon copy notations in the form illustrated on page 99.

	Words
October 21, 19--	3

	Words
Mr. N. K. Lenz, Office Manager	10
Product Development Corporation	16
1799 Woodburn Street	20
Covington, KY 41014	24

Dear Mr. Lenz:	28

Thank you for calling on us when you needed ^{36} additional office help recently. We hope you ^{46} liked Dianne O'Bannon's work as much as she ^{54} enjoyed working in your Sales Department. ^{63}

Although you have used only our stenographic ^{72} services so far, we have a number of people ^{81} qualified in other work areas: machine cal- ^{89} culation, data processing, accounting, and ^{98} duplicating. Please give us the opportunity ^{107} to serve you whenever peak work loads make ^{116} on-the-premises assistance desirable. ^{123}

The enclosed booklet describes the educational ^{133} and experience backgrounds of several mem- ^{141} bers of our traveling work force. These ^{149} thumbnail summaries are typical of those we ^{158} have on file for most of our "temporary assis- ^{167} tants." If we don't have on our regular staff ^{176} an employee who meets the requirements of ^{185} the job, we'll tell you so and try to find one ^{194} who does. You can depend on Office Aides! ^{203}

Sincerely yours, ^{206}

William R. Hathaway, Jr. ^{211}
Work Relations Coordinator ^{217}

slr ^{218}

Problem 3

If time permits, type two 1' writings on the opening lines and two 1' writings on the closing lines of Style Letter 2, page 99. Then type a 5' writing on the entire letter.

LESSON 164

164A Preparatory Practice [5] *each line at least three times*

Alphabet	My very quick expeditions to the African jungles will end in Zanzibar.
Figure-symbol	Use two dollar signs in such expressions: $169 to $350; $270 or $480.
Long words	The copying processes shown were verifax, thermography, and photocopy.
Fluency	The job is to use the right word in the right place at the right time.
	| 1 | 2 | 3 | 4 | 5 | 6 | 7 | 8 | 9 | 10 | 11 | 12 | 13 | 14 |

164B Growth Index [15] *two 5′* control-level *writings; figure* nwam

All letters are used.

		GWAM 1′	5′	
¶ 1	Seventy years ago we were living in a horse-and-buggy era; the	13	3	64
1.6 SI	conveniences of modern society were undeveloped. People who recall	26	5	67
5.8 AWL	those bygone days of uncertain, hazardous safaris over muddy roads may	40	8	70
75% HFW	question whether they were really alive at all. It is likely safe to	54	11	72
	believe that few are hankering to trade their present situation for a	68	14	75
	return to the good old days.	74	15	76
¶ 2	Today we are able to travel on our superhighways in luxury and ease	13	17	79
1.6 SI	or jet through the air at supersonic speeds. We can use fewer hours to	28	20	82
5.8 AWL	cross the continent than it formerly took for a shopping tour. Our	41	23	85
75% HFW	accomplishments in travel, as well as in any of a dozen other areas we	56	26	87
	can mention, have become possible largely through constantly increas-	69	29	90
	ing requirements of the consumer.	76	30	92
¶ 3	A consumer of goods plays a vital role in our economy. Without him	14	33	94
1.6 SI	to buy what is placed on the market, our economic system would surely	28	35	97
5.8 AWL	fail. In addition to the part he plays in buying goods, the consumer	42	38	100
75% HFW	has what is perhaps an even more significant function: By his wishes	56	41	103
	and demands, he indicates direction to the industrial world. He helps	70	44	105
	decide what commodities are manufactured.	78	46	107
¶ 4	At one time, manufacturers produced goods with hardly any attempt	13	48	110
1.6 SI	to discover what the buying public really wanted to buy. This rather	27	51	113
5.8 AWL	foolish procedure is surely no longer the case. A producer in today's	41	54	115
75% HFW	economy who scorns the needs and desires of his customers does so at	55	57	118
	his own risk. To be successful in a highly competitive market, he must	70	59	121
	serve the whims and caprices of the potential buyer.	80	62	123
1′ GWAM	| 1 | 2 | 3 | 4 | 5 | 6 | 7 | 8 | 9 | 10 | 11 | 12 | 13 | 14 |			
5′ GWAM	| 1 | 2 | 3 |			

LESSON 58

58A Preparatory Practice ⑦ *each line three times; then 1' writings on Line 4*

Alphabet   Jenny Nixon left my squad last week and gave back a prize she had won.

Figures   Gary reported on the following rooms: 6, 10, 18, 25, 27, 39, and 140.

Figure-symbol   Was his 4-year lease (May 23 expiration) renewed May 10 at a 5% boost?

Fluency   When the profit statement is in good form, take it to the tax auditor.

| 1 | 2 | 3 | 4 | 5 | 6 | 7 | 8 | 9 | 10 | 11 | 12 | 13 | 14 |

58B Technique Practice: Response Patterns ⑦ *each line once from the book, twice from dictation*

which is | of these | of course | amount of | number of | some of | part of | on our
it will | have to | for this | that this | at this | on this | to this | this letter
this matter | this time | that this | that it | so that | hope that | it was | if we
there are | it would | for this | that it | in order | will not | as you | thank you
as well | as well as | as soon | as soon as | we will | we will be | thank you for

58C Addressing a Large Envelope and Folding a Letter ⑥

Large envelopes (No. 10) are preferred for letters with enclosures and for letters of two or more pages.

Begin the address 2½″ from the top edge and 4″ from the left edge of the envelope. This placement meets the POD read-zone requirements for optical scanning, as illustrated below. The Post Office Department directs that *all* addresses be SS, regardless of the number of lines.

DO: Type an envelope from the illustration.

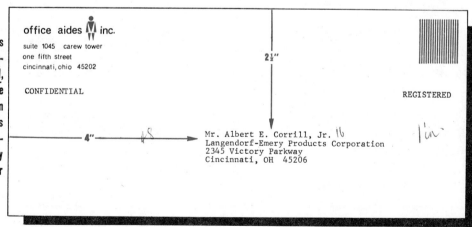

Type addressee notations (Hold for Arrival, Personal, Please Forward, and the like) a triple space below the return address and 3 spaces from left edge of envelope. The notations may be either underlined or typed in all capitals.

office aides inc.
suite 1045   carew tower
one fifth street
cincinnati, ohio 45202

CONFIDENTIAL

2½″

REGISTERED

Mr. Albert E. Corrill, Jr.
Langendorf-Emery Products Corporation
2345 Victory Parkway
Cincinnati, OH 45206

Begin mailing notations (AIRMAIL, SPECIAL DELIVERY, REGISTERED, and the like) below the stamp position and at least 3 line spaces above the envelope address. The notations should be typed in all capitals.

FOLDING A LETTER FOR A LARGE ENVELOPE

Step 1. With the letter face up on the desk, fold slightly less than one third of the letterhead up toward the top.

Step 2. Fold down the top of the letter to within ½″ of the bottom fold.

Step 3. Insert the letter into the envelope with the last crease toward the bottom of the envelope and with the last fold up.

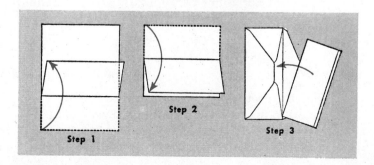

Step 1

Step 2

Step 3

Job 1: Approval Copy of a Cost Sheet

Prepare an approval copy of the form shown below; from it type a hectograph master so that the form can be duplicated. Side margins of 1½″ are suggested. You might also set the right margin to lock the machine where you want your lines to end. Center vertically. Indent the *total* lines 10 spaces from the left margin.

Words

TYPEWRITING PRODUCTION COST SHEET   7

Name of Typist _____   18

Date _____ Job Number _____ Page _____   29

Class Designation _____   40
                                                                63

Cost of all paper used to complete job: 71

_____ sheets at .02 a sheet $_____   80

Cost of carbon paper: 85

_____ sheets at .03 a sheet   _____   94

Charges for working time: 99

Time job was started: _____   105

Time job was finished: _____   112

Total minutes: _____ x .03   _____   120

Cost of writer's time (standardized):   2.50   132

Miscellaneous costs (standardized):   .05   143

Other costs (estimated):   _____   151

TOTAL JOB COST $_____   157

Signature of Typist _____   168

Note. The word count for this job will vary with the typists' use of the underline key for blank lines.

Job 2: Duplicating a Cost Sheet

Using the hectograph master prepared for Job 1, duplicate 30 to 50 copies of the form for your use in computing costs for future jobs. Save the master so that additional copies can be made as needed. Store the master carefully. To avoid smudging the carbon impression, dispose of the carbon sheet and fasten the second sheet to the back of the master in its original position.

58D Problem Typing: Business Letters with Large Envelopes ⓵⓪ *full sheets; Line: 60;* *date on Line 14*

Prepare two carbon copies and address a large envelope for each of the following letters. Erase and correct any errors you make as you type.

In Problem 1, note the use of *Mrs.* to indicate the dictator's marital status. In Problem 2, note that the listed items are indented 5 spaces from the left margin, are single-spaced with double spacing preceding and following; note, too, that two spaces follow the periods after the numbers. *Be sure to:* set a tabulator stop to indent the date and the closing lines; reset the left margin to type the listed items.

Problem 1

	Words
October 22, 19-- | Dr. Dorothy Crunk, Chair-	8
man | Department of Business Studies | Gate-	16
way Community College | Cincinnati, OH	23
45218 | Dear Dr. Crunk: |	28

We are processing the employment applica- 36
tion of Miss Arlene Spencer, who lists you as 45
one of her references. She completed her 53
training in your department this past June. 62

Our Office Aides must move frequently from 71
one assignment to another; therefore, a pros- 80
pective aide should possess great adaptability, 89
the ability to adjust immediately not only to 99
new situations but also to new employers and 108
to new co-workers. One of our interviewers 116
wonders whether Miss Spencer would be able 125
to adapt quickly enough. 130

Do your work-experience records contain any 139
information that would be helpful to us in 148
assessing Miss Spencer's likelihood of success 157
as one of our Office Aides? We shall appre- 166
ciate your giving us this information either 175
on the enclosed form or by telephone. 182

Sincerely yours, \| (Mrs.) Rhoda L. Lee \| 190
Personnel Officer \| lkd \| Enclosure \| cc Mr. 198
William R. Hathaway, Jr. 202/223*

*Includes envelope address.

Problem 2

	Words
October 22, 19-- | Mrs. Ellen K. Burroughs	8
9 Franklin Street | Middletown, OH 45042	16
Dear Mrs. Burroughs: |	21

If you will complete the enclosed work- 28
preference record and return it to us in the 37
postpaid envelope supplied for your conve- 46
nience, we shall place your name on our regis- 55
ter as an Office Aide. 59

Please fill in the form completely. It provides 69
spaces for you to indicate (among other items 78
of information): 82

  1. The date of your availability for 90
     assignment 92
  2. Your preference in work location 100
  3. Your preference in type of business 108
     operation 110

We are pleased to have you join our growing 119
staff of temporary office assistants. Upon 128
your success rests our own. We shall do 136
whatever we can to assure that mutual 144
success. 146

Sincerely yours, \| (Mrs.) Rhoda L. Lee \| Per- 154
sonnel Officer \| lkd \| Enclosure 159/172

Problem 3

Type the letter of Problem 2 again, but with the following changes:

	Words
Address: Miss Deborah Chisenhall	8
5687 Cincinnati Pike	12
Dayton, OH 45449	16
Salutation: Dear Miss Chisenhall:	20
Dictator: (Miss) Loraine Dorsey	153
Official Title: Personnel Assistant	157
Reference Line: Use your own initials	160/172

LESSON 59

59A Preparatory Practice ⑦ *each line three times; then 1' writings on Line 4*

Alphabet   David O. Whaley hopes to have a quick jet flight to Brazil next month.
Figures   Dial 926-5718 or 926-5739 to obtain your copy of this 40-page booklet.
Figure-symbol Won't the B & B (Bixler & Barnes) stock pay 4%, plus a $2.30 dividend?
Fluency   If you wish to write well, use those words that we all can understand.
| 1 | 2 | 3 | 4 | 5 | 6 | 7 | 8 | 9 | 10 | 11 | 12 | 13 | 14 |

Words

(No word count is given for the heading.)
(¶ 1) The Communications Committee is 6
happy to present its report suggesting some 15
simple methods for improving written com- 23
munications. (¶ 2) We are especially indebted 31
to the division managers who submitted their 40

Words

ideas for consideration. Where several sug- 48
gestions were closely related, they were com- 57
bined and adapted to the form used in this 66
report. (¶ 3) We hope the brief suggestions 74
presented will be helpful to all personnel en- 83
gaged in writing business communications. 91/102

Job 2: Approval Copy of Committee Report

Unbound manuscript style; indent enumerations from both margins; DS between items

Words

IMPROVING WRITTEN COMMUNICATIONS 7
George V. Bayly Company 11
(¶ 1) The growing concern of top manage- 18
ment in improving communications is appar- 26
ent in many of our leading publications. More 36
and more firms are beginning to realize how 44
losses in prestige and profits may result from 54
poor writing practices. The cost is often very 63
high. (¶ 2) The letter writer must become 71
competent in this vital area. He can improve 80
his communications abilities through careful 89
preparation and serious practice. The follow- 98
ing pointers can be of valuable assistance: 107

Words

1. Have before you the letter to be answered. 117
2. Collect all necessary data before you begin. 127
3. Make a brief outline, either mentally or with 137
a pencil, of the major points you wish to in- 145
clude in your message. 4. Organize these 154
points into the logical order of presentation. 164
5. Picture your reader as you write. 6. Use 173
clear, simple, courteous language. 7. Write 182
naturally, as if you were talking to your 191
reader. 8. Get to the heart of your message 200
quickly. 9. Remember that courtesy pays divi- 209
dends and that rudeness and disrespect do not. 218

Job 3: Composing an Interoffice Memorandum

Compose a short memorandum from you to the committee that prepared the Job 2 report. Provide an appropriate subject line. Express your appreciation for the report, and suggest some additional pointers that you believe might be added to the list that was given in the report.

LESSON 163

163A Preparatory Practice [5] *each line at least three times*

Alphabet	Jack Squires won the rich prize by driving many extra hours last fall.
Figures	The 396 boys labored at least 7,840 hours for 125 different employers.
Combination	Automatically or electrically typewritten letters must go first class.
Fluency	It is said that men who succeed are able to learn from their failures.

| 1 | 2 | 3 | 4 | 5 | 6 | 7 | 8 | 9 | 10 | 11 | 12 | 13 | 14 |

163B Paragraph Guided Writings [10] *use 155F, page 268, as directed*

59B Skill-Transfer Typing ⑦ *Line: 60; each line for a 1' writing; compare gwam*

		Words
Straight copy	Can their van move the six heavy zinc boxes for the foreman?	12
Statistical copy	My Order #736 totals $528.90 and must be shipped by June 14.	12
Rough draft	The artist worked (steadily on) in#spite of the *stifling* heat.	12
Script	*Ed expected the quiz to be very difficult for the nine boys.*	12

| 1 | 2 | 3 | 4 | 5 | 6 | 7 | 8 | 9 | 10 | 11 | 12 |

59C Drill on Tabulating ⑥

USE: Half sheet; 60-space line; SS; 1½" top margin.
DO: Center horizontally the table of Problem 1, 59D, below, leaving 6 spaces between columns. As a centered main heading, use MAILING CHARGES. Repeat, if time permits. **Goal:** To improve use of the tabulator and skill in aligning figures.

59D Problem Typing: Business Letters and Postal Card ㉚

FOR LETTERS: Line 60; date on Line 14; 1 cc; envelope of appropriate size; errors corrected; substitute your initials for xx in the reference line.

Problem 1

	Words
October 23, 19–– | Dr. Michael R. Mc-	7
Donough | 6832 Dixie Highway | Hamilton,	14
OH 45014 | Dear Dr. McDonough: |	20

	Words
The letters introducing your new physical fit-	29
ness program to a selected sample of athletic	39
coaches were typed, folded, and mailed last	47
week. The various charges are listed below:	56

		Words
Typing Letters	$56.70	61
Addressing Envelopes	2.70	66
Folding, Stuffing, and Stamping	1.75	76
Postage	9.00	79
	$70.15	79

	Words
We are pleased to have had the opportunity	88
to assist you. The changes we worked out	96
together should result in a greater number of	105
responses. Please let us know how many re-	114
turns come in.	117

	Words
By the time you are ready to prepare a com-	125
plete promotion, we shall have a battery of	134
four Auto-Typists installed. The cost per letter	144
should therefore be less. In addition, the Auto-	154
Typists eliminate the need for error correction	163
on the final copies.	168

	Words
Sincerely yours, | John D. Morganroth |	175
Assistant Sales Manager | xx	180/193

Problem 2

	Words
October 23, 19–– | Miss Jean G. Hanna, Dean |	8
Tri-State College of Business | 15 N.W. River-	17
side Drive | Evansville, IN 47708 | Dear	25
Miss Hanna:	27

	Words
We are pleased to send you today a compli-	35
mentary copy of our communications layout	44
guide	45

	Words
STYLED TO THE READER'S TASTE	51

	Words
This little booklet has become a popular item	60
on the shelves of many college bookstores.	69

	Words
After you have used the guide as a reference	78
for a few days, you will probably want each of	87
your secretarial students to have one. It is	96
obtainable at $1.50 a copy from Business	105
Books, Inc., 5101 Madison Road, Cincinnati,	113
Ohio 45227.	116

	Words
Thank you for your interest in our communi-	124
cations practices. We shall be pleased to re-	133
ceive any comments and suggestions you may	142
have for the improvement of our layout guide.	151

	Words
Sincerely yours, | Randall B. Parkhurst | Com-	160
munications Director | xx	164/184

Problem 3

Type and address a postal card to *Mr. R. B. Dunn, Manager* \| *Central College Store* \| *Louisville, KY 40212.* Use the date and ¶s 1 and 2 of Problem 2 for the message. Supply an appropriate salutation; omit the complimentary close and type OFFICE AIDES, INC. in all caps a triple space below the message.

Job 2: Approval Copy of Memorandum

Plain paper; 1" top and side margins; type the headings SS

Words

TO: Board of Directors FROM: Wayne A. 8
Young, President DATE: June 8, 19-- SUB- 16
JECT: Meeting of June 15 (¶ 1) The Board of 24
Directors will meet on Friday, June 15. (¶ 2) 32
There are a number of items that must be 40
considered before our meeting date in July. 49
It is imperative that the special committee 58
reports be presented for criticism so that any 68
suggested revisions can be considered by the 77
committees next week. Action must be taken, 86
too, on two new resolutions that will affect 95
our operations greatly during the coming 103
months. (¶ 3) The meeting will begin 109
promptly at 1:30 in the Board Room. A copy 118
of the agenda is enclosed for your information. 130

Job 3: Preparing a Hectograph Master

1. Prepare a hectograph master from the approval copy of Job 2; maintain 1" top and side margins.
2. After proofreading and correcting the master copy, run 15 clear copies.

LESSON 162

162A Preparatory Practice (5) *each line at least three times*

Alphabet The men glazed calyxes of blue flowers on pink antique jars and vases.

Figures Type dimensions in figures: 175 ft. 10 in. by 239 ft. 8 in. by 46 ft.

Rhythm The auditor signed his name to the audits for eight firms in the city.

Fluency Power is not revealed by striking hard or often, but by striking true.

| 1 | 2 | 3 | 4 | 5 | 6 | 7 | 8 | 9 | 10 | 11 | 12 | 13 | 14 |

162B Skill-Comparison Typing (10) *1' writings on each line; compare* gwam

Balanced hand A sense of contentment comes with our knowing that work is done right.

Direct reaches William Allen Abbott, the assessor, took my letter to the office, too.

Direct reaches If June Ceece is hungry, she must try Min's grape sherbet for dessert.

Right hand John, he pointed out, found a lump of molybdenum high on our mountain.

Left hand We read that tax rates on traded cars seem to have swerved toward 25%.

| 1 | 2 | 3 | 4 | 5 | 6 | 7 | 8 | 9 | 10 | 11 | 12 | 13 | 14 |

162C Production Typing: Committee Report; Interoffice Memorandums (35)

Job 1: Approval Copy of Interoffice Memorandum

On a half sheet, type the interoffice memorandum on page 278. Direct the memorandum to all department heads from the Communications Committee. Word the subject line appropriately.

Use the current date. List the Committee members: Robin Alcorn, Chairman; Stephen J. Scott; and Chris L. Rainey at the left margin, a triple space below the message.

LESSON 60

60A   Preparatory Practice ⑦ *each line three times; then 1' writings on Line 4*

Alphabet   Max landed a few quick jabs, but they weren't enough to stop Vic Zola!

Figures   Check my record: May 7, 25 letters; May 8, 24; May 9, 28; May 10, 36.

Figure-symbol   Use 1/2 and 1/4--not ½ and ¼--with such fractions as 5/6, 3/8, or 7/9.

Fluency   To turn a fast buck is the only goal of a number of our newer members.
              | 1 | 2 | 3 | 4 | 5 | 6 | 7 | 8 | 9 | 10 | 11 | 12 | 13 | 14 |

60B   Building Speed and Control ⑬ *two 1' writings on each ¶; then two 3' writings on both ¶s*

All letters are used.

		GWAM	
		1'	3'

¶ 1
1.4 SI
5.4 AWL
85% HFW

You would not expect a sizable response to a mailing late in the   13 | 4 | 40

spring of a letter promoting snow tires; nor should you expect a let-   27 | 9 | 44

ter written in less than standard language to be effective if it has   41 | 14 | 49

been mailed to a group of college professors.   50 | 17 | 52

¶ 2
1.4 SI
5.4 AWL
85% HFW

A good knowledge of words is vital, of course; but so is a clear   13 | 21 | 56

knowledge of the reader. It is quite important that you style your   27 | 25 | 61

message to your reader's taste and direct it to his vocabulary level.   41 | 30 | 65

The writer is just half of the communication process; the reader is   54 | 35 | 70

the other.   56 | 36 | 71

1' GWAM | 1 | 2 | 3 | 4 | 5 | 6 | 7 | 8 | 9 | 10 | 11 | 12 | 13 | 14 |
3' GWAM | 1 | 2 | 3 | 4 | 5 |

60C   Problem Typing Review ㉚

1. Make pencil notations of the problems and page numbers given at the right.
2. Type each problem once, correcting any errors you make, unless you are directed by your instructor not to do so.
3. Address an envelope for each letter typed. Fold and insert the letters.

Pages 98–99, 56C, Style Letter 2
Page 101, 57D, Problem 2
Page 103, 58D, Problem 2
Page 104, 59D, Problem 3

LESSON 61

61A   Preparatory Practice ⑦ *each line three times; then 1' writings on Line 4*

Alphabet   Jack Craven planned six spots for Roz, but she quit my show in August.

Figures   Industrial stocks moved up 5.89; rails, down 2.47; utilities, up 1.63.

Figure-symbol   Did Ned pay $4.81 to $4.95 (less 6% discount) for 37 ft. of #260 wire?

Fluency   If a job squeeze is on, get the most from the edge you have right now.
              | 1 | 2 | 3 | 4 | 5 | 6 | 7 | 8 | 9 | 10 | 11 | 12 | 13 | 14 |

161B Word Division ⑩

Use the backspace-centering method for arranging the tabulation. Then as you type each word, insert a hyphen at the most appropriate word-division place, assuming that the bell rang as the first letter of the word was typed. If a word should not be divided, type it without a hyphen.

friendly	article	couldn't	oriental
inasmuch	business	various	anticipation
education	ideal	question	gratitude
creation	written	aviation	impossible

161C Production Typing: Hectograph (Spirit) Duplication ㉟

Typing Leaders. After the first item in a column, alternate a space and a period to a point 2 or 3 spaces short of the longest item in the next column. Note whether you type the periods on odd or even cylinder-scale numbers; align subsequent rows by starting them in like manner; end all rows at the same point.

Job 1: Approval Copy of Agenda

Full sheet; center vertically and horizontally; 70-space line; use spaced leaders between columns

	Words
YOUNG MANUFACTURING COMPANY	6
Agenda for Meeting of the Board of Directors	15
June 15, 19--	17
1. Call to Order . . . . Wayne A. Young	31
2. Reading and Approval of Minutes . . . . . Clay A. Lewis	44
3. Reports of Officers	49
President's Report . . . . Wayne A. Young	61
First Vice-President's Report . . . . . . Darwin R. Sampson	74
Treasurer's Report . . . . Henry D. Rico	86
4. Reports of Special Committees	93
Report on Personnel Policy . . . . . . James F. Harvard	105
Report on Foreign Markets . . . . Douglas James	117
Report on Rate Revision . . . . F. Eugene Young	130
5. Dividend Declaration . . . . John L. Johnston	143
6. New Business	147
Presentation of Resolution on	153
Cumulative Voting . . . . David H. Van Zant	165
Presentation of Resolution to	171
Amend Stock Option Plan . . . . . . Charles L. Wrigley	184
7. Adjournment	187

All letters are used.

			GWAM 1'	5'

¶ 1
1.4 SI
5.4 AWL
85% HFW

What we say and how we say it influence the people to whom we talk | 13 | 3 | 34

and write. Their reactions to us and our ideas are greatly influenced by | 28 | 6 | 37

our language. Therefore, how we think and express our ideas will | 41 | 8 | 39

vitally affect the success of our daily lives. | 51 | 10 | 41

¶ 2
1.4 SI
5.4 AWL
85% HFW

All major positions in the modern business world require an ability | 14 | 13 | 44

to write well. The bigger the job, the more vital the writing skill. | 28 | 16 | 47

Sooner than you expect, you may have an opportunity for such a job. Are | 42 | 19 | 49

you ready to do the writing a top job demands? | 52 | 20 | 51

¶ 3
1.4 SI
5.4 AWL
85% HFW

The flair some people seem to show in writing usually results from | 13 | 23 | 54

years of careful effort. As you try to analyze the letters of others and | 28 | 26 | 57

to write some yourself, you can develop your own flair. In fact, flair | 43 | 29 | 60

may be little more than word skill well applied. | 52 | 31 | 62

1' GWAM | 1 | 2 | 3 | 4 | 5 | 6 | 7 | 8 | 9 | 10 | 11 | 12 | 13 | 14 |
5' GWAM | 1 | 2 | 3 |

61C Problem Typing Measurement ㉚ *Line: 60; date, Line 16; 2 cc's; envelope; errors corrected*

Get Ready to Type . . . . . 4'
Timed Production . . . . 20'
Proofread . . . . 6'

1. Assemble needed supplies: 3 letterheads, 2 carbon sheets, 6 copy sheets, 3 envelopes.

2. Get ready to type; when told to begin, type as many problems as you can in 20 minutes.

Problem 1

	Words
October 24, 19--	Mr. J. Evan Richards	Apollo Tool & Die Works	1818 Sherman	15
Avenue	Norwood, OH 45212	Dear Mr. Richards:		24

Thank you for telephoning this morning to discuss with us the possibility of our | 40
providing some temporary secretarial help during the months of December and | 56
January. We shall be glad to work with you in any way that will be beneficial. | 72

The enclosed brochure describes our objectives and functions and outlines briefly | 88
our methods of operation. The table of pay rates for various classifications of | 104
employees will give you a good idea of the cost of the work you want to have done. | 121

Mr. Ronald J. Seybold, one of our work relations coordinators, will call you | 137
early next week to arrange an appointment to consider your job requirements in | 152
detail. You'll find him quite capable in matching the worker to the job. | 167

Sincerely yours, | John D. Morganroth | Assistant Sales Manager | xx | Enclosure | | 182
cc Mr. Ronald J. Seybold | 187/204

Job 3: Interoffice Memorandum

Decide spaces between columns for tabulation; use no abbreviations; provide columnar headings (third column is the loan number)

Words

TO: Arthur Beach, Controller **FROM:** Don 6
Raymondo, Credit Manager **DATE:** (*current*) 14
SUBJECT: Delinquent Accounts (¶ 1) The 19
following borrowers, all from Knoxville, Ten- 27
nessee, are delinquent in their accounts by 36
two payments. (¶ 2) When the accounts first 44
became delinquent, we sent our customary 52
letter; and to date we have received no replies. 62
Accordingly, we shall mail our second letter 71
today. If no response is received in the next 80
10 days, we will proceed with our usual course 90
of action. 92

				Words
V. L. Lee	Delden Road	3460	$194	99
Cyrus Bay	135 Depot Ave.	3859	226	106
Jay Lake	2189 Doll Ave.	4172	631	113
Boyd Crane	975 Eads Ave.	5094	845	120
D. E. Love	862 Deva Drive	5748	312	127
A. A. Acre	434 Dunn St.	7623	753	134
Ben M. Key	800 E Drive	9047	548	141
Ray McGee	Donna Lane	9521	477	147

Job 4: Fill-Ins on Form Letters

Use your typewriter to fill in the current date, name and address, appropriate salutation, loan number, and amount due on 8 of the form letters duplicated in Job 2. The necessary information is given in Job 3. Observe the following steps:

1. Place a form letter in your typewriter. Set the left margin even with the left margin of the letter.
2. Type the date about 12 lines from the top of the sheet in a position that is consistent with the style of letter you have used.
3. Turn back from the first mimeographed line of the letter the correct number of lines to type the address and salutation. Use a personal title with each name. The ZIP Code designation for Knoxville, Tennessee (TN) is 379. Add to it the zone code for the appropriate street: 15 (Doll), 17 (Depot), 18 (Delden), 20 (Deva, Donna, Dunn, E, and Eads), as shown in the U.S. Post Office Department ZIP Code Directory.
4. Type the loan number and the amount due in the appropriate blanks. (Use this form: $194.00.)
5. Try to match the shade of the duplicating ink by using a lighter or heavier stroke as necessary.

Job 5: Chain-Feeding Envelopes

Using a chain-feeding procedure, address an envelope for each of the 8 letters prepared in Job 4. Use the appropriate personal title with each name. Fold and insert the letters in the proper envelopes.

LESSON 161

161A Preparatory Practice [5] *each line at least three times*

Alphabet Jay could give Mr. Ball only a week for his reply to the new tax quiz.

Figures Members of 15 clubs came to the 7:30 meeting held at 2849 86th Street.

Right hand Only you and John Hiplo may make the trip to look for Jim in Honolulu.

Fluency Learn to do the work that ought to be done whether you like it or not.

| 1 | 2 | 3 | 4 | 5 | 6 | 7 | 8 | 9 | 10 | 11 | 12 | 13 | 14 |

Words

October 24, 19--| Miss Sally Hickenlooper| 31 Pine Ridge Drive| Indianapolis, 15
IN 46260| Dear Sally: 20

Mrs. Lee has asked me to send you the following payroll record forms to be com- 35
pleted before you report for work November 15: 45

1. Employee's Withholding Exemption Certificate 55
2. Health-Hospitalization Insurance Application 64
3. Personal Data Card 69

We certainly are pleased that you have decided to become an Office Aide when 84
you move to Cincinnati next month. You will like Cincinnati, I know; and we 100
shall do whatever we can to make your adjustment to new surroundings smooth 115
and pleasant. 118

As soon as your Cincinnati telephone is installed, please call and give me the 134
number so that we can plan an unofficial welcome for you to the Queen City. 149

Cordially yours, | (Miss) Shirley Biggs | Secretary to Mrs. Lee | xx | Enclo- 163
sures| cc Mrs. Rhoda L. Lee 168/181

Problem 3

Retype the letter of Problem 2, but address it to:

    Miss Darlene Higgins
    3800 Brentwood Court
    Columbus, OH   43213

Supply an appropriate salutation and change the date in ¶ 1 to November 22. Prepare a carbon copy for Mrs. Rhoda L. Lee and type the carbon copy notation on the letter.

● **Self-Improvement Practice** *Line: 60; date on Line 16*

Words

October 28, 19 -- (to 5) 3

Mr. Jay Bainbridge, *Manager* 9
54 Cleveland Avenue *Electrical Supply Company* 14
Milford, ~~Ohio~~ 45150 18
(OH) 22

Dear Mr. Bainbridge : 26

    Here are the *hourly* pay rates for the ~~3 categories~~ *three classifications* of temporary employees we 44
discussed on the telephone today: 49

    Senior Stenographer $3.00 54
    Keypunch Operator 2.70 59
    Clerk-Typist 2.60 63

As you indicated on the telephone, our rates are *somewhat* higher than those of some of the 81
other agencies in this area. Apparently they *know* what their services are worth, and 98
so do we. We have yet to have an employer tell us that an Office Aide did not 114
give a day's work for a day's pay. ¶ May we have the opportunity of placing one or 131
more of our highly trained workers in your company *soon*. 142

    Sincerely yours, 145

    John D. Morganroth/Assistant Sales Manager 154/172

xx

159-160A Preparatory Practice [5] *each line at least three times*

Alphabet — Any mobility expert can quickly adjust to the severe freezing weather.

Figures — Sociology 217 will meet from 8:30 to 9:45 daily in Room 601, Rud Hall.

Rhythm — The busy chairman felt it his duty to handle their problem with vigor.

Fluency — We must visualize specific goals if we wish to achieve enviable skill.

| 1 | 2 | 3 | 4 | 5 | 6 | 7 | 8 | 9 | 10 | 11 | 12 | 13 | 14 |

159-160B Paragraph Guided Writings [10] *use 155F, page 268, as directed*

Production Typing Information

PREPARING MATERIAL FOR DUPLICATION

As a rule, type an approval copy of a letter or report to be duplicated. This is particularly true of material to be stenciled. Check the copy twice; once for accuracy of typing and once for accuracy of style.

For best results in typing copy for duplication, clean the type; then type with a normal, staccato touch. Errors can be corrected, but correcting procedures depend upon the supplies being used. Follow closely all directions given by your instructor.

159-160C Production Typing: Stencil Duplication [35]

Job 1: Approval Copy of Letter to Be Mimeographed

1½" side margins; open punctuation; blocked subject line

Type a copy of the following form letter on plain paper, omitting the date, inside address, salutation, loan number, and amount due. Leave spaces for these items to be filled in after the stencil is run. (Leave 6 spaces after the dollar sign in ¶ 1.)

Words

SUBJECT: Loan No. (¶ 1) We wrote you 7
last month regarding the delinquency of pay- 16
ments on your loan. As yet, we have received 25
neither a remittance nor a reply. Two install- 34
ments, amounting to $, are now due. 43
(¶ 2) It has always been our policy to be 50
lenient whenever possible; we feel, however, 59
that we are entitled to some explanation when 68
payments are not made on time. (¶ 3) Can you 76
make a substantial payment on your account 85
within ten days? If not, we shall have to re- 94
quest the trustees to institute sales proceed- 103
ings in accordance with the terms of your trust 113
deed. The expense of this action will, of 121
course, be chargeable to you. (¶ 4) We ear- 129
nestly hope that you will give this account 137
your prompt attention and avoid the expense 146
and inconvenience of the action mentioned 155
above. Very truly yours COLBY FINANCIAL 163
ASSOCIATION Eugene Blaut, Secretary 171

Job 2: Stencil from Approved Copy of Letter

Prepare a stencil from the approval copy that you typed as Job 1; then run fifteen clear copies. Information for filling the blanks on the duplicated copies will be provided in Jobs 3 and 4, page 275.

Purpose. The purpose of the 10 lessons of this section is to increase your communication skills through the medium of personal and business reports and to provide additional composing opportunities.

Machine Adjustments. Line: 70, unless otherwise directed; SS drills; DS timed writing ¶s and indent first line of each ¶ 5 spaces; DS manuscripts or reports.

Self-Improvement Practice. Type the script and rough draft items on pages 110, 111, 118, 122, or the Self-Improvement Practice items on page 126.

LESSON 62

62A Preparatory Practice ⑦ *each line three times; then 1' writings on Lines 2 and 4*

Alphabet — Professor Henry King announced a major quiz will be given next Monday.
Figures — These 80 scouts, 12 men, and 67 donkeys were loaded with 3,945 pounds.
Figure-symbol — Miller & Southby (local grocers) were selling bananas for 12¢ a pound.
Fluency — He will do well to try one or more of the very fine pens for the work.

| 1 | 2 | 3 | 4 | 5 | 6 | 7 | 8 | 9 | 10 | 11 | 12 | 13 | 14 |

62B Technique Practice: Stroking ⑩ *each line three or more times*

Balanced-hand — Did the chairman say the visit of the men will aid the endowment fund?
Adjacent — As Sadie has said, few can excel the many points Myrna Powell has won.
One-hand — In my opinion, it was foolish to race up that hill as fast as you did.
Hyphen — Here is an up-to-date reference for those out-of-this-world questions.
Roman numerals — Type Roman numerals in capital letters: I (1), IV, (4), V (5), X (10).

| 1 | 2 | 3 | 4 | 5 | 6 | 7 | 8 | 9 | 10 | 11 | 12 | 13 | 14 |

62C Speed and Control Building ⑩

1. Type a 1' writing on the following ¶. Determine *gwam*. Then add 4 *gwam* to this rate for a new goal.
2. Type two 1' guided *speed* writings, trying to reach the new goal. If you attain it on the first or second attempt, add 4 more *gwam* for the next writing. Use a 15" guide call.
3. Reduce your last goal rate by 2 *gwam* for the next guided writing.
4. Type two 1' guided *control* writings on the ¶, trying to reduce your errors. If you make more than 2 errors on the first writing, reduce your speed by 2 more *gwam* for the next writing.
5. Type a 2' writing. Determine *gwam* and errors.

All letters are used.

1.4 SI
5.4 AWL
85% HFW

	2' GWAM
Some workers can't do anything unless they are told just what to	7 / 53
do and how to do it. They may be good at routine jobs, but they are	13 / 60
limited by their lack of imagination, creativity, and the urge to ex-	20 / 67
plore new methods of doing things. Even great skill isn't adequate,	27 / 74
because quick hands must be guided by a reflective head--a fact many	34 / 80
workers often fail to recognize. Learn now to match your skills with	41 / 87
a desire to "find a better way" of doing your work.	46 / 93

2' GWAM | 1 | 2 | 3 | 4 | 5 | 6 | 7 |

Job 1: Short Letter

*Modified block style with
blocked ¶s; 1 carbon copy*

	Words
october 4, 19–– miss angela mercurio 987 modoc	9
avenue stockton ca 95204 dear miss mercurio	19
(¶ 1) Last October Jennie Mercer bought two	26
best-selling novels and read them both the	35
same day. She loved the books, but she com-	43
pletely forgot our One-Day Fall Coat Sale; so	53
Jennie Mercer spent another winter in her	61
old coat. (¶ 2) Don't be a Jennie Mercer.	69
Next Thursday is the day. Prices will be re-	77
duced 25 to 50 percent. (Confidentially, that's	87
why it's just a one-day sale––two days would	96
ruin us!) (¶ 3) So, c'mon over and join your	104
budget-wise friends. That's next Thursday,	113
remember; and we'll be watching for you.	121
sincerely yours ralph e fleming manager	130/142

Job 2: Average-Length Letter with Subject Line

*Modified block style with blocked ¶s; decide place-
ment and style of subject line; no carbon copy*

	Words
mr marcus e simpson 346 francis avenue hart-	9
ford ct 06106 dear mr simpson subject your	19
lawn, mr simpson (¶ 1) This is one of fifty	27
personal letters we are mailing this week to	36
Hartford men who we think are sincerely in-	45
terested in beautiful lawns. How was your	53
name selected? It's really very simple. (¶ 2)	62
Last year we contacted local dealers for the	71
names of regular customers who had pur-	78
chased Laine's Lawn Nutrient. This informa-	87
tion indicated to us that these folks were con-	96
cerned about the health of their grass. Then	105
we called on the nurseries in the vicinity for	115
the names of townspeople who had purchased	123
bedding plants. These people, we knew, liked	132
to tinker about in the outdoors. The dealers	142
were happy to cooperate with us in supplying	151
the names when they found out why we	158
wanted them. And now it is time to let you	167

	Words
in on the secret. (¶ 3) We have completed our	175
research on a new product, Laine's NuGren,	184
that will vitalize grass by encouraging deeper-	193
growing roots and healthier stem stock. Now	202
we want fifty Hartford residents to test	210
NuGren; we want YOU to test NuGren. A	218
50-pound bag is yours absolutely free from	228
your area merchant who handles Laine's prod-	237
ucts. Just hand him the enclosed card. (¶ 4)	245
A few weeks after you have applied NuGren	254
to your lawn, fill out and return to us the ques-	263
tionnaire the dealer gives you. The rest is up	273
to us. sincerely yours john j pruitt area	282
manager (*Don't forget to type the enclosure*	286/
notation.)	298

Job 3: Average-Length Letter with Subject Line

*Modified block style with blocked ¶s; decide
style of letter and subject line; 1 carbon copy*

	Words
mr alexander k zeitler 3641 arroyo seco drive	10
san jose ca 95125 dear mr zeitler subject good	20
newspaper reading (¶ 1) We want to place	28
your name in our copy of Who's Who Among	39
Well-Read People in San Jose. (¶ 2) That	52
"book" now contains the names of all sub-	60
scribers to the San Jose News–Herald. You	71
see, our subscribers are among the best-read	80
people in this city––in the state––in the coun-	90
try! (¶ 3) The News–Herald is delivered	99
every morning, just before breakfast, right at	109
the front door; and what better way is there	118
to start the day than with a good newspaper?	127
Whatever news you need for the day––about	135
special sales, entertainment, finance, sports,	145
society, politics––is all in the News–Herald;	156
and it's "right off the wire." (¶ 4) Wouldn't	164
you like to have your name in our copy of	173
Who's Who Among Well-Read People in San	189
Jose? All you need do is fill out and mail the	199
enclosed card. sincerely yours wesley e carter	209
circulation manager	216/230

ALIGNING ARABIC AND ROMAN NUMERALS

Align columns of Arabic and Roman numerals at the right. To provide the proper spacing between the columns of Arabic and Roman numerals, set each tabulator stop for the number of spaces needed between columns *plus* the number of spaces required to type the longest line in the column.

SPACING BETWEEN RELATED AND UNRELATED COLUMNS

Spacing may vary between columns depending on their relationship. In the following manuscript, for example, related columns (1-2, 3-4, 5-6) are typed closer together for quick identification of the relationship between the columns; but unrelated columns (2-3, 4-5) are more widely separated.

Full sheet; 1½″ top margin; 65-space line; 5-space ¶ indention; DS the ¶s; SS the table and outline; spaces between columns as indicated

---

ARABIC AND ROMAN NUMERALS IN OUTLINES

Words 8

TS

Use Roman numerals to identify major divisions of outlines; | 20

capital letters to identify subheadings; and Arabic numerals to | 32

identify items under subheadings. Study the Arabic and Roman nu- | 45

merals listed below: | 50

DS

SPACING KEY	9	1	I		6	VI		15	XV		53
		2	II		7	VII		40	XL		56
		3 4	III	10	8 4	VIII	10	50 4	L	9	61
		4	IV		9	IX		60	LX		64
		5	V		10	X		100	C		68

Type topic outlines without punctuation at the ends of lines | 80

(except for abbreviations), but type sentence outlines with appro- | 94

priate punctuation at line endings. | 101

There are several acceptable styles for capitalizing headings | i13

and subheadings. The style illustrated below (showing headings in | 127

descending order of importance) is one of the most widely used. | 139

TS

TOPIC OUTLINE | 142

TS

I.   CAPITALIZING HEADINGS IN OUTLINES | 150

DS

Reset margin→A.   Major Headings in All Caps | 156
B.   Important Words of First-Order Subheadings Capitalized | 168
C.   Only First Word of Second-Order Subheadings Capitalized | 180

DS

II.   SPACING OUTLINES | 185

DS

A.   Horizontal Spacing | 189
Set tab →1.   Title typed solid or as a spread heading | 199
2.   Other headings typed solid | 205
3.   Identifying numerals and letters followed by 2 spaces | 217
B.   Vertical Spacing | 221
1.   Title followed by a triple space | 228
2.   Main headings (except the first) preceded by a double space, followed by a double space | 240 248
3.   All subheading items single-spaced | 256

depend to a great extent on the way typists 72
address envelopes. Typists, therefore, are 81
urged to prepare them as follows: (¶ 2) 1. 89
Use only the block form with single spacing. 98
(¶ 3) 2. Abbreviate the state name with the 106
approved two-letter abbreviation without in- 114
ternal spacing and without punctuation; then 123
space twice and type the ZIP Code. (¶ 4) 131
3. To be read by the Optical Character 139
Reader, the address must be higher than 1/2 147
inch but no higher than 3 inches from the 156
bottom edge of the envelope, a "read-zone" 164
of 2 1/2 vertical inches. The following specifi- 174
cations will result in read-zone address place- 183
ment: No. 10 (large) envelope, 2 1/2 inches 192
from top edge, 4 inches from left edge; No. 201

6 3/4 (small) envelope, 2 inches from top, 210
2 1/2 inches from left. (¶ 5) 4. Multiple-line 218
addresses pose no problem if, consistently, the 228
final line contains the city, state, and ZIP Code. 238
(¶ 6) 5. In anticipation of the possible reading 247
of street names by the Optical Character 255
Reader in the future, typists are asked also to 265
begin the next-to-last line with the street num- 276
ber followed by the street name. Other items 286
(an apartment number, for example) may be 295
placed at the end of this line or on a separate 305
line above it. (¶ 7) 6. The efficiency of the 313
Optical Character Reader is enhanced by the 322
use of a black typewriter ribbon of good in- 331
tensity on a white envelope. 336

Addressing Envelopes

Examples of recommended styles for addressing envelopes for use with the Post Office Department's Optical Character Reader are shown below. Notice that only two-letter state abbreviations are used, with no abbreviation period. Two blank spaces usually separate the state abbreviation and the ZIP Code.

Charles A. Cox, M.D.
390 Ferry Street
Little Rock, AR   72202

Mr. David E. Furgrow
Wellington Apartments
380 Shasta Drive, North
Milwaukee, WI   53209

Miss Ann Glenn
98 Lewis Street, Apt. A
Richmond, VA   23231

Note. The inside address is usually identical with the envelope address.

LESSON 158

158A   Preparatory Practice (5) *each line at least three times*

Alphabet   The moving experts quickly adjusted ten gauges before the water froze.
Figures   The house is 35 feet by 47 feet, but the lot measures 168 by 209 feet.
Left hand It was rare when I agreed to pay him extra wages for addressing cards.
Fluency   The chairman will talk to all of us about handling the tough problems.
| 1 | 2 | 3 | 4 | 5 | 6 | 7 | 8 | 9 | 10 | 11 | 12 | 13 | 14 |

158B   Skill-Comparison Typing (5) *each line of 158A above for a 1' writing; compare gwam*

158C   Squeezing and Spreading Letters (5)

Type the sentences shown below. Make corrections by squeezing or spreading letters.

Any man who does only lit tle things losesthe capacity for big things.
Never in the his tory of the world hve so many owed so much to so few.
A gentleman has the good senseto disagree without being disagree able.
| 1 | 2 | 3 | 4 | 5 | 6 | 7 | 8 | 9 | 10 | 11 | 12 | 13 | 14 |

63A   Preparatory Practice ⑦ *each line three times; then 1' writings on Lines 2 and 4*

Alphabet   She will give any quaint excuse for making bold jaunts to polar zones.

Figures   I timed my 5 winners at 146, 137, 128, 116, and 109 wpm, respectively.

Symbols   Do not divide "don't" or "wasn't" (contractions) at the end of a line.

Fluency   You will find that you can do a lot of work if you will plan the work.
              | 1 | 2 | 3 | 4 | 5 | 6 | 7 | 8 | 9 | 10 | 11 | 12 | 13 | 14 |

63B   Technique Practice: Response Patterns ⑩ *each line at least three times*

Balanced-hand   Six or eight of their men lent a hand with the work of the city audit.

Combination   Their union steward may draft a formal statement to the next chairman.

Double letters Lynn will see that Britt sends the letter to your office by next week.

One-hand   Did you arrive after I set the minimum rate based on average earnings?

One-hand   I was not at union headquarters when a new wage contract was defeated.
                | 1 | 2 | 3 | 4 | 5 | 6 | 7 | 8 | 9 | 10 | 11 | 12 | 13 | 14 |

63C   Typing from Script ⑧ *line: 65; DS*

1. Type each of the following ¶s as a 1' writing. Determine *gwam* and errors.

2. Type a 3' writing on both ¶s combined. Repeat the first ¶ if necessary. Determine *gwam* and errors.

All letters are used.

	GWAM	
	1'	3'

To simplify your first typing of manuscripts, up to now all your reports were typed with a uniform 65-space line, regardless of whether your machine had pica- or elite-size type. Next, you will learn to arrange reports according to standard conventions of manuscript layout, based on number of inches in the margins instead of number of spaces in the writing line.

12	4	54
25	8	58
38	13	63
51	17	67
65	22	72
73	24	74

When standard conventions are followed, pica and elite solutions will differ somewhat. If 1-inch side margins are used, for example, an elite line will contain 78 spaces while a pica line will contain only 65 spaces. As a result, considerably more copy can be placed on a page of elite type. Be quick to learn the placement points for reports just as you have for other problems.

12	28	78
25	33	83
38	37	87
51	41	91
64	46	95
77	50	100

1' GWAM | 1 | 2 | 3 | 4 | 5 | 6 | 7 | 8 | 9 | 10 | 11 | 12 | 13 |
3' GWAM | 1 | 2 | 3 | 4 | 5 |

Job 1: Tabulation with Carbon Copy

*SS; decide spaces between columns; use either **exact** placement **or** reading position*

TWO-LETTER ZIP ABBREVIATIONS				Words
				6
For Use with ZIP Code				10
state				
Alabama	AL	Montana	MT	15
Alaska	AK	Nebraska	NE	19
Arizona	AZ	Nevada	NV	23
Arkansas	AR	New Hampshire	NH	29
California	CA	New Jersey	NJ	35
Canal Zone	CZ	New Mexico	NM	40
Colorado	CO	New York	NY	45
Connecticut	CT	North Carolina	NC	52
Delaware	DE	North Dakota	ND	57
District of Columbia	DC	Ohio	OH	64
Florida	FL	Oklahoma	OK	68
Georgia	GA	Oregon	OR	72
Guam	GU	Pennsylvania	PA	77
Hawaii	HI	Puerto Rico	PR	82
Idaho	ID	Rhode Island	RI	87
Illinois	IL	South Carolina	SC	93
Indiana	IN	South Dakota	SD	99
Iowa	IA	Tennessee	TN	103
Kansas	KS	Texas	TX	107
Kentucky	KY	Utah	UT	111
Louisiana	LA	Vermont	VT	115
Maine	ME	Virginia	VA	119
Maryland	MD	Virgin Islands	VI	125
Massachusetts	MA	Washington	WA	132
Michigan	MI	West Virginia	WV	137
Minnesota	MN	Wisconsin	WI	143
Mississippi	MS	Wyoming	WY	148
Missouri	MO			150

Job 2: Interoffice Memorandum with Carbon Copy

1" side margins; SS; block paragraphs; indent numbered items from both margins

	Words
TO: All Typists **FROM:** A. J. Davis **DATE:**	5
(current) **SUBJECT:** New Mailing Procedures	12
(¶1) The United States Post Office, in an	20
effort to cope with the ever-expanding volume	29
of first-class mail, has begun the use of Opti-	38
cal Character Readers (OCR's) to read ad-	46
dresses and to sort mail electronically.	55
The efficiency of the system, however, will	63

Problem 1: Poem

Half sheet, long side at left; line: 45; SS; 2" top margin; center title in ALL CAPS

	Words
I Asked and Received TS	4
I asked for bread,	8
He gave me a field to plow --	14
A field to seed and tend and spray,	21
To care for day by day --	26
And I have bread now. DS	31
I asked for money,	34
He gave me work to do --	39
Work most exacting, demanding,	45
With horizons ever expanding --	52
Now I have money, too. DS	56
I asked for honors,	60
He gave me a choice to make --	67
The easy wrong or the hard right,	73
Honor or honors for which to fight --	81
He leadeth me: Honors without honor I forsake.	90

Problem 2: Centering "Spread" Titles

HOW TO CENTER A "S P R E A D" TITLE

1. From the center of the paper, backspace once for each letter except the last one in the heading and once for each space between words.
2. Type the title, spacing once between the letters and three times between the words.

Half sheet, short side at left; 2" top margin; DS; center each "spread" title shown below. The first one is given in correct form.

	Words
C E N T E R I N G H E A D I N G S	7
TYPING TITLES AND HEADINGS	13
TYPING REPORT OUTLINES	17
TYPING REPORT MANUSCRIPTS	22
CENTERING OVER WRITING LINE	28
CENTERING ON SPECIAL-SIZE PAPER	34

Problem 3: Outline of Manuscript Form

Full sheet; line: 70; SS; 2½" top margin

	Words
U N B O U N D A N D T O P B O U N D M A N U S C R I P T S TS	13
I. EASE OF READING AIDED BY MARGINS AND SPACING DS	23
A. Margins	25
1. Bottom and side: 1"	30
2. Top, first page: unbound, 1½ or 2"; topbound, 2 or 2½"	42
3. Top, other pages: unbound, 1"; topbound, 1½"	53
B. Spacing	55
1. Body of manuscript double-spaced	63
2. Paragraphs indented 5, 7, or 10 spaces uniformly	73
3. Quoted material of 4 or more lines single-spaced	84
a. Indented 5 spaces from both margins	93
b. Quotation marks permissible but not required	104
C. Page Numbers	107
1. First page: centered ½" from bottom edge of paper	119
2. Other pages, unbound: even with right margin ½" from top	131
3. Other pages, topbound: same as for the first page DS	142
II. CLARITY AIDED BY HEADINGS AND SUBHEADINGS DS	153
A. Main Headings	156
1. Centered in all capital letters	164
2. Followed by triple space	170
B. First-Order Subheadings	175
1. Typed on separate line even with left margin, underlined	188
2. Preceded by triple space and followed by double space	200
C. Second-Order Subheadings	205
1. Indented as first line of paragraph, underlined	216
2. Preceded by double space	222

156C Technique Improvement: Stroking [10] *each line at least three times*

First six lines: Use the response pattern suggested. **Last two lines:** Type on the control level.

1	Word recognition	Keep your book at the right side so you can see it well when you type.
2	Word recognition	It is not hard to do good work if you will make up your mind to do it.
3	Stroke	Can he discriminate between fact and principle, evidence and argument?
4	Stroke	Executives prepared for retirement psychologically and sociologically.
5	Combination	A microfilm camera will now film both sides of records simultaneously.
6	Combination	If you will work diligently, you are bound to improve your efficiency.
7	Direct reaches	Many of the mementos my brother collected were brought to Grady Thumb.
8	Double letters	They cannot suggest shipping small baggage by express for three weeks.
		| 1 | 2 | 3 | 4 | 5 | 6 | 7 | 8 | 9 | 10 | 11 | 12 | 13 | 14 |

156D Sentence Guided Writings [10] *two 1′ writings on each sentence with the call of the guide*

		GWAM 15″	12″	10″
1	It makes a difference whether they go into a thing to win or to drift.	56	70	84
2	There is no easy road to learning; the price of learning is hard work.	56	70	84
3	The real work of this world is not done by people who watch the clock.	56	70	84
4	One good way to gain high speed in typing is to cut out waste motions.	56	70	84
	| 1 | 2 | 3 | 4 | 5 | 6 | 7 | 8 | 9 | 10 | 11 | 12 | 13 | 14 |			

156E Composing at the Typewriter [10]

Compose a brief paragraph with the opening sentence, "It sometimes takes courage to make a decision." When you have finished, make as many corrections and retype as much of the paragraph as time allows.

LESSON 157

157A Preparatory Practice [5] *each line at least three times*

Alphabet	This Juarez plaza was extremely quiet and dark for an October evening.
Figures	Consult pages 157, 264, 398, and 406 for other details on those items.
Rhythm	The giant flakes did not melt, so they kept their usual size and form.
Fluency	The world bestows its big prizes upon the ones who do their work well.
	| 1 | 2 | 3 | 4 | 5 | 6 | 7 | 8 | 9 | 10 | 11 | 12 | 13 | 14 |

157B Paragraph Guided Writings [10] *use 155F, page 268, as directed*

64A Preparatory Practice ⑦ *each line three times; then 1' writings on Lines 3 and 4*

Alphabet   The qualities of the mined zinc keep varying with the job excavations.

Figures   Here is Rothman's order for 50M of Form CZ1234 and 20M of Form WX6789.

Figure-symbol   Perform the calculation of (134 x 569) – (127 x 45) on the calculator.

Fluency   It is easy to give advice to others but not always so easy to take it.

| 1 | 2 | 3 | 4 | 5 | 6 | 7 | 8 | 9 | 10 | 11 | 12 | 13 | 14 |

64B Technique Practice: Machine Manipulations ⑦ *each line at least twice*

Center
↓

Tabulator
and return   Try not to pause at the end of the
line before you return.

Tabulator   three ☐4☐ 3 ☐4☐ five ☐4☐ 5 ☐4☐ seven ☐4☐ ☐4☐ eleven ☐4☐ 11 ☐4☐ fifteen ☐4☐ 15

Shift keys   Send Fields & Marshall ten copies of the new book by Niels and Atwood.

Space bar   If it is convenient, may I see you at the next meeting of the members?

Shift lock   Underline or ALL CAP addressee notations: Hold for Arrival, PERSONAL.

| 1 | 2 | 3 | 4 | 5 | 6 | 7 | 8 | 9 | 10 | 11 | 12 | 13 | 14 |

64C Composing at the Typewriter ⑩

1. Study the poem given as Problem 1, page 111, and decide what it means to you. Make notes.

2. Compose and type a paragraph, giving your interpretation of the poem. Proofread; correct; retype.

64D Typing Superscripts and Subscripts ⑩

A *superscript* is a figure or symbol typed above the line of writing; a *subscript*, a figure or symbol typed below. Use the ratchet release (automatic line finder) to position the carriage to the desired position.

To Type a Footnote Reference Figure (Superscript): (1) Operate the ratchet release; (2) turn the cylinder *backward* (toward you); (3) type the figure, then return the lever to normal position.

To Type a Chemistry Symbol (Subscript): (1) Operate the ratchet release; (2) turn the cylinder *forward* (away from you); (3) type the figure and return the lever to its position.

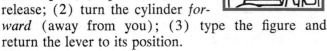

DRILL PROCEDURE

1. Type a 1" line, using the underline key.

2. Operate the ratchet release and move the cylinder *forward* (away from you) about 1".

3. Type another 1" line.

4. Return the lever to normal position; move the cylinder back to the first line; gauge the line and type over it.

5. Type the sentences given below, typing the superscript and the subscripts as directed at the left.

According to a Typewriting News article, "The ZIP Code should appear on the line with the names of the city and state."[1]

The symbol for sodium carbonate is Na_2CO_3.

Preliminary Information

The jobs in this section are typical of those you might be asked to do in a general office. You are already familiar with many of them because you have typed similar problems before. Complete directions for every job, therefore, may not always be given. When specific instructions are not provided, you will need to make basic decisions yourself. You are ready to do so. The following guide will help you.

(1) Common Sense. Let your artistic sense of balance and taste help to indicate how a job should be placed on a page for the utmost in attractiveness and utility. Learn to use margins and spacing to greatest advantage. Visualize how a job should look before you begin typing. Don't be satisfied just to finish a job. Accept responsibility for a job and do it well. Work independently.

(2) Basic Knowledge. You have learned much about typewriting procedures by carefully following the directions given you. Now is the time to rely on what you have learned and put it to use. Trust your knowledge. You have, for example, learned to use open and mixed punctuation forms with business letters. You may use the one you choose, but you can't use them both in the same letter. Make the choice; then be sure you follow it consistently.

(3) References. When seriously in doubt, check your book or ask your instructor for suggestions. For example, you may be directed in a job to use a subject line; but you are uncertain about just which forms are acceptable. Your textbook will explain that you may block it, indent to paragraph point, or center it; you may type it in all caps or simply capitalize the first letter. The typist usually makes such decisions.

If you make some procedural mistakes as you type the jobs that follow, learn from your mistakes; in so doing you will learn to be a professional.

LESSON 156

156A Preparatory Practice (5) *each line three or more times*

Alphabet	With a fixed goal in mind, quickly size up a job before making a move.
Figures	Only 789 of the 1,453 students solved more than 260 of these problems.
Balanced hand	This is the work the chairman told them to do, and they can do it now.
Fluency	The care they give their tools may indicate the quality of their work.
	| 1 | 2 | 3 | 4 | 5 | 6 | 7 | 8 | 9 | 10 | 11 | 12 | 13 | 14 |

156B Communication Aid: Proofreading (15)

Full sheet; 70-space line; 5-space ¶ indentions; DS

1. As you type the paragraph, make all necessary corrections. Check your work with your instructor.
2. Using the textbook copy again, type three 2′ writings on the *control level.*

All letters are used.

	GWAM 1′	2′	
the Zone Improvement Program, or "ZIP Code, has two elementary	13	7	66
objectives: (1) to give speedier service while (2 keeping expenses	27	14	73
at a minimum. when ZIP Code is not used, every letter must be read by	41	21	80
6 or 7 post office employees in order to route it properly? ZIP Code	55	28	87
not only reduces the number of times addresses must be read it shortens	69	35	95
the time to do whatever reading is still necessary and it cuts costs	83	42	102
by saving time. now, with the advent of optical scanning machinery that	98	49	109
will "read" 36000 pieces of mail an hour even quicker delivery at a	112	56	116
sensible cost will soon be feasible.	119	60	119

1′ GWAM | 1 | 2 | 3 | 4 | 5 | 6 | 7 | 8 | 9 | 10 | 11 | 12 | 13 | 14 |
2′ GWAM | 1 | 2 | 3 | 4 | 5 | 6 | 7 |

Problem 1: Unbound Manuscript

*Top margin: pica, 1½"; elite, 2";
side margins: 1" (10 pica spaces;
12 elite spaces); spacing: double;
SS and indent listed items 5
spaces from both margins*

Miniature models of both the pica and the elite solutions are given at the right. *Do not type from the models;* work from the copy given at the bottom of the page.

Problem 2: Topbound Manuscript

If time permits, retype Problem 1 as a topbound manuscript. Omit the last sentence of ¶ 2, including the quotation.

PICA

ELITE

	Words
THE SPEAKER'S DILEMMA	4

The inexperienced public speaker is faced with a real problem in deciding upon — 20
the method of delivery to use. The beginner usually feels more secure if he type- — 37
writes the speech in advance and actually reads the copy word for word. The big — 53
weakness in this, of course, is that audience contact is difficult to maintain. — 69

Most experienced speakers deliver their speeches extemporaneously from a pre- — 84
pared outline. The novice without a script, however, fears that he will "fall on — 101
his face." He is conscious of the point which was made so well by the orator — 117
Demosthenes of ancient Greece: "A vessel is known by the sound, whether it be — 132
cracked or not; so men are proved by their speech, whether they be wise or foolish." — 150

As a compromise, the beginner should probably use a typewritten script; but — 165
he should attempt to extemporize, and he should use the script only when he feels — 181
the need to do so. With experience, he will depend upon a script less and less. — 198

Aside from the decision regarding the form and the extent of notes to use, — 213
the speaker's dilemma includes other elements: — 222

    1. To gesture or not to gesture. — 227
    2. To inject humor or "play it straight." — 236
    3. To illustrate with examples or merely describe. — 246
    4. To visualize or merely vocalize. — 253

In general, visual aids and illustrative examples not only make a talk more — 269
interesting, but also encourage the speaker into natural animation and the use of — 285
spontaneous gestures. — 289

155E Building Accuracy ⑩

Use the paragraphs in 155F. Place a check mark in the margin of each ¶ that you have typed without error. If time remains when you have completed typing the ¶s, retype those in which you made an error. When time is called, total your check marks and place the number at the top of the page.

155F Paragraph Guided Writings ⑩

1. Choose a ¶ to use as a speed goal. Type two 1' writings at the set speed.
2. Use the next succeeding ¶ for three 1' writings at the speed indicated. (If ¶ 6 was your goal, try to exceed its rate in the third and fourth writings.)
3. Type your goal ¶ again for two 1' writings. Type with improved accuracy. Compare *gwam*.

		GWAM	
		1'	5'

¶1
1.6 SI
5.8 AWL
75% HFW
32 words
(64 wam)

You can find sincere, lasting happiness in various walks of life; | 13 | 3 | 52
luckily, it is your disposition, not your position, that makes you a | 27 | 5 | 55
happy or an unhappy person. | 32 | 6 | 56

¶2
1.6 SI
5.8 AWL
75% HFW
37 words
(74 wam)

The fellows that long for social acceptance will endeavor to per- | 13 | 9 | 58
fect the knack of holding a good conversation. In actuality, they will | 27 | 12 | 61
remember, hopefully, to let it go once in a while. | 37 | 14 | 63

¶3
1.6 SI
5.8 AWL
75% HFW
38 words
(76 wam)

One who questions an opinion is canny; one who quarrels with plain | 13 | 17 | 66
facts is a fool; but anybody who recognizes the difference between cold | 28 | 20 | 69
facts and sheer opinion is likely to be perceptive. | 38 | 22 | 71

¶4
1.6 SI
5.8 AWL
75% HFW
42 words
(84 wam)

Many people are open-minded; they usually see two points of view in | 14 | 24 | 74
an argument––the erroneous one and theirs. Hence, it is necessary to | 28 | 27 | 76
realize that often the broadest utterance comes from the narrowest mind. | 42 | 30 | 79

1.6 SI
5.8 AWL
75% HFW
46 words
(92 wam)

If you want efficiency and reliability, you will find them if you | 13 | 33 | 82
find a busy man. We are apparently divided into one group that accom- | 27 | 35 | 85
plishes and one group that can't be bothered. Join the busy group; the | 42 | 38 | 88
competition is lighter. | 46 | 39 | 89

¶6
1.6 SI
5.8 AWL
75% HFW
51 words
(102 wam)

For every lad who exhibits a tiny spark of genius, one can easily | 13 | 42 | 91
spot a dozen others who are experiencing serious ignition trouble. If | 27 | 45 | 94
you belong to the latter group, stop looking for easy solutions to your | 42 | 48 | 97
problems. Begin searching for the right ones. | 51 | 49 | 99

1' GWAM | 1 | 2 | 3 | 4 | 5 | 6 | 7 | 8 | 9 | 10 | 11 | 12 | 13 | 14 |
5' GWAM | 1 | 2 | 3 |

LESSON 65

65A Preparatory Practice ⑦ *each line three times; then 1' writings on Lines 2 and 4*

Alphabet   Kip Judge has a very large screen he will bring for my quiz next week.

Figures   In 1959, 302 clerks were working here; in 1964, 734; and in 1969, 928.

Figure-symbol   Zeno's sold 2,479 meals @ $1.75 per plate and 860 pieces of pie @ 35¢.

Fluency   The very time to try again and to do our best is when we want to stop.

| 1 | 2 | 3 | 4 | 5 | 6 | 7 | 8 | 9 | 10 | 11 | 12 | 13 | 14 |

65B Preparing a Page-End Indicator ⑩

A page-end indicator is a standard 8½" x 11" sheet on which the numbers 1 to 33 have been typed vertically line by line from the top edge along the right side of the upper half while the numbers 33 to 1 are similarly typed on the lower half. Such an indicator is a useful device for typing manuscripts. It is particularly helpful in estimating the space needed for footnotes at the bottom of a page.

PROCEDURE

Insert a full sheet of paper. At the right edge of the sheet type the figure 1 in the first line space from the top edge, the figure 2 in the next space, and so on until you type the figure 33. In the next line space, repeat the figure 33; in the next space type 32, and so on down to figure 1 in the last line space on the page.

• *Keep your page-end indicator sheet for later use.*

DRILL

Place the page-end indicator sheet back of and extending slightly to the right of a full sheet. Insert these sheets into the typewriter and on the bottom half type the following words centered on Lines 24, 18, and 12, respectively:

horizontal

vertical

center

65C Problem Typing: Outline and Footnotes ㉝

Problem 1: Outline

Line: 70; SS; start on Line 20, using page-end indicator

	Words
LEFTBOUND MANUSCRIPTS WITH FOOTNOTES	7
TS	
I. MARGINS FOR MANUSCRIPTS BOUND AT LEFT	16
DS	
A. Top Margin	19
1. First page, 1½ or 2 inches	25
2. Other pages, 1 inch	30
B. Side and Bottom Margins (All Pages)	38
1. Left side, 1½ inches	43
2. Right side, 1 inch	48
3. Bottom, 1 inch	52
II. FOOTNOTES FOR ALL MANUSCRIPTS	60
A. Numbering	63
1. Reference figure at end of citation or quotation	74
2. Footnote (same reference figure) on page with quotation	86
B. Spacing	89
1. Separated from text or body by 1½-inch underline, preceded by a single space and followed by a double space	100 / 112
2. Single-spaced, separated by double spacing	122

SECTION 26 TYPING IN A GENERAL OFFICE

LESSONS 155–164

Drill Copy: Full sheet; 70-space line; SS.

Paragraph Copy: Full sheet; 70-space line; DS; 5-space ¶ indention.

Production Copy: For letters, use the modified block style with block ¶s, the current date (if one is not given), and your reference initials. Choose a style of punctuation; correct errors; make copies as directed; address envelopes.

Special Supplies Needed: Letterheads or full sheets; interoffice communication forms; executive-size stationery; carbon sheets; second sheets; envelopes of appropriate size; stencil; hectograph masters.

LESSON 155

155A Preparatory Practice (5) *each line three or more times*

Alphabet	Becky joined Felix at The Palace even though it was time for her quiz.
Figures	Please order 301 pens, 495 erasers, 672 pencils, and 189 carbon packs.
Long words	His professional characteristics now satisfied executive requirements.
Fluency	If our work is worth doing, it is worth doing as well as we can do it.

| 1 | 2 | 3 | 4 | 5 | 6 | 7 | 8 | 9 | 10 | 11 | 12 | 13 | 14 |

155B Skill-Comparison Typing (5) *each line of 155A above for a 1′ writing; compare* gwam

155C Squeezing Letters; Typing Symbols (10)

Follow the directions given in the left column. Type each line twice.

1. **Erasing and Correcting Errors.** Type the line as given; then erase and correct errors.

   Proofread all werk carefully before
   you remove it form teh typewriter.

2. **Squeezing Letters to Correct Errors.** Type the sentence; then erase and squeeze the letters *cor* and *ave* to type the words *correct* and *have*.

   Corect any mistakes you may hav
   missed when you were typing the job.

3. **Typing Special Symbols.** Type the sentences using special symbols.

   We know that water freezes at 32° Fahrenheit.
   Here is the solution: 20 × 2 ÷ 5 + 15 = 23.

155D Action Typing (10) *type twice; as you type, follow the instructions of the ¶*

Words

When you finish typing this sentence, center horizontally by the 13
backspace-centering method in all capitals the following items: 26

spirit duplication 30
ink (or stencil) duplication 36
offset duplication 39

Center and type as a spread heading in all capitals the following 53
title: 54

planning the office layout 65

Center the following title, capitalizing only the first letter of 78
each word. Then underline the entire title. 87

skills that pay dividends 97

Problem 2: Portion of a Manuscript Page with Footnotes

Full sheet and page-end indicator;
DS; 5-space ¶ indention; side
margins: 1½" left, 1" right

DO: Type the first line opposite Line 25 of the bottom half of the indicator sheet to maintain a 1" bottom margin. Follow the steps given at the right in typing reference figures for footnotes.

TYPING SUPERIOR FIGURES FOR FOOTNOTE REFERENCES

1. Move the ratchet release (automatic line finder) forward.
2. Move the cylinder back (toward you) a half space.
3. Type the superior figure.
4. Return the ratchet release and cylinder to their regular positions.
5. Continue typing.

• *Do not type copy line for line; listen for bell to return at line endings.*

PICA

```
                                                                    25
  new building.  Each of these situations involves uncertainty,     24
                                                                    23
  and each of them is essentially a prediction of an outcome.        22
                                                                    21
      "The study of probability began around three hundred          20
                                                                    19
  years ago."1  According to Encyclopaedia Britannica, Jakob         18
                                                                    17
  Bernoulli--a Swiss mathematician--"can be regarded as the          16
                                                                    15
  father of probability theory as a branch of mathematics."2        14
                                                                    13
  ─────────                                                         12
    1George W. Snedecor and William G. Cochran, Statistical         11
  Methods (6th ed.; Ames, Iowa:  The Iowa State University          10
  Press, 1967), p. 199.                                              9
    2"Probability," Encyclopaedia Britannica (1968), XVIII,          8
                                                                     7
  570.                                                               6
                                                                     5
                                                                     4
                          1                                          3
                                                                     2
                                                                     1
```

ELITE

```
                                                                    25
      scheduled completion of a new building.  Each of these situations in-   24
                                                                    23
  volves uncertainty, and each of them is essentially a prediction of an       22
                                                                    21
  outcome.                                                           20
                                                                    19
      "The study of probability began around three hundred years ago."1        18
                                                                    17
  According to Encyclopaedia Britannica, Jakob Bernoulli--a Swiss mathe-        16
                                                                    15
  matician--"can be regarded as the father of probability theory as a          14
                                                                    13
  branch of mathematics."2                                          12
  ─────────                                                         11
    1George W. Snedecor and William G. Cochran, Statistical Methods  10
  (6th ed.; Ames, Iowa:  The Iowa State University Press, 1967), p. 199.        9
                                                                     8
    2"Probability," Encyclopaedia Britannica (1968), XVIII, 570.     7
                                                                     6
                                                                     5
                                                                     4
                          1                                          3
                                                                     2
                                                                     1
```

Begin Elite Line with

Begin Pica Line with

	Words
scheduled completion of a new building. Each of these situations involves	13
uncertainty, and each of them is essentially a prediction of an outcome.	30
"The study of probability began around three hundred years ago."[1] According to Encyclopaedia Britannica, Jakob Bernoulli—a Swiss mathematician—	44
	64
"can be regarded as the father of probability theory as a branch of mathe-	79
matics."[2]	81
SS 1½"	85
DS	
[1]George W. Snedecor and William G. Cochran, Statistical Methods (6th	101
ed.; Ames, Iowa: The Iowa State University Press, 1967), p. 199.	114
DS	
[2]"Probability," Encyclopaedia Britannica (1968), XVIII, 570.	131

Problem 3: Portion of a Manuscript Page with Footnotes

Full sheet; margins: 1" side and bottom; begin on
Line 33; leave extra space between body and foot-
note divider line to maintain a 1" bottom margin.

Retype the copy of Problem 2 as an unbound manuscript with footnotes. If the last page of a manuscript is less than a page, place footnotes at bottom of page.

154C Technique Practice [5] *each line twice without error*

1	Long words	Please offer your suggestions concerning bibliographic materials used.
2	3d, 4th fingers	We saw at least six fellows who were watching our opening performance.
3	Long reaches	My brother showed nerve in interrupting with his unnecessary opinions.
4	One hand	In Kim's opinion, the wages in our trade are in excess of the average.

| 1 | 2 | 3 | 4 | 5 | 6 | 7 | 8 | 9 | 10 | 11 | 12 | 13 | 14 |

154D Production Skill Checkup: Letter with Tabulated Report [25]

Problem 1: Letter with Tabulated Report

Modified block with block ¶s; open punctuation

Words

mr whitney grenwald office manager crave- 8
more manufacturing company 3890 o'shaugh- 16
nessy avenue huntsville al 35801 dear mr 25
grenwald (¶ 1) At the meeting in Gary, you 33
asked about the standards for computing 41
office production costs I mentioned in my talk 50
and about their usefulness in reducing costs. 59
These standards were established two years 68
ago when Lombard and Peck were retained to 77
conduct time and motion studies for our com- 85
pany. They are listed below. *(SS the items* 91
and leave 8 spaces between columns.)

		Words
Business Letters	39 wam	96
Envelopes	26 wam	100
Manuscripts (with footnotes)	23 wam	107
Manuscripts (without footnotes)	38 wam	115
Simple Rough Drafts	21 wam	120
Simple Tabulated Reports	16 wam	126
Spirit Masters	38 wam	131
Stencils	26 wam	134

Words

(¶ 2) The figures have proven most useful to 142
us in deciding what methods to use in pro- 150
ducing office copy. In some instances, for 159
example, we have decided that recent tech- 167
nological advances such as copying machines 176
produce duplicates that are less expensive 184
than typist-produced copies. In other cases, 194
we have decided to standardize certain forms 203
and procedures in order to reduce time- 210
consuming computations and manipulations. 219
Still further, known skill differences have 228
prompted us to allocate work among our typ- 236
ists more judiciously and with better results. 246
(¶ 3) I must tell you, however, that these fig- 254
ures have value only in the computation of 262
costs and should not, because of the inclusion 272
of various cost-effective factors in their cal- 281
culation, be used to evaluate performance. 289
yours very truly b l duffy office manager 299/322

Problem 2: Tabulation

Type as a 2-column table with columnar headings the list of standards given in the letter in Problem 1. Use a full sheet of paper, reading position, and double spacing for the body of the table. Leave 8 spaces between columns. Center horizontally on the sheet the heading SHAWNEE MANUFACTURING COMPANY and the subheading Minimum Typewriting Speeds for Computing Office Production Costs. Center the column heads Job and Standard over the columns.

LESSON 66

66A Preparatory Practice (7) *each line three times; then 1' writings on Lines 3 and 4*

Alphabet   Sidney will keep the olive jaguar if he acquires extra cash from Buzz.

Figures   The new numbers are: Janet, 841-2937; Fred, 261-5200; Eric, 831-4129.

Figure-symbol   The $6\frac{1}{2}\%$ interest of $81.08 on my $1,247.35 note (dated May 29) is due.

Fluency   Most of us, whether young or old, have potential that is never tapped.

| 1 | 2 | 3 | 4 | 5 | 6 | 7 | 8 | 9 | 10 | 11 | 12 | 13 | 14 |

66B Control Building: Long Words (5) *each line three times at your control rate*

Ken has described several business applications of probability theory.

Probability studies are particularly helpful in effective forecasting.

Analysis of the experimental data provides an estimate of probability.

| 1 | 2 | 3 | 4 | 5 | 6 | 7 | 8 | 9 | 10 | 11 | 12 | 13 | 14 |

66C Growth Index (8) *one 5' writing; determine* gwam *and errors*

All letters are used.

	GWAM 1'	5'

¶ 1
1.4 SI
5.4 AWL
85% HFW

Text	1'	5'
A good business letter is a work of art, and the knack of writ-	13	3 54
ing such a letter is usually learned best through actual experience.	27	5 57
But experience does not always teach with zeal, and quite often this	41	8 60
is a very slow way to learn. In order to add to this vital skill more	55	11 63
quickly, therefore, the wise student will study what those who are	68	14 65
judges in the field have found to be the basic rules for effective	82	16 68
letter writing.	85	17 69

¶ 2
1.4 SI
5.4 AWL
85% HFW

The first such rule tells you to present in each statement just	13	20 71
one principal or main thought. This is the way to assure unity in your	27	22 74
letters. The next rule suggests that you connect all parts of your	41	25 77
message clearly and logically by the expert use of words; that is, make	55	28 80
the entire message stick together. The final rule urges you to direct	69	31 82
the attention of the reader to the key points of the letter; that is,	83	34 85
to give your message power.	89	35 86

¶ 3
1.4 SI
5.4 AWL
85% HFW

To apply the basic rules with success, it is imperative that you	13	37 89
plan your letter by developing a topic outline of what you wish to	26	40 92
say. At the beginning of the outline include a strong, hard-hitting	40	43 94
sentence that will quickly grasp the attention of the reader. At the	54	46 97
end of the outline add a sentence that will end the letter on a warm,	68	48 100
friendly note. Throughout the plan, try to see the situation as the	82	51 102
reader does.	84	52 103

1' GWAM | 1 | 2 | 3 | 4 | 5 | 6 | 7 | 8 | 9 | 10 | 11 | 12 | 13 | 14 |
5' GWAM | 1 | 2 | 3 |

154A Preparatory Practice (5) *each line at least three times*

Alphabet	The judge gave back the extra prize quickly when my show was finished.
Figures	In 1967, we received 2,865 letters and 340 postcards asking for gifts.
Long reaches	My uncle undoubtedly hunted for hundreds of unknown uniforms annually.
Fluency	Men will always profit from the goal of helping others solve problems.
	| 1 | 2 | 3 | 4 | 5 | 6 | 7 | 8 | 9 | 10 | 11 | 12 | 13 | 14 |

154B Straight-Copy Skill Checkup (15) *two 5′* control-level *writings; figure* nwam

All letters are used.

		GWAM 1′	GWAM 5′	
¶ 1	The ultimate achievement of a business venture is based on its	13	3	72
1.6 SI	written communications. Naturally, letters have a vital part to play,	27	5	75
5.8 AWL	as do any such frequently used written forms as tables, news releases,	41	8	77
75% HFW	memoranda, or the telefax. A business needs timely, factual informa-	55	11	80
	tion; and what is said, how it is expressed, and the way it looks are	69	14	83
	all a part of the art of a capable typist. Proper handling of informa-	83	17	86
	tion is his job.	86	17	86
¶ 2	Billions of pages of typed material are produced annually in the	13	20	89
1.6 SI	United States, and on such pages the business of the nation is consum-	27	23	92
5.8 AWL	mated. Thus, the acquisition of fine typewriting ability can furnish	41	25	95
75% HFW	one of the surest roads to the company office; and young people with	55	28	97
	ambition for office work will strive to become fast, accurate typists	69	31	100
	who are very proud of the quality and of the quantity of typed work	82	34	103
	they can produce.	86	34	104
¶ 3	We must be cognizant, of course, that typing speed alone is not	13	37	106
1.6 SI	enough evidence of employability. Skill is important, but a true aware-	27	40	109
5.8 AWL	ness of sound office procedure is also needed. A mastery of the mys-	41	43	112
75% HFW	teries of the English language also cannot be overlooked nor can the	55	45	115
	question of personality. In other words, then, no employer wants to hire	70	48	117
	just one more skillful person; he needs a well-rounded employee to add	84	51	120
	to his group.	86	52	121
¶ 4	Regardless of which area of work you eventually enter, your typing	13	54	124
1.6 SI	skill should be an asset. It can help you gain, hold, perform, and even	28	57	126
5.8 AWL	earn promotion in your job. Typewriting is not simply a vocational	42	60	129
75% HFW	skill; it has personal applications, also. Though it is true that many	56	63	132
	people are paid for their typing ability, the fact that this skill can	70	66	135
	be used in ways either related or unrelated to professional work is an	84	69	138
	added attraction.	88	69	138
1′ GWAM	| 1 | 2 | 3 | 4 | 5 | 6 | 7 | 8 | 9 | 10 | 11 | 12 | 13 | 14 |			
5′ GWAM	| 1 | 2 | 3 |			

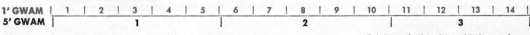

NWAM (Net Words a Minute) = 5′ GWAM — 2 for each error or $\frac{\text{Total words typed — 10 for each error}}{\text{Number of minutes in writing}}$

66D Problem Typing: Letter with Table; Portions of Second Page of Manuscript (30)

Problem 1: Letter with Table

Modified block, blocked ¶s; mixed punctuation; line: 65; date on Line 16; center listed items with 6 spaces between columns; address envelope

	Words
(*Current date*) Mr. Philip G. Morris	Quality	9
Foods, Inc.	67 Canterbury Street	Worches-	17
ter, MA 01610	Dear Mr. Morris:	(¶ 1)	24
Several weeks ago you asked me to let you	32
know when we increased the number of food	41
lines we are able to offer our customers. Just	50
this month we secured the franchise to sell	59
many of the products of Top Foods, Ltd.	67

	Words
(¶ 2) Early next week I shall stop to see you	75
to explain the delivery schedule for these new	85
products. In the meantime, the two items	93
listed below will illustrate that the products	102
are priced right.	106

24-can case of yellow cling peaches	$6.50	115
48-can case of creamed white corn	7.50	123

	Words
(¶ 3) If you need additional information be-	130
fore I arrive, please write me or call me collect	140
at (617) 821-3940.	Sincerely yours,	Richard	149
B. Higgenbotham	Assistant Sales Manager		157
xx	158

Problem 2: Drill on Typing Portion of Second Page of Manuscript with Footnote

PICA

ELITE

Type the following copy as page 2 of a leftbound manuscript (1″ top margin with the page number on Line 4). Use your page-end indicator sheet.

Since this second page is not full, space down appropriately to type the footnote in order to maintain a 1″ bottom margin.

	Words
In an article entitled "It's More Probable Than You Think," Martin Gardner	15
illustrated some remarkable examples of probability. One of them is what mathe-	31
maticians call the birthday paradox. The birthday paradox predicts that out of	47
a group of 23 people, the chances are more than even that of their 23 birthdays,	63
two will fall on the same date.[3]	70

Space down to Line 20 of your indicator sheet.

	Words
Modern business management depends heavily upon the predictions of proba-	84
bility studies for such decisions as:	92
1. Determining desirable inventory levels.	101
2. Planning new products.	107
3. Estimating rate of growth.	113
4. Determining market potential.	120
	124
[3]Martin Gardner, "It's More Probable Than You Think," Reader's Digest	141
(November, 1967), p. 108.	146

Problem: Unbound Manuscript

1. Leave a 2-inch top margin on page 1. For other margins and style see RG page ix.
2. Use the heading BUSINESS LETTERS.
3. Type the footnotes at the bottom of the pages on which references to them are made (RG page ix)

	Words
(¶ 1) A good business letter is seldom noted	14
for its remarkableness. Even the careful re-	20
searcher will have difficulty finding one in	29
literary anthologies. Speakers rarely quote	38
from them. If one is found in a museum, it	47
was placed there because of the historical	55
significance of its signature. Yet we should	65
realize that business letters are documents of	74
power. (*SS; indent quoted ¶ 5 spaces from each*	76
margin.) People do not aspire to the fame re-	83
served almost wholly in these days for writers	92
of fiction. But writers of letters convey more	102
thoughts to more people in a week than fiction	111
writers do in a year. They move more people	120
to action. They give more people pleasure.	129
They conduct the nation's business.[1] (*end of*	136
quotation) (¶3) Business letters are rather ordi-	143
nary documents. Simply stated, they are a	151
functional medium for commercial communi-	159
cation. If well written, they adhere to the	168
"Rule of the Three C's"—Clear, Concise, and	177
Correct. They are generally intended to evoke	187
a favorable response. For that reason, anyone	196
who has anything to do with the preparation	205
of business letters must take every precaution	214
to see that this goal is met; and one of the	223
more important persons contributing to the	232
writing of business letters is the typist. (¶ 4)	241
The recipient of a letter forms an impression	250
from its appearance before he begins to read	259
the message. A well-placed letter with clean,	268
even typescript will make a favorable impres-	277
sion and will encourage the recipient to read	286
with care and attention.[2]	291

Important Parts of the Business Letter	307
(¶ 5) Date. The typist dates the letter. Dates	316
are important in business, for filed correspon-	325
dence forms a chronological history that can	334
have significant value. The date on a letter	344

	Words
may have legal implications, also. (¶ 6)	351
Address. The typist provides the proper spell-	362
ing of the name and the correct address of the	371
recipient. The correct spelling of a name is a	381
compliment; certainly it indicates thoughtful-	390
ness. An incorrect address will delay delivery	399
of the letter. (¶ 7) Body of the letter. As	411
the body of the letter is being typed, the typist	421
must be alert for mistakes of any kind. Punc-	430
tuation must be inserted, spelling must be	439
checked, and paragraphing must be provided.	448
If there is doubt about anything in the letter,	458
it must be double-checked for accuracy. The	467
typist must take a personal interest in each	476
letter typed. (¶ 8) Enclosures. A good typist	486
pays special attention to enclosures. What	495
can be more disconcerting to the recipient	504
than to read that he should take some prompt	513
action as indicated by an enclosure—and not	522
be able to find the enclosure! (¶ 9) Copies.	531
A sufficient number of clear copies should be	541
made to send to each person with a legitimate	550
interest in its contents, and the reader should	559
be notified that copies have been sent.	568
(¶ 10) Business letters deserve careful study.	576
Whether it will be your job to compose them	585
or to type them, the effort has but one pur-	593
pose—a clear, concise, correct letter that will	603
bring results. (*Indent quoted ¶.*) (¶ 11) Everyone	608
in the company who in some way aids in the	617
preparation of letters . . . must be fully appre-	626
ciative of the value of doing each part of the	636
task in a businesslike manner and using stan-	644
dards that result in quality work.[3]	651

---

[1] "About Writing Letters," The Royal Bank of Canada Monthly Letter, Vol. 49, No. 3 (March, 1968), p. 1. (*32 words*)

[2] Peter L. Agnew, James R. Meehan, and William R. Pasewark, Clerical Office Practice (4th ed.; Cincinnati: South-Western Publishing Co., 1967), p. 387. (*39 words*)

[3] Ibid. (*6 words*)

LESSON 67

67A Preparatory Practice ⑦ *each line three times; then 1' writings on Lines 2 and 4*

Alphabet   Just how much should Greg Zahn expect to pay for five weeks in Quebec?

Figures   The ZIP Codes are: Alan, 53190; Dwayne, 74104; Ed, 27403; Sam, 60178.

Figure-symbol   Interest accumulated in 1968 to $432.57 when the rate increased by ½%.

Fluency   As you get to know a man, you get to know his good points most of all.

| 1 | 2 | 3 | 4 | 5 | 6 | 7 | 8 | 9 | 10 | 11 | 12 | 13 | 14 |

67B Typing from Rough Draft ⑧ *type twice with 1" top and side margins*

Words

The *following* guides ~~that follow~~ will be useful in ~~the~~ preparation   10

of manuscripts of two (pages ⎡or more⎤):   17

1. Never end a page with a hyphened word / ^or have^ ~~Avoid having~~   27
   more than two consecutive lines end with a hyphen*ed word*.   39

2. ~~Avoid having~~ *Never have* only one line of a paragraph at the bot-   50
   tom or at the top of a page.   56

3. Type ea*ch* footnote on the *same* page ~~with~~ *as* it's reference   67
   figure. (Another acceptable practice is to place *all*   78
   footnotes at the end of the manuscript.)   87

4. Type the page number on the s*e*cond/~~sheet~~ *page* and subse-   98
   quent ones at the right margin a half inch from the   108
   top, unless the report is to be topbound, in which case   120
   center the number a half inch from the bottom edge   130
   of the sheet.   133

67C Centering Over the Line of Writing ⑩

TO CENTER OVER LINE OF WRITING

To center over the line of writing (as a title in a leftbound manuscript), follow these steps:

1. Determine the center of the line:
   a. Note on the platen or paper-bail scale the numbers where the left and right margins are set.
   b. Add these two figures.
   c. Divide the sum by 2.

2. From the center of the line, backspace *once* for each *two* typewriter characters and spaces

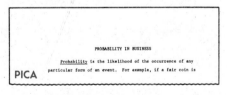

PICA

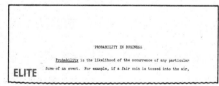

ELITE

in the heading to be centered; begin to type where backspacing ends.

DO:

1. Set margin stops for typing a leftbound manuscript.

2. Beginning on Line 13, type two lines from the copy given below.

3. Using Steps 1 and 2 at the left, center the heading PROBABILITY IN BUSINESS over the line of writing.

4. Compare your copy with the appropriate model at the left.

5. Repeat Steps 1-4, above. See if you can complete the drill more quickly this time.

Probability is the likelihood of the occurrence of any particular form of an event. For example, if a fair coin is tossed into the air,

Problem 2: Executive-Size Letter and Interoffice Memorandum

Type the letter twice as follows:

1. Executive-size stationery (7¼- by 10½-inch); 1-inch side margins; open punctuation; 10-space ¶ indention
2. Interoffice memorandum; 1-inch side margins; make all necessary adaptations to the interoffice form; add subject line *Schenectady Reservations*

Words

mr a g smith district manager banner publish- 13
ing company inc 1376 clinton street schenec- 22
tady ny 12305 dear mr smith (¶ 1) Thank you 30
for your offer to help me with my transporta- 39
tion and hotel reservations. My reservations 48
have been made, subject to contingencies, of 57
course. If I should need any help, I shall let 66
you know. My hotel reservation in Schenec- 75
tady is at the Schenectady Hilton, which I 83
understand is in a convenient location in your 93
part of town. (¶ 2) I shall call you on Mon- 100
day or Tuesday of next week so that we can 109
set an exact time for our conference. I am 118
looking forward to seeing you soon. sincerely 127
yours russel d mayes vice-president 135/157

LESSON 153

153A Preparatory Practice (5) *each line at least three times*

Alphabet Elizabeth M. Jefferson became perplexed when the fog quickly moved in.

Figures Flight 97 arrives in Erie at 4:35 a.m. Flight 68 arrives at 1:30 p.m.

Long words Technological discoveries have contributed greatly to our advancement.

Fluency Everything will come to the man who waits––if he works while he waits.

| 1 | 2 | 3 | 4 | 5 | 6 | 7 | 8 | 9 | 10 | 11 | 12 | 13 | 14 |

153B Communication Aid: Proofreading (5) *make all corrections as you type*

1 to reserve this room however my lyon must send the hotal a deposit

2 on the other hand you may write to the erie topeka or reno offices

3 if an interview is not feasable write a strong letter of application

4 now is the time to take action but counsel hasnt filed a tax report

5 please read this letter mr davis then send it to mr john woodward

6 i sincerely hope though that his last minute reports are up to date

7 he send his order last week however it just arrived in todays mail

8 he filed an up to date report of course with the manager mr miles

9 a childs world is a make believe world an adults is one of reality

10 ronald jones worked for us from november 18 1967 to august 25 1968

| 1 | 2 | 3 | 4 | 5 | 6 | 7 | 8 | 9 | 10 | 11 | 12 | 13 | 14 |

Side margins: 1½″ left, 1″ right; top margin on page 1: 1½″ pica, 2″ elite; top margin on page 2: 1″ for both pica and elite type

Type the following copy as a two-page manuscript to be bound at the left. Center the title over the *line of writing.*

Use your page-end indicator sheet to guide you in placing the heading on the first page, the page number on the second page, and the footnotes.

	Words
PROBABILITY IN BUSINESS	5

Probability is the likelihood of the occurrence of any particular form of an event. For | 15, 25
example, if a fair coin is tossed into the air, | 34
one of two events will occur——the coin will | 43
turn up either heads or tails. Most persons | 52
would assume that these two events are equally | 62
likely to occur. | 65

There are many instances in which it is | 73
impossible to determine the probabilities so | 82
readily in advance. If a number of trials are | 92
made, however, the analysis of the experimental data will give a relative frequency that can | 100, 110
be used as an estimate of the probability. | 119

The concept of probability is particularly | 128
useful in business when there is a situation | 137
for which the outcome is uncertain: the likelihood that a new product will be successful | 146, 155
or that rain will prevent the scheduled completion of a new building. Each of these situations involves uncertainty, and each of them | 163, 173, 182
is essentially a prediction of an outcome. | 190

"The study of probability began around | 198
three hundred years ago."[1] According to | 206
Encyclopaedia Britannica, Jakob Bernoulli—— | 220
a Swiss mathematician——"can be regarded as | 228
the father of probability theory as a branch of | 238
mathematics."[2] | 241

In an article entitled "It's More Probable | 250
Than You Think," Martin Gardner illustrated | 259
some remarkable examples of probability. | 267
One of them is what mathematicians call the | 276
birthday paradox. The birthday paradox pre- | 284

dicts that out of a group of 23 people, the | 293
chances are more than even that of their 23 | 302
birthdays, two will fall on the same date.[3] | 311

In another illustration of probability, the | 320
Life Science Library on Mathematics cites coincidental deaths of three presidents of the | 336, 346
United States. John Adams, James Monroe, | 353
and Thomas Jefferson, for example, all died on | 362
the Fourth of July——Adams and Jefferson in | 371
1826, Monroe in 1831.[4] Furthermore, two of | 380
our presidents share the same birth dates: | 389
James K. Polk and Warren G. Harding—— | 396
November 2. | 399

Among the first applications of probability were those involving games of chance, | 406, 415
and we still study "gaming theory." One of | 424
the first business applications of probability | 433
was made by insurance companies whose risks | 442
were determined by mortality tables. | 450

Modern business management depends | 457
heavily upon the predictions of probability | 465
studies for such decisions as: | 472

1. Determining desirable inventory levels. | 479, 481
2. Planning new products. | 486
3. Estimating rate of growth. | 493
4. Determining market potential. | 500

[1] George W. Snedecor and William G. Cochran, Statistical Methods (6th ed.; Ames, Iowa: The Iowa State University Press, 1967), p. 199. *(34 words)*

[2] "Probability," Encyclopaedia Britannica (1968), XVIII, 570. *(17 words)*

[3] Martin Gardner, "It's More Probable Than You Think," Reader's Digest (November, 1967), p. 108. *(26 words)*

[4] David Gergamini, Life Science Library on Mathematics (New York: Time, Inc., 1963), p. 143. *(25 words)*

LESSON 152

152A Preparatory Practice (5) *each line at least three times*

Alphabet	Jack and Harve did not question Jeff Mowrey about his puzzling excuse.
Figures	In 1968, 537 firms adopted the Donaldson Plan; 402 are still using it.
Drill on pol	The policy of the police was never to discuss politicians or politics.
Fluency	The key to earning the respect of your friends is to respect yourself.

| 1 | 2 | 3 | 4 | 5 | 6 | 7 | 8 | 9 | 10 | 11 | 12 | 13 | 14 |

152B Statistical Typing (10)

2 full sheets; center vertically and horizontally; DS; erase and correct errors

Type two tabulations, centering the title STATISTICAL TYPING over each one. Decide the number of spaces between columns. Use the backspace-from-center method (RG page x)

1. A three-column tabulation, using the first three columns only
2. A four-column tabulation, using all four columns

				Words 3-col.	Words 4-col.
1234	3456	5678	7890	3	4
1357	2468	3479	4680	6	8
5791	6802	7913	9135	9	12
2938	3849	4756	1000	12	16
1739	6402	5800	5060	15	20
1805	0993	1406	1072	18	24
3112	1111	2121	2211	21	28
4423	4224	6232	3323	24	32
6546	5335	8344	6444	27	36
7660	7577	9565	8556	30	40

152C Production Skill Checkup: Letter Styles; Executive-Size Letter; Interoffice Memorandum (35)

Problem 1: Letters in Modified Block and AMS Simplified Styles *2 carbon copies*

Type each letter twice as follows:

1. Modified block style; indented ¶s; mixed punctuation; block subject; postscript (RG page v)
2. AMS Simplified style (RG page v); make all necessary changes

Words

(First word count includes 3 words for the date.)

mr robert s beyer president atlas company 12
incorporated 7640 casablanca avenue st peters- 21
burg fl 33706 dear mr beyer subject the ab- 31
607 calculator (¶ 1) Last Monday it was our 39
pleasure to demonstrate to your Orlando office 48
staff our new AB-607 calculator. I am sure 57
the employees there experienced something 65
totally new in the smooth, fast handling of 74
basic computational work. (¶ 2) The AB-607 82
is the calculator with a memory. With the 90
AB-607, ten-digit constants can be stored in 99
the machine and recalled for instant reuse in 108
problems of addition, subtraction, multiplica- 117
tion, or division. (¶ 3) To understand fully 125
how it frees your attention to concentrate on 135
end results, you should really put it through 144
its paces yourself. Complete and return the 153
enclosed card, and our salesman will promptly 161
arrange a demonstration at your conven- 170
ience. sincerely yours gerald rogers sales 179
manager enclosure cc mr p t kelly *(postscript)* 186
The AB-607 is available at no increase in price 199
over the 600. 198/218

68A Preparatory Practice [7] *each line three times; then 1′ writings on Lines 3 and 4*

Alphabet	As the bus sped away, Dave Jantz made a quick lunge for the exit door.
Figures	They asked each of us to type these formulas: H_2O, H_2SO_4, and Na_2CO_3.
Figure-symbol	She told everyone to type math formulas like this: $X^2 = 3Y - (Z + 5)$.
Fluency	Every chairman can save a lot of effort if he will just plan his work.
	| 1 | 2 | 3 | 4 | 5 | 6 | 7 | 8 | 9 | 10 | 11 | 12 | 13 | 14 |

68B Skill-Transfer Typing [8]

1. Type a 2′ writing on each ¶ below. Determine *gwam*. Compare rates. Identify slower ¶.
2. Type two 1′ writings on the ¶ on which you had fewer *gwam*. Try to equal the better 2′ rate.

		GWAM 1′	GWAM 2′
¶ 1	One of the dreams of our present system of education is to bring	13	7
1.4 SI	the school to the student. A number of plans are being used to make	27	13
5.4 AWL	this dream come true. First, the state university in each of many	40	20
85% HFW	states has set up one or more local centers. Second, some states have	54	27
	added two or three new colleges to their state college systems. Third,	69	34
	a great number of junior colleges and technical schools have been	82	41
	started in both urban and suburban areas. Thus, more and more students	97	48
	can commute and do not have to live on the campus. The cost of going	111	55
	to school can thereby be reduced.	117	59
¶ 2	In 1960 there were about 1,300 colleges in the U.S. in which one	13	7
1.4 SI	could earn a degree: universities, senior colleges, and special schools.	28	14
5.4 AWL	In all, well over 3,500,000 full-time and part-time students were taking	43	21
85% HFW	courses of one kind or another in such colleges. At the same time there	58	29
	were more than 500 two-year junior or community colleges in which more	72	36
	than 400,000 were enrolled for study. By the end of the decade the four-	87	43
	year colleges had grown so that just over 4,000,000 full-time and more	101	50
	than 1,000,000 part-time students were enrolled as the two-year colleges	115	57
	shot up to more than 1,500,000 full-time and part-time students.	128	64
1′ GWAM	| 1 | 2 | 3 | 4 | 5 | 6 | 7 | 8 | 9 | 10 | 11 | 12 | 13 | 14 |		
2′ GWAM	| 1 | 2 | 3 | 4 | 5 | 6 | 7 |		

68C Special Footnotes [5]

When two footnotes contain references to the same work and one follows the other without intervening footnotes, use *Ibid.*, the abbreviation for *ibidem* (meaning in the same place), and the exact page number for the second footnote *if it differs from the first one.*

When a footnote refers to a different page in a work already cited and one or more footnotes separate it from the first one, use the author's name and the notation *op. cit.*, the abbreviation for *opere citato* (meaning in the work cited), with the appropriate page number. If the reference is to precisely the same page covered by a reference not immediately preceding, use the author's name and *loc. cit.*, the abbreviation for *loco citato* (meaning in the same place), without the page number.

DO: Use your page-end indicator behind a full sheet of paper. On Line 18 at the bottom of the page, type the underline and the following footnotes.

---

[3]Richard A. Lester, Manpower Planning in a Free Society (Princeton: Princeton University Press, 1966), p. 205.

[4]Ibid.

[5]Ibid., p. 210.

[6]Haggblade, loc. cit.

[7]Rohrer, op. cit., p. 56.

Problem 1: Letter Parts

2 full sheets; 60-space line; 1½" top margin; SS; TS between items

Correct and type the copy in the right column as directed in the left column.

1. **Address and Salutation.** Use open punctuation (RG page v).

mr c e hines president lee paper company 4526 lynnhaven drive toledo oh 43609 dear mr hines

2. **Address with Attention Line.** Use mixed punctuation (RG pages v and vii).

owen & morehouse brothers 3875 harrington avenue st joseph mo 64504 attention mr paul t pretzlaff gentlemen

3. **Letter with Blocked Subject Heading.** Use open punctuation (RG page vii).

dear mr cline subject the national economy

4. **Letter with Centered Subject Heading.** Use open punctuation (RG page vii).

gentlemen subject an investment in education

5. **Closing Lines.** Block style; mixed punctuation; enclosure notation (RG page vii).

very truly yours briggs manufacturing company louis e graziano accountant jl enclosures 2

6. **Closing Lines with Carbon Copy Notation.** Modified block style; mixed punctuation (RG page v).

very truly yours vice-president gkmallard/jmt cc mr donald e fetterman mr russell l ogden

7. **Second-Page Heading.** Use the horizontal form (RG page vii).

mr w d rusciello 2 current date

8. **Second-Page Heading.** Use the block form (RG page vii).

packaging corporation of america 2 current date

Problem 2: Letters in Block and Modified Block Styles

Type the letter twice as follows:
1. Block style; open punctuation (RG page v)
2. Modified block style; blocked ¶s; mixed punctuation (RG page v)
3. Capitalize and punctuate the heading and closing lines.

	Words
may 9, 19— freatman & roberts inc 387 com-	9
monwealth avenue savannah ga 31407 atten-	17
tion mr. albert c freatman gentlemen (¶ 1)	25
You are indeed correct in assuming that the	34
coverage outlined in your letter of May 5 is	43
included under your comprehensive policy	51
with us. It will not be necessary for you to	60
continue this protection with Allied Mutual.	69
(¶ 2) We are returning your Allied Mutual	76

	Words
policy so that you may send it back to them.	86
Also included is a note explaining that you	94
wish the policy terminated with no further	103
charge. (¶ 3) With both policies in force, you	111
would have duplicate coverage; and each in-	120
surance company would pay only half of each	129
claim. Thank you for calling this matter to	138
our attention before you paid your premium.	147
(¶ 4) Please let us know if you have further	154
questions regarding your insurance with our	163
company. very sincerely yours c h dalton gen-	173
eral agent (*your initials*) enclosures 2	178/198

(The boldface number includes the word count for the envelope.)

Problem 1: Two-Page Leftbound Manuscript

Top margin: pica, 1½"; elite, 2"; indent quotations and enumerated items 5 spaces from left and right margins; SS quotations; SS lines of each enumerated item, but DS between items.

Typing the Ellipsis: The omission of words from a quotation is shown by an *ellipsis*, which is typed with three alternating periods and spaces, or four if the end of a sentence is included in the omission (as illustrated in the quoted paragraphs below).

	Words
ADDRESSING FOR OCR	4

The ZIP Code system of mail sorting was 12
started by the Post Office Department on 20
July 1, 1963. After only a few years, ZIP 29
Codes are now being used in envelope ad- 36
dresses by a vast majority of mailers, both 45
business and personal. The widespread use of 54
ZIP Codes has helped to hold down mailing 63
charges. As President Johnson has said: 71

> The ZIP Code system is effective, 78
> efficient, and essential to a modern 85
> postal system . . . . By holding down 93
> the cost of handling each individual 100
> piece of mail, ZIP Code benefits not 108
> only mail users, but also the tax- 114
> payers . . . .[1] 118

ZIP has now been combined with the Opti- 125
cal Character Reader (OCR) to provide elec- 134
tronic mail sorting for a sizable portion of 143
business mail in several major cities.[2] 151

According to the Post Office Department, 159
OCR's are now in use in eight major cities: 168
Boston, Chicago, Detroit, Houston, Los 176
Angeles, New York, Philadelphia, and San 184
Francisco.[3] Some of these cities have more 193
than one OCR. 196

The POD suggests the following general 204
guides for addressing envelopes to be compat- 212
ible to OCR's reading habits:[4] 219

1. The address must be prepared in a 226
type style the OCR can read accu- 233
rately. Both pica and elite type- 239
writer type are ideal; script-like type 247
is not. 249
2. All lines of the address should be 257
blocked at the left. 263
3. All addresses are preferably single- 272
spaced (including two- and three- 279
line ones for uniformity). 284
4. The bottom line of the address must 292
contain the city and state names and 300
the ZIP Code. The state name may 306
be spelled in full or abbreviated ac- 314
cording to the standard abbrevia- 320

tions of the special two-letter 330
abbreviations.

5. The next-to-last line of the address 338
should be reserved for the street ad- 345
dress or the Post Office box number, 352
if either is known. 357
6. The address should be surrounded 364
by white space, as follows: 1/2 inch 372
above, 5/8 inch to the left, and the 379
entire space below and to the right. 387
In other words, the OCR read zone 393
must be clear of all but the address. 401

Some purists have lamented such "tam- 403
pering" with long-observed rules of envelope 417
addressing, suggesting that the POD recom- 426
mendations represent too great a departure 434
from "convention." In overall effect, however, 444
the changes are not really drastic; at the same 453
time, they result in quite readable addresses. 463
Furthermore, as Robinson has pointed out: 472

> If the foregoing guides result in 478
> address placement that is less artisti- 486
> cally balanced than functional, re- 493
> member that speed and accuracy in 500
> mail handling are more important 506
> than beauty of envelopes . . . .[5] 513

[1]National ZIP Code Directory, POD Publication 65 (Washington, D.C.: Post Office Department, 1968), p. iii. (*31 words*)
[2]Jerry W. Robinson, "The Marriage of ZIP and OCR," Typewriting News (Spring, 1969), p. 3. (*21 words*)
[3]Addressing for the Optical Character Reader, POD Publication 114 (Washington, D.C.: Post Office Department, 1968), p. i. (*33 words*)
[4]Ibid., pp. 3-6. (*4 words*)
[5]Robinson, op. cit., p. 4. (*10 words*)

Problem 2: Manuscript with Table

Retype page 2 of Problem 1, adding the following copy to make a three-page manuscript:

	Words

The following table may be used as a 302
guide for addressing envelopes and postal 310
cards. Its use will result in acceptable address 320
placement for OCR sorting. Column 1 gives 329
the kind of mailing piece (small envelope, 337
large envelope, or postal card); Column 2, the 347
distance between the top of the envelope or 355
card and the first line of the address; and Col- 365
umn 3, the distance from the left edge of the 374
envelope or card to the horizontal beginning 383
of the address.[6] 387

Small Envelope	2"	2½"	391
Large Envelope	2½"	4"	395
Postal Card	2"	2"	399

[6]Robinson, loc. cit. (*20 words*)

SECTION BASIC AND PRODUCTION SKILLS CHECKUP

LESSONS 151–154

Section 25 provides a checkup on basic skills and problems of earlier lessons. If you have difficulty with a task, refer to the page listed at the end of directions.

Drill Copy: Full sheet; 70-space line; SS.

Timed Writings and Paragraph Writings: Full sheet; 70-space line; 5-space ¶ indention; DS.

Letter Copy: Current date, 1 carbon copy (unless specified otherwise); your reference initials; correct errors.

Special Supplies Needed: Letterheads (or full sheets), interoffice memorandum forms; carbon paper; file copy sheets; second sheets; and envelopes of the appropriate size.

LESSON 151

151A Preparatory Practice (5) *each line at least three times*

Alphabet	Guy Crumley planned to review the book and relax just before the quiz.
Figures	Flight 907 left for Kansas City at 5:38 a.m. with 24 men and 61 women.
Shift keys	Wilbur Pollard and Roy Granville went to the World's Fair in Montreal.
Fluency	A quick way to gain your own goals is to aid your friends with theirs.
	| 1 | 2 | 3 | 4 | 5 | 6 | 7 | 8 | 9 | 10 | 11 | 12 | 13 | 14 |

151B Timed Writing (10) *two 3′ writings; compare* gwam

All letters are used in each ¶.

		GWAM 1′	3′
¶ 1 1.6 SI 5.8 AWL 75% HFW	Let us examine a pertinent point. Probably you realize you have	13	4
	come a long way in studying to become a proficient typist. Maybe by	27	9
	now you can type rapidly with accuracy. You have studied diverse let-	41	14
	ter styles and punctuation forms and can use them expertly. You have	55	18
	learned to position items attractively on a page. What more is there	69	23
	to master? Analyze carefully; trust your judgment. What reply can you	83	28
	make to such a query?	87	28
¶ 2 1.6 SI 5.8 AWL 75% HFW	Further study in typewriting can aid you to achieve several desir-	13	33
	able goals. For example, supplemental drill can aid you to type faster	28	38
	with more accuracy than you do now. Intricate problems will denote for	42	43
	you just what can be expected of a vocational typist. As you learn to	56	48
	make basic decisions, so will you type independently and without refer-	70	53
	ral to any definite directions; and you can learn to organize work.	84	57
	Yes, there is more to learn--quite a lot more.	93	60

1′ GWAM | 1 | 2 | 3 | 4 | 5 | 6 | 7 | 8 | 9 | 10 | 11 | 12 | 13 | 14 |
3′ GWAM | 1 | 2 | 3 | 4 | 5 |

LESSON 69

69A Preparatory Practice ⑦ *each line three times; then 1' writings on Lines 3 and 4*

Alphabet   John had a puzzled look when Bix requested a very special song for me.

Figures   Precincts 29, 30, and 31 report 1,928, 754, and 637 votes cast so far.

Figure-symbol   Cindy asked Dick, "Doesn't the sum of 8 3/4 and 9 4/5 equal 18 11/20?"

Fluency   Television woos many a person away from the things he should be doing.

| 1 | 2 | 3 | 4 | 5 | 6 | 7 | 8 | 9 | 10 | 11 | 12 | 13 | 14 |

69B Skill-Transfer Typing ⑧

1. Type a 2' writing on each ¶ below. Determine *gwam*. Compare rates. Identify slower ¶.

2. Type two 1' writings on the ¶ on which you had fewer *gwam*. Try to equal the better 2' rate.

		GWAM	
		1'	2'

¶1
1.4 SI
5.4 AWL
85% HFW

It is true that there is just as much competition in business today as fifty years ago? A lot of many folks do not think there is. They say competition is much less in evidence now than before. They allude to what they consider to be a great growth in companies that once were small and to the increasing merging of firms one with another. They point also, too, to the rise in government control and in taxes, two a factor that limits competition to some extent.

     12 · 6 · 52
     25 · 13 · 58
     38 · 19 · 65
     53 · 26 · 72
     70 · 35 · 80
     86 · 43 · 88
     91 · 45 · 91

¶2
1.4 SI
5.4 AWL
85% HFW

Yet, one point of view stands out. Competition in the last few decades seems to have become more intense: in terms of prices, in terms of services, and in terms of products. Is it because of huge firms or in spite of them? That is a moot question. However, a demand for better products and a need to refine the methods of production have made more acute the need for firms to combine all resources in a unique way to produce products at competitive prices.

     14 · 7 · 53
     30 · 15 · 61
     46 · 23 · 69
     62 · 31 · 77
     78 · 39 · 85
     92 · 46 · 92

69C Composing and Typing from Rough Draft ⑩

DO: Type the portion of the manuscript as given; then describe what happens to you when you type a timed writing. Make corrections; then retype the manuscript from your corrected copy.

MIND AND BODY

(¶ 1) If proof is needed that the mind has a far-reaching influence upon the body, just watch me type. The psychiatrists must have had my typing in mind when they wrote:

(¶ 2) The relationship between body and mind is continuous and intimate. . . . Mind and body are so closely connected . . . not even a single thought or mood can come into existence without being reflected in the physical organism.[1]

(¶ 3) I type quite well, as a rule; but when I hear, "Get ready for a 5-minute writing, please," my emotions take over my typing motions and *(Describe how you feel and how you type when taking a timed writing.)*

---

[1]Edward A. Strecker and Kenneth E. Appel, <u>Discovering Ourselves</u> (New York: The Macmillan Company, 1962), pp. 12-13.

Problem 3: Outline

2" top margin; see p. 185

Words

STOCKS

1

I. COMMON STOCK

5

  A. No Fixed Dividends

9

  B. Voting Privilege Usually

15

II. PREFERRED STOCK

20

  A. Dividends Usually Paid First

27

    1. Cumulative (unpaid dividends accumulate)

36

    2. Noncumulative (dividends in arrears not paid)

46

    3. Participating (sharing residual dividends with common stockholders)

58
61

    4. Nonparticipating (receiving only agreed percent of dividends)

72
75

  B. Voting Privilege Usually Absent

82

III. STOCK VALUES

87

  A. Par Value Stock

91

  B. No Par Value Stock

96

  C. Market Value of Stock

101

  D. Book Value of Stock

106

IV. STOCKHOLDERS MEETING

112

  A. Usually Held Annually

117

  B. Elections Conducted

122

    1. Board elected by stockholders

129

      a. Personal vote

133

      b. Proxy

136

    2. Officers elected later by Board

143

Problem 4: Purchase Order

See p. 225

Words

Ordered From Meade Sports Goods Company 417 Hooper Street Norfolk, VA 25313   13
Order No. 1879 **Date** (*current*) **Terms** 1/10, n/30 F.O.B. Richmond **Ship Via** Gold   23
Star Trucking Lines   27

Quantity	Cat. No.	Description	Price	Total	
12	SR129	Marsh's Jet Spin Reels	9.72	116.64	36
10	SR135	Marsh's Buddy Lightweight Spin Reels	7.12	71.20	48
8	SR136	Bing's Spinlite Special Spin Reels	17.82	142.56	59
18	SR140	Aladdin's Freespeed Spin Reels	9.17	165.06	70
16	SR142	Zig's Spin Wondereels	10.73	171.68	79
6	TB607	Aladdin Aluminum Tackle Boxes	6.40	38.40	89 90
				705.54	91

Problem 1: Poem

Half sheet, long side at left;
line: 35; begin on Line 13

	Words
A SERMON IN RHYME	4

	Words
If you have a friend worth loving,	11
Love him. Yes, and let him know	17
That you love him, ere life's evening	25
Tinge his brow with sunset glow.	32
Why should good words ne'er be said	39
Of a friend till he is dead?	45
If you hear a song that thrills you,	52
Sung by any child of song,	58
Praise it. Do not let the singer	65
Wait deserved praises long.	71
Why should one who thrills your heart	78
Lack the joy you may impart?	84
--Daniel Webster Hoyt	88

Problem 2: Outline

Half sheet, long side at left; begin on
Line 10; line: 40; spread the heading

	Words
SEEDING A LAWN	6
I. PREPARING THE SOIL	10
A. Breaking Up and Pulverizing Soil	18
1. Spade	20
2. Power tiller	23
B. Soaking Area To Be Planted	29
C. Adding Nutrients	34
II. SMOOTHING OUT THE SEEDBED	41
A. Leveling the Soil	45
B. Cutting Off High Spots	50
1. "Homemade" drag	55
2. Roller	57
3. Rake	59
III. SEEDING AND PROTECTING THE LAWN AREA	68
A. Using Mechanical Seeder	74
B. Adding Protective Cover	79
1. Straw	82
2. Cloth	84
C. Sprinkling To Set Seed	89

Problem 3: Unbound Manuscript

Full sheet; DS; 5-space ¶ in-
dention; 1½" or 2" top margin

● Underline italicized items.

	Words
TYPING SPECIAL SYMBOLS AND SIGNS	7

(¶ 1) Type the hyphen with a space before [14] and after it for a minus sign (6 – 2). The [23] small *x* with a space before and after it can be [32] used for the multiplication sign (2 x 6). Use [42] the quotation mark (") for inches, seconds, [51] and ditto; and the apostrophe (') for feet or [60] minutes. Type the symbol for "Care of" with [69] the small c, diagonal, and small o (c/o). Type [79] the dash with two hyphens without spacing [87] before or after them (May 6--Wednesday). [96] (¶ 2) Many symbols or signs not on the stan- [103] dard typewriter keyboard can be made by [111] combining characters. To type the exclama- [119] tion point, type the period; backspace; and [128] type the apostrophe (!). For a plus sign, type [138] the diagonal; backspace; and type the hyphen [146] (+). For a division sign, type a hyphen; [154] backspace; and type a colon (÷). (¶ 3) Sym- [162] bols are raised (superscripts) or lowered (sub- [171] scripts) from the writing line by using the [180] ratchet release and the cylinder. To type the [190] degree symbol, for example: Operate the [198] ratchet release; turn the cylinder *toward* you [208] slightly; then type a small o (68°). (¶ 4) [216] When typing chemistry symbols, the sub- [224] scripts must be lowered from the line of writ- [233] ing. Type the symbol in all capitals, *leaving* [243] *space for the subscripts*; then backspace to the [258] space for the first subscript; operate the [266] ratchet release; and turn the cylinder a half [276] space *away* from you; type the first subscript [286] --then space to the second blank space and [294] type the second subscript; and so on. Type [303] the following chemistry symbols: $MgSO_4$ and [312] Na_2CO_3. [313]

Note. One-page manuscripts are not numbered.

Type for 25 minutes. Erase and correct errors. You will need an interoffice memorandum form, a purchase order, and full sheets of blank paper. When time is called, compute your *n-pram*.

Problem 1: Interoffice Memorandum with Table

SS body; see p. 179

		Words
TO: David E. Moore	DATE: (Current)	6
FROM: Robert Daniels		9
SUBJECT: Bonding Agents	FILE: IM–A–768	14

As a result of our recent article in Ceramics, we have had many — 28
inquiries from people associated with the building industry about the rela- — 43
tive qualities of the three leading brands of adhesives now on the market. — 58

In response to these inquiries, we have conducted tests on these — 71
brands—–Belmont, Luxor, and Dye's—–with results as shown below. — 84

COMPARATIVE QUALITIES OF THREE BONDING AGENTS — 94

	Belmont	Luxor	Dye's	
	Belmont	Luxor	Dye's	101
Waterproof	Excellent	Average	Poor	108
Water Resistance	Excellent	Excellent	Excellent	118
Flexibility	Average	Poor	Poor	124
Bonding Strength	Excellent	Average	Average	132
Workability	Excellent	Poor	Excellent	140

The excellence of the Belmont product is evident, but it should be — 153
kept in mind that its price is about three times that of the other two. — 168
You may use this information in whatever ways will serve you best. — 181
Complete information about the tests is available from our office. — 196

Problem 2: Table with Horizontal Rules

Full sheet; SS; decide spaces between columns; add horizontal rules; see p. 204

REGISTRATION OF COPYRIGHTS BY SELECTED MEDIA — 9

1950 to 1965 — 12

Subject Matter of Copyright	1950	1960	1965	Words
				40
Subject Matter of Copyright	1950	1960	1965	48
				62
Total	210,564	243,926	293,617	69
Books	50,456	60,034	76,098	74
Periodicals	55,436	64,204	78,307	81
Lectures, Sermons, Addresses	1,007	835	848	91
Musical Compositions	52,309	65,558	80,881	99
Works of Art	4,013	5,271	5,735	106
Drawings or Plastic Works of				112
Scientific or Technical Character	1,316	768	1,239	123
Photographs	1,143	842	860	129
Motion Picture Photoplays	782	2,755	2,536	139
				153

Source: U.S. Bureau of the Census, Statistical Abstract of the United — 174
States: 1966 (87th ed.; Washington: U.S. Government Printing — 189
Office, 1966), p. 526. — 194

LESSON 70

70A Preparatory Practice (7) *each line three times; then 1′ writings on Lines 3 and 4*

Alphabet	Five quick zebras formed a phalanx, viewing a young jackal with alarm.
Figures	Invoice Nos. 4571 and 8692 were both paid last month by Check No. 301.
Figure-symbol	I am requesting 9 seats @ $2.60, 8 seats @ $3.20, and 7 seats @ $4.15.
Fluency	To look for the right job is far better than to look for just any job.

| 1 | 2 | 3 | 4 | 5 | 6 | 7 | 8 | 9 | 10 | 11 | 12 | 13 | 14 |

70B Technique Practice: Machine Manipulation (8) *each line at least three times*

Tabulator	automation [5] computers [5] probability [5] prediction [5] electronic
Shift lock	Order the magazine Saturday Review and two copies of the book ELECTRA.
Backspacer	Be careful of your use of Ibid., loc. cit., and op. cit. in footnotes.
Ratchet release	Raise the temperature of the H_2O to 212°; lower the H_2SO_4 to just 72°.
Margin release	←5 It is not enough to think that you can; you must take the next step and prove it.

| 1 | 2 | 3 | 4 | 5 | 6 | 7 | 8 | 9 | 10 | 11 | 12 | 13 | 14 |

70C Skill-Transfer Typing (5) *each paragraph repeated for a 1′ writing; compare* gwam

		1′ GWAM
Straight copy	Striking the keys when you type is not the same thing as striking	13
	a golf ball, for in typing you do not follow through.	24
Rough draft	In typping you must uose a quick sharp strock and pull the finger	13
	just slightly toard the palm ofyour hand	22
Script	You should realize the power that is yours by typing with	12
	quiet hands and arms that are almost free of motion.	22
Statistical	If you are typing 35-45 gwam, can you add 2 or 3 gwam to your	12
	rate by the end of the term? Just 5 days remain!	22

70D Problem Typing Review (30)

Get Ready to Type . . . . 2′
Timed Production . . . . 23′
Final Proofreading . . . . 5′

DO: Type each of the problems listed at the right. Type the problems as directed, except that you will prepare a carbon copy of each one and will correct errors as you type.

Problems To Be Typed

Page	Lesson Part No.	Problem No.
109	62D	—
111	63D	1
115	65C	2
117	66D	2
118	67C	—
120	68C	—

LESSON 150

150A Preparatory Practice ⑤ *each line three or more times*

Alphabet	Elizabeth Jacks should mix five quarts of gray paint for Hugh Budwell.
Figure-symbol	The blue sedan (Model 950--315 hp) has a Blue Book value of $2,786.40.
One hand	Drews was requested to decrease the minimum number of pollution tests.
Fluency	The first and last rule of writing clear copy is knowing your subject.

| 1 | 2 | 3 | 4 | 5 | 6 | 7 | 8 | 9 | 10 | 11 | 12 | 13 | 14 |

150B Growth Index ⑩ *one 5′ writing; compute* nwam

All letters are used.

		GWAM 1′	5′	
¶ 1 1.5 SI 5.6 AWL 80% HFW	Credit is a vital sales tool. Without it, many companies could	13	3	57
	not stay in business. Often the more credit firms grant, the larger	27	5	59
	will be their total annual sales. This principle is based on the	40	8	62
	fact that a credit sale is easier to make than a cash sale. Statistics	54	11	65
	show that a credit buyer gets more and in larger amounts. A credit	68	14	68
	customer is usually a steady one. All sales must be profitable, however,	83	17	70
	and this calls for good business credit.	91	18	72
¶ 2 1.5 SI 5.6 AWL 80% HFW	What is credit? It is the ability a buyer has to acquire goods	13	21	75
	or services from a seller in exchange for his word to pay a specific	27	23	77
	amount at a specific future time. Thus, firms do not grant credit; they	41	26	80
	accept it. Companies offer their goods or services. The buyer, on the	56	29	83
	other hand, either offers cash or his credit. If he offers credit,	69	32	86
	you either accept or reject his credit and business. Either decision is	84	35	89
	basically yours to render.	89	36	90
¶ 3 1.5 SI 5.6 AWL 80% HFW	Firms, in appraising a buyer as a credit risk, examine him from	13	38	92
	four angles. The first of these is his character. His former dealings	27	41	95
	are analyzed and judged. One writer said, "It is more important to	41	44	98
	know a customer's philosophy than his income. If he is a scoundrel,	55	47	101
	there is no need to continue." Those who have the desire to pay their	69	50	104
	bills generally have the ability. Finally, the debtor's memory should be	84	53	107
	as good as that of the creditor.	90	54	109

1′ GWAM | 1 | 2 | 3 | 4 | 5 | 6 | 7 | 8 | 9 | 10 | 11 | 12 | 13 | 14 |
5′ GWAM | 1 | 2 | 3 |

LESSON 71

71A Preparatory Practice (7) *each line three times; then 1′ writings on Lines 3 and 4*

Alphabet	Laziness vexed Jack, but he built his physique by lifting more weight.
Figures	A survey on June 7, 1968, listed the population of the town at 23,540.
Figure-symbol	Serial #81547 was stamped on the engine; Model #2193 (R) was below it.
Fluency	Of the six major elements, I think the first is most important by far.
	| 1 | 2 | 3 | 4 | 5 | 6 | 7 | 8 | 9 | 10 | 11 | 12 | 13 | 14 |

71B Growth Index (7) *a 5′ writing; determine* gwam *and errors*

All letters are used.

		GWAM 1′	5′	
¶ 1	Discipline of conduct is a condition of life that will be with us	13	3	51
1.4 SI	as long as we live. When we are children, our parents and our teachers	28	6	54
5.4 AWL	guide our conduct and establish our discipline. A boy, for instance, who	42	8	57
85% HFW	wishes to become an expert athlete must be made to discipline himself	56	11	60
	through daily practice and work to perfect his style. Also, a girl who	71	14	63
	has a desire to become a fine pianist must be urged to discipline her-	85	17	65
	self to follow set hours and methods of practice in order to do well.	99	20	68
¶ 2	As the years pass, however, each of us realizes more and more that	13	22	71
1.4 SI	the discipline must come from within. No longer can we depend upon our	28	25	74
5.4 AWL	parents and teachers to goad us into appropriate action; we must employ	42	28	77
85% HFW	our own self-discipline. To be successful in college, for example, we	56	31	79
	must develop good study habits and stay with them. To be a success in	71	34	82
	business, we must plan our own work and make that plan work. As we grow	85	37	85
	older, we must discipline ourselves to put work before personal enjoy-	99	40	88
	ment. There is a time for work and a time for play, and each requires	113	42	91
	its own discipline of conduct. Finally, the time comes when we must	127	45	94
	discipline ourselves to the freedoms as well as to the demands of our	141	47	96
	own old age.	144	48	97

1′ GWAM | 1 | 2 | 3 | 4 | 5 | 6 | 7 | 8 | 9 | 10 | 11 | 12 | 13 | 14 |
5′ GWAM | 1 | 2 | 3 |

71C Problem Typing Measurement: Outline and Manuscript (36)

Get Ready to Type . . . . 2′
Timed Production . . . . 30′
Final Proofreading . . . . 4′

Problem 1: Two-Page Leftbound Manuscript

Full sheets; top margin: 1½″ pica; 2″ elite; errors corrected

Words

THE MACHINE AGE OFFICE 5

Automation, which greatly increases 14
man's ability to use tools, and computers, 24
which multiply his ability to do mental work, 33
must rank with nuclear energy as the most 42
important developments of our age. Com- 50
puters were originally developed by scientists 59
and engineers to aid in the solution of prob- 68
lems involving large amounts of computation.[1] 77
Today, computers are being utilized in data 86
processing departments in business to the 94
great benefit of everyone. This is true because 104
"the tremendous speed and accuracy of data 113
processing equipment make possible the pro- 121
duction of the myriad reports and documents 130
required in a modern business operation."[2] 139

Everyone in today's business world is af- 147
fected in some way by computers and elec- 155
tronic data processing. According to the Data 164
Processing Management Association, elec- 172
tronic data processing has become a necessary 181
and integral part of our existence.[3] Those who 191
work in business offices are affected by 199
mechanical and automated processes both 207
directly and indirectly. As an example, Hanna, 217
Popham, and Beamer point out: 223

> The modern office uses many 228
> machines and facilities in processing 238
> data. Some of them--typewriters, 246

directors' meetings are held once a month. 106
The fees for meetings attended are $450 for 115
non-employee directors. Employee directors 123
do not receive any fees. (¶4) The 12 nomi- 131
nees for directors were elected. 138

Proposal to Limit Charitable Contributions
155

(¶5) In commenting on this proposal, one 162
stockholder stated that contributions before 171
taxes were equal to approximately 6½ cents a 180
share and to only 3¼ cents after taxes. He 189
stated that he was very happy to give in this 198
manner. The proposal was defeated by a vote 207
of 1,510 votes for and 17,161 votes against. 216
(¶6) At the meeting of the Board of Direc- 223
tors, which followed the stockholders meeting, 233
all officers were reelected to their positions. 243

Ralph C. Morris   Eugene Bailey 249
Chairman of the Board   President 255

Problem 2: Last Page of Leftbound Manuscript

This is page 6 (last page) of report; see p. 185

This is page 6 (last page) of report; see p. 185

Words

(¶1) While tremendous advances have been 7
made in science and technology, our knowl- 15
edge of how to develop and employ men lags 24
far behind. Frank H. Cassell, Director of the 33
United States Employment Service, summed 41
up the present state of affairs in this way: 51
"We can create miracles from molecules, but 59
we are only beginning to get some grasp of 68
what people can do if given the right oppor- 77
tunity and incentive to develop their talents." [5] 87
The need to develop our manpower is today's 95
new frontier. (¶2) We often judge a nation's 104
greatness by its art, scientific achievements, 113
and raw materials. While there is nothing 122
wrong with this method of assessing a nation's 131
leadership, there is a new measure that sur- 140
passes all others. That measure is the state 149
of a nation's manpower. (¶3) We have only 156
recently begun to recognize the real value of 165
investing in people. As a result, education is 171
being thought of as our greatest industry. Its 185
products are the human resources of this 193
nation.[6] 195

[5] Frank H. Cassell, "Manpower––Today's Frontier," California Management Review (Spring, 1968), p. 3. (*29 words*)
[6] Ronald Gross and Judith Murphy, The Revolution in the Schools (New York: Harcourt, Brace & World, Inc., 1964), p. 8. (*28 words*)

Problem 3: Letter on Executive-Size Stationery (7¼" by 10½")

Modified block; open punctuation

Words

(*Current date*) mr ira m hammond jr 3712 9
elfindale street springfield mo 65804 dear mr 19
hammond (¶1) Thank you for selecting the 26
Manor Hotel as your home away from home. 34
It was a pleasure to have you with us. (¶2) 42
You will help us greatly if you give us your 51
frank opinion of our facilities and service. We 61
recognize how important it is for all our em- 70
ployees to give friendly, efficient service and 80
for all equipment to be in faultless condition. 89
(¶3) Compliments will be passed on to em- 96
ployees; constructive criticism will be given 106
our immediate attention. cordially julius 114
weaver chairman of the board 120/134

Problem 4: Agenda for Meeting

DS between items; arrange attractively on full sheet

Words

ARCADE SOCIETY 3

Agenda for Meeting, April 9, 19–– 10

1. Call to Order 13
2. Minutes of March Meeting 19
3. President's Report on Plans to Revise Mem- 28
   bership Regulations 32
4. Treasurer's Report 37
5. Report of Committee on Scholarships on 45
   Contributions Received for Aid of For- 53
   eign Students in American Schools 60
6. Report of Progress on Plans for the An- 68
   nual Dinner Meeting in June by the 75
   Program Committee 79
7. Adjournment 82

duplicators, copiers, and calculators — 253
——the secretary uses regularly in her — 261
work. Others——punched-card equip- — 267
ment, tape-activated machines, and — 274
the electronic computer——may or — 281
may not be operated by the secre- — 287
tary, but they are important to her — 294
work.[4] — 296

Data processing is not a new process; it — 304
has been operating for centuries. Nor is the — 313
mechanical processing of data a new develop- — 322
ment. In fact, from the digital computer on — 331
his hands and feet, man has progressed — 339
through the abacus, the simple adding ma- — 347
chine, the electric calculator, and the elec- — 355
tronic calculator to the modern electronic — 364
computer. — 366

Increasing dependence upon data is a — 374
phenomenon of modern business. Information — 382
from all parts of an industrial complex are — 391
channeled into its central offices. Other data — 401
are researched and collected, statistics are — 410
organized into meaningful tables and graphs, — 419
and reports are prepared for others to study, — 428
evaluate, and act upon. Few areas offer the — 437
secretary greater opportunity to prove her — 446
value as an administrative assistant.[5] — 454

[1]E. Wainright Martin, Jr., Electronic Data Processing (Rev. ed.; Homewood, Illinois: Richard D. Irwin, Inc., 1965), p. 3. (33 words)

[2]Clarence B. Randall and Sally Weimer Burgley, Systems & Procedures for Business Data Processing (2d ed.; Cincinnati: South-Western Publishing Co., 1968), p. 79. (42 words)

[3]Data Processing Management Association, Automatic Data Processing (Englewood Cliffs, N.J.: Prentice-Hall, Inc., 1966), pp. 11-14. (31 words)

[4]J Marshall Hanna, Estelle L. Popham, and Esther K. Beamer, Secretarial Procedures and Administration (5th ed.; Cincinnati: South-Western Publishing Co., 1968), p. 428. (44 words)

[5]Ibid., p. 427. (4 words)

Problem 2: Outline

Half sheet, long side at left; line: 45; 1" top margin

	Words
PROCEDURES OF DATA HANDLING	6
I. RECORDING DATA	9
A. Original Source Documents	15
B. Preparing Cards and Tapes	21
II. CLASSIFYING DATA	27
A. Using Alphabetic Code	32
B. Using Numeric Code	37
C. Using Alphanumeric Code	42
III. CREATING NEW DATA	48
A. Programming to Manipulate Data	55
B. Performing Arithmetic Operations	63
1. Addition	66
2. Subtraction	70
3. Multiplication	75
4. Division	78
IV. SORTING DATA	83
V. SUMMARIZING DATA	88
A. Consolidating Data	92
B. Providing for Information Retrieval	100

Problem 3: Composing

Compose as you type in unbound manuscript form a two- or three-paragraph statement of your understanding of the effects of computers and automation on your chosen field of work. Proofread and correct your copy; then type a final copy using THE COMPUTER AND I as a heading.

Self-Improvement Practice

If you complete the problem typing any day before the period ends, select from the following statements a topic for an interpretative composition.

For each topic selected, *compose as you type* one or two paragraphs giving your interpretation of the statement. If time permits, type a corrected copy.

1. The years teach much which the days never know. ——Emerson
2. Thoughts are but dreams till their effects be tried. ——Shakespeare
3. At any age, to be only a member of a group is to be less than a complete person. ——Stoddard
4. Responsibility is the price every man must pay for freedom. ——Hamilton
5. There are two kinds of fools. One says, "This is old, therefore it is good." The other says, "This is new, therefore it is better." ——Inge

Problem 3: Block Style Letter

Open punctuation; 1 carbon copy

Words

walter l davis esq. washburn, hosler & locke 13
936 commerce building springfield mo 65821 22
dear mr davis (¶ 1) This letter confirms our 29
telephone conversation of this morning in 38
which you and your firm were appointed our 47
legal representatives in the case of Ramsey v. 56
Worthington. (¶ 2) I am having a complete 63
list of our transactions with both litigants 72
documented, and a copy of it will be sent to 81
you. Mr. McLeeds has withdrawn completely 90
from the case; he will give you his files. If 99
you need still further information, let me 108
know personally. sincerely yours irvin h dia- 117
mond president cc mr raymond mcleeds 125/144

Problem 4: Modified Block Letter with Table

Indented ¶s; open punctuation

Words

bond–moore sports equipment company 1475 11
kilvington avenue nashville tn 37211 atten- 24
tion sales department gentlemen (¶ 1) Will 32
you please send us a quotation for the follow- 41
ing merchandise as soon as possible. All 49
prices should be quoted f.o.b. our store. 58

14 doz.	Lead Bass Casting Sinkers	64
50 pkgs.	Nylon Snelled Fang Hooks	71
8 doz.	Standard June Bug Spinners	78
12 doz.	Standard Trolling Spinners	85

(¶ 2) Please state all terms clearly, noting 93
quantity and cash discounts. yours very truly 102
durston & wallace burton e stanley director 111
of purchases 114/130

LESSON 149

149A Preparatory Practice [5] *each line three or more times*

Alphabet Jack and Beth Powell may take a quiz next week if the board gives one.

Figure-symbol O'Dell paid $729.38 (less 10%) for Model #4560 at Birdwell & Smothers.

Vowels Despite his diet, he ate various pieces of chocolate candy and sweets.

Fluency We know that success comes to the men who are too busy to look for it.

| 1 | 2 | 3 | 4 | 5 | 6 | 7 | 8 | 9 | 10 | 11 | 12 | 13 | 14 |

149B Production Skill Building [10] *type 142B, page 246, as directed*

149C Production Measurement: Reports [35] *errors corrected; figure* n-pram

Type for 25 minutes. Correct errors. To type the problems in this lesson, you will need three full sheets of blank paper. When time is called, compute your *n-pram.*

Problem 1: Partial Report of Stockholders Meeting

Unbound manuscript form; SS; see p. 241

Words

REPORT OF MORRIS MOTORS 5
STOCKHOLDERS MEETING 9

(¶ 1) The 25th Annual Meeting of Morris 16
Motors stockholders was called to order by 24
Ralph C. Morris, Chairman of the Board of 33
Directors, who presided. Mr. Morris wel- 41
comed the stockholders present at the meet- 49
ing as well as several officers. 56

Election of Directors 65

(¶ 2) The 12 nominees named in the proxy 72
statement were nominated. (¶ 3) A stock- 78
holder inquired as to the number of directors' 88
meetings and fees paid. Mr. Morris said that 97

SECTION 11 REVIEW: Basic and Problem Skills

LESSONS 72–73

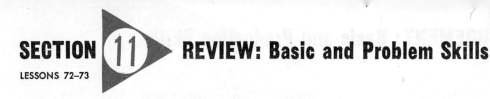

Purpose. The purpose of the two lessons of this section is to review the work of the preceding 71 lessons in preparation for the measurement activities of Section 12.

Machine Adjustments. Unless otherwise directed, use a 70-space line and SS. Be alert to required changes in line length and spacing in the checkup and review portions of the lessons.

LESSON 72

72A Preparatory Practice [5] *each line twice; then 1′ writings on Line 4*

Alphabet	Jud Vance says the quest for great power may take extra zeal by Irwin.
Figures	Our store has three locations: 38-40 Main; 2756 Oakland; 1396 Beamer.
Figure-symbol	Jay insured his car, Engine #P41738295J, on Mutual Policy #A2134-J-67.
Fluency	She works with great vigor on the eight land forms for the city panel.
	| 1 | 2 | 3 | 4 | 5 | 6 | 7 | 8 | 9 | 10 | 11 | 12 | 13 | 14 |

72B Basic Operations Checkup [13] *line: exactly 50; each item on a separate half sheet*

1. **Shift Keys and Shift Lock.** Begin on Line 10. DS the following paragraph:

   Dr. Gail Evans is the author of TEACHERS ALL. In addition, she has contributed numerous articles to the periodical Modern Education. Her latest is entitled "The Current Status of Auto-Instruction." She will lecture tonight at 8 p.m. in Hinkle Hall.

2. **Typing Outside the Margins.** Type on Line 17. Begin the sentence given below 7 spaces outside the left margin. When the bell rings, continue typing and complete the sentence on one line.

   Are you drinking at the fountain of knowledge or merely gargling?

3. **Typing Roman Numerals.** Begin on Line 8. DS the Roman numerals **I.** through **X.** in a column at the left margin.

4. **Margin Release and Backspacing.** Reset the left margin 4 spaces to the right. Begin on Line 12. SS the following numbered items; DS between them. Use the margin release and backspacer to position the numbers.

   1. Operate the margin release key, then backspace four times to type the number.
   2. Begin the second line of an enumerated item at the same point where the first line begins.

5. **Automatic Line Finder.** Reset the left margin for a 50-space line. Begin on Line 12. DS the following sentence, using the line finder (ratchet release) to type the superscripts and the subscripts.

   Decrease the temperature of the H_2SO_4 to 0° centigrade or 32° Fahrenheit.

6. **Aligning and Typing Over.** Reinsert the paragraph typed as Item 1; gauge the line and letter; type over the first and last lines.

72C Problem Layout Review [32]

Supplies Needed: half sheets, 2; postal cards, 2; full sheets, 1; small envelopes, 1

Make a typewritten list of the problems listed at the right in order of textbook page number. Put the list in a convenient place for easy reference.

Type each problem as directed, except that you will prepare a carbon copy of each one and correct any errors you make as you type.

Problems To Be Typed

Page No.	Lesson Part No.	Problem No.
59	34C	1
61–62	36C	2
70–71	41C	1, 3
87	51C	1

SECTION 24 MEASU... and Pr...duction Skills

LESSONS 148–150

Unless otherwise directed, follow these ...
Drill Copy: Full sheet; 70-space line; ...
Production Copy: When complete directions are not given, use your own judgment. Make your work neat ...d attractive. Correct your errors.
Page References: When appropriate, reference is given for a quick review of problem procedures. No extra time is allowed for reference, however.

LESSON 148

148A Preparatory Practice (5) *each line three or more times*

Alphabet	Pizarro's powerful army unjustly vanquished the boxed-in Inca kingdom.
Figure-symbol	Our Check #75921 for $340.68, covering your Invoice #537, is enclosed.
Long reaches	Only the hungry baby's babbling disturbed the dignity of the ceremony.
Fluency	Until we meet the problem, we do not need to worry about its solution.
	| 1 | 2 | 3 | 4 | 5 | 6 | 7 | 8 | 9 | 10 | 11 | 12 | 13 | 14 |

148B Paragraph Guided Writings for Speed (10) *type 128D, page 221, as directed*

148C Production Measurement: Communication Forms (35)

Materials: To complete the problems in this lesson, you will need letterheads, carbon paper, onionskin, and envelopes.

Type for 25 minutes. Use the current date and your initials. Correct your errors. Make a carbon copy and address an envelope for each letter. When time is called, compute the *n-pram.*

Problem 1: Modified Block Letter

Mixed punctuation; centered subject line

Words

mr john s scranton vice-president cantwell 12
and cramm's 878 amber street houston tx 21
77022 dear mr scranton subject: el rancho 29
patio furniture (¶ 1) Thank you for meeting 37
with me yesterday to discuss our new line of 46
furniture, El Rancho Patio. (¶ 2) When I re- 53
turned to my office this morning, I told our 62
sales manager, Mr. John Bartel, that your 71
store was considering an adoption of the El 79
Rancho line. He was, of course, pleased and 88
authorized me to offer you a 5 percent dis- 97
count on your initial order. (¶ 3) I shall be 105
in Houston next month and shall telephone 113
you then to learn if I can give you any fur- 122
ther information about the El Rancho Patio 130
line. sincerely yours miles a brookhart sales 140
representative A copy of our Manufacturer's 150
Warranty is enclosed. 154/172

Problem 2: AMS Simplified Letter

Open punctuation; see p. 176

Words

mr frank c green 898 evergreen drive augusta 13
ga 30904 policy no 743891 (¶ 1) Our records 21
reveal the very gratifying fact that the final 30
premium payment for your policy has been 38
received. You now have a contract that is 47
paid in full. May we congratulate you upon 56
the attainment of this objective, which you 65
planned so many years ago. (¶ 2) If at any 72
time you should desire information concern- 81
ing this policy or assistance in connection with 90
your insurance estate, please call on us. Our 100
services are always at your disposal. (¶ 3) So 108
that our records may always be up to date, 117
Mr. Green, we shall appreciate your notifying 126
us promptly of any change in your address. 135
victor m young – vice-president cc mr george 145
thom agent 147/158

LESSON 73

73A Preparatory Practice [5] *each line twice; then 1′ writings on Line 4*

Alphabet	Vaughn Dixon acquired the prize job with a large firm just like yours.
Figures	Order 25 each of Cat. Nos. 273J, 596C, 3140V, and 836M from Eban, Inc.
Figure-symbol	Send payment notices on these accounts: #4128, $57.90; #6329, $84.50.
Fluency	Hand the proxy statement to the chairman so their title can be signed.

| 1 | 2 | 3 | 4 | 5 | 6 | 7 | 8 | 9 | 10 | 11 | 12 | 13 | 14 |

73B Basic Operations Checkup [13]

1. **Centering Vertically and Horizontally.** Center the following announcement vertically and each line horizontally on a half sheet (8½″ by 5½″). Use double spacing.

BUSINESS-ECONOMICS CLUB

Regular Monthly Meeting

January 23, 3 p.m.

Royce Hall, Room 132

Speaker: Dr. L. N. Reeves

Topic: "Business in Education"

2. **Centering on Special-Size Paper.** Insert a half sheet with the long side at the left. Center the announcement of Item 1 again both vertically and horizontally. Use *triple* spacing and place the copy in *reading* position.

3. **Centering on a Postal Card.** DS and center the Item 1 announcement vertically and horizontally on a postal card (or paper cut 5½″ x 3¼″).

4. **Centering Columnar Headings.** First, on a half sheet, type the 3 columnar entries shown below, leaving 8 spaces between them. Then center the following headings over Columns 1, 2, and 3, respectively:

Advertising Medium	1960	1970
Radio-Television Spots	$ 75,000	$100,000

5. **Listening for the Bell; Word Division.** Use a half sheet and double spacing. Set the margin stops for a 60-space line, adding 5 spaces to the right margin for the ringing of the bell. Be guided by the bell to return the carriage as you type the following paragraph. Use the margin release, and divide words as necessary to maintain a reasonably uniform right margin.

Listening for the typewriter bell as a guide for returning to start the new line requires that you know the fundamental guides for dividing words. Without this important knowledge, you are quite likely to have less-than-attractive right-hand margins.

73C Problem Layout Review [32]

Supplies Needed: half sheets, 2; full sheets, 2; envelopes: large, 2; small, 1; letterheads, 2

Make a typewritten list of the problems listed at the right in order of textbook page number. Put the list in a convenient place for easy reference.

Type each problem as directed, except that you will prepare a carbon copy of each one and correct any errors you make as you type.

Problems To Be Typed

Page No.	Lesson Part No.	Problem No.
94–95	54C	2
101	57D	1
103	58D	2
104	59D	1
119	67D	—

LESSON 147

147A Preparatory Practice (5) *each line three or more times*

Alphabet   This unique, exciting bazaar was planned by Jack, Velma, and Florence.

Figure-symbol   For $274.31 (plus tax), Mr. Stone can take UAL Flight 580 at 6:19 a.m.

Outside reaches   Zeno mopped his brow, then powered the axe halfway through the quartz.

Fluency   Assuming you retire at 60, you are now preparing for 40 years of work.
| 1 | 2 | 3 | 4 | 5 | 6 | 7 | 8 | 9 | 10 | 11 | 12 | 13 | 14 |

147B Growth Index (15) *Use 141B, page 244, for two 5' writings; compute nwam on better one*

147C Sentence Guided Writings (10)

Type two or more 1' writings on each sentence with the guide called each 15, 12, or 10 seconds. Try completing a sentence and returning your carriage as the guides are called.

		GWAM		
		15"	12"	10"
1	I was pleased to hear from you about the position open in your office.	56	70	84
2	Thank you for giving me the opportunity to talk to you about this job.	56	70	84
3	I shall try to live up to the high standards of your firm in this job.	56	70	84
4	Thank you for the offer of a position on the sales staff of your firm.	56	70	84

| 1 | 2 | 3 | 4 | 5 | 6 | 7 | 8 | 9 | 10 | 11 | 12 | 13 | 14 |

147D Communication Aid: Composing (20)

1. Type the paragraph below.
2. In a second paragraph, accept the offer. Restate the offer and the beginning date of employment. Indicate your pleasure at having been selected.
3. Proofread Paragraph 1, marking it for correction.
4. Edit and correct your paragraph; then retype both paragraphs.

I am pleased to offer you a position in our Accounting Department at a beginning monthly salary of $500. If you accept this offer, your employment is to start on Monday, June 5, at 8:15 a.m. Your duties will be in the general area of bookkeeping and accounting. As I told you during your interview, we expect this position to develop into one of head of our Credit Department. Our firm is a rapidly growing one, so the opportunities for advancement are very good for the right man. Please let me know if you will accept my offer.

SECTION 12 MEASUREMENT: Basic and Problem Skills

LESSONS 74–75

Purpose. The purpose of this section of two lessons is to measure the basic and problem skills you have developed as well as your knowledge of problem layout and machine manipulations.

Machine Adjustments. Unless otherwise directed, use a 70-space line and SS. Be alert to required changes in line length and spacing in the measurement portions of the lessons.

LESSON 74

74A Preparatory Practice (5) *each line twice; then 1′ writings on Line 4*

Alphabet	Helga Veek expects just as sizable a drop in my new quota as in Fay's.
Figures	Process the following orders immediately: M127485, M304621, and N219.
Figure-symbol	Invoices #B4178 and #L3956 (less 2%) require a net payment of $697.40.
Fluency	They may award the contract to a downtown auditor at the minimum rate.

| 1 | 2 | 3 | 4 | 5 | 6 | 7 | 8 | 9 | 10 | 11 | 12 | 13 | 14 |

74B Growth Index (10) *DS one 5′ writing; then 1′ writings as time permits*

All letters are used.

		GWAM 1′	GWAM 5′	
¶ 1	You have learned a great deal about typing in only a few months.	13	3	44
1.4 SI 5.4 AWL 85% HFW	You may not be striking all keys as rapidly or as precisely yet as you	27	5	47
	want to, but you have begun a sturdy foundation upon which you can	41	8	49
	build even more skill. Like any other skill, typing demands continued	55	11	52
	effort to be maintained or improved; so set aside daily practice time.	69	14	55
¶ 2	If you proceed with the typing sequence in college, your practice	13	16	58
1.4 SI 5.4 AWL 85% HFW	time will be scheduled for you. Even so, you will find that a bit of	27	19	61
	extra practice each day may be just enough to push your new skill into	41	22	63
	a prize grade category. Even if you do not continue with formal typing	56	25	66
	instruction, you can add greatly to your skill all by yourself.	68	27	69
¶ 3	A timed effort is superior to an untimed one. Timing supplies a	13	30	71
1.4 SI 5.4 AWL 85% HFW	little desirable pressure; it also helps to inform you just how well	27	33	74
	you are doing. In school, your teacher times you. If you practice on	41	36	77
	your own, you ought to work under time pressure then, too. A timing	55	38	80
	record or tape is an effective device to use for this very fine purpose.	69	41	83

1′ GWAM | 1 | 2 | 3 | 4 | 5 | 6 | 7 | 8 | 9 | 10 | 11 | 12 | 13 | 14 |
5′ GWAM | 1 | 2 | 3 |

74C Problem Typing Measurement (35)

Get Ready to Type	*4′*
Timed Production	*25′*
Final Proofreading	*6′*

Supplies Needed: half sheet, 1; postal card, 1; letterhead, 1; full sheets, 4

Turn to page 131 and begin to type the problems given there. When time is called, complete the line you are typing, remove the paper from the machine, and retain all your work. In Lesson 75 you will continue with the problems at the point you stopped in Lesson 74. *Erase and correct all errors as you type.*

NELSON & SONS COMPANY

Application for Employment

1185 LOUISE STREET   WICHITA, KANSAS 67203   316-123-7117

■ ■

PLEASE TYPE

Date __June 15, 19--__

Name _____ David _____ Charles _____ Edward _____
       Last   *First*   *Middle* 852-3000

Address __254 Slaton Hall, Bentley Coll., Wichita, KS__ __67207__ Telephone Number __Ext. 148__
     Street and Number   *City*   *State*   *ZIP Code*

Position Desired __Clerk__   Social Security No. __799-23-1864__

                (During   (Summer)

How Long Have You Lived at the Above Address? __2 years__ school term)   Do You Live with Your Parents? __Yes__
                                                                   Yes/No

Date and Place of Birth __June__ __4__ __1948__ __Topeka__ __Kansas__   Citizen of United States? __Yes__
               Month   *Day*   *Year*   *City*   *State*   *Yes/No*

Weight __185__   Height __5__ __11__   Right or Left Handed __Left__
      Pounds   *Feet*   *Inches*

                                                No. of Dependents

Single (X)   Married ( )   Widowed ( )   Separated ( )   Divorced ( )   Other than Self _____

EDUCATION

	School Name	Address	Major	From Year	To Year	Grad. Degree
Grammar	Fullbright Element.	Topeka, Kansas		1954	1962	Diploma
High School	Holcomb High School	Topeka, Kansas	Gen'l Course	1962	1966	Diploma
Business						
Evening						
University or College	Bentley College	Wichita, Kansas	Office Mgt.	1966		
Other						

PREVIOUS EMPLOYMENT

From Mo. Yr.	To Mo. Yr.	Name and Address of Employer	Position	Salary	Reason for Leaving
June 1964	Sept. 1966	Okewa Youth Camp Coffeyville, Kansas	Assistant to Director	$25 week	Returned to school
Sept. 1966	Sept. 1967	Williamson's Bookstore Wichita, Kansas	Salesclerk	$1.50 hour	New position
Sept. 1967		Bentley College Wichita, Kansas	Student Assistant to Professor	$1.75 hour	

PERSONAL REFERENCES *

Name	Address	Occupation
Mr. Bruce Tobey	Holcomb High School Topeka, Kansas	Principal
Dr. Frank I. Ellis	College of Bus. Admin. Bentley Coll., Wichita, KS	Chairman
Mr. B. V. Dalton	Okewa Youth Camp Coffeyville, Kansas	Director

* If you have never been employed, give names of two responsible persons (not relatives) to whom we can refer.

Signature *Charles E. David*

Model Copy of an Application Blank

LESSON 75

75A Preparatory Practice (5) *each line twice; then 1' writings on Line 4*

Alphabet   Jack Hibler may request the new ZIP Codes from Gwen Jevon next Monday.

Figures   Pay Invoice No. J2148375, but be sure to deduct Credit Memo No. C6490.

Figure-symbol   This 9- by 12-foot carpet is marked $587 but sells for $463 this week.

Fluency   He is aware of the unusual contract to be awarded the big trade union.

| 1 | 2 | 3 | 4 | 5 | 6 | 7 | 8 | 9 | 10 | 11 | 12 | 13 | 14 |

75B Skill-Comparison Typing (7) *each line for a 1' writing; compare gwam*

Balanced-hand   The six girls may go to the city to work with the auditor of the firm.

Double letters   Ella was puzzled by the letter that followed the offer of a free book.

Adjacent keys   I saw Lew Polk strike out on a pop fly, but he still leads all others.

One-hand   Rated only average, my test car drew no awards in a few races at Lynn.

Row 1   Zeal or zest can bring much more success next time than luck ever can.

Consecutive   To excel my gym record, Cecil must surpass my skill in the broad jump.

| 1 | 2 | 3 | 4 | 5 | 6 | 7 | 8 | 9 | 10 | 11 | 12 | 13 | 14 |

75C Growth Index (8) *DS one 5' writing; determine gwam and errors*

All letters are used.

		GWAM	
		1'	5'

¶1
1.4 SI
5.4 AWL
85% HFW

Will you be a dropout, or will you hang tight and finish college?   13   3 | 45
A high percentage of students who enter college do not stay to complete   28   6 | 48
a degree. A majority of these leave college during the first year or   42   8 | 50
two after entry. Most of those who make it through the first two years   56   11 | 53
manage to stay with it until they have met all diploma requirements.   70   14 | 56

¶2
1.4 SI
5.4 AWL
85% HFW

Students give a wide variety of reasons for dropping out of school.   14   17 | 59
Among them are marriage, lack of money, and desire for a well-paying   28   19 | 61
job. Not so often given but just as real are: not seeing how the   41   22 | 64
courses being offered prepare for life goals, not adjusting to a new   55   25 | 67
kind of society, and not getting passing grades in all courses.   67   27 | 69

¶3
1.4 SI
5.4 AWL
85% HFW

Are you content with college now and pleased with all you have so   13   30 | 72
far accomplished? If not, compare your personal goals with the aims   27   33 | 75
of the program of courses you are now pursuing. If the two don't mesh,   41   36 | 78
try some other program before you give up. The prize of success and   55   38 | 80
satisfaction may be as near as the next section of the general catalog   69   41 | 83
of your college.   73   42 | 84

1' GWAM | 1 | 2 | 3 | 4 | 5 | 6 | 7 | 8 | 9 | 10 | 11 | 12 | 13 | 14 |
5' GWAM | 1 | 2 | 3 |

75D Problem Typing Measurement (30) *continue typing the problems on pages 131-133*

146A Preparatory Practice [5] *each line three or more times*

Alphabet	Parker says this exciting jazz was arranged from lovely baroque music.
Figure-symbol	The report for 1968 showed a profit of $327,450, or a net gain of 17%.
One hand	In my opinion, the mill weavers should request oil for the extra loom.
Fluency	In letters the thought is central, and it should be clearly expressed.
	| 1 | 2 | 3 | 4 | 5 | 6 | 7 | 8 | 9 | 10 | 11 | 12 | 13 | 14 |

146B Communication Aid: Spelling [5]

1. Type these commonly misspelled words twice; study the words as you type them.
2. Close your book; type the words from your instructor's dictation. Check your work.

chosen confident committee balance calendar buoyant chaperon conquered

committing coming copies indictment existence experience guard hurried

abrupt absorbent accelerate accessory accommodate acknowledgment fiery

146C Technique Improvement: Combination Response [10] *each line 5 times; flowing rhythm*

1	The past is of use to us only as it can make the life of today fuller.
2	Being a leader is largely a matter of knowing how to work with people.
3	It makes a difference whether they go into a thing to win or to drift.
4	The will to win is a big aid to all the men who want to do big things.
5	The final games are to be played by two of the best teams in the city.
	| 1 | 2 | 3 | 4 | 5 | 6 | 7 | 8 | 9 | 10 | 11 | 12 | 13 | 14 |

146D Production Typing: Completing an Application Blank [30]

Problem 1: Letter Returning Form

Type this letter as a personal business letter. Decide on the letter style and form of punctuation.

	Words
Room 254, Slaton Hall Bentley College	8
Wichita, KS 67207 June 15, 19-- Mr. Lyle	16
C. Nelson, President Nelson & Sons Company	25
1185 Louise Street Wichita, KS 67203 Dear	33
Mr. Nelson (¶ 1) Thank you for asking me	41
to visit with you in your office last Thursday.	50
I enjoyed discussing employment possibilities	60
with you. Touring your plant was an un-	67
expected pleasure. (¶ 2) The application form	76
you asked me to complete is enclosed. It	84
appears to be complete; but if there is any	93
further information you would like to have,	102
please let me know. (¶ 3) If you decide you	109
want me to take the tests you mentioned, I	118
can make arrangements to do so when it is	126
convenient for you. Sincerely yours Charles	135
E. David Enclosure	139/172

Problem 2: Typing an Application Form

Type a copy of the application form shown on page 252. Arrange your copy carefully; keep your typing just above the printed lines. Try to have your typing as free of errors as possible.

Problem 3: Personal Application Form

Complete another application form. This time, assume *you* are the applicant. Use the information you would give an employer.

Problem 1: Memo Announcement

Use a half sheet; line: 60; top margin: 1½″. Correct your errors as you type memo at the right.

Problem 2: Card Announcement

Type the message of Problem 1 as a postal card announcement. Type the talk title in cap and lowercase letters enclosed in quotation marks as part of the final sentence of ¶ 1. As a signature line use Ron Allen, PDK Secretary. Use your college residence address for the card address.

January 3, 19--   3

A distinguished educator, Dr. Raymond S.   11
McNeil of Educational Technology, Inc., will   20
be the speaker at the next regular meeting of   30
Phi Delta Kappa. His subject will be   37

INSTRUCTIONAL STRATEGIES   42

The meeting will be on Wednesday, February   51
15, at 4:30 p.m. in the Little Theater of the   60
Cathedral of Learning. Be certain to hear this   69
eminent scholar.   73

Problem 3: Personal Letter

Prepare a corrected copy of the following letter. Use modified block style; blocked ¶s; mixed punctuation; line: 60; *date* on Line 16. Prepare a carbon copy. Address a small envelope. Correct your errors as you type. **Note.** The use of parentheses with "Miss" or "Mrs." in a typewritten signature is optional.

Words

2920 Scioto Hall   3
Cincinnati, Ohio   45219   8
January 3, 19--   11

College

L.
Mr. Paul Ritchie   15
~~School~~ of Education   20
University of Cincinnati   25
Cincinnati, Ohio 45219   29

Dear Mr. Ritchie: 33

My word record for the month of December is given below. It   45
includes time spent typing course outlines and lecture nootes   58
as well as time devoted to reading final examinations.   69

December 10   2 hours   73
December 11   3 hours   77
December 14   8 hours   81
December 16   5 hours   85
December 17   6 hours   89

(shall) Since I shall be doing full-time student teaching next quarter   101
and ~~will~~ not often be on campus, will you please have my check   114
mail to me at the address shown above?   122

I appreciate (the opportunity very much) of working with you as   135
a teaching and office assistant. That experience will be al-   147
most as valuable, I believe, as my student teaching activity.   160

Sincerely yours,   163

Miss Mary Riga   166

Problem 2: Personal Data Sheet

2" top margin; 60-space line; uniform vertical spacing

DATA SHEET — 2

Charles E. David — 5

Address — 8

254 Slaton Hall — 11
Bentley College — 14
Wichita, Kansas   67207 — 19
Telephone: 852–3000, Extension 148 — 26

Personal Information — 34

Age, 20. Single. Weight, 185 pounds. Height, 5 feet 11 inches. — 47

Education — 51

Graduate, General Course, Holcomb High School, Topeka, Kansas. — 64
Sophomore, Office Management, Bentley College, Wichita, Kansas. — 77

Experience — 80

Assistant to Director, Okewa Youth Camp, for two summers. — 92
Salesclerk, Williamson's Bookstore, on Saturdays for one year. — 105
Student Assistant to Doctor Erwin M. Keithley, Professor of Communications, Bentley College, for one year. — 118 / 127

References — 131

Mr. Bruce Tobey, Principal, Holcomb High School, Topeka, Kansas. — 144
Dr. Frank I. Ellis, Chairman, College of Business Administration, Bentley College, Wichita, Kansas. — 157 / 164
Mr. B. V. Dalton, Director, Okewa Youth Camp, Coffeyville, Kansas. — 178
Mr. Larry Bond, Manager, Williamson's Bookstore, Wichita, Kansas. — 191

LESSON 145

145A   Preparatory Practice (5) *each line three or more times*

Alphabet   Jack Foxe quizzed the two players about the length of an average game.

Figure-symbol He wrote, "Sell 875 @ $63\frac{1}{4}$¢ ea., 130 @ $29\frac{1}{4}$¢, and the remainder @ $49\frac{1}{2}$¢."

Double letters The committee expressed a desire to have your bookkeeper's assistance.

Fluency   It takes a great deal more than just an age of 21 to make a man of us.

| 1 | 2 | 3 | 4 | 5 | 6 | 7 | 8 | 9 | 10 | 11 | 12 | 13 | 14 |

145B   Building Control (15) *type 103B, page 183, as directed*

145C   Production Typing: Composing Letter of Application and Data Sheet (30)

Problem 1

Compose and type a letter of application for a job you would like to have for the summer. Assume a friend has told you of the opening. The firm to which you are applying is George Johnson & Son Company (provide a local address).

Problem 2

Construct and type a data sheet to accompany your letter. Use your own name, address, and qualifications in the data sheet. Arrange the data neatly on a full sheet of paper.

Problem 4: Business Letter

Modified block; blocked ¶s; mixed punctuation; line: 60; date on Line 16; 2 cc's; correct errors; envelope

Note. A color bar (|) has been given to aid you in arranging the opening and closing lines.

Words

January 4, 19-- | Mrs. Kathryn Townsend | John Marshall Junior High School | 14
Noble and Marion Streets | Houston, TX   77009 | Dear Mrs. Townsend: 27

After many years of extensive research and study by eminent scientists throughout   44
the world, we are pleased to announce the publication of our richly illustrated   60
series   61

THE MYSTERIES OF THE EARTH   66

This series was designed especially for junior high school students. The text   82
has been written in easy, concise language so the ideas can be grasped quickly   98
by young students. Your students will find this series exciting and interesting.   115

We are sure you will want this series for your library. We are, therefore, send-   131
ing you, free of charge, a copy of the first volume. Examine it carefully; then   147
order the series quickly so you will have the books for the beginning of your   163
next school year.   166

Sincerely yours, | J. Mark Atkinson | Assistant Sales Manager | *your initials* | 179
cc Dr. Elwood J. Foley, Principal   185

Problem 5: Table

Reading position on full sheet; 4 spaces between columns; SS each pair of lines; DS between pairs of lines

Center the columnar headings over the longest line in each column. Prepare a carbon copy; correct errors.

Words

DAY-BY-DAY LOG OF APOLLO 8   5

(December 21-27, 1968)   10

Activity	EST	Date	
Blastoff from cape Kennedy	7:51 a.m.	December 21	26
Left earth's gravity for moon	10:41 a.m.	December 21	37
Passed the midpoint of flight	3:08 a.m.	December 22	47
First live telecast from spacraft	3:01 p.m.	December 22	58
Second telecast from spacecraft	2:58 p.m.	December 23	69
Entered moon's gravitational field	3:30 p.m.	December 23	80
Engine fired to drop craft into orbit	4:05 a.m.	December 24	92
Telecast on ninth orbit of moon	9:31 p.m.	December 24	102
Engine fired to boost craft out of orbit	1:10 a.m.	December 25	115
Fifth TV transmission from spacecraft	4:15 a.m.	December 25	126
Made midcourse correction	7:09 a.m.	December 26	136
Final live telecast from spacecraft	3:52 p.m.	December 26	147
Spacecraft reentered earth's atmosphere	10:41 a.m.	December 26	160
Splash down in Pacific off Honolulu	10:51 a.m.	December 27	171

144A Preparatory Practice (5) *each line three or more times*

Alphabet	We quickly brought the extra juice the five puzzled athletes demanded.
Figure-symbol	The policy is #8763–412590–N*. (The "N" shows two types of coverage.)
Drill on ea	These ears of corn are easier to eat than were the ears I ate earlier.
Fluency	Often it is the person who knows everything who has the most to learn.

| 1 | 2 | 3 | 4 | 5 | 6 | 7 | 8 | 9 | 10 | 11 | 12 | 13 | 14 |

144B Sentence Guided Writings (10)

Type two or more 1′ writings on each sentence with the guide called each 15, 12, or 10 seconds. Try completing a sentence and returning your carriage as the guides are called.

		GWAM 15″	12″	10″
1	I know that I can do the work with a little more ease each day I type.	56	70	84
2	Many a man has done well at the last hour because he would not let go.	56	70	84
3	I should hold my eyes on the copy at all times if I am to build skill.	56	70	84
4	You must keep your arms and wrists quiet; let the fingers do the work.	56	70	84

| 1 | 2 | 3 | 4 | 5 | 6 | 7 | 8 | 9 | 10 | 11 | 12 | 13 | 14 |

144C Paragraph Guided Writings (10) *type 83B, page 146, as directed*

144D Production Typing: Letter of Application and Data Sheet (25)

Problem 1: Letter of Application

Type this letter as a personal business letter. Decide on the letter style and form of punctuation.

	Words
Room 254, Slaton Hall/Bentley College	8
Wichita, KS 67207 June 10, 19–– Mr. Lyle	16
C. Nelson, President Nelson & Sons Company	25
1185 Louise Street Wichita, KS 67203 Dear	33
Mr. Nelson (¶ 1) Mr. Harry Carlton has told	41
me that you usually hire several college stu-	50
dents to work for your company during the	58
summer. He suggested that I write to you	67
and ask to be considered for a job this sum-	75
mer. (¶ 2) I am 20 years old and a sophomore	83
at Bentley College, where my studies are con-	92
centrated in the area of office management.	101
Both my high school and college grades have	110
been average or better. My extracurricular	119
activities include membership on the college	128
football, track, and debating teams. In high	137
school, I was coeditor of the school news-	145
paper; I work as a reporter on the college	154
paper. (¶ 3) Mr. Carlton informed me that	161
you expect your employees to be punctual,	170
reliable, and industrious. He explained also	179
that the work can be strenuous. I am not	187
afraid of hard work, Mr. Nelson; my health	196
is excellent; and I have always engaged in	204
physical activity. (¶ 4) I am eager to explain	213
to you personally why I want a job this sum-	221
mer and why I would particularly like to work	231
for your company. My telephone number is	239
852–3000, Extension 148. A personal data	247
sheet is enclosed. Sincerely yours Charles E.	257
David Enclosure	261/282

Problem 6: Report Manuscript

Side margins: 1½" left, 1" right;
top margin: 1½" pica, 2" elite

Type the following copy as a two-page leftbound manuscript.

Prepare a carbon copy. Erase and correct errors as you type.

	Words
THE RETURN OF MAN	4

At 10:42 a.m. (EST) Saturday, December 21, 1968, from Cape Kennedy, Florida,   19
Apollo 8 burst the bonds of earth, riding a mighty Saturn 5 rocket and carrying   35
American astronauts Borman, Lovell, and Anders into interplanetary space on man's   51
first voyage around the moon.[1] At 10:51 a.m. (EST) the following Friday, after   67
six days in space (orbiting the moon ten times), the Apollo 8 astronauts blazed   83
perfectly to a bull's-eye predawn splashdown about a thousand miles from Honolulu   100
and only 2½-3 miles from the aircraft carrier U.S.S. Yorktown, the pickup vessel.   116
The astronauts were safe, sound, and happy at the end of the half-million-mile   132
Christmas journey, an odyssey unprecedented in the annals of man.[2] Man had indeed   149
gone to the "forbidding, desolate moon" and returned safely to the "good earth."   165

In their six-day voyage, the Apollo 8 crew established a flock of new space-   180
travel records, including: 186

1. First men to travel so far from earth (233,000 miles) §§   197
2. First men to enter moon's gravitational pull §§   207
3. First men to orbit moon and see its back side §§   217
4. A new speed record for man (nearly 25,000 mph)[3]   227

Not since the voyage of Columbus (epitomizing the Renaissance) has any single   243
exploration done so much to enlarge the horizons of man. But aside from the fact   259
that this epic achievement will be celebrated for as long as men honor the bravery   276
and skill of other men, we earthlings can only guess at the long-range significance   293
of the flight.   296

The central lesson of Apollo 8 seems clear and unmistakable, however: If man   311
can elevate his moral and ethical concepts to reach his scientific achievements,   327
then no problems of famine, disease, or war are insoluble. The central difficulty   344
in solving these human problems is that a relatively limited number of thinkers and   361
technicians working with sophisticated electronic computers and mechanical devices   378
are not sufficient to create an equally needed public conscience. Only education   394
can do that—from kindergarten through college. Such education must be provided   410
by an army of teachers who are capable of harmonizing an idealistic philosophy with   427
a realistic understanding of and point of view toward the problems in relation to   443
our economic, political, and technical ability to solve them.   456

   459

[1] The Cincinnati Post and Times–Star (December 21, 1968), p. 1.   479

[2] Ibid. (December 27, 1968), p. 1.   487

[3] Fred M. Harmon, "The Great Triumph in Space," U.S. News & World Report,   506
Vol. 66, No. 1 (January 6, 1969), p. 9.   514

143C Production Typing ㉕

Problem 1: Memorandum to Graduates

Full sheet; 1" side margins

Words

TO: Business School Graduates **FROM:** Arthur — 7
L. Carlson, Dean **DATE:** (*Current*) **SUBJECT:** — 13
Application Letters (¶ 1) In writing applica- — 21
tion letters, use plain white paper of good — 30
grade. Type your letters. Do not use hotel, — 39
club, or fraternity stationery. Never use the — 48
letterhead of the business in which you may — 57
now be employed. Your letters should be — 65
neatly typed, as they will reflect your profes- — 74
sional standards. (¶ 2) In a direct, opening — 82
statement, apply for the position. If you have — 92
learned of the opening from an acquaintance — 101
of the employer, use his name. A personal — 109
touch is always helpful. (¶ 3) State your — 116
understanding of the requirements of the posi- — 125
tion. A short, direct statement or two will — 134
suffice. (¶ 4) Show how your education and — 142
experience match the requirements of the job. — 151
From your qualifications, choose the facts that — 161
will convince the employer you can handle the — 170
position. Hold back details that are not rele- — 179
vant. (¶ 5) Show some of your personality. — 187
Tell the employer why you are interested in — 196
his type of business. Give only such personal — 205
details as you think may be of interest to him. — 215
(¶ 6) Give at least three references. Indicate — 224
that you have been given permission to use — 232
their names. Generally, give both business — 241
and personal references. (¶ 7) Finally, request — 250
an interview. Tell the employer how and — 258
when he may reach you. — 263

Problem 2: Letter Inquiring about Opening

Using the current date, your address, and your
name, write this letter as a personal business letter.
Decide on the letter style and form of punctuation.

Words

mr irving l stone attorney-at-law broadway — 21
building spokane wa 99203 dear mr stone — 29
(¶ 1) Do you anticipate an opening in your — 37
office for a secretarial assistant? If you do, — 46
I should like to make formal application for — 55
the position. (¶ 2) I shall be graduated from — 63
Spokane College this June with a major in — 72
business. I can — 75

type — 76
take dictation — 79
arrange appointments — 84
handle routine office duties — 89

(¶ 3) I have held a number of typing, steno- — 97
graphic, and secretarial positions in campus — 106
and Spokane offices during the summer — 113
months. This experience has been most benefi- — 122
cial, especially in helping me to decide on a — 132
legal secretarial career. (¶ 4) A reply will be — 140
most appreciated. If you expect to have an — 149
opening in your office, I can arrange to see — 158
you at your convenience. very truly yours — 167
(*your name*) — 171/196

Problem 3: Request for Letter of Reference

Same procedure as in Problem 2

Words

mr leonard m pierce president pierson-brick — 21
company 8315 marquette street spokane wa — 29
99204 dear mr pierce (¶ 1) Will you please — 37
write a letter of reference for me to Mr. Irving — 47
L. Stone, Attorney-at-Law, Broadway Build- — 55
ing, Spokane, Washington 99203. I am ap- — 63
plying for a secretarial position in Mr. Stone's — 73
office and believe that my experience as a — 81
stenographer in your office last summer will — 90
carry a great deal of weight. (¶ 2) I believe — 99
that Mr. Stone would be most interested in — 107
knowing when I worked for you, in what — 115
capacity, and how well I handled my duties. — 124
I shall appreciate your writing this letter for — 134
me. very truly yours (*your name*) — 142/173

SECTION 13 BASIC AND PROBLEM SKILLS CHECKUP

LESSONS 76–79

Purpose. This section checks on your ability to operate a typewriter and to type samples of the problems covered in earlier lessons.

Machine Adjustments. Unless otherwise directed, use a 70-space line and single spacing for the drills. Follow the other directions carefully.

LESSON 76

76A Preparatory Practice [5] *each line three or more times*

Alphabet	The missile, its jets blazing, flew unswervingly; it exploded quickly.
Figure-symbol	Model #7006, marked $528.11, is selling for $435.99--a loss of $92.12.
Capitals	Senator John Poe visited the United States Naval Academy in Annapolis.
Fluency	No problem that we tackle is ever so big as the problem that we dodge.
	| 1 | 2 | 3 | 4 | 5 | 6 | 7 | 8 | 9 | 10 | 11 | 12 | 13 | 14 |

76B Typewriter Operation Checkup [10] *perform each operation as directed below*

1. **Paper Guide.** Set the paper guide at 0 (or whatever setting is appropriate for the typewriter you are using). See page iii if your typewriter needs a different setting.
2. **Margins.** Set the margin stops for a 50-space line; then a 60-space line; then a 70-space line.
3. **Paper Bail and Card Holders.** Have the card holders in "up" position. Raise the paper bail; twirl a sheet of paper into the typewriter; replace the paper bail. Work quickly.
4. **Line-Space Regulator.** Set the line-space regulator for double spacing.
5. **Touch Regulator.** (a) Set the touch regulator at its lowest setting; then type the following sentence:

   A sheet of paper that is 11 inches long will hold 66 horizontal lines.

   (b) Set the regulator at a medium setting and retype the sentence. (c) Set the regulator at its highest setting. Type the sentence again. (d) Set the regulator at the point you prefer.
6. **Paper Release.** Operate the paper release and remove the paper from the typewriter. Return the release to its normal position. Practice inserting and removing the paper several times.

76C Problem Checkup: Manuscripts; Word Division [35] *25′ timing; circle errors; figure* g-pram

$$\text{G-PRAM (gross production rate a minute)} = \frac{\text{Gross (total) words typed}}{\text{Length (in minutes) of writing}}$$

Problem 1: Unbound Manuscript

Margins: 2″ top; 1″ side; DS; 5-space ¶ indention

Words

CHANGING TYPEWRITERS 4

• Triple-space

(¶ 1) Sometime during your training you may 12
be assigned to a make of typewriter you have 21
not used before. While each make has its indi- 30
vidual characteristics, basic skill requirements 40
are the same for all of them; and you should 49
be able to change from one make to another 58
with a minimum of difficulty. (¶ 2) Changing 66
from a nonelectric to an electric typewriter 76
can provide a different kind of experience. 84
The basic skill needed is still the same, but 93
you must adapt techniques to the instant 101

142C Skill-Comparison Typing [20] *two 1′ writings on each sentence; compare* gwam

Goal	The top men in a firm work with people as well as they work with jobs.
Figures	Express dimensions in figures: 15 feet by 13 feet 7 inches by 2 feet.
Long reaches	We filed an application for the funds before reading the announcement.
Shift keys	Larry Rohy and Walter Zahl will go to Quincy, Patterson, and Santa Fe.
Long words	He is likely to influence the next generation of intellectual leaders.
Double letters	Gregg will succeed in getting the committee's letters to their office.
Hyphen	Our vice-president is on a far-reaching trip to get all-round players.
One hand	In my opinion, minimum wage rates were agreed upon in Edwards in July.
	| 1 | 2 | 3 | 4 | 5 | 6 | 7 | 8 | 9 | 10 | 11 | 12 | 13 | 14 |

142D Communication Aid: Composing [15]

1. Type the paragraph below.
2. In a second paragraph, grant the appointment on the date specified. Set a time for the appointment and indicate that it can be changed if not convenient.
3. Proofread Paragraph 1, marking it for correction.
4. Edit and correct your paragraph; then retype both paragraphs.

I shall be in Cleveland on Friday, May 5, and should like to see you for a few minutes if your appointment calendar permits. The reason for this request is that I should like to look into employment opportunities in your company. I am graduating from the School of Business, Ohio State University, with a major in advertising, and am desirous of bringing my qualifications to your attention.

LESSON 143

143A Preparatory Practice [5] *each line three or more times*

Alphabet	Willard Young packed a dozen quarts of plum jam in the box for Violet.
Figures	The 29 vessels--marked "Circa 1780 B. C."--were 245 to 360 years older.
Adjacent keys	Freddy needed his cooperation in order to start the logs rolling away.
Fluency	It does not take long for the man with push to pass the man with pull.
	| 1 | 2 | 3 | 4 | 5 | 6 | 7 | 8 | 9 | 10 | 11 | 12 | 13 | 14 |

143B Skill-Comparison Typing [20] *type 142C, above, as directed*

response of the electric machine. You may be 110
startled to find a number of extra characters 119
popping up in unexpected places, the machine 128
may "run away" from you once or twice, or 137
strange things may happen as you use the 145
wrong keys; but these mishaps usually right 154
themselves in a few days. (¶ 3) Remember 161
that it is the way of human nature to resist 170
any kind of change. Adjustments to new 178
situations require much time and patience. If 187
you work more slowly at first, however, think- 197
ing carefully about the location of new keys 206
and parts and trying to develop stroking 214
power to match that required by the new 222
machine, you will be back in top form in a 230
few days. But keep in mind that it is up to 240
you to adapt to the new machine—the ma- 248
chine cannot adapt to you. 253

Problem 2: Unbound Manuscript with Footnote

*Margins: 2" top; 1" side; DS; SS and indent quo-
tation 5 spaces from both margins; SS footnote;
leave extra space between body and footnote
divider line to maintain a 1" bottom margin*

TIME-SHARING   Words 3

TS

(¶ 1) One of the most important develop- 9
ments since the computer was introduced is 18
time-sharing. It makes instant data processing 27
available to companies of all sizes at low cost. 37
(¶ 2) Lewis E. Lachter writes as follows: 45

(¶ 3) There are time-sharing sys- 50
tems today where as many as 100 per- 57
sons are using a single computer at 64
one time. Each individual feels he 71
has exclusive use of the computer, 78
and with the tremendous capacity of 86
the hardware involved, he essentially 93
does.[1] 95

(¶ 4) Banks and large industrial and engineer- 103
ing companies are the big users of time- 111

sharing. More medium and small firms will 119
be using time-sharing as costs go down and 128
additional computers become available. 135

   139

[1]Lewis E. Lachter, "Closer Manager/ 146
EDP Interaction," Administrative Manage- 158
ment (January, 1968), p. 21. 165

Problem 3: Numbered Items

*Margins: 2" top; 1" side; SS; DS between num-
bered items; indent them 5 spaces from left margin*

WORD DIVISION   Words 3

Divide—   5

1. Words between syllables only. 11
2. Hyphenated words and compounds at 19
   hyphens only. 22
3. Words by putting as much as possible 30
   of the word on the first line to suggest 38
   the completed word. 42
4. A word of three or more syllables at a 51
   one-letter syllable. Type the one-letter 59
   syllable on the first line unless it is part 68
   of such terminations as ible, able, or 78
   ical, in which case carry it to the sec- 86
   ond line. If a one-letter syllable pre- 94
   cedes a second one-letter syllable, 101
   divide between them. 105

Do not— 107

5. Separate a one-letter syllable at the 116
   beginning or end of a word. 121
6. Separate a two-letter syllable at the 130
   end of a word. 133
7. Divide the last word on a page. 140

Avoid if possible— 144

8. Separating a two-letter syllable at the 153
   beginning of a word. 157
9. Dividing words at the ends of two or 165
   more consecutive lines or a word at 172
   the end of the last complete line of a 180
   paragraph. 182

SECTION 23 PREPARING FOR EMPLOYMENT APPLICATION

LESSONS 142–147

Unless otherwise directed, follow these procedures in Section 23:

Drill Copy: Full sheet; 70-space line; SS.
Production Copy: When complete directions are not given, use your own judgment. Make your work as neat and attractive as possible. When you are asked to type letters, use the style and punctuation you prefer. Address envelopes as needed. Correct your errors. You need not make carbon copies.

LESSON 142

142A Preparatory Practice (5) *each line three or more times*

Alphabet	Daniel Joyer's macabre mask, "Banquo's Ghost," won five or six prizes.
Figure-symbol	At the meeting, 289,356 stockholders (70%) voted "no" on Proposal #14.
Second row	Jason thanked the Highland laddies and lassies for dancing the flings.
Fluency	The nation's future lies in the plans and actions of its young people.

| 1 | 2 | 3 | 4 | 5 | 6 | 7 | 8 | 9 | 10 | 11 | 12 | 13 | 14 |

142B Production Skill Building (10) *two 3′ writings; compute* gwam *on each*

Unbound manuscript form

Words

We are shifting inthis county from a product-oriented cul- 12
ture to one of an idea-oriented one. Education is being though 27
of of as our great industty. Do you wonder, for more people 39
any
are engaged in this indus try then in/other: 51 million students 53
teachers
and 2 million instructors on a full-time bases, and the number 65
is growing. Our country's outlay for education is $50 billion 78
a year and so is exceeded only by our expenditure for devense. 90
recently
Economies have only/begun to recognize the real value 103
of investing in people. A trained man or woman has a caiptal 116
value in the economy that should be considered along with plant, 129
equipment, and inventories. 135
Many economists are now stressing emphasizing education as 144
the key to our economic and social advance. They tPace all the 157
greatness of America, not along tovast, naturall resources, but 169
to foresigjted invest men in human capitol. as wells More than 180
anyone in history, we in the United States hitched our star to 196
Education. 198

LESSON 77

77A Preparatory Practice (5) *each line three or more times*

Alphabet	Brazilian Judge Frank Wavo is quietly confirming the risk of smallpox.
Figure-symbol	Mark Invoice 118299 "350 sets @ 67¢ a set, less 2 4/5% cash discount."
Direct reaches	Myron Trumble tried to unlock the gate in front of the deserted house.
Fluency	The future is not with the job; it is with the one who holds that job.

| 1 | 2 | 3 | 4 | 5 | 6 | 7 | 8 | 9 | 10 | 11 | 12 | 13 | 14 |

77B Typewriter Operation Checkup (10) *perform each operation; then type four 1′ writings on the lines in No. 3*

Full sheet; 1½″ top margin; DS; DS twice between writings

1. **Carriage-Release Levers and Tab Clear Key.** Locate these parts on your typewriter. Use them to clear any tabulator stops now set on your machine.
2. **Tab Set Key.** Set a tabulator stop at the center of the paper.
3. **Tabulator and Backspace Key.** Tabulate to the center of the paper; use the backspace key to center each of the following titles horizontally:

The Development of Young Data Processors
A Plan to Stop the Gold Drain
Look What's Happening to Glass!
GENERAL PREDICTIONS ABOUT COMPUTER USES

77C Problem Checkup: Memorandum; Announcement; Postal Card (35) *25′ timing; circle errors; figure* g-pram

Proofreader's Marks

Mark	Meaning	Example	Mark	Meaning	Example
^	insert	for my ^new car	⊏	move to left	⊏ A man earns
℘	delete	us ~~all~~ to go	⊐	move to right	Le⊐arn the names
∽ or tr	transpose	to (quickly)(go)	≡	capitalize	south; South; south
lc	lower-case letters	the /Manager	ds	double spacing	ds → 1 2
⁀	close up space	could see h er	ss	single spacing	ss → 1 2
ital	change to italic	the Journal of	¶	paragraph	
#	add space	inthe house			

Problem 1: Rough Draft of a Memorandum

Half sheet; 1″ top margin; 1″ side margins; current date; block style

Words

Current date *3 blank lines here* 3

Subject: Office copiers 8

The i deal copier *would* produce dry copys *ies* in lessthan a ~~minute~~ *second* 21
at less than a penny a copy. It sould be compact, ues uncoatedd 34
paper, *and* reproduces all colors. In ad dition, it would be Simple, *lc* 47
silent, odorless, and durable. ¶Even if such a copier *were* available, 61
many managers would not ~~use them~~ *buy it*. They would recognize that, while 74
they only needed some of its feat ures, they would have to pay for 87
all of them. 90

141C   Production Measurement ㉚ *20' writing; erase and correct all errors*

Problem 1: Letter on Executive-Size Paper

(Sheet 7¼" by 10½")

	Words
(Current date) mr hunter a langley area man-	9
ager mott supply company 802 touchstone	17
avenue dayton oh 45427 dear hunter (¶ 1)	25
For months we have watched our costs rise	34
and have waited patiently for them to return	43
to normal. Apparently we have waited too	51
long, for our current monthly report shows	60
a net loss. Therefore, we must increase some	69
of our prices, effective the first of next month.	79
(¶ 2) Please look over the proposed price in-	87
creases and the short advertisement we plan	96
to send with the new price list. Both are	104
enclosed. We want your frank comments.	112
(¶ 3) You may notify your customers that our	120
prices will be advanced soon; we can accept	129
orders at our present rates, however, for the	138
remainder of this month only. sincerely yours	148
b f savage vice-president enclosures 2	156/175

Problem 2: Program of Meeting

Half sheet (5½" by 8½")

	Words
MANAGEMENT SOCIETY ANNUAL MEETING	7
Longfellow Hotel, Niagara Falls	13
October 10, 19--	17
10:00 a.m. Cascade Room	21
Opening Statements	25
Richard Adams, President, Manage-	32
ment Society	34
Address: "Consumer Innovators"	41
Herbert Simon, Professor of Com-	47
puter Sciences, Purdue University,	54
Lafayette, Indiana	58
Open Forum	61
Leader: Oscar B. Osborne, Market-	67
ing Consultant, Rochester, New York	75
12:30 p.m. Viewpoint Dining Room	82
Luncheon and Introduction of Visitors	90
Address: "Technological Obsolescence"	98
Benjamin L. Gerber, Management	104
Consultant, Buffalo, New York	110
Business Meeting	114
3:15 p.m. Adjournment	119

Problem 3: Partial Notice of Meeting of Stockholders

	Words
CREST MOTORS CORPORATION	5
Notice of Annual Meeting of Stockholders	13
To Be Held April 16, 19--	18
(¶ 1) PLEASE TAKE NOTICE that the annual	25
meeting of the stockholders of Crest Motors	34
Corporation will be held on Friday, the 16th	43
day of April, 19--, at two o'clock in the after-	53
noon, at 123 Washington Boulevard, Detroit,	61
Michigan. (¶ 2) The annual meeting will be	69
held for the purpose of electing seven direc-	80
tors and for the purpose of considering and	87
acting upon the proposals set forth in the	95
attached Proxy Statement. (¶ 3) The record	103
of stockholders entitled to vote at said meet-	112
ing will be taken at the close of business,	121
April 5, 19--.	124
By Order of the Board of Directors	131
Edward E. Fardo, Secretary	136

Problem 4: Partial Report of Stockholders Meeting

	Words
REPORT OF STOCKHOLDERS MEETING	6
(¶ 1) The regular annual meeting of stock-	13
holders was held in Detroit, Michigan, on	22
April 16, 19--. The number of votes cast by	31
proxy or in person was equal to 89.4% of the	40
outstanding common stock. The following	48
action was taken at the meeting:	55
(1) Election of the following directors:	63
John E. Baldwin Clyde McGraw	69
Alfred Glasser, Jr. David Roche	75
F. E. Henricks A. B. Schmidt	81
Norman Snyder	84
(2) Approval of proposals to increase the	94
number of shares of common stock	100
from 10,000,000 shares to 15,000,000	108
shares.	109
(¶ 2) At the meeting of the Board of Direc-	117
tors which followed the stockholders meeting,	126
Mr. Fred Hillary, Assistant Vice-President,	134
was elected Vice-President. All other officers	144
were reelected to their positions.	151
Harvey Doyle Thomas Sorrell	157
Chairman of the Board President	163

Problem 2: Centered Announcement

Half sheet; DS; center problem vertically and each line horizontally

Words

THE WAGNER–PERKINS PUBLISHING COMPANY 8
invites you to a 11
CONTINENTAL BRUNCH 15
served continuously from 11 a.m. to 1 p.m. 23
CABANA ROOM OF THE HOTEL EL DORADO 30
(*use next Wednesday's date*) 33

Problem 3: Centered Announcement

Full sheet; center Problem 2 in reading position (2 lines higher than if it were centered exactly); TS

Problem 4: Postal Card

48-space line; SS; block style; current date; address the card to yourself; use your surname in salutation

Words

We were very much pleased to receive your 16
subscription to TRAVEL. We look forward to 24
having you as a regular reader for many years 33
to come. 35

If you have any questions about your subscrip- 44
tion, please write us. Again, thanks. 52

TRAVEL Magazine 55/67

LESSON 78

78A Preparatory Practice (5) *each line three or more times*

Alphabet	This capital, Byzantium, was subjected to six very frightening quakes.
Figure-symbol	He said, "Ship 14 #872 lamps, listed at $39.50 less 6% cash discount."
Long reaches	My uncle, Jimmy Bricklin, mumbled sadly, "My TV must be broken again."
Fluency	One step a day takes me on the way to the place I want to be some day.
	| 1 | 2 | 3 | 4 | 5 | 6 | 7 | 8 | 9 | 10 | 11 | 12 | 13 | 14 |

78B Typewriter Operation Checkup (10) *perform each operation as directed below*

Full sheet; 70-space line; DS; 1½" top margin

1. **Margin-Release Key.** Type Sentence 1 below. Turn the cylinder forward about five lines; depress the margin-release key; move the carriage to the extreme left. Erase *may*. Return to original typing position; type *can* in the erased space.
2. **Ratchet Release.** Type Sentence 2. Operate the ratchet release; turn the cylinder forward about three inches. Disengage the ratchet release and turn the cylinder back to the line of writing. Type over the sentence.
3. **Variable Line Spacer.** Type Sentence 2. Operate the variable line spacer and turn the cylinder forward about three inches. With the variable line spacer still depressed, return as accurately as you can to the writing line and release the variable line spacer. Type over the sentence.
4. **Bell and Margin Lock.** Space forward 20 spaces from where you have set the left margin. Type Sentence 3 until you hear the bell ring. Count the number of spaces between the ringing of the bell and the locking of the machine. Consider this number when you set your right margin stop.

Sentence 1	Both pica and elite type may be measured six lines to a vertical inch.
Sentence 2	A sheet of paper 8½ inches wide will hold 102 elite or 85 pica spaces.
Sentence 3	For a 1-inch top margin on a page, you should begin to type on Line 7.
	| 1 | 2 | 3 | 4 | 5 | 6 | 7 | 8 | 9 | 10 | 11 | 12 | 13 | 14 |

140C Production Skill Building (30)

Make pencil notations of the problems at the right to be typed for 20 minutes. When time is called, compute your *n-pram.*	Page 237, 136C, Problem 1 Page 239, 137D, Problem 1 Page 240, 138D, Problem 1 Page 241, 138D, Problem 2

LESSON 141

141A Preparatory Practice (5) *each line three or more times*

Alphabet	His proclivity to work explains his fine grade on a major botany quiz.
Figure-symbol	Ray Cook sent 530 bills in 1968, reducing his bad debts losses $8,427.
First row	Has Maxine Mazon or Bob Vanz, members of this club, climbed Mt. Blanc?
Fluency	This is a good week to do all the things you promised to do last week.
	| 1 | 2 | 3 | 4 | 5 | 6 | 7 | 8 | 9 | 10 | 11 | 12 | 13 | 14 |

141B Growth Index (15) *two 5′ writings; compute* nwam *on the better one*

All letters are used.

		GWAM 1′	5′	
¶ 1 1.5 SI 5.6 AWL 80% HFW	Why is learning to ride bicycles such a difficult task? Actually,	13	3	57
	there is nothing new to learn. We learned body balance, pedaling, and	28	6	59
	steering at a very early age; therefore, we have all the required skills	42	8	62
	necessary to stay on a bicycle from the very first day. Most of us must	57	11	65
	practice riding the tricky bicycle several times before we are really	71	14	68
	successful. Why? If we have the ability needed, why can't we do the	85	17	71
	job on our first attempt?	90	18	72
¶ 2 1.5 SI 5.6 AWL 80% HFW	We can fail at a task when we have no confidence in our ability.	13	21	75
	Those who expect to succeed, will ride a bicycle; those who can but are	28	23	77
	not certain they can, will tumble off. Surely, the difference between	42	26	80
	those who succeed and those who fail is the quality of confidence.	55	29	83
	Confidence will propel us forward, unafraid. Naturally, overconfidence	70	32	86
	is foolish; but many times it is wiser to bite off more than we can	83	35	87
	chew than to die of malnutrition.	90	36	90
¶ 3 1.5 SI 5.6 AWL 80% HFW	Confidence is a tilt of the chin; his friend, Determination, a	13	38	92
	gleam in the eye. Learn to recognize both of these qualities. To-	26	41	95
	gether, they are a formidable team. They can help you reach the	39	44	98
	goals that many another person can only philosophize about. The slo-	53	47	100
	gans, "I can because I know that I can" and "I will," should be	66	49	103
	memorized and recited frequently. Using the aid of the two slogans,	79	52	106
	you can attempt a really great job; and you will win.	90	54	108
1′ GWAM	| 1 | 2 | 3 | 4 | 5 | 6 | 7 | 8 | 9 | 10 | 11 | 12 | 13 | 14 |			
5′ GWAM	| 1 | 2 | 3 |			

78C Problem Checkup: Letter Styles and Outline ㉟ 25' timing; circle errors; determine g-pram

Problem 1: Personal Business Letter in Modified Block Style with Open Punctuation

Full sheet; 65-space line; open punctuation; date on Line 14 from top; address on 4th line below date

	Words
4201 Broadway | Portland, Oregon 97232 |	8
April 15, 19-- | London & Bond Insurance	15
Co., Ltd. | 515 West Sixth Street | Los	23
Angeles, California* 90014 | Gentlemen	30
(¶ 1) Thank you for your comments about	37
the article I wrote for The Office. My origi-	48
nal manuscript contained answers to your	56
questions about typing envelopes, but limita-	65
tions of space did not permit them to be	73
included. I can, however, summarize my rec-	82
ommendations for you. (¶ 2) On a small en-	89
velope type the address (blocked and single-	98

*Always leave 2 spaces between the state name or abbreviation and the ZIP Code.

	Words
spaced) 2 inches from the top and 2 1/2 inches	107
from the left edge of the envelope. On a	116
large envelope type the address in this style	125
2 1/2 inches from the top and 4 inches from	134
the left edge of the envelope. (¶ 3) Type	141
mailing notations (such as AIRMAIL) below	149
the stamp and at least 3 line spaces above the	159
envelope address. Type the return address	167
(blocked and single-spaced) on Line 2 from	176
the top of the envelope and 3 spaces from the	185
left edge. Type addressee notations (such as	194
Please Forward) a triple space below the re-	203
turn address and 3 spaces from the left edge	212
of the envelope. (¶ 4) I hope the guides are	220
helpful. Please write to me again if there is	229
any further information I can provide. | Very	238
truly yours | Henry S. Baxter	244

Problem 2: Business Letter in Modified Block Style with Mixed Punctuation

Letterhead (or full sheet); 60-space line; mixed punctuation; date on Line 18 from top; address on 4th line below date*

	Words
Current date | Dr. William Biel | 3420 Viola	9
Street | Danville, IL 61832 | Dear Dr.	16
Biel (¶ 1) Will you take just a minute or	24
two to do us a favor? We need your answers	32
to a few questions about the banks in your	41
area. This is one way that banking services	50
can be improved to serve you better. (¶ 2)	58
The enclosed questionnaire is very short––it	67
will take less than five minutes of your time.	76
Please fill it out and return it to us in the	85
envelope provided. (¶ 3) Gibbs Associates is	93
a public opinion polling firm and is the Mid-	102
west affiliate of Elmo Popper in New York.	111
We are members of the Chicago Better Busi-	119
ness Bureau and have been serving clients in	128
this area for a number of years. (¶ 4) Thank	136
you for your help. | Sincerely yours | William	145
F. Gibbs | President | (Your initials) Enclosures	152

*Insert the necessary punctuation when mixed punctuation is specified even though it does not appear in the copy.

GIBBS ASSOCIATES

330 N. Michigan Avenue
Chicago, IL 60601

Midwest Affiliate of Elmo Popper, New York

Current date

Dr. William Biel
3420 Viola Street
Danville, IL 61832

Dear Dr. Biel:

Will you take just a minute or two to do us a favor? We need your answers to a few questions about the banks in your area. This is one way that banking services can be improved to serve you better.

The enclosed questionnaire is very short--it will take less than five minutes of your time. Please fill it out and return it to us in the envelope provided.

Gibbs Associates is a public opinion polling firm and is the Midwest affiliate of Elmo Popper in New York. We are members of the Chicago Better Business Bureau and have been serving clients in this area for a number of years.

Thank you for your help.

Sincerely yours,

William F. Gibbs

William F. Gibbs
President

bdf

Enclosures

Modified Block Style with Mixed Punctuation

Problem 2: Amendments to Constitution and Bylaws

Unbound report form; SS descriptive copy; DS and TS between parts as indicated

2
TS

	Words
PROPOSED AMENDMENTS AND REVISIONS TO	7
THE CONSTITUTION AND BYLAWS	13

DS

1"
m'gs.
line 14

Stockton Chapter, Management Society   20

TS

Amendment 1   25

DS

All references within the Constitution   33
and Bylaws to the word "National" shall be   41
changed to read "International."   48

TS

Amendment 2   53

DS

Center
ARTICLE I – OFFICERS AND DIRECTORS   60

DS

Section 1. Shall be amended as follows: 68

DS

Officers – The officers of this chapter shall   79
be President, a First Vice-President, a Sec-   87
ond Vice-President, Secretary, and Treasurer,   97
all of whom shall be members exofficio of the   106
Board of Directors.   110

DS

Section 3. Shall be amended as follows: 118

DS

Nominations – The Advisory, Long-   127
Range Planning, and Nominating Committee   135
shall submit, to the Chapter at the next regu-   142
lar meeting prior to the April annual meeting,   154
a report placing in nomination one candidate   163
for each office to be filled by election.   171

DS

Section 8. Shall be amended as follows: 180

Duties of Vice-Presidents – In the ab-   192
sence of the President, the First Vice-President   202
shall perform all the duties of the office of   211
President. He shall also have such other   220
powers and duties as the Board of Directors   228
may delegate to him.   233

TS

Amendment 3   237

C.

ARTICLE II – COMMITTEES   242

Section 1. Shall be amended as follows: 250

Standing Committees: The President   261
shall appoint the following committees from   270
the members of the Chapter: 276

a. A Program Committee shall make all   284
arrangements for regular meetings of the   292
Chapter as well as coordinate special pro-   300
grams through a Program Services Commit-   308
tee.   309

b. A Membership Committee shall solicit   317
and investigate applications for membership   326
and recommend to the Board whether they   334
be accepted or declined in accordance with   342
provisions of Article IV of the Bylaws.   350

LESSON 140

140A Preparatory Practice ⑤ *each line three or more times*

Alphabet   Jeffrey Belkman awarded five prizes to the aquatic experts in Georgia.

Figure-symbol * Billed as "285 sets @ 76¢ a set," the listing caused a $149.03 error.

Inside keys   Mighty heights jut from the five beautiful, but formidable, mountains.

Fluency   Do the little things well, and the big things take care of themselves.
               | 1 | 2 | 3 | 4 | 5 | 6 | 7 | 8 | 9 | 10 | 11 | 12 | 13 | 14 |

140B Guided Paragraph Writings for Speed and Control ⑮ *135E, page 235, as directed*

Problem 3: Outline

Full sheet; 40-space line; 2″ top margin

	Words
THE OFFICE OF 1984	4
TS	
I. SHORTAGE OF ADMINISTRATIVE MANAGERS	12
DS	
A. Four Times as Many Needed	18
B. Protection from Recruiting Raids	25
C. New Forms of Compensation	31
DS	
II. NEW JOBS	35
A. Office Technicians	40
B. Governmental Relations Experts	47
III. OBSOLETE JOBS	52
A. Middle Management Personnel	58
1. Quality control experts	65
2. Insurance underwriters	71
B. Two Million to Lose Jobs	77
IV. NEW KINDS OF COMPENSATION	84
A. New Stock Option Programs	90
B. Multiple Fringe Benefits	96
C. Loss-of-Job Insurance	101
D. Nonmonetary Alternatives	107
E. Individualization of Income	113
V. NEW MANAGEMENT ACTIVITIES	120
A. Development of Job Standards	126
B. Research on Salary Plans	132
C. Emphasis on Needs and Opportuni-	139
ties Rather than Programs	145
D. Personnel Transfer and Retraining	153
E. Creation of New Jobs	158
VI. MECHANIZATION	163
A. Increased Use of Computers	169
B. Improved Communication Systems	176

LESSON 79

79A Preparatory Practice (5) *each line three or more times*

Alphabet	Ezra Weber likes the piquancy of orange juice mixed with clover honey.
Figure-symbol	In 1968, storms delayed delivery of 4,370 tons (25% of all shipments).
Third row	Our pitcher, Quentin, threw three powerful pitches and won the series.
Fluency	There are many more trapdoors to the bottom than shortcuts to the top.

| 1 | 2 | 3 | 4 | 5 | 6 | 7 | 8 | 9 | 10 | 11 | 12 | 13 | 14 |

79B Technique Improvement: Stroking (20)

1. Type each sentence three times.
2. Type a 1′ writing on each sentence. Type on the *control* level.

Control Level: When the purpose of your typing is to type with ease and control, drop back in rate and type on the *control level.*

1	Shift keys	Barry and Keith Johnson met in Mexico City in July or early in August.
2	Long reaches	The men received a number of summaries of the stormy political report.
3	Double letters	All his possessions have been transferred to your home in Tallahassee.
4	One hand	As Johnny Carver asserted, Fred was regarded as carefree and careless.
5	Balanced hand	The men may visit the ruins in the ancient city if they get the forms.
6	3d and 4th fingers	As Alex pointed out in his paper, the essay questions were quite easy.
7	Hyphen	They found this to be an up-to-date plan for out-of-town credit sales.
8	Direct reaches	Gregg Bright hunted with Cedric Nunis in the jungle around this river.

| 1 | 2 | 3 | 4 | 5 | 6 | 7 | 8 | 9 | 10 | 11 | 12 | 13 | 14 |

139B Production Skill Building ⑮ *two 5' writings; compute gwam*

Words

As a spokesman for management, I am happy to welcome   11

you as a stockholder in Budlong Financial Corporation. We   22

appreciate your expressions of confidence in this company and   35

assure you we intend to continue our role as one of the national's leading   49

financial institutions.   54

[As you probably know, our subsidiaries make an im-   64

portant contribution to the financial and industrial structure of the   78

American and Canadian economies. In putting money to work   90

usefully, our subsidiaries advance well over six million dol-   102

lars a year to consumers and business organizations for the   114

fulfillment of their needs. We financed major retail pur-   125

chases to families and lent them money directly. We also   137

provide a broad range of financing, factoring, and leasing   149

services to industry. We provide installment financing for   161

parents, covering school and college expenses, and construct   173

and lease college dormitories and dining halls.   182

We also insure automobiles against collision and other damages   195

and write life, health, and accident insurance.   204

The Annual meetings of stockholders takes place on the forth Tuesday   218

in April. We hope you will be able to attend the meetings   230

in the future. For those who cannot attend, a report on the   242

proceedings will be sent to all stockholders after each meeting.   255

Your questions or comments about activities will always be   267

most welcome.   270

139C Production Typing ㉚

Problem 1: Letter on Executive-Size Stationery (7¼" by 10½")

Type 139B as the body of a letter to Mr. Stephen Corcoran, 5778 Nantuckett Avenue, Durham, NC 27703. The sender is M. D. Sundeen, President. Use the current date, an appropriate salutation, and a complimentary close. Center the letter on executive-size stationery. Leave 1" side margins. *(298/310 words)*

79C Straight-Copy Checkup (15) *two 5′ control-level writings; figure gwam on the better writing*

Full sheet; 70-space line; DS; 5-space ¶ indention

When you type on the control level, drop back in rate and work for ease and precision of stroking.

All letters are used.

	GWAM		
	1′	5′	

¶ 1
1.5 SI
5.6 AWL
80% HFW

The serious student who wishes to enter the business world should — 13 | 3 | 56
utilize his school years to develop the traits, skills, and know-how — 27 | 5 | 59
that are generally demanded of all those who want to attain success in — 41 | 8 | 62
it. The student should recognize, for example, the importance of neat, — 56 | 11 | 65
suitable clothing and good grooming. He should learn that if he wishes — 70 | 14 | 68
to get very far in an office job, he must be able to dress well--even — 84 | 17 | 70
on a limited budget. — 88 | 18 | 71

¶ 2
1.5 SI
5.6 AWL
80% HFW

The student who desires to find a job in the business world will — 13 | 20 | 74
also learn how to express himself in clear, appropriate language. This — 27 | 23 | 77
ability is usually placed at the top of the list of those most needed — 41 | 26 | 80
by the graduate. As a result, he will build his vocabulary with the — 55 | 29 | 82
aid of a dictionary whenever he can. He will learn to spell, and to — 69 | 31 | 85
structure and punctuate his sentences. He will know that writing and — 83 | 34 | 88
speaking skills can be acquired with practice. — 92 | 36 | 90

¶ 3
1.5 SI
5.6 AWL
80% HFW

The able student with an office position as his ultimate goal will — 13 | 39 | 92
learn how to act as well as look the part. While correct clothes and — 27 | 42 | 95
meticulous grooming are important, so are good posture, the right — 41 | 44 | 98
attitude, and a pleasant voice. There are few employers, however, who — 55 | 47 | 101
select an attractive package that has but little of value in it, so the — 69 | 50 | 104
more ability a student has, the better will be his chances of getting — 83 | 53 | 106
the job he really desires. — 88 | 54 | 107

1′ GWAM | 1 | 2 | 3 | 4 | 5 | 6 | 7 | 8 | 9 | 10 | 11 | 12 | 13 | 14 |
5′ GWAM | 1 | 2 | 3 |

79D Skill-Comparison and Transfer Typing (10) *two 1′ writings on each sentence; compare gwam*

		Words
Goal	Most men can do better work with machines than without them.	12
Shift keys	Kathy Dow will visit Lisbon, Rome, and Florence this summer.	12
Rough draft	Far of us quit To many men stop loking for a job when they find a job to do. work we #	12
Script	A scientist knows that he who fears failure seldom succeeds.	12

LESSON 79   **Section 13: Basic and Problem Skills Checkup**   **140**

Problem 2: Board Minutes

1 original; ~~1 carbon copy~~; SS; leftbound manuscript form

Words

MINUTES OF THE MEETING OF THE BOARD OF DIRECTORS 10

DS

August 18, 19–– 13

TS

A special meeting of the Board of Directors was held on Friday, 26
August 18, 19––. Members present were Messrs. Bradley, Dawson, 39
Glidden, Holstein, May, McClintock, Roberts, and Wahl. Members absent 53
were Messrs. Lipscomb and Puckett. 60

The Chairman stated that the purpose of the meeting was to con- 73
sider the offer of merger with the Dodge Bank and Trust Company. 86
Statements of Condition of the Merchants State Bank and Dodge Bank 99
and Trust Company as of August 1, 19––, were placed in the hands of 113
each member present. Copies of these statements are attached and are 127
made a part of these Minutes. 133

According to the terms of the proposed merger, holders of shares 146
of Dodge Bank and Trust Company will receive shares of the combined 160
bank on a share-for-share basis, and holders of shares of the Merchants 174
State Bank will retain their present shares. Holders of common stock of 189
the Dodge Bank and Trust Company may, at their option, receive in 202
cash $62 for each share of common stock held. 211

After a careful study and discussion of the terms of the proposed 224
merger, the members of the Board present unanimously voted to direct 238
the President to notify the stockholders of the terms of the proposed 252
merger and of the Board recommendation that this merger be approved. 266

There being no further business, the meeting was adjourned at 279
4:15 p.m. 281

Respectfully submitted, 286

Secretary 287

LESSON 139

139A Preparatory Practice (5) *each line at least three times*

Alphabet — We must analyze and prove the exact question before the judge asks it.

Figure-symbol — Your Invoice #246–80 says, "Pay this total: $57.91." We paid $57.39.

Long reaches — My boy, "Sunny," is excited about the 60 rabbits he raised as a hobby.

Fluency — On the other hand, everyone who is on the level has his ups and downs.

| 1 | 2 | 3 | 4 | 5 | 6 | 7 | 8 | 9 | 10 | 11 | 12 | 13 | 14 |

SECTION 14 BUSINESS LETTERS

LESSONS 80–87

Unless otherwise directed, proceed as follows:
Drill Copy: Full sheet; 70-space line; SS.
Paragraph Copy: Full sheet; 70-space line; DS; 5-space ¶ indention.

Production Copy: Letterhead (or full sheet); current date (unless given); your reference initials; erase and correct your errors. Letter form, carbon copies, and envelopes should be used as indicated.

LESSON 80

80A Preparatory Practice (5) *each line at least three times*

Alphabet	The vast exodus of workingmen was probably just one equalizing factor.
Figure-symbol	Lee & Dun's price, \$53.40, is 2½ times as high as their 1967–68 price.
First row	Can Mr. Van Bux, the banker, visualize our volume six months from now?
Fluency	A right approach to work that must be done cuts the size of most jobs.

| 1 | 2 | 3 | 4 | 5 | 6 | 7 | 8 | 9 | 10 | 11 | 12 | 13 | 14 |

80B Communication Aid: Spelling (5)

1. Type these commonly misspelled words twice; study the words as you type them.
2. Close your book; type the words from the dictation of your instructor. Check your work.

chosen confident committee balance calendar buoyant chaperon conquered
temperament statement studying shining similar familiar humorous chord
committing coming copies indictment existence experience guard hurried

| 1 | 2 | 3 | 4 | 5 | 6 | 7 | 8 | 9 | 10 | 11 | 12 | 13 | 14 |

80C Technique Improvement: Response Patterns (23)

1. Type each sentence three times.
2. Type a 1′ writing on each. Use the response pattern indicated.

Stroke: See, think, and type difficult combinations letter by letter.

Word: See, think, and type short, easy words as word wholes.

Combination: Type short, easy words as word wholes; type difficult combinations letter by letter. Blend the two into a smooth typing rhythm.

1	Stroke	Their response to the recent campaign went far beyond my expectations.
2	Stroke	Educational budgets of large companies often exceed those of colleges.
3	Word	When he knows that a thing should be done, he can find a way to do it.
4	Word	We all know that he can do the work the way it can and should be done.
5	Combination	They know that in the long run this project will yield useful results.
6	Combination	No one, however, believes that we need to leave the outcome to chance.
7	Combination	Except for what is marked, they will be glad to accept their shipment.
8	Combination	If he has some time sometime this afternoon, we can discuss his plans.

| 1 | 2 | 3 | 4 | 5 | 6 | 7 | 8 | 9 | 10 | 11 | 12 | 13 | 14 |

LESSON 138

138A Preparatory Practice [5] *each line three or more times*

Alphabet Always loquacious, Hazel gave Pam her subject for the next day's talk.

Figure-symbol For a $30\frac{1}{2}\%$ discount, call Mr. Hanna at this number: 271–6598, Ext. 4.

Quiet hands The piquant taste of the lemonade temporarily slakes our heavy thirst.

Fluency Please keep in mind that your stroking must be sharp, clean, and even.

| 1 | 2 | 3 | 4 | 5 | 6 | 7 | 8 | 9 | 10 | 11 | 12 | 13 | 14 |

138B Communication Aid: Composing [15]

1. Type the paragraph below.
2. In a second paragraph, accept the invitation. Indicate the title of your presentation.
3. Proofread Paragraph 1, marking it for correction.
4. Edit and correct your paragraph; then retype both paragraphs.

Will you please speak to the members of Delta Pi Epsilon at a dinner meeting on Wednesday, October 14, 19--. The meeting is set for the Victory Room of Robaires, 4296 Melrose Avenue. We plan to have dinner at 6:30, and your talk will follow immediately. Delta Pi Epsilon is an honorary fraternity devoted to the improvement of business and economic education. You may select your own topic. I shall appreciate hearing from you soon.

138C Building Speed and Control [5] *137C, page 238, as directed*

138D Production Typing [25]

Problem 1: Letter on Executive-Size Stationery (7¼″ by 10½″)

Type the following letter on executive-size stationery. When stationery is narrower than the regular 8½″ width, regulate line length by setting appropriate margins. Such letter margins are usually 1″ wide.

Words

august 18 19-- mr vernon e caster president 10
dodge bank and trust company dodge wi 54625 19
dear mr caster (¶ 1) At a special meeting of 26
our Board of Directors held today, the terms 36
of the offer of a merger between the Mer- 44
chants State Bank and Dodge Bank and Trust 53
Company were thoroughly explored. (¶ 2) It 60
is the unanimous recommendation of our 68
Board of Directors that the terms of the pro- 77
posed merger be approved, and I have been 85
directed to notify the holders of shares of 94
common stock in the Merchants State Bank 102
of a special meeting to be held on September 111
30 for the purpose of voting on the proposed 120
merger. (¶ 3) In carrying out the directions 128
of the Board of Directors, I do so with confi- 137
dence that this proposed merger will be to the 147
mutual advantage of all holders of stock in 156
both banks. I look forward with much inter- 164
est to working with you as one of the officers 174
of the resulting institution. cordially yours 183
j d may president 188/203

80D Building Speed (17) *use* combination response

1. Type two 1′ writings on each ¶.   **2.** Type two 3′ writings on all ¶s.   **3.** Compute *gwam* for each writing.

All letters are used.

		GWAM	
		1′	3′

¶1
1.5 SI
5.6 AWL
80% HFW

Summarizing is a powerful study tool. To develop it, you must learn to condense into one or two short paragraphs the contents of an entire textbook chapter. This ability will separate the men from the boys on a quiz. A summary should contain in your own words the main ideas in the material you have covered.

13 | 4 | 74
27 | 9 | 78
40 | 13 | 83
54 | 18 | 88
62 | 21 | 90

¶2
1.5 SI
5.6 AWL
80% HFW

Outlining is another practical aid to learning, as it will help you build the ability to think logically. When you outline, you summarize the text of a chapter and arrange ideas on a scale that shows the importance of one point to another. Just practice outlining the material you read. If you do, you will grow in the ability to think.

14 | 25 | 95
28 | 30 | 100
42 | 35 | 104
56 | 39 | 109
68 | 43 | 113

¶3
1.5 SI
5.6 AWL
80% HFW

One authority in the learning field recommends the use of a question outline. It is one in which the terse notes normally included in an outline are replaced by questions on the significant points covered in a chapter. If you try this aid, you will learn that it would require almost fiendish ingenuity on the part of an instructor to design a set of questions which you did not anticipate.

13 | 48 | 117
27 | 52 | 122
41 | 57 | 127
55 | 62 | 131
69 | 66 | 136
79 | 70 | 139

1′ GWAM | 1 | 2 | 3 | 4 | 5 | 6 | 7 | 8 | 9 | 10 | 11 | 12 | 13 | 14 |
3′ GWAM | 1 | 2 | 3 | 4 | 5 |

LESSON 81

81A Preparatory Practice (5) *each line at least three times*

Alphabet   They have excused a man who plagiarized quotes from books or journals.

Figure-symbol   Roman & O'Hare's 5% discount ($27.50) reduced our 1968 total to $433.

Hyphen   They cannot re-cover the chair for your son-in-law with that material.

Fluency   The worker who takes pride in his work seldom needs to do a job twice.

| 1 | 2 | 3 | 4 | 5 | 6 | 7 | 8 | 9 | 10 | 11 | 12 | 13 | 14 |

81B Technique Improvement: Response Patterns (10) *two 1′ writings on each line*

1   Stroke   New concepts and techniques are being tested to deal with the project.

2   Word   The man who knows and knows that he knows is a man who will do things.

3   Combination   Either you or I can go. Neither of us has a session during that hour.

4   Combination   The power of positive thought is, moreover, more than a clever slogan.

| 1 | 2 | 3 | 4 | 5 | 6 | 7 | 8 | 9 | 10 | 11 | 12 | 13 | 14 |

137D Production Typing 25

Problem 1: Program of Meeting

Type a copy of the following program. Plan your work so that the program will be attractively placed on a single page. Correct your errors.

1 col.

	Words
MADISON ACCOUNTANTS ASSOCIATION	6
Continental Hotel, Madison DS	12
November 10, 19-- DS	15
TS	
3:00 p.m. Copenhagen Room	20
Address: "Tax Laws and the Accountant"	28
Ernest B. Towner, Comptroller, National	36
Tractor Co., Milwaukee	41
Panel Discussion	45
Harold Fields, Senior Partner, Fields,	53
Gunther & Jackson, Madison; George	60
Gentry, Lawyer, Green Bay; Ralph M.	68
Kinney, Chief Accountant, Hooker &	75
Sons, Madison	78
5:15 p.m. Rio de Janerio Room	84
Social Hour	87

	Words
6:00 p.m. Quebec Room	91
Buffet Dinner	94
7:30 p.m. Copenhagen Room	98
Address: "Court Decisions on Taxes"	106
Alex M. Pfeiffer, Partner, Price & Pfeif-	114
fer, Madison	117
Panel Discussion	121
William Gibbs, President, Gibbs Manu-	128
facturing Co., Madison; Wilmert Perkins,	137
Comptroller, Hunter-Miller Company,	144
Milwaukee; Sydney B. Phillips, Vice-	152
President, Webb Aerospace Corporation,	160
Madison; Thomas Justiz, Tax Consultant,	168
Chicago	170
Open Forum Discussion	175

Problem 2: Speech (First Part)

This is the first part of a speech that Mr. Bernard Gladstone, President of Marvel Motors, will deliver at a meeting of the stockholders. Type in unbound manuscript form. Use triple spacing and 10-space paragraph indentions for easy reading. Correct your errors. Prepare a title for the speech. Leave 3 blank spaces after the title.

	Words
To the Members of the Marvel Family:	8

(¶ 1) Since I came to work for Marvel Motors in 1930, vast changes have taken place in our Company, the environment in which it operates, and the standards of success that we have set for ourselves. (¶ 2) We had our fair share of problems in the ensuing years. In 1930, Marvel Motors, with 19 percent of the market, was just starting to gain momentum as a successful competitor. The economy was booming, but there were prophets of gloom in those days, too. (¶ 3) I recall a statement made by a nationally known economist in the middle 1920's who said, "One car per family is the measure of ultimate use of the automobile for the same reason that one bathtub and one telephone serve the needs of the family unit." This type of pessimistic vision led to his prediction in 1927 that the number of vehicles on the road at that time--22 million cars and trucks--represented the saturation point for motor vehicles in this country. (¶ 4) Today--some 40 years after the saturation point for motor vehicles in this country had been estimated at 22 million--we have over 88 million vehicles on the roads and a growing demand that continues to push the figures higher. (¶ 5) The results of our performance during the past year have been made available to you through our Annual Report. Because demand for automotive products fluctuates from year to year, we can obtain a better indication of both short- and long-term performance by analyzing a longer time span. With this in mind, let us review the past year in relation to our performance over the past 10 years. This is a representative period during which substantial growth was realized by Marvel Motors and the automotive industry.

Information on Typing Letters

Stationery

Business letters are usually typed on 8½- by 11-inch letterhead stationery. For letters of more than one page, plain paper of the same size, color, and quality as the letterhead is usually used for the additional pages. Onionskin or manifold paper is used for carbon copies. Smaller letterheads of 8½ by 5½ or 5½ by 8½ may be used for short letters.

Letter Placement

Some offices use standard side margins for all letters. Others vary the side margins according to letter length. The longer the letter, the narrower the margins. Office typists place letters by judgment. A placement table, such as the one given below, plus practice, will help you develop this intuitive sense. Disregard the table as soon as possible.

How to Use the Placement Table

Column 5 tells you on what line from the top edge of the paper to type the date for business letters of various lengths.

In business letters, the first line of the address is typed on the 4th line space below the date.

Note that each 50-word increase in average-length letters (101-300 words) calls for two fewer line spaces between the top of the paper and the date line.

Letters in which the space between the top edge of the letterhead and the first line of the address approximately equals the space between the last line of the body and the bottom edge appear to be well centered.

Letters that contain such special features as attention and subject lines, long quotations, enumerations, tables, and the like may require adjustment in the date-line placement. Also, when a deep letterhead makes it impossible to type the date on the designated line, type it a double space below the last letterhead line.

Column 3 tells you how wide the side margins should be for letters of different lengths. Note that letters of 101-300 words take 1½-inch margins. Since most letters you type will be of average length, you should get to know the adjustments for these letters quite well in a short time.

Letter Placement Table

(1) Letter Classification		(2) 5-Stroke Words in Letter Body	(3) Side Margins	(4) Margin Description	(5) Date Line Position (From Top Edge of Paper)
Short		Up to 100	2″	Wide	Line 20
Average	1	101 – 150	1½″	Standard	18
	2	151 – 200	1½″	"	16
	3	201 – 250	1½″	"	14
	4	251 – 300	1½″	"	12
Long		301 – 350	1″	Narrow	12
Two-page		More than 350	1″	Narrow	12

Date Line

The *horizontal* placement of the date line depends on the style of letter being typed, design of the letterhead, office preference, or a combination of these factors.

Block Style. Type date at left margin.

Other Styles. Begin date at center point or type it even with right margin. In this book, the first practice is generally preferred and used.

Business Letters Typed on Plain Paper

If plain paper is used as a letterhead substitute, space down from the top of the paper to type the date as suggested in the foregoing table.

Personal Business Letters Typed on Plain Paper

Deduct 2 lines from the figures given in Column 5 of the Letter Placement Table. Type the return address at this point, followed by the date.

137B Communication Aid: Parentheses (15)

Full sheet; 1½" top margin; 70-space line; SS with DS between items

1. Type the heading, PARENTHESES.
2. Type the rules and examples given below (with numbers); underline the side headings.
3. Compose and type four sentences, each sentence illustrating one rule. Number these sentences to correspond with the rules.

Words

2

Rules 5

(1) Use parentheses to set off parenthetical or explanatory matter. 18

(2) Use parentheses when an amount expressed in words is followed by 32
the same amount in figures. 38

(3) Parentheses may be used to enclose item enumerations. 49

(4) A punctuation mark follows the second parenthesis if it punctuates 64
the sentence as a whole. 69

(5) A punctuation mark is placed inside the parentheses if it applies to 83
the parenthetical material. 89

(6) A reference in parentheses at the end of a sentence is placed before 104
the period unless it is a complete sentence in itself. 115

Examples 118

(1) Ralph (my cousin) lives in the capital city of Arizona (Phoenix). 132

(2) I can sell my home to them for thirty thousand dollars ($30,000). 146

(3) John set three goals: (1) speed, (2) control, and (3) good form. 160

(4) I will call him (the lawyer, I mean), but I shall call you first. 174

(5) Bring the late report with you. (We have a copy of the old one.) 188

(6) You will find the pictures you desire in the new book (page 137). 202

Other Examples 208

137C Building Speed and Control (5)

1. Type two 1′ writings on the *exploration level.* Compute *gwam* on the better one. All letters are used.
2. Type two 1′ writings on the *control level.* Compute *nwam* on the better one. Compare the *gwam* and *nwam* rates.

All letters are used.

1.4 SI
5.6 AWL
85% HFW

Some persons do not believe that time is important. They appear to have an excess of it; and, as a consequence, they become quite bored and lazy. They forget to realize that every minute contains a potential meant just for them. Minutes inexorably change into days; days rapidly turn into months and years; and Time copies the history of our lives. We write another page every day. What kind of story is it? What kind of story will it be? Only Time and you will determine.

Consultants in Business Practices
PERRY & DERRICK, INC.
111 Lincoln Park / Newark, New Jersey 07102 / Telephone 201-227-0453

	Words in Parts	5' GWAM

Begin date at center on Line 12

February 15, 19-- ~~DS~~ *can vary* | 4 | 1

Mailing notation AIRMAIL | 5 | 1
DS

Address
Miss Evelyn Terry, Office Manager | 12 | 2
Standard Steel Equipment Company | 19 | 3
270 - 53d Street | 22 | 4
Brooklyn, NY 11232 | 26 | 5
DS

Salutation Dear Miss Terry | 29 | 6
DS

The booklet you requested about letter format is en- | 40 | 8
closed. The format features described are those adopted | 51 | 10
by this company. This letter follows them. | 60 | 12

The first line of each paragraph is indented five | 10 | 14
spaces. The date, complimentary close, company name, | 21 | 16
Body and the dictator's name are started at the center point | 32 | 18
of the paper. We use open punctuation. In this style, | 43 | 21
punctuation marks are omitted after the date, address, | 54 | 23
salutation, and closing lines unless an abbreviation is | 65 | 25
used, in which case the period is typed as part of the | 76 | 27
abbreviation. | 79 | 28

Although we do not usually show the company name | 89 | 30
in the closing lines, we have done so here to illustrate | 100 | 32
for you the correct handling of it. Since the dictator's | 112 | 34
name is typed in the closing lines, only the typist's | 123 | 36
initials are used in the reference notation. | 131 | 38

Special mailing notations are typed in all capital | 142 | 40
letters at the left margin, a double space below the date. | 153 | 43

After you have had an opportunity to examine your | 10 | 45
copy of Styling Business Letters, I shall appreciate | 25 | 48
your sending us your impressions of it. | 33 | 49

Complimentary close Sincerely yours | 36 | 50
DS

Company name PERRY & DERRICK, INC. | 41 | 51

Richard S. Perry *3 blank lines*

Typed name
and official title Richard S. Perry, Manager *(4th line space)* | 46 | 52
DS

Reference
initials mev | 47 | 52
DS
Enclosure
notation Enclosure | 49 | 52

STYLE LETTER 3: *Modified Block with Indented Paragraphs and Open Punctuation (Typed in Pica Type)*

136C Production Typing: Typing on Half-Size Stationery; Chain-Feeding Envelopes (30)

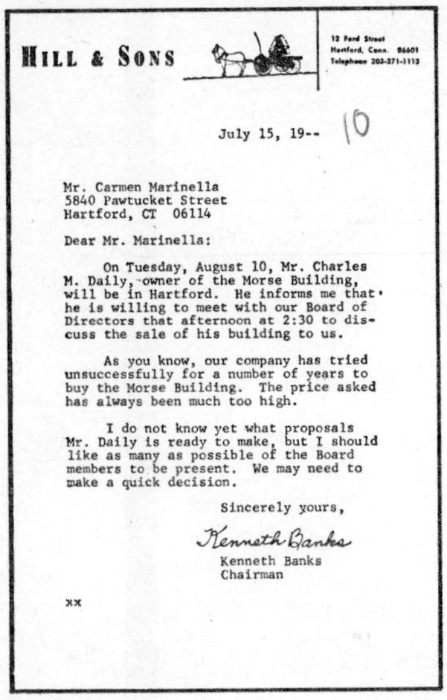

HILL & SONS

12 Ford Street
Hartford, Conn. 06601
Telephone 203-271-1112

July 15, 19--

Mr. Carmen Marinella
5840 Pawtucket Street
Hartford, CT 06114

Dear Mr. Marinella:

On Tuesday, August 10, Mr. Charles M. Daily, owner of the Morse Building, will be in Hartford. He informs me that he is willing to meet with our Board of Directors that afternoon at 2:30 to discuss the sale of his building to us.

As you know, our company has tried unsuccessfully for a number of years to buy the Morse Building. The price asked has always been much too high.

I do not know yet what proposals Mr. Daily is ready to make, but I should like as many as possible of the Board members to be present. We may need to make a quick decision.

Sincerely yours,

Kenneth Banks
Chairman

xx

Letter on Half-Size Stationery

Problem 1: Letter Typed on 5½- by 8½-inch Stationery

¾" side margins; date on Line 10

Words

july 15, 19-- mr carmen marinella 5840 pawtucket street hartford 13
ct 06114 dear mr marinella (¶ 1) On Tuesday, August 10, Mr. 25
Charles M. Daily, owner of the Morse Building, will be in Hartford. 39
He informs me that he is willing to meet with our Board of Directors 53
that afternoon at 2:30 to discuss the sale of his building to us. (¶ 2) 66
As you know, our company has tried unsuccessfully for a number of 79
years to buy the Morse Building. The price asked has always been 92
much too high. (¶ 3) I do not yet know what proposals Mr. Daily 104
is ready to make, but I should like as many as possible of the Board 118
members to be present. We may need to make a quick decision. 131
sincerely yours kenneth banks chairman 139/151

Problem 2: Letter Typed on Half-Size Stationery

Type the letter in Problem 1 again. Address it to the first name on the list in Problem 3. (*150 words*)

Problem 3: Chain-Feeding Envelopes

Chain-feed fourteen small envelopes, typing two for each of the following addresses. Feed seven of the envelopes by Method 1 (back-feeding) and seven by Method 2 (front-feeding). (See page 236.) Add a personal title to each name.

richard s anderson 84090 pelham road hartford ct 06107
george l burke 9321 beardsley street bridgeport ct 06607
l v campbell 548 alcazar street new brunswick nj 08904
carmen marinella 5840 pawtucket street hartford ct 06114
martin c morales 3196 mediterraneo san juan pr 00924
randolph x scott 3458½ passaic street newark nj 07104
john scott williams 2992 colfax avenue e | elizabeth nj 07204

LESSON 137

137A Preparatory Practice (5) *each line three or more times*

Alphabet	In waves, jagged ice chunks quickly excised big lumps of frozen earth.
Figure-symbol	The note said, "The problem is 37 x 96 — 458; time: 1′ 20″ /s/ John."
Capitals	I moved from Elm Street, Orange, Texas, to Pine Avenue, Red Oak, Iowa.
Fluency	A man needs work to do, and there is work in the world for each of us.

| 1 | 2 | 3 | 4 | 5 | 6 | 7 | 8 | 9 | 10 | 11 | 12 | 13 | 14 |

81C Production Orientation and Skill Building (35)

Problem 1

1. Type the letter on page 144 in the style shown. The body contains 217 five-stroke words. Consult the table for placement directions, taking into account the additional lines required for the company name in the closing and for the enclosure notation.

2. Type on the *exploration level*; do not correct errors.

3. With a pencil, mark the corrections that need to be made.

Problem 2

1. On plain paper type a 5' writing on the letter from your corrected copy. Do not correct your typing errors. Compute *g-pram*.

$$\text{G-PRAM} = \frac{\text{Gross (total) words typed}}{\text{Length (in minutes) of writing}}$$

2. Type the letter again on the *control level*. Erase and correct your errors as you type.

LESSON 82

82A Preparatory Practice (5) *each line at least three times*

Alphabet
The exact propinquity of the moving red object was quickly recognized.

Figure-symbol
Memo #38 says, "Bel & Bel's May 27 order ($1,694.50) is a cash order."

Double letters
Miss Poole, from Tallahassee, will see Tennessee and Mississippi soon.

Fluency
Training is learning the rules; experience is learning the exceptions.
| 1 | 2 | 3 | 4 | 5 | 6 | 7 | 8 | 9 | 10 | 11 | 12 | 13 | 14 |

82B Production Skill Building (15)

Using the letter on page 144, type the writings described at the right on the *control level*. Do not erase and correct your errors. Compute *g-pram* for each writing.

1. Type three 1' writings on the date, mailing notation, address, salutation, and the first paragraph.

2. Type three 1' writings on the last paragraph, complimentary close, company name, dictator's name and title, reference initials, and enclosure notation.

3. Type a 5' writing on the entire letter.

82C Production Typing: Letters in Modified Block Style (30)

Problem 1

Letter placement table on p. 143; 134 words; indented ¶s; open punctuation

	Words
Mr. James T. Bolder | Placement Director |	11
Underwood Community College | Dyke, VA	18
22935 | Dear Mr. Bolder | (¶ 1) Our office	25
staff begins summer vacations June 1, and we	34
usually rotate our vacations so that only	42
a few people are away from the office during	51
any one week. Even so, we are often short-	60

	Words
handed during our busiest season. (¶ 2) To	67
rectify this situation, we want to hire two or	77
three temporary employees for the months of	86
June, July, and August. Such replacements will	95
need above-average office skills and should,	104
since they will be moved from job to job,	113
be adaptable to change. Naturally, we will	121
provide any necessary job instruction. (¶ 3) If	130
you can recommend several students who are	139
looking for summer work, we shall be happy	147
to make arrangements with them for inter-	155
views. | Very truly yours | W. P. Stone,	163
Office Manager	167

LESSON 136

136A Preparatory Practice [5] *each line three or more times*

Alphabet	The misty jungle quivered as herds of zebra panicked in excited waves.
Figure-symbol	"My rate of return," he says, "can be 32½% ($1,385 ÷ $4,260) by 1979."
Long words	The secured obligation includes extension of my original indebtedness.
Fluency	Lucky is the man who has a clear idea of what he wants his life to be.
	| 1 | 2 | 3 | 4 | 5 | 6 | 7 | 8 | 9 | 10 | 11 | 12 | 13 | 14 |

136B Communication Aid: Composing [15]

1. Type the paragraph below.
2. In a second paragraph, acknowledge the request. Indicate that the booklet is being sent. No charge.
3. Proofread Paragraph 1, marking it for correction.
4. Edit and correct your paragraph; then retype both paragraphs.

I understand that you publish a booklet with the interesting title Joint Tenancy: Can It Work for You? I am a student in the Law School of the University of Washington and should very much appreciate receiving a copy of this booklet from you. If there is a charge for it, let me know. I shall send a check to you.

Chain-Feeding Envelopes

METHOD 1—BACK FEEDING

Stack the envelopes *face up* on the left side of the typewriter.

Insert the first envelope to typing position; place a second envelope behind the cylinder in the "feed" position.

Address the first envelope. As you twirl the first envelope out of the machine with the right hand, feed another envelope in the "feed" position with the left hand.

As the first envelope is removed, the second envelope will be moved into typewriting position. Continue the "chain" by placing a new envelope in the "feed" position each time the addressed envelope is removed.*

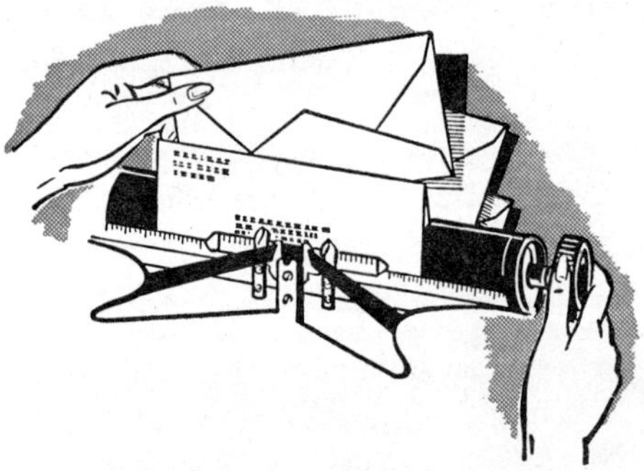

Back-Feeding Envelopes

METHOD 2—FRONT FEEDING

Stack the envelopes face down, flap toward you, on the left side of the typewriter.

Address the first envelope; then roll it back (toward you) until a half inch shows above the alignment scale.

Insert the next envelope from the front, placing it between the first envelope and the cylinder.

Turn the cylinder back to remove the first envelope and to position the second one. Continue the "chain" by feeding all envelopes from the front of the cylinder.

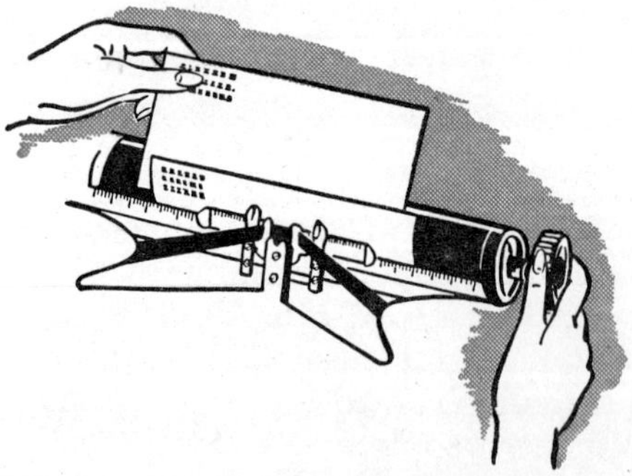

Front-Feeding Envelopes

**Some typewriters require three envelopes simultaneously around the platen for backfeeding. When this is necessary, insert an envelope between the bottom of the preceding envelope and the platen.*

Problem 2

88 words; mixed punctuation; indented ¶s

Words

Miss Betty N. Toland | 135 Madison Avenue | 11
Portsmouth, VA 23704 | Dear Miss Toland | 19
(¶ 1) Our office has received a request from a 27
firm in Alexandria asking for the names of 36
persons who might be interested in working 45
for them during the summer. (¶ 2) If you 52
are still looking for summer employment, will 61
you please complete the enclosed card and 69
return it promptly to our office. Be sure to 79
list both your local and Alexandria addresses. 88
(¶ 3) When the company has received your 95
records, someone will contact you to arrange 104
for an interview. Sincerely yours | James T. 113
Bolder | Placement Director | Enclosure 121

Problem 3

73 words; mixed punctuation; indented ¶s

Words

Mr. W. P. Stone, Office Manager | Atlantic 11
Fruit Company, Inc. | 1323 Spring Valley 19
Drive | Alexandria, VA 22312 | Dear Mr. 26
Stone | (¶ 1) Thank you for writing to us 34
inquiring about students who are seeking sum- 42
mer employment. (¶ 2) I am enclosing per- 49
sonnel record cards for three of our students 59
who are planning to spend this summer in 67
Alexandria. They should be well qualified for 76
the type of employment you mentioned. Our 85
faculty recommends them. (¶ 3) If we can 92
help you further, please write to us again. 101
Very truly yours | James T. Bolder | Place- 109
ment Director | Enclosures 114

LESSON 83

83A Preparatory Practice [5] *each line at least three times*

Alphabet	David Cox, the lazy, obsequious janitor, is working for small payment.
Figure-symbol	Our contract, #785–03, dated March 12, 1968, allows us a $4\frac{1}{2}$% discount.
Inside keys	Phillip Dexter requested them to apply for the quiz questions quickly.
Fluency	We do not have time to do a job right––but we find time to do it over.
	| 1 | 2 | 3 | 4 | 5 | 6 | 7 | 8 | 9 | 10 | 11 | 12 | 13 | 14 |

83B Paragraph Guided Writings [10]

1. Type four 1′ writings on the *exploration level.* Record *gwam* for the best writing.
2. Type three 1′ writings on the *control level.* Record *gwam* for the most accurate writing.

1.5 SI
5.6 AWL
80% HFW

A man's ability to reason and his capacity to solve problems are closely related to the number of words he knows. Most experts agree, however, that memorizing new words will do very little to add to your mental stature. If word knowledge is retained, a large vocabulary will make it possible for you to understand and assimilate more. Keep in minu, cnough, that a man is not smart because he has a good vocabulary. It is the other way around.

135D Technique Improvement: Stroking ⑩ *three or more correct copies of each line*

Double letters	Bill Hubbard asked Gregg Mann about a funny old man from Apple Valley.
Long reaches	Many young people eat their lunch at Myron Brigg's Cafe in Huntsville.
Long words	Specialists can edit and continue developing programming instructions.
3d and 4th fingers	Opal was puzzled by the quaint antique pots she saw in the old piazza.
One hand	Brad was aware, as we were, that the trade union exaggerated its case.
Balanced hand	The man must give some thought to his work if he is to profit from it.

`| 1 | 2 | 3 | 4 | 5 | 6 | 7 | 8 | 9 | 10 | 11 | 12 | 13 | 14 |`

135E Guided Paragraph Writings for Speed and Control ⑮

1. Type a 2' writing to establish your base rate.
2. Type three 2' writings with the call of the ½' guides at exactly your base rate.

3. Set a goal that is about 10 words higher than your base rate. Type two 2' writings; try to reach your new goal on each writing.

	GWAM		
	2'	3'	

¶1
1.5 SI
5.6 AWL
80% HFW

Men who know how a skill is acquired do not deny the vital need for rapid finger action. It is wrong, however, to think that motions alone can develop typewriting speed. Smooth typing at a fast rate is an end result of many things done extremely well. A typing student will soon learn that reading habits, posture, and attitude are necessary parts of a total performance. Without them, rapid finger action has little effect on the rate of speed.

2'	3'	
6	4	64
13	9	69
20	14	73
27	18	78
34	23	83
41	28	87
45	30	90

¶2
1.5 SI
5.6 AWL
80% HFW

An expert typist will, for example, read copy very carefully. His eyes follow the lines at an even rate. Typists who look away from the copy frequently lack the requisite continuity in typing, and speed is reduced materially. Do not read too far ahead. Focus on just a word or two at a time. When you come to a long, difficult word, type as you read each letter or syllable. Good reading habits can help to produce better typewriting results.

2'	3'	
52	34	94
59	39	99
66	44	104
73	48	108
80	53	113
87	58	118
90	60	120

2' GWAM `| 1 | 2 | 3 | 4 | 5 | 6 | 7 |`
3' GWAM `| 1 | 2 | 3 | 4 | 5 |`

Information on Addressing Envelopes

To hasten the sorting and distribution of first-class mail, the U.S. Post Office Department now uses Optical Character Readers to read electronically the ZIP Code and the name of the city and to sort the letters into appropriate bins. This agency asks that the following directions be observed.

Placement. The city and state line is optically scanned. The address lines must be higher than ½ inch from the bottom of the envelope, but no higher than 3 inches from the bottom. This 2½-inch "read zone" is 8 inches long, and it must not be closer than 1 inch to either the right or left edges of the envelope.

Extraneous information, regardless of its nature, will not interfere with reading if it is placed above the address block. The space below the address block should be kept completely clear to the bottom of the envelope.

Spacing. The address lines should be arranged in block form. Typing in single-space style is recommended by the Post Office Department.

The city and state names and the ZIP Code should appear in that sequence on the bottom line. Four-line addresses may be used so long as the city line complies with the foregoing placement directions.

State Abbreviations. The Post Office Department recommends the use of two-letter abbreviations for state names. Approved forms appear on page viii. These abbreviations should be typed in all caps, without an ending period.

In the typing of names of states in letter addresses, the recommended practice is to type the two-letter state abbreviations and ZIP Codes. If the ZIP Code is not known or available, the state name is spelled in full or typed according to the standard abbreviation.

Notations. Postal directions (such as AIRMAIL, SPECIAL DELIVERY, etc.) are typed in capitals below the stamp and at least 3 line spaces above the address. Addressee instructions (*Hold for Arrival, Please Forward, Personal*, etc.) should be typed a triple space below the return address and 3 spaces from the left edge of the envelope. Addressee instructions may be either underlined or typed in all capitals.

If it is not convenient to locate account numbers, dates, attention lines, and other similar items outside the read zone, they may be entered on any line of the address block above the street name or box number.

Personal Titles. Always use an appropriate personal title on a letter, envelope, or card addressed to an individual. When a woman's marital status is not known, use *Miss* as the personal title. (The abbreviation *Ms.* may also be used.)

Small Envelope. Use a small envelope (6½ by 3⅝ inches) for a one-page letter without enclosures.

Large Envelope. Use a large envelope (9½ by 4⅛ inches) for a letter of more than one page and for those with enclosures.

Observe the addresses on the small and large envelopes illustrated below. The notations indicate recommended placement for good appearance. At the same time the addresses appear in the read zones.

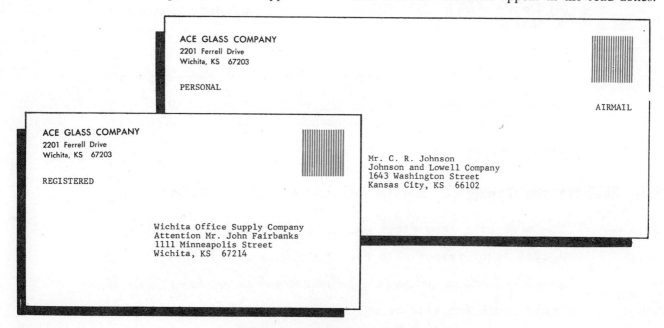

SECTION 22 EXECUTIVE COMMUNICATIONS

LESSONS 135–141

Unless otherwise directed, follow these procedures for Section 22:
Drill Copy: Full sheet; 70-space line, SS.
Paragraph Copy: Full sheet; 70-space line, DS.
Production Typing: When complete directions are not given, use your own judgment. Make your work as neat and attractive as possible. When you are asked to type letters, use the style of punctuation you prefer; but use your own reference initials. Correct all errors. You need not make carbon copies.

Special Materials: Executive-size stationary and large and small envelopes (you will decide which to use) are needed to complete the problems in this section.

LESSON 135

135A Preparatory Practice (5) *each line three or more times*

Alphabet	Using a sextant, Jeff quickly realized the big ship was slowly moving.
Figures	Operator 26 in Reno wants you to call Area Code 702, 463-8591 at once.
Capitals	The Senator from the state of Vermont, Carl O. McGee, spoke at 12 p.m.
Fluency	Do you agree with men who think that life will begin at the age of 40?
	| 1 | 2 | 3 | 4 | 5 | 6 | 7 | 8 | 9 | 10 | 11 | 12 | 13 | 14 |

135B Communication Aid: Abbreviations (10) *as directed in 122C, page 212; type a heading*

Full sheet; 1½" top margin; 70-space line; SS with DS between items

	Words
	3
Rules	5
(1) Type in full names of states when they stand alone.	16
(2) Names of months should not be abbreviated.	26
(3) Names of cities should not be abbreviated.	35
(4) Do not space in abbreviations containing periods, but space between	49
initials.	52
Examples	55
(1) We spent the fall in Minnesota (not Minn.) as originally planned.	69
(2) The meetings have been set for February 15, April 10, and June 2.	83
(3) Our representatives will be in Chicago, New York, and Washington.	97
(4) Mr. E. L. Bossart left for Minneapolis at 9:30 a.m. on Wednesday.	111
Other Examples	117

135C Skill-Transfer Typing (10) *two 1' writings on each sentence; compare* gwam

		Words
Goal	The star of a show sings one song too few, not one too many.	12
Rough draft	A idea isnot rasponsable for the poeple whom beleve it. (handwritten corrections: n, #, e, i, &, i, in)	12
Script	Counting time is not nearly so important as making it count.	12
Figures	Their check for $137 brought the total collected to $892.50.	12

83C Production Typing: Modified Block Style Letters ㉟

Beginning with this lesson, vertical lines are no longer used to indicate opening and closing line endings. Arrange these lines correctly. In addition, add punctuation marks where needed.

An official title may follow the name of the addressee; it may be on a line with the company name; or it may be on a line by itself. (See page 149.)

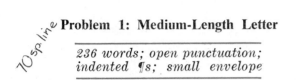

Problem 1: Medium-Length Letter

236 words; open punctuation; indented ¶s; small envelope

	Words
Mr. James T. Bolder Placement Director	11
Underwood Community College Dyke, VA	18
22935 Dear Mr. Bolder (¶ 1) Some time ago	25
I wrote to you asking for the names of stu-	34
dents who wanted summer work, and you sent	42
the names of three people to me. We have	51
tested these students; perhaps you would be	60
interested in our conclusions. (¶ 2) Miss	67
Toland did well on the tests. She needed	75
more time than the others to transcribe her	84
shorthand notes; but her letter was neat,	93
properly placed, and correct in style. She	101
began the filing tests slowly, but her speed	110
increased as she became acquainted with the	119
procedures. (¶ 3) Mr. Martin took his short-	127
hand notes rapidly, and he transcribed them	136
quickly and accurately. His letter was free of	145
errors. He did well with the machines test,	154
but he was much slower than the others at	163
filing. (¶ 4) Miss Basset is one of the fastest	171
shorthand writers we have ever tested; but	180
her transcript contained misspellings and	188
other inaccuracies. The letter was not attrac-	198
tively placed on the page, and her typing was	207
not so neat as that of the others. She was	216
fast (but not accurate) on the filing and the	225
machines tests. (¶ 5) Although we had	231
planned to hire only one student, we hired	240
two--Miss Toland and Mr. Martin. Thank	248
you for providing us with the type of employ-	257
ees we need. Very truly yours W. P. Stone,	266
Office Manager	269/285

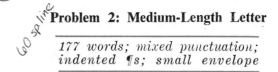

Problem 2: Medium-Length Letter

177 words; mixed punctuation; indented ¶s; small envelope

	Words
Mr. L. W. West Farmer, West & Lincoln	11
133 Byer Street Edwardsville, VA 22456	19
Dear Mr. West (¶ 1) Miss Lorna Basset,	26
about whom you inquired in your recent let-	34
ter, is a student at our school. Her record	43
indicates she should be graduated in January.	52
(¶ 2) Always a friendly and cooperative	59
person, Miss Basset accepts responsibility	68
willingly; she has been both secretary and	76
president of the Arts Club on our campus.	85
She dresses neatly and tastefully. Her grades	94
are average; she attends her classes regularly.	104
(¶ 3) According to her teachers, Miss Basset	112
is a very rapid, enthusiastic worker. She	121
writes shorthand and types at very high rates	130
of speed, but her letters are not always neat	139
and accurate. (¶ 4) It would appear to us that	147
Miss Basset has an excellent potential for a	156
job that provides additional training and help-	166
ful supervision. We therefore recommend her	175
to you for summer work, with the thought	183
that she might return to you as a full-time	192
employee when she finishes school. Sincerely	201
yours James T. Bolder Placement Director	210/225

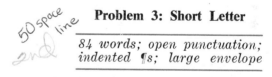

Problem 3: Short Letter

84 words; open punctuation; indented ¶s; large envelope

	Words
June 27, 19-- Professor Fred R. Saxton 461	9
Washington Avenue Iowa City, IA 52240	16
Dear Professor Saxton (¶ 1) A promotion	23
plan for the book PRODUCTION PROCEDURES	31
is enclosed for your approval. You will recall	41
that our contract provides for your approval	50
of promotion plans. (¶ 2) When all final	57
proofreading is finished late in October, PRO-	66
DUCTION PROCEDURES will probably be ready	75
to go to press; but plans to promote the book	83
should be settled before August 1. May we	92
therefore have your prompt approval for each	101
plan we suggest. Very truly yours Edward	110
Caster Senior Editor Enclosure	117/130

Problem 2: Invoice

Type in duplicate

Words

Sold To Pacific Builders Supply Co. 31553 Gladstone Blvd. Riverside,   12
CA 92504 **Terms** Net 30 days **Date** September 20, 19—— **Our Order**   20
No. 5777 **Your Order No.** N14899 **Shipped By** Express   24

Quantity	Description	Cat. No.	Unit Price	Amount	
12	Regulation shuffleboard sets	1893-N	17.50	210.00	35
20	Master 6-ball croquet sets	1821-N	21.25	425.00	45
6	Big league archery sets	2106-E.	24.70	148.20	54
10	Steel and aluminum golf carts	1956-G	23.60	236.00	65
3 doz.	League-style official baseballs	0056-B	18.20 doz.	54.60	78 / 80
Checked By (*Your Initials*)				1,073.80	82

Problem 3: Credit Memorandum

Type a credit memorandum from Harper Brothers Sports Equipment to William E. Lodge Company, 14932 Virginia Way, Ogden, UT 84403. **Date:** September 28, 19——. **No.** 554. The entries are as follows:

Words
17

Quantity	Cat. No.	Description	Unit Price	Total	
2	1893-N	Regulation shuffleboard sets	17.50	35.00	27
3	1821-N	Master 6-ball croquet sets	21.25	63.75	36
1	1956-G	Steel and aluminum golf cart	23.60	23.60	46 / 48
				122.35	49

Problem 4: Statement of Account

Type a statement of account from Harper Brothers Sports Equipment to William E. Lodge Company, 14932 Virginia Way, Ogden, UT 84403. **Date:** September 30, 19——. The entries are as follows:

Words
16

Date	Items	Debits	Credits	Balance Due	
Sept. 1	Balance			425.50	21
8	Payment on account		425.50	00	28
12	Invoice #5215	829.30		829.30	34
20	Invoice #5777	122.35		951.65	40
28	Credit Memorandum #554		122.35	829.30	48

84A   Preparatory Practice ⑤ *each line at least three times*

Alphabet   Jeff York amazed us by stating his quixotic view of the labor problem.

Figure-symbol   On May 27, 1964, George paid Sedge–Brown $513.02, just $4.98 too much.

Inside keys   Five navy tugs tried to enter the harbor before fog ruined visibility.

Fluency   The man who keeps his eyes fixed on his goal can walk a straight path.

| 1 | 2 | 3 | 4 | 5 | 6 | 7 | 8 | 9 | 10 | 11 | 12 | 13 | 14 |

84B   Building Speed and Control ⑩

1. Type three 1' writings on the *exploration level*.
2. Type three 1' writings on the *control level*.

3. Compute *gwam*. Record the rate of your most accurate and your fastest writings.

1.5 SI
5.6 AWL
80% HFW

Carbon paper, with the glossy side down, is placed on a sheet of plain paper. Second sheets of thin paper are generally used for carbon copies. The letterhead paper is then laid on the carbon paper, and the several sheets are inserted into the typewriter so that the face of the letterhead is toward the writer. The dull side of the carbon paper will be toward you when the sheets are inserted in proper position for typing.

| 1 | 2 | 3 | 4 | 5 | 6 | 7 | 8 | 9 | 10 | 11 | 12 | 13 | 14 |

Problem Typing Information

MAILING NOTATION IN A LETTER

If a special mailing notation is used in a letter, type it at the left margin midway between the date and the first line of the inside address. If the notation is to be typed on the carbon copy only, insert a piece of heavy paper between the ribbon and the original (first) sheet. The paper should be thick enough to prevent the imprint of the type from showing on the original sheet.

TITLES IN THE ADDRESS

Use a personal title (*Mr., Mrs., Miss.*, etc.) in the address when the letter is to an individual. An official title (indicating the position held) may be typed (1) on the line with the name, (2) on the line with the company name, or (3) on a separate line. Capitalize the title. Use the style that will give the best balanced lines.

May 31, 19--

Mailing notation   REGISTERED MAIL

Title on line with name
```
Mr. E. P. Johnson, Manager
Smith Real Estate Company
1001 Kansas Avenue
Omaha, NE   68110
```

Title on line with company name
```
Mr. Lawrence P. Robertson
Manager, Ohio Tractors, Inc.
2200 Greensburg Road
Canton, OH  44720
```

Title on separate line
```
Miss Anne K. Taylor
Dean of Women
North Idaho Junior College
Coeur d'Alene, ID  83814
```

134B Communication Index [5] *each sentence once; figure* nwam

Full sheet; 2″ top margin; 70-space line; DS

Punctuate and capitalize these sentences as you type them. Do not number them. Read a sentence through before you start typing it.

1 if this is true said the speaker our country is safe and strong

2 mr william raymond jr of ames iowa will address the camera club

3 we left fort worth texas however on saturday january 10 at 8 a m

4 when john goodmans report arrived we studied its contents carefully

5 we received the bird guide but its too expensive may we use yours

6 if we go to europe in january we shall visit london paris and rome

7 we ordered a 12 foot case a 10 foot case is too narrow for the study

8 ted morris car has been parked near the grand hotel for several days

134C Growth Index [10] *5-minute writing on 127B, page 219*

134D Production Measurement [30] *errors corrected; figure* n-pram

Type the following problems for 20 minutes. Make one carbon copy of each problem. You will be scored on the number of problems finished.

Problem 1: Purchase Order

					Words
To Harper Brothers Sports Equipment, 38908 Washington Street, Jersey					13
City, NJ 07302 **Order No.** N14899 **Date** September 12, 19-- **Terms**					21
Net 30 days **Ship Via** Express					25
Quantity	**Cat. No.**	**Description**	**Price**	**Total**	
12	1893-N	Regulation shuffleboard sets	17.50	210.00	36
20	1821-N	Master 6-ball croquet sets	21.25	425.00	46
6	2106-E	Big league archery sets	24.70	148.20	55
10	1956-G	Steel and aluminum golf carts	23.60	236.00	66
3 doz.	0056-B	League-style official baseballs	18.20 doz.	54.60	79 80
				1,073.80	82

Problem 1: Enclosure for Problem 2

Margins: 2″ top; 1″ side; 5-space ¶ indention; DS; SS and indent numbered ¶s from side margins

	Words
ERASING ON CARBON COPIES	5

TS

(¶ 1) Erase and correct all typing errors. Use   13
a hard eraser in correcting errors on the origi-   23
nal copy. A soft eraser works best on carbon   32
copies. In correcting errors when carbon cop-   41
ies have been made, proceed as follows: 50

1. Move the carriage to the extreme   57
   right or left so that the eraser   64
   crumbs will not fall into the   70
   machine.   72

DS

2. Place a small card directly behind   80
   the original. Erase the error on   87
   the original copy.   91
3. Transfer the card behind the first   100
   carbon copy, and erase that copy.   107
4. Continue erasing all carbon copies   115
   in this manner, moving from front   122
   to back.   124
5. Strike the correct key or keys   132
   lightly. Repeat the stroking until   139
   the desired shading is achieved.   145

Problem 2

166 words; open punctuation; indented ¶s; 1 carbon copy; large envelope

	Words

Miss Lori Bellmont, Secretary Webster Allen   12
Corporation 1700 Broadway Denver, CO   19
80202 Dear Miss Bellmont (¶ 1) I am en-   26
closing the report you requested on erasing   34
on carbon copies. It is one we distribute to   44
all office personnel who use typewriters in our   53
company. I hope you will find it helpful.   62
(¶ 2) Some of our typists use correction   69
cover-ups that are principally of two types: 78
chalk-coated paper or liquid correction fluid.   88
Both applications are quite satisfactory. (¶ 3)   96
When using the chalk-coated paper, place the   105

coated side down over the error. Retype the   114
error in order to transfer the chalk dust to   123
the incorrectly typed characters. Remove the   132
paper and type in your correction. (¶ 4)   139
Liquid correction fluid looks much like white   149
or colored nail polish and is available in   157
shades to match various colors of paper.   166
Choose a tint to blend with the paper you are   175
using. Paint over the error, let the fluid dry,   185
then type the copy desired. Sincerely yours   194
Alphonso Lopez Office Manager Enclosure   202/220

Problem 3: Company Name in Closing Lines

92 words; open punctuation; block ¶s; 1 carbon copy; large envelope

If the company name appears in the closing lines, type it in all capitals, a double space below the complimentary close as shown in the illustration. The name of the writer is then typed on the 4th line space below the company name.

```
            Yours very truly

            CONTINENTAL PROTECTION CO.


            William E. Hathaway, Jr.
            District Manager

xx

Enclosure
```

	Words

Mr. Ernest L. Hawthorne 1365 Peachtree   11
Street Atlanta, GA 30309 Dear Mr. Haw-   19
thorne (¶ 1) A man buys life insurance so   26
that he is provided with protection, but he   35
may discover one day that he has not needed   43
this kind of protection. Of what possible use   53
is his policy to him? (¶ 2) This question (and   61
others like it) is answered in our novel book-   70
let *Insurance in Action*, which is enclosed.   83
Our agent, Mr. Vince Bradley, will be glad   92
to answer any additional questions confront-   100
ing you. Call him; his number is in your tele-   109
phone book. Yours very truly CONTINEN-   117
TAL PROTECTION CO. William E. Hathaway,   125
Jr. District Manager Enclosure   132/144

133B Skill-Comparison Typing [5] *1′ writings on each line of 133A, page 230; compare* gwam

133C Communication Aid: Capitalization [10] *as directed in 122C, page 212; type a heading*

Full sheet; 1½″ top margin; 70-space line; SS with DS between items

Words

3

Rules 5

(1) As a rule, capitalize nouns preceding a figure. The word page is 20
usually not capitalized, however, unless it begins a sentence. 33

(2) Capitalize only the first word of a complimentary close. 45

(3) All titles appearing in the address and closing lines of business 59
letters should be capitalized. 65

(4) Capitalize a title that precedes a name or that is used to refer to 80
a specific person. Titles appearing elsewhere may be written with- 94
out a capital, unless the title is one of high distinction. 105

Examples 109

(1) Each case is fully explained in Volume III, Chapter 12, page 207. 123

(2) Capitalize first words of complimentary closes: Sincerely yours. 137

(3) Capitalize titles in letter addresses: Mr. John Lowe, Treasurer. 151

(4) On Monday, President Fred Barnes had lunch with the club manager. 165

Other Examples 170

133D Production Skill Building [30] *errors corrected; figure* n-pram

Make a pencil notation of the problems at the right to be typed as a 20-minute writing. Make one carbon copy of each form. Finish as many of the problems as you can. Compute *n-pram.*

Page 223, 129D, Problem 2
Page 226, 130D, Problem 3
Page 227, 131D, Problem 3
Page 230, 132D, Problem 3

LESSON 134

134A Preparatory Practice [5] *each line at least three times*

Alphabet	Frankly, it would be an amazing experience just to visit with a queen.
Figure-symbol	In 1957, our profits were $37,461.05; this year, they are $189,227.13.
Outside keys	Professor Lopez' quiz in law was two hours long; still, we all passed.
Fluency	The man who wants to be a leader would do well to learn how to follow.
	| 1 | 2 | 3 | 4 | 5 | 6 | 7 | 8 | 9 | 10 | 11 | 12 | 13 | 14 |

LESSON 85

85A Preparatory Practice [5] *each line at least three times*

Alphabet	We hope Mr. Frazier will quickly adjourn the executive board meetings.
Figure-symbol	Memo #7091 said: Buy 25½ dozen @ 46¢ and 38½ dozen @ 27¢ immediately.
Long words	Management development must challenge the manager to question success.
Fluency	Hard work can often help a person overcome many handicaps he may have.

| 1 | 2 | 3 | 4 | 5 | 6 | 7 | 8 | 9 | 10 | 11 | 12 | 13 | 14 |

85B Production Skill Builder [15] *type two 5′ writings on the letter on page 144; compute* g-pram.

85C Production Typing: Modified Block Style with Variations [30]

Letters of Two or More Pages

Use plain paper for the second and subsequent pages of letters. Begin the heading about an inch from the top edge of the sheet. Type the heading at the left margin in *block form* or in the *horizontal form* (one-line arrangement).

Leave 3 blank lines between the heading and the first line of the resumed letter; use the same side margins as for preceding page.

Note. Do not resume the body of a letter with the last part of a divided word. Include at least two lines of a paragraph at the bottom of a page and at least two lines at the top of the succeeding page.

```
Mr. Allen N. Newton
Page 2
March 18, 19--

Write or call your nearest Ramton representative for information
```

```
Mr. Allen N. Newton            2            March 18, 19--

Write or call your nearest Ramton representative for information
```

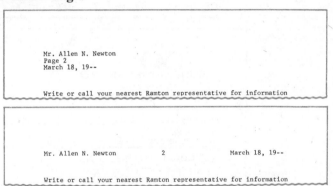

Headings for Letters of Two or More Pages—Block Form and Horizontal Form

Problem 1: Two-Page Letter

422 words; open punctuation; block ¶s; 1 carbon copy; large envelope

Words

March 18, 19-- Mr. Allen N. Newton, 7
Vice-President Bedford-Lowe, Ltd. 450 15
Massachusetts Avenue Niagara Falls, NY 23
14305 Dear Mr. Newton (¶ 1) The Harlowe 30
National Bank, a multimillion dollar institu- 38
tion serving New York City and Long Island 47
City, is one of the first banks to establish 56
separate budgets for its 24 branches and 40 65
departments. This step requires the prepara- 74
tion of a complex monthly budget report, 82
which resulted in a three-day headache for the 91
Accounting Department each month. This 99
was the case, at any rate, until a Ramton 200 109
electric printing calculator turned the entire 118
operation into a routine one-hour job. (¶ 2) 126
With the Ramton 200, a monthly budget sum- 134
mation for each branch can be programmed 142
by mathematical functions once. The Ramton 151
200 then continues to perform the operations 160
automatically while variables such as deposits, 170
rates, and loans are fed into it. The results 179
are printed on paper tape for verification and 189
filing. As a consequence, the budgets go out 198
three days to a week earlier. (¶ 3) The Ram- 205
ton's ability to do difficult calculations in 215
milliseconds makes it invaluable to Harlowe 223
National in other ways. It can be programmed 233
to compound interest on a continual daily 241
basis. Moreover, it can prepare a last-minute 250
analysis of future profits for each branch and 260
department. With conventional methods, this 269
operation would have taken all night. The 277
Ramton 200 has the job done in an hour. 286
(¶ 4) All arithmetic functions are performed 293
by touching figures on the simple control keys. 303

Problem 3: Statement of Account

Type in duplicate

Words

Date June 30, 19-- **To** Pacific Builders Supply Co. 31553 Gladstone Blvd. 13
Riverside, CA 92504 17

Date	Items	Debits	Credits	Balance Due	Words
June 1	Balance			3,571.60	22
10	Payment on account		3,571.60	00	30
15	Invoice #47221	952.17		952.17	37
20	Invoice #47592	1,181.40		2,133.57	44
24	Credit Memorandum #524		181.40	1,952.17	53

Problem 4: Voucher Check

Type in duplicate the following voucher check. Use the variable line spacer to bring the ruled lines on the check into proper typing position.

pb
PACIFIC BUILDERS SUPPLY CO.
31553 Gladstone Blvd.
Riverside, California 92504

16–310
1219

July 2 19 -- No. 4982 3

PAY to the order of Burdett Building Corporation $ 952.17 13

Nine hundred fifty-two and 17/100---------------------------------- Dollars 27

WEST COAST NATIONAL BANK
LOS ANGELES, CALIFORNIA 90006

⑆1219⑈0320⑆ 143 0602 46⑈

Treasurer, PACIFIC BUILDERS SUPPLY CO.

Detach This Stub Before
Cashing This Check

TO Burdett Building Corporation 33
1348 Cactus Road, East 38
Phoenix, AZ 85022 41

IN PAYMENT OF THE FOLLOWING INVOICES:

Date	Invoice	Amount	Words
6/15/--	#47221	952.17	46

pb
PACIFIC BUILDERS SUPPLY CO.
31553 Gladstone Blvd.
Riverside, California 92504

LESSON 133

133A Preparatory Practice (5) *each line at least three times*

Alphabet Medical experts frequently view smoking as a major hazard to the body.

Figure-symbol Its weight is 36#; height, 2′ 8″; Length, 27′ 9″; code number, 14–10 *.

Direct reaches Dee longed to troll for muskellunge, so Polly swerved to deeper water.

Fluency There are many elements that combine to produce finer typing outcomes.

| 1 | 2 | 3 | 4 | 5 | 6 | 7 | 8 | 9 | 10 | 11 | 12 | 13 | 14 |

Words

Multiplication and division are both fully auto- 313
matic. You simply index the figures, touch 321
the control keys, and there's your answer-- 330
printed on tape. For all its simplicity, the 339
Ramton 200 is a full-fledged calculator. It has 349
an automatic constant multiplier, automatic 358
divisor alignment, and automatic retention of 367
quotient. (¶ 5) Ramton makes and sells more 375
different kinds of calculators than any other 384
company in the world. You are thus assured 393
of finding the right calculator for your par- 402
ticular operation without having to pay for 410
more computing sophistication than you actu- 419
ally need. (¶ 6) Write or call your nearest 427
Ramton representative for information on the 436
full line of full-value Ramton calculators. You 446
can bank on them. Yours very truly RAMTON 454
MACHINES, INC. Joseph Keane, Sales Man- 462
ager 463/484

Problem 2: Writer's Name Omitted in Closing Lines

94 words; date of letter, January 12; open punctuation; indented ¶s; 1 carbon copy; large envelope

When the writer's name is not included in the closing lines, type his initials before yours at the end of the letter, thus: WSB:*your initials*

Words

Mr. J. Harmon Roberts Station Manager 11
Radio Station WRNC Euclid, OH 44123 18
Dear Mr. Roberts (¶ 1) With this letter we 26
are enclosing five copies of a two-minute com- 35
mercial message we should like to have pre- 43
sented on the air from your studio at 10:58 52
a.m. for 14 consecutive days, commencing 60
with the first Monday of next month. If pos- 69
sible, we should like to have the announce- 77
ment read by Stan Givens of your announcing 86
staff. (¶ 2) It is our understanding that the 94
time for this spot announcement is part of 103
that we contracted for in our agreement of 112
January 2 with you. Very truly yours Ad- 120
vertising Manager WSB:*your initials* Enclo- 126
sures 5 127/142

LESSON 86

86A Preparatory Practice (5) *each line at least three times*

Alphabet	Major Forbes quickly recognized the power of an auxiliary naval force.
Figure-symbol	By buying the stock at 124¼ and selling it at 86½, Lance lost $395.70.
Capitals	The President of the United States visited Chicago, Omaha, and Tucson.
Fluency	If you can succeed the first time, it is time to try something harder.

| 1 | 2 | 3 | 4 | 5 | 6 | 7 | 8 | 9 | 10 | 11 | 12 | 13 | 14 |

86B Building Speed and Control (10) *type 84B, page 149, as directed there*

86C Production Skill Building: Letters in Modified Block Style (35)

Type these problems as a 25′ writing. Correct your errors. Type a carbon copy and an appropriate envelope for each letter. Compute your *n-pram.*

Page 148, 83C, Problem 2
Page 150, 84C, Problem 2
Page 150, 84C, Problem 3
Page 152, 85C, Problem 2, above

N-PRAM (NET PRODUCTION RATE A MINUTE)

N-pram refers to the rate on production copy on which errors are erased and corrected.

PENALTIES FOR ERRORS:

Deduct 10 words....... for each error not erased on an original copy

Deduct 5 words........ for each error not erased on a carbon copy

$$\text{N-PRAM} = \frac{\text{Gross (total) words} - \text{Penalties}}{\text{Length (in minutes) of writing}}$$

Problem 1: Credit M...

Robinson, op. cit., p. 4.

Type in duplicate   *Type in duplicate*

Credit Memorandum

BB **Burdett Building Corporation**

No. 359

Date May 15, 19--

1348 Cactus Road, East
Phoenix, Arizona 85022
Telephone 322-1960

To Pacific Builders Supply Co.
31553 Gladstone Blvd.
Riverside, CA 92504

YOUR ACCOUNT HAS BEEN CREDITED FOR:

Quantity	Description	Cat.No.	Unit Price	Amount
2	Radiant wall heaters	9352	9.95	19.90
1 ctn.	Embossed wood vinyl asbestos tile	1200	11.15	11.15
1	Oven wood-fan	3280	17.45	17.45
				48.50

Words
1
3
9
13
17
25
37
44
46
47

Statement of Account

BB **Burdett Building Corporation**

Date May 31, 19--

To   Pacific Builders Supply Co.
31553 Gladstone Blvd.
Riverside, CA 92504

1348 Cactus Road, East
Phoenix, Arizona 85022
Telephone 322-1960

Date	Items	Debits	Credits	Balance Due
May 1	Balance			130.00
1	Invoice #45172	3,272.00		3,402.00
10	Invoice #45340	718.10		4,120.10
15	Credit Memorandum #359		48.50	4,071.60
20	Payment on account		500.00	3,571.60

Words
3
8
13
17
22
29
36
45
52

87A Preparatory Practice (5) *each line at least three times*

Alphabet	Walter expects to have two dozen tickets for the July banquet meeting.
Figure-symbol	To work this problem: Add (+) 186,549 to 327,060; subtract (–) 3,672.
Third row	They went to her party, for they were quite sure Betty would be there.
Fluency	Believe about half of what you hear––and be sure it is the right half.

| 1 | 2 | 3 | 4 | 5 | 6 | 7 | 8 | 9 | 10 | 11 | 12 | 13 | 14 |

87B Growth Index (15) *two 5′* control-level *writings; figure* gwam *on better writing*

All letters are used.

		GWAM 1′	5′	
¶ 1 1.5 SI 5.6 AWL 80% HFW	Communication experts agree that the average letter costs about	13	3	58
	two and a half dollars to produce. Included in the cost are the time	26	5	61
	of the dictator and typist, paper, postage, and fixed charges, such	40	8	63
	as wear and tear on the equipment used in the process. With costs go-	54	11	66
	ing sky high, every avenue must be explored to keep them in check. Pro-	69	14	69
	ficiency of the staff can be upgraded, and all possible steps must be	83	17	72
	taken to reduce the cost of "getting out the mail."	93	19	74
¶ 2 1.5 SI 5.6 AWL 80% HFW	When executives study some of the communications going through	13	21	77
	the mails, they may wonder if letters are worth what they cost. Very	27	24	79
	likely, many are not. The ability to write can be acquired. The	40	27	82
	principles of clear writing can be mastered by almost anybody. One	53	29	85
	must first be able to gather and organize the data he needs; then he	67	32	87
	must know how to put his data into words that convey exactly what he	81	35	90
	wants to say. Those who write letters should become skillful in the art.	96	38	93
¶ 3 1.5 SI 5.6 AWL 80% HFW	Finally, every effort must be made by the staff to cut costs.	13	40	96
	The experts say that a majority of letters are about thirty percent	26	43	98
	longer than necessary, and long letters are usually very fuzzy. Clarity	41	46	101
	and brevity go hand in hand. Analyze the letters you write. With a	55	49	104
	pencil, strike out the words and phrases that are not needed. Rewrite	69	51	107
	the letter. Does not its meaning shine through more lively and clearly?	84	54	110
	It is a way to cut costs.	89	55	111

1′ GWAM | 1 | 2 | 3 | 4 | 5 | 6 | 7 | 8 | 9 | 10 | 11 | 12 | 13 | 14 |
5′ GWAM | 1 | 2 | 3 |

87C Production Measurement: Business Letters (30) *20′ timing; errors corrected; compute* n-pram

Type the four letters on page 154. Make a carbon copy of each letter. Address an envelope of appropriate size for each letter.

132A Preparatory Practice (5) *each line at least three times*

Alphabet	Jack Fledger will accompany me when I visit the quaint, exotic bazaar.
Figure-symbol	They may deduct a discount of 3 1/3% ($124.80) from our Invoice #9567.
Double letters	Sherry's committee passed coffee and cocoa at the Mississippi meeting.
Fluency	Remember that very few men are experts in more than one or two fields.
	| 1 | 2 | 3 | 4 | 5 | 6 | 7 | 8 | 9 | 10 | 11 | 12 | 13 | 14 |

132B Skill-Comparison Typing (5) *two 1' writings on each of Lines 1 and 4 of 132A; compare* gwam

132C Communication Aid: Capitalization (10) *as directed in 122C, page 212; type a heading*

Full sheet; 1½" top margin; 70-space line; SS with DS between items

Words

3

Rules 5

(1) Capitalize the first word of a complete quotation. Do not capital- 19
ize a quotation resumed within a sentence. 28
(2) Capitalize the first word following a colon if that word begins a 42
sentence. 44
(3) Capitalize adjectives or common nouns that are used as a part of 58
proper names. Do not capitalize geographic terms if they are used 72
in the plural. 75
(4) Capitalize words derived from proper nouns unless these words have 89
acquired independent, common meanings. 97

Examples 101

(1) "He is suffering," the critic said, "from paralysis of analysis." 115
(2) Use this rule: Capitalize principal words in titles of articles. 129
(3) We camped on Cedar and June lakes on our way to Ellis State Park. 143
(4) He had their lovely oriental rug cleaned by Tim Lee, an Oriental. 157

Other Examples 162

Production Typing Information

WINDOW ENVELOPES

Window envelopes have transparent or cut-out openings in the lower center, through which the address typed on a letter, an invoice, or other business forms can be seen.

FOLDING A HALF-SIZE SHEET FOR A WINDOW ENVELOPE

Keep in mind that the complete address must show through the window in the envelope. Fold a full-page form from the top down fully two thirds the length of the paper; then fold back the required distance to make the address come to the correct position. Fold a half sheet through the center, keeping the typewritten side on the outside. Insert the paper into the envelope with the address side toward the front.

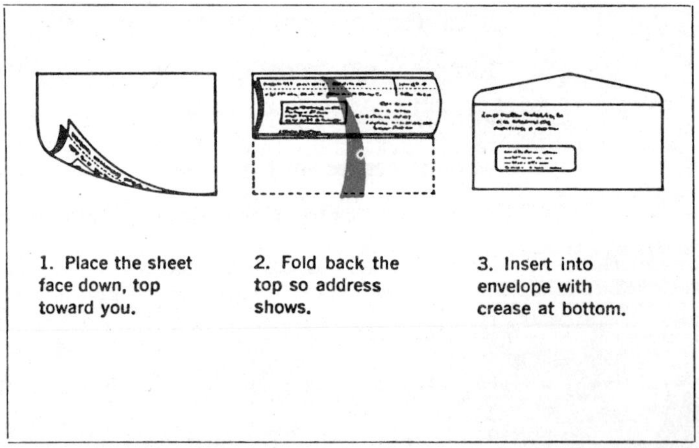
1. Place the sheet face down, top toward you.
2. Fold back the top so address shows.
3. Insert into envelope with crease at bottom.

Folding a Half-Size Form for a Window Envelope

Problem 1

138 words; mixed punctuation; modified block; indented ¶s

Words

Mr. Franklin R. Stern 158 South Maple 11
Road Odin, IL 62870 Dear Mr. Stern 18
(¶ 1) Thank you for permitting us to open 25
one of our charge accounts in your name. 34
We appreciate your patronage. (¶ 2) Our 41
credit manager tells me that you have selected 50
the Budget Account type of credit service. 59
Your choice is a wise one; the Budget Account 67
count allows a generous 90 days for payment, 76
with only one third of the account to be pay- 85
able the tenth of each month following a pur- 93
chase. Terms such as these are one of the 102
privileges we provide for our customers; and 111
there is, of course, no charge of any kind for 120
them. (¶ 3) We sincerely hope this will be 128
the beginning of a long and pleasant friend- 137
ship. If at any time you have a suggestion for 146
improving our service, please let us hear from 156
you. Cordially yours DIAMOND & COULTER 164
L. S. Roost, Manager 169/180

Problem 2

104 words; open punctuation; modified block; indented ¶s; reference initials not needed

Words

Miss Betty N. Toland 135 Madison Avenue 11
Portsmouth, VA 23704 Dear Miss Toland 19
(¶ 1) Will you please complete as soon as 26
possible the enclosed personnel record card 35
and return it to this office. We must have the 44
card before we can include your name on our 53
payroll. (¶ 2) Print all information clearly, 61
and be certain to include your full name and 70
address and your social security number. 79
In addition, let us know how you wish to 87
handle your salary check. You may either 95
get it at the payroll office or have it sent to 105
your bank for deposit. (¶ 3) We are pleased 113
to know you will be working with us this 121
summer. Sincerely yours (Miss) Fern Ann 129
Royal Payroll Clerk Enclosure 135/147

Problem 3

129 words; open punctuation; modified block; block ¶s; writer's initials: HVL

Words

Miss Charlene Marie Lampel 1204 Spring 11
Garden Drive Aurora, IL 60538 Dear Miss 19
Lampel (¶ 1) Our records indicate that checks 27
drawn to your order in payment of dividends 36
on stock of this Corporation, as described on 45
the enclosed application, have not been paid 54
by the bank on which the checks were drawn. 63
(¶ 2) If the dividend checks are in your pos- 71
session, we request that they be cashed or 79
deposited promptly. If they have been lost or 89
destroyed, please complete and execute the 97
enclosed application and return it to us. Upon 107
receipt of the application, we shall arrange for 116
the issuance of replacement checks, provided 125
your application is found to be in good order. 135
(¶ 3) For your convenience, a return envelope 143
requiring no postage is enclosed. Very truly 152
yours Assistant Secretary Enclosures 2 161/174

Problem 4

117 words; open punctuation; modified block; block ¶s

Words

Mr. William Senn Bell Advertising Manager 12
McMillan & Smith, Inc. 901 Euclid Avenue 20
Cleveland, OH 44115 Dear Mr. Bell (¶ 1) 27
Thank you for sending us your spot commer- 35
cial to broadcast for 14 consecutive days, com- 44
mencing with the first Monday of next month. 53
Stan Givens will record your message, and it 62
will be played at 10:58 in the morning on 71
each of the requested days. (¶ 2) We are 78
pleased to announce that Mr. Paul Jacks will 87
join our staff next week as our advertising 96
consultant. He has handled radio advertising 105
accounts for more than ten years and is highly 114
adept in finding out if advertising campaigns 124
are worth what they cost. He will be glad 132
to help you with any advertising problems 141
you may have. Cordially yours J. Harmon 149
Roberts Station Manager 154/175

Type in duplicate

Problem 1: Invoice

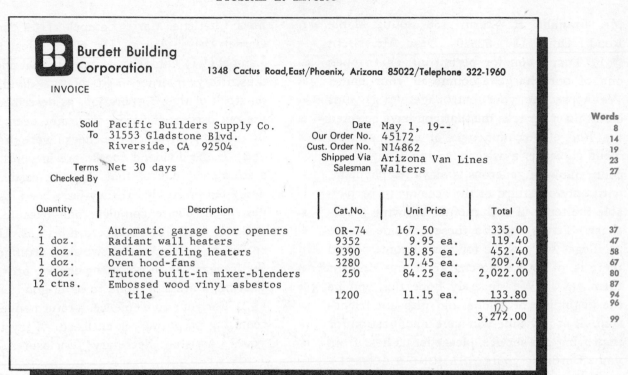

					Words
BB Burdett Building Corporation	1348 Cactus Road, East/Phoenix, Arizona 85022/Telephone 322-1960				

INVOICE

			Words
Sold To	Pacific Builders Supply Co.	Date May 1, 19--	8
	31553 Gladstone Blvd.	Our Order No. 45172	14
	Riverside, CA 92504	Cust. Order No. N14862	19
		Shipped Via Arizona Van Lines	23
Terms	Net 30 days	Salesman Walters	27
Checked By			

Quantity	Description	Cat. No.	Unit Price	Total	
2	Automatic garage door openers	OR-74	167.50	335.00	37
1 doz.	Radiant wall heaters	9352	9.95 ea.	119.40	47
2 doz.	Radiant ceiling heaters	9390	18.85 ea.	452.40	58
1 doz.	Oven hood-fans	3280	17.45 ea.	209.40	67
2 doz.	Trutone built-in mixer-blenders	250	84.25 ea.	2,022.00	80
12 ctns.	Embossed wood vinyl asbestos tile	1200	11.15 ea.	133.80	87 / 94
					96
				3,272.00	99

Problem 2: Confirmation Letter

1. Compose and type a letter to Pacific Builders Supply Co. Thank them for their Order No. N14888, of April 25 (Problem 3, p. 226). Indicate that there will be a very brief delay due to a temporary shortage of some of the items. The number of the invoice for this order is given in Problem 3 below.

2. Type the letter on a full sheet; select the letter and punctuation style. Date the letter May 4.

Problem 3: Invoice

Type in duplicate

	Words
Sold To Pacific Builders Supply Co. 31553 Gladstone Blvd. Riverside,	12
CA 92504 **Terms** Net 30 days **Date** May 10, 19-- **Our Order No.** 45340	20
Your Order No. N14888 **Shipped By** Redman Van Lines	25

Quantity	Description	Cat. No.	Unit Price	Amount	
6 rolls	Asphalt felt, 30 lb.	1311	3.15 ea.	18.90	35
12 gals.	Wood preservative		2.50 ea.	30.00	44
8 rolls	Rosin sized sheathing, 20 lb.		2.50 ea.	20.00	55
6	Ceiling exhaust fans	8310	27.95 ea.	167.70	64
6	Wall exhaust fans	8510	32.75 ea.	196.50	73
1 doz.	Outdoor lights, brass	M-153	23.75 ea.	285.00	83 / 84
Checked By (Your Initials) **Salesman** Walters				718.10	88

SECTION 15 BUSINESS LETTERS WITH SPECIAL FEATURES

LESSONS 88–94

Unless otherwise directed, proceed as follows:
Drill Copy: Full sheet; 70-space line; SS.
Paragraph Copy: Full sheet; 70-space line; DS; 5-space ¶ indention.

Production Copy: Letterhead (or full sheet), current date (unless given), and your reference initials should be used. Erase and correct errors. Prepare carbon copies and envelopes of appropriate size.

LESSON 88

88A Preparatory Practice (5) *each line at least three times*

Alphabet	Czar Alexei quickly delivered his bellicose judgment on foreign power.
Figure-symbol	Didn't Invoice #87456–90 allow us a 3 1/5% discount––or was it 3 2/5%?
Double letters	The committee added bookkeeping and speech to the school's curriculum.
Fluency	Habits are like muscles––the more we use them, the stronger they grow.

| 1 | 2 | 3 | 4 | 5 | 6 | 7 | 8 | 9 | 10 | 11 | 12 | 13 | 14 |

88B Skill-Comparison Typing (15) *three 1′ writings on each ¶; compare* gwam *and number of errors on the writings*

All letters are used.

GWAM 1′ | 5′

¶ 1 — 1.3 SI, 5.2 AWL, 90% HFW

Mark Twain once wrote that nothing so needs to be changed as the 13 3 56
habits of others. What he referred to, no doubt, was the wasteful, 27 5 59
unfriendly habits all men get into from time to time. Generally, most 41 8 62
people have many excellent habits, also; and these can prove to be of 55 11 64
use. If a good habit is set, it is as hard to change as a bad one. In 69 14 67
your daily typing practice, it will pay you to give all your attention 83 17 70
to building the right kind of habits. 91 18 72

¶ 2 — 1.5 SI, 5.6 AWL, 80% HFW

Is your vocabulary all you want it to be? If you are like the 13 21 74
majority of us, it will call for improvement. You can begin at once 26 23 77
to utilize words that are unfamiliar and to integrate them into your 40 26 80
normal speech. Try reading aloud from well-written books or articles; 54 29 82
such reading will make you pronounce the words you may skip. Look 68 32 85
for unique words that have appeal. Learn any meanings that they 81 34 88
convey; then practice using them very diligently. 91 36 90

¶ 3 — 1.7 SI, 6.0 AWL, 70% HFW

The soybean is a life capsule for a greatly overpopulated world. 13 39 92
It is used in animal feeds that help multiply the production of such 27 42 95
items as filet mignons, drumsticks, and pork chops. As a food ingredi- 41 45 98
ent, a field that has scarcely been scratched, it increases the produc- 57 48 101
tion of many of our top supermarket delicacies. This ubiquitous legume 71 50 104
is one of the best food multipliers for any community popping with people. 86 53 107

1′ GWAM | 1 | 2 | 3 | 4 | 5 | 6 | 7 | 8 | 9 | 10 | 11 | 12 | 13 | 14 |
5′ GWAM | 1 | 2 | 3 |

Problem 3: Purchase Order

Type in duplicate

Words

To Burdett Building Corporation, 1348 Cactus Road, East, Phoenix, AZ 13
85022 **Order No.** N14888 **Date** April 25, 19-- **Terms** n/30 **Ship Via** Red- 21
man Van Lines 23

Quantity	Cat. No.	Description	Price	Total	Words
6 rolls	1311	Asphalt felt, 30 lb.	3.15 ea.	18.90	34
12 gals.		Wood preservative	2.50 ea.	30.00	43
8 rolls		Rosin sized sheathing, 20 lb.	2.50 ea.	20.00	54
6	8310	Ceiling exhaust fans	27.95 ea.	167.70	63
6	8510	Wall exhaust fans	32.75 ea.	196.50	71
1 doz.	M-153	Outdoor lights, brass	23.75 ea.	285.00	81 83
				718.10	84

LESSON 131

131A Preparatory Practice [5] *each line at least three times*

Alphabet Next, we quickly moved the jig-saw puzzle to a large table near a fan.
Figure-symbol In Footnote (*) say, "Our bid of 3½¢ more in 1967 has paid $4,680.52."
Long words The nonadaptive organization was often insensitive to its environment.
Fluency We all make mistakes; they will help us if we try to profit from them.

| 1 | 2 | 3 | 4 | 5 | 6 | 7 | 8 | 9 | 10 | 11 | 12 | 13 | 14 |

131B Skill-Comparison Typing [5] *two 1' writings on each of Lines 1 and 4 of 131A; compare* gwam

131C Communication Aid: Capitalization [10] *as directed in 122C, page 212; type a heading*

Full sheet; 1½" top margin; 70-space line; SS with DS between items

Words

3

Rules 5

(1) Capitalize names of the days of the week, months, and holidays; do 19
not capitalize names of seasons unless they are personified. 32
(2) Capitalize names of regions; do not capitalize nouns or adjectives 46
indicating direction. 51
(3) Capitalize names of organizations, clubs, and their derivatives. 65
Capitalize names of things with specific individuality that are used 79
as proper names. 82
(4) Capitalize names of specific courses; do not capitalize such names 95
when they are used to denote common divisions of knowledge. 109

Examples 112

(1) I can arrange for a showing of fall styles on Tuesday, August 28. 126
(2) I landed in eastern France after I had crossed the Arctic Circle. 140
(3) The Rotary Club met in the Jeffrey Room of the Continental Hotel. 154
(4) You must write shorthand well, so please enroll for Shorthand II. 168

Other Examples 174

88C Manipulative Drill: Correcting Copy by "Squeezing" or "Spreading" Letters ⑮

"SQUEEZING" AN OMITTED LETTER WITHIN A WORD

First, erase the word.

Typewriters Without Half-Space Mechanism: "Squeeze" letters into available space by using backspace key and typing as explained at the left.

Typewriters with Half-Space Mechanism: Position carriage in the space preceding erased word; then:

1. Depress and hold down space bar; strike first letter of erased word.
2. Release space bar, press it down again and hold it; strike second letter of erased word. Continue in this manner until the correction is made.

Electric Typewriters, but Not the Selectric: Use same process as for squeezing at the beginning or end of a word.

"SQUEEZING" AN OMITTED LETTER AT THE BEGINNING OR AT THE END OF A WORD

Typewriters Without Half-Space Mechanism: Move carriage to the space or letter following omission. Depress backspace key halfway and hold it in position as you type omitted letter.

Typewriters with Half-Space Mechanism: Move carriage to last space before omission. Depress and hold down space bar; type omitted letter.

Electric Typewriters: Move carriage to proper position for inserting omitted letter. Hold carriage in position as you type the letter.

"SQUEEZING" AND "SPREADING" OF LETTERS ON THE SELECTRIC TYPEWRITER

A detailed explanation of these two operations is given on page xii of the Reference Guide.

"SPREADING" TO CORRECT A WORD WITH AN ADDED LETTER

First, erase the word.

Typewriters Without Half-Space Mechanism: Space twice after word preceding error; then:

1. Depress backspace key halfway; strike first letter of erased word; release backspace key, and hit space bar once.
2. Depress backspace key halfway; strike second letter of erased word. Continue in this manner until correction is made.

Typewriters with Half-Space Mechanism: Position carriage for first letter of erased word; then:

1. Depress and hold down space bar; strike the first letter.
2. Release space bar; press and hold it down; strike the second letter. Continue in this manner until the correction is made.

Electric Typewriters: Spreading is not feasible on electric machines.

PROCEDURE Study the explanatory material carefully. Then, type the problem sentences exactly as they are shown at the right and make the corrections by "squeezing" or "spreading." Compare your corrected sentences with those illustrated below. Repeat if time permits.

```
Friday was a very busy day for the staff.
The edition was well worth his effort.
Several of them worked until six o'clock.
The boys checked every page of the issue.
```

SENTENCE 4 Add *s* to *boy*.

1 Friday was a very usy day for he staff.

2 Thhe edition was welll worth his effort.

3 Several of thm worked untl six o'clock.

4 The boy checked every pag of the issue.

88D Skill-Comparison and Transfer Typing ⑮ *three 1' writings on each sentence; compare gwam*

		Words
Goal	Nothing is so rare as the use of a word in its true meaning.	12
One hand	John Plum traced the baggage to my street address in Waseca.	12
Rough draft	We are pleased glad to write to your about this new, unique book.	12
Script	His success depends on his ability to work well with others.	12

Examples

(1) Did he read "A New Asia"? I called, "Strike while others sleep!" 116

(2) The title of this fine article is "Principles of Office Systems." 130

(3) Chapter V, entitled "The Nature of Learning," is one I have read. 144

(4) I am using as a guide the pictures that appear in Office Systems. 161

Other Examples 167

130D Production Typing: Purchase Orders; Confirmation Card ㉕

Problem 1: Purchase Order

Type in duplicate

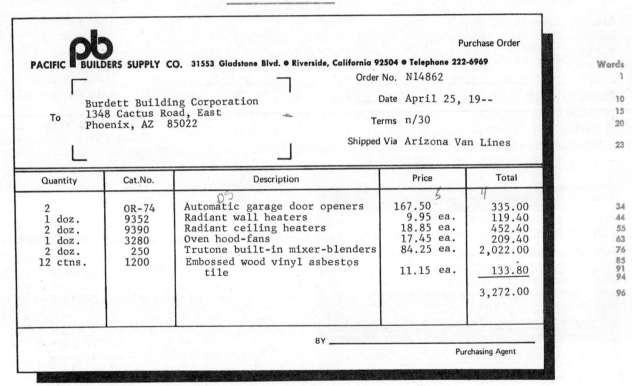

				Words

PACIFIC BUILDERS SUPPLY CO. 31553 Gladstone Blvd. ● Riverside, California 92504 ● Telephone 222-6969

Purchase Order

Order No. N14862 — 1

To Burdett Building Corporation
1348 Cactus Road, East
Phoenix, AZ 85022

Date April 25, 19-- — 10

Terms n/30 — 15 / 20

Shipped Via Arizona Van Lines — 23

Quantity	Cat.No.	Description	Price	Total	Words
2	OR-74	Automatic garage door openers	167.50	335.00	34
1 doz.	9352	Radiant wall heaters	9.95 ea.	119.40	44
2 doz.	9390	Radiant ceiling heaters	18.85 ea.	452.40	55
1 doz.	3280	Oven hood-fans	17.45 ea.	209.40	63
2 doz.	250	Trutone built-in mixer-blenders	84.25 ea.	2,022.00	76
12 ctns.	1200	Embossed wood vinyl asbestos tile	11.15 ea.	133.80	85 / 91 / 94
				3,272.00	96

BY _____
Purchasing Agent

Problem 2: Confirmation Card

Type the confirmation message on a postal card; see p. 178 for placement directions

Words

April 28, 19-- Gentlemen (¶) Thank you for 8
your Order No. N14862 of April 25, 19--. 16
This order will be shipped immediately. If 25
you should need to write or call us about it, 34
please refer to our Invoice No. 45172. BUR- 43
DETT BUILDING CORPORATION *Address on* 48
card: Pacific Builders Supply Co. 31553 Glad- 56
stone Blvd. Riverside, CA 92504 62

LESSON 89

89A Preparatory Practice [5] *each line three or more times*

Alphabet	Al Gray became exhilarated as we kept justifying his five quiz scores.
Figure-symbol	A & D Mine sold 8,764 tons of #130 coal (259 more tons than in March).
Inside keys	The navy frigates fought the battle for fifteen hours before retiring.
Fluency	One of our most wonderful experiences is to find that work can be fun.

| 1 | 2 | 3 | 4 | 5 | 6 | 7 | 8 | 9 | 10 | 11 | 12 | 13 | 14 |

89B Communication Pretest: Capitalization and Punctuation [15]

Full sheet; DS; 3″ top margin

Type each sentence once as you capitalize and punctuate it. Do not number the sentences.

Later lessons of this division contain rules and other aids to help you build communication skill. Correcting the following sentences will give you an opportunity to assess your present knowledge of capitalization and punctuation.

Sentence 8: Type the title of the play in all capital letters. Titles of plays may also be underlined or enclosed in quotation marks (with principal words capitalized).

1 from july 10 1967 to july 20 1968 we built and sold 49 new houses

2 a short simple explanation of the process we use appears in the book

3 the man we hire for this position must be alert reliable and honest

4 this book which has just been published is very helpful to teachers

5 when we finish the job we plan to take a short vacation trip to iowa

6 we have the funds but we are reluctant to buy your wire recorder now

7 in 1967 32 books were added to our price list in 1968 18 pamphlets

8 miss lees my secretary picked up our tickets for the play king lear

9 after closing the exhibit mr hamilton will send the books to peoria

10 it is true however that these cuts do not affect our office workers

Production Typing Information

ATTENTION LINE IN A LETTER

While the attention line is still used, there is a growing preference for addressing a letter to an individual or department rather than to the company. When the attention line is used, type it a double space below the inside address and a double space above the salutation. Since it is part of the address, the recommended placement is at the left margin. The attention line may also be centered.

```
                    January 14, 19--

Elliott Plastics, Inc.
1025 West Hazel
New Haven, CT  06511

Attention Research Director

Gentlemen
```

Problem 3: Purchase Requisition

Type in duplicate

Words

Requisition No.: 1017 **Date:** April 22, 19-- **Date Required:** May 10, 19-- 7

Deliver to: Leonard B. Murphy **Location:** Department #47 **Job. No.:** 95 14

Quantity	Description	Words
6 rolls	Asphalt felt, 30 lb., No. 1311	22
12 gals.	Wood preservative	27
8 rolls	Rosin sized sheathing, 20 lb.	35
6	Ceiling exhaust fans, Model 8310	42
6	Wall exhaust fans, Model 8510	48
1 doz.	Outdoor lights, brass, Model M-153	57

LESSON 130

130A Preparatory Practice [5] *each line at least three times*

Alphabet	Six cold, quivering monkeys from the jungle had been put in warm zoos.
Figure-symbol	Bond #7365024 will not be called until 1978, and it pays 5¼% interest.
First row	Mr. Newman discovered zinc, bauxite, and miscellaneous minerals there.
Fluency	A good criticism is the kind that makes you feel you have been helped.
	| 1 | 2 | 3 | 4 | 5 | 6 | 7 | 8 | 9 | 10 | 11 | 12 | 13 | 14 |

130B Paragraph Guided Writings for Rate Control [10]

1. Type 128D, page 221, for three 1′ writings at 40 words a minute.
2. Type three 1′ writings at 60 words a minute. Try to hit your goal on the exact letter as time is called. The quarter or half minutes may be called to guide you.

130C Communication Aid: Quotation Marks [10] *as directed in 122C, page 212; type a heading*

Full sheet; 1½″ top margin; 70-space line; SS with DS between items

Words

3

Rules 5

(1) Place question marks or exclamation points inside quotation marks 19
when they are part of the quotation; place them outside when they 33
refer to the entire sentence, of which the quotation is but a part. 47

(2) Use quotation marks to enclose the titles of magazine articles, 60
reports, and lectures. 65

(3) Use quotation marks to enclose subdivisions of published work. 78

(4) Underline or type in all capitals titles of books, booklets, news- 92
papers, magazines, and theses. 99

(Continued on page 225)

89C Production Typing: Attention Lines; Mailing and Enclosure Notations ㉚

Problem 1: Letter with Attention Line

132 words; open punctuation; modified block;* attention line at left margin

A letter addressed to a firm but containing an attention line should use the salutation *Gentlemen*.

	Words
January 14, 19–– Elliott Plastics, Inc. 1025	9
West Hazel New Haven, CT 06511 Atten-	17
tion Research Director Gentlemen (¶ 1) We	24
are currently engaged in research for the Gov-	33
ernment space program, and the project we are	42
working on involves the construction of cer-	51
tain new space vehicles. We are hoping you	60
can help us with a problem we now face.	68
(¶ 2) We urgently need a highly viscous sub-	75
stance that retains its adhesive quality under	85
extreme conditions and that has a marked	93
degree of flexibility. No glue now on the	102
market can meet our specifications. (¶ 3) We	110
shall be grateful if you will immediately notify	119
us if your firm is doing any research that could	128
result in the type of cementing material we	137
need. One of our men can fly to New Haven for	147
further discussions with you at any time. Sin-	156
cerely yours M. E. Borman Chief Technician	165/177

use colon

*Unless indented paragraphs are specified, modified block form requires block paragraphs.

Problem 2: Letter with Attention Line and Mailing and Enclosure Notations

120 words; mixed punctuation; modified block; centered attention line; mailing notation (see p. 144); carbon copy

	Words
January 17, 19–– AIRMAIL Brant Aircraft, Inc.	9
56 Chevoit Drive Chattanooga, TN 37411	17
Attention Mr. M. E. Borman, Chief Techni-	25
cian Gentlemen (¶ 1) Your letter about re-	33
search in adhesives has been referred to me	42
for reply. (¶ 2) Until the first of June, our	50
laboratory had been at work on adhesives re-	59
search; but since we gained most of the goals	68
we set out to reach, the project was ended	77

	Words
and another begun. The problem confronting	85
you was not seriously studied at any time by	94
our group. (¶ 3) The products we perfected	102
are all patented, and they are on the market.	111
They were surely among those you tested;	120
their names are typed on the enclosed card.	129
(¶ 4) We regret we cannot help you with your	136
problem. We can, however, offer you access	145
to any of our files. Very truly yours Oscar E.	155
Battle Director of Research Enclosure	163/175

Problem 3: Letter with Attention Line and Multiple Enclosure Notation

172 words; open punctuation; modified block; indented ¶s; attention line at left margin; carbon copy

	Words
January 20, 19–– Brant Aircraft, Inc. 56	8
Chevoit Drive Chattanooga, TN 37411	16
Attention Chief Technician Gentlemen (¶ 1)	23
I have discovered through discussions with	32
my customers that your firm is trying to	40
locate a gripping substance or device that has	49
exceptional flexibility under extreme condi-	58
tions. (¶ 2) I have represented fastening	65
manufacturers for 28 years; and, to the best	74
of my knowledge, there is no glue that will	83
do that kind of job. To find such a glue has	92
been the object of many researches, all of	101
which show that any "flexible fixative" lacks	110
strength and holding power. (¶ 3) Have you	118
thought of using rivets or pins instead of	126
glue? Our company markets many fine fas-	134
teners that can expand and contract with little	144
danger of breaking. They are available; they	153
are inexpensive; and they may well be the	162
solution to your problem. (¶ 4) I am enclos-	169
ing copies of our price lists and will stop at	179
your offices next week to explain the prin-	187
ciples involved and answer questions. Very	196
truly yours J. Donald Carr Eastern Repre-	204
sentative Enclosures: 4 price lists	212/224

be omitted in columnar tabulations of figures 119
where the ruling separates the dollars from 128
the cents. It is customary to use abbrevia- 136
tions such as gal., ft., ea., %, # for No., and 148
other similar special abbreviations. Names of 157
months may be abbreviated when limited 165
space on the form makes this desirable. (¶ 4) 173
Single-space invoices, statements, and similar 183
forms (such as credit memorandums, purchase 192
requisitions, purchase orders, etc.) unless you 201
have three or fewer lines, in which case use 210
double spacing. (¶ 5) When more than one 217

line is required for the description on a form, 227
type the description on successive lines (single- 237
space and indent the second line 3 spaces). 246
(¶ 6) There is no hard-and-fast rule on spac- 253
ing data in columns. Generally, the longest 262
line in each column, except the one in which 271
the items are listed or described, is centered 281
by eye measurement under the column head- 289
ing. Centering by exact methods is not re- 297
quired or recommended. Begin the description 306
items about 2 spaces to the right of the ruled 316
line. 317

Problem 2: Purchase Requisition

Type in duplicate

PURCHASE REQUISITION	
PACIFIC pb BUILDERS SUPPLY CO. 31553 Gladstone Blvd. ● Riverside, California 92504 ● Telephone 222-6969	

		Words
Deliver To Lee Bolden	Requisition No. 1012	3
Location Department #42	Date April 20, 19--	5
Job No. 72	Date Required May 10, 19--	12

Quantity	Description	
2	Automatic garage door openers, Model OR-74	21
1 doz.	Radiant wall heaters, Model 9352	38
2 doz.	Radiant ceiling heaters, Model 9390	45
1 doz.	Oven hood-fans, Model 3280	55
2 doz.	Trutone built-in mixer-blenders, Model 205	29
12 ctns.	Embossed wood vinyl asbestos tile, Model 1200	66

Approximate center

Tab 2 spaces from rule

Purchasing Agent

LESSON 90

90A Preparatory Practice [5] *each line three or more times*

Alphabet — The truculent Javanese quickly exhibited zeal for more fighting power.

Figure-symbol — The * on page 358 of The Story of 1760 refers you to pages 74 and 209.

Quiet hands — The populace celebrated the queen's birthday--she was 66 in September.

Fluency — Believe in luck; but the harder you work, the more luck you will have.

| 1 | 2 | 3 | 4 | 5 | 6 | 7 | 8 | 9 | 10 | 11 | 12 | 13 | 14 |

90B Communication Aid: Comma [20]

Full sheet; 1½″ top margin; 70-space line; SS with DS between items

1. For the heading, type COMMA.
2. Type the rules and examples given below (with numbers); underline the side headings.
3. Compose and type six sentences, each sentence illustrating one rule. Number these sentences to correspond with the rules.

Words

Rules 3

DS

DS

(1) In citing a date within a sentence, set off the year with commas. 17

(2) When two or more adjectives modify a noun, separate them by commas 32
if they bear equal relationship to the noun. 41

• Space once after the parenthesis

(3) Words in a series are separated by commas. 50

(4) Use a comma after a dependent clause that precedes its principal 64
clause. 66

(5) Use commas to set off a nonrestrictive appositive, but do not set 80
off a restrictive appositive. 86

(6) When two unrelated groups of figures come together, separate them 100
with a comma. 103

TS

Examples 106

DS

(1) On May 24, 1969, we transferred our account to a bank in Phoenix. 120
(2) This firm is known to all of us for giving honest, alert service. 134
(3) They like to receive letters that are short, clear, and friendly. 148
(4) When you learn the facts, you will change your mind about my car. 162
(5) Mr. Poe, our manager, is ill. He has read the book COST SYSTEMS. 176
(6) In 1967, 135 firms used this plan. During 1968, 32 discarded it. 190

TS

Other Examples (*Compose six sentences, each sentence illustrating one rule.*) 196

DS

Production Typing Information

SUBJECT LINE

A *subject line*, when used, is typed a double space below the salutation. In the block style or the AMS Simplified letter style (page 176), the subject line is typed even with the left margin. In other styles it may be typed (1) even with the left margin, (2) at paragraph point, or (3) centered.

The word *Subject*, when used in the subject line, is followed by a colon and is typed in all capitals or with only the first letter capitalized. It may also be omitted (as in the AMS Simplified letter style).

```
                                    March 9, 19--

AIRMAIL - SPECIAL DELIVERY

Dr. Henry L. Allen
Town House Hotel
271 Continental Drive
Minneapolis, MN  55430

Dear Henry:

                 SUBJECT:  Bold Journey Project

        Last week I wrote to General Hunt telling him of
our lack of progress in solving the adhesives problem.
```

Centered Subject Line in a Letter

129A Preparatory Practice [5] *each line at least three times*

Alphabet	Zelma Wayne helped mix a quart of orange juice to serve for breakfast.
Figure-symbol	The item was numbered 749/830/12 **. The simplified number is 749–56 *.
One hand	The greatest act we ever saw was the Savage Lion of Sweetwater, Texas.
Fluency	Any man has difficulty guiding another further than he himself can go.
	| 1 | 2 | 3 | 4 | 5 | 6 | 7 | 8 | 9 | 10 | 11 | 12 | 13 | 14 |

129B Paragraph Guided Writings for Control [10]

1. Type 128D, page 221, for 1′ to establish your base rate.
2. Set a goal 8 to 10 words lower than your base rate.
3. On five 1′ writings, type no faster than your goal. Try for errorless copies. The quarter or half minutes may be called to guide you.

129C Communication Aid: Quotation Marks [10] *as directed in 122C, page 212; type a heading*

Full sheet; 1½″ top margin; SS with DS between items; 70-space line

Words

3

Rules 5

(1) Use quotation marks to enclose a direct quotation. 16
(2) When a quotation is broken by such expressions as he said, enclose 32
both parts of the quotation with quotation marks. 42
(3) Place periods or commas inside the ending quotation mark. 55
(4) Place semicolons or colons outside the quotation mark. 66

Examples 70

(1) This man wrote, "Happiness is not the end of life; character is." 84
(2) "Great minds," Irving wrote, "have purposes; others have wishes." 98
(3) "What we need," Harry said, "is dirtier hands and cleaner minds." 112
(4) She said, "I listen for facts"; I know she concentrates on ideas. 126

Other Examples 132

129D Production Typing: Interoffice Memorandum; Purchase Requisition [25]

Problem 1: Interoffice Memorandum

Full sheet; 1″ side margins; SS

Words

TO: My Vacation Replacement **FROM:** The 5
Secretary to the Purchasing Agent **DATE:** 12
(*Current*) **FILE:** AOO **SUBJECT:** Business 18
Forms (¶ 1) As I shall not have an opportu- 25
nity to meet and talk with you before you 34
begin working in Mr. Frank's office during 42
my vacation, I think it will be helpful if I 51
explain briefly how business forms are to be 60
typed. (¶ 2) Make full use of the tabulator 68
mechanism to insure proper alignment of fig- 77
ures in the columns and to speed up your 85
work. Space forward for short amounts; back- 93
space for long amounts. (¶ 3) Periods may 101
be omitted after abbreviations, and they may 110

90C Production Typing: Letters with Subject and Attention Lines [25]

When a long company name appears in the closing lines of a letter, as in Problem 2, begin the closing lines 5 or more spaces to the left of the center point.

Problem 1

129 words; open punctuation; modified block; indented ¶s; centered subject line; carbon copy

Words

March 9, 19-- AIRMAIL - SPECIAL DELIVERY 8
Dr. Henry L. Allen Town House Hotel 271 16
Continental Drive Minneapolis, MN 55430 24
Dear Henry SUBJECT: Bold Journey Project 33
(¶ 1) Last week I wrote to General Hunt 40
telling him of our lack of progress in solving 49
the adhesives problem. I asked him for one 58
more month to extend our research. (¶ 2) 65
This morning I received a reply from him in 74
which he bluntly states that we may have no 83
extension of time, and he says that we will be 92
held to our contract as it now stands. (¶ 3) 100
Will you therefore finish the work you are 109
now doing and return at once. You must be 117
here before Monday; for if we stop the Mengl 126
study, you must help us decide what areas we 135
should begin to explore next. (¶ 4) I am 142
sending you a Xerox copy of General Hunt's 151
letter so that you will appreciate fully 159
our position. Sincerely yours M. E. Bor- 167
man Chief Technician Enclosure 174/190

Problem 2

114 words; open punctuation; modified block; attention and subject lines at left margin; carbon copy

Words

March 9, 19-- Brant Aircraft, Inc. 56 Chevoit 9
Drive Chattanooga, TN 37411 Attention De- 17
partment of Research Gentlemen Subject: 26
Bold Journey Project (¶ 1) The Federal 32
Space Administration has proposed that we 40
replace your company on the contract for the 49
Bold Journey Project. They have stressed 58
that time is of the utmost importance. (¶ 2) 66
If we agree to undertake this project, are you 75
willing to let us have as soon as possible all 85
the data you have collected? This action will 94
avoid any duplication of effort. It will also be 104
helpful if you will allow our Director of Re- 113
search, Dr. Conrad Miller, to work with your 122
staff for a few days to become familiar with 131
the problems involved. He would, of course, 140
work at our expense. (¶ 3) We shall appre- 147
ciate a prompt reply. Sincerely yours MIDLAND- 157
CONTINENTAL AIRFLIGHT CO. Guy S. Wear, 165
President 167/179

LESSON 91

91A Preparatory Practice [5] *each line three or more times*

Alphabet	Six books on safe driving, due July 2, will emphasize crash equipment.
Figure-symbol	The note ("27¢ for stamps") was among receipts of $3,680.94 on May 15.
Long words	Punctuation, pronunciation, and enunciation show communication skills.
Fluency	Each of us has 24 hours in his day; what we do with them is important.
	| 1 | 2 | 3 | 4 | 5 | 6 | 7 | 8 | 9 | 10 | 11 | 12 | 13 | 14 |

91B Building Speed [10] *1' writing on each ¶, 88B, page 155; then a 3' writing on all ¶s; compute* gwam

SECTION 21 BUSINESS FORMS

LESSONS 128–134

Drill Copy: Full sheet; 70-space line; SS.
Paragraph Copy: Full sheet; 70-space line; DS; 5-space ¶ indention.
Production Copy: Follow carefully the directions given with each problem; erase and correct errors.

Special Materials: Use printed forms if they are available, or half sheets of paper with the typewritten material arranged as it would be on printed forms. *Do not type headings that would be printed on the forms.*

LESSON 128

128A Preparatory Practice [5] *each line at least three times*

Alphabet	Would John Knox have kept Mary, Queen of Scots, from Elizabeth's grip?
Figure-symbol	How can B/O & H, Inc., meet accounts of $217,463 and $58,900 by May 1?
Long words	If an additional air-conditioning duct is needed, it can be installed.
Fluency	Hard luck is composed of equal portions of laziness and poor judgment.
	| 1 | 2 | 3 | 4 | 5 | 6 | 7 | 8 | 9 | 10 | 11 | 12 | 13 | 14 |

128B Skill-Comparison Typing [10] *type each line of 128A for two 1′ writings; compare* gwam

128C Technique Improvement: Stroking [10] *type each line of 121B, page 210, as directed*

128D Paragraph Guided Writings for Speed [10]

1. Type for 1′ to establish your base rate.
2. Set a goal 8 to 10 words higher than your base rate.
3. Type five 1′ writings. Try to reach your new goal in each minute. Quarter or half minutes may be called to guide you.

1.5 SI
5.6 AWL
80% HFW

Another grand old product is being threatened with obsolescence. This time it is thread. Because of higher labor costs, many of the makers of garments are increasing their use of "fusing" or other adhesive techniques. A leader in the field reports that within a very few years, almost all the garments made will be partially or wholly fused. In a short time, thus, when anyone says he feels as if he is coming unglued, he may really mean it.

| 1 | 2 | 3 | 4 | 5 | 6 | 7 | 8 | 9 | 10 | 11 | 12 | 13 | 14 |

128E Building Control [15]

Use the ¶s of 127B, page 219. Type two 1′ *control-level* writings on each ¶; then a 5′ writing on all three ¶s combined.

REPLY REFERENCE NOTATION

Some writers ask that a reply to a letter mention a file or case number. If the letterhead indicates a printed position for this information (usually at the top of the letterhead), supply it. If not, type the reply reference notation as you would type a subject line (page 159). The word *Reference* or *Re:* may be typed before the notation.

```
Dear Sir

          Reference:  Your File #31-082

    The Federal Space Administration has granted us a
10-day extension on our contract for the Bold Journey
Project.  We now believe we shall be able to satisfy the
contract, and assignment to you will not be necessary.

                                 Very truly yours


                                 M. E. Borman
                                 Chief Technician

xx

cc Mr. Guy S. Wear
```

CARBON COPY NOTATION

Carbon copies of letters are occasionally sent to interested persons. The carbon copy notation informs the addressee to whom copies were sent and is typed a double space below the reference initials line or the last typed line at the left margin.

91C Production Typing: Special Notations (35)

Problem 1: Letter with Mailing and Reply Reference and Enclosure Notations

96 words; mixed punctuation; modified block; reply reference notation at left margin; carbon copy

Words
SPECIAL DELIVERY Mr. Leo J. Richards, Man- 12
ager Gunther Plumbing Company 7412 Ore- 20
gon Trail Youngstown, OH 44512 Dear Mr. 28
Richards Re: File #202-B (¶ 1) Enclosed are 36
three copies of the contract we revised some 45
days ago when we met in the office of Stephen- 54
son and Volk. Please fill in the missing infor- 64
mation required on pages 2 and 3, and return 73
the original and one copy of the contract to 82
us. (¶ 2) As soon as possible, please obtain 90
a bond and send it to us in triplicate. (¶ 3) 98
Enclosed with this letter is an insurance form 107
in triplicate. Please have your insurance car- 117
rier complete these forms and mail them 125
directly to us. Very truly yours JAMES INDUS- 134
TRIES, INC. David E. Cork General Manager 143
Enclosures 6 146/168

Problem 2: Letter with Reply Reference and Carbon Copy Notations

135 words; open punctuation; modified block; indented ¶s; centered reply reference notation; 2 carbon copies

Words
March 11, 19-- Mr. Jerry E. Wagner, Presi- 8
dent Apex Electronics Corporation 8100 La- 16
verne Avenue Oklahoma City, OK 73135 24
Dear Sir Reference: Your File #31-082 (¶ 1) 32
The Federal Space Administration has granted 41
us a 10-day extension on our contract for the 50
Bold Journey Project. We now believe we 58
shall be able to satisfy the contract, and 67
assignment to you will not be necessary. 75
(¶ 2) We received a letter similar to yours 83
from the Northeast National Airflight Com- 91
pany, of Saginaw, Michigan. The Space Ad- 99
ministration had apparently planned to assign 108
our contract for the Bold Journey Project to 117
two companies, yours and Northeast National 126
Airflight. (¶ 3) If we should not be able to 134
meet our new deadline, as we now believe we 143
can, we shall be quite willing to give your 152
company and the Northeast National Airflight 161
Company all the help we can. Very truly 169
yours M. E. Borman Chief Technician cc Mr. 178
Guy S. Wear 180/201

Problem 3: Composing a Letter

Write a letter for Mr. Richard's signature (Problem 1). Use file reference notation and punctuation style you desire. Indicate that original and one copy of contract are enclosed with information inserted as requested. Indicate, also, that bond will be obtained shortly and that insurance forms have already been sent to carrier.

Address letter to Mr. David E. Cork General Manager James Industries, Inc. 81912 Valentine Drive Dayton, OH 45431

Problem 1: Modified Block Letter

101 words; open punctuation

Words

mr marvin s hardwick 310 national avenue 12
montgomery al 36105 dear marvin (¶1) 18
The following list shows the shipments of 27
Chemtox made to Kingway & Company last 35
year. All invoices were paid by them within 44
the 30-day discount period. 49

Order No.	Date	Amount	
LA-517032-M	April 7	$3,605.22	64
LA-517099-M	April 9	814.79	70
LA-517322-M	June 6	40.00	75
LA-517846-M	August 1	175.23	82 / 84
Total		$4,635.24	88

Order No. / Date / Amount — 58

(¶2) I suggest you call on Mr. Chambers, 95
the Kingway & Company purchasing officer. 104
Find out, if you can, why we have not had an 112
order from them since last August. sincerely 122
harold brookings sales manager 128/140

Problem 2: Interoffice Memorandum

Full sheet; SS; current date

Words

TO: Clark Yardley FROM: Norbert L. Peoples 5
DATE: *Current* SUBJECT: Commissions 10
Earned by Salesmen (¶1) As you know, the 18
Company pays a 5 percent commission on all 26
sales exceeding the quota set for each sales- 35
man. Commissions earned during the last 43
month are as follows: 48

Salesmen	Commissions	
Brooks, Harvey	$250	62
Casady, F. A.	425	65
Diamond, George	130	69
Flowers, Hunter	325	73
Moody, Charles A.	250	78
Willis, Bernard	325	82

Salesmen / Commissions — 57

(¶2) The commissions are paid on net sales. 90
The amounts included do not include amounts 98
added for sales taxes, and discounts are 107
deducted. 109

Problem 3: Page 4 of Manuscript

Leftbound report; paragraphs DS; table SS

Words

(¶1) The Borough of Alden has the most 7
highly developed business district in its trad- 16
ing area. The following tabulation shows the 25
type and number of services it offers: 33

TYPE AND NUMBER OF SERVICES IN ALDEN AREA		
Food stores	11	45
Eating places	14	48
General merchandise	2	53
Apparel	12	55
Furniture, appliances	8	60
Gasoline stations	12	64
Lumber, building, hardware stores	6	71
Drugstores	4	74
Other retail stores	12	79
Personal services	23	83
Auto repair shops	8	87
Merchant wholesalers	6	92
Other wholesalers	1	97
Photography studios	2	100
Paint stores	3	104

TYPE AND NUMBER OF SERVICES — 39
IN ALDEN AREA — 42

(¶2) Included in the above establishments 111
are several large wholesale, retail, and service 121
chains that have located in and around Alden. 131
A new One-Trip Market is located in a plaza 139
that has recently been built about two miles 148
east of town. 151

(¶3) There are other businesses in the Alden 159
area which, although they employ fewer peo- 168
ple, are important because of their diversity. 177
There are (1) the Federal Bakery, (2) David- 186
son Wood Products, (3) the Alden Gazette, 194
(4) the Alden Concrete Company, (5) Selec- 203
tron Metal Products Company, (6) Mills 210
Technical Institute, (7) Leads Manufacturing 219
Company, and (8) Preston Builders, Inc. 227
These companies are now working at 75 per- 236
cent of capacity. 239

LESSON 92

92A Preparatory Practice [5] *each line at least three times*

Alphabet	Ezra quickly fixed the broken vase with just mucilage and brown paper.
Figure-symbol	Ken's stock, bought at 135½, sold for 248¼ in the 1966–67 bull market.
Adjacent keys	There were three points on Kili's eastern slope free of rough weather.
Fluency	All of us need a lot of pushing and guiding if we are to do good work.

| 1 | 2 | 3 | 4 | 5 | 6 | 7 | 8 | 9 | 10 | 11 | 12 | 13 | 14 |

92B Communication Aid: Comma [20]

Full sheet; 1½" top margin; 70-space line; SS with DS between items

1. For the heading, type COMMA.
2. Type the rules and examples given below (with numbers); underline the side headings.
3. Compose and type six sentences, each sentence illustrating one rule. Number these sentences to correspond with the rules.

Words

Rules 3

DS

(1) Use commas to set off a nonrestrictive clause. 14

(2) Use a comma to separate coordinate clauses joined by one of the 27
pure conjunctions (and, but, for, or, neither, nor). 38

(3) Use a comma to point off an introductory phrase containing a verb. 52

(4) Use commas to set off parenthetic words, phrases, and clauses that 66
may be omitted without harming the structure of the sentence. 79

(5) Use commas to set off words of direct address. 89

(6) Use a comma to separate city and state names. 99

TS

Examples 103

DS

(1) This trip, which is recommended in all guide books, costs little. 117

(2) A position is open, but I cannot interview anyone to fill it yet. 131

(3) To qualify for a job, he must know how to write forceful letters. 145

(4) This is one job, for example, on which she can use expert advice. 159

(5) Thank you, Mr. Cole, for sending the portraits to me so promptly. 173

(6) Our annual meeting will be held in Cleveland, Ohio, on August 21. 187

TS

Other Examples *(Compose six sentences, each sentence illustrating one rule.)* 192

DS

Production Typing Information

POSTSCRIPT

Type the postscript a double space below the reference initials line or the last typed line. The postscript need not be preceded by the letters "P.S."; it is indented or blocked to agree with the style used in other paragraphs of the letter.

```
                                  H. R. Wilkins, President

xx

Enclosure

So that your employees will be taking no chances, we shall
accept the return of any boats not satisfactory and make
a full refund.  We guarantee your complete satisfaction.
```

LESSON 127

127A Preparatory Practice [5] *each line three or more times*

Alphabet	Six big jet planes flew over the Azores and quickly landed in Morocco.
Figures	She traveled about 726,894 miles, logging 1,530¼ hours of flying time.
Drill on vowels	Every trainee receives a special certificate at graduation ceremonies.
Fluency	Discuss business in the office; outside it, talk about something else.
	| 1 | 2 | 3 | 4 | 5 | 6 | 7 | 8 | 9 | 10 | 11 | 12 | 13 | 14 |

127B Growth Index [15] *type one 5′* control level *writing on each ¶*

All letters are included.

		GWAM 1′	5′	
¶ 1 1.5 SI	Literally, dozens of studies have been made of the reasons that	13	3	58
5.6 AWL	office workers fail in their jobs. With but very few exceptions, the	27	5	61
80% HFW	reports we have show that failure is due to a lack of personal qualities	41	8	64
	needed for a job. Weak office skills are an infrequent cause of dis-	55	11	66
	missal. The case is very clear. Loyalty, good work habits, and the	69	14	69
	ability to work well with others are essential for success in an office	83	16	72
	job.	84	17	73
¶ 2 1.5 SI	Efficiency in the basic office skills is fundamental. Let there	13	19	75
5.6 AWL	be no doubt on this point. A person, for example, who is unable to	27	22	78
80% HFW	type, spell, proofread, or solve simple arithmetic problems would	40	25	80
	likely not get a typing job in the first place. The idea that is being	54	28	83
	presented here, however, is that the ability to type is not enough. A	68	31	86
	typist is expected to bring to the job a number of impeccable personal	83	33	89
	qualities that permit him to use his skill in typing to best advantage.	97	36	92
¶ 3 1.5 SI	Courtesy is a superb example of a quality that is essential in	13	39	94
5.6 AWL	office work. It determines just how well we can get along with the	26	41	97
80% HFW	people with whom we work. Reflect on your own experiences for a	39	44	100
	moment. Is it not true that the people to whom you have been sincerely	54	47	103
	courteous have been courteous to you? Is it not true, too, that your suc-	69	50	106
	cess is measured by what others think of you? Courtesy has many satisfy-	83	53	108
	ing rewards. Everyone agrees that it is indispensable in office work.	97	56	111
1′ GWAM	| 1 | 2 | 3 | 4 | 5 | 6 | 7 | 8 | 9 | 10 | 11 | 12 | 13 | 14 |			
5′ GWAM	| 1 | 2 | 3 |			

127C Production Measurement [30] *errors corrected; figure* n-pram

Type as many of the problems as you can in 20 minutes. Correct all errors. Do not make carbon copies.

Problem 1

128 words; mixed punctuation; modified block; centered attention line; capitalize and punctuate as you type

	Words
burton & nelson industries inc 319 jefferson	12
drive durham nc 27705 attention purchas-	21
ing agent gentlemen (¶ 1) Here is your	28
opportunity to make it possible for your em-	37
ployees to buy for their children at wholesale	46
price a toy sailboat of rare design. Place the	56
enclosed folder on your bulletin board or show	65
it to your employees, accumulate the individ-	72
ual orders, and send them to us. (¶ 2) We	81
shall bill the boats at $36 per dozen, 2%	90
10 days, f.o.b. Lansing, Michigan. The price	99
of each boat is thus $3, which is just half of	108
what they would cost in retail stores. More	117
than a hundred thousand of these boats have	126
been sold in retail stores at prices ranging	135
from $6 to $8.75. (¶ 3) We look forward to	143
receiving your order soon. We can fill it im-	152
mediately. very truly yours maddox specialty	161
company h r wilkins, president enclosure	171
(*Postscript*) So that your employees will be	177
taking no chances, we shall accept the return	186
of any boats not satisfactory and make a	194
full refund. We guarantee your complete	202
satisfaction.	205/219

Problem 2

116 words; open punctuation; modified block; attention and reply reference notations at left margin

	Words
springfield seed & bulb company 8271 dart-	11
mouth road springfield ma 01106 attention	20
mr will jackson gentlemen re order no. 281	29
(¶1) Please cancel Order No. 281. We shall	37
replace it with another order, which you will	46
receive from us in a day or two. (¶ 2) Our	54
first order is out of line with the current de-	63

	Words
mand for seeds and bulbs. Our sales have	72
been far below our expectations, and we do	80
not want to overstock. (¶ 3) Our supply of	88
your brochure PLANTING HINTS TO GROWERS	97
is very nearly exhausted. Our customers tell	105
us that it is very helpful. They like the	114
clear, practical explanations and vivid il-	122
lustrations. Will you please send us another	132
box of 500 copies. I can assure that we	140
shall put them to good use. very truly yours	150
garden supplies inc robert thompson, manager	159/174

Problem 3

82 words; open punctuation; modified block; attention and reply reference notations at left margin

	Words
airmail berkshire contracting company 931	11
clayton avenue evansville in 47715 attention	21
mr d b anderson gentlemen reference file no	30
3155 (¶ 1) Two copies of a contract with the	38
Evansville Mortgage Company, 17511 Elm-	46
hurst Drive, Evansville, are enclosed for the	55
installation of plumbing equipment. Please	64
sign the owner's copy of the contract and	72
return it to us as soon as possible. (¶ 2) The	81
specifications for the installation are attached	90
to the contractor's copy of the contract. We	100
can send you an additional set of the specifica-	109
tions if you need them. very truly yours	118
moore engineering company fred morris,	125
architect enclosures 2	130/144

Problem 4: Composing a Letter

Write a letter for Mr. Anderson's signature (Problem 3). Use file reference notation and punctuation style you desire. Indicate that the signed copy of the contract is enclosed. Ask Mr. Morris to send an additional set of specifications.

Address letter to: Mr. Fred Morris Architect Moore Engineering Company 3147 Colonial Avenue Evansville, IN 47710

LESSON 126

126A Preparatory Practice [5] *each line three or more times*

Alphabet	Don forgot to cover Kay's jonquil; he expected below-zero temperature.
Figure-symbol	About 17 2/3 percent of the 16,450 men have read George Orwell's 1984.
Adjacent keys	Fred tried to decide just how much of the old junk might be destroyed.
Fluency	Do not use a long word when there is a short one you know you can use.

| 1 | 2 | 3 | 4 | 5 | 6 | 7 | 8 | 9 | 10 | 11 | 12 | 13 | 14 |

126B Communication Aid: Numbers [10] *as directed in 122C, page 212*

Full sheet; 1½" top margin; SS with DS between items; 70-space line

Words

NUMBERS 2

Rules 4

(1) Numbers preceded by nouns are usually expressed in figures. 17
(2) Express measures, weights, and dimensions in figures. 28
(3) In business letters, the percent sign (%) is preferred when it is 42
preceded by definite figures. With approximations and in most 55
formal writings, percent is preferred. 63
(4) Spell names of small-numbered avenues and streets (ten and under). 77
Type house numbers in figures, except for house number One. 90

Examples 93

(1) We found the exact quotation in Volume VIII, Section 4, page 191. 107
(2) The box Ralph sent measured 7 ft. 6 in. and weighed 45 lbs. 3 oz. 121
(3) About 85 percent of all loans will bring a return of 6% interest. 135
(4) They have moved from One 125th Street to 1830 North First Street. 149

Other Examples 155

126C Tabulation Skill Builder [5]

Type two 2′ writings on the following short table. Allow 10 spaces between the columns. You need not center the table vertically. Type the two writings on one page. Compute *gwam* by dividing words by 2.

Words

LIFETIME ANNUAL MEAN INCOME--1963 7

Males 25-64 Years Old 11

		Words
Elementary school dropout	$ 3,641	18
Elementary school graduate	4,921	25
High school dropout	5,592	30
High school graduate	6,693	36
College dropout	7,839	40
College graduate	10,062	45

126D Production Skill Building [30] *errors corrected; figure* n-pram

Make pencil notations of the problems at the right to be typed for a 20′ writing. Figure your *n-pram.*

Page 214, 123D, Problem 1
Page 216, 124D, Problem 1
Page 217, 125C, Production Typing

LESSON 93

93A Preparatory Practice [5] *each line at least three times*

Alphabet	All of his money exhausted, lazy Jacques is now verging on bankruptcy.
Figure-symbol	The fractions 1/9, 5/45, and 7/63 are proper fractions. What is 80/2?
Quiet hands	The very first jet plane flight was made in 1942 in an XP-59 Aircomet.
Fluency	A smile will cut your load in half; a frown only heaps up your burden.
	| 1 | 2 | 3 | 4 | 5 | 6 | 7 | 8 | 9 | 10 | 11 | 12 | 13 | 14 |

93B Manipulative Drill: Tabulation [10]

2 half sheets; DS; 10 spaces between columns; type in exact center

1. Review the steps for horizontal placement of columns given at the right.
2. Tabulate the words; study spellings as you type.
3. Close your book; type the words from dictation.

Columns

			Words
advice	beacon	chagrin	4
commitments	judgment	losing	10
missile	misspelling	muscles	16
permitting	personal	personnel	22
privileges	promptly	recognize	28
recommend	separate	similar	33
subtle	traveled	vertical	38

Intercolumns

HORIZONTAL PLACEMENT OF COLUMNS

1. Move margin stops to ends of scale; clear tabulator rack.
2. From center of page backspace 1 space for each 2 letters and spaces in longest line of each column and for each 2 spaces left between columns. Set *left margin stop* at this point.

   Note. Carry forward to the intercolumn the extra space that may occur at the end of the longest line of a column; to the next column the extra space that may occur in an intercolumn. If an extra space occurs at the end of the longest line of the final column, drop it.
3. From left margin stop, space forward *once* for each letter and space in longest line of first column and for each space to be left between first and second columns. Set a *tab stop* at this point for the second column. Follow a similar procedure for additional columns.

93C Skill-Comparison and Transfer Typing [5] *one 1′ writing on each sentence; compare* gwam

		Words
Goal	She knows that every time she speaks, her mind is on parade.	12
Figures	Our plant can produce 5,973 gallons of paint every 24 hours.	12
Rough draft	We ~~were~~ are ple~~s~~ased to wel come you~~r~~ to ou~~t~~r fam~~li~~ily of stock # owners.	12
Script	Please write or call if we can be of any further assistance.	12

93D Production Skill Building: Business Letters with Special Features [30] *20′ timing; errors corrected; figure* n-pram

Make a pencil notation of the problems listed at the right. Type each letter with a carbon copy, and address an envelope for each letter. Arrange your material conveniently; work continuously.

Page 158, 89C, Problem 2
Page 160, 90C, Problem 2
Page 161, 91C, Problem 2
Page 163, 92C, Problem 3

LESSON 94

94A Preparatory Practice (5) *each line three or more times*

Alphabet   The vicious mix-up was quickly organized by those foreign journalists.

Figure-symbol   By waiting until May 30, he paid 5½% instead of 2¼%, losing $1,479.86.

Double letters   The embarrassed bookkeeper will be accessible and can accommodate you.

Fluency   We may have a second chance, but it is never so good as the first one.

| 1 | 2 | 3 | 4 | 5 | 6 | 7 | 8 | 9 | 10 | 11 | 12 | 13 | 14 |

94B Growth Index (15) *two 5' control level writings; figure gwam on better writing*

All letters are used.

	GWAM 1'	5'

¶1
1.5 SI
5.6 AWL
80% HFW

All letters convey two messages. One is expressed in words; the other, by the impression it makes on the reader. The second is the hidden quality you put into an envelope each time you mail a letter. The written message is important; let there be no doubt on this point. A letter must say what it should, and it should say it clearly and suc- cinctly. Nobody likes to receive fuzzy letters in which ideas defy interpretation. A clear letter is usually a welcome caller.

13 | 3 | 60
27 | 6 | 62
41 | 8 | 65
55 | 11 | 68
69 | 14 | 71
83 | 17 | 74
95 | 19 | 76

¶2
1.5 SI
5.6 AWL
80% HFW

Almost everyone disapproves of men or women who overdress or who do not dress appropriately for their calling. As a writer remarked, "I hate to see men overdressed; a man ought to look like he is put to- gether by accident, not added up on purpose." How you dress is very important; so are the letters you send out to represent you. They should reflect a company at its very best. Letters gain admittance more easily than callers, but this privilege should not be abused.

13 | 22 | 79
27 | 24 | 81
41 | 27 | 84
55 | 30 | 87
68 | 33 | 90
82 | 35 | 92
95 | 38 | 95

¶3
1.5 SI
5.6 AWL
80% HFW

In an office setting, you must be observant of the many hidden qualities that are part of any good letter. A firm will often be judged on the typing and on the care you take in spelling, punctuating, and proofreading your work. Somehow, a letter that is faulty in these basic points does not impress a reader with the purpose of its message. The letters you type must express the dignity and sincerity with which a company conducts business affairs.

13 | 41 | 98
26 | 43 | 100
40 | 46 | 103
54 | 49 | 106
69 | 52 | 109
83 | 55 | 112
94 | 57 | 114

1' GWAM | 1 | 2 | 3 | 4 | 5 | 6 | 7 | 8 | 9 | 10 | 11 | 12 | 13 | 14 |
5' GWAM | 1 | 2 | 3 |

94C Production Measurement: Business Letters with Special Features (30) *20' timing; errors cor- rected; compute n-pram*

Type the four letters on page 166. Make a carbon copy of each letter. Address an envelope of appropriate size for each letter.

124D Production Typing: Correspondence with Tabulated Reports [30]

Problem 1: Interoffice Memorandum

Full sheet; 1" side margins; DS; indent ¶s; SS quotation in ¶ 2; SS tabulated report

Words

TO: Henry Wagner, Director of Research 7
FROM: John D. Neff, Production Manager 14
DATE: *(Current)* 17
SUBJECT: Retesting Copper Alloy #17 22

(¶ 1) According to Dr. Maetinson's report, 29
the failure of our tests on CS17 was due to 38
a mistake in formula application. Dr. Maetin- 47
son says that the correct formula for use in 56
our basic procedure (Step 6) should have been 65
the Benzloff formula: $M^2/M + 14_s = P_s$. 74
The thermal exposure should have been 1900° 82
F. instead of 1750° F. Dr. Maetinson 90
explains: 92

(¶ 2) An attempt to apply the Craig- 98
Towne formula [the one we used] in tests 107
such as this is understandable; but the differ- 116
ence between the formulas [the Benzloff and 125
the Craig–Towne], although small, was criti- 133
cal in the CS17 tests. (¶ 3) The complete 141
Maetinson report is in my office, and copies 150
of it will be sent to you as soon as they can 159
be made. (¶ 4) Will you please review all 166
computations for CS17 promptly and have 174
materials and staff ready for new tests at 9:30 184
on the following mornings next week. 191

TS

CS17 REVISED TEST SCHEDULE 197

TS

Test	Day	Director	Words
		DS	203
Stress	Monday	Dr. Carlson	209
Thermal	Tuesday	Dr. Koontz	214
Flexibility	Wednesday	Mr. Kunselman	221
Tension	Thursday	Mr. Joseph	227
Corrosion	Friday	Mr. Recupero	233

Problem 2: Letter with Tabulated Report

Decide on letter and punctuation style; estimate length of letter.

Words

mr theodore m byers 331 fernwood avenue 11
trenton nj 08610 dear mr byers reference 21
escrow #768 (¶ 1) The Lexington Guarantee 28
Building & Loan Association has deposited 36
with us in escrow Deed of Reconveyance and 45
Stanford Fire Insurance Policy No. 44380, 53
subject to the payment of the following: 62

		Words
Principal balance	$2,663.49	67
Interest	4.14	71
Trustee's fee on reconveyance	3.00	77
		81
Total	$2,670.63	85

(¶ 2) Additional interest is to be paid at the 94
rate of 52 cents per diem from July 1, 19––, 103
to date of receipt of a final settlement. yours 112
very truly frank d hill real estate department 123/135

LESSON 125

125A Preparatory Practice [5] *each line three or more times*

Alphabet Jack now realizes that his brusque expletives often frightened my dog.

Figure-symbol L/P, Inc., 7521½ Hone Road, grossed 2¼% more ($2,348.60) than in 1968.

Double letters Miss Capp occasionally allows Babbette a banana for dessert at dinner.

Fluency If a thing is right, stand up for it; if it is wrong, try changing it.

| 1 | 2 | 3 | 4 | 5 | 6 | 7 | 8 | 9 | 10 | 11 | 12 | 13 | 14 |

125B Building Speed [15] *type two 1' writings on each ¶ of 121D, page 211; compute* gwam *on the better writing of each pair*

Problem 1

134 words; open punctuation; modified block; centered subject line

	Words
Dr. William E. Kerr 52 Tally Ho Lane Alexandria, VA 22307 Dear Dr. Kerr SUBJECT: Challenge to Trophy Fishermen (¶ 1) Early last month, I had the opportunity of presenting our story on Arctic fishing at Great Pine Lodge, Great Bear Lake, Northwest Territories, to your Lions Club. I hope that I properly conveyed the story of what it's like to fish in the fourth largest freshwater lake in all of North America. (¶ 2) Dr. Kerr, I am enclosing a copy of our new 20-page color brochure. Possibly this folder can provide additional information to you and your friends when discussing Arctic fishing in the Northwest Territory. (¶ 3) If there is any additional information you desire, please call or write. Thank you again for allowing me to tell you about fishing on Great Bear Lake. Sincerely yours GREAT PINE LODGE Jim Castle General Manager Enclosure	11 20 27 36 45 54 62 71 81 89 97 106 115 124 132 141 150 158 167 173/185

Problem 2

119 words; mixed punctuation; modified block; attention line and reply reference notation at left margin

	Words
Property Management Company 7294 El Miradero Avenue Glendale, CA 91201 Attention Mr. Leonard Carpenter Gentlemen Re: File #842-N (¶1) Yesterday we examined the Formica tops on the backbars in the Royal Hotel Drugstore and found that four pieces, amounting to 19 linear feet, should be replaced. (¶ 2) We suggest that the Formica be eliminated underneath the coffee urns and that two urn pans be used between the Formica sections instead. This new arrangement will eliminate any future trouble with the Formica top. (¶ 3) We offer to build, deliver, and install the Formica tops and the two Monel Metal urn pans for the sum of $170. We can do this work almost immediately. Please let us know soon if you want us to make these repairs. Very truly yours Harley Davidson Chief Engineer cc Mr. Richard Perry	10 19 28 34 44 52 61 68 77 86 95 103 112 120 128 136 145 154 163/184

Problem 3

119 words; open punctuation; modified block with indented ¶s; centered subject line; capitalize and punctuate

	Words
airmail mr michael wunsch, office manager langston–forbes chemical company 15 roosevelt avenue, e.	tacoma wa 98404 dear mr wunsch subject membership roster (¶ 1) As in 1968, the firm of Epson–Alexandre has been authorized to photograph our members for the new membership roster for 1969–1970. (¶ 2) A representative of Epson–Alexandre will contact you to arrange a mutually convenient appointment to take your photograph for this purpose. (¶ 3) Your consent to be photographed will not obligate you in any way. You may obtain personal portraits from the several proofs which will be shown you, but only if you so desire. (¶ 4) The value of our roster depends on the amount of membership participation in this project. Our goal is to obtain a photograph of every member. sincerely yours arthur mcintosh director	12 20 29 36 45 54 62 69 78 87 94 103 112 120 129 137 147 155 164/186

Problem 4

95 words; mixed punctuation; modified block; capitalize and punctuate; writer's initials: JDD

	Words
mr and mrs dwayne schramm 39 mound view court topeka ks 66614 dear mr and mrs schramm (¶ 1) Are you interested in knowing the present market value of your lovely home? (¶ 2) We have never before experienced a greater demand for fine homes in your prestige area; and, needless to say, obtainable prices are startling. (¶ 3) If you will be kind enough to return the enclosed card, we shall be glad to make an appointment at your convenience. Please be assured that our professional opinion will be given entirely in confidence and without obligation. sincerely yours greater topeka investment company vice-president enclosure	11 20 27 36 43 52 62 70 79 88 97 106 119 127 132/145

Problem 2: Modified Block Letter with Two Tables

138 words; mixed punctuation; decide on spaces between columns

Words

mcarthur furniture store 23141 rock island 12
road ft. lauderdale fl 33311 Gentlemen (¶ 1) 20
In accordance with your order No. 990, we are 29
shipping to you today the following rugs: 38

12	9′ x 12′ Wiltons	42
7	9′ x 12′ Broadlooms	46
1	6′ x 14′ Axminster	51
10	8′ x 14′ Wiltons	55

(¶ 2) Each rug is separately wrapped; and, 62
following your special instructions, the Broad- 71
loom rugs bear the following tag: 78

		Words
Weight	86#	81
Size	9′ x 12′	83
Fringe	4″	85
Type	Broadloom	88
Color	(Gray, blue, or coral)	94

(¶ 3) We hope these rugs will be entirely 101
satisfactory. Our company has been weaving 110
fine carpets for over 75 years, and to our 119
knowledge we have not lost a customer be- 126
cause of unsatisfactory workmanship or poor 135
service. (¶ 4) Accept our sincere thanks for 143
this first order. We promise you the best of 152
service in the years ahead. Very truly yours 162
sanders rug company wendell e baines 169
president 172/187

LESSON 124

124A Preparatory Practice [5] *each line three or more times*

Alphabet Examine Herb's work; judge for quality; recognize needed improvements.

Figure-symbol Type: "Buy 2,850 pins @ 43½¢ each for the 1969 and 1970 conventions."

One Hand We referred only a minimum number of monopoly cases to my legal staff.

Fluency Do not hesitate to say, "I don't know"; it can save many explanations.

| 1 | 2 | 3 | 4 | 5 | 6 | 7 | 8 | 9 | 10 | 11 | 12 | 13 | 14 |

124B Communication Aid: Symbols [10]

Full sheet; DS; 14 spaces between columns; center in reading position

OTHER MEANINGS FOR PRESENT CHARACTERS

Caret (insert)	Diagonal	for/pictures
Times	x (lower case)	62 x 18
Minus	Hyphen	25 - 15
Signed	Diagonals, s	/s/ J. R. Stout
Pounds	Number sign	100# of coal
Feet	Apostrophe	9' x 12'
Minute	Apostrophe	5' writing
Inch or inches	Quotation mark	8½" x 11"
Second	Quotation mark	3" warning
Ditto	Quotation mark	John Bellen, Erie
		E. S. Brior, "

124C Technique Improvement: Stroking [5] *type a 1′ writing on each of the first four lines of 121B, page 210*

SECTION 16 SPECIAL COMMUNICATION FORMS

LESSONS 95–102

Unless otherwise directed, proceed as follows:
Drill Copy: Full sheet; 70-space line; SS.
Paragraph Copy: Full sheet; 70-space line; DS; 5-space ¶ indention.

Production Typing: Follow specific directions given with each problem; correct errors.
Materials Needed: Letterheads (or full sheets); carbon sheets; file copy sheets; Desk-Fax and interoffice communication forms; envelopes of appropriate size.

LESSON 95

95A Preparatory Practice [5] *each line three or more times*

Alphabet	Mazie was probably enjoying her quiet visit to Cape Cod for six weeks.
Figure-symbol	Exactly 25.167% of the solids (384 pounds) must be added at 10:29 a.m.
Home row	Daylight was fading; Hal adjusted the waning little spark of gaslight.
Fluency	Although the turtle took just one step at a time, he gained the prize.

| 1 | 2 | 3 | 4 | 5 | 6 | 7 | 8 | 9 | 10 | 11 | 12 | 13 | 14 |

95B Building Speed and Control [20]

1. Type a 1′ writing on each paragraph on the *exploration level.*
2. Type a 1′ writing on each paragraph on the *control level.*
3. Type two 5′ writings on all paragraphs on the *control level.* Figure *gwam.*

All letters are used.

		GWAM 1′	5′	
¶ 1 1.5 SI 5.6 AWL 80% HFW	There are only a half dozen operating parts of a typewriter that	13	3	59
	are used frequently. You can add several words to your rate by using	27	5	62
	expertly any one of the six. Getting high typing rates is more often	41	8	64
	a case of eliminating useless motions than working more rapidly. Just	55	11	67
	analyze what you do when you use the shift and tabular keys, the space	69	14	70
	bar, the carriage return, the margin release, or backspace key. Note	83	17	73
	the movements you make. Cut out any that are not necessary.	95	19	75
¶ 2 1.5 SI 5.6 AWL 80% HFW	Manipulating the shift is part of typing. You should employ the	13	22	78
	correct method in shifting for a capital. If you are using a standard	27	24	81
	machine, hold your left elbow in regular position, stretch the little	41	27	83
	finger to the shift key, depress and hold down until the capital has been	56	30	86
	struck and released. If you do an inadequate job or have a capital sus-	70	33	89
	pended in midair or only partly visible, there is a better way to type.	85	36	92
	Practice until you improve.	90	37	93
¶ 3 1.5 SI 5.6 AWL 80% HFW	Do you begin without a pause after a carriage return is made on	13	40	96
	a manual typewriter? If not, practice to improve. When you return	26	42	99
	the carriage, use a short throw with the elbow held close to the body.	41	45	101
	When a return is completed, drop the hand to normal position, and	54	48	104
	begin typing on the next line without pausing. The entire operation	68	51	107
	takes only split seconds; and it will, if you practice the techniques	82	53	110
	correctly.	96	56	112

1′ GWAM | 1 | 2 | 3 | 4 | 5 | 6 | 7 | 8 | 9 | 10 | 11 | 12 | 13 | 14 |
5′ GWAM | 1 | 2 | 3 |

123B Skill-Comparison Typing (5) *type a 1' writing on each line of 123A, page 213; compare rates*

123C Communication Aid: Symbols (10)

Full sheet; DS; 8 spaces between columns; center in reading position

CONSTRUCTING SPECIAL SYMBOLS   ← triple-space

Plus	Diagonal; backspace; hyphen	$\neq$
Divided by	Hyphen; backspace; colon	$\div$
Left bracket	Diagonal; backspace; underline; roll cylinder back one line; underline	[
Right bracket	Underline; diagonal; backspace; roll cylinder back one line; underline	]
Exponent	Ratchet release, number	25^4
Degrees	Ratchet release, o (lower case)	75°
Superior	Ratchet release, figure or letter	be seen.[1]
Inferior	Ratchet release, figure or letter	H_2O
Equals	Ratchet release, hyphens	=

123D Production Typing: Letters with Tabulated Reports (30)

Problem 1: Modified Block Letter

214 words; open punctuation; decide on spaces between columns

	Words
March 12, 19-- Mr. George Stanton 104	8
Logan Crescent West	Yorkton, Saskatche-	15
wan	CANADA Dear Mr. Stanton (¶ 1) You	22
will be glad to know that Bond–Handley's re-	30
turn on net shipments for the year just past	39
was about 11 percent. This figure compares	48
very favorably with about 10 percent for the	57
previous year. Included in net earnings of the	66
year is a nonrecurring net gain of $821,200	75
from forward sales of pound sterling to pro-	83
tect our interest in Bond–Lanham, Limited.	92
(¶ 2) In November, the Board of Directors	99
declared a 3-for-2 stock split and increased	108
the regular quarterly dividend from an ad-	116
justed 26 cents to 30 cents per share after the	126
split. The financial highlights of the year are	136
as follows:	138

DS

		Words
Net shipments	$108,449,883.00	145
Net earnings	11,449,948.00	150
Earnings per share	2.01	157
Dividends per share	1.20	164
Book value per share	13.38	171
Working capital	58,290,766.00	177
Shareholders' investment	76,373,015.00	184

DS

	Words
(¶ 3) The Company continues to make a major	192
commitment to its expanded product develop-	200
ment program, which accounts for an increas-	209
ingly large percentage of new business and	218
backlog. The rate of incoming orders in the	227
past several months indicates that improved	235
shipments and earnings may be expected dur-	244
ing the coming year. (¶ 4) On behalf of the	252
directors, I extend thanks to all the share-	260
holders for their support. Sincerely yours	269
Benjamin V. Hornsberger Chairman and	276
President	279/293

Handwritten notes: "8 spaces", "tabs 35, 79", "8 spaces", "ds", "line 21", "14-88", "13 8 36 8 9", "margin 27 tab: 61", "24 10 15 DS", "line 12 20-85 or ?", "when letter includes table – shorten margins?"

95C Skill-Comparison and Transfer Typing [5]

Type each sentence as a 1′ writing with the 15″ call of the line ending. Try to reach the rates set on the goal sentence when you type succeeding sentences.

		GWAM 15″ Guide	Words in Line
Goal sentence	The talent of success is nothing more than doing what you can do well.	56	14
Hyphens	The well-known speaker talked about up-to-date methods in office work.	56	14
Double letters	Ann can now notify all her classes that the 22 books will arrive soon.	56	14
Figures	We can now ship 147 of the 593 wall fixtures you ordered on August 27.	56	14

95D Technique Improvement: Response Patterns [10] *each line three times on the response level indicated*

1	Stroke	Several residents mailed Form X, thereby establishing legal residence.
2	Stroke	These discrepancies were immediately corrected by improved scheduling.
3	Stroke	Mae inquired at local stationery stores for stationary light fixtures.
4	Word	She will take an ad in your paper if you will add one more line to it.
5	Word	No problem is so big that it lacks an answer. Learn to think clearly.
6	Word	This is the kind of work I like to do and the work I can do very well.
7	Combination	I know their themes were not submitted; there are no more papers here.
8	Combination	Some people will try anything once; others will try it once too often.
9	Combination	To make your work look neat, keep the right margin as even as you can.

| 1 | 2 | 3 | 4 | 5 | 6 | 7 | 8 | 9 | 10 | 11 | 12 | 13 | 14 |

95E Manipulative Drill: Tabulation [10]

2 half sheets; DS; 8 spaces between columns; type in exact center

1. If necessary, review the steps for horizontal placement of columns, 93B, p. 164.
2. Tabulate the words; study spellings as you type.
3. Close your book; type the words from dictation.

			Words
access	adjourn	analyzed	5
allotment	commitments	convey	11
dictionary	dilemma	disappointed	17
exceptions	exhibited	extension	23
familiarize	grateful	receive	29
referred	schedule	stymied	34
vehicles	vicious	visibility	40

LESSON 96

96A Preparatory Practice [5] *each line three or more times*

Alphabet	The jarring impact of the earthquake paralyzed six old Bavarian towns.
Figure-symbol	Change Ray's total (19½) to 20; add it to Ann's totals (357 and 684½).
Second row	Ask Gladys if she has a half tank of gas; she has less than she knows.
Fluency	He would rather do one thing really well than do many things half way.

| 1 | 2 | 3 | 4 | 5 | 6 | 7 | 8 | 9 | 10 | 11 | 12 | 13 | 14 |

122D Production Skill Building: Letters with Tables [25]

Problem 1: Modified Block Letter

139 words; open punctuation

Type the letter for two 5′ writings. No carbon copies; no erasures. Compute *gwam.*

	Words Prob. 1	Words Prob. 3
March 20, 19–– Mr. Thomas B. Washington 2200 Franklin Road Newport	13	13
News, VA 23601 Dear Mr. Washington	21	21
(¶ 1) Of the 68 wells drilled last year in which we had full or part interest,	35	35
18 were exploratory. We found 4 oil and gas-distillate pools, 1 gas	49	49
field, and 3 additional oil and gas zones under established producing	63	63
fields. (¶ 2) The attached table shows you the number of acres in which	76	76
we have an interest in various oil fields or regions.	88	88
		130
(¶ 3) In addition to our interest in the foregoing regions, we hold leases,	102	144
options, or operating rights on 15,000 acres in Alaska. On the Kenai	116	158
Peninsula, where Alaska's first major oil discovery was made, we hold	130	172
5,000 acres, some within six miles of the discovery well. (¶ 4) Inquiries	143	185
and comments about our activities are always welcome from our stock-	157	199
holders.	159	201
Very truly yours AMERICAN PETROLEUM COMPANY Donald A. Barret	172	214
Executive Vice-President	177/193	219/235

Problem 2: Table

SS; 6 spaces between columns; type timed writings on one sheet

Type the table at the left below for two 1′ writings. No erasures. Compute *gwam.*

		Words
Ship Shoal	10,100	4
Southeast Timbalier	1,200	9
Bay Marchand	2,500	13
Bastian Bay	1,725	16
Azalea	12,700	19
Eugene Island, Dome	3,200	25
Eugene Island, Shark	1,200	30
North Henderson	250	34
Wolfe Creek	1,400	38
North Hitchcook	950	42

Problem 3: Letter with Table

1. Insert the table at the left after ¶ 2 of the letter in Problem 1. Make the necessary change in the wording of ¶ 2.
2. Type two 5′ writings on the combined problems. Compute *gwam.*

Note: Adjust, by judgment, the margins and the spacing between the top of the paper and the date for this problem to center the letter attractively.

LESSON 123

123A Preparatory Practice [5] *each line at least three times*

Alphabet Explain quietly how Dickens vilified Ebenezer Scrooge or Jacob Marley.

Figure-symbol Your memo #83-40 (dated May 25) mistakenly cites "16 prs. @ 79¢ a pr."

Capitals Mary, Jack, and Sarah Jane visited St. Paul, Minnesota, last November.

Fluency I will give most of my time to work; it must be a worthy contribution.

| 1 | 2 | 3 | 4 | 5 | 6 | 7 | 8 | 9 | 10 | 11 | 12 | 13 | 14 |

96B Skill-Comparison and Transfer Typing (10) *two 1' writings on each sentence, 95C, page 168, without the call of the guide; compare rates*

96C Communication Pretest: Punctuation Marks (10)

Full sheet; 2" top margin; DS; 70-space line

The following sentences will pretest your knowledge of the punctuation marks to be studied in this section. As you type, make necessary corrections and insert the punctuation marks emphasized at the left of the sentences.

1	Terminal punctuation	may i hear from you soon about this matter so that i may file a claim
2	Terminal punctuation	does mr jackson know how long this young man has worked in my office
3	Exclamation point	get on the bandwagon hurry remember the contest ends this tuesday
4	Semicolon	i ordered those pens a month ago i have not received any of them yet
5	Semicolon	i saw the notice on the board last month therefore i was forewarned
6	Semicolon	if he goes he will drive but since he is busy he may not go at all
7	Hyphen	twenty five of the men will report for work before the end of the day
8	Hyphen	i know that the machine is available for a 10 20 or 30 day period
9	Hyphen	lewis has a free and easy manner on his weekly coast to coast program
10	Dashes	sympathy the kind we all treasure is two hearts tugging at one load

| 1 | 2 | 3 | 4 | 5 | 6 | 7 | 8 | 9 | 10 | 11 | 12 | 13 | 14 |

96D Production Typing: Manuscript and Telegram (25)

Problem 1: Unbound Manuscript

Type in unbound manuscript form with a 2" top margin; number the pages. If necessary, refer to directions on page 185.

PREPARING TELEGRAMS

TS

(¶ 1) Almost all telegrams are transmitted to Western Union offices by telephone, teleprinter, or Desk-Fax. When they are transmitted by telephone or teleprinter, one or more copies of the message are typed on plain paper for the files. The file copy should show the class of service specified, account to be charged if other than that of the sender, date and time the message was filed, name and address of the recipient, message, sender's name and possibly his title, and reference initials of the typist. The form in which these data are typed on the paper is flexible. (¶ 2) Desk-Fax (or Telefax) machines are installed in companies that send and receive a large number of messages. When this service is used, telegrams are typed on special forms that are later placed on the cylinder of the transmitter. An electronic eye then scans the message and flashes it to a similar machine located at the nearest telegraph center, which in turn flashes it to its destination. The Desk-Fax also receives telegrams by the same process. (¶ 3) The senders of domestic messages (those communicated within the continental United States) have two classes of service available:

SS and indent numbered items 5 spaces from both margins

1. Full-Rate Telegram. This is the speediest service available. The minimum

Full sheet; 1½" top margin; 70-space line; SS with DS between items

1. Type the heading.
2. Type the rules and examples given below (with numbers); underline the side headings.

3. Compose and type four sentences, each sentence illustrating one rule. Number these sentences to correspond with the rules.

Words

NUMBERS

2

Rules

4

(1) Numbers ten and under are generally spelled out; numbers eleven and above are written in figures.

17

24

(2) When several numbers are used in the same context, all numbers should be typed the same way, either in figures or spelled, except that any number that begins a sentence must be spelled.

38

51

65

(3) As a general rule, spell the shorter of two numbers used together.

77

(4) Isolated fractions are usually spelled, but a series of fractions is written in figures.

92

96

Examples

99

(1) He bought six bananas and two pints of cream to make the dessert.

113

(2) Sixty-five people (57 men, 5 boys, and 3 women) climbed Mt. Hood.

127

(3) Order No. 135 was for two 50-gallon drums and 27 ten-gallon cans.

141

(4) Almost one fourth of the job is finished. Add 1/2, 3/7, and 5/8.

155

Other Examples

161

Production Typing Information

TABULATED REPORTS IN WRITTEN COMMUNICATIONS

When space permits, indent a table from both margins. Single-space the tabulated material. For a table with a centered heading, triple-space before the heading and after the last line. For a table without a centered heading, double-space before the first and after the last lines.

For letters up to 200 words (containing a report), use 1½-inch side margins; for letters over 200 words, use 1-inch side margins. In addition, reduce the space between the top edge of the paper and the date line by one or two lines for each line in the table. This is a rough guide; your judgment should prevail.

As a rule, use the backspacing method for deciding on the placement of columns.

Shortcut for Placement of Simple Two-Column Tables. For simple two-column tabulations, set a tab stop for the first column 5 to 10 spaces to the right of the left margin. For the second column, backspace 5 to 10 spaces for the indention from the right margin and 1 space for each letter and space in the longest columnar entry; then set a tab stop for the right column. Be careful, however, not to have columns too far apart for easy reading.

ADJUSTMENTS IN VERTICAL PLACEMENT OF LETTERS

You may occasionally find that you have misjudged the length of a letter and that it is going to be either too high or too low on the page. The following suggestions for condensing or expanding letters may be used to help you solve such letter-placement problems.

Condensing. To condense a letter that is extremely long:

1. Reduce the space allowed for a signature.
2. Omit the company name (if one is used) in the closing lines.
3. Type the reference initials on the same line as the writer's typewritten name.

Expanding. To expand letters that are extremely short:

1. Allow 2 blank lines between the letter body and the complimentary close.
2. Type the reference initials 4 to 6 spaces below the dictator's name.
3. Allow more blank lines for the penwritten signature.

charge is based on 15 words. For longer messages, a charge is made for each additional word. (The former day letter service has been discontinued.)

2. Overnight Telegram. Overnight telegrams may be sent any time up to midnight for delivery the next morning. The minimum charge is based on 100 words. For longer messages, a charge is made for each additional word.

(¶ 4) There are a few important points to keep in mind in preparing a telegram. The class of service desired, the point of origin, and the date should be indicated. One complete address is free. The address on a telegram should thus include all the information that will be helpful in locating the addressee quickly. Even a telephone number or the business title of the addressee may be used without charge. The ZIP Code need not be included. (¶ 5) Only one signature may be included without extra charge. A title, name of department, or name of firm may be added. The name of the city from which a message is sent is shown without charge in the date line of the delivered message.

Problem 2: File Copy of Telegram

Full sheet; 2" top margin; DS; 60-space line

Type a copy of the following telegram. The illustration below is in acceptable form. Type the heading TELEGRAM at the top, as shown.

TELEGRAM Telegram May 2, 19––, 9 a.m. William B. Biggs, President Pacific Industries, Inc. 41892 Van Ness Boulevard San Francisco, California (¶) Arriving San Francisco Wednesday. Can you meet me to discuss supplying materials for the Wilmott contract? Quick delivery vital. Telegraph reply. Charles Holman, Manager Monarch Builders, Inc. (*your initials as typist*)

```
                    T E L E G R A M

Telegram

May 2, 19--, 9 a.m.

William B. Biggs, President
Pacific Industries, Inc.
41892 Van Ness Boulevard
San Francisco, California

Arriving San Francisco Wednesday.  Can you meet me to discuss

supplying materials for the Wilmott contract?  Quick delivery

vital.  Telegraph reply.

                              Charles Holman, Manager
                              Monarch Builders, Inc.

xx
```

File Copy of Telegram on Plain Paper

LESSON 97

97A Preparatory Practice [5] *each line three or more times*

Alphabet	Our quiz grades quickly improved, but we failed the June examinations.
Figure-symbol	I wrote, "P & L Co., 936 Oak St., 1,840 prs. @ 72¢ per pr. (less 5%)."
Capitals	D. H. Achs, P. G. Hasko, and R. I. Quinn live in Salt Lake City, Utah.
Fluency	We must prepare ourselves for work that must be done in the year 2000.

| 1 | 2 | 3 | 4 | 5 | 6 | 7 | 8 | 9 | 10 | 11 | 12 | 13 | 14 |

97B Communication Aid: Terminal Punctuation [15]

Full sheet; 1½" top margin; SS with DS between items; 70-space line

1. For the heading, use TERMINAL PUNCTUATION.
2. Type the rules and examples (with numbers) on page 171.
3. Compose and type an additional sentence to illustrate further each rule. Number these sentences to correspond with the rules.

121D Building Speed and Control (25)

1. Type two 5' writings—the first on the *exploration level*; the second on the *control level*.
2. Compute *gwam*. Compare rates on the two writings.
3. Type, without timing, until you make an error.
4. Type three times the line in which you made the error; continue until you complete the three ¶s.

All letters are used.

	GWAM	
	1'	5'

¶ 1
1.5 SI
5.6 AWL
80% HFW

The words a business writer uses must be active and alive. A letter that contains ordinary, dated words gets little attention. Such letters make us feel that we have been cheated. Strong, forceful words give an impression of a lively, vital writer with an important message on his mind. He utilizes short words and on occasion a unique word to drive home a unique point. No one expects a letter writer to be a novelist, but he can be interesting.

1'	5'	
12	2	59
27	5	62
41	8	65
55	11	68
69	14	70
83	17	73
90	18	75

¶ 2
1.5 SI
5.6 AWL
80% HFW

When you compose technical papers, you will discover that the initial writing is rarely your best one. Your papers may be readable all right, but usually there are several areas that lack polish. An excellent first step, therefore, is to record your opinions on paper as quickly as possible. You can then edit and revise as needed. Read your paper aloud; if it sounds good to you, it will probably sound good to your reader. Time will not permit you to be overly fussy. Know when to polish--and when to finish.

1'	5'	
12	21	77
26	23	80
40	26	83
54	29	85
67	31	88
82	34	91
96	37	94
103	39	95

¶ 3
1.5 SI
5.6 AWL
80% HFW

A man should have some special qualities to be an effective business writer. He should be adjustable; he should know how to size up people; he must be courteous and sincere; and he should have at his command an adequate supply of words that he can utilize to get across his ideas. If he can explain complex technical problems and provide sensible solutions to them in a sincere, direct way, he will be equal to the demands of business writing.

1'	5'	
13	41	98
27	44	101
40	47	103
54	50	106
68	52	109
82	55	112
89	57	113

1' GWAM | 1 | 2 | 3 | 4 | 5 | 6 | 7 | 8 | 9 | 10 | 11 | 12 | 13 | 14 |
5' GWAM | 1 | 2 | 3 |

LESSON 122

122A Preparatory Practice (5) *each line three or more times*

Alphabet   Jerry will exchange zinc for quicksilver because of price adjustments.

Figure-symbol That policy, #7639–858–42–RJ* (issued February 16, 1960), has expired.

Outside keys   The six dazed, weary antelopes walked slowly down the westward slopes.

Fluency   Learn what you can today; experience will be a most demanding teacher.

| 1 | 2 | 3 | 4 | 5 | 6 | 7 | 8 | 9 | 10 | 11 | 12 | 13 | 14 |

122B Skill-Comparison Typing (10) *two 1' writings on each line of 122A; compare gwam*

Space once after the parenthesis

Rules
DS

(1) A complete sentence has a period for terminal punctuation. — 19

(2) A request in the form of a question is usually punctuated with a — 33
period. — 35
DS

(3) Use a question mark after a direct question--not after an indirect — 49
question. — 51

(4) Use an exclamation point after a word, a phrase, or a sentence to — 65
indicate strong emotion or to carry sharp emphasis. — 76
TS

Examples
DS — 79

(1) The mastery of an art requires technical proficiency and insight. — 93

(2) Will you please have Mr. Johns sign the six copies of the report. — 107

(3) When did you hire her? He asked how long she has worked for you. — 121

(4) Your sales met your quota! Congratulations! You earned a bonus! — 135
TS

Other Examples (*Compose four sentences, each sentence illustrating one rule.*) — 141

97C Production Typing: Telegrams (30)

Problem 1: File Copy of Telegram

Full sheet; 2" top margin; 60-space line; DS message; style shown on p. 170; add heading TELEGRAM

Telegram May 2, 19--, 1 p.m. Gerald M. Marshfield Crystal Supply Company 700 Post Road St. Louis, Missouri (¶) Meeting with Holman Wednesday to consider supplying materials for Wilmott contract. Assemble Monarch Builders order we discussed for prompt shipment. Will advise. William B. Biggs, President Pacific Industries, Inc. (*your initials as typist*)

Problem 2: File Copy of Overnight Telegram

Directions given for Problem 1

Overnight telegram May 2, 19--, 3:30 p.m. William B. Biggs, President Pacific Industries, Inc. 41892 Van Ness Boulevard San Francisco, California (¶) Inventory of Smo-lite needed for Wilmott contract depleted. Remainder of order can be on cars and ready to leave within 24 hours. Advise. Charles Holman, Manager Monarch Builders, Inc. (*your initials as typist*)

Problem 3: Telefax Message

Type the Telefax message illustrated below. Make one carbon copy.

Call Letters. These identify Desk-Fax station.

Class of Service. Indicate by letters NL or NL (Col) if the overnight message is sent collect. If FR or no letters appear, messages are sent full rate.

Type only within outlined border.

Typist's reference initials may be typed at the left margin.

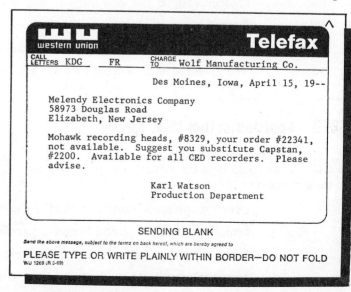

western union **Telefax**

CALL LETTERS KDG   FR   CHARGE TO Wolf Manufacturing Co.

Des Moines, Iowa, April 15, 19--

Melendy Electronics Company
58973 Douglas Road
Elizabeth, New Jersey

Mohawk recording heads, #8329, your order #22341, not available. Suggest you substitute Capstan, #2200. Available for all CED recorders. Please advise.

Karl Watson
Production Department

SENDING BLANK

Send the above message, subject to the terms on back hereof, which are hereby agreed to

PLEASE TYPE OR WRITE PLAINLY WITHIN BORDER—DO NOT FOLD
WU 1269 (R 5-69)

SECTION 20 COMMUNICATIONS WITH TABLES

LESSONS 121–127

Unless otherwise directed, proceed as follows:

Drill Copy: Full sheet; 70-space line; SS.

Paragraph Copy: Full sheet; 70-space line; DS; 5-space ¶ indention.

Production Copy: For letters, use the current date (unless one is given); your reference initials. Carbon copies are optional; correct all errors. Capitalize, space, and punctuate opening and closing lines.
Materials Needed: Letterheads or full sheets; interoffice communication forms.

LESSON 121

121A Preparatory Practice [5] *each line three or more times*

Alphabet	I realized the heavily boxed "junk" from a shipwreck was antique gold.
Figure-symbol	B & B, Inc.'s orders (#189K to 207K) for $\frac{1}{2}$ and $\frac{1}{4}$ lots total $4,536.63.
First row	Ancient, wizened men circled the bubbling mixture, exorcising a demon.
Fluency	It is the things you do, not yourself, that you should take seriously.
	| 1 | 2 | 3 | 4 | 5 | 6 | 7 | 8 | 9 | 10 | 11 | 12 | 13 | 14 |

121B Technique Improvement: Stroking [10]

Type each line three times on the *control level.* Hold your arms and hands quiet. Center the stroking action in your fingers.

1	awa	The police are aware of this unpopular policy. They await your reply.
2	pol	The politician is away. He won the popularity award in this district.
3	Long reaches	Under this new system, all their employees receive annuities annually.
4	Long reaches	I may prepare a summary of my lumber and linoleum purchases this year.
5	Double letters	It occurred to the committee that a fall meeting would be unnecessary.
6	Double letters	Lowell succeeded in getting the proof, although the fee was excessive.
7	One hand	Fred saw John in Honolulu. He agreed to charge only the minimum rate.
8	One hand	We referred Rex Vetter to your address on West Union Street in Joplin.
		| 1 | 2 | 3 | 4 | 5 | 6 | 7 | 8 | 9 | 10 | 11 | 12 | 13 | 14 |

121C Communication Aid: Spelling [10]

1. Type each line twice.
2. Close your book; type the words from your instructor's dictation.
3. Check your work.
4. Retype any words in which you made an error.

overrun pronunciation parallel recede tiring usage weird safety liable
omissions neither perseverance persistent paralysis pageant occurrence
forty nineteen fifty miniature marries optimism persuade replies occur
temperament statement studying shining similar familiar humorous chord

Problem 4: Desk-Fax Message

Type in Desk-Fax form, with one carbon copy.

Call Letters: KDG **Full rate; no service designation needed. Charge to:** Wolf Manufacturing Co. Des Moines, Iowa, April 17, 19-- Virgil Carter Company 2002 Speedway Moline, Illinois (¶) Submit best price on 12 #2200 magnetic core matrices with 256 bit capacity. Ben Byrom General Manager

Problem 5: Desk-Fax Message

Type in Desk-Fax form, with one carbon copy.

Call Letters: KDG **Class of Service:** NL **Charge to:** Wolf Manufacturing Co. Des Moines, Iowa, April 18, 19-- General Precision, Inc. 732 Washington Avenue Pleasantville, New York (¶) Send dates of employment and evaluation of Kenneth Tom who is applicant for senior programmer position. Ben Byrom General Manager

LESSON 98

98A Preparatory Practice [5] *each line three or more times*

Alphabet	Jim Flack was required to pay the tax on the zinc souvenirs he bought.
Figure-symbol	Terms of the May 6 invoice for $497.85 are 2/10, n/30. Pay it May 15.
Long words	Secretary Newenhall's noncommittal responses delighted his detractors.
Fluency	When you can type 60 words a minute with but a few errors, try for 65.
	| 1 | 2 | 3 | 4 | 5 | 6 | 7 | 8 | 9 | 10 | 11 | 12 | 13 | 14 |

98B Communication Aid: Semicolon and Colon [15]

Full sheet; 1½" top margin; SS with DS between items; 70-space line

Type the following material as directed in 97B, page 170, except that you will use the heading SEMICOLON AND COLON.

Words

SEMICOLON AND COLON 4

Rules 6

(1) Use a semicolon between the clauses of a compound sentence when no 20
conjunction is used. 24

(2) Use a semicolon between the clauses of a compound sentence that are 39
joined by a conjunctive adverb (however, therefore, etc.). 51

(3) Use a semicolon to separate the clauses of a compound sentence when 65
one or both members are punctuated with commas. 75

(4) Use a colon to introduce an enumeration or listing. 86

TS

Examples 89

(1) The statements did not come with his letter; they may come today. 104

(2) We had engine trouble; consequently, we could not arrive in time. 118

(3) You may take Fay, Helen, and John; and the others will go by bus. 132

(4) Please ship us the following parts: fuse box, light, and switch. 146

TS

Other Examples *(Compose four sentences, each sentence illustrating one rule.)* 151

Problem 1

ADVERTISING EXPENDITURES: 1950 and 1966

(Figures in Millions)

Medium	1950	1966
Newspapers	$2,076	$ 4,895
Radio	605	1,001
Television	171	2,784
Magazines	515	1,291
Farm Papers	21	34
Direct Mail	803	2,454
Business Papers	251	712
Outdoor	143	178
Miscellaneous	1,125	3,253
Totals	$5,710	$16,602

Source: Reader's Digest Almanac, 1968.

Problem 2

U.S. PRESIDENTS AND THEIR TERMS

Since 1900

Theodore Roosevelt	1901 – 1909
William Howard Taft	1909 – 1913
Thomas Woodrow Wilson	1913 – 1921
Warren Gamaliel Harding	1921 – 1923
John Calvin Coolidge	1923 – 1929
Herbert Clark Hoover	1929 – 1933
Franklin Delano Roosevelt	1933 – 1945
Harry S Truman	1945 – 1953
Dwight David Eisenhower	1953 – 1961
John Fitzgerald Kennedy	1961 – 1963
Lyndon Baines Johnson	1963 – 1969
Richard Milhous Nixon	1969 –

Problem 3

PROJECTED CHANGES IN DISTRIBUTION
OF EMPLOYMENT

Major Occupational Groups

Group	1964	1975	Change
Farm	6.3	3.9	—21.0%
Service	13.2	14.1	35.0
White Collar	44.2	48.3	38.0
Blue Collar	36.3	33.7	17.0

Source: U.S. Department of Labor, America's
Industrial and Occupational Manpower
Requirements, 1964-1975.

Problem 4

Arrange in columns; add $ sign where needed

PERSONAL EXPENDITURES

(Figures in Millions)

Group	Amount
Food and Tobacco	115,446
Clothing; Accessories; Jewelry	48,406
Personal Care	8,215
Housing	67,135
Household Operation	66,658
Medical Care	31,250
Personal Business	23,992
Transportation	55,607
Recreation	28,673
Private Education and Research	6,667
Religious and Welfare Activities	6,475
Foreign Travel and Remittances	3,384
Total Personal Outlay	461,908

Source: The World Almanac, 1968.

98C Production Typing: Block Style Letter [30]

Problem 1: Style Letter

Study Style Letter 4, page 174. Observe its characteristics and the placement of letter parts. Type the letter on letterhead or plain paper. There are 153 words in the body of the letter.

Problem 2: Block Letter

158 words; open punctuation; block style

Words
February 15, 19-- Mr. George Jefferson 3412 9
Litchfield Place Spokane, WA 99208 Dear 17
Mr. Jefferson (¶ 1) Just announce that you 24
are moving, and you may have to do a lot of 33
talking to convince your teen-ager that she 42
can find new friends in her new community. 51
(¶ 2) American understands deeply the per- 58
sonal problems of moving, because we have 66
moved more families from familiar old friends 75
to interesting new ones than any other van 84
line in the world. (¶ 3) We also understand 92
how to be most helpful at this trying time. 101
While you do what you can about personal 109
matters, we do our best to relieve you of con- 118
cerns about the move itself. We advise you 127
about all the details of moving, and we han- 136
dle your things as if we owned them. (¶ 4) 143
When the cares of moving start piling up on 152
you, dial your American agent. He knows 160
how to change your outlook on moving. We 169
move families, not just furniture. Yours very 178
truly Wilson T. Bryant Vice-President 186/199

Problem 3: Block Letter with Attention Line

207 words; open punctuation; block style; attention line at left

Words
February 15, 19-- Hal E. Webb, Inc. 356 8
Alvarado Houston, TX 77035 Attention 16
Mr. Joel Rich Gentlemen (¶ 1) The all- 22
electric concept proves itself again, this time 32
in the beautiful Del Amo Financial Center. 40
This financial complex is one more important 49
addition to the long list of all-electric projects 59
owned and operated by major corporations. 68
(¶ 2) Electric space-conditioning systems can 76
save builders 30 to 50 percent in first-cost 85
installation. In most cases, expensive stacks, 95
flues, and vents are eliminated, often saving 104
the equivalent in space of whole floors. Be- 113
sides, there is more freedom of design in all- 122
electric buildings. Less room is required for 131
the main space-conditioning plant, resulting 141
in a low first-cost, minimum-maintenance 149
building with very competitive per square foot 158
operating costs. (¶ 3) Del Amo Financial 166
Center, Allen Boyd, Architect, is just one of 175
the hundreds of case histories of all-electric 184
buildings in Texas. We shall be glad to show 193
you how to apply the all-electric concept to 202
your commercial or industrial building project 212
for remarkable savings. Write for free book- 221
let containing sample plans. Very truly yours 230
SOUTHERN TEXAS COMPANY Glen V. Ritter, 239
Chief Engineer 242/256

LESSON 99

99A Preparatory Practice [5] *each line three or more times*

Alphabet	Prometheus gave fire to man; he was quickly judged and exiled by Zeus.
Figure-symbol	*Whytt & Kane used a 1967 estimate of 32½ percent (4,580 square feet).
Hand position	Could you balance two dimes on the backs of your hands while you type?
Fluency	A good idea is just a thought unless we change it to words and action.

| 1 | 2 | 3 | 4 | 5 | 6 | 7 | 8 | 9 | 10 | 11 | 12 | 13 | 14 |

LESSON 119

119A Preparatory Practice [5] *each line three or more times*

Alphabet	Dank fog hid unlit objects; expressway driving became quite hazardous.
Figure-symbol	*List does not include Day & Company's Policy #87–6230–WE–1954 (paid).
Third row	We were there two weeks earlier; point out where you were living then.
Fluency	A man who is just minutes late each day loses hours of work in a year.

| 1 | 2 | 3 | 4 | 5 | 6 | 7 | 8 | 9 | 10 | 11 | 12 | 13 | 14 |

119B Technique Improvement: Response Patterns [15] *each line at least three times*

1	Word-recognition	A plan will help you do the things you should when you should do them.
2	Stroke	Several important inventions and discoveries changed their operations.
3	Combination	There is nothing dangerous about the great movement that is under way.
4	Word-recognition	Who can know the great things he can do until he tries to do his best?
5	Stroke	Of all the major forms of mass transportation, the pipeline is unique.
6	Combination	A pipeline merely stands still and lets the freight do all the moving.
7	Word-recognition	The will to win is a big aid to all the men who want to do big things.
8	Stroke	Mt. Blanc tunnel represents an engineering feat of heroic proportions.
9	Combination	No one is so futile as he who will not or cannot control his thoughts.

| 1 | 2 | 3 | 4 | 5 | 6 | 7 | 8 | 9 | 10 | 11 | 12 | 13 | 14 |

119C Production Skill Building [30]

Make a notation of the problems listed at the right to be typed for a 20′ writing. Type them until time is called. Compute your *n-pram*.

Page 202, 115D, Problem 1
Page 205, 116D, Problem 2
Page 206, 117C, Problem 1

LESSON 120

120A Preparatory Practice [5] *each line three or more times*

Alphabet	Mary Turner quickly ate the extra pizza we had saved for Jane Boering.
Figure-symbol	Lee & Cowl's 14¼% discount applies to your $27,630 and $58,909 orders.
Adjacent keys	We were pleased to allow her to point out her real reasons for asking.
Fluency	A man who makes many mistakes in his work can be a very costly worker.

| 1 | 2 | 3 | 4 | 5 | 6 | 7 | 8 | 9 | 10 | 11 | 12 | 13 | 14 |

120B Growth Index [15] *two 5′ writings on 112B, page 196; figure* nwam *(net words a minute) on the better writing.*

To figure NWAM—

1. Determine *gwam*.
2. Deduct from *gwam* 2 for each error.

120C Production Measurement [30] *type for 20 minutes; compute* n-pram

1. Use a full sheet, reading position, and double spacing for each problem.
2. Decide on spaces between columns.
3. Erase and correct all errors.

BUSINESS WRITING, INCORPORATED

Communications  *Consultants*

2203 CEDAR DRIVE, E. / HICKSVILLE, NEW YORK 11804 / 212-869-2560

	Words in Parts	Total Words
February 12, 19--	4	4
Miss Margaret Lamson	8	8
62200 Beacon Hill Road	12	12
Waterbury, CT 06716	17	17
Dear Miss Lamson	20	20
Thank you for your letter of February 5 requesting a copy	32	32
of our Letter Writing Manual. I regret that this manual	44	44
is not yet in printed form. The mimeographed copies cur-	55	55
rently available are restricted to use in our offices.	67	67
We have adopted the block form illustrated in this letter.	12	79
You will observe that machine adjustments are simpler, re-	24	91
sulting in a saving of much time by the typist. The date,	36	103
address, salutation, and closing lines all begin at the	47	114
left margin. Paragraphs are blocked also. The form is	58	125
used in many business offices.	65	131
You should get a copy of our Letter Writing Manual in a	11	143
few weeks. There is no charge for the manual. We hope	22	154
you will find it useful. Please write me again if I can	34	165
send you any additional information.	41	173
Sincerely yours	45	176
S. James Whitmore		
S. James Whitmore	48	180
President	50	182
rsk	51	183

STYLE LETTER 4: *Block Style (Typed in Pica Type)*

LESSON 118

118A Preparatory Practice ⑤ *each line three or more times*

Alphabet   Max Jackson left the quiz show early to give Mable a prize he had won.

Figures   Of the 1,670 dispensers made by Employee #8492, 158 could not be OK'd.

Double letters   The officers will meet with the committee to discuss the class dinner.

Fluency   Even though your rate varies, try to strike all keys with equal force.

| 1 | 2 | 3 | 4 | 5 | 6 | 7 | 8 | 9 | 10 | 11 | 12 | 13 | 14 |

118B Building Speed ⑮ *type 113B, page 198, as directed there*

118C Production Typing: Tabulated Reports ㉚

Problem 1: Multiline Columnar Headings

Full sheet; DS; reading position; decide on spaces between columns

To center the heading over the second and third columns: (1) Move the carriage to the first stroke in the second column; note the number on the scale. (2) Move the carriage to the last stroke in the third column; note the number on the scale. (3) Add the two numbers; divide by 2 to find the center of the column, the point from which the backspacing begins.

			Words
SUNFLOWER TRANSPORTATION COMPANY			7
Long-Term Debt			10
	December		SS 13
First Mortgage Bonds	**1968**	**1969**	25
3 1/8% series due 1976	$50,000	$50,000	33
3 7/8% series due 1976	45,000	47,000	40
4 1/8% series due 1980	70,000	82,500	48
4 3/8% series due 1982	60,500	68,000	55
5 1/2% series due 1982	55,000	57,000	63
5 1/8% series due 1984	90,000	94,500	70
5 1/4% series due 1984	82,500	84,000	77
5 3/4% series due 1988	77,500	85,000	85
5 7/8% series due 1988	55,500	64,500	92
6 1/4% series due 1990	63,000	72,500	100
6 1/2% series due 1990	92,000	91,500	107

Problem 2: Multiline Headings

Full sheet; DS; reading position; decide on spaces between columns; SS 2-line main heading; do not abbreviate any words

			Words
NATIONWIDE WEEKLY SALARY DATA			6
FOR SELECTED EDP JOBS			10
	Established Ranges		SS 18
	Average	**Average**	28
Job Title	**Low**	**High**	31
Lead Systems Analyst	$201	$273	37
Senior Systems Analyst	180	249	44
Junior Systems Analyst	149	207	50
Lead Programmer	176	242	55
Senior Programmer	154	210	60
Junior Programmer	126	173	65
Lead Computer Operator	138	186	71
Senior Computer Operator	138	186	78
Junior Computer Operator	100	134	84
Tab Equip. Manager	144	194	90
Lead Tab Equip. Operator	114	150	98
Senior Tab Equip. Operator	99	131	105
Junior Tab Equip. Operator	89	116	113
Keypunch Supervisor	110	148	118
Lead Keypunch Operator	95	124	125
Senior Keypunch Operator	85	111	131
Junior Keypunch Operator	77	99	138
			142

Source: "EDP Salary Study—1968," *Business*   152
Automation (June, 1968), pp. 40-41.   161

Full sheet; 1½" top margin; SS with DS between items; 70-space line

	Words
COLON AND HYPHEN	3

Rules 6

(1) Use a colon to introduce a question or long quotation. 17

(2) Two spaces follow a colon except when it is used to separate hours 32
and minutes or the initials in the reference line of a letter. As a 46
rule, use figures with a.m. and p.m. 54

(3) Use a hyphen in compound numerals from twenty-one to ninety-nine. 68

(4) Retain the hyphen in a series of hyphenations with the same ending. 83

Examples 86

(1) The question is this: What experience is necessary for the jobs? 100

(2) We finished the tour at 12:45 p.m. and left the city at 5:26 p.m. 114

(3) Approximately thirty-seven of the forty-eight delegates attended. 128

(4) All 15- and 20-day trips to Maine have been temporarily canceled. 142

Other Examples *(Compose four sentences, each sentence illustrating one rule.)* 148

99C Production Typing: AMS Simplified Letter ㉚

Problem 1: Style Letter

Type the letter on page 176. There are 175 words in the body of the letter.

Problem 2: AMS Letter

178 words; AMS simplified style

	Words
Mr. W. A. Lynn, Sales Manager Kerr Manu-	11
facturing Company 4715 Headford Avenue	19
Waterloo, IA 50701 PREPARATION OF A	26
MARKET SURVEY (¶1) Store owners, gen-	32
eral merchandise managers, and buyers need	41
to know every good furniture manufacturer	49
in the market. In order to be of service to	58
them, we are now preparing a MARKET SUR-	66
VEY that will be distributed to stores sub-	74
scribing to our service. (¶2) A similar survey	83
was sent to our subscribers two years ago.	92
Many furniture manufacturers also found this	101
survey to be instrumental in acquiring new	109
business. There is no expense involved on	118
your part; our services are paid for by the	127
stores we represent. (¶3) If your company	134
wishes to be listed in the MARKET SURVEY,	143
please give us the following information:	151

	Words
1. A complete description of furniture manu-	160
factured. 2. Patterns and designs recently de-	170
veloped. 3. Dates and terms of delivery;	178
services rendered. (¶4) We should like to	186
have this information soon, as we intend to	195
go to press in six weeks. Your cooperation	203
in this matter will be deeply appreciated.	212
ROBERT ADAIR – PRESIDENT	218/237

Problem 3: AMS Letter

77 words; capitalize and punctuate

	Words
march 12, 19–– mr lawrence l crawford busi-	9
ness education department university of mary-	18
land college park md 20742 condensation of	27
your excellent article (¶1) I think you will	35
be pleased to know, Mr. Crawford, that we	43
have selected your excellent article, "Revo-	52
lutionary Changes in Our Schools," which	60
appeared in the January issue of Business	70
Education Forum, for condensation in a com-	81
ing issue of The School Digest. (¶2) Full	92
credit will be given to you and to the Forum.	103
I am sure that our readers will find your arti-	112
cle most worthwhile. jerome c peterson man-	121
aging editor	124/144

Problem 1: Report with Uneven Columns and Totals

Full sheet; DS; reading position; decide spaces between columns

Words

BERNARD LUSKIN WEAR   4

First Quarter Departmental Sales   11

Department	January	February	March	
Shoes	$ 840.12	$ 660.13	$ 489.90	32
Dresses and Lingerie	3,487.37	3,200.34	4,591.25	43
Hats	660.14	860.25	940.46	48
Coats	1,027.78	2,806.50	2,175.70	56
Jewelry	89.48	95.35	103.36	61
Gloves and Handbags	376.24	350.80	421.56	70
Sweaters and Blouses	385.67	435.78	497.90	78
Furs	816.57	730.69	500.89	83 / 91
Totals	$7,683.37	$9,139.84	$9,721.02	101

(column header underscores: January, February, March — 23)

Type total line immediately under last amount; double-space and type total.

Problem 2: Tabulated Report from Corrected Script

Full sheet; DS; reading position; decide spaces between columns

Words

Midland Packaged Foods *all caps*   5

Sales Promotion Costs   9

Item	1968	1969	
Circulars	$10,472	$12,800	21
Letters (Automatic)	830	750	26
Samples	11,733	8,105	32
Direct Mail	3,489	5,400	37
Exhibits and Demonstrations	980	825	44
Prizes	279	370	47
Midland News *all caps*	3,483	4,762	53
Misc. Costs *spell out*	552	418	59 / 64
Totals	$33,598	$31,698	68

BUSINESS WRITING, INCORPORATED

Communications 🌐 *Consultants*

2203 CEDAR DRIVE, E. / HICKSVILLE, NEW YORK 11804 / 212-869-2560

	Words in Parts	Total Words

Begin all lines at left margin

October 5, 19-- ¹⁴

| | 3 | 3 |

Address at least 3 blank line spaces below date

Mr. S. W. Jackson, Manager
North American Cement Corp.
39501 Bartlett Avenue
Boston, MA 02129

	9	9
	14	14
	19	19
	22	22

Salutation omitted

Subject line in all capital letters with a triple space before and after it

AMS SIMPLIFIED STYLE

| | 26 | 26 |

This letter is typed in the timesaving simplified style
recommended by the Administrative Management Society.
To type a letter in the AMS style, follow these steps:

	38	38
	49	49
	60	60

1. Use block format with blocked paragraphs.

| | 9 | 69 |

2. Omit the salutation and complimentary close.

| | 19 | 79 |

Enumerated items at left margin; if items are not numbered, indent 5 spaces

3. Include a subject heading and type it in ALL CAPS a
   triple space below the address; triple-space from
   the subject line to the first line of the body.

	30	90
	41	101
	51	111

4. Type enumerated items at the left margin; indent
   unnumbered listed items five spaces.

| | 61 | 121 |
| | 69 | 129 |

5. Type the writer's name and title in ALL CAPS at least
   four line spaces below the letter body.

| | 80 | 140 |
| | 89 | 149 |

6. Type the reference initials (typist's only) a double
   space below the writer's name.

| | 100 | 160 |
| | 107 | 167 |

Correspondents in your company will like the AMS simplified letter style not only for the "eye appeal" it gives
letters but also because it reduces letter-writing costs.

	11	178
	23	190
	35	201

Complimentary close omitted

S. James Whitmore

S. JAMES WHITMORE - PRESIDENT

| | 41 | 207 |

akb

| | 41 | 208 |

Writer's name and title in all capital letters at least 3 blank line spaces below letter body

STYLE LETTER 5: *AMS Simplified Letter Style (Typed in Pica Type)*

The Administrative Management Society (formerly known as the National Office Management Association or NOMA) has adopted a simplified letter for use in business correspondence. Style Letter 5, above, is an example of the recommended form. Study the features of this style carefully. (This letter is typed in pica type.)

Problem 2: Report with Horizontal Rulings

Full sheet; DS; reading position; decide spaces between columns; add horizontal rulings as in Problem 1; put the source note below the bottom rule

			Words
DOMESTIC EXPORTS BY COMMODITY GROUPS			7
Figures in Millions of Dollars			14
			38
Commodity	1960	1965	42
Food and Live Animals	2,662	4,004	55
Beverages and Tobacco	483	517	62
Crude Materials, Except Fuels	2,777	2,856	69
Mineral Fuels	814	947	77
Animal and Vegetable Oils and Fats	307	471	83
Chemicals	1,816	2,402	92
Machinery and Transport Equipment	7,011	10,016	97
Other Manufactured Goods	4,076	4,840	106
Other Transactions	450	952	114
			120
Source: Statistical Abstract of the United States, 1966.			133
			153

LESSON 117

117A Preparatory Practice [5] *each line three or more times*

Alphabet — Jealous of Banquo, MacBeth, vainly prizing a crown, executed the king.

Figure-symbol — Clee & Gray's sales, $68,490.23, are 5/17 greater than five years ago.

Direct reaches — I decided my funny brindle puppy, "Mimi," could jump on my TV program.

Fluency — We can begin to worry if we discover our work is not worth our salary.

| 1 | 2 | 3 | 4 | 5 | 6 | 7 | 8 | 9 | 10 | 11 | 12 | 13 | 14 |

117B Communication Aid: Apostrophe [10] *as directed in 114C, page 199*

Full sheet; 1½" top margin; 70-space line; SS with DS between items

Words

APOSTROPHE 2

Rules 4

(1) Add 's to form the plural of numbers and letters (7's, five's). 18
(2) Use the apostrophe to show omission of figures (class of '65). 32
(3) Use the apostrophe to show omission of letters in abbreviations 45
(Rob't, Marg't, Sec'y). No period follows such abbreviations. 58
(4) Use single quotation marks (apostrophe) for quotes within quotes. 72

Examples 76

(1) The teacher gave 5 A's, 7 B's, and 30 C's to a class of 42 girls. 90
(2) The dinner meeting for the class of '66 will be held on Thursday. 104
(3) The minutes of the meeting were signed "Charles S. Clark, Sec'y." 118
(4) Mr. Kromer said, "I heard them say to your sister, 'It is time.' " 132

Other Examples 137

LESSON 100

100A Preparatory Practice [5] *each line three or more times*

Alphabet	The Maharajah's quixotic group visited Auckland, New Zealand, briefly.
Figure-symbol	Type on Line 49, "137 pens @ $26.80 ea., less 5½%. Ship immediately."
Double letters	Ann Lee's well-written letters will soon arrive in the committee room.
Fluency	To type rapidly, hold the arms quiet and make the fingers do the work.
	| 1 | 2 | 3 | 4 | 5 | 6 | 7 | 8 | 9 | 10 | 11 | 12 | 13 | 14 |

100B Communication Aid: Hyphen and Dash [15] *as directed in 97B, page 170*

Full sheet; 1½" top margin; SS with DS between items; 70-space line

	Words
HYPHEN AND DASH	3
Rules	5
(1) Use a hyphen to join compound adjectives preceding a noun.	18
(2) Use a dash (--) to indicate a sudden change in thought.	30
(3) Use a dash (--) for emphasis to set off an appositive.	42
(4) Use a dash (--) to introduce the name of an author when it follows	56
a direct quotation.	60
Examples	64
(1) The well-known statesman has been appointed for a four-year term.	78
(2) The best way--perhaps the only way--to have friends is to be one.	92
(3) Your stars--freedom, opportunity, faith--are bright and constant.	106
(4) "The Road to Freedom, while narrow, is a two-way street."--Gross.	120
Other Examples (*Compose four sentences, each sentence illustrating one rule.*)	125

100C Manipulative Drill: Aligning Columns at the Right [5] *repeat if time permits*

Full sheet; 2" top margin

1. Type the first column, aligning the items at the right 2 inches from the extreme left of the sheet according to the explanatory material at the right.
2. Type the second and third columns in the same way at the positions indicated. Do not tabulate from column to column.

ALIGNING COLUMNS AT THE RIGHT

1. Type the first listed item in its desired position.
2. On the next line, position the carriage one space to the right of the last letter (or mark of punctuation) of the item above.
3. Backspace once for each stroke in the second item (including any marks of punctuation).
4. Type the second item. Repeat procedure for any subsequent items.

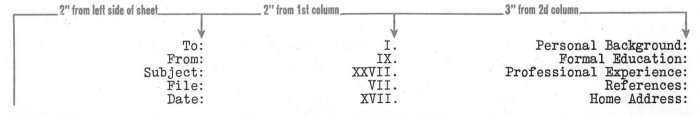

2" from left side of sheet — 2" from 1st column — 3" from 2d column

```
                     To:             I.        Personal Background:
                   From:            IX.          Formal Education:
                Subject:         XXVII.  Professional Experience:
                   File:           VII.                References:
                   Date:          XVII.              Home Address:
```

116C Production Skill Building (5)

Type the report on page 202, as directed on that page. Plan and type as much of the problem as you can in 4 minutes.

Type on the *control level.* When time is called, compute *g-pram.* Good: 6 to 10 words.

116D Production Typing: Report with Horizontal Rulings (30)

Problem 1: Report with Horizontal Rulings

Full sheet; DS; reading position; decide spaces between columns

Guides for typing table can be found on page 200.

			Words
	ORIENTATION SCHEDULE		4
DS →			
	February		6
DS →			
	═══════════════		27
DS →			
Topic	Leader	Date	30
SS →			
───────────			41
DS →			
Customer Relations	Johnson	2	51
Personnel Policies	Endicott	4	57
Company History	Endicott	3	63
Employee Benefits	Endicott	5	68
Products We Make	Goodman	9	74
Company Social Programs	Sanchez	10	81
Company Organization	Taylor	11	87
Branch Operations	Taylor	12	93
Letter Writing Techniques	Perkins	13	100
File It and Find It	MacMillan	20	107
Questions and Answers	Staff	21	113
Suggestion System	Goodman	23	119
Training Programs	Endicott	24	125
The Computer Center	Wagner	25	131
Safety First	Serron	27	137
A Word from Our President	Fischer	28	144
SS →			
───────────			154

Problem 1: Interoffice Memorandum

Type memorandum on page 179; 1" left and right margins; carbon copy on a plain sheet

If an interoffice memorandum form is not available, use a full sheet of plain paper and type headings for the special sections as shown on the illustration on page 179.

Problem 2: Interoffice Memorandum

Interoffice memorandum form or plain sheet; SS; 1" left and right margins; no carbon copy; company mail envelope

	Words
TO: Wilbur B. Maxwell, Regional Manager	7
FROM: George H. Hannah, Sales Manager	14
DATE: May 10, 19-- **SUBJECT:** Automobiles	19
(¶ 1) In assigning water systems specialists	26
to the various districts on the East Coast, we	36
will need very soon two new automobiles.	44
One of them is for W. R. Nelson, District #3;	53
the other for John Burns, District #5. I sug-	62
gest that we obtain authorization to buy the	71
two automobiles needed. (¶ 2) Tudor sedans	79
will be satisfactory for these men. I believe	88
authorization should cover the purchase of	97
one of the lighter makes. We can then take	106
whatever make is available in the small car	115
class. (¶ 3) The two men will be ready to go	123
into their territories about the middle of June.	133
We should have the cars by that time.	141/150

Problem 3: Interoffice Memorandum

Interoffice memorandum form or plain sheet; SS; 1" left and right margins; 3 carbon copies

List on one line the three names to whom the memorandum is being sent.

	Words
TO: Harvey Smith, Frank L. Stevens, Mar-	7
vin Kahn **FROM:** John A. Rohr, Regional	13
Manager **DATE:** May 15, 19-- **SUBJECT:** Sale	18
of Overstocked Materials (¶ 1) It has come	25
to my attention that with the current high	34
levels of inventories, some of our divisional	43
offices are disposing of overstocked materials	53
to local customers at greatly reduced prices.	62
Perhaps it would be well for a divisional office	72
to circularize other divisional offices before	81
disposing of usable stock. In this way we can	91
take care of the needs of our offices before	100
disposing of our stock. (¶ 2) I am eager to	107
have your inventories balanced as rapidly as	116
possible and do not wish to slow down the	125
sale or disposal of surplus materials. I shall,	135
however, appreciate your sending a circular	143
letter to other divisions before surplus mate-	153
rials are sold.	156

Problem 4: Postal Card

48-space line; block style; SS; address the card to yourself; add salutation with your name

A message placed on a postal card must be brief, and the sender may find it necessary to omit any "extras" that fail to contribute directly to his main thought. He will usually include, however, the date, his typed name (except when writing to a friend), and a return address, printed or typed on the address side of the card. S. James Whitmore, President

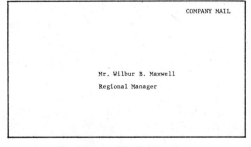

Company Mail Envelope

Postal Card—Address Side   **Postal Card—Message Side**

Problem 2: Rough Draft of Tabulated Report

Full sheet; DS; reading position; decide spaces between columns

Words

ALL-TIME BEST SELLERS ← DS 4
Nonfiction 7

TS

Title → Center over column	Date	Copies	Words
The pocket books of Baby And Child Crae (are)	1946	19,076,822	24
Better Homes and Gardens Cook Book	1930	11,325,299	34
Pockett Atlas	1071 (1917)	12,000,000 (11)	40
Bettey Crocker's Cook Book (Picture)	1950	7,000,000*	50
How To Win A friend and Inluence People	19(73)	6 578,314	61
101 Famous Poems	1917 (6)	6 000,000*	68
English-Spanish, Spanish-English Dictionary	1948	4,567,000 (5,899,000)	74 / 80
Profiles in Corage	19(65)	5,498,651	87
Roget's pocket Thesauras	1923	5 416,857	95

98

DS — Source: 70 Years of Best Sellers, 1895-1965, 1968). Alice Payne Hackett, (New York: R.R. Bowker Co., 126
DS — *Estimated. 128

LESSON 116

116A Preparatory Practice (5) *each line three or more times*

Alphabet	Jim quickly played the exciting pizzicato movement from Boccio's work.
Figure-symbol	My new figures show a 1,235,780 increase, or 469½% more than expected.
Inside keys	The Ghurka rug was torn five times before Mr. Hunter finally fixed it.
Fluency	For a lazy man, each hour of each day seems to have 120 weary minutes.

| 1 | 2 | 3 | 4 | 5 | 6 | 7 | 8 | 9 | 10 | 11 | 12 | 13 | 14 |

116B Communication Aid: Apostrophe (10) *as directed in 114C, page 199*

Full sheet; 1½" top margin; 70-space line; SS with DS between items

Words

APOSTROPHE 2

Rules 4

(1) Company and organization names sometimes omit the apostrophe. 18
(2) It is better not to use the possessive form for inanimate objects, 32
but business sanctions the possessive with day, month, year, etc. 45
(3) Use 'd to form the past and past participle of coined words. 58
(4) Do not use an apostrophe if a preposition follows a possessive noun. 73

Examples 76

(1) She walked from Wilson's Department Store to Citizens State Bank. 90
(2) It's true that eight years' work was destroyed in one day's time. 104
(3) The office manager X'd out the last line; then he OK'd the cable. 118
(4) Fred has had ten years of experience as manager of Eckert Studio. 132

Other Examples 138

BUSINESS WRITING, INCORPORATED

HICKSVILLE, NEW YORK 11804   INTEROFFICE COMMUNICATION

Words

Printed headings

TO: Conrad V. Tilton, Sales Department   7

FROM: Eva L. Burnside, Training Supervisor   14

DATE: July 27, 19--   17

SUBJECT: Company Correspondence   22

Salutation omitted

1-inch side margins

Correspondence within our company is typed on this special inter-office form. The general purpose of this form is to provide a rapid, convenient means of preparing the communications that are exchanged by the various members of this organization. As you can see from the printed headings, information can be set up quickly. Only essential information is included.   35 / 47 / 61 / 73 / 86 / 96

Observe that titles, full addresses, the salutation, the compli-mentary close, and the signature are omitted. The inclusion of a subject heading is highly recommended. It will immediately tell the reader what subject is treated in the memorandum. The subject heading is also an aid in filing the communication.   109 / 122 / 135 / 148 / 159

All interoffice messages, regardless of length, should be typed with one-inch left and right margins. Generally, messages should be single-spaced, with double spacing between paragraphs. Short messages may be double-spaced if desired. The message should be typed in block form with blocked paragraphs. A triple space should separate the first line of the message from the subject heading.   172 / 185 / 198 / 212 / 224 / 236 / 238

The initials of only the typist should be typed a double space below the last line of the message. Notations regarding enclo-sures and carbon copy distribution should be included; and if included, they should be typed in the same position they occupy in regular correspondence.   251 / 264 / 276 / 289 / 294

When an envelope is needed, the notation COMPANY MAIL is typed in the space normally used for the postage stamp. The address is then typed on the envelope in the position normally occupied by the address. The recipient's name and his departmental designa-tion should be given.   308 / 320 / 333 / 346 / 350

Closing lines omitted
Typist's initials

cy   351

cc Ethel Bergman, Administrative Assistant   360
    Sales Department   363

STYLE LETTER 6: *Interoffice Communication Style (Typed in Pica Type)*

115B Communication Aid: Apostrophe [10] *as directed in 114C, page 199*

Full sheet; 1½" top margin; 70-space line; SS with DS between items

Words

APOSTROPHE 2

Rules 4

(1) When common possession is to be shown for two or more persons, 18
use 's with the last name only. 25

(2) Possessive pronouns do not take an apostrophe. It's is a contraction 40
for it is. The apostrophe is used in contractions. 52

(3) When a proper name of one syllable ends in s, add 's for possession. 67

(4) Add only an apostrophe to a proper name of more than one syllable 81
that ends in s to show possession. 88

Examples 92

(1) Van and Bert's mother is in England; Jane's mother is in Austria. 106

(2) The book is hers. Its cover is torn, so wrap the book with care. 120

(3) Bess's talk on antiques was better organized than James's report. 134

(4) Carl Williams' store is only one block from Vince Meadows' house. 148

Other Examples 154

115C Production Skill Building [5]

Full sheet; DS; 16 spaces between columns

As you are timed for 4 minutes, make machine adjustments and type the columns of the tabulated report illustrated on page 201. Type on the *control level.*

115D Production Typing: Tabulated Reports [30]

Full sheet; DS; reading position; 8 spaces between columns

Problem 1: Three-Column Report

			Words
ALL-TIME BEST SELLERS			4
TS			
Title	Author	No. Sold	13
DS			
Peyton Place	Metalious	9,919,785	19
In His Steps	Sheldon	8,065,000 *	26
God's Little Acre	Caldwell	8,061,812	33
Gone with the Wind	Mitchell	6,978,211	41
Lady Chatterley's Lover	Lawrence	6,326,470	49
The Carpetbaggers	Robbins	5,563,841	56
Exodus	Uris	5,473,710	61
I, the Jury	Spillane	5,390,105	67
To Kill a Mockingbird	Lee	5,363,909	74
The Wonderful Wizard of Oz	Baum	5,000,000 *	83

SS→
______________ 87
DS→

Source: Alice Payne Hackett, 70 Years of Best Sellers, 1895–1965 (New 108
York: R. R. Bowker Co., 1968). 114

* Estimated. 117

LESSON 101

101A Preparatory Practice [5] *each line three or more times*

Alphabet	Mr. Black's quizzical expression mystified the judges and the viewers.
Figure-symbol	Dan's note read, "On May 29, we will pay (at 6% interest) $13,784.50."
Adjacent reaches	We were excited and frightened; we looked like three dreaded warriors.
Fluency	Some people feel it is easier to be critical than it is to be helpful.
	| 1 | 2 | 3 | 4 | 5 | 6 | 7 | 8 | 9 | 10 | 11 | 12 | 13 | 14 |

101B Communication Aid: Spelling [5]

1. Type these commonly misspelled words twice; study the words as you type them.
2. Close your book; type the words from your instructor's dictation; check your work.

consensus cylinder deferred deficient dissatisfied embarrass erroneous

gratuity guarantee haphazard height imitation inaugurate issuing suing

exaggerate exorbitant facsimile fiend fluorescent foreign fulfill lien

101C Technique Improvement: Stroking [10] *two 1' writings on each line*

Long reaches	This is a very effective symbol; we have been using it for many years.
Double letters	It will be unnecessary to pay Mr. Tratt a commission in the beginning.
One hand	Face the facts; you can win an award only if you exceed Jim's average.
Balanced hand	Our neighbor and his visitor may take a dirigible to the ancient city.
	| 1 | 2 | 3 | 4 | 5 | 6 | 7 | 8 | 9 | 10 | 11 | 12 | 13 | 14 |

101D Production Skill Building: Special Communication Forms [30] *20' timing; errors corrected; figure* n-pram

Make a pencil notation of the problems listed at the right. Follow the directions indicated for each problem. Repeat the problems if time permits.

Page 173, 98C, Problem 2
Page 175, 99C, Problem 2
Page 178, 100D, Problem 3
Page 178, 100D, Problem 4

LESSON 102

102A Preparatory Practice [5] *each line three or more times*

Alphabet	The buzzing, jumping insects quieted, for it was exactly five o'clock.
Figure-symbol	Compute: 640 pairs @ 38½¢ and 975 sets @ 12½¢; allow a 14½% discount.
Hand position	All of us need to study and understand our economic system thoroughly.
Fluency	Fix your eyes on the book; trust your mind and fingers to do the work.
	| 1 | 2 | 3 | 4 | 5 | 6 | 7 | 8 | 9 | 10 | 11 | 12 | 13 | 14 |

		Words in Columns	Total Words

1
2
3
4
5
6
7
8
9 ←———Main heading———→   FORMADEX DISTRIBUTORS   4
10   DS
11 ←——Secondary heading——→   Video Tapes   7
12   TS
13
14 ←——Columnar headings——→ Company   Location   13
15   DS

Company	Location	Words in Columns	Total Words
Electronics Service Company	Phoenix	7	20
Evenview Television Systems	Hollywood	15	28
AVF Communications, Inc.	Santa Barbara	23	36
Elsco Colorado, Inc.	Denver	28	41
Audio Video Industries, Inc.	Miami	35	48
Lock Audio Associates	Atlanta	41	54
Electronic Equipment, Inc.	Chicago	48	61
Lake Systems Corporation	Boston	55	68
General TV Network	Detroit	60	73
Dayton Communications	Dayton	66	79

KEY   28   14   13

26
27
28
29
30
31
32
33

114D Production Typing: Two-Column Tabulated Report ㉚

Problem 1

Half sheet; exact center; SS; 14 spaces between columns

After studying the information on page 200, type the tabulated report shown above.

Problem 2

If time remains, type the problem again. Omit the secondary heading and leave 10 spaces between columns. (*76 words*)

LESSON 115

115A Preparatory Practice ⑤ *each line three or more times*

Alphabet   The bold Viking queen came for her topaz, aquamarine, and onyx jewels.

Figure-symbol   Invoice #46–891 lists credit terms of 2½/15, n/30. We can save $7.49.

Long words   We can outline the economic implications and technical specifications.

Fluency   Learning to live with others might be as hard on them as it is on you.

| 1 | 2 | 3 | 4 | 5 | 6 | 7 | 8 | 9 | 10 | 11 | 12 | 13 | 14 |

102B Communication Index: Capitalization and Punctuation (5) *capitalize and punctuate as you type*

1 her car bearing a washington license is parked in a no parking zone

2 will you please ask about their low priced one and two bedroom units

3 fifty one of the men had first or second class cabins for the cruise

4 a chemist in fact any scientist could analyze these strange fluids

5 joe who owns an old bus drives to tucson and it takes him 15 hours

| 1 | 2 | 3 | 4 | 5 | 6 | 7 | 8 | 9 | 10 | 11 | 12 | 13 | 14 |

102C Growth Index (10) *one 1′ and one 5′ writing; figure* gwam

All letters are used.

		GWAM 1′	5′	
¶ 1 1.5 SI 5.6 AWL 80% HFW	You must remember that success is not achieved by lying awake at	13	3	58
	night, but by being awake in the daytime. Generally, the men who get	27	5	60
	ahead in any calling analyze their working methods. They compare them	41	8	63
	with the techniques used by celebrated experts in their chosen fields.	56	11	66
	So it must be with you in typewriting or any other course you may be	70	14	69
	taking. Study the methods you are using; be quick to perfect the tech-	84	17	72
	niques that may improve your work.	91	18	73
¶ 2 1.5 SI 5.6 AWL 80% HFW	The space bar is used very frequently in typewriting. One in every	14	21	76
	five strokes is handled by your right thumb. Strike the bar with very	28	24	79
	quick down-and-in movements. Keep your wrist steady as you control the	42	27	82
	bar. Ideally, the stroke is associated with the word just completed, not	57	30	85
	as a separate operation. Give very careful attention to operating the	71	32	87
	various other parts of your machine. Sooner or later, you will discover	86	35	90
	that you do more as you learn to do less.	94	37	92
¶ 3 1.5 SI 5.6 AWL 80% HFW	If you use a manual typewriter, study very carefully the way you	13	40	95
	return the carriage. Obviously, you must return it with adequate energy	28	42	97
	to get it back to the left margin. Keep the fingers of your right hand	42	45	100
	in position over the home keys. Quickly move the left hand to the return	57	48	103
	lever. Move it forward far enough to take up the slack; then throw the	71	51	106
	carriage with a very quick movement of the wrist. Return the left hand;	85	54	109
	resume typing immediately.	90	55	110

1′ GWAM | 1 | 2 | 3 | 4 | 5 | 6 | 7 | 8 | 9 | 10 | 11 | 12 | 13 | 14 |
5 GWAM | 1 | 2 | 3 |

Production Typing Information

VERTICAL PLACEMENT OF TABULATIONS

Exact. Count total lines to be used, including spaces between lines; subtract total from lines available; divide remainder by 2 (ignore fractions). Leave this number of blank lines at the top of the sheet.

Reading Position. Type material two lines above what has been computed as exact center.

Alternate Method. Insert the paper; roll it to the vertical center. Roll the cylinder back (toward you) once for every two lines in the copy to be typed. This will place the copy in exact vertical center. To type a problem in reading position, roll the cylinder back two additional lines.

Spacing after Headings. Leave one blank line between a main and a secondary heading and between a columnar heading and its column. Leave two blank lines after a main heading if a secondary heading is not used, or after a secondary heading when a main heading and a secondary heading are both used.

HORIBONTAL PLACEMENT OF TABULATIONS

Headings. After spacing down to allow for the top margin as determined by vertical placement computations, center the main heading; double-space and center the secondary heading (if one is used); then triple-space.

Columns. Note the longest item in each column (if a columnar heading is the longest item, count it as such unless judgment indicates otherwise). Decide the number of spaces to leave between columns.

Backspace from the center of the page once for every two spaces in the longest item in each column and once for every two spaces between all the columns. At the point where you finish backspacing, set the left margin stop for the first column.

From the left margin, space forward once for every stroke in the longest item of the first column and once for each space between the first and second columns. Set the first tab stop. Follow this same procedure for setting tab stops for the remaining columns.

Columnar Headings. Center columnar headings over the columns. When a heading has been counted as the longest item in a column, it may be necessary to reset the tab stop in order to center the column under the heading.

There are several methods of centering columnar headings over a column, but probably the easiest way is to add the figures from the cylinder scale for the first and last strokes in the column. Dividing this sum by 2 will result in the center point of the column.

Columnar headings are usually underlined.

HORIZONTAL RULINGS

Horizontal lines are often used in tabulated reports to set off the columnar headings. A double line is usually placed above columnar headings and a single line below them. A single line is also placed under the last line of the report. These lines can be the exact width of the report, or they can extend several spaces on each side of it.

To type rulings the exact width of the report, first determine the placement of columns. When you set the tab stop for the last column, continue spacing forward one space for each stroke in the longest item in that column. Immediately after stroking for the last stroke in this item, move the right margin stop so that the typewriter will lock at that point. Rulings can then be typed across the page until the carriage locks.

Double Lines. Double-space from the last line of the heading; type the first of the double lines; then operate the variable line spacer; move the cylinder forward slightly; type the second line. Double-space between this double line and the columnar headings.

Single Lines. Single-space from columnar headings; type a single line. Double-space after this line before typing columnar entries.

Single-space after typing the last columnar entries and type a single line.

Source Note (If Used). Double-space from the single line; type the source note at the left margin or indent 3 to 5 spaces.

TABULATOR STOPS FOR UNEVEN COLUMNS

Uneven Columns. When columns contain amounts of figures of uneven length, set the tab stop at a point that will take care of the greatest number of entries. After tabulating, backspace for longer items or space forward for shorter ones.

Dollar Signs. In a money column, type a dollar sign before the first amount in the column and before the total (if one is shown). Place the dollar sign before the first amount and the total, typed so that it will be one space to the left of the longest amount in the column.

Totals. Totals are treated as a part of the column. To make them easier to read, totals are usually separated by a double space from the column.

102D: Production Measurement: Special Communication Forms ㉚ 20' timing; errors corrected; figure n-pram

Problem 1: Block Style Letter

124 words; open punctuation;
block style; model on page 174

	Words
January 10, 19-- Mr. Harry M. Bing, Man-	8
ager Continental Supply Company 3331 Sher-	16
wood Street Boise, ID 83706 Dear Mr.	24
Bing (¶1) We never upset the balance of	31
nature. When we cut the drawer facing for	39
an IDEAL desk pedestal, we cut from the same	48
piece of walnut or teak. In that way, the	57
beauty of the grain pattern doesn't get lost.	66
(¶2) Most desk manufacturers run the grain	74
across. They get more drawers out of a piece	83
of wood, but they lose nature's design. (¶3)	91
At IDEAL, we pay so much attention to the	100
little things that the big ones take care of	109
themselves--like smoothly gliding drawers,	117
flawless finishes, and rattleproof construction.	127
(¶4) Why not see what we mean at your	134
IDEAL branch or dealer showroom? He is	142
listed in the Yellow Pages. Very truly yours	151
Sanford Thurber, Sales Manager	158/176

Problem 2: AMS Letter

123 words; open punctuation; AMS simplified letter
style; model on page 176; capitalize and punctuate

	Words
january 10, 19-- mr d c vasquez vice-president	10
orient importers inc 3151½ livingston avenue	20
niagara falls ny 14303 the choice is yours	29
(¶1) There are two kinds of belt dictating	36
machines--magnetic and visible. We are the	45
only company that offers both. Since we	53
make both, we are perfectly content to let	62
you make your own choice. It is easy to	70
be objective when you have no axe to grind.	79
(¶2) You can choose our DICTATION-MASTER	86
Magnetic and get a reusable dictation belt that	96
lets you erase and correct your own mistakes.	105
Or you can choose our DICTATION-MASTER	113
Visible that lets you find your place instantly	123
and makes a permanent record of your dicta-	131
tion. (¶3) A telephone call will get a	138
DICTATION-MASTER representative right over	147
to help you make your choice. lawrence wood-	155
side sales manager	160/181

Problem 3: Interoffice Memorandum

Interoffice memo form; SS the message; 1" side
margins; model on p. 179; interoffice envelope

	Words
TO: Henry O. McGraw, Personnel Director	7
FROM: H. B. Layne, Training Supervisor	14
DATE: July 30, 19-- **SUBJECT:** Placement of	19
Trainees (¶) On August 1, two trainees	26
(presently working in the Duplicating Depart-	35
ment) will have satisfactorily completed their	45
training with a sufficient amount of skill in	54
order to be eligible for jobs on our regular	63
staff as soon as suitable vacancies occur.	72
These trainees are Lynn Roget, a clerk-typist	81
who speaks French fluently, and Donna Far-	89
num, a stenographer.	94/103

Problem 4: File Copy of Telegram

Full sheet; 2" top margin;
60-space line; DS message

	Words
TELEGRAM Telegram January 12, 19--, 11:30	8
a.m. Herman Brode, President National	16
Dynamics, Inc. 3119 Monroe Street Ports-	24
mouth, Virginia (¶) Inventories at capacity	32
or over. Confident we can furnish supplies as	41
needed for Gulf Bridge structure. Sufficient	50
cable for two bridges. Marvin Hunter, Man-	59
ager National Cable Corporation (*your initials*	66
as typist)	

Problem 5: Postal Card

48-space line; block style; SS; address
card to Harry M. Bing (Problem 1)

	Words
January 20, 19-- Dear Mr. Bing (¶) You are	8
very cordially invited to a demonstration of	17
IDEAL'S new "feed itself" Copier. You just set	26
the dial for the number of copies you want.	35
When all copies are made, the IDEAL shuts	44
itself off. It has many other new features.	53
You will want to see them. Sanford Thurber,	62
Sales Manager *Return address on card:* Ideal	65/83
Office Equipment Co. 4114 Rose Street, Boise,	
ID 83703	

113D Technique Improvement: Response Patterns [15] *each line five times*

Stroke	Most prominent executives possess superior facility in communications.
Word	What is done is done--we learn from the past, but we cannot change it.
Combination	Desire for personal growth can lead a man to the books he should read.
Combination	A young man who wants to go to the top learns to express himself well.
Combination	Although it may seem longer, it pays to do a job right the first time.
	| 1 | 2 | 3 | 4 | 5 | 6 | 7 | 8 | 9 | 10 | 11 | 12 | 13 | 14 |

LESSON 114

114A Preparatory Practice [5] *each line three or more times*

Alphabet	Fred McBee's organization works hard extirpating juvenile delinquency.
Figure-symbol	The invoice cited "24 doz. prs. #5083 shoes @ $17.39 (less 65¢) a pr."
Adjacent keys	We were assured Polk Power Saws were proper saws to cut sides 32 x 45.
Fluency	Your personality might get you a job, but skills must hold it for you.
	| 1 | 2 | 3 | 4 | 5 | 6 | 7 | 8 | 9 | 10 | 11 | 12 | 13 | 14 |

114B Skill-Comparison Typing [5] *each line for 1′; compare rates*

Goal sentence	He is sure to say that you can gain ability by meeting difficult jobs.
Hyphen	The well-to-do manager solicited the funds in a door-to-door campaign.
Weak finger	Only I was quite puzzled by his apparent lack of aptitude for the job.
	| 1 | 2 | 3 | 4 | 5 | 6 | 7 | 8 | 9 | 10 | 11 | 12 | 13 | 14 |

114C Communication Aid: Apostrophe [10]

Full sheet; 1½″ top margin; 70-space line; SS with DS between items

1. For the heading, type APOSTROPHE.
2. Type the rules and examples given below (with numbers); underline the side headings.
3. Compose and type four sentences, each sentence illustrating one rule. Number these sentences to correspond with the rules.

Words

APOSTROPHE 2

Rules 4

(1) The singular possessive is usually formed by adding 's; but for words 19
having more than one syllable and ending in s, only the apostrophe 33
is added. 35

(2) When plural nouns do not end in s, add 's to form the possessive. 50

(3) Add only the apostrophe to form the possessive of plural nouns ending 65
in s. 66

(4) The possessive of initials, abbreviations, etc., is formed with 's. 81

Examples 84

(1) The Countess' son (my boss's uncle) financed all his boy's trips. 98

(2) Children's shoes and women's robes are on sale at the local shop. 112

(3) The girls' shoes and boys' coats will be shipped by fast express. 126

(4) William Wright, Jr.'s signature must appear on the YMCA's checks. 140

Other Examples 146

SECTION 17 TECHNICAL PAPERS AND BUSINESS REPORTS

LESSONS 103–110

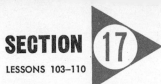

Unless otherwise directed, proceed as follows:
Drill Copy: Full sheet; 70-space line; SS.
Paragraph Copy: Full sheet; 70-space line; DS; 5-space ¶ indention.

Production Copy: Follow directions given with the problems. Erase and correct errors.

LESSON 103

103A Preparatory Practice (5) *each line three or more times*

Alphabet	James Forrest's proxy quickly voted to recognize the required bylaws.
Figure-symbol	Felt & Blane's address is 7290 East 356th Street (Telephone 452–8134).
Quiet hands	Popular Queen Paula saw the purple azaleas on display at my dormitory.
Fluency	We should learn to spell, because we will have to do it all our lives.

| 1 | 2 | 3 | 4 | 5 | 6 | 7 | 8 | 9 | 10 | 11 | 12 | 13 | 14 |

103B Building Control (15) *two 1′ control level writings on each ¶; then two 3′ writings on all ¶s*

All letters are used.

		GWAM 1′	3′	
¶ 1 1.5 SI 5.6 AWL 80% HFW	The adage, "Give credit when credit is due," means that credit can	13	4	72
	be granted to deserving customers; if not merited, it must be denied.	28	9	77
	Another policy can mean financial loss. A man's character is crucial in	42	14	81
	credit matters, as is his power to pay. Can he pay? There is no sure	57	19	86
	answer, but business ability and honor must be weighed.	68	23	90
¶ 2 1.5 SI 5.6 AWL 80% HFW	In addition to character and power to pay, the resources of the	13	27	94
	man must be examined. If he has adequate assets available, you can	26	31	98
	expect him to pay all his bills when they become due. If the capital	40	36	103
	in the owner's name comes primarily from earnings, he is usually a good	55	41	108
	charge risk. Earning reports must be analyzed with caution.	67	45	112
¶ 3 1.5 SI 5.6 AWL 80% HFW	Finally, the general condition of the industry in which a man is	13	49	116
	engaged must be weighed. It is not enough to judge a man's credit	26	54	121
	potential by the three C's of credit: character, capacity, and capital.	41	59	126
	All factors must be looked at in the light of the economic conditions	55	63	131
	that prevail, for many elements are part of the total picture.	68	67	135

1′ GWAM | 1 | 2 | 3 | 4 | 5 | 6 | 7 | 8 | 9 | 10 | 11 | 12 | 13 | 14 |
3′ GWAM | 1 | 2 | 3 | 4 | 5 |

SECTION 19 TABLES

LESSONS 113–120

Unless otherwise directed, proceed as follows:
Drill Copy: Full sheet; 70-space line; SS.
Paragraph Copy: Full sheet; 70-space line; DS; 5-space ¶ indention.

Production Copy: Follow directions for each problem. You need not make carbon copies of the problems in this section.

LESSON 113

113A Preparatory Practice (5) *each line three or more times*

Alphabet	Howard Long paid the tax on five quarts of gray paint for Jack Bozman.
Figure-symbol	The footnote (*) refers to p. 230 of Vol. 45, the May 27, 1968, issue.
Outside keys	Paul X. Wazo passed the quiz; he knew (at last) "Vox populi, vox Dei."
Fluency	The busy worker knows that 60 minutes in an hour is never enough time.

| 1 | 2 | 3 | 4 | 5 | 6 | 7 | 8 | 9 | 10 | 11 | 12 | 13 | 14 |

113B Building Speed (15)

1. Type three ½′ writings; reach for 30 or more words in that time.
2. Type three 1′ writings; reach for 60 or more words.
3. Type three 1½′ writings; reach for 90 or more words.

The goals are marked in the copy.

1.5 SI
5.6 AWL
80% HFW

1′ GWAM

As you begin to type, make very certain you are sitting in a 12
proper position. Sit well back in the chair; keep your feet flat on 26
the floor for good [30] equilibrium. Position the copy so that you can read 41
it easily. Adjust the typewriter, the desk, and the chair until they 55
are in a suitable position [60] in accordance with your height. Be alert, 69
but be comfortable. In conclusion, approach each task with a positive 83
attitude. You can improve your typing [90] ability by adding to the cer- 96
tainty with which you work. 102

1′ GWAM | 1 | 2 | 3 | 4 | 5 | 6 | 7 | 8 | 9 | 10 | 11 | 12 | 13 | 14 |

113C Technique Improvement: Tabulating (15) *type the drill three times on one sheet*

Full sheet; 3″ top margin; SS; decide spaces between columns

			Words
31,730	53,108	45,041	4
16,235	27,372	13,132	8
52,546	25,153	75,784	13
76,317	42,768	47,465	17
98,900	68,985	38,479	21
17,480	10,356	47,925	25

103C Technique Improvement: Typing by Combination Response [15]

each sentence three times; repeat a line on which you have made more than one error

1 Use two hyphens to type the dash--without space before and after them.

2 Either you or I can go. Neither of us has a session during that hour.

3 "We shall go tomorrow," said John. "We will go right now!" I shouted.

4 As I rode farther up the trail, I tried to analyze my problem further.

5 I am anxious about the last test, but I am eager to take the next one.

| 1 | 2 | 3 | 4 | 5 | 6 | 7 | 8 | 9 | 10 | 11 | 12 | 13 | 14 |

103D Skill-Comparison and Transfer Typing [15] *two 1′ writings on each sentence*

Try reaching the rates set on the goal sentence in typing succeeding sentences. Type additional writings on the sentence on which you need to make the most improvement.

			Words
1	Goal sentence	Just initial and return the enclosed order form to us today.	12
2	Weak fingers	I was puzzled by his apparent lack of aptitude for this job.	12
3	Direct reaches	Trudy hummed a hymn on the great stage and had fun doing so.	12
4	Rough draft	Ple^a^se wri te ^if^ you have ~~some~~ any ques ti ons a bout ~~the~~ our op~~p~~erations.	12
5	Script	*We appreciate the confidence you have placed in our company.*	12

LESSON 104

104A Preparatory Practice [5] *each line three or more times*

Alphabet — In a truly amazing way, John's books quickly verified his tax reports.

Figure-symbol — The tags marked * say: "Sell @ $17.89 each or @ $5,326.40 a carload."

Drill on a, u — Thousands of us order sauerkraut to inaugurate an auspicious New Year.

Fluency — Finish the job; in most cases it is the final half that really counts.

| 1 | 2 | 3 | 4 | 5 | 6 | 7 | 8 | 9 | 10 | 11 | 12 | 13 | 14 |

104B Skill-Comparison and Transfer Typing [15] *two 1′ writings on each sentence in 103D, above; compare* gwam

104C Production Typing: Outline [30]

2 full sheets; 6″ writing line; 2″ top margin

1. Type the outline on page 185. As a reminder to leave about a 1″ bottom margin on the first page, make a light pencil mark about 1½″ from the bottom edge. (Erase the mark later.) Center the page number on the first page ½″ from the bottom of the page.

2. On the second page, type the page number, 2, in the upper right corner even with the right margin ½″ from the top of the page. Begin typing the copy for the second page on Line 7.

line 4

Two spaces follow the period after lettered or numbered divisions in an outline.

Problem 2: Last Page of Leftbound Manuscript

Last page, page 6, of leftbound report; see p. 185 for correct form; prepare footnotes from information given

	Words
Classification Systems	9

(¶ 1) The orderly classification of books in a library constitutes an interesting study. The clay tablets discovered in the Assyrian library of Ashurbanipal, 688 to 626 B.C., were grouped under two headings: those dealing with the earth and those dealing with the heavens. Early Jesuit libraries classified their collections under two headings also. On the shelves of one side of the library were the beautifully bound books of the conformists. On the shelves of the other side were the black bound books of the heretics. These early systems had one thing in common: they were based on the contents of the books. This is the way books are classified today.[6] (¶ 2) To avoid confusion, libraries use one of the standard classification systems that have been developed. There are three such systems in use today. They are the Dewey Decimal System, the Cutter System, and the Library of Congress System. (¶ 3) According to Johnson, a classification system has three major functions: (1) to provide a uniform "shorthand" system for indicating the contents of a book, (2) to group books treating similar subjects under the same headings, and (3) to facilitate the physical organization of books on library shelves.[7]

Footnote Information: The material for both footnotes was paraphrased from page 6 of H. Webster Johnson's book, *How To Use the Business Library*, Third Edition, 1964, published by the South-Western Publishing Company, Cincinnati. (*35 words*)

Problem 3: Outline

Full sheet; 2" top and left margins (see p. 185 for correct form)

Add outline designations; indent, space, capitalize, and punctuate the outline correctly.

	Words
how to use the library	5
I. locating books	8
library card catalog	13
information on card	18
author's name	22
title of reference	27
subject of book	32
call number	35
organization of cards	41
cumulative book index	50
list of books in print	56
information included	61
publisher's weekly	69
list of books by week of issue	76
description of subject treated	83
II. classification systems	90
dewey decimal system	95
most widely used	99
based on progressive use of numbers	108
major groupings	112
000--general works	117
100--philosophy	121
200--religion	125
300--social sciences; sociology	133
400--philology	137
500--pure science	142
600--useful arts	147
700--fine arts; recreation	153
800--literature	158
900--history	161
library of congress system	168
cutter system	171

TYPING MANUSCRIPTS AND REPORTS

TS

Align Roman
numerals at
the right ——————

I. MARGINS — 9

Reset margin —————— DS

   A. Unbound Manuscripts and Reports — 16

1st tab stop ——————→ 1. Top: first page, 1½ or 2 inches; other pages, 1 inch — 28

      2. Sides and bottom: 1 inch — 34

   B. Manuscripts and Reports Bound at the Left — 43

      1. Top: first page, 1½ or 2 inches; other pages, 1 inch — 55

      2. Sides: 1½ inches at the left; 1 inch at the right — 66

      3. Bottom: 1 inch — 70

   C. Manuscripts and Reports Bound at the Top — 79

      1. Top: first page, 2 or 2½ inches; other pages, 1½ inches — 92

      2. Sides and bottom: 1 inch — 98

↓——Backspace   DS

II. SPACING — 101

   A. Body — 103

      1. Double-spaced with 5-, 7-, or 10-space paragraph indentions — 116

      2. Quoted material of 4 or more lines single-spaced and indented 5 spaces — 131

2nd tab stop ——————→ from both margins; quotation marks permissible but not required — 145

      3. Tabulated material: single-spaced — 153

   B. Footnotes — 155

      1. Numbered consecutively throughout report, or in books numbering — 169

      started anew with each chapter — 176

      2. Identified by superior figures typed ½ space above the line of writing — 191

      3. Separated from the last line of manuscript by a divider line, approxi- — 206

      mately 1½ inches in length; divider line preceded by a single vertical — 221

      space and followed by a double space — 229

      4. Indented and single-spaced with a double space between footnotes — 243

Determine ——→ **III. HEADINGS AND SUBHEADINGS** — 250
when to
begin the
next page

   A. Main Heading — 254

      1. Centered in all capital letters over the writing line — 265

      2. Followed by a triple space — 272

   B. First-Order Subheadings (Side Headings) — 281

      1. Typed at left margin on separate line and underlined — 292

      2. Main words started with capital letters — 301

      3. Preceded by triple space and followed by double space — 313

   C. Second-Order Subheadings (Paragraph Headings) — 323

      1. Indented as first line of paragraph and underlined — 334

      2. Usually, only first word capitalized — 342

      3. Preceded by a double space — 349

IV. PAGINATION (PAGE NUMBERING) — 356

   A. Unbound and Leftbound Manuscripts and Reports — 366

      1. First page: centered ½ inch from bottom of page — 377

      2. Other pages: on the fourth line even with right margin — 389

   B. Topbound Manuscripts and Reports — 397

      1. All pages: centered ½ inch from bottom edge of paper — 409

      2. Page number separated from text or footnote by at least a triple space — 424

      (A partially filled page will require more than a triple space.) — 437

All letters are used.

	GWAM		
	1'		5'

¶ 1
1.5 SI
5.6 AWL
80% HFW

The goal of a methods modernization program is to find a better way to accomplish the required tasks. The theoretical objective is to find the best way to do a particular job. Many tasks have been studied again and again, and some really significant improvements have been developed. As job requirements change and new tools and goods are produced with which to do a task, new methods will be found by modern man that will ultimately lead to a better way.

14	3	56
28	6	58
43	9	61
57	11	64
71	14	67
85	17	70
92	18	71

¶ 2
1.5 SI
5.6 AWL
80% HFW

Most large companies hire or train analysts to do methods improvement work. When this is not done, enthusiasm in improvement lags because no one has been designated to inject interest in it. In large firms, the selection of a methods analyst is justified. The person must not only direct methods studies of his own, but he must train the workers how to simplify their jobs. As a rule, this plan leads to a better way.

13	21	74
28	24	77
42	27	80
56	30	82
70	32	85
84	35	88

¶ 3
1.5 SI
5.6 AWL
80% HFW

One special tool that methods experts use to study work procedures is the flow chart. It is simply nothing more than a picture of each step through which a paper goes in order to process the particular data. Every step is shown by a symbol. A symbol indicates what operation takes place and what machine, if any, is needed to handle it. With a chart before them, analysts can visualize the total job and discover better ways of doing it.

13	38	91
27	41	93
41	43	96
55	46	99
68	49	102
82	52	104
88	53	106

```
1' GWAM | 1 | 2 | 3 | 4 | 5 | 6 | 7 | 8 | 9 | 10 | 11 | 12 | 13 | 14 |
5' GWAM |       1       |       2       |       3       |
```

112C Production Measurement: Rough Draft; Leftbound Manuscript; Outline (30)

20' for typing; errors corrected; compute n-pram

Problem 1: Rough Draft

Leftbound manuscript form; 2" top margin (see p. 185 for correct form)

	Words
	3

The Dictionary

A good dictionary contains all of the principal words in a language. Such a book, sometimes called a lexicon, is equipped with words that are currently acceptible as good usage. Those words are called the standard words; that is, they are words that a speaker or writer would normally use. These are several hundred thousand standard words; and consequently, a good dictionary contains many words that the typical person sees or heard rarely. It is a recognized fact that most people have [only an "average" vocabulary with "understandable" pronunciation. In fact, and average college student might be embarassed to discover he is familiar with the meaning and pronunciation of fewer less than then one tenth of all the works in his language.

| 14 |
| 28 |
| 41 |
| 56 |
| 69 |
| 80 |
| 93 |
| 104 |
| 118 |
| 130 |
| 142 |
| 151 |

LESSON 105

105A Preparatory Practice [5] *each line three or more times*

Alphabet	After a week's probe, the lazy jury acquitted 27 men of evading taxes.
Figure-symbol	Models #823–7 and #495–1 are available at discounts of from 6% to 10%.
One hand	Polly Young and Jon Cassavetes were dressed for the "Lollipop Minuet."
Fluency	Just one ounce of appreciation is often worth many pounds of pressure.
	| 1 | 2 | 3 | 4 | 5 | 6 | 7 | 8 | 9 | 10 | 11 | 12 | 13 | 14 |

105B Sentence Guided Writings [10]

Type two or more 1′ writings on each sentence with the guide called each 15, 12, or 10 seconds. Try completing a sentence and returning your carriage as the guide is called.

		GWAM 15″	12″	10″
1	If they agree to this proposal, we can send them a corrected contract.	56	70	84
2	Anyone who works in this company must be skillful as well as pleasant.	56	70	84
3	To erase an error near the end of a page, roll the paper down, not up.	56	70	84
4	The talent of success is nothing more than doing what you can do well.	56	70	84
	| 1 | 2 | 3 | 4 | 5 | 6 | 7 | 8 | 9 | 10 | 11 | 12 | 13 | 14 |			

105C Production Typing: Topbound Manuscript with Footnotes [35]

1. Before you type the manuscript on pages 187-188, read the material carefully so that you will understand its content.
2. Type the manuscript in topbound form (see page 185) with a 2″ top margin for the first page and a 1½″ top margin for succeeding pages. Use a 5-space paragraph indention. Number the pages.
3. Type each footnote on the page on which the reference appears even though all footnotes are given at the end of the report in the problem. Be sure to leave enough space at the bottom of a page for the 1-inch margin and footnotes. Number the footnotes from 1 up throughout the manuscript.
4. The illustration at the right shows the second page of the manuscript (typed in pica type).

Note. You will not complete this problem in this lesson; additional time is given in Lessons 106 and 107.

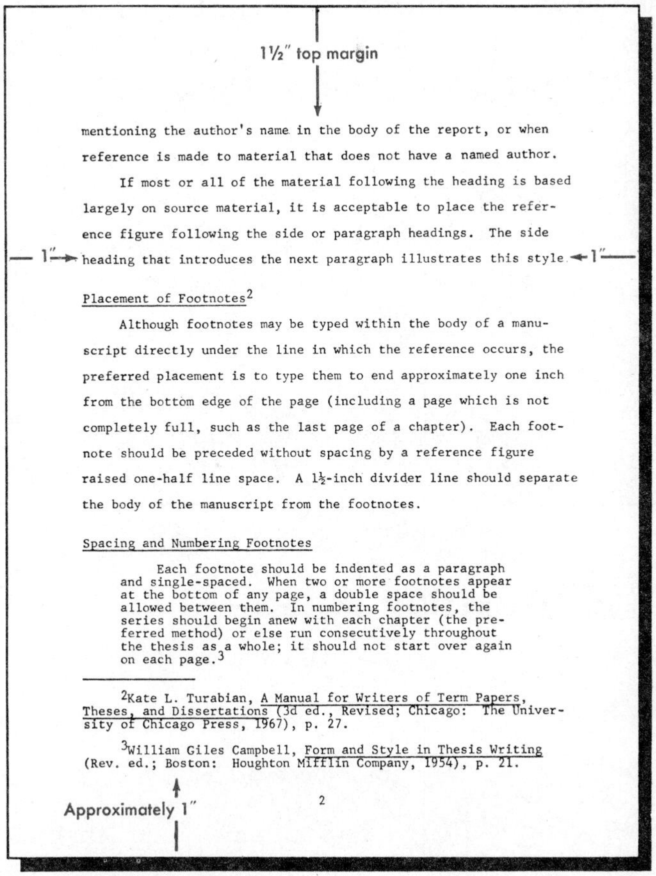

mentioning the author's name in the body of the report, or when reference is made to material that does not have a named author.

If most or all of the material following the heading is based largely on source material, it is acceptable to place the reference figure following the side or paragraph headings. The side heading that introduces the next paragraph illustrates this style.

Placement of Footnotes[2]

Although footnotes may be typed within the body of a manuscript directly under the line in which the reference occurs, the preferred placement is to type them to end approximately one inch from the bottom edge of the page (including a page which is not completely full, such as the last page of a chapter). Each footnote should be preceded without spacing by a reference figure raised one-half line space. A 1½-inch divider line should separate the body of the manuscript from the footnotes.

Spacing and Numbering Footnotes

Each footnote should be indented as a paragraph and single-spaced. When two or more footnotes appear at the bottom of any page, a double space should be allowed between them. In numbering footnotes, the series should begin anew with each chapter (the preferred method) or else run consecutively throughout the thesis as a whole; it should not start over again on each page.[3]

[2]Kate L. Turabian, A Manual for Writers of Term Papers, Theses, and Dissertations (3d ed., Revised; Chicago: The University of Chicago Press, 1967), p. 27.

[3]William Giles Campbell, Form and Style in Thesis Writing (Rev. ed.; Boston: Houghton Mifflin Company, 1954), p. 21.

2

Problem 2: Modified Block Style Letter with Reply Reference and Carbon Copy Notations

125 words; mixed punctuation; centered reply reference; 2 carbon copies

Words

mr louis la croix, chief engineer south bend 12
building corporation 22100 bernice street south 22
bend in 46637 dear mr la croix reference, con- 31
tract #1322 (¶ 1) You may begin work on the 39
property at 5522 Berkley Place, South Bend. 48
Please notify us when trenches have been dug 57
and forms have been placed so that we may 65
inspect them before the foundation is poured. 75
(¶ 2) At least 24 hours before requesting pay- 83
ment under the building loan agreement, 91
please call for an inspection. The expense of 100
a second inspection, if one is necessary, must 109
be borne by the contractor. (¶ 3) It will be 117
necessary for you to obtain, at this office, 126
receipt forms which must be signed by sub- 135
contractors and material dealers as payments 144
are made. If you wish, call us; and we shall 153
send the forms to you by mail. yours very 161
truly roy l calhoun chief architect cc mr 171
thomas best 173/195

Problem 3: AMS Simplified Letter with Mailing and Enclosure Notations

114 words; open punctuation; airmail notation; 1 carbon copy

Words

mr mason brown president brown–scranton 13
advertising agency 3412 longfellow street 22
allentown pa 18104 you get less with fore- 30
most (¶ 1) You get a lot less with a Fore- 37
most Dictation System. There are no belts, 46
no tapes, no discs to adjust. You just pick up 56
the simple handset and dictate. (¶ 2) A light 64
comes on at your secretary's desk. To tran- 72
scribe, she slips on a tiny headset and types-- 82
even as you dictate--if she wishes. If she is 91
busy, Foremost will store the recorded mate- 100
rial until later, automatically. Result? You 109
get less confusion, less frustration, more at- 118
tention, and more accomplished. (¶ 3) Read 127
the enclosed folder; then ask your Foremost 135
dealer to install a set for a week's free trial. 145
charles b whitcomb sales manager enclosure 154/175

Problem 4: Interoffice Memorandum

Full sheet; SS message

Words

TO: All Division Managers **FROM:** Avril 6
Burnstein, Controller **DATE:** (*current*) **SUB-** 13
JECT: Foremost Dictation Sets Available 20
(¶ 1) Foremost Dictation Sets are now avail- 27
able to all division managers. This system has 37
been checked out in my office and found to be 46
very efficient. I suggest that you see the set 56
in my office before you decide to order one. 65
The attached folder gives you details. (¶ 2) 73
If you wish, we can install a dictation set in 82
your office for a trial period. Installation of a 93
set takes but a few minutes. Enclosure 101

LESSON 112

112A Preparatory Practice [5] *each line three or more times*

Alphabet	The Jazz Quintet will play excellent background music for a new movie.
Figure-symbol	The problems are 276 ÷ 13 and 845 ÷ 90; set them up this way: 13)276.
Double letters	My committee addressed letters to Miss Barbara Serere, 77 Hill Street.
Fluency	The things at which men laugh often tell you the kind of men they are.
	| 1 | 2 | 3 | 4 | 5 | 6 | 7 | 8 | 9 | 10 | 11 | 12 | 13 | 14 |

FOOTNOTE GUIDES

TS

Words

(1) The guides for handling footnotes and footnote references in this report are based on a careful study of standard reference works, such as those by the University of Chicago Press, Turabian, Campbell, Harbrace, and Perrin. While these authorities do not agree with one another on all points of style, the guides recommended in this report are based on majority practice.

TS

Placement of Footnote Reference Figures

DS

(¶ 2) Footnote reference figures (superscripts) should be placed in a manuscript so that the least interruption in thought results. Four placements of footnote reference figures are in common use. They are described below. (¶ 3) The preferred practice is to place the reference figure at the end of material that is directly or indirectly quoted or paraphrased.[1] An almost equally acceptable practice is to place the reference figure at the end of the statement that introduces directly quoted material. (4) A less acceptable practice, but one enjoying considerable use, is to place the reference figure after the name of the author of the reference. A major disadvantage of this practice is the inconsistency that results if references are made to materials without mentioning the author's name in the body of the report, or when reference is made to material that does not have a named author. (5) If most or all of the material following the heading is based largely on source material, it is acceptable to place the reference figure following the side or paragraph headings. The side heading that introduces the next paragraph illustrates this style.

Placement of Footnotes [2]

Words

(¶ 6) Although footnotes may be typed within the body of a manuscript directly under the line in which the reference occurs, the preferred placement is to type them to end approximately one inch from the bottom edge of the page (including a page which is not completely full, such as the last page of a chapter). Each footnote should be preceded without spacing by a reference figure raised one-half line space. A 1½-inch divider line should separate the body of the manuscript from the footnotes.

Spacing and Numbering Footnotes

DS; SS the ¶

(¶ 7) Each footnote should be indented as a paragraph and single-spaced. When two or more footnotes appear at the bottom of any page, a double space should be allowed between them. In numbering footnotes, the series should begin anew with each chapter (the preferred method) or else run consecutively throughout the thesis as a whole; it should not start over again on each page.[3]

(¶ 8) Two or more short footnotes may be typed on one line if they are separated by at least two blank spaces. In no instance, however, may a footnote so begun be continued on a second line. (¶ 9) Lengthy footnotes containing explanatory material may be continued to the foot of the next page, above any footnotes for that page. They should be broken in the middle of a sentence to make it obvious that the footnote is incomplete.

Form of Footnotes

(¶ 10) The footnotes that follow represent the consensus of authorities for basic style and defensible compromise of differences on points on which some authorities disagree. (¶ 11) There is a generally accepted, brief form of footnote that can be used when a complete

SECTION 18 MEASUREMENT: Basic and Production Skills

LESSONS 111–112

Production Measurement

You will be directed to type representative problems from prior lessons. Follow the original directions for each problem. Since these problems are timed, get ready to type quickly. Use the current date if none is given; your reference initials; appropriate envelope; erase and correct errors. Unless otherwise directed, follow this procedure:

Drill Copy: Full sheet; 70-space line; SS.
Paragraph Copy: Full sheet, 70-space line; DS; 5-space ¶ indention.

Materials Needed

Letterheads (or full sheets); carbon sheets; file copy sheets; interoffice communication forms (if available); envelopes of appropriate size.

$$\text{N-PRAM} = \frac{\text{Gross (total) words} - \text{Penalties}}{\text{Length (in minutes) of writing}}$$

Penalties for Errors: Deduct 10 words for each error not erased on an original copy; deduct 5 words for each error not erased on a carbon copy.

LESSON 111

111A Preparatory Practice [5] *each line three or more times*

Alphabet	We quickly proved the existence of the glazed lamp you just described.
Figure-symbol	Cox & Conan's office, 3450 Cord Street, opened May 12, 1967, at 8 a.m.
Drill on i, o	Ohio's position as a contributor to this nation's growth is improving.
Fluency	Each of us will steer his ship by the star he has chosen to guide him.

| 1 | 2 | 3 | 4 | 5 | 6 | 7 | 8 | 9 | 10 | 11 | 12 | 13 | 14 |

111B Building Speed [15] *type 109C, page 191, as directed there*

111C Production Measurement: Business Letters [30] *20′ timing; errors corrected; figure* n-pram

Problem 1: Block Style Letter with Subject Line, Enclosure Notation, and Postscript

116 words; open punctuation; blocked subject line; carbon copy

Words

miss sue fremont lowell-grant agency 7751 12
highland drive salt lake city ut 84121 20
dear miss fremont subject susan longlade con- 29
cert (¶ 1) The contract you sent us for the 37
Susan Longlade concert was signed this morn- 45
ing. We are retaining one copy for our files; 55
the original is enclosed. (¶ 2) The Arts Board 63
has asked me to express to you its sincere 72
gratitude for obtaining this engagement for 81
us. We are most pleased to add Mlle. Long- 89
lade's program to our list of winter perform- 98
ances, which now includes Alfred Stone, the 107
McKinley Dancers, Fern Madison, and Do- 115
menica Leschenko. (¶ 3) If there is anything 123
I can do to help with the local arrangements 132
for the Longlade concert, please let me know. 141
I shall be glad to help. Sincerely yours martin 151
v kenton chairman arts board enclosure: 160
signed contract (Postscript) Please send photo- 167
graphs and publicity on Susan Longlade for 175
use in our promotion of the concert. 183/199

bibliography is included with the report. This 673
form is illustrated in normal footnote position 682
in Footnote 4 below.[4] (¶ 12) The complete 690
footnote for a book reference is given in Foot- 699
note 1. Observe the footnote style used when 708
reference is made to a work for which no au- 717
thor is given.[5] (¶ 13) When reference must be 725
made to an article appearing in a magazine, 733
the form illustrated in Footnote 6 is recom- 742
mended.[6] When no author is given for a 750
magazine article and when the volume and 758
issue number are not known or given, the 766
form illustrated in Footnote 7 is preferred.[7] 776
(¶ 14) Governmental agencies acting as au- 783
thors are listed with the largest body first, 792
followed by its division and subdivision in 801
order. For printed works available from the 810
U.S. Government Printing Office, the facts of 819
publication are as shown.[8] (¶ 15) For refer- 826
ences to lectures and speeches, the pertinent 835
available facts are placed in parentheses after 845
the name of the speaker and the title of the 854
lecture or speech.[9] Unpublished reports, min- 863
utes, letters, and the like, are credited infor- 872
mally by showing the available facts in logical 882
order without parentheses.[10] (¶ 16) When 889
two footnotes contain references to the same 898
work and one follows the other without inter- 906
vening footnotes, use Ibid., the abbreviation 916
for ibidem (in the same place), and the exact 927
page number for the second footnote if it 935
differs from the first one.[11] (¶ 17) When a 943
footnote refers to a different page in a work 952
already cited and one or two footnotes sepa- 961
rate it from the first one, use the author's 970
name and the notation op. cit., the abbrevia- 980
tion for opere citato (meaning in the work 991
cited), with the page number, instead of re- 999
peating the name of the publication and other 1009
identifying data.[12] (¶ 18) If the footnote ref- 1017
erence is to precisely the same matter covered 1026
by a reference not immediately preceding, use 1035

the author's name and loc. cit., the abbrevia- 1046
tion for loco citato (meaning in the place 1057
cited). Page numbers do not follow the form 1066
loc. cit. for the simple reason that they are 1077
unnecessary.[13] 1079

SS and type divider line
DS to footnotes

[1] Peyton Hurt, Bibliography and Footnotes (Rev. ed.; Berkeley: University of California Press, 1963), p. 61. (30 words)

[2] Kate L. Turabian, A Manual for Writers
of Term Papers, Theses, and Dissertations
(3d ed., Revised; Chicago: The University of
Chicago Press, 1967), p. 27. (46 words)

[3] William Giles Campbell, Form and Style
in Thesis Writing (Rev. ed.; Boston: Houghton Mifflin Company, 1954), p. 21. (26 words)

[4] Bruce Bliven, Jr., The Wonderful Writing Machine, p. 25. (21 words)

[5] Life Insurance Fact Book (New York:
Institute of Life Insurance, 1957), p. 30. (21
words)

[6] George A. W. Boehm, "How They Pre-
dict the Economic Future," Think, Vol.
XXXIII, No. 4 (July-August, 1967), p. 8. (24
words)

[7] "Office Services in an Age of Sophistication," Administrative Management (November, 1967), pp. 20-26. (25 words)

[8] U.S. Bureau of the Census, Statistical
Abstract of the United States: 1966 (87th
ed.; Washington: U.S. Government Printing
Office, 1966), p. 66. (38 words)

[9] Lainie Koslyn, "Profile of a Secretary"
(From a lecture to the National Secretaries
Association, Honolulu, March 18, 1968). (29
words)

[10] From a letter written by Margaret
MacMillan to Judy Bennett, April 5, 1967. (15
words)

[11] Ibid., p. 2. (4 words)

[12] Bruce Bliven, op. cit., p. 52. (8 words)

[13] William Giles Campbell, loc. cit. (9
words)

¶ Large] company*ies* will *rent or* buy th*eir* machines; small ones will ad*o*pt   151

time-sharing plans by#which for as little *as* $350 they will#be able   165

to use *a* computer*s* 25 hours a month. Packaged programs *covering* ~~for~~ ac-   176

counting procedures for *a variety of* industries will#be # *available* at relatively small   195

cost. Virtually ever*y*one in the office will, *be expected to* know how to use *the* ~~a~~   207

computer.   209

←────────────── Copying Duplication Machines   220

     Machines us*ing* the electrostatic *copying* process will *continue to* dominate   235
the field. An off⁀set duplication machine has been developed,   248
however, that can print on both sides of a sheet in one opera-   260
tion. In addition, a new mimeograph stencil has been developed   273
ds that can be inserted with the original copy into a copier.   285
no¶ The copier cuts the stencil in a matter of seconds. Costs   297
of copying equipment, now quite high, will go down. Plans are   309
currently under way to ma⁀ke*t* a "family copier" very short⁀ly   321
for less than $30. The books and magazines of the future may   334
not be prepared on big presses, bound, and mailed the way th*ey*   346
are today. According to Kleinschrod: 354

     ¶ Page] ima*g*es may be stored on super-miniaturized   364
     microfiche--some catalog publishers are doing this   374
     already--to be mailed far less expensively in small   384
     thin envelopes. You then ask the system for en-   394
     larged h*a*rd copies of only those pages that inter-   404
     est you.²   406

Triple-space

Problems Created by Machine⁀ry   418

     The \most pressing/ ~~two~~ problems *reported* by administrative managers   431

in connection with the a*d*vent of *the* Office Machine age are break-   444

[downs and inadequately trained *operators* ~~people~~. Office *machines* ~~equipment~~ of   457

the 1970's will be *more* complex. extensive traini*ng* will be need*ed*   470

to \ *o*perate them, \many and\ skilled technic*i*ans will be needed   482

to ~~maintain them.~~ *keep them in repair.*   487

─────────────────
¹ Kleinschrod, \Walter/ "Office Services in an Age of Sophistication," Administrative Management (November, 1967), pp. 20-26. *(34 words)*

     ² Ibid., p. 24.   *(7 words)*

LESSON 106

106A Preparatory Practice [5] *each line three or more times*

Alphabet — Equip the tug Zyma B for work and expect her to be judged serviceable.

Figure-symbol — In 1925, A & E Company's net sales were $283,490; in 1968, $6,708,351.

One hand — The sea breezes were piling up the waves into great rolling mountains.

Fluency — We can always do more good by being good than we can in any other way.

| 1 | 2 | 3 | 4 | 5 | 6 | 7 | 8 | 9 | 10 | 11 | 12 | 13 | 14 |

106B Building Control [15] *(12′ timing)*

Working for 12 minutes, type as many errorless copies of ¶ 1, page 183, as you can. Type from the textbook. Score 1 point for each errorless copy of the paragraph. A score of 2 is *acceptable*; 3, *good*; 4, *very good*; 5 or above, *excellent*.

106C Production Typing: Topbound Manuscript with Footnotes [30] *continue typing 105C, pages 186-188*

LESSON 107

107A Preparatory Practice [5] *each line three or more times*

Alphabet — Subsequently, Jack wouldn't have a copy of my magazine, The Executive.

Figure-symbol — King & Wynn collected $6,582, plus 4½% interest, less $137.90 in fees.

Long words — Vehicular traffic commenced utilizing the enormous structure Thursday.

Fluency — The trouble with a temper is that it can be lost when we need it most.

| 1 | 2 | 3 | 4 | 5 | 6 | 7 | 8 | 9 | 10 | 11 | 12 | 13 | 14 |

107B Building Control [15] *(12′ timing)*

Working for 12 minutes, type as many errorless copies of ¶ 2, page 183, as you can. Type from the textbook. Score 1 point for each errorless copy of the paragraph. A score of 2 is *acceptable*; 3, *good*; 4, *very good*; 5 or above, *excellent*.

107C Production Typing: Topbound Manuscript with Footnotes [30] *continue typing 105C, pages 186-188*

LESSON 108

108A Preparatory Practice [5] *each line three or more times*

Alphabet — Excessive assignments will often quickly jeopardize both joy and zeal.

Figure-symbol — The * before the A & Z firm name denotes 1968 sales exceeded $234,750.

Inside keys — Janet has just finished tying over fifty bright ribbons on your gifts.

Fluency — It should be reward enough just to know you have done the right thing.

| 1 | 2 | 3 | 4 | 5 | 6 | 7 | 8 | 9 | 10 | 11 | 12 | 13 | 14 |

109D Problem Skill Building [20]

Problem 1: Outline

Type a 10′ writing on 104C, pages 184 and 185. Correct errors; figure *g-pram.*

Problem 2: Bibliography

Type a 5′ writing on 108C, page 190. Correct errors; figure *g-pram.*

LESSON 110

110A Preparatory Practice [5] *each line three or more times*

Alphabet	We were quickly exhausted, proving no match for zebra in wild jungles.
Figure-symbol	Our $1,906.47 payment saved us 37¼ cents (.3725) on each of 138 items.
Drill on a, e	Kathleen Allen has read "The Faerie Queen"; maybe she is rereading it.
Fluency	Our education starts before age 6; it should not end until we pass 96.
	| 1 | 2 | 3 | 4 | 5 | 6 | 7 | 8 | 9 | 10 | 11 | 12 | 13 | 14 |

110B Growth Index [15] *type two 5′* control-level *writings on ¶s of 102C, page 181; compute* gwam *on the better writing*

110C Production Measurement: Rough Draft of a Leftbound Manuscript [30] *20′ timing; figure* n-pram*; repeat if time permits*

Leftbound manuscript form; 2″ top margin (see p. 185 for correct form)

Words

2″ top

The Machine-Age Office) center 5

¶ What highly-sophisticated machines are being ysed in ~~in~~ this coun- 13

try's offices? What ~~questions~~ problems are ~~this~~ these machines presenting 29

and ~~who~~ how are these problems being solved? These are the ques- 41

tions with which this paper deals. The ~~findings~~ answers to these questions are based on a na- 58

tional survey of 500 administrative managers.[1] 68

Computers (Triple-space) 71

All those taking part in this study assert that computers will ~~surely~~ 84

become an indispensable part of the office in the 1970's. Com- 97

puters are now in their ~~3d~~ third generation, and ~~the~~ ~~4th~~ fourth generation ma- 110

chines are just emerging. The ~~third~~ fourth generation computers will be 124

characterized by "firmware," a term denoting packaged programs. 137

108B   Building Control ⑮ *(12' timing)*

Working for 12 minutes, type as many errorless copies of ¶ 3, 103B, page 183, as you can. Type from the textbook. Score 1 point for each errorless copy of the paragraph. A score of 2 is *acceptable*; 3, *good*; 4, *very good*; 5 or above, *excellent*.

108C   Production Typing: Bibliography and Title Page ㉚

Problem 1: Bibliography

Topbound manuscript form; same margins as on p. 1; SS with DS between entries

Type the bibliography below to accompany the manuscript typed as 105C, pages 186-188. Start the first line of each entry at the left margin; set a tab stop to indent the second and succeeding lines 5 spaces. Remember to type the appropriate manuscript page number.

	BIBLIOGRAPHY	Words
	TS	3
One-author book	Bliven, Bruce, Jr. The Wonderful Writing Machine. New York: Random House, 1954.	23 / 25
Magazine article	Boehm, George A. W. "How They Predict the Economic Future," Think. Vol. XXXIII, No. 4 (July-August, 1967), pp. 8-11.	40 / 50
One-author book	Campbell, William Giles. Form and Style in Thesis Writing, Rev. ed. Boston: Houghton Mifflin Company, 1954.	71 / 79
Two-author book	Erlich, Eugene, and Daniel Murphy. Writing and Researching Term Papers and Reports. New York: Bantam Books, 1964.	97 / 108
One-author book	Hurt, Peyton. Bibliography and Footnotes, Rev. ed. Berkeley: University of California Press, 1963.	127 / 133
Lecture notes	Koslyn, Lainie. "Profile of a Secretary." From a lecture to the National Secretaries Association, Honolulu, March 18, 1968.	148 / 158
No author listed	Life Insurance Fact Book. New York: Institute of Life Insurance, 1957.	177 / 178
Letter reference	MacMillan, Margaret. Letter written to Judy Bennett, April 5, 1967.	192
Ignore a, an, or the in alphabetizing	A Manual of Style, 12th ed. Chicago: The University of Chicago Press, 1969.	210 / 211
Magazine article	"Office Services in an Age of Sophistication," Administrative Management. (November, 1967), pp. 20-26.	229 / 237
Author and editors cited	Perrin, Porter G. Writer's Guide and Index to English, 4th ed., prepared and edited by Karl W. Dykema and Wilma R. Ebbitt. Chicago: Scott, Foresman and Company, 1965.	259 / 273 / 278
Government publication	Style Manual. Washington: U.S. Government Printing Office, 1967.	294
One-author book	Turabian, Kate L. A Manual for Writers of Term Papers, Theses, and Dissertations, 3d ed., rev. Chicago: The University of Chicago Press, 1967.	319 / 335 / 336
Government publication	U.S. Bureau of the Census. Statistical Abstract of the United States: 1966, 87th ed. Washington: U.S. Government Printing Office, 1966.	358 / 373

Problem 2: Title Page

1. Center and space on a full sheet of paper the lines at the right as directed.
2. When you have finished typing the title page, arrange all your papers in this order:

   Title page (this problem)
   Manuscript pages (105C, pages 187 and 188)
   Bibliography page (Problem 1, page 190)

3. Fasten all the sheets together at the top.

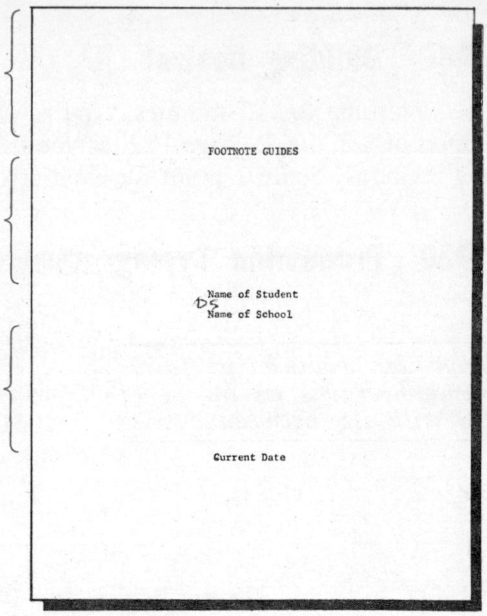

2½″
FOOTNOTE GUIDES
2½″
Name of Student
DS
Name of School
2½″
Current Date

LESSON 109

109A Preparatory Practice [5] *each line three or more times*

Alphabet	I know that an extreme Quebec blizzard may be jeopardizing four lives.
Figure-symbol	Corley & Wellman sent us Check #723 (dated November 19) for $4,867.50.
Long words	The audio-visual environment offers unique opportunities for research.
Fluency	The more they leave to chance the less chance they have of getting it.

| 1 | 2 | 3 | 4 | 5 | 6 | 7 | 8 | 9 | 10 | 11 | 12 | 13 | 14 |

109B Sentence Guided Writings [10] *type 105B, page 186, as directed there*

109C Building Speed [15]

1. Type two ½′ writings; reach for 30 or more words in that time.
2. Type two 1′ writings; reach for 60 or more words.
3. Type two 1½′ writings; reach for 90 or more words.
4. Type two 2′ writings; try to complete the paragraph.
5. If you complete the paragraph, begin it again. The goals are marked in the copy.

All letters are included.

		Words
	Men who hold jobs with high salaries and who enjoy greater social	13
	prestige appear to have a common attribute. They can express a thought,	28
	an idea, or a concept in exact words. They know how to create vivid	42
1.5 SI	effects with the words they use. They have an adequate vocabulary, and	56
5.6 AWL 80% HFW	they know how to use it to obtain the results they want. In addition,	71
	they must have something more than a hazy notion of their subject. The	85
	blunt truth is that recognition and prosperity seem to come more easily	99
	to the men who have sufficient word power to express their ideas in	113
	clear, accurate, and convincing ways.	120

REFERENCE GUIDE

TYPEWRITER OPERATIVE PARTS

Typewriters have similar operative parts, the names of which vary somewhat from typewriter to typewriter even when the function is the same. These similar operative parts are identified in the four segments of a typewriter given below and on page ii. Each segment is a composite and not an exact segment of any one typewriter. For this reason, the exact location of a part identified in the segment may be slightly different from that on your typewriter; but the differences are, for the most part, few and slight.

Extra parts that are peculiar to the typewriter you operate can be identified by reference to the instructional booklet distributed by the manufacturer of the typewriter. This booklet can be very helpful to you because all its content is directed to the operation of one specific make of machine.

In using the illustrations, follow the line from the number to the part location. Know the function of each part, as explained in the textbook, and learn to operate it with maximum efficiency.

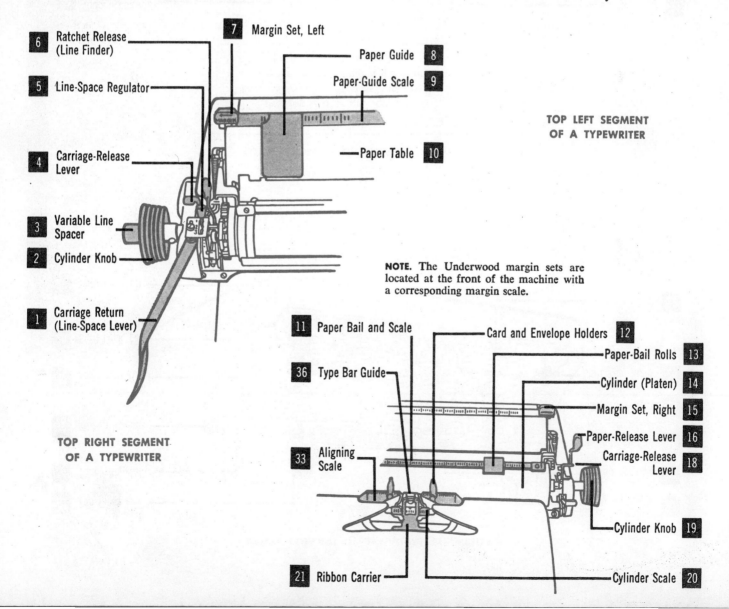

6 Ratchet Release (Line Finder)

7 Margin Set, Left

8 Paper Guide

9 Paper-Guide Scale

5 Line-Space Regulator

4 Carriage-Release Lever

10 Paper Table

TOP LEFT SEGMENT OF A TYPEWRITER

3 Variable Line Spacer

2 Cylinder Knob

NOTE. The Underwood margin sets are located at the front of the machine with a corresponding margin scale.

1 Carriage Return (Line-Space Lever)

11 Paper Bail and Scale

12 Card and Envelope Holders

13 Paper-Bail Rolls

36 Type Bar Guide

14 Cylinder (Platen)

15 Margin Set, Right

16 Paper-Release Lever

18 Carriage-Release Lever

TOP RIGHT SEGMENT OF A TYPEWRITER

33 Aligning Scale

19 Cylinder Knob

21 Ribbon Carrier

20 Cylinder Scale

LOWER SEGMENT OF A MANUAL TYPEWRITER

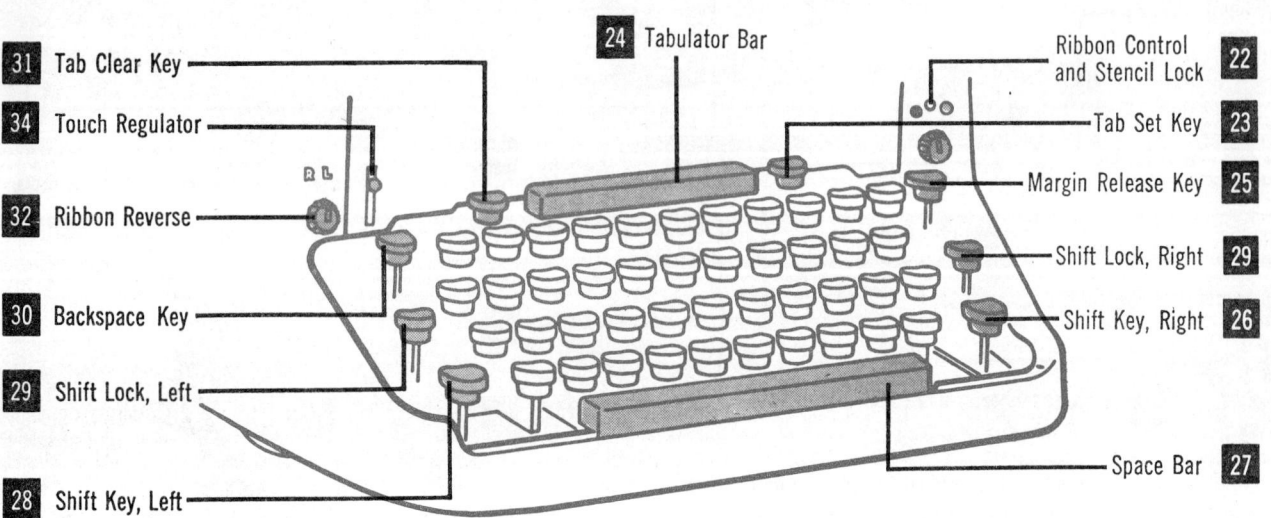

31 Tab Clear Key

34 Touch Regulator

32 Ribbon Reverse

30 Backspace Key

29 Shift Lock, Left

28 Shift Key, Left

24 Tabulator Bar

22 Ribbon Control and Stencil Lock

23 Tab Set Key

25 Margin Release Key

29 Shift Lock, Right

26 Shift Key, Right

27 Space Bar

LOWER SEGMENT OF AN ELECTRIC TYPEWRITER

> ### CHECK YOUR TYPEWRITER TO SEE IF:
> **1.** The position is different for: ¢ @ * _ (underline)
> **2.** These keys have "repeat" action: *backspace, space bar, carriage return, hyphen-underline*
> **3.** Extra keys are used: **+ = ! 1**

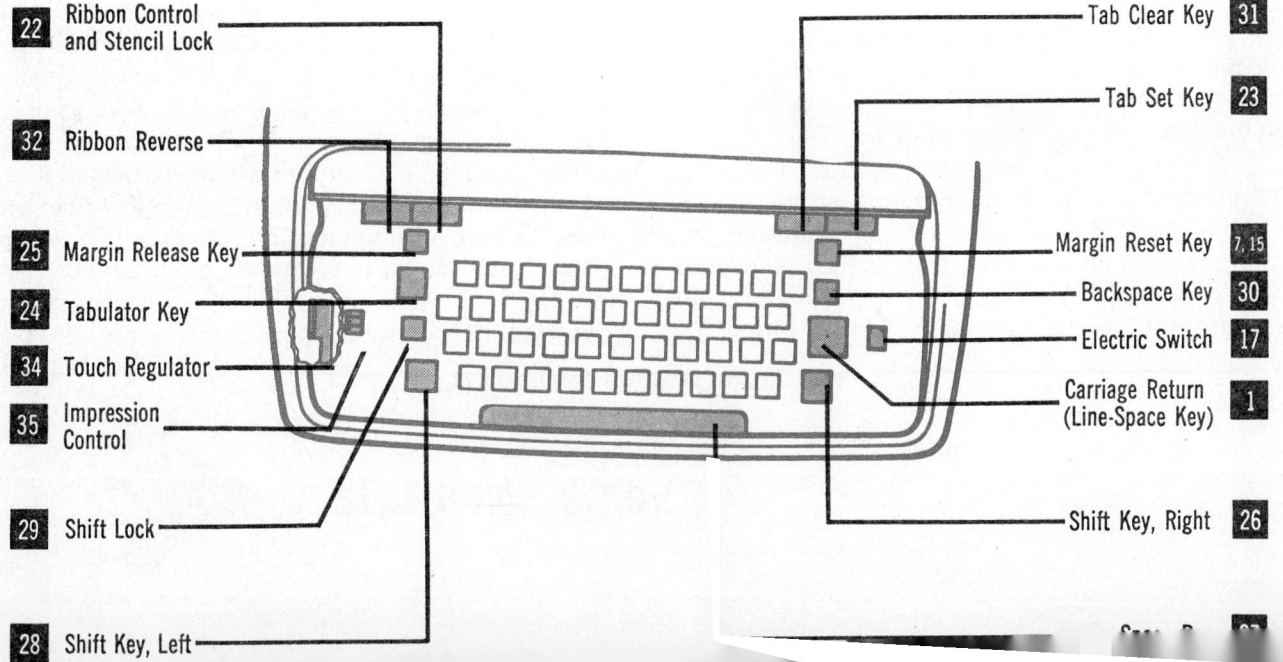

22 Ribbon Control and Stencil Lock

32 Ribbon Reverse

25 Margin Release Key

24 Tabulator Key

34 Touch Regulator

35 Impression Control

29 Shift Lock

28 Shift Key, Left

31 Tab Clear Key

23 Tab Set Key

7, 15 Margin Reset Key

30 Backspace Key

17 Electric Switch

1 Carriage Return (Line-Space Key)

26 Shift Key, Right

PAPER GUIDE AND CENTERING POINT

Typewriters are of three types in regard to setting the paper guide and arriving at the center point.

Type 1: ROYAL, OLYMPIA, AND SMITH-CORONA "SECRETARIAL 250" ELECTRIC

Set the paper guide on 0 on the paper-guide scale. When 8½" by 11" paper is inserted with the left edge against the guide, the centering point will be 42 for pica and 51 (or 50 for convenience) for elite machines.

Type 2: IBM MODEL D, AND REMINGTON

The fixed centering point is 0 for both pica and elite machines. Marks on the paper-guide scale aid the typist in setting the paper guide to center paper correctly.

Type 3: SMITH-CORONA NON-ELECTRIC, R. C. ALLEN, IBM SELECTRIC, AND UNDERWOOD

A variety of marks appear on the paper table or copy-guide scale to aid the typist in setting the paper-guide scale for automatic centering of 8½" by 11" paper. Marks on the paper-bail scale indicate the center point of the paper.

If no marks appear on the paper-bail scale to indicate the center point of the paper, insert the paper after the paper guide has been set. Add the carriage scale reading on the left edge of the paper to the reading at the right edge. Divide this sum by 2 to arrive at the center point.

STANDARD DIRECTIONS APPLYING TO ALL TYPEWRITERS

On every typewriter, there is at least one scale, usually the cylinder scale (20), that reads from 0 at the left to 85 or more at the right, depending on the width of the carriage and style of type—either pica or elite. The spaces on this scale are matched to the spacing mechanism on the typewriter.

To simplify direction giving, your instructor may ask you to insert paper into your machine so that the left edge corresponds to 0 on the carriage scale. The center point on 8½" by 11" paper will then be 42 on the carriage scale for a pica machine or 51 (or 50 for convenience) on an elite machine.

If this procedure is adopted, adjust the paper guide to the left edge of your paper after it is inserted with the left edge at 0 on the carriage scale. Note the position of the paper guide. Move it to this point at the beginning of each class period.

SETTING THE MARGIN STOPS

PLANNING THE MARGIN STOPS (7, 15)

To center typed material horizontally, set stops for the left and right margins. Typewriters differ in their mechanical adjustments and the bell rings at different points on different typewriters; but the carriage locks at the point where the right margin stop is set. After the bell rings, there will be from 6 to 11 or more spaces before the carriage locks, some machines allowing more but none fewer than 6 spaces.

Test out your typewriter and determine the number of spaces the bell rings before the carriage locks. Take this into consideration when setting the right margin stop. Since the ringing of the bell is a cue to return the carriage, set the right stop 3 to 7 spaces beyond the desired line ending so the ringing will come at approximately 3 spaces before the point at which you want the line to end.

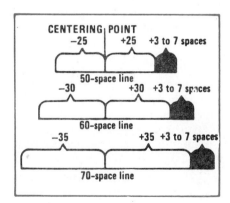

MECHANICS OF SETTING MARGIN STOPS

IBM "MODEL D" AND UNDERWOOD ELECTRIC

To Set Left Margin Stop: Move the carriage to the left margin stop by depressing the return key. Depress and hold down the margin reset key as you move the carriage to the desired new margin position; then release the margin reset key.

To Set Right Margin Stop: Move the carriage until it is against the right margin stop. Depress and hold down the margin reset key as you move the carriage to the desired new margin position; then release the margin reset key.

IBM "SELECTRIC"

To Set Left and Right Margin Stops: Push in on the appropriate stop and slide it to the correct position on the margin scale; release the stop. Use the space bar to move the carrier out of the way when setting a margin stop to the right of the carrier's present location.

(Continued on page iv)

SETTING MARGIN STOPS (Continued)

OLYMPIA AND UNDERWOOD NONELECTRIC

To Set Left and Right Margin Stops: Move the left and right margin stops to the desired position on the front scale for the Underwood typewriter and on the scale in back of the Olympia.

The Underwood typewriter has margin indicators (solid geometric shapes) on the front scale to indicate balanced margin set positions. The Olympia has an easy-to-see red line, on the upright plastic guide, to indicate exact position of setting.

REMINGTON ELECTRIC AND NONELECTRIC

To Set Left and Right Margin Stops: Move the left margin stop to the desired position to begin the line of writing. Move the stop for the right margin to the desired position to set the right margin stop.

SMITH-CORONA ELECTRIC

To Set Left and Right Margin Stops: Depress the left carriage-release button and the left margin button and move the carriage to the desired location for the left margin stop; release the two buttons simultaneously. Use a similar operation to set the stop for the right margin.

ROYAL ELECTRIC AND NONELECTRIC

To Set the Left Margin Stop: Pull forward the left margin lever, move the carriage to the desired point, and release the lever. Set the right margin the same way, using the right margin lever.

SMITH-CORONA NONELECTRIC AND R. C. ALLEN

To Set the Left Margin Stop: Move the carriage to the desired point and touch the left margin button or key.

Set the right margin stop the same way, using the right margin button or key.

Another Method: While holding down the button or key, move the carriage to the point desired; then release the button or key.

KNOW YOUR TYPEWRITER

Your machine may have timesaving features not included in this discussion of operating parts. Learn these features from a study of the manufacturer's pamphlet which describes and illustrates the operating parts of the typewriter you are using. You can get this pamphlet without cost from the manufacturer of your typewriter. The pamphlet will have many ideas for your operative improvement.

CHANGING TYPEWRITER RIBBONS

Techniques for changing ribbons vary from machine to machine. The steps that follow are basic to all machines:

1. Wind the ribbon on one spool, usually the right one.
2. Raise and lock the ribbon carrier as follows: Depress the shift lock. Set the ribbon control for typing on the lower portion of the ribbon. Depress and lock any two central keys, such as y and t.
3. Remove the ribbon from the carrier. Remove both spools.
4. Hook the new ribbon on the empty spool and wind several inches of new ribbon on it. Be sure the ribbon winds and unwinds in the proper direction.
5. Place both spools on their holders. Thread the ribbon through the ribbon carrier.
6. Release the shift lock. Return the ribbon indicator to type on the upper portion of the ribbon. Unlock the two keys.
7. Clean the keys if necessary to make your work clear and sharp.

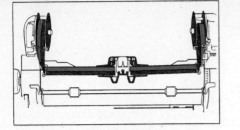

Electric

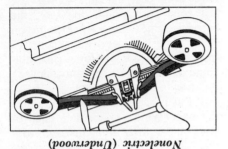

Nonelectric (Underwood)

Path of the Ribbon as It Winds and Unwinds on the Two Spools

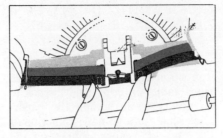

Ribbon Threaded Through the Ribbon-Carrier Mechanism

office aides inc

suite 1045 carew tower one fifth street cincinnati,ohio 45202 telephone(513)271-8811

October 20, 19--

Republic Supply Company
2670 Queen City Avenue
Cincinnati, OH 45238

Attention Miss Janet Wellington

Gentlemen:

The modified block style has some distinctive features, as
shown by this letter and described in the enclosed pamphlet.

The date, complimentary close, and name and official title of
the dictator are begun at the horizontal center of the page.
These can be placed correctly with one tabulator adjustment.

Special lines (reference, enclosure, and carbon copy notations)
are placed at the left margin, a double space below the last
of the closing lines. If the dictator's name is part of the
closing lines, only the typist's initials are required in the
reference. If the dictator's initials are used, they precede
those of the typist and are usually typed in capital letters.

The modified block style, about which you inquired yesterday,
is widely used by the clients for whom we prepare letters.
We think you will like it, too.

Sincerely yours,

Randall B. Parkhurst

Randall B. Parkhurst
Communications Director

lkd

Enclosure

cc Mr. John R. Rodgers, Jr.

Modified Block, Blocked ¶s, Mixed

PD Consultants in Business Practices
PERRY & DERRICK, INC.

111 Lincoln Park / Newark, New Jersey 07102 / Telephone 201-227-0453

February 15, 19--

AIRMAIL

Miss Evelyn Terry, Office Manager
Standard Steel Equipment Company
270 - 53d Street
Brooklyn, NY 11232

Dear Miss Terry

The booklet you requested about letter format is enclosed. The format features described are those adopted
by this company. This letter follows them.

The first line of each paragraph is indented five
spaces. The date, complimentary close, company name,
and the dictator's name are started at the center point
of the paper. We use open punctuation. In this style,
punctuation marks are omitted after the date, address,
salutation, and closing lines unless an abbreviation is
used, in which case the period is typed as part of the
abbreviation.

Although we do not usually show the company name
in the closing lines, we have done so here to illustrate
for you the correct handling of it. Since the dictator's
name is typed in the closing lines, only the typist's
initials are used in the reference notation.

Special mailing notations are typed in all capital
letters at the left margin, a double space below the date.

After you have had an opportunity to examine your
copy of Styling Business Letters, I shall appreciate
your sending us your impressions of it.

Sincerely yours

PERRY & DERRICK, INC.

Richard S. Perry

Richard S. Perry, Manager

mev

Enclosure

Modified Block, Indented ¶s, Open

BUSINESS WRITING, INCORPORATED

Communications Consultants

2203 CEDAR DRIVE, E. / HICKSVILLE, NEW YORK 11804 / 212-869-2560

February 12, 19--

Miss Margaret Lamson
62200 Beacon Hill Road
Waterbury, CT 06716

Dear Miss Lamson

SUBJECT: Letter Writing Manual

Thank you for your letter of February 5 requesting a copy
of our Letter Writing Manual. I regret that this manual
is not yet in printed form. The mimeographed copies currently available are restricted to use in our offices.

We have adopted the block form illustrated in this letter.
You will observe that machine adjustments are simpler, resulting in a saving of much time by the typist. The date,
address, salutation, and closing lines all begin at the
left margin. Paragraphs are blocked also. The form is
used in many business offices.

You should get a copy of our Letter Writing Manual in a
few weeks. There is no charge for the manual. We hope
you will find it useful. Please write me again if I can
send you any additional information.

Sincerely yours

S. James Whitmore

S. James Whitmore
President

rsk

Block, Open

BUSINESS WRITING, INCORPORATED

Communications Consultants

2203 CEDAR DRIVE, E. / HICKSVILLE, NEW YORK 11804 / 212-869-2560

October 5, 19--

Mr. S. W. Jackson, Manager
North American Cement Corp.
39501 Bartlett Avenue
Boston, MA 02129

AMS SIMPLIFIED STYLE

This letter is typed in the timesaving simplified style
recommended by the Administrative Management Society.
To type a letter in the AMS style, follow these steps:

1. Use block format with blocked paragraphs.

2. Omit the salutation and complimentary close.

3. Include a subject heading and type it in ALL CAPS a
   triple space below the address; triple-space from
   the subject line to the first line of the body.

4. Type enumerated items at the left margin; indent
   unnumbered listed items five spaces.

5. Type the writer's name and title in ALL CAPS at least
   four line spaces below the letter body.

6. Type the reference initials (typist's only) a double
   space below the writer's name.

Correspondents in your company will like the AMS simplified letter style not only for the "eye appeal" it gives
letters but also because it reduces letter-writing costs.

S. James Whitmore

S. JAMES WHITMORE - PRESIDENT

akb

AMS Simplified

ADDRESSING ENVELOPES

Address Placement and Spacing. Block the address lines; use single spacing. Type the city and state names and ZIP Code in that sequence on the bottom line.

For a small envelope, start the address lines 2″ from the top and 2½″ from the left edge.

For a large envelope, start the address lines 2½″ from the top and 4″ from the left edge.

State Abbreviations. When the ZIP Code is known, use the 2-letter abbreviation (page viii) in all caps, without a period. Type the ZIP Code 2 spaces after the abbreviation. If the ZIP Code is not known, type the state name in full or use the standard abbreviation.

Notations. Type postal directions, such as AIRMAIL and SPECIAL DELIVERY, below the space required for the stamp. Type HOLD FOR ARRIVAL, PERSONAL, PLEASE FORWARD, etc., a triple space below the return address and 3 spaces from the left edge.

Return Address. Type the return address on the second line from the top and 3 spaces from the left edge.

Small Envelope

> OSHKOSH CRAFTSMEN, INC.
> 573 Lexington Avenue
> New York, New York 10022
>
> PERSONAL   2″
>
>   2½″   Mr. Maurice L. Egan, President
>   National Fastener Company, Inc.
>   252 Mayhill Street
>   Saddle Brook, NJ 07662

Large Envelope

> OSHKOSH CRAFTSMEN, INC.
> 573 Lexington Avenue
> New York, New York 10022
>
>   2½″   SPECIAL DELIVERY
>
>   4″   Taylor Investment Service
>   Attention Mr. John Douglass
>   220 Newbury Street
>   Boston, MA 02116

FOLDING-AND-INSERTING PROCEDURE FOR ENVELOPES

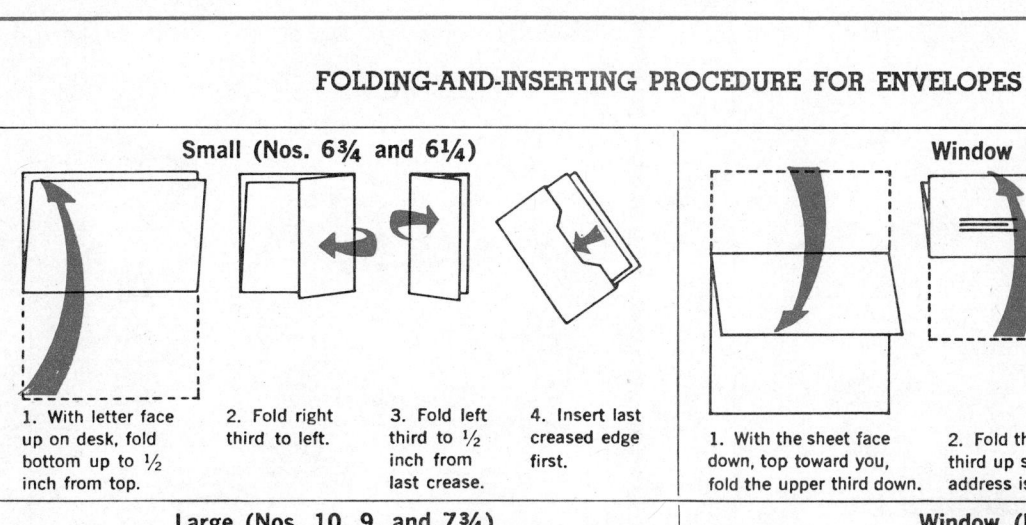

Small (Nos. 6¾ and 6¼)

1. With letter face up on desk, fold bottom up to ½ inch from top.
2. Fold right third to left.
3. Fold left third to ½ inch from last crease.
4. Insert last creased edge first.

Window (Letter)

1. With the sheet face down, top toward you, fold the upper third down.
2. Fold the lower third up so the address is showing.
3. Insert the sheet into the envelope with the last crease at the bottom.

Large (Nos. 10, 9, and 7¾)

1. With the letter face up, fold slightly less than one third of the letterhead up toward the top.
2. Fold down the top of the letterhead to within ½ inch of the bottom fold.
3. Insert the letter into the envelope with the last crease toward the bottom of the envelope.

Window (Invoice)

1. Place the sheet face down, top toward you.
2. Fold back the top so address shows.
3. Insert into envelope with crease at bottom.

LETTER-PLACEMENT POINTERS

Margins and Date Placement. Some offices use standard side margins for all letters. Others vary the side margins according to letter length, as is the case in the following guide:

5-Stroke Words in Letter Body	Side Margins	Date Line
Up to 100	2″	20
101 – 300	1½″	18–12*
Over 300	1″	12

*Date line is moved up 2 line spaces for each additional 50 words.

The horizontal placement of the date depends on the style of letter, design of the letterhead, or a combination of these factors.

Block and AMS Simplified Styles: Type the date at the left margin.

Modified Block Style: Begin date at center point or type it even with right margin.

Address. Type the first line of the address on the fourth line space below the date. Type an official title, when used, on either the first or second line, whichever gives better balance.

Attention Line. Type an attention line, when used, on the second line below the letter address and a double space above the salutation. Type it at the left margin (preferred), or center it.

Subject Line. Type a subject line on the second line below the salutation. In block or AMS Simplified styles, type the subject line even with the left margin. In other styles, type it even with the left margin, at paragraph point, or centered.

Type the word *Subject* in all capitals or with only the first letter capitalized, or omit it (as in the AMS Simplified style).

Company Name in Closing. When the company name is included in the closing, type it in all caps on the second line below the complimentary close.

Typewritten Name and Official Title. Type the name of the writer of a letter and his official title on the 4th line space below the complimentary close, or on the 4th line space below the company name when it is used. Type the writer's name and his official title on the same line, or type the title below the writer's name.

Enclosure Notation. Type an enclosure notation (*Enc.* or *Enclosure*) on the second line space below the reference initials.

Two-Page Letters. Include at least two lines of a paragraph at the bottom of the first page and at least two lines at the top of the second page of a two-page letter. Do the same for any letter of more than one page.

Begin the heading on continuation pages an inch from the top edge of the sheet. You may use either the block or horizontal form. Leave 2 blank lines between the heading and the first line of the resumed letter; use the same side margins as for the first page.

Second-Page Headings

Mr. A. C. Dow Page 2 May 6, 19--	**Block Form**

Horizontal Form

Mr. A. C. Dow   2   May 6, 19--

GUIDES FOR WORD DIVISION

Divide—

1. Words between syllables only.

2. Hyphenated words and compounds at hyphens only.

3. Words so that *cial*, *tial*, *cion*, *sion*, or *tion* are retained as a unit.

4. A word of three or more syllables at a one-letter syllable. Type the one-letter syllable on the first line unless it is part of such terminations as *ible*, *able*, or *ical*, in which case carry it to the second line. If two one-letter syllables come together, divide between them.

5. A word in which the final consonant is doubled when a suffix is added between the double letters, as *control-ling*.

6. A word that ends in double letters after the double letters when a suffix is added, as *will-ing*.

Do not—

7. Divide a word of five or fewer letters.

8. Separate a one-letter syllable at the beginning or end of a word.

9. Separate a two-letter syllable at the end of a word.

10. Divide the last word on a page.

11. Separate a syllable without a vowel from the rest of a word, as *would-n't*.

Avoid if possible—

12. Separating a two-letter syllable at the beginning of a word.

13. Dividing words at the ends of more than two successive lines.

14. Dividing abbreviations, numbers, and proper names; but a surname may be separated from the initials or given name, when necessary.

TWO-LETTER ABBREVIATIONS FOR STATE, DISTRICT, AND TERRITORY NAMES

These two-letter abbreviations, recommended by the U.S. Post Office Department, should be used for business addresses for which ZIP Codes are known and used.

Alabama	AL
Alaska	AK
Arizona	AZ
Arkansas	AR
California	CA
Canal Zone	CZ
Colorado	CO
Connecticut	CT
Delaware	DE
District of Columbia	DC
Florida	FL
Georgia	GA
Guam	GU
Hawaii	HI
Idaho	ID

Illinois	IL
Indiana	IN
Iowa	IA
Kansas	KS
Kentucky	KY
Louisiana	LA
Maine	ME
Maryland	MD
Massachusetts	MA
Michigan	MI
Minnesota	MN
Mississippi	MS
Missouri	MO
Montana	MT
Nebraska	NE
Nevada	NV
New Hampshire	NH
New Jersey	NJ
New Mexico	NM
New York	NY

North Carolina	NC
North Dakota	ND
Ohio	OH
Oklahoma	OK
Oregon	OR
Pennsylvania	PA
Puerto Rico	PR
Rhode Island	RI
South Carolina	SC
South Dakota	SD
Tennessee	TN
Texas	TX
Utah	UT
Vermont	VT
Virgin Islands	VI
Virginia	VA
Washington	WA
West Virginia	WV
Wisconsin	WI
Wyoming	WY

ASSEMBLING A CARBON PACK

METHOD 1 (Desk Assembly)

1. Place the sheet ("second" or "file copy sheet") on which the carbon copy is to be made flat on the desk; then place a carbon sheet, *carbon (glossy) side down*, on top of the sheet. Add the original sheet (letterhead or plain sheet) on top of the carbon sheet.

   Note. For each carbon copy desired, add one set (the "second" or "file copy sheet" and a carbon sheet).

2. Pick up the carbon pack and turn it so the second sheets and the glossy sides of the carbon sheets face you.

3. Straighten the pack by tapping the top of the sheets gently on the desk.

4. Insert the pack by holding it firmly in one hand while turning the cylinder slowly with the other.

METHOD 2 (Machine Assembly)

1. Assemble paper for insertion into the typewriter (original sheet on top; second sheets beneath).

2. Insert paper, turning the cylinder until the sheets are gripped slightly by the feed rolls; then lay all but the last sheet over the top of the machine.

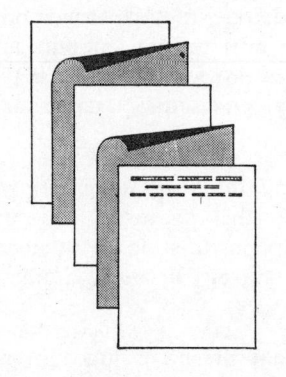

Deck Assembly of a Carbon Pack

3. Place carbon sheets between the sheets of paper with the *glossy side toward you*. Flip each sheet back as you add each carbon.

4. Roll the pack into typing position.

REMOVING THE CARBON SHEETS

Because carbon sheets do not extend to the top edge of the paper in the machine assembly of a carbon pack, the sheets can be easily removed by pulling them out all at one time as you hold the left top edge of

GUIDES FOR INSERTING A CARBON PACK

1. *To keep sheets straight when feeding*, place pack under an envelope flap or in the fold of a plain sheet of paper.

2. *To "start" the carbon pack:*
   (a) Release the paper-release lever,
   (b) Feed the pack around the cylinder until sheets appear at the front; then
   (c) Reset the paper-release lever.
   (d) After the pack is inserted, remove the envelope or paper fold.

3. *To avoid wrinkling*, release and reset the paper-release lever after the pack has been partially inserted.

Machine Assembly of

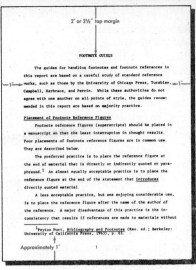

First Page, Topbound

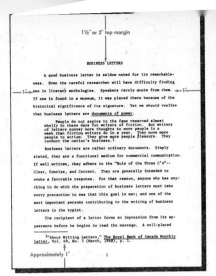

First Page, Unbound

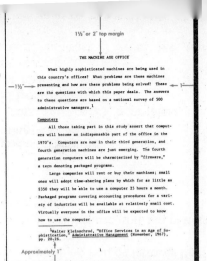

First Page, Leftbound

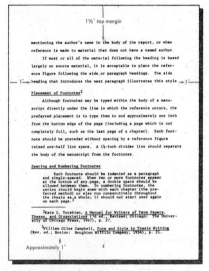

Second Page, Topbound

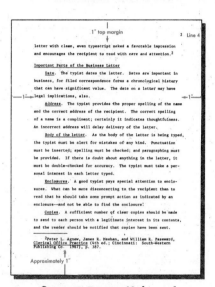

Second Page, Unbound

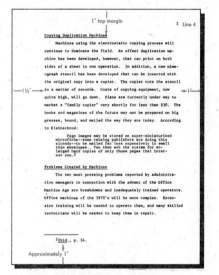

Second Page, Leftbound

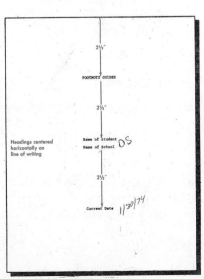

Title Page

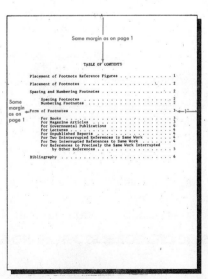

Table of Contents

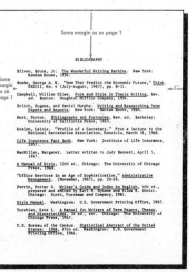

Bibliography

CORRECTION SYMBOLS (PROOFREADERS' MARKS)

Sometimes typed or printed copy may be corrected with proofreaders' marks. The typist must be able to interpret correctly these marks in retyping the corrected copy or *rough draft* as it may be called. The most commonly used proofreaders' marks are shown below.

Symbol	Meaning
‖	Align type
Cap or ≡	Capitalize
⌒	Close up
(delete mark)	Delete
ds	Double-space
=/	Hyphen
∧	Insert
∨	Insert apostrophe
⊙	Insert colon
(comma mark)	Insert comma
⊙	Insert period
?/	Insert question mark
∨∨	Insert quotation marks
; or ;/	Insert semicolon
⚡ or #	Insert space
#>	Insert space between lines
Stet	Let it stand (ignore correction)
(bracket)	Move to left
(bracket)	Move to right
no ¶ [	No new paragraph
¶	Paragraph
ss	Single-space
#	Space
SP	Spell out
═══	Straighten line
∿ or tr	Transpose
ts	Triple-space
────	Underline
l.c.	Use lower case

CENTERING SUMMARY

HORIZONTAL CENTERING

From the center, backspace once for each two letters, figures, spaces, and punctuation marks in the heading or line to be centered. (In backspacing, disregard an odd or leftover stroke.) Start typing where the backspacing ends.

HORIZONTAL CENTERING—SPREAD HEADINGS

1. From the center, backspace once for each letter except the last one in the heading and once for each space between words.
2. In typing the heading, space once after each letter or character and three times between words.

VERTICAL CENTERING
BACKSPACE-FROM-CENTER METHOD

1. Move the paper to vertical center: 34th line space for a full sheet; 17th li...

2. Roll the platen back once for each two lines (including blank lines). Ignore an odd or leftover line. Start typing where the spacing ends.
3. For reading position on a full sheet, roll the platen back 2 additional line spaces.

VERTICAL CENTERING
MATHEMATICAL METHOD

1. Count lines and blank line spaces in problem.
2. Subtract lines used from lines on sheet.
3. Divide by 2 to get top and bottom margins. If a fraction results, disregard it.
4. For reading position, subtract 2 from the top margin.
5. Space down from top edge of paper 1 more th...

TABULATION SUMMARY

VERTICAL PLACEMENT

For vertical placement of tables, use either the backspace-from-center or the mathematical method explained on page x.

Spacing after Headings. Leave one blank line between a main and a secondary heading. Leave two blank lines after a secondary heading. If a secondary heading is not used, leave two blank lines after a main heading.

Leave one blank line between a columnar heading and its column.

HORIZONTAL PLACEMENT OF TABULATIONS

Columns. Note the longest item in each column. (If a columnar heading is the longest item, count it as such unless judgment indicates otherwise.) Decide the number of spaces to leave between columns, preferably an even number.

Backspace from the center of the paper once for every two spaces in the longest item in each column and once for every two spaces between all the columns. At the point where you finish backspacing, set the left margin stop for the first column.

From the left margin, space forward once for every stroke in the longest item of the first column and once for each space between the first and second columns. Set the first tab stop. Follow this same procedure for setting tab stops for the remaining columns.

Columnar Headings. Center the columnar headings over the columns.

When a heading has been counted as the longest item in a column, it will usually be necessary to reset the tab stop in order to center the column under the heading.

There are several methods of centering columnar headings over a column, but probably the easiest way is to add the first and last strokes in the column. Divide this sum by 2 to get the center point of the column. Columnar headings are usually underlined.

HORIZONTAL RULINGS

Horizontal lines are often used in a tabulated report to set off columnar headings. A double line is usually placed above columnar headings and a single line below them. A single line is also placed under the last line of the report. These lines can be the exact width of the report, or they can extend several spaces on each side of it.

To type rulings the exact width of the table, first determine the placement of columns. When you set the tab stop for the last column continue spacing forward one space for each stroke in the longest item in that column. Immediately after stroking for the last stroke in this item, move the right margin stop so that the typewriter will lock at this point. Rulings can then be typed across the page until the carriage locks.

Placement of Double Lines. After typing the secondary heading, double-space; type the first of the double lines; then operate the variable line spacer; move the cylinder forward slightly; type the second line. Double-space between this line and the columnar headings.

Placement of Single Lines. After typing the columnar headings, single-space; type a single line; then double-space to the first columnar entries. Single-space after typing the last columnar entries and type a single line.

Source Note (If Used). Double-space from the single line; type the source note at the left margin or indent 3 to 5 spaces.

TABULATOR STOPS FOR UNEVEN COLUMNS

Uneven Columns. When columns contain amounts of figures of uneven length, set the tab stop at a point that will take care of the greatest number of entries. After tabulating, backspace for longer items or space forward for shorter ones.

Dollar Signs. In a money column, type a dollar sign before the first amount in the column and before the total (if one is shown). Place the dollar sign before the first amount and the total, typed so that it will be one space to the left of the longest amount in the column (usually the total).

Totals. To make them easier to read, totals are usually separated by a double space from the column. Type the total line immediately under the last amount in the column. Do not space before typing the total line.

DRAWING RULED LINES

To Draw Horizontal Lines: Place the pencil point through the cardholder (or on the type bar guide above the ribbon); depress the carriage-release lever to draw the carriage across the line.

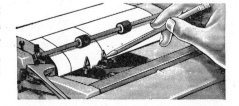

To Draw Vertical Lines: Operate the line finder. Place the pencil point or pen through the cardholder (or on the type bar guide above the ribbon). Roll the platen up the page until you have a line of the desired length. Remove the pen or pencil and reset the line finder.

HOW TO ERASE AND CORRECT ERRORS

Using an Eraser Shield

1. Depress margin-release key and move carriage to extreme left or right to prevent eraser crumbs from falling into the typing mechanism.
2. To avoid disturbing the paper alignment of the type, turn the cylinder forward if the erasure is to be made on the upper two thirds of the paper; backward, on the lower third of the paper.
3. To erase on the original sheet, lift the paper bail out of the way, and place a 5″ x 3″ card *in front of* the first carbon sheet. Use an eraser shield to protect the writing that is not to be erased. Brush the eraser crumbs away from the typewriter.
4. Move the protective card in front of the second carbon, if more than one copy is being made. Erase the errors on the carbon copy with a soft (or pencil) eraser first, then with the hard typewriter eraser used in erasing on the original copy.
5. When the error has been erased on all copies, remove the protective card, position the carriage to the proper point, and type the necessary correction.

SQUEEZING AND SPREADING OF LETTERS

In correcting errors, it is often possible to "squeeze" omitted letters into half spaces or to "spread" letters to fill out spaces.

1. *An omitted letter at the beginning or end of a word:*

   Error: an omitte letter
   Correction: an omittedletter

Corrective steps:

1. Move carriage to the letter *e*.
2. Depress and hold down the space bar; strike the letter *d*.

Note. On an electric typewriter, it may be necessary to hold the carriage by hand at the half-space point.

2. *An omitted letter within a word:*

   Error: a leter within
   Correction: a letter within

Corrective steps:

1. Erase the incorrect word.
2. Position the carriage at the space after the letter *a*.
3. Press down and hold the space bar; strike the letter *l*.
4. Release the space bar, then press it down again and hold it; strike the next letter.
5. Repeat the process for any additional letters.

3. *Addition of a letter within a word:*

   Error: a lettter within
   Correction: a letter with...

Corrective steps:

1. Erase the incorrect word.
2. Position the carriage as if you were going to type the letter *l* in its regular position following the space.
3. Press down and hold the space bar; strike the letter *l*.
4. Release the space bar; then repeat the process for each remaining letter.

IBM SELECTRIC TYPEWRITER

When making corrections, you may locate the horizontal position of the typing element by using either the black line on the clear view card holder (circled at right) or the red arrow on the margin scale. If you use the card holder as your indicator, position the black line at the point on the paper at which you want to insert the new character. Then return to the line of type and insert the correction.

Crowding Letters

Error: the ordr today
Correction: the order today

To crowd the "e" into "ordr," erase the final "r." Backspace until the black line on the card holder is over the space formerly occupied by the final "r." Place the palm of the right hand on the top of the front cover.

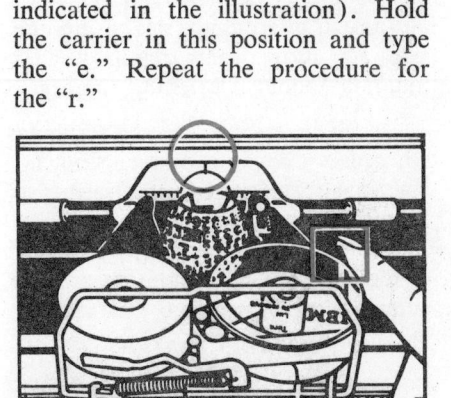

LEFT against the carrier position post with your finger until the black line is moved back one-half space (as indicated in the illustration). Hold the carrier in this position and type the "e." Repeat the procedure for the "r."

Spreading Letters

Error: He will send
Correction: He can send

To replace "will" with "can," first erase "will." Type "c" in place of "w" and type "n" in place of final "l."

Position the black line on the card holder over the position occupied by the first "l." Place the palm of the right hand on the top of the front cover. Reach under the cover and press left against the carrier position post with your finger until the black line of the card holder is directly between the "i" and "l." Type "a." Re-